REAL ESTATE DEVELOPMENT LAW

Second Edition

■ ■ ■

Rick Daley

AMERICAN CASEBOOK SERIES®

WEST
ACADEMIC
PUBLISHING

American Casebook Series is a trademark registered in the U.S. Patent and Trademark Office.

© 2011 Thomson Reuters
© 2017 LEG, Inc. d/b/a West Academic
    444 Cedar Street, Suite 700
    St. Paul, MN 55101
    1-877-888-1330

West, West Academic Publishing, and West Academic are trademarks of West Publishing Corporation, used under license.

Printed in the United States of America

ISBN: 978-1-68328-126-9

This book is dedicated to my wife Sandy—my best friend and the love of my life. In the inestimable words of Bob Dylan—

"You're the other half of what I am,
you're the missing piece
And I love you more than ever
with that love that doesn't cease."[1]

---

1   Bob Dylan, *Wedding Song, on* PLANET WAVES (Asylum Records 1974).

PREFACE TO THE SECOND EDITION

When the folks at West Academic approached me last year about writing a second edition of my 2011 REAL ESTATE DEVELOPMENT LAW text, my initial reaction was to say "thanks, but no thanks." The truth is that I never thought I would write a book of any kind, let alone a second edition of a law book. After further reflection, I decided to step back in the fray and produce a second edition of the book for three reasons—(1) I thought doing so would give me the chance to fine tune and correct some of the mistakes I made on the first go-round, (2) I wanted to broaden the book's audience to include not just law students, but also aspiring transactional business lawyers, and (3) I was planning to retire from teaching at the Moritz College of Law at The Ohio State University and my wife was desperately afraid that I would sit around in my bathrobe all day drinking wine and binging on Netflix. So for all those reasons (but mostly the last one), I found myself back at the keyboard trying to bang out a slightly bigger and hopefully much better second edition of REAL ESTATE DEVELOPMENT LAW.

Let me start out by reiterating the point I made in the preface to the original book—that is this book is being written from a practical and not a scholarly perspective. Over the years, I have been called by a lot of different names—most of them couched in mildly profane terms to take due note of my natural wit and mental acuity. However, rest assured that the word "scholar" has never before been uttered in the same sentence as "Rick Daley." Although I had the privilege of being a member of the faculty of a wonderful law school like Moritz for a full ten years, the fact of the matter is that my knowledge of the topic of this book was wholly formed by my 25+years representing real estate developers, first as a lawyer in private practice and then as in-house counsel. The voice in which this book is written is, therefore, undeniably and without choice that of a practicing lawyer.

While this book is not filled with scholarly analysis or insightful legal queries, neither is it intended to be a primer on the technical aspects of real estate development law. Rather, the focus is on examining why the real estate development lawyer takes certain positions and how a real estate development lawyer's actions and judgments serve to enhance (or detract from) the ultimate success of a real estate deal.

Let me make several comments about the style, approach, and organization of this book.

- For the most part, the topics addressed in this book are examined from the viewpoint of the lawyer representing a real estate developer. The competing perspectives of the other players in the real estate development process are, however, highlighted when and where appropriate.

- Real estate development law is not a discrete substantive area of the law, but rather it is an amalgamation of a multitude of legal disciplines that a real estate development lawyer must master if he is to successfully represent his client. Therefore, this book explores not just traditional real estate topics, such as the leasing, acquisition, and conveyance of real property, but also issues related to tax, partnership, bankruptcy, environmental, finance, zoning, construction, and public law.

- A mantra that is repeated often in this book is that "if you want to succeed as a real estate development lawyer, you first need to understand the real estate development business." As such, the first three chapters of this book are devoted to an exploration of the real estate development business, including a full chapter on what the real estate development lawyer needs to know about the economics of a real estate development project.

- The role played by the real estate development lawyer is examined during each of the ten stages of a real estate project, beginning with the acquisition of the land on which the project will be developed and ending with the ultimate sale of the project.

- I strongly believe that the best way to appreciate the lawyer's role in the real estate development process is to look at that process against the backdrop of a "real world" case study. I have chosen as the primary case study a 350-acre mixed use project located in Orlando, Florida, having over two million square feet of developed office space, two apartment complexes, two hotels, and a neighborhood retail center. I worked on this deal (the "Heathrow International Business Center") over a ten-year period during my stint as Executive Vice President and General Counsel of The Pizzuti Companies.

- The heart and soul of real estate development law is represented by the documents prepared, reviewed, and negotiated by the real estate development lawyer. A significant part of this book is dedicated to (1) looking at the key provisions of those legal documents that evidence the real estate development deal, and (2) discussing how those provisions can be structured and manipulated to serve the legitimate business needs of the real estate development lawyer's client. The Document Appendix to this book includes a number of standard transactional documents that a real estate development lawyer encounters during the course of the representation of a developer.

- I have made a conscious attempt to sprinkle throughout the book *"Practice Tips"* that I learned during my career. The tips are not intended to be intellectually inspiring or particularly insightful—just useful.

- Terms of art commonly used by developers and their lawyers are highlighted in ***boldface italicized print*** when they first appear in the text and are then further defined in the Glossary of Terms that appears at the end of the book.

- The practice of transactional business law does not lend itself to absolutes or legal imperatives. As a result, the text is liberally sprinkled with terms like "typically," "normally," and "customarily."

- In addition to updating and cleaning up the original text, I have added to this second edition narratives on a variety of current topics and strategies related to the real estate development process, including portfolio joint ventures, crowdfunding, mezzanine debt, build-to-suit leases, limited liability general and limited partnerships, the New Markets Tax Credit, the EB–5 immigration program, the Basel III Rule, the Credit Retention Risk Rule, and the Dodd-Frank Wall Street Reform and Consumer Protection Act. I have also reworked major portions of the text to incorporate lessons that I learned while trying to explain financial, business, and legal concepts to the hundreds of impressionable law school students that I had the privilege of teaching during my stint as a senior lecturer at the Moritz College of Law. My hope is that the end result of the revisions and additions I have made in this second edition is a text that is conceptually tighter and more readily understood.

I would be remiss if I didn't take the time to list some of the people who have directed and inspired me during my professional career. Thanks to all of my early mentors (particularly Dave Sidor, Jim King, Jim Mulroy, and Kim Swanson), my friends and colleagues at The Pizzuti Companies (including Cliff Aiken, Jim Cramer, Dean Kissos, Jim Miller, and Scott West) and to all those lawyers who showed me the right way to practice law (Jim Seay, Dick Murphey, and Fred Smith among a long list of exemplary professionals). A special thank you goes to Ron Pizzuti, who, by rescuing me from private practice, provided me with the platform to expand my talents and make some money along the way.

I also want to express appreciation to all my buddies who helped me out during my years in academia by agreeing to speak to my students—thanks Brian Ellis, Dave Conrad, Paul Ghidotti, David Fisher, Dan Bailey, Bob Weiler, Franz Geiger, Gina Ormond, Janice Gresko, Brett Kaufman, Jay Devore, Brent Miller, Ken Krebs, Pat Dugan, and Bob Schottenstein, among others. Finally, I must acknowledge and thank two very special people without whom this book would never have been written—Ken and Paula Zeisler. But for their initial idea to sponsor a course at Moritz on real estate development law, I would never have had the opportunity to live my dream of waking up every morning to work on a book (albeit one with few plot twists and zero creativity).

RICK DALEY

June 1, 2017

ABOUT THE AUTHOR

Rick is a 1978 graduate of The Ohio State University Moritz College of Law. Following graduation, he spent 12 years in private practice, first as an associate and principal with the Columbus firm of Murphey, Young & Smith and then as a partner in the international firm of Squire, Sanders & Dempsey. During his 12 years of law firm practice, Rick represented a wide variety of closely held corporate clients, with a special emphasis on the representation of real estate developers. In 1990, Rick left Squire, Sanders & Dempsey to become executive vice president and general counsel of The Pizzuti Companies, a real estate development company headquartered in Columbus with offices in Chicago, Orlando, and Indianapolis. For the next 13 years, Rick served in the dual role of lawyer and business principal in connection with The Pizzuti Companies' development, leasing, and financing of more than 20 million square feet of Class A office and industrial projects throughout the Midwest and Southeast regions of the United States.

Rick retired from The Pizzuti Companies in 2003 and spent three years providing legal and business consulting services to private developers and corporate real estate departments. He became a full-time member of the Moritz College of Law faculty in the fall of 2006. In 2013, students gave Rick the Morgan Shipman Outstanding Professor Award. In 2014, he received the Provost's Award for Distinguished Teaching by a Lecturer and was inducted into the Academy of Teaching at The Ohio State University. Rick retired from Moritz in the fall of 2016 and now spends his time guest lecturing at Moritz and the Fisher College of Business and auditing courses at Ohio State on topics that are much more interesting than real estate development law.

SUMMARY OF CONTENTS

TABLE OF CONTENTS

Chapter 7. Stage 3: Forming and Capitalizing the Project Entity 213

TABLE OF CONTENTS **xxi**

REAL ESTATE DEVELOPMENT LAW

Second Edition

CHAPTER 1

WHAT IS REAL ESTATE DEVELOPMENT LAW?

▪ ▪ ▪

I. INTRODUCTION

The logical place to start this book is with a nice, tidy definition of exactly what is meant by the term "real estate development law." Try as I might, I have yet to come up with such a definition.

Most areas of the practice can be defined by reference to the substantive body of law that serves as the foundation for the practitioner's day-to-day activities. For example, we all think we have a pretty good idea of what securities law is all about—that is, a legal specialty that is centered on the application of the Securities Act of 1933 and the Securities Exchange Act of 1934. The same goes for most other defined areas of the practice— environmental law, estate planning, tax law, criminal law, etc. The well-defined bodies of law that serve as the context for those practice areas are summarized and explicated in legal treatises that line the walls of libraries in every law firm and law school in this country.

One can scan the shelves of those law libraries without ever finding a single book (save this one) wholly dedicated to the topic of real estate development law. The reason for this is quite simple—real estate development law is a practice area that is defined not by matters of substantive law, but rather by the business activities of the lawyer's client. In essence, real estate development law is nothing more than a massing of all those legal disciplines that a lawyer must call upon when seeking to help a real estate developer achieve its business objectives.

Real estate developers are impatient folks who have no tolerance for the rigor or niceties of legal specialties. As a young lawyer, I once made the mistake of pointing out to a developer client that its proposed project triggered a host of complex legal issues crossing several distinct practice areas. The developer looked me in the eye and said, "Son, I don't really care which way the wind is blowing, just bring the damn ship in."

Real estate development law is, therefore, all the "stuff" that a lawyer must know in order to help the developer client "bring the ship in." On any given project, a real estate development lawyer may be called upon to advise a developer not only on traditional real estate law topics, such as

1

the acquisition, leasing, and conveyance of real property, but also on matters involving all of the following legal disciplines:

- Tax law (federal, state, and local);

- Finance law;

- Contract law;

- Corporate, partnership, and limited liability company law;

- Securities law;

- Environmental law;

- Bankruptcy law;

- Government relations and public law;

- Land use and zoning law;

- Insurance law;

- Construction law; and

- Litigation (hopefully, precious little of this one).

Let me quickly dispense with the notion that a real estate development lawyer has the luxury of doing nothing other than managing so-called "experts" in each of the above disciplines. The economics of the real estate development business simply do not lend themselves to the use of a phalanx of lawyers, each of whom is a specialist in a discrete area of the law. The lead real estate development lawyer must have a strong working knowledge of each of the legal disciplines that comprise the area of real estate development law. Without such a broad working knowledge, the real estate development lawyer will simply not be able to help his client "bring the ship in."

It is not, however, enough for a real estate development lawyer to master all of the areas of the law listed above. Dick Murphey, a brilliant lawyer and one of my senior partners, once told me that a good business lawyer must first understand the client's business. Dick's point was that it is the business lawyer's job to not only keep the client out of trouble, but also to create a legal platform to permit the client to achieve its business objectives—in other words, make money and grow and stabilize its business. There is no area of business law where my former partner's wise words ring more true than that of real estate development law. A lawyer who purports to be an expert in all of the legal disciplines noted above will be an abysmal failure as a real estate development lawyer unless the lawyer is equally adept at understanding the business goals of the developer. A "legal expert" who disdains the practical day-to-day functioning of the client's business may end up being a highly sought out speaker at bar association functions, but that same expert will not be equipped to help the client achieve its business objectives—and for that reason, the "expert" will never be a successful transactional business lawyer.

If you take only one thing from this book, it should be this:

If you want to succeed as a real estate development lawyer, you first need to understand the real estate development business.

II. THE REAL ESTATE DEVELOPMENT BUSINESS

At its essence, real estate development is the process of crafting solutions to satisfy the real estate needs of a defined customer class (be it a fantastically prosperous global corporation or the ordinary Joe who lives down the street). The process starts with the developer identifying an unsatisfied customer need. Once that need is identified, the developer's job then becomes taking an unproductive vacant tract of land and manipulating it in some fashion (by subdividing it, rezoning it, building a building on it, etc.) to satisfy the customer's needs. This process of marrying a customer's real estate needs with a newly-created real estate product is what the real estate development business is all about.

The value-add for which the developer is ultimately compensated is twofold:

- Its correct identification of the customer's unsatisfied real estate need; and

- Its design and execution of a business plan to meet the customer's need in a cost-effective and otherwise appropriate manner.

This description of the real estate development business sounds much like that of any other business—that is, the business owner must divine the nature of the customer's demand and then figure out a way to supply a product that best meets that demand. There are, however, two unique characteristics of the real estate development business that distinguish it from other business models.

- The real estate development business is, by its very essence, a *LONG-TERM* endeavor. Once the developer devises its business plan for the project, it then has to construct the building that is at the center of that business plan. The construction period of a commercial real estate project can last anywhere from six months (for a small warehouse building) to five years or more (for a major mixed use development). Moreover, the life cycle of a developer's participation in a development project often spans a period of ten to 20 years after the construction of the project is completed.

- The real estate business is also an extremely *CAPITAL INTENSIVE* business. The cost of developing a 100,000-square-foot suburban office building typically runs anywhere from $10–$40 million, depending on the level of the building's finishes and the geographical market in which the building is located. The real kicker is that all of these costs have to be funded by the developer *UPFRONT* before the developer has any defined sense of whether the project will prove to be a success.

The long-term and capital intensive nature of the real estate development business stands in stark contrast to most other consumer-based business ventures. Take for example, a small women's apparel store where the store owner buys 20 red sweaters, puts them on display at the front of the store, and then waits to see if its customers gobble the sweaters up or move on to the next store. The store owner finds out in a matter of days or weeks whether the red sweaters are a hit. If they are, the store owner orders more sweaters. If the sweaters are not a hit, the store owner writes of its investment in the 20 sweaters (maybe a thousand dollars) and moves on to its next marketing effort.

Contrast this with the situation faced by the suburban office building developer mentioned earlier in this section. The developer has to spend somewhere around $20 million at the inception of its office project before the developer knows the extent to which its targeted customers will like the project. In addition, it is quite likely that the developer will not know with any degree of certainty whether its project is a financial success for at least a few years after construction of the office building is completed (and, in many cases, ten to 20 years later).

So while the real estate development business is, at its core, much like every other business, the long-term and capital intensive nature of the real estate development business ratchets up both the quality and quantity of the business risk faced by the developer. If the developer makes a mistake in identifying its customer's need or in designing and implementing a business plan to satisfy that need, then the developer will suffer for a long time and in a very big way. As is discussed *ad nauseum* in the rest of this book, it is the real estate development lawyer's job to recognize and then mitigate the outsized risks that are an inherent part of the developer's business.

A. WHO ARE THE DEVELOPER'S CUSTOMERS?

Like any other business, the real estate development business is driven by the needs, attitudes, likes, and dislikes of its customers. The old saw about "build it and they will come" never was true and certainly holds no sway in today's dynamic global economy. The bankruptcy court records are replete with stories of real estate developers who ignored the basic needs of their customers, and, instead, became obsessed with building their dream projects in pioneering locations. No matter how beautiful or creative a particular real estate project may be, it will not work unless a customer deems it worthy of plunking down its real cash for the right to use or own that project.

Who then are the real estate developer's customers? The developer's customers can be broken down into two broad categories.

- *Tenants*—These are the folks who are willing to pay rent to *USE* for a specified period of time all or a portion of a project created by the developer. Banks, law firms, technology companies, and other private sector tenants are the lifeblood of office buildings, warehouses, shopping centers, and other commercial real estate projects.

- *Buyers*—These are the people who want to *OWN* the developer's project, because they believe that owning real estate is a good investment. These buyers (commonly referred to as ***institutional investors***) generally come from the ranks of life insurance companies, pension plans, equity funds, sovereign wealth funds, and other financial institutions, both domestic and foreign, that have huge sums of money to invest in real estate each year.

The focus of this book is on the development of commercial real estate projects that meet the needs of two distinct classes of customers—(1) tenants from the private sector, and (2) buyers from the ranks of the institutional investor community. The success of a real estate development project is largely predicated upon the developer's ability to create a product that simultaneously satisfies the needs of each of these customers.

Sam Walton, the founder of Walmart once said that "There is only one boss; the customer. And he can fire everybody in the company from the chairman on down, simply by spending his money somewhere else."[1] The real estate developer needs to accept and embrace the fact that there are two customers that can fire the developer—both the developer's tenants and its institutional investors.

B. WHAT ARE THE CUSTOMERS' NEEDS?

The needs of a real estate developer's customers are subject to many of the same societal shifts and attitudinal changes that characterize the needs of the customers of any other business. Due to the lag time in the

---

[1] Sam Walton, https://www.brainyquote.com/search_results.html?q=sam+walton.

development and construction of a real estate project, the life cycle of a trend in the real estate business is usually longer than in other businesses. But make no mistake about it, trends do exist in the real estate business and any developer who ignores those trends will see its projects end up in the same trash heap as the pet rock and the beehive hair-do. Again, it is not the size, beauty, or location of the product created by the developer that is important, but rather whether the created product appropriately meets the needs of the targeted customer class.

What then are the needs of the developer's two customers—that is, the private sector tenant and the institutional investor? The next section of this chapter looks at the general real estate needs of each of those customers.

1.   Private Sector Businesses as Tenants

Private sector businesses usually opt to satisfy their real estate needs by leasing product created by developers. There are, of course, many exceptions to this general rule. By way of example, a company might choose to own a real estate project if the project must be highly customized to suit the company's unique operational needs—for example, a manufacturing plant or a research and development facility. The norm, however, is for companies to meet their real estate needs by leasing and not owning that real estate. As such, the focus of this text is on a private sector business being a tenant customer of the real estate developer.

There are two basic reasons that support a company's decision to lease (rather than own) the real estate it needs to operate its business.[2]

- It costs less for a company to lease real estate than it does for it to own the same real estate (at least in the short-term). Private sector companies generally want to preserve their financial resources to fund the operation and growth of their core businesses and not the acquisition and ownership of real estate.

---

[2]   *See* WILLIAM B. BRUEGGEMAN AND JEFFREY D. FISHER, REAL ESTATE FINANCE AND INVESTMENTS 494–499 (14th ed. 2011) for a discussion of additional factors that a company weighs when making its lease vs. own decision. One factor that historically worked in favor of a company's decision to lease rather than own real estate was the fact that under pre-2016 generally accepted accounting principles a company's lease of space for its business operations rarely had any impact on the company's balance sheet. *See id.* at 498. However, on February 25, 2016, the Financial Accounting Standards Board laid waste to the "no balance sheet impact" rule by issuing Accounting Standards Update 2016–02, Leases (Topic 842). Under that ASU, a tenant will need to reflect its lease of real estate as both an asset and a liability on its balance sheet. Because tenants do not need to implement the changes required under the ASU until at the earliest 2019, no definitive statement can be made at this point on whether the issuance of the ASU will cause companies to rethink their customary commitment to leasing rather than owning real estate. At least anecdotally, it appears that most practitioners and accountants believe that the new lease accounting rules will not usher in any fundamental change in the lease vs. own decision faced by private sector businesses.

- For similar reasons, companies generally do not want to deploy their human resources to deal with the myriad of operational and financial issues and risks involved with the ownership of real estate—for example, the replacement of a leaky roof, the retrofitting of an obsolete air conditioning system, or the disposition of unwanted real estate assets. It is easier for a company to lease real estate and leave all of those risks to developers or financial institutions who are accustomed to dealing with real estate issues. A common refrain voiced by private sector companies is that "We are in the business of selling widgets and not in the real estate business."

At the risk of stating the obvious, it is the rent paid by the tenants of a real estate project that creates the value inherent in that project. The rent must be sufficient to cover the project's expenses, plus provide a profit to the developer to compensate it for the entrepreneurial risk it took in developing the project in the first instance. While no real estate project is risk-free, the real estate developer can significantly ameliorate the risk of a real estate project by leasing it as soon as possible to creditworthy tenants. With this tenet in mind, it is easy to see why developers thirst for the opportunity to have creditworthy private sector companies as tenants in their projects.

2. Institutional Investors as Buyers

Life insurance companies, pension plans, and other foreign and domestic financial institutions have vast cash resources that they need to invest to achieve the financial return targets set by their governing boards. The managers of these institutional portfolios seek to diversify their investments among different asset classes (for example, stocks, bonds, commodities, and real estate), so that they can avoid compounding the risk associated with the poor financial performance of any one class of assets.

Institutional investors look for two things when they invest in real estate:

- Current operating profits represented by the excess of rents over property expenses (*net operating income*); and

- An increase in the value of the real estate over the investor's cost of acquiring and carrying that asset (*residual value*).

The price the institutional investor is willing to pay for a real estate asset is directly tied not only to the amount of the net operating income and residual value flowing from that asset, but also to the relative predictability that the projected income and value will be realized. Stated differently, the more confident the investor is that the expected income and value will be achieved, the higher the price the investor will pay for the underlying asset. To the extent the investor believes that the asset's achievement of the projected financial performance is somewhat risky, the acquisition price will be reduced accordingly. At some point, the investor's lack of confidence in the predictability of the asset's financial performance may lead the investor to decide to back away from making any investment in the subject real estate asset.

Institutional investors seek to lessen the risk associated with their real estate investments by insisting that any project acquired by them be an ***institutional-grade property***. An institutional-grade real estate project is one where:

- The creditworthiness of the project's tenant roster is sufficiently solid as to give the investor comfort that the expected income stream from the project will be realized; and

- The project location, design, and quality of construction are such that it is reasonable to assume that replacement tenants will be found if and when the existing tenants vacate the project.

The price that an investor is willing to pay for a particular real estate asset is directly tied to where that asset falls on the institutional-grade continuum.

An institutional investor's purchase of a project is almost always the developer's ultimate ***exit strategy*** for that project. The concept of an exit strategy is developed at much greater length in *Chapter 12—Stages 8–10: Selecting an Exit Strategy* (see pages 593–596). At this point, what is important to keep in mind is that the institutional investor's purchase of the developer's created project provides the developer with an opportunity (1) to wring out the last dollar of profit from its created project, and (2) to end all the developer's risk on that project.

The real estate developer must at all times during the course of its development of a particular project keep in mind not only the needs and wants of the tenants it is wooing for that project, but also the needs and wants of the investors who will provide the developer with its exit strategy for that project. If the developer disregards the needs of the institutional investor community by failing to develop an institutional-grade property, then the developer's exit strategy might disappear. An otherwise well-executed project can very quickly fall into the "loser" category if the absence of an exit strategy leaves the developer in limbo and, hence, exposes the profitability of its project to erosion from unanticipated future market risks.

C. WHAT ARE THE CUSTOMERS' PRODUCT TYPES?

The prior section of this chapter talked in general terms about the identity and needs of the real estate developer's customers. That discussion intentionally avoided any reference to the specific nature of the real estate product and, instead, focused on the process whereby a real estate developer identifies an unsatisfied need of a customer and then creates a product to meet that customer's needs. It is that process that defines the real estate development business. The building constructed by the developer is simply a by-product of the development process.

Having made that philosophical point (perhaps once too often), it is important to take note of the various product types created by real estate developers. Set forth below is a chart that identifies (1) the general types of products created by real estate developers (referred to in the remainder of this book as *projects*), and (2) the class of customers typically served by those projects. The listed product types are limited to those commercial real estate projects that are traditionally viewed as being institutional-grade and, hence, subject to acquisition by the previously-discussed institutional investor. In the vernacular used in this book, the term "commercial real estate" does not include "for sale" residential projects, such as single family residences or condominiums, because the customer base (private consumers) and the economic drivers (sales price) of those projects are markedly different from those of the other types of commercial real estate projects that are the focus of this book. In addition, the identification in the following chart of the "customers served" addresses only the direct user of the listed project type. The other "customer served" by each project type is, of course, the institutional investor who is a potential buyer of these institutional-grade projects.

Type of Project	Customers Served by Project
Office • Downtown Office Buildings • Suburban Office Buildings	Private Sector Businesses
Industrial • Warehouses • Manufacturing/R&D Facilities	Private Sector Businesses
Retail • Regional Malls • Neighborhood Strip Centers • Lifestyle Centers • Big Box Centers	Private Sector Businesses and Private Consumers
Multi-family Residential Apartments	Private Consumers
Hospitality • Hotels • Restaurants	Private Sector Businesses and Private Consumers
Mixed Use (a combination of more than one of the above project types)	Private Sector Businesses and Private Consumers

The above table is not intended to be an exhaustive listing of all the project types currently being developed by real estate developers. Rather, it is merely an attempt to highlight the principal project categories that have historically attracted the attention of the institutional real estate investor.

One development activity that is not specifically highlighted in the above list is land development.[3] While land development is an essential component of the real estate development business, it is not one that typically attracts institutional investor capital. Land development is the process of taking a vacant parcel of land and readying it for the construction of **vertical improvements** (developer-speak for buildings).

---

[3] Land development is to be sharply contrasted with land speculation where an individual or company buys land hoping that the land will significantly increase in value in the future, at which time the owner will quickly sell it for a profit. Land speculators do not attempt to add value to the land through their development efforts, but simply make a market bet that something will occur in the future that will make the purchased land more valuable.

The developer adds value to the vacant parcel by: subdividing the parcel into smaller usable tracts; extending roads, utilities, and other infrastructure throughout the parcel; and securing all governmental approvals required for the development of the parcel.[4] Land development can occur as a free-standing development activity (with the land developer selling off the developable tracts to other vertical improvement developers or users) or as a necessary adjunct for the development of a vertical improvement project on the land. For the purposes of this book, it is assumed that the developer's land development efforts are a precursor to its development of a vertical improvement project on the land.

III. PLAYERS IN THE REAL ESTATE DEVELOPMENT PROCESS

The development of a real estate project requires the coordinated efforts of a number of real estate professionals. The role the developer plays in the process is analogous to the role of the conductor of a symphony orchestra. It is the developer's job to select the various members of the orchestra (the "players" described below); to provide them with the sheet music for the performance (the overall development plan); and to coordinate the nature, timing, and scope of the performance of each of the players. Upon the completion of a successful performance, the conductor takes a bow amidst a standing ovation—and the real estate developer makes a hefty deposit of cash at its local bank.

In his book about the demise of the Olympia and York real estate company, Peter Foster neatly sums up the developer's role in the following manner:

> They are not necessarily architects or contractors, engineers or financiers, but their skill lies in bringing these specialties together to satisfy the demands of those who need space to carry out their businesses. They do not draw up blueprints or erect steel or pour concrete, but they cause these things to happen.[5]

Every real estate development project has as its genesis a developer-generated vision of how to best satisfy a real estate need of a targeted class of customers. Sinclair Lewis characterized this "vision" in the following caustic terms in his book *Babbitt*:

> Babbitt spoke well—and often—at these orgies of commercial righteousness about the "realtor's function as a seer of the future

---

[4] For an excellent exposition of how a developer can add value to land by its development activities, *see* John D. Hastie, *Real Estate Acquisition, Development and Disposition form the Developer's Perspective*, in ALI-ABA COURSE OF STUDY MATERIALS, MODERN REAL ESTATE TRANSACTIONS: PRACTICAL STRATEGIES FOR REAL ESTATE ACQUISITION, DISPOSITION, AND OWNERSHIP, Course No. SS–012, 16–19 (July 2010).

[5] PETER FOSTER, TOWERS OF DEBT: THE RISE AND FALL OF THE REICHMANNS 19 (1993).

development of the community, and as a prophetic engineer clearing the pathway for inevitable changes"—which meant that a real estate broker could make money by guessing which way the town would grow. This guessing he called Vision.[6]

The stereotypical real estate developer is Charlie Croker, the lead character in Tom Wolfe's book *A Man in Full*.[7] Charlie was an ex-All American football player, who was able to parlay his status as an athletic hero and an all-round "good old boy" into the creation of a real estate empire and the acquisition of all the toys symbolic of his position at the top of the real estate heap. Unfortunately for Charlie, he forgot about the "customer" thing, fell in love with a real estate product (a pioneering high-rise office building far outside the Atlanta business district), and ended up having all of his toys auctioned off to the highest bidder by his lender.

Today's real estate developers (at least the successful ones) are a far cry from the Charlie Croker and Babbit stereotypes. The business is now dominated by Harvard and Duke MBA grads (and I dare say a fair number of law school grads) and not by glad-handers and back-slappers like Charlie Croker. The "vision" possessed by today's developer is not simply a matter of Babbit's gut instinct (although I would be remiss if I did not recognize the importance of an "educated gut" in the development business), but more a function of a detailed analysis of demographics, logistics, financial returns, and market research. The aspiring real estate development lawyer is, therefore, forewarned that the lawyer's future client is likely to be someone who can not only talk about "dirt", but is also equally conversant on the topics of discounted cash flow, commercial mortgage backed securities, preferred returns, and tax increment financing.

The developer is charged not only with defining the vision of the development plan, but also with executing that development plan. The following is a brief description of the various players whose activities and contributions must be orchestrated by the developer during the real estate development process.

A. DESIGN PROFESSIONALS

Once the developer crystallizes its vision for satisfying the needs of its customer, it must turn to architects, engineers, and land planners to give life and definition to that vision. These design professionals, working in close concert with the developer, create preliminary schematic plans for the design and structure of the project. Once the preliminary plans are approved by the developer, the designers (usually headed by the architect) then prepare a more detailed set of plans and specifications that serve as the blueprint for the execution of the project. The plans and specifications

---

    [6]   SINCLAIR LEWIS, BABBIT 40 (1922).

    [7]   TOM WOLFE, A MAN IN FULL (1998).

are a fluid set of documents that are modified over time to reflect changes to make the project more cost-effective and to better hone in on satisfying both the perceived and actual needs of the customer. During the construction of the project, the architect's role shifts from that of a designer to that of an inspector, as it fulfills the responsibility of seeing to it that the project, as actually constructed, conforms to the design plan approved by the developer.

B. CONSTRUCTION PROFESSIONALS

The construction of the project envisioned in the architect's plans and specifications is the job of construction professionals who generally fall into one of the following three sub-categories.

- *Contractor*—The contractor is the person who has the overall responsibility for constructing the project in accordance with the plans and specifications. While the contractor's specific title may vary depending on the specific structure of its contractual arrangement with the developer (general contractor, construction manager, and design-builder are the most common position titles), its job remains the same—to construct the project on time, on budget, and in strict accordance with the approved plans and specifications. Once the plans and specifications are completed (ideally with significant input from the contractor), the contractor's task is to prepare a construction cost budget and a construction schedule. If approved by the developer, the submitted budget and schedule then become the bible for the project, with the contractor being contractually committed to build the project on budget and on time.

- *Subcontractors*—Subcontractors are the trade groups that are charged with performing the actual work of constructing the project. Examples of customary trades found on a commercial real estate project are site excavators, plumbers, electricians, steel erectors, cement contractors, landscapers, drywallers, and roofers. Each subcontractor enters into a contractual arrangement directly with the contractor, with such arrangement obligating the subcontractor to perform its piece of the work at the cost and within the time frame specified in the bid it submitted at the inception of the construction project.

- *Suppliers*—Suppliers provide the materials and supplies needed by the contractor and subcontractors to perform their respective construction tasks. Examples of construction firms falling into this sub-category are steel fabricators, concrete suppliers, and window and door companies.

C. FINANCE PROFESSIONALS

As noted earlier in this chapter, the value of a commercial real estate project is dictated not by its wonderful location or creative design, but rather by the financial returns it produces for the developer and its institutional investors—specifically, the project's net operating income and residual value. As a result, it should not be surprising that financial analysts and accountants are key players in the development of a real estate project. Financial analysts and accountants are responsible for creating, validating, and vetting both the projected and the actual financial performance of a commercial real estate project (both pre-tax and after-tax). They also are central forces supporting the developer's securing of debt and equity financing for the project on the best available price and terms (often referred to with equal parts admiration and derision as "financial engineering").

D. RISK MANAGERS

Real estate projects are rife with risk, ranging from the most basic (being that the project misses the mark in its attempt to meet an unsatisfied customer need) to those involving a specific aspect of the execution of the project development plan (for example, the risk that the project is not completed on time and on budget). As is discussed at great length later in this book, the management of these risks is the special province of the real estate development lawyer who must not only identify all of the potential risks of a particular project, but must then also try to hedge the developer's risk through a combination of creative deal structuring and accomplished document drafting. There are, however, a number of specific project risks that can be addressed through the receipt of insurance or certifications from the following third party risk managers.

- *Property Insurers*—Insurance companies provide insurance protecting the developer from risks associated with damage to the project from fire and other casualties both during and after the construction of the project. Liability insurance protecting the developer from exposure to lawsuits for the traditional "slip and fall" and other on-site injuries and property damage can also be obtained from insurance companies.

- *Title Insurers*—Forty years ago, a developer's comfort that it had good title to its land was generally provided in the form of a title abstract put together by a sole practitioner. The abstract purported to show all the title documents found with respect to the parcel of land in the county courthouse. The protection afforded by such an abstract was only as good as the malpractice coverage maintained by the preparer of the title abstract (which was usually minimal at best). Today, the quality of title to real estate is insured by mammoth title insurance companies who are obligated to compensate the real estate owner for any loss incurred if title to the real estate ends up falling short of the title quality insured by the title insurance company. The receipt of title insurance is an essential component of every commercial real estate transaction.

- *Surveyors*—A surveyor provides the developer with a visual depiction of the boundaries of the land that the developer is buying and the location of any roadways, utility lines, and other improvements located on the developer's land and adjacent land parcels. The survey, when read in conjunction with the title policy provided by the title insurance company, serves to confirm that the size, location, and character of the land are consistent with the developer's overall development plan for the land.

- *Environmental Firms*—A standard part of every real estate acquisition is the receipt of an environmental assessment from a qualified environmental firm certifying that the property is free of any environmental contaminants or other hazardous substances (or if, any such contaminant or substance is present, a statement as to the identity, location, and concentration of such contaminant or substance). The receipt of a well-crafted, environmental certification from a qualified and financially-sound environmental firm goes a long way toward ameliorating the project risk associated with adverse environmental conditions. A development of fairly recent vintage is environmental insurance issued by an insurance company that is designed to protect the landowner from various types of environmental risk.

- *Wetland Consultants*—Wetlands are now recognized as being an integral part of our ecosystem. Laws have been adopted that protect the destruction or alteration of areas falling with the definition of "protected wetlands." There are few occurrences that have a more deleterious impact on the budget and schedule of a development project than a determination that the developer's construction activities have improperly disturbed a wetlands area. As a result, it is now part of the developer's standard pre-acquisition checklist to receive a certification from a qualified wetlands consultant that the parcel to be acquired does not infringe on any protected wetlands.

- *Appraisers*—Every development project has at its core a projection of the fair market value of the project. Central to the validity of that value projection are the financial and demographic assumptions made by the developer concerning matters such as the amount of the rent that it will be able to collect from its tenants, the length of time it will take to fully lease the project, and the expense of operating the project in the future. Developers are a fairly confident lot who do not believe that they need any third party confirmation concerning the accuracy of their financial projections. Banks and other financial institutions that provide the developer with the funds necessary to develop its projects tend not to be quite as sanguine about the rectitude of the developer's financial assumptions. Lenders routinely require, as a condition to the making of a real estate loan, that a qualified appraiser issue an appraisal report confirming the accuracy of the developer's financial projections. While an appraisal is not a guaranty of project value, it does provide comfort to the lender (and also indirectly to the developer) that the project's economics have a solid basis in financial and market reality.

E. LENDERS

Simply stated, developers love to use "other people's money" when they develop real estate projects. In the typical real estate deal, 70–90% of the project's development costs are funded through a construction loan obtained by the developer (although in the years immediately following the Great Recession of 2008, that loan-to-cost ratio dropped dramatically to 40–60%).

The construction loan is almost always secured by a first mortgage on the subject real estate and is typically for a term of 24–36 months (being the time period generally considered sufficient to complete construction and fully lease the project to rent-paying tenants). Construction loans are generally fully *recourse* to the developer or another creditworthy entity affiliated with the developer (meaning that all of that entity's assets can be attacked to pay off the loan). Commercial banks are the usual providers of construction loans.

Once the project is fully leased, the developer customarily turns to a permanent lender to provide the funds necessary to pay off the short-term construction loan. In contrast to construction debt, permanent debt is generally *nonrecourse* to the developer (meaning that the developer is not personally liable for the repayment of the loan) and has a term of five to ten years. Historically, the primary providers of permanent debt have been insurance companies, pension plans, and other financial institutions.

Construction and permanent loans are the traditional forms of debt used to finance the development, ownership, and operation of commercial real estate projects. There are, however, countless other loan arrangements used to finance real estate projects. Among the techniques that are most in vogue in the current lending environment are mezzanine debt, securitized loans, and tax-exempt bond financing. Those arrangements are all designed to give the developer greater options and more flexibility when structuring the financing of its project development costs.

F.   INVESTORS

This chapter has already discussed at some length the role that institutional investors (life insurance companies, pension plans, and other financial institutions) play as a customer of the real estate developer. As stated in that earlier discussion, the institutional investor's purchase of a completed real estate project represents the ultimate exit strategy for the developer. The investor's purchase of the project can take many forms, ranging from the outright purchase of fee simple title to the project to the investor's formation of a joint venture with the developer. In a real estate joint venture, the developer usually cashes out a portion of its interest in the project, but retains a limited interest in the project's future financial performance.

As noted earlier, developers generally finance the majority of their development costs with construction debt. The remaining project costs are funded with equity provided either by the developer or by third party investors. Historically, the only investors who were willing to provide the developer with upfront equity were the developer's "family and friends"— for example, doctors, dentists, in-laws, and golfing buddies. Institutional investors were reluctant to invest in a project before the income stream from committed project tenants was fully stabilized. However, as institutional investors continue to chase ways to increase the yield on their real estate investments, it has become much more commonplace for the institutional investor to invest in development projects from their inception, thereby giving the developer yet another avenue to satisfy its desire to use "other people's money" to finance its development activities.

G.   OPERATORS

Once construction of a real estate project is completed (and, in reality, even before then), the developer has to ensure that the following two distinct functions are properly performed.

- *Leasing*—The responsibility for performing this function is generally assigned to a licensed real estate broker (commonly referred to as a *listing broker*) whose job it is to find tenants to lease space in the developer's project. This is the real estate developer's version of the marketing department found in other businesses.

- *Property Management*—Every completed project needs someone to make sure that the toilets flush, building security is maintained, and the rent is collected. These tasks are generally assigned to a *property manager*.

The developer may either hire independent brokerage and property management firms or hire people on the developer's own payroll to perform these two tasks. The decision as to which of these alternatives to select is largely a matter of the developer's personal preference and business style. Small development companies often choose to outsource these two jobs to third parties. This permits the developer to offload to others the ongoing cost of paying the overhead and other general administrative expenses of the personnel required to perform the leasing and management functions. As the developer's business grows, operating and cost efficiencies are often achieved by pulling those functions in-house.

H. ECONOMIC DEVELOPMENT OFFICERS

Prior to the 1990's, governmental officials were seldom, if ever, viewed as positive contributors to a real estate development project. Rather, they were perceived as obstacles that the developer had to overcome in order to bring its development project to fruition. However, over the last 20+ years, it has suddenly dawned on appointed and elected officials that one way to augment a state or local government's revenue base (without having to raise taxes on the citizenry) is to entice developers to build job-producing projects within the government's geographic boundaries. This recognition has caused virtually every political subdivision in the country to create a new staff position for an economic development officer. It is the economic development officer's job to put together a menu of tax abatements, grants, and other financial and governmental incentives to entice a developer to build its project in a particular locale. A government's decision to incentivize a private development project often proves to be the difference between a project that never gets off the ground and one that becomes a tremendous success.

I.   PUBLIC SECTOR

The involvement of the public sector in the real estate development process is highlighted in the following quote:

Private sector real estate developers have a public sector partner in every deal—no exceptions—whether or not they choose to recognize that partner. The government—federal, state, and local—controls the U.S. system of capitalism under which private developers operate. Real estate development is a highly regulated process. Property law, public infrastructure, financial market rules, zoning, building permits, and impact fees are all part of the public sector's realm. . . . [I]f developers do not work hand in hand with local governments, giving them the same amount of respect and attention they would give a private sector partner delays and problems are likely to occur. . . . Time is money in real estate development, and overlooking or antagonizing . . . public partners often costs a developer time, which translates into more interest payments and more significant costs. More important, the public sector can permanently delay a developer and can even change the rules in the middle of the game. . . . For these reasons, it pays for private developers to treat the public sector as a partner from the outset. The partnership is like a marriage: it can take many forms, but if it fails, it is painful.[8]

J. LAWYERS

Oh yeah, I almost forgot to mention one last player in the real estate development process—the real estate development lawyer.

IV. THE REAL ESTATE DEVELOPMENT LAWYER

A real estate development lawyer's job is to represent the interests of the developer in all aspects of the real estate development process. In this respect, the role of the real estate development lawyer is similar to the role played by a merger and acquisition specialist, securities lawyer, or any other transactional business lawyer. The lawyer assumes primary responsibility for papering the terms and conditions of the client's business transaction and advising the client on how best to deal with the various business and legal risks inherent in that transaction.

A real estate development lawyer's practice is, however, markedly different in a number of respects from the practices of other transactional business lawyers.

- The real estate development lawyer is involved in virtually every aspect of his client's business. A banking lawyer handling a structured financing arrangement for a retail clothing store has little, if any, reason to be overly involved with or knowledgeable about the client's core business. Because the real estate development business is essentially nothing more than an endless stream of legal transactions, the real estate development lawyer is continually immersed

---

[8] MIKE E. MILES, GAYLE L. BERENS, AND MARC A. WEISS, REAL ESTATE DEVELOPMENT, PRINCIPLES AND PROCESS 12–13 (4th ed. 2007).

in the developer's business activities. As such, the mantra introduced at the inception of this chapter about the necessity of understanding the client's business takes on heightened significance for the real estate development lawyer.

- A real estate development lawyer must be proficient in a number of legal fields in order to effectively represent his client. The practices of most transactional lawyers involve specializing in one limited area of the law—for example, securities law for the lawyer mentioned above who is handling a debt offering for a retail client. That degree of specialization is not feasible for a real estate development lawyer. The nature of the real estate development business is such that a lawyer representing a developer must have a thorough comprehension of a broad array of legal disciplines, including real estate, tax, securities, finance, environmental, bankruptcy, zoning, construction, and partnership law.

- A real estate development lawyer generally must "go it alone" in representing a developer. Unlike a merger or a securities offering, most real estate development deals cannot support an army of highly-specialized lawyers. Both the economics and intertwining nature of the various components of the real estate development process dictate that the real estate development lawyer not only assume direct hands-on responsibility for the structuring of the development deal, but also for the deal's execution.

- A real estate development lawyer's actions can have a dramatic impact on the profitability (or lack thereof) of a developer's development project. The lawyer handling the clothing merchant's debt offering does not have any real impact on how many sweaters the client sells. It is the color, style, and composition of the sweater that dictates the profit the client derives from its sweater sales. In the real estate development business, it is as much the developer's skill in managing the risks inherent in the development process as it is the nature of the product produced by that process that ultimately dictates how much money the developer makes on the project. The real estate lawyer's efforts have a direct impact on the quality of the developer's risk management efforts and, hence, on the overall success of the developer's project.

The differences noted above between the practice of the real estate development lawyer and that of other types of transactional business lawyers are intended to be just that—differences between practice types, without any value judgments being made as to which practice type is more interesting, challenging, or lucrative. "Beauty truly is in the eye of the beholder" when it comes to a young lawyer's selection of a practice area. As a lawyer who has spent my entire career representing developers, I do, however, admit to a bias in favor of real estate development law.

A. THE REAL ESTATE DEVELOPMENT LAWYER'S ROLES

The real estate development lawyer plays a wide variety of roles in the representation of a developer. Each of those roles requires the lawyer to learn and continually fine-tune a diverse set of skills.

1. Advisor

I love to read trashy lawyer novels for the pure escape value of reading about lawyers who not only devise ingenious legal strategies, but also end up physically taking down the bad guy. I find the following passage in the Steve Martini novel *Double Tap* to be wonderfully descriptive of the essence of being a transactional business lawyer.

> What do you think I should do? You can hurdle the bar exam and sally forth to spend decades in front of the bench. You can deflect thunderbolts tossed by the gods in black robes and do battle daily with other lawyers. But in the end it is this question posed by [a client] that is the riddle most feared by every attorney I have ever met.[9]

Rest assured that your developer client will frequently ask you that fear-inducing question—what do you think I should do? Moreover, the question will not be limited to so-called "legal" issues on which you can wax eloquently for hours without ever coming to any real conclusion. No, the developer is much more likely to ask you the dreaded "what do you think I should do" question about fundamental business issues, such as whether the developer should waive the contingencies in a purchase contract and proceed to close on the purchase of a multi-million dollar parcel of land. While the real estate development lawyer cannot make the decision for the developer, the lawyer must be willing to step up and give honest, unvarnished advice when the developer asks for it. Trust me when I tell you that developers do not tolerate lawyers who are incapable of providing direct answers to the client's equally direct questions. When the inevitable question is asked by your client, just keep in mind the admonition leveled at me by the client I mentioned at the outset of this chapter—"Frankly son, I don't care which way the wind is blowing, just bring the damn ship in."

---

[9] STEVE MARTINI, DOUBLE TAP 182 (2005).

2. Deal Designer

The real estate development lawyer is responsible for concocting the deal design and structure for a real estate project. The structure ultimately put in place by the lawyer must be tax-efficient and consistent with the developer's tolerance for risk. The structure must also effectively integrate all of the developer's relationships with the other project participants—that is, lenders, investors, construction professionals, etc. Finally, the selected structure must provide the developer with an acceptable exit strategy at each stage of the deal. The development of the right deal design requires the lawyer to marshal not only a thorough working knowledge of real estate, tax, and partnership law concepts, but also a full understanding of the client's business and financial condition.

3. Risk vs. Reward Analyst

As mentioned earlier in this chapter, the success of any real estate project is dependent on how well the developer manages project risk. The real estate development lawyer should take the lead in identifying and then dealing with all project risks in a fashion that is appropriate within the context of the particular deal. This does not mean that it is the lawyer's role to eliminate all risks attendant to a particular real estate project. In truth, the only way to eliminate all project risks is to kill the deal—something that bad lawyers do way too often. The real estate development lawyer's job is to lead the developer through a risk-reward analysis, so that the risks ultimately taken by the developer are reasonably justifiable in light of the potential rewards to be derived by the developer from its participation in the project.

4. Negotiator

The real estate development lawyer usually serves as the developer's chief negotiator on all deal issues (legal and business). In performing this role, the lawyer must put aside the competitive drive to "win" every issue and instead focus on those issues that are essential to the developer being in a position to move forward with the project. Nowhere is the concept of a "win-win" outcome of more consequence than in the context of a real estate development deal. In an effort to produce such a "win-win" result, it is incumbent upon the real estate development lawyer to not only understand the developer's business objectives, but also those of the business person and lawyer sitting on the other side of the table.

5. Drafter

If a lawyer is going to be successful in the practice of real estate development law, the lawyer must master the art of communicating in writing in a clear and concise manner. One only needs to look at the mounds of documents cluttering the table at a real estate closing to realize that a real estate development lawyer without exceptional drafting skills is like a singer with laryngitis.

6. Enforcer

Every client occasionally needs its lawyer to act as the "bad cop" when trying to enforce the provisions of a contract. It is crucial for the real estate development lawyer to keep this fact in mind when designing the structure of the client's development deal. As stated by one noted development lawyer:

> If the transaction was structured and the documents prepared with enforcement in mind, [litigating the documents] will present no major trauma for the attorney or the client; if not, both of them might be in for major surprises.[10]

B. TEN CHARACTERISTICS OF A SUCCESSFUL REAL ESTATE DEVELOPMENT LAWYER

The following are ten characteristics that any successful real estate development lawyer must possess.

- The lawyer must have a sound understanding of the entirety of the business deal and, in particular, the project economics of that deal.

- The lawyer must have a solid working knowledge of the multiple legal disciplines that impact a real estate development deal—that is, real estate, tax, finance, contract, securities, environmental, bankruptcy, public, zoning, insurance, construction, and public law.

- The lawyer must be able to communicate the developer's positions in writing in a clear, concise, and strategic manner.

- The lawyer must be a *deal maker* and not a *deal killer.*

- The lawyer must be able establish and maintain solid mutually respectful working relationships with all of the players in the real estate development process.

- The lawyer must never hide behind the law when the developer asks for advice.

- The lawyer must avoid the temptation to show off by overlawyering a deal.

- The lawyer must have both the judgment and the inclination to make quick decisions.

---

[10] *See* HASTIE, *supra* note 4, at 13.

- The lawyer must feel comfortable working alone, without the safety net provided by the presence of an army of supporting lawyers.

- The lawyer must understand that success is measured not by the brilliance and creativity of the lawyer's deal structure or by the comprehensiveness of the lawyer's documents, but rather by how well the deal structure and documents serve the client's business objectives.

Practice Tip #1-1: Why Be a Real Estate Development Lawyer?

It is no doubt apparent by now that I thoroughly enjoyed my career as a real estate development lawyer. I had a blast representing developers (they are definitely interesting folks) and made a few bucks along the way. But I do not want you to just take my word about how cool it is to be a real estate development lawyer. Here are several reasons why you might want to think about a career in real estate development law.

- *The fundamentals of the real estate development business model are strong and enduring (which is a good thing for a lawyer who represents developers). People and businesses will always need shelter to live and work. The nature of that shelter will continue to evolve as technology becomes an ever-increasing part of our daily lives and the millennials replace the baby boomers as the dominant consumer generation—but shelter of some type will still be needed.*

- *Real estate is an attractive investment alternative to institutional investors. While real estate is certainly a cyclical industry (witness what happened during the Great Recession of 2008), the industry always makes a comeback once the supply and demand curves attain an acceptable equilibrium. From the perspective of the institutional investor community, investing in real estate produces a better yield than an investment in Treasury notes and a less volatile return than an investment in stocks and bonds.*

- *The real estate development business is local in nature and cannot be successfully conducted or dominated from a high-rise office on Wall Street. The "local" nature of the business means that there will always be plenty of work for real estate development lawyers in each geographic market.*

- *Similarly, the real estate development business is not capable of being outsourced to areas outside of the United States.*

"Boots on the ground" are an essential component of the real estate development business.

- *The real estate development business really is a "big deal." The Census Bureau's estimate of spending on new construction in the United States in 2016 is $1.182 trillion, with the commercial real estate sector contributing almost $430 billion of that amount.*[11]

- *As you will better appreciate when you read the remaining chapters of this text, the real estate development business is intensely legal in nature. The business is an endless stream of legal transactions ranging from the initial acquisition of the project land, to the construction, leasing, and financing of vertical improvements, and, ultimately, to the sale of the project. It falls to the real estate development lawyer to negotiate and paper the deal at each stage of the project's development. This is especially true in the increasingly complex arena of the commercial real estate practice. All this means one very important thing for the real estate development lawyer—FEES and plenty of them, and, if you get lucky, maybe a right to participate in the venture's profits.*

- *You do not have to slave away at a BigLaw shop with hundreds of other lawyers to practice real estate development law. In fact, the most successful real estate lawyers I know practice with small boutique firms where jeans and t-shirts are the norm rather than a suit and tie.*

- *You get to visit construction sites and wear a hard hat.*

- *Finally, working with and around real estate developers is a hoot. A developer is the embodiment of the entrepreneurial spirit—bright, creative, and fun-loving. The best part is that the lawyer on occasion gets to drive by a building and say to family members "I helped make that." Top that one litigators.*

V. SUMMARY

There is no precise definition of the area of practice known as real estate development law. At its most basic level, real estate development law is the compendium of knowledge and skills that a lawyer must possess in order to help a real estate developer achieve its business goals. A real estate development lawyer must have not only a thorough understanding

---

[11] *See* CENSUS BUREAU OF THE DEPARTMENT OF TREASURY, CENSUS BUREAU NEWS—VALUE OF CONSTRUCTION PUT IN PLACE AT A GLANCE (November 1, 2016), available at https://www.census.gov/construction/c30/pdf/pr201611.pdf (last visited on January 19, 2017).

of a number of substantive areas of the law, but also a solid working knowledge of the development business. Always remember the mantra—*If you want to succeed as a real estate development lawyer, you must first understand the real estate development business.*

CHAPTER 2

THE TEN STAGES OF A REAL ESTATE DEVELOPMENT PROJECT

■ ■ ■

I. INTRODUCTION

Chapter 1 touched upon the roles a real estate development lawyer plays in representing a developer. That discussion necessarily started with an examination of the business of real estate development. The real estate development business is, in essence, made up of a series of real estate projects, each of which is a micro-business in and of itself.

This chapter takes a look in a more specific and focused manner at what a real estate development lawyer actually does in the course of the lawyer's practice. That inquiry is prefaced with an examination of the nature and scope of the business activity that is supported by the real estate development lawyer's efforts—that is, the real estate project. For the purposes of this chapter, a "real estate project" means an institutional-grade commercial real estate project that is leased to private sector business tenants. The discussion in this chapter is, however, equally applicable to other types of real estate development projects—for example, the construction of a four-unit apartment building adjacent to a college campus.

II. WHAT IS A REAL ESTATE PROJECT?

Each real estate project developed by a real estate developer is, in effect, a separate business. Some projects involve the development of a single building for one customer. Such projects can have duration of two years or less and often have a fully-dedicated development staff of only one or two people. Then there are projects that consist of the development of a massive mixed use site for a multitude of customers, involving the developer's expenditure of hundreds of millions of dollars. Those projects can take upwards of ten years to complete and frequently require a fully-dedicated development staff of ten or more people.

Regardless of its size, each real estate project starts in the same fashion—by the developer identifying an unsatisfied need of a targeted customer or customer class and then coming up with an idea of how best to satisfy that need. Once the developer devises its initial vision for a particular project, the project then advances through a series of stages that, by and large, are consistent for every project regardless of product type or location. Those stages are the focus of the remainder of this chapter.

III. THE TEN STAGES OF A REAL ESTATE DEVELOPMENT PROJECT

Many books and articles have been written about the various elements and stages of a real estate development project. Most of those works are written from the perspective of the real estate developer and, hence, are heavily weighted toward the stages of a project's life cycle having to do with the developer's formulation of its initial vision and its subsequent testing of that vision to determine the feasibility of moving forward with the development project. For real estate purists, the classic definition of feasibility was proffered by James A. Grasskamp in 1972, when he wrote that a "real estate project is 'feasible' when the real estate analyst determines that there is a reasonable likelihood of satisfying explicit objectives when a selected course of action is tested for fit to a context of specific constraints and limited resources."[1] Developers tend to reduce this definition to a more simple statement of feasibility—"the deal works."

The vision and feasibility stages of the real estate development process are uniquely the province of the developer as entrepreneur and visionary. The lawyer (almost by definition, neither a visionary, nor an entrepreneur) rarely plays anything but a minor peripheral role in these initial two stages of the real estate development process.

The lawyer's role starts once the developer has come up with its initial idea for the project and reached at least a preliminary conclusion as to the project's feasibility. From the perspective of the real estate development lawyer, the ten stages of a real estate development project are as follows:

1. Gaining control of the site;

2. Securing essential governmental approvals and incentives;

3. Forming and capitalizing the project entity;

4. Closing the land acquisition;

5. Securing construction financing;

6. Designing and constructing the project;

7. Negotiating the project lease;

8. Executing an interim exit strategy;

---

[1] James A. Grasskamp, *A Rational Approach to Feasibility Analysis*, APPRAISAL JOURNAL 515 (1972).

9.   Operating the project; and

10. Selling the project.

These ten stages are present in every real estate project. They do not, however, occur in a neat sequential order. It is a rare deal, indeed, where at least three of the stages do not converge and play themselves out over exactly the same period of time. By way of example, it is far from unusual for the real estate development lawyer to be negotiating a contract with a landowner seeking control of the site at the exact same time the lawyer is negotiating a construction loan commitment with a bank and the specifics of a tax abatement package with representatives of the local municipality. The overlapping and relative fluidity of these development stages is yet another reason why the real estate developer lawyer must gain an early and thorough understanding of all the components of the underlying business deal.

The pages that follow examine in summary fashion each of the ten stages of a real estate development project. That examination first focuses on the developer's business objectives and then moves on to a discussion of the lawyer's activities in support of those business objectives.

A. STAGE 1: GAINING CONTROL OF THE SITE

Developer's Business Objectives. It is assumed for the purposes of this discussion that the developer has already selected a site that it believes is an ideal (or at least acceptable) location for the creation of a project to satisfy the needs of its targeted customer. Once that site is selected, the developer's business objective is to gain control of that site as quickly and cheaply as possible.

It is quite likely at this stage of the project's life that the developer has made only a preliminary decision of the feasibility of the project. While the developer may feel pretty good about the location of the site and the existence of the customer's unsatisfied real estate need, the developer has probably not yet worked out the final project economics, secured debt or equity financing, or actually locked down a customer for the project. All the developer knows is that the project has potential if it is located on the selected site. The developer's goal at this stage of the game is simply to tie up the site long enough to permit the developer to do all those things that are necessary to permit it to reach a final conclusion on whether the project is a "go" or a "no go." What the developer has in mind when he tells his lawyer to "tie up" the site is the taking of whatever minimal actions are required to prevent the developer's competitors from swooping in to gain control of the land and, therefore, capture the project's potential. Gaining legal control of the site and not actually buying the site is the developer's objective in Stage 1.

Lawyer's Job. This stage is where the real estate development lawyer has the first opportunity to add value to the developer's project. The lawyer's activities during this stage are as follows.

- *Learn the Business Deal*—Before putting pen to paper (or, in today's world, "fingers to keyboard"), the real estate development lawyer must first acquire a solid working knowledge of all aspects of the developer's project, including the project's targeted customer, product type, financial projections, and development schedule.

- *Prepare the What-If List*—This is where the lawyer's value-add shines at its brightest. It falls to the real estate development lawyer to go through the mental gymnastics of identifying all those foreseeable events and conditions, the occurrence or existence of which could lead the developer to decide to scrap the project. These are what my first mentor called *WHAT-IFS*: what if the land is not zoned for commercial development; what if hazardous substances are found on the site; what if title to the land is unmarketable, etc. Once the what-ifs are identified, the lawyer must then figure out how best to protect the client from the occurrence of the negative event or circumstance by either (1) identifying a method to confirm the non-existence of the event or circumstance in the subject project (for example, by requiring the receipt of a clean environmental report certifying that no adverse environmental condition exists on the land), or (2) providing an acceptable exit strategy for the client if a negative event or circumstance is found to exist in the project (for example, the grant to the developer of a right to terminate its obligation to purchase the land if an adverse environmental condition is found to exist on the land).

- *Select the Right Form of Contract*—Purchase agreements are a lot like clothing, in that there is no one agreement that is right for every occasion. Just as one would not wear flannel pajamas to a wedding, the real estate development lawyer should not use a 100-page *killer form*, purchase agreement to paper the developer's purchase of a two-acre tract from an unsophisticated landowner.

- *Prepare and Negotiate a Contract That Serves the Client's Business Objective*—In preparing the purchase contract, the real estate development lawyer must always keep in mind what the client's business objective is at this stage of the project—that is, to gain legal control of the land long enough to permit the developer to figure out if the project is feasible. Preparing a contract that serves this business objective, while at the same time protecting the client from the existence of the dreaded "what-ifs," is an art form that must be mastered by any lawyer who aspires to success in the real estate development field.

B. STAGE 2: SECURING GOVERNMENTAL APPROVALS AND INCENTIVES

Developer's Business Objectives. Before the developer purchases the land, it wants to have in hand all governmental approvals that are essential to the developer's decision to move forward with the development of the project. The identity of the "essential" governmental approvals varies from deal to deal, depending on the uniqueness of the deal and the political climate in the jurisdiction in which the project is situated. At the bare minimum, the developer wants confirmation that the property is zoned to permit its development in the contemplated manner and that any governmental incentives needed to make the project's economics work are in place (for example, the grant of a tax abatement or the government's agreement to fund the construction of needed off-site infrastructure). In an ideal world, the developer will have received all requisite governmental approvals prior to its purchase of the land (culminating in the issuance of a building permit for the full construction of the project). However, the real estate developer does not live in an ideal world and is almost always willing to proceed with the land purchase, before its receipt of those governmental approvals that are either perfunctory in nature or that the developer's experience tells it will eventually be issued without controversy or unreasonable delay.

Lawyer's Job. This is the one stage where the extent of the real estate development lawyer's participation can vary a great deal from project to project. The real estate development lawyer must first sit down with the developer to determine which governmental approvals fall into the "essential" category mentioned above. It is quite common for the developer to take the lead in securing those governmental approvals that, while essential to the project, are not perceived to be the subject of much political controversy. Unfortunately, in today's politically divisive culture, very few governmental actions fall into the noncontroversial category. It is the real estate development lawyer's job to be sufficiently well-versed in the legal parameters surrounding the sought after governmental approval, so that the lawyer can come to the client's rescue if and when things get sticky. If things get really sticky (for example, if the developer wants to build a Walmart superstore adjacent to a high-end residential subdivision), then the developer should strongly consider bringing in political muscle in the form of separate zoning counsel who can leverage a pre-existing relationship with the local politicos to secure the desired approval. A good zoning lawyer possesses a unique combination of the networking skills of a lobbyist and the analytical and presentation skills of a litigator. While it is important for the real estate development lawyer to have a thorough understanding of zoning law and procedure, it is equally important for the real estate development lawyer to know when to turn matters over to a full-time zoning lawyer.

C. STAGE 3: FORMING AND CAPITALIZING THE PROJECT ENTITY

Developer's Business Objectives. Few developers profess to be experts when it comes to structuring either the entity that will own the project or the manner in which outside equity investors will participate in that entity. Developers do, however, have very specific expectations (some might say "demands" is a better word choice) as to the outcome of that structuring:

- The structure must be "tax efficient" (lawyer-speak for the developer's desire to minimize the tax it pays on the profits generated from the real estate project);

- The structure must limit the developer's personal liability for project risks;

- The structure must vest as much decision-making control as possible with the developer (developers give whole new meaning to the term "control freak"); and

- The structure must result in the investment by outside equity providers being "cheap capital" (meaning that the financial return paid to the outside equity providers is as low as possible and, in all events, less than the return paid to the developer if the project is successful).

Lawyer's Job. At Stage 2, the development lawyer is much more a tax, securities, corporate, and partnership lawyer than a real estate lawyer. It is this project stage, more than any other, that demands that the development lawyer have a full and effective understanding of the economics of the subject real estate project. The development lawyer must first select the proper form of the legal entity that will own the project. The lawyer must then draft legal documents to govern (1) the manner in which the entity is capitalized and managed, and (2) the way in which the project's profits and losses are allocated among the developer and its outside equity investors. In doing so, the development lawyer must be mindful of meeting the expectations of the developer, no matter how unrealistic certain of those expectations may be. The real estate development lawyer must also seek to imbue the entity's governing documents with sufficient flexibility to cover the future twists and turns in the project's development and the maturation of the relationship between the developer and the equity investor. Designing appropriate exit strategies to deal with those twists and turns is one of the development lawyer's biggest challenges during this project stage.

D. STAGE 4: CLOSING THE LAND ACQUISITION

Developer's Business Objectives. The closing of the land acquisition is the watershed moment when the developer effectively makes the decision to proceed with the project. Before it commits the funding necessary to acquire the land, the developer must have first reached a comfort level that the project is feasible—that is, that the rewards of moving forward with the project sufficiently outweigh the risks associated with the project. Once the decision has been made that the project is feasible, it then is time for the developer to begin executing its development plan for the project. In most situations, that means closing on the purchase of the land and promptly beginning construction of the project.

Lawyer's Job. As the keeper of the what-if list, it is the real estate development lawyer's job to make sure that all the conditions specified in the purchase contract have been met to the developer's reasonable satisfaction. These conditions include (1) the successful conclusion of all project due diligence, (2) the determination that title to the land is marketable, (3) the securing of all requisite governmental approvals for the project, (4) the validation of the truth of all representations and warranties made in the contract by the land seller, and (5) the occurrence of all other events specifically identified as conditions precedent to the developer's obligation in the purchase contract. If all the contractual conditions have been satisfied, the real estate development lawyer must next turn to orchestrating all of the moving parts and players that make up a real estate closing. Much of what a lawyer does in preparing for and then effecting the land acquisition closing is more logistical than legal in nature. The closing checklist, which itemizes all those things that have to be done and all those documents that have to be executed and delivered at or before closing, is the lawyer's best friend during the closing process. As one author so aptly put it when describing why clients turn over the closing process to their lawyers—"Lawyers are diligent, obsessive and careful."[2] While these characteristics sometimes get in the way in one's personal life, they are the perfect skills for the real estate development lawyer to possess when serving as the coordinator of the closing process.

E. STAGE 5: OBTAINING CONSTRUCTION FINANCING

Developer's Business Objectives. Most developers try to fund somewhere between 70–90% of their development costs with construction debt obtained from a commercial bank or other financial institution. The

---

2   *See* JOSHUA STEIN, A PRACTICAL GUIDE TO REAL ESTATE 173 (2001).

developer wants to achieve three basic goals when securing construction financing for the project:

- It wants the cost of the debt to be as cheap as possible;

- It wants to be able to draw down on the construction loan when and as necessary to pay its development costs; and

- It wants to try to limit its personal liability on the construction debt.

Lawyer's Job. The focus of the lawyer's attention during the course of negotiating the construction loan documents is threefold—(1) addressing all those specific situations where the funding needs of the developer's project are at odds with the standard loan disbursement provisions of the documents (for example, the funding of the developer's fees upfront and not pro rata over the construction term), (2) inserting as much flexibility as reasonably practicable in the loan documents, so that the developer can respond in an effective manner to unexpected developments during the construction period (for example, reserving the right to use cost savings in one category of construction expense to fund budget busts in another category), and (3) including provisions in the loan documents that seek to limit the circumstances under which the developer will be personally liable for the repayment of the loan (for example, providing that the loan becomes partially non-recourse to the developer upon the leasing of a stated portion of the project to creditworthy tenants). It is imperative that the real estate development lawyer understand not only the business objectives of the developer, but also those of the lender. By understanding the perspectives of both parties, the development lawyer is better equipped to successfully negotiate changes to the loan documents that serve the developer's interests without eviscerating the legitimate business needs of the lender.

F. STAGE 6: DESIGNING AND CONSTRUCTING THE PROJECT

Developer's Business Objectives. The developer has two objectives during Stage 6:

- The creation of a project design that is aesthetically and functionally attractive to both potential users of the project and institutional investors; and

- The completion of project construction on budget and on time.

Achieving these two objectives requires the developer to be extremely hands on during this stage of the project, meeting at least weekly with both the project architect and contractor to review the progress of construction and prepare an action plan to address any unexpected developments.

Lawyer's Job. It falls to the real estate development lawyer to prepare contracts with all of the design and construction professionals (principally the architect and general contractor). The contracts must spell out in a consistent and complete manner the respective roles and responsibilities of every person who participates in the design and construction of the project. The documents should also make it clear that the developer (and not the architect or the contractor) is the final arbiter of all decisions that need to be made during this project stage. Finally, it is the real estate development lawyer's job to add sufficient teeth to the documents to incentivize the design and construction professionals to complete construction of the project on time, on budget, and in full accordance with the project design selected by the developer.

G. STAGE 7: NEGOTIATING THE PROJECT LEASE

Developer's Business Objectives. The prior six project stages are all centered on the cost side of the developer's business. Stage 7 is where the developer makes its money. The profitability of a project is directly tied to the developer's success in meeting the following three leasing objectives:

- The project should be leased to creditworthy tenants at rents that are consistent with or better than the project's initial financial projections;

- The lease-up of the project should occur within the time frames set forth in the project's business plan; and

- The project should be leased on business and legal terms that are consistent with the expectations of the developer's "other customer"—that is, the institutional investor who will ultimately invest either debt or equity in the project.

The developer's profit on the project will suffer if it fails to meet any of these objectives.

Lawyer's Job. During Stage 7, the real estate development lawyer becomes an integral part of the developer's marketing team. In Stages 1 through 6, the developer is the consumer (buying land, seeking governmental approvals, securing construction financing, etc.). At the leasing stage, the developer is selling its product to its customer. The last thing a developer needs at this crucial money-making stage of the project is a lawyer who revels in playing the role of a hard-ass by preparing the most egregious, one-sided lease imaginable and then being intractable in a fervent resolve to win the negotiation of every point in the lease document. Tenants have choices and one choice they often make is not to deal with a developer that is represented by a lawyer who chooses to kill and not make deals.

Conversely, a lawyer can add real value to the developer's project if the lawyer:

- Prepares a relatively short lease document that covers the essential deal points and protects the developer's legitimate business interests, but is still readable and relatively user-friendly;

- Focuses the lease negotiations on those provisions that make or save the developer real money (for example, the rent, operating expense reimbursement, and tenant improvement provisions) and limits the amount of time spent on the negotiation of relatively insignificant legal issues (for example, the attempt to craft a pluperfect subordination or eminent domain clause);

- Makes sure that the terms of the lease conform to the expectations and requirements of the institutional investor community; and

- Includes provisions that make the lease easier (and therefore, more cost effective) for the developer's property manager to administer.

A real estate development lawyer who follows these four simple rules will make money for the developer in both the short-term and the long-term.

H. STAGE 8: EXECUTING AN INTERIM EXIT STRATEGY

Developer's Business Objectives. Once the project is fully leased and cash flowing, the developer faces the question of what to do next—should it sell the project outright or should it retain full or partial ownership of the project for a further period of time.

- *Sale of Project*—The advantages of a quick project sale are that (1) it puts cash into the pocket of the developer in an amount equal to the sum of its capital contributions to the venture, plus the incremental value of the project over its development costs, and (2) it eliminates any risk that a future occurrence (for example, a tenant bankruptcy or a downturn in the economy) will erode the profit inherent in the project. An outright sale of the project is, however, a taxable event and subjects the developer to income tax on the excess of the project's sales price over the project's adjusted tax basis (which, at this early stage in the project's history, is generally equal to the project's development costs). Developers who regularly opt to sell a project as soon as it is leased and cash flowing are called ***merchant builders***.

- ***Retention of Ownership***—Many developers prefer to hold on to projects for an extended period of time, in order to take advantage of both (1) the continuing positive cash flow produced from the project, and (2) the anticipated increase in the value of the project over time. By doing so, the developer postpones the imposition of any tax on the project's profit until the date of the project's ultimate sale. The retention of an ownership interest in the project does, however, subject the developer to the ongoing risk that something will happen in the future that decreases (or wholly eliminates) both the project's positive cash flow and its incremental value. A developer can try to limit this risk by retaining only partial ownership of the project. Developers who regularly opt to hold on to the ownership of all or a part of their projects for an extended period of time are referred to in the real estate industry as ***portfolio builders***.

If the developer decides to retain an ownership position in the project, it should seek to pay off its construction loan as soon as possible after the project is fully leased. The typical construction loan has three features that do not comport with the developer's continuing ownership of a fully-leased project:

- The developer (or one of its affiliates) is personally liable for the repayment of the construction loan;

- The interest rate of a construction loan is a variable rate that is subject to increase if the financial index to which it is tied increases (for example, the prime rate or the London Interbank Offered Rate); and

- The loan term matures shortly after the completion of the project (usually no more than one or two years after completion).

A developer who wants to retain ownership of a project (in full or in part) can do so and still pay off the construction loan by (1) replacing the construction loan with a permanent non-recourse loan, (2) contributing the project to a newly-formed joint venture with an institutional investor, with the investor making a cash contribution to the venture sufficient to retire any construction debt, or (3) a combination of (1) and (2). Under each of these alternatives, the developer positions itself to continue to enjoy the economic benefits from the project (positive cash flow in the short-term and continuing appreciation in the value of the project in the long-term). A developer who wishes to cash out a significant part of its equity in the project (represented by both its initial cash contribution to the project and its interest in the incremental value of the project over its development costs) will likely choose either alternative (2) or (3). If the developer has no particular desire or need to have its equity in the project returned, then the developer is more apt to refinance the project with a permanent nonrecourse loan and retain ownership of 100% of the project.

Lawyer's Job. At this stage, the real estate development lawyer's first mission is to advise the developer as to which of the available interim exit strategies will best achieve the developer's business objectives. In order to render effective advice on this topic, the development lawyer must be well-versed not only on the economics of the subject project, but also on the economics of the developer's business as a whole. The development lawyer must also determine if there is an outside equity investor who must approve the implementation of an interim exit strategy (and, if there is, what options are available to the developer if the investor fails to approve the developer's selected strategy). Finally, the development lawyer must once again put on a tax lawyer hat to make sure that the selected exit strategy does not result in any unexpected tax consequences to the developer or its equity investors. Once the decision is made as to which interim exit strategy will be implemented, the real fun starts for the real estate development lawyer. Regardless which interim exit strategy is selected, the legal documents required to evidence the transaction are sure to be complex and voluminous—two words that are music to the lawyer's ears.

I.   STAGE 9: OPERATING THE PROJECT

Developer's Business Objectives. The developer's economic desires for the project during this operational stage are relatively simple and straightforward—(1) to maximize and stabilize the project's annual cash flow, and (2) to enhance the long-term residual value of the project. In order to actualize these goals, the developer wants its project operations to proceed in accordance with the following guiding principles:

- Keep the project full with tenants paying rent at or above the budgeted level;

- Hold project expenses at or below the budgeted level;

- Maintain the project in a good condition and order of repair; and

- Keep both its tenants and equity investors happy.

The job of keeping the project full usually falls to a licensed real estate broker, while the remaining three tasks are assigned to a property manager. Whether the developer staffs these roles internally or externally is largely a matter of the developer's personal preference and business style.

Lawyer's Job. If the developer opts to staff project operations externally (that is, by outsourcing these functions to independent third parties), then the development lawyer must put together agreements retaining the broker and property manager. Those agreements should clearly delineate what is expected from the broker and the property manager and should be for relatively short terms, so that the developer can go a different direction if the third party's performance is not acceptable. During the operations stage, the development lawyer also assumes the role of a legal handyman, taking on whatever legal matters might arise with respect to the day-to-day management of the project. By way of example, the development lawyer might have to deal with a tenant bankruptcy one day and with an on-site environmental spill the next.

J. STAGE 10: SELLING THE PROJECT

Developer's Business Objective. Forget about the maxim that real estate is all about "location, location, location." The reality is that timing is an equally important contributor to the ultimate success of a real estate project. The developer's business objective at this final project stage is quite simple—to maximize its profit by picking the optimal time to sell the project. Selecting that optimal date is, however, much more of an art than it is a science. There are many considerations that factor into the determination of when a project should be sold. The most important consideration is market timing—that is, selling the project at a time when the demand for commercial real estate like the project is at its peak, thereby maximizing the purchase price that an institutional investor will pay for the project. Project-specific conditions also influence the selection of the time when a project should be marketed for sale. By way of example, it would not be advisable to try to sell a project at a time when the project's anchor tenant has only one year left on its lease term (because of the uncertainty about the future income stream generated from the project). Conversely, a project that has no leases expiring for the next five years would be an ideal candidate for sale. The art of selecting the optimal time to put a project up for sale involves balancing the general state of the economy with the project-specific conditions that also impact a project's marketability.

The upshot of this timing dilemma is that a developer who waits too long to pull the trigger on its project sale may end up seeing all of the value of its project permanently eroded during a lengthy downturn in the real estate markets. The moral of this story is that the successful developer should err on the side of selling its project too early rather than too late.

Lawyer's Job. In the first instance, it is the real estate development lawyer's job to create the legal flexibility to permit the developer to sell its project when the developer decides that the time is right to do so. Developers do not take kindly to hearing from their lawyers that the provision of a lease, financing agreement, or other legal document makes the sale of a project at the time selected by the developer infeasible (by way of example, a project mortgage might include a prepayment penalty that requires the developer to pay a hefty additional sum to its lender if the project is sold early in the loan term). The real estate development lawyer's mission is to anticipate the developer's ultimate sale of the project by creating contractual exits for the developer at each of the prior nine project stages.

The project sale also presents the real estate development lawyer with a unique and interesting opportunity to have a significant body of the lawyer's work product scrutinized and critiqued by an army of lawyers, accountants, and other real estate professionals retained by the buyer to perform due diligence on the project. A key part of a buyer's due diligence consists of a review of legal documents, such as project leases, reciprocal easement agreements, and title conditions and restrictions. Legal documents that create uncertainty about the predictability of the project's future income stream have a direct negative impact on the purchase price an investor will pay for the project. Examples of such circumstances are a lease that does not clearly set forth the rent applicable to a tenant's extension term or a lease that leaves up in the air the issue of whether the landlord or the tenant has the obligation to pay for any required upgrading of the project's heating and air conditioning system.

To the extent the real estate development lawyer performed well in the prior nine project stages, this process will be relatively painless for the development lawyer (and maybe even a bit rewarding). To the extent the development lawyer failed to do the job in those earlier stages, the lawyer will get to witness first-hand the economic impact that poor lawyering has on the value of a real estate project.

IV. SUMMARY

This chapter laid the groundwork for the remainder of this book by identifying the ten stages of the lawyer's participation in a real estate development project. The role played by the real estate development lawyer during each of those ten stages of a development project is examined in much more detail in later chapters of this book.

CHAPTER 3

WHAT THE REAL ESTATE DEVELOPMENT LAWYER NEEDS TO KNOW ABOUT PROJECT ECONOMICS

■ ■ ■

I. INTRODUCTION

The mantra for this book is *if you want to succeed as a real estate development lawyer, you first need to understand the real estate development business.* With that admonition in mind, Chapter 1 examined the nature of the real estate development business and the various players who are involved in that business. Chapter 2 looked at the ten stages of a real estate development project. This chapter concludes the initial study of the business aspects of real estate development by examining the fundamentals of project economics.

The following topics are covered in this chapter:

- The reasons the real estate development lawyer should care about project economics;
- The basic concepts of net operating income and residual value;
- The funding of development costs with construction debt and equity contributions;
- The risk/return parameters that define the financial expectations of the construction lender and the equity investor;
- The status of commercial real estate as an "investable asset";
- The concept of financial leverage;
- The theory of the time value of money; and
- The methodologies used to value real estate projects.

As was the case in Chapters 1 and 2, the discussion of project economics is viewed primarily from the perspective of the real estate development lawyer.

II. WHY SHOULD A REAL ESTATE DEVELOPMENT LAWYER CARE ABOUT PROJECT ECONOMICS?

By now you are probably asking yourself a couple of questions.

• Why is this crazy author making me learn about economics?

• Isn't that what accountants and financial analysts are for?

While I will refrain from commenting on my mental state or hazarding a guess as to the relative usefulness of accountants or financial analysts, I am happy to try to answer the fundamental question—"Why should a real estate development lawyer care about project economics?"

The discussion of project economics properly starts with the concepts embodied in the following quotes from two well-regarded books on real estate finance.

> Valuation is a function of the future *INCOME STREAM* and the *RISK* associated with that stream.[1]

> An investor who buys a particular property is in effect buying a set of *ASSUMPTIONS* about the ability of the property to generate *CASH FLOWS OVER THE PERIOD* and the likely *MARKET VALUE OF THE PROPERTY AT THE END OF THE HOLDING PERIOD.* That the physical structure is tangential to the investment decision is sometimes difficult for students to grasp. But soundness of construction, distinguished architecture and harmonious surroundings are relevant to the investment decision only to the extent those factors affect the flow of benefits from ownership and control.[2]

The common thread running through both of these quotes is that the value of commercial real estate is a function not of the project's location, design, or construction, but rather of the income stream generated from that project. This concept is markedly different from the way in which residential real estate is valued, where factors such as the number of bedrooms/bathrooms, the school district in which the house is located, and the level of the interior and exterior finishes carry the day. When it comes

---

[1] *See* MICHAEL E. MILES, GAYLE L. BERENS, AND MARC A. WEISS, REAL ESTATE DEVELOPMENT: PRINCIPLES AND PROCESS 93, emphasis added (3rd ed. 2000). Michael E. Miles, together with two different co-authors, has issued two subsequent editions of REAL ESTATE DEVELOPMENT: PRINCIPLES AND PROCESS TEXT. *See* MIKE E. MILES, LAURENCE M. NETHERTON, AND ADRIENNE SCHMITZ, REAL ESTATE DEVELOPMENT: PRINCIPLES AND PROCESS (4th ed. 2007); and MIKE E. MILES, LAURENCE M. NETHERTON, AND ADRIENNE SCHMITZ, REAL ESTATE DEVELOPMENT: PRINCIPLES AND PROCESS (5th ed. 2015). While both of the later editions of the book are fine expositions on the development process, I find the discussion of project economics in the third edition of the textbook to be better suited for transactional business lawyers who are the target audience for this book. For that reason, the references in this book to Dr. Miles textbook will be to the third edition of that textbook.

[2] *See* GAYLON E. GREER AND MICHAEL D. FARRELL, INVESTMENT ANALYSIS FOR REAL ESTATE DECISIONS 16–17, emphasis added (2nd ed. 1988).

to commercial real estate, those factors are, in the words of Dr. Greer, "tangential" to the primary value determinant—that is, the income stream produced by the project.

It should, therefore, come as little surprise that the first thing that an institutional investor wants to see when deciding whether it will buy a project and, if so, what it will pay for that project, is not a photograph of the building, the project plans and specifications, or even the demographics for the market in which the project is located. No, what the institutional investor is most interested in are the project leases. The institutional investor knows that the leases define both the amount of the income stream generated from a project and the various risks associated with the investor's receipt of that income stream.

Given the fact that the single most important determinant of the value of a real estate project is the work product of the real estate development lawyer, it seems rather obvious why the lawyer should feel compelled to learn something about project economics. The following are four additional reasons why an aspiring real estate development lawyer should read the remainder of this chapter.

- An essential element of the structuring of any real estate development deal is the allocation of a project's economic benefits and risks among the various providers of capital to the project—that is, the developer, the lender, and the outside equity investors. Without a sound understanding of project economics, the lawyer will be at a loss in seeking to properly allocate those benefits and risks among the parties.

- As stated at the outset of this chapter, the value of a project is not determined by the quality of its construction or design (the "bricks and mortar" equation), but rather is a function of two things—(1) the project's current income stream (represented by the lease), and (2) the sales proceeds realized upon the ultimate disposition of the project (represented by the sales contract). The real estate development lawyer is a key participant in both the leasing of the project and its ultimate sale. As a result, there is perhaps no other industry where the profitability of the client's business is more closely tied to the lawyer's job performance.

- Real estate documents in today's marketplace are filled with financial formulas and definitions. A real estate development lawyer who understands project economics can add real value to the client's deal by manipulating those definitions and formulas in a manner that redounds to the client's benefit.

- Developers love lawyers who speak their lingo.

III. REAL ESTATE ECONOMICS 101

The lawyer's course in real estate economics begins with a reiteration of the prior statement that the value of a commercial real estate project is a function of two basic economic concepts:

- The *net operating income* generated from the project; and
- The *residual value* of the project.

The next section of this chapter takes a brief look at each of these concepts.

A. NET OPERATING INCOME

Net operating income (NOI) is the term used to measure the current income stream generated by a project. Net operating income is defined as follows:

Net operating income = Gross revenues − Operating expenses.

Gross revenues are the sum of all rents, operating expense reimbursements, parking fees, and other income received by the owner of the project. *Operating expenses* are all those expenses that are paid by the owner to operate and maintain the project, including real estate taxes, janitorial fees, maintenance and repair costs, insurance premiums, utility costs, and property management fees. Expressly excluded from the definition of "operating expenses" are the principal and interest paid on the project debt and capital expenditures (for example, leasing commissions and the cost of adding to or replacing the structural components of the project).

When calculating a project's net operating income, an institutional investor commonly adds two fictional line item expenses to its calculation, both of which have the effect of decreasing a project's net operating income—(1) a so-called *vacancy allowance* to reflect the investor's expectation of the normal vacancy and uncollectable rents associated with a project (typically an amount equal to 5% of the total projected gross revenues), and (2) a so-called *structural reserve* to reflect the average cost of repairing and replacing the project's structural components over the life of the project (typically an amount equal to $.05–.10 per square foot contained within the project, depending upon the age and physical condition of the project). The existence and amounts of these two reserves varies depending upon the provisions of the project's lease and the investor's perception of the project's risk.

B. RESIDUAL VALUE

Residual value is the cash produced on the sale of the project. For this purpose, residual value is defined as follows:

Residual value = Gross sales proceeds – selling expenses.

Gross sales proceeds are generally equal to the purchase price payable on the sale of the project. ***Selling expenses*** are those transactional costs that reduce the amount of cash available for distribution to the project participants (that is, the developer and its lender and equity investors) and include real estate brokerage commissions, legal fees, and title insurance premiums.

C. USE OF NOI AND RESIDUAL VALUE

A project's net operating income and residual value are the cash sources used by the project owner (1) to repay the funds advanced by the lender, developer, and equity investors to pay the costs of developing the project, and (2) to pay an additional return (that is, profit) to those parties to compensate them for the risks they took in funding the development costs. The amount and timing of the payments to be received by these three categories of fund providers are directly linked to the risk taken by the provider when the funds were committed to the project. The adage "the greater the risk, the greater the return" certainly holds true in the real estate development business.

At this point, let's pause to highlight the meaning of the word ***return***—a term that is used frequently in both this chapter and the rest of this book. "Return" is a term used to evaluate the relative success of a real estate project. Owners of a real estate project (be it the developer or an outside equity investor) talk about two types of "returns"—***return on*** their project investment and the ***return of*** their project investment. In the terminology of the stock or bond markets, "return on" is the dividend/interest that the investor receives periodically throughout the term of its ownership of the stock/bond, and "return of" is the repatriation to the investor of the original amount of its investment at the time of the sale of the stock or the redemption of the bond.

If a real estate investor receives a full return of its investment in a project, then any cash it receives from a return on its investment represents the profit on the investor's investment. The cash profit received by a real estate investor is commonly referred to as the investor's ***net cash flow*** and consists of the sum of (1) the investor's ***net cash flow from operations*** over the duration of the investor's ownership of the project, plus (2) the ***net sales proceeds*** received by the investor following the sale of the project. "Net cash flow from operations" is generally equal to the project's NOI minus the project's debt service payments and capital expenditures, and "net sales proceeds" equal the project's gross sales proceeds minus any selling expenses and the full pay-off of all project debt. As is discussed later in this chapter, all of these return calculations are ***before tax returns***—meaning that they are calculated without taking into consideration any state, local, or federal income taxes payable by the investor as a result of its ownership of the project.

Of course, if the sum of all cash distributions received by an investor from a real estate project (both "return on" and "return of" distributions) is less than the amount of investor's original investment, then the investor has a net loss on its investment—a regrettable circumstance that Will Rogers was undoubtedly referring to when he purportedly remarked that "I am not so much concerned with the return on capital as I am with the return of capital."[3]

Practice Tip #3-1: Remember It's All Make Believe

Michelle Obama once said that she became a lawyer for the same reason that all people become lawyers—because she was bad at math.[4] It is not my intention in this Practice Tip to contest that assertion (although I do believe that the former First Lady's point is at least somewhat debatable). I am confident that any lawyer can gain a basic understanding of the project economics discussed in this chapter as long as the lawyer is open to remembering a few simple formulas and buying a financial calculator.

What the lawyer must also appreciate is that the numbers that a real estate developer and its lender and equity investors bandy about when talking about a real estate development project are not real—they are all make believe. As noted in one of the quotes that led off this chapter, the numbers are based on assumptions made by the developer. They are merely financial projections of what might happen down the road. Until a project is fully leased and cash flowing (hopefully at the conclusion of Stage 7 of the project), the project's value is ephemeral at best—no more valuable than the piece of paper on which the financial projections are written. It is the real estate development lawyer's job to help the developer "make it real."

IV. THE FUNDING OF DEVELOPMENT COSTS

The funds used to pay the costs of developing a real estate project come from three principal sources—(1) the project lender, (2) the developer, and (3) the outside equity investors. This section examines the risk and return expectations and requirements of each of these funding sources. As a

---

[3] Randolph W. Forsyth, *Will Rogers Would Understand These Markets*, BARRONS (August 21, 2007), http://www.barrons.com/articles/SB118762200063402876.

[4] *See* Katherine Skiba, *Michelle Obama Stresses Importance of Girls Pursuing STEM*, CHICAGO TRIBUNE, September 25, 2011, http://www.chicagotribune.com/news/local/breaking/chi-michelle-obama-stresses-important-of-girls-pusuing-science-math-technology-20110926-story.html.

stepping off point for that discussion, one first needs to gain an appreciation for the cost categories that are included in the development cost budget.

A. DEVELOPMENT COST BUDGET

The development cost budget must include all those costs that are directly related to the development of a real estate project (referred to in the remainder of this chapter as *development costs*). There are three basic categories of development costs.

- *Land costs* are the costs incurred by the developer in connection with its acquisition and ownership of the land on which the developer's project is located.

- *Hard costs* are those costs that are incurred directly in connection with the construction of the building, the build-out of the tenant space, and the making of other site improvements, and include the contractor's fee and the cost of all labor and materials provided to the project.

- *Soft costs* are all those costs, other than hard costs, that would not have been incurred but for the development of the subject project. Soft costs include the following:

  o Interest, fees, and other carrying charges paid on any loan secured to acquire the land or construct the building;

  o Fees paid to architects, engineers, and other design professionals;

  o Appraisal fees, title insurance premiums, and surveying costs;

  o Due diligence costs paid to environmental consultants, soils engineers, land planners, etc.;

  o Real estate brokerage and leasing commissions;

  o Impact fees and other governmental charges;

  o Advertising and other marketing costs;

  o Legal fees;

  o Construction period operating expenses, such as real estate taxes, insurance premiums, and utility charges;

  o An operating reserve to fund the projected deficit in the project's net operating income during the period after completion of construction, but before the project is sufficiently leased to cover the project's operating expenses;

o   A contingency reserve to cover any unexpected costs incurred during the development process; and

o   Development fees paid to the developer.[5]

B. CONSTRUCTION FINANCING

The developer typically funds 70–90% of its project development costs through a construction loan. Commercial banks are the biggest suppliers of construction loans in the United States. The risk/return parameters of the typical construction loan are described below.

1.   Risks Faced by Construction Lender

Construction lenders face two basic risks:

- The risk that construction of the project is not completed on budget and on time; and

- The risk that, even if completed on budget and on-time, the project does not produce sufficient cash flow or possess sufficient value to pay off the construction loan.

The construction lender is the least risk tolerant of the three main funding sources for the typical real estate development project (the other two being the developer and its outside equity investors). The construction lender seeks to mitigate its lending risk in a number of ways, including those discussed below.

- ***Requiring a First Mortgage on Project***—The primary way that the construction lender limits its risk exposure is by securing the repayment of its loan with a first mortgage on the project. If a default occurs under the construction loan, then the construction lender can foreclose on the project and, if necessary, contract with a third party for the completion of the project. It should be noted, however, that a sale of an uncompleted project at foreclosure rarely produces sufficient cash to cover the full amount of the outstanding construction debt. The construction lender is, therefore, often left with little choice but to protect its loan position by completing construction of the project.

---

[5]   The developer's fees are not only a component of the project's overall development costs, but also a source of the financial return garnered by the developer from its participation in the project. The fact that the construction lender and outside equity investors are customarily responsible for funding the vast majority of the developer's fees leads to a natural tension between the developer and its lender and outside investors concerning both the amount of the development fee and the time at which it is paid to the developer. *See infra* Chapter 5, pages 297–299, and Chapter 9, pages 393–395 for a further discussion of this point.

- *Receiving Personal Guaranties from Developer*—The construction lender further addresses the risk inherent in a construction loan by requiring the developer (or a creditworthy affiliate of the developer) to provide the lender with personal guaranties that the project will be completed on budget and on time (a "completion guaranty") and that all principal and interest on the loan will be paid when due (a "payment guaranty").

- *Limiting the Length of the Loan Term*—The construction lender does not want to take long-term risk on the project. For this reason, most construction loans are for a term of no more than 36 months. The relatively short term of the construction loan forces the borrower to either sell the project prior to the maturity of the construction loan or obtain a permanent loan to refinance its construction loan position.

- *Limiting the Loan Amount*—The most obvious way that a construction lender can limit its risk is by reducing the amount of its loan. As noted earlier, a lender typically seeks to mitigate its loan risk by loaning less than all of a project's development costs (the *loan-to-cost ratio (LTC)* that is historically in the 70–90% range). The next section of this chapter explores three other tests commonly used by a construction lender to limit the amount of the construction loan and, hence, the construction lender's risk that the loan is not fully repaid by the developer.

2. Loan Ratios

A construction lender relies on three other ratios to place a ceiling on the amount of its construction loan—(1) the *loan-to-value ratio (LTV)*, (2) the *debt service coverage ratio (DSC)*, and (3) the *debt yield ratio (DY)*.[6] The first such ratio (LTV) limits the loan amount by reference to the projected residual value of the developer's project, while the other two ratios (DSC and DY) limit the loan amount by reference to the projected net operating income of that project.

- *LTV Ratio*—The loan-to-value ratio is a test that a construction lender uses to determine whether its collateral for the repayment of the loan (the first mortgage on the

---

[6]   *See generally* DAVID C. LING AND WAYNE R. ARCHER, REAL ESTATE PRINCIPLES: A VALUE APPROACH, 446–448 (3rd ed. 2010); PHILLIP T. KOLBE AND GAYLON E. GREER, INVESTMENT ANALYSIS FOR REAL ESTATE INVESTORS, 135–138 (7th ed. 2009); Carl Circo, *Real Estate Project Valuation and Underwriting Metrics—A Refresher*, in ACREL NEWSLETTER 4, 5–6 (April 2010); Thomas A. Hauser, *Debt Markets—Dead, Delayed or Dynamic: Current Factors Influencing Real Estate Finance*, in ACREL PAPERS, Tab 2, 5 (Fall 2016); and Thomas F. Kaufman, *Real Estate Metrics—Presentation Slides*, in ALI-CLE Modern Real Estate Transactions, Course SYOO6 1059 (August 2016).

project) will produce sufficient value to pay off the loan if the lender should have to foreclose on the project. Most lenders use an LTV ratio in the vicinity of 60–80%. A construction loan made at a 70% LTV means that the maximum amount of the construction loan is 70% of the project's projected value at stabilization (that is, when the project is fully leased and cash flowing). The value differential (that is, the 30% by which the projected value exceeds the loan amount) is the "cushion" that the construction lender relies on to lessen its risk exposure on the construction loan.[7]

- ***DSC Ratio***—The use of a debt service coverage ratio is designed to give the lender comfort that the expected income stream from the project will be sufficient to permit the developer to pay all debt service payments when and as they become due during the term of the construction loan. Most lenders use a debt service coverage ratio of somewhere between 1.20 and 1.40. A construction loan made at a DSC of 1.30 means that the projected net operating income from the project must be at least 130% of the debt service the developer is required to pay on its construction loan. This 30% differential gives the lender comfort that the project should produce sufficient cash flow to service its debt.

Once the maximum debt service the project can support is determined by applying the DSC ratio, the maximum loan amount can then be determined by using what lenders commonly refer to as a ***mortgage constant***. A mortgage constant is the percentage of an original loan that must be paid every year to repay all principal and interest over a stated period of time (commonly referred to as the ***amortization period***). To calculate the mortgage constant, the lender must first make certain assumptions about the interest rate payable on the loan and the time period over which the loan is to be amortized. Once those assumptions are made, the determination of the mortgage constant is simply a matter of doing the math.[8] The maximum loan amount supported by a particular project under the DSC test is equal to the project's maximum debt service (determined

---

[7] *See* MILES, *supra* note 1, at 84.

[8] For those compulsive mathematicians in the reading audience, a monthly mortgage constant can be calculated using a hand-held calculator by solving for payment (PMT), where PV = $1; FV = 0; n = the number of months in the selected amortization period; and i = the stated interest rate payable under the loan (divided by 12—accomplished by using the "g" key on an HP 12–C calculator). *See* WILLIAM B. BRUEGGEMAN AND JEFFREY D. FISHER, REAL ESTATE FINANCE AND INVESTMENTS 85 (14th ed. 2011).

by dividing the project's projected NOI, by the stipulated DSC ratio), divided by the mortgage constant.[9]

- *Debt Yield Ratio*—The debt yield ratio is a loan test that is being relied on more and more by today's lenders to insulate them from the risk that a financed project will not have sufficient income and value to pay off the lender's project loan. A loan's debt value ratio is calculated by dividing the project's projected NOI at stabilization by the principal amount of the construction loan. By way of example, if the projected annual NOI for a project is $2 million, then the maximum loan amount that a lender applying a 10% DY ratio would be willing to make is $20 million (the NOI of $2 million ÷ the 10% DY ratio). The straightforward debt yield test is designed to alleviate the lender's risk that the application of the LTV and DSC ratios could produce an unreasonably high loan amount in a real estate environment characterized by high values and low interest rates (both of which are present in the current real estate market).[10]

- *Application of LTV, DSC, and DY Ratios*—The operation of the LTV, DSC, and DY tests is illustrated by the following example.

Example 3-1: Assume that a project being underwritten by a construction lender has the following financial characteristics:

- Total development costs of $4,200,000;

- Projected stabilized value of $5,000,000; and

- Projected annual net operating income of $450,000.

Further assume that the lender proposes to set its maximum loan amount for the project by employing a LTV ratio of 80%, a DSC ratio of 1.20 (using a mortgage constant of 10%),[11] and a DY ratio of 11%.

With all these assumptions in mind, the maximum loan amount under the LTV test is $4 million [project value of $5 million, multiplied by the 80% LTV ratio]. The maximum loan amount produced under the DSC test is $3.75 million [(NOI of $450,000, divided by the 1.2 DSC ratio), divided by the mortgage constant of 10%]. The application of the 11% DY ratio

---

[9]   *See* KOLBE, *supra* note 6, at 137.

[10]   *See* HAUSER, *supra* note 6, at 5; and KAUFMAN, *supra* note 6, at 1067.

[11]   A 10% mortgage constant is produced by the use of an assumed annual interest rate of 8% and an assumed amortization period of 20 years. For those untrusting souls, the assumed interest rate and amortization period can be run through the formula set forth in note 8, *supra*, to produce a monthly mortgage constant of .0084. That monthly figure is then multiplied by 12 to produce an annual mortgage constant of 10.04% (which, for the purposes of the textual illustration, has been rounded down to 10%).

produces a maximum loan amount of $4.09 million (the annual NOI of $450,000, divided by the 11% DY ratio). A construction lender, being the risk averse animal that it is, almost always sets the loan amount at the lower of the three maximum loan amounts produced by the LTV, DSC, and DY tests ($3.75 million in this example).

The LTV, DSC, and DY tests are also commonly used by permanent lenders to determine the maximum amount of a permanent loan that made on a project. Construction lenders regularly canvass the permanent lender community to determine what LTV, DSC, and DY ratios are being used to set the principal amount of permanent loans. By keeping abreast of what is going on in the permanent loan market, the construction lender tries to ensure that it does not make a construction loan on a project in an amount in excess of that which a permanent lender will make on that same project once it is completed and leased in accordance with the developer's initial projections. Unlike the construction lender, the permanent lender has the relative luxury of applying the LTV, DSC, and DY tests based on actual net operating income numbers and not on those projected by the developer in advance of the development of the project. As such, the making of a permanent loan is an inherently less risky activity than is the making of a construction loan.

Practice Tip #3-2: The Aftermath of the 2008 Recession

In the run-up to the Great Recession of 2008, lenders were regularly maxing out the principal amounts of their real estate loans by using wildly aggressive LTC, LTV, DSC, and DY ratios. The end result was an over-leveraging of the real estate markets (particularly the residential market). Enter the Great Recession of 2008 that was triggered in large measure by the recklessness of the real estate capital markets (again, especially prevalent in the residential debt market).[12]

In the immediate aftermath of the 2008 dislocation in both the U.S. economy generally and the commercial real estate economy specifically, lenders simply stopped making real estate loans. As the commercial real estate market began to stabilize a bit in 2011, lenders started once again to make commercial real estate loans, but on vastly more conservative terms. Loans were made only to the most creditworthy real estate owners and then only for projects that were fully leased and cash flowing. In the last few years, real estate lenders have loosened their underwriting standards and

---

[12] For a very interesting discussion of the causes and consequences of the 2008 recession, *see* ANTHONY DOWNS, REAL ESTATE AND THE FINANCIAL CRISIS: HOW TURMOIL IN THE CAPITAL MARKETS IS RESTRUCTURING REAL ESTATE FINANCE (2009).

debt dollars are now flowing freely to all commercial real estate projects (both new developments and existing projects).

The following table highlights anecdotal evidence (culled primarily from my conversations with real estate practitioners) of sample debt ratios commonly used by commercial real estate lenders in each of the years 2006, 2011, and 2016.

Loan Ratio	2006	2011	2016
Loan-to-Cost Ratio	75–95%	40–60%	65–85%
Loan-to-Value Ratio	70–85%	50–65%	60–75%
Debt Service Coverage Ratio	1.1–1.3	1.5–1.7	1.2–1.4
Debt Yield Ratio	7–10%	15–18%	12–15%

What the above table illustrates is how commercial real estate lenders react to cycles in the commercial real estate industry by ramping up loan amounts in boom times, ratcheting them back in down times, and modulating them in periods of perceived stability. This is, of course, exactly the reaction that one would expect to see in the commercial lending markets. The one side note that should be made is that commercial lenders are almost always reactive and not predictive in their lending practices. For that reason, the market typically sees changes in lender's underwriting practices toward the end and not at the beginning of a real estate cycle.

The figures on the comparative loan ratios used by commercial lenders in good times, bad times, and OK times also highlight an ongoing issue that lenders face when making real estate loans whose terms span across real estate cycles—specifically, can a loan made using underwriting practices in Year One later be refinanced using underwriting practices in vogue two, three, or more years later? By way of example, take a $10 million construction loan made in 2006 using a LTC ratio of 90%, an LTV ratio of 80%, a DSC ratio of 1.2%, and a DY ratio of 9% (all of which were certainly not out of character during the go-go days of 2002–2007).[13] *What happens to that loan when the borrower seeks to refinance in 2009 when the real estate debt markets are totally shut down? Let's assume that the borrower is able to get the construction lender to extend the maturity date of the construction loan until 2011. What happens to the borrower's $10 million loan when the application of the loan ratios prevailing in 2011 support a loan of only $6 million—$4 million short of the amount needed to pay off*

---

[13] In this example, the $10 million loan amount was determined by applying the four loan ratios to a project having a cost of $11.11 million, a projected value at stabilization of $12.5 million, a projected annual NOI of $900,000, and a mortgage constant of 7.5%

the original 2006 construction loan?[14] *The answer to both of those questions is that the borrower better be flush with cash to pay off the refinancing gap (few were in the aftermath of the onset of the Great Recession) or have a lender who accepts the "extend and pretend" philosophy that most lenders were forced to embrace in the years following 2008.*

The "extend and pretend" practice was described in the Wall Street Journal as being "a technique for dealing with business borrowers who can't repay loans coming due: Give them more time, hoping things improve and they repay later."[15] *A more jaundiced commentator might prefer this definition of "extend and pretend" found in the Urban Dictionary—"A temporary solution to a severe hangover which involves addressing the condition with another round of heavy drinking: this method is not necessarily a cure to a hangover, only a postponement of the inevitable."*[16]

Despite the derisive nature of the Urban Dictionary definition, the fact is that "extend and pretend" worked out OK for those lenders who were willing and able to continue to "extend and pretend" the high-octane loans they made in the lead-up to the Great Recession until the real estate markets started to revive in 2014 and the years thereafter. Less patient lenders ended up taking big write-downs on their books by foreclosing on projects that could no longer support the level of the loans made in the period from 2003 to 2007.

Looking at the plight of commercial real estate lenders in the aftermath of the Great Recession is an extreme way to illustrate the inherent risk that a real estate lender makes each time it makes a term loan secured by a real estate project. What works for a lender in 2017 may or may not work when the loan matures three, five, seven, or ten years later. In the words of Yogi Berra, "It's tough to make predictions, especially about the future."[17]

---

3. Return Expectations of the Construction Lender

The construction lender's return for taking the risk of making a construction loan is represented by the interest payments it receives under

---

[14]   A $6 million loan could be produced by assuming that (a) the loan ratios prevailing in 2011 are an LTC of 55%, an LTV of 50%, a DSC of 1.7, and a DY of 15%, and (b) the project is still has a total cost of $11.11 million, an annual stabilized NOI of $900,000, a value of $12.5 million, and a mortgage constant of 7.5%. Given the dislocation in the real estate market during the Great Recession, it is extremely doubtful that the assumptions listed in clause (a) would have remained true in 2011—making the borrower's refinancing position even more untenable.

[15]   Carrick Mollenkamp and Lingling Wei, *To Fix Sour Property Deals, Lenders "Extend and Pretend,"* WALL STREET JOURNAL (July 7, 2010), http://www.wsj.com/articles/SB10001424052748 704764404575286882690834088.

[16]   URBAN DICTIONARY, www.urbandictionary.com/define.php?term=extend+and+pretend (last visited on January 23, 2017).

[17]   YOGI BERRA, http://www.goodreads.com/quotes/261863-it-s-tough-to-make-predictions-especially-about-the-future.

the loan. The construction lender typically passes through to the borrower all of the costs incurred by the lender in connection with the making of its construction loan, thereby preserving the interest paid on its loan as the lender's true economic return. The costs customarily passed on to the borrower include the lender's legal fees, appraisal costs, title insurance premiums, and construction inspection costs. Construction lenders also frequently charge upfront "loan origination" fees, which, as little more than prepaid interest, serve to augment the lender's return on its construction loan.

The construction lender makes its money off of the spread between its **cost of funds**[18] and the interest rate it receives on its project loan. A construction lender's "cost of funds" is a factor of (a) the interest rate it needs to pay on money deposited with it by its depositor customers, and (b) the interest rate it needs to pay on any money borrowed by it from the Federal Reserve Bank or any other source.

Reduced to its simplest and most basic statement, a bank makes money when it receives a deposit from a customer for a CD paying 2% and then takes that deposit and uses it to make a construction loan to a developer at an interest rate of 6%. The bank's positive return in this scenario is, however, wholly dependent on the developer being able to pay off the construction loan at maturity. The uncertainty that this desired outcome will occur is the risk that was addressed in the preceding section of this chapter. While a construction lender always requires a positive spread between the rate of interest charged on a construction loan and its cost of funds (it is, after all, in the business of making money), the size of that spread varies depending on the lender's perception of its risk in making the loan. This is just another way of saying that the lender expects a return commensurate with its assumed risk. Put in real world terms, the interest rate charged on a project that is 100% pre-leased to Microsoft will be significantly lower than the interest rate charged on a project where no pre-leasing exists.

Another risk faced by a construction lender is that a change in the economy occurs during the term of the construction loan that increases the lender's cost of funds above that which existed when the loan was closed. The construction lender addresses this risk by requiring that the interest rate payable under its construction loan must be adjusted from time to time to reflect an increase in a financial index selected by the lender. The prime rate, the federal funds rate, and the London Inter-bank Offered Rate (**LIBOR**) are examples of benchmarks commonly used for this purpose by construction lenders.

---

[18] *See* LING, *supra* note 6 at 221 and 641. There are a number of indexes that track the average "cost of funds" of lending institutions—*see e.g.*, the 11th District Monthly Weighted Average Cost of Funds Index, available online at http://www.fhlbsf.com.

C. EQUITY CONTRIBUTIONS

Construction debt usually covers somewhere between 70–90% of a project's development costs. That leaves 10–30% of the development costs to be funded through equity contributions made to the project by the developer and its outside equity investors. The terms *equity* and *capital* are used interchangeably throughout this chapter to refer to cash or other property contributed by the developer and its outside equity investors to the entity that owns the real estate development project. Also for the purposes of this chapter, no sharp distinction is drawn between the treatment of the equity contributed by the developer versus that of the equity contributed by the outside equity investors. That distinction, which is a central component of the developer's business plan, is discussed at length in Chapter 7 of this book (see pages 259–280).

The developer almost always makes some level of equity contribution to the project. Large, national developers often contribute 100% of the equity needed to fund the gap between the amount of the construction loan and the project's total development costs. Even in those projects where the vast majority of the needed equity is provided by outside investors, the outside investors normally insist that the developer make a significant equity contribution to the venture to ensure that the developer has a stake in seeing to it that the project is successful. In the language of the real estate industry, this is known as requiring that the developer have *skin in the game*.

Who are the outside equity investors that serve as an additional source for the funding of a project's development costs? On smaller projects, they tend to fall into the category of "family and friends" of the developer. On larger projects, the bulk of the outside capital is provided by the type of institutional investors discussed in Chapter 1 of this book—for example, life insurance companies, pension funds, equity funds, and other financial institutions. Regardless whether the investor is the developer's family dentist or a life insurance company, all capital providers share a common investment goal—they want to "achieve the maximum ownership interest and share of returns from the development while making the minimum possible financial exposure."[19]

By making an equity investment in a project, the equity investor is effectively buying a share of the project's net operating income and residual value. The following excerpt from a respected real estate finance textbook nicely illustrates this point.

> The price an investor is prepared to pay for a defined property interest depends in part upon the amount and timing of . . . anticipated cash flows; how much will be received, and when? It

---

[19] *See* MILES, *supra* note 1, at 48.

depends also on the degree of confidence with which expectations are held and the investor's tolerance for bearing risk. The final variable is the attractiveness of alternative opportunities.[20]

The next three sections of this chapter look at (1) the risks associated with the making of an equity investment in a real estate development project, (2) the commensurate economic return demanded by the equity investor, and (3) the position occupied by real estate in the panoply of investment alternatives available to an equity investor.

1.   Risks Faced by the Equity Investor

The equity investor faces the same basic project risks that are faced by the construction lender—that is, (1) the risk that the project is not completed on budget and on time, and (2) the risk that, even if the project is completed on budget and on time, the project does not produce sufficient cash flow or possess sufficient value to pay the projected economic return to the equity investor (which, for the purpose of this discussion, includes the developer). The level of risk associated with the making of an equity investment in a real estate project is, however, significantly greater than that associated with the making of a construction loan. The reasons the equity investor has a heightened level of risk are discussed below.

- *No Fixed Obligation to Repay*—Unlike the loan dollars advanced by the construction lender, the funds committed by the outside capital provider are truly at risk with the success of the project. There is no fixed obligation on the part of the project owner or any other person to repay either the investor's contributed capital or any return on that capital.

- *No Security for Repayment*—In return for its equity contribution, the investor receives an ownership interest in the entity that owns the real estate project. It does not, however, receive any collateral interest in the underlying project to secure its hope of receiving a return of its equity contribution or a share of the project's cash flow.

- *No Cushion for Repayment*—The previous discussion of the construction lender's risk profile spoke about the lender's attempt to mitigate its risk by using certain lending tests to create "cushions" between the value of the project and the amount of the construction loan (the loan-to-value test) and the project's cash flow and the lender's debt service payments (the debt service coverage and debt yield tests). No such cushion exists for the capital provider, who, in effect, is the construction lender's cushion. The capital provider gets paid only after all requisite principal and interest payments are

---

[20]   *See* KOLBE, *supra* note 6, at 6.

made to the construction lender. Moreover, the only way that the capital provider will receive any profit from its investment is if the project ultimately has a value in excess of its accrued development costs (which include any unexpected cash deficits generated by the project). In effect, the investor gets the project's "leftover" net operating income and residual value after the lender first gets its fixed share of that net operating income and residual value.

- *Lack of Marketability for Equity Interests*—There is no ready market for the sale of equity interests in private real estate projects. The owner of stock in a publicly-traded company can cut its losses by selling its stock when it sees the company beginning to lose value. The investor in a private real estate project has almost no ability whatsoever to limit its loss in that fashion.[21]

2. Return Expectations of the Equity Investor

The risk assumed by the equity investor is much greater than that assumed by the construction lender. As such, the return expectations of the equity investor are much higher than those of the construction lender.

In order to fully appreciate how the risk/return continuum plays out in the context of a real estate project, one must take a look at three standard economic return measurements.

- *Return on Total Costs*—This return standard measures the overall productivity of the project. A project's return on total costs is equal to the project's stabilized net operating income, divided by the project's total development costs. In Example 3-1, it was assumed that a project produced annual net operating income of $450,000 and that the project's aggregate development costs were $4.2 million. Using these same assumptions, the project's overall rate of return would be 10.71% (the NOI of $450,000, divided by the development costs of $4,200,000). This 10.71% project return must then be divided between the two principal funding sources for the project—that is, the construction lender and the equity

---

[21] The creation of publicly-traded real estate investment trusts has permitted the small investor to purchase a highly marketable equity ownership interest in real estate. A real estate investment trust or "REIT," such as Simon Property Group Inc., ProLogis, and Duke Realty Corp. owns vast portfolios of commercial real estate. By definition, however, a REIT must have at least 100 shareholders and, therefore, is not an entity suited for the garden variety closely-held real estate development venture that is the subject of this book. For a general discussion of the REIT ownership vehicle, *see* Robert G. Gottlieb, *How REITS Are Different from other Real Estate Investments*, 31 PRACTICAL REAL ESTATE LAWYER 49 (January 2015).

investors (which again, for this purpose, includes both the developer and its outside equity investors).

- *Return on Debt*—The construction lender's return on its advancement of the construction loan proceeds is roughly equal to the rate of interest being charged on the construction loan. In Example 3-1, the return on debt would be the 8% interest rated charged to the project by the construction lender.

- *Return on Equity*—This financial standard measures the return to the equity investor and is often referred to as the *cash on cash return*. The return on equity is equal to the cash that is available for distribution to the equity investors (commonly referred to as *before tax cash flow*), divided by the total capital contributed to the project by the investors. For this purpose, before tax cash flow is equal to the project's net operating income, less (1) the debt service payments required to be paid to the project lender, and (2) those other project costs that are not part of the operating expense component of the project's net operating income—for example, the cost of replacing a roof or acquiring additional land. This calculation is consistent with the requirement that the project's cash flow must first be applied to the payment of the project's debt service costs, before any cash distributions are made to the equity investors.

The following example shows how an investor's return on equity is calculated.

Example 3-2: Assume the following facts produced under the prior Example 3-1:

- Total development costs $4,200,000
- Construction loan amount $3,750,000
- Amount of invested equity $450,000
- Annual NOI $450,000
- Annual debt service $375,000

Under these facts, the project's before tax cash flow is $75,000 (the annual NOI of $450,000, minus the annual debt service of $375,000) and the project's return on equity is 16.67% (the before tax cash flow of $75,000, divided by the amount of the investor's invested equity of $450,000).

D. DEBT VS. EQUITY RETURNS

The relative return expectations of the construction lender and the equity investor are nicely highlighted in Example 3-2. Under the facts of that example, the project's return on total costs is 10.71% (the annual NOI of $450,000, divided by the total development costs of $4.2 million). The construction lender's return on its debt is 8% (the assumed interest rate on the lender's construction loan), and the investor's return on equity is 16.67%.

The disparity in the returns of the construction lender and the equity investors mirrors the disparity in the risks taken by those parties in funding their respective shares of the project's development costs. The greater risk assumed by the equity investor justifies the greater return paid to the equity investor.

The higher level of risk assumed by the equity investor is further underscored by making one minor change to the facts of Example 3-2. If it is assumed that the actual NOI from the project is only $375,000 (and not $450,000 as initially projected by the developer), the lender's return on debt is 8%, while the investor's return on equity is 0%.

[handwritten margin note: Once loan is paid off, does investor get paid?]

Under that scenario, the entirety of the project's net operating income ($375,000) is used to pay debt service on the loan (the loan amount of $3,750,000, multiplied by the mortgage constant of 10%), leaving no cash whatsoever for distribution to the investor. The lender's return remains fixed at its 8% interest rate and the investor bears the full brunt of the risk of a decrease in the project's net operating income. Therefore, while the equity investor achieves a higher return on its contribution to the project than does the lender if the project is successful, the tables are turned in the construction lender's favor if the project is not as successful as originally projected. This is proof positive of the workings of the risk-return formulation.

V. FINANCIAL LEVERAGE

As noted previously, the majority of a real estate project's development costs are usually funded with debt. The use of borrowed funds to finance a project is called *leverage*.

From the equity investor's perspective, there are two fundamental advantages of the use of leverage to fund a project's development costs.

- Leverage permits the equity investor to diversify its real estate investments by funding 10–30% of the development costs in several deals, rather than 100% of those costs in just one project. This diversification lowers the investor's real estate risk by permitting it to spread that risk over several different projects.

- Leverage can be used to increase the investor's percentage return on equity.

A.   IMPACT OF LEVERAGE ON RETURN ON EQUITY

Leverage, if properly used, can significantly increase the financial return to the equity investor. This point is illustrated by revisiting three economic concepts discussed earlier in this chapter:

- *Return on Total Costs*—The stabilized net operating income of the project divided by its total development costs;

- *Mortgage Constant*—The percentage of the loan amount that is required to be paid annually to fully repay all principal and interest over an assumed amortization period; and

- *Return on Equity*—The investor's before tax cash flow, divided by its equity contributions.

With these concepts in mind, three basic propositions can be stated concerning the impact of leverage on a real estate development deal:[22]

- *Proposition #1*—If the project has no leverage whatsoever (that is, all development costs are funded by capital contributions from equity investors), then the investor's return on equity is identical to the project's return on total costs;

- *Proposition #2*—So long as the project's return on total costs is greater than the mortgage constant on the project debt, the use of leverage serves to increase the investor's return on equity (so-called *positive leverage*); and

- *Proposition #3*—Conversely, once the mortgage constant exceeds the project's return on total costs, the use of further leverage causes the investor's return on equity to decrease (*negative leverage*).

The impact financial leverage has on an investor's equity return can best be understood by going back to the example that has been used throughout this chapter. Remember that the return on total costs for the hypothetical project addressed in Examples 3-1 and 3-2 was 10.71%. Proposition #1 provides that a wholly unleveraged project (that is, one funded 100% with equity contributions) produces a return on equity to the investor at the same 10.71% level. The return on equity for the hypothetical investor in Example 3-2 was 16.67%. The placement of debt on the project of $3,750,000 caused the investor's return on equity to increase by almost

---

[22] *See generally* David GELTNER, NORMAN G. MILLER, JIM CLAYTON, AND PIET EICHOLTZ, COMMERCIAL REAL ESTATE ANALYSIS AND INVESTMENTS 310 (2nd ed. 2007; BRUEGGEMAN, *supra* note 8, at 349–354; LING, *supra* note 6, at 136–141; and Circo, *supra* note 6, at 5 (April 2010).

6%. This is true because, under proposition #2, the hypothetical project produced a return on cost (10.71%) that was higher than the mortgage constant (10%) applicable to the project debt—hence the project's leverage was positive.

What happens if the leverage on the hypothetical project is increased by an additional $250,000 to $4 million? The answer is that the increased leverage continues to enhance the investor's returns as long as the cost of the debt (represented by the mortgage constant) remains less than the project's return on total costs. The result, however, is markedly different if the lender decides that the higher loan amount merits an increase in its interest rate from 8 to 9% (to compensate the lender for the additional risk of making the higher loan). The impact of this interest rate increase is that the project's mortgage constant goes from 10% to 10.8%. At this leverage level, the project has fallen over the precipice of negative leverage because the project's return on total costs (10.71%) is less than the mortgage constant on the project debt (10.8%).

Under proposition #3, an increase in the assumed leverage to $4 million, coupled with an increase in the interest rate to 9%, should result in a reduction in the investor's return on equity—which it does, decreasing the investor's return on equity from 16.67% to 9%. The investor's return on equity of 9% is calculated as follows: the investor's before tax cash flow of $18,000 (the excess of the project's NOI of $450,000 over its debt service of $432,000—produced by multiplying the project debt of $4 million, by the mortgage constant of 10.8%), divided by the investor's $200,000 capital contributions (the difference between the project's total development costs of $4.2 million and the $4 million principal amount of the project's construction debt).

Reducing the leverage on the hypothetical project from $3.75 million to $3.5 million should, consistent with the principle enunciated in proposition #2, cause a reduction in the investor's return on equity (because the project still has positive leverage at the $3.75 million debt level). Under Proposition #2, the $250,000 reduction in the project's leverage causes the investor's return on equity to fall from 16.67% to 14.29%. The investor's return on equity of 14.29% is calculated as follows: Investor's before tax cash flow of $100,000 (the excess of the project's NOI of $450,000 over its debt service of $350,000—produced by multiplying the project debt of $3.5 million, by the mortgage constant of 10%), divided by Investor's $700,000 capital contributions (the difference between the project's total development costs of $4.2 million and the $3.5 million principal amount of the project's construction debt).

B. CAUTIONARY WORDS OF WISDOM

The preceding discussion seems to indicate that determining the proper amount of leverage for a project is simply a matter of math. All one has to do is to run the numbers to reach the leverage level that maximizes the return on equity to the investor. In the vernacular of the real estate investor, this mathematical process is called "chasing yield."

However, pushing up leverage levels to chase yield has non-mathematical consequences due to the always lurking presence of the "r" word—that is, risk. The greater the leverage, the greater the risk that (1) the project's net operating income will not be sufficient to cover the project's debt service, and (2) the project's residual value will be less than the amount of the project debt. The re-introduction of the concept of risk might cause either (or both) of the lender and the investor to resist increasing the amount of debt on the project— even if the incremental debt theoretically constitutes positive leverage. The characterization of leverage as being positive or negative relates strictly to the math of the return on equity calculation and has nothing to do with qualitative levels of project risk.

The developer must also remember that the viability of the financial calculations discussed in this section is totally dependent on the accuracy of the projections and assumptions on which such calculations are based. If the developer's zest to increase its return on equity causes it to overstate its projected net operating income, the fact that its calculations show that leverage is still mathematically positive will be of little import in the ensuing work-out negotiations with the construction lender and the outside equity investor.

There are other real world consequences to increasing leverage on a deal. The interest rate charged on a construction loan having a loan-to-value ratio of 90% is likely be higher than the interest rate charged on a loan on the same project that has a loan-to-value ratio of 60%. The construction lender is also much more likely to be inclined to place stringent conditions on its loan disbursements under the 90% LTV loan than it is under a lower-leveraged project, including, for example, the imposition of a condition that no disbursements will be made until at least 50% of the project is leased to creditworthy tenants. When chasing yield, the developer must be cognizant of both the economic and non-economic deal changes that may be triggered by an increase in the project's leverage ratio.

There are two other factors that may cause the equity investors to make an investment decision that runs counter to the pure math of positive and negative leverage.

- *Scarcity of Capital*—If the investors are running low on cash or simply want to spread their cash over a wider range of projects, they may opt to increase the amount of the project's leverage even if the math shows that the resulting debt increase moves the project's leverage into the "negative" category. From the perspective of a cash-poor investor, a reduced equity return of 15% is better than the alternative return of 0% that would be produced if the project cannot move forward at a lower leverage level.

- *Lack of Comparable Alternative Investments*—Similarly, if the investors do not have any other place to invest their money to achieve a return comparable to the return achievable on the subject real estate project, they may opt to decrease the amount of the project's leverage even if math shows that the resulting decrease in the amount of the project's positive leverage reduces the investors' returns on equity. From the investor's perspective, a reduced equity return of 12% on an investment of $4 million is better than an equity return of 15% on an investment of $3 million if the investors' remaining available funds of $1 million must be invested in Treasury Notes at a 1% annual yield.

VI. AFTER-TAX ECONOMIC RETURNS

All of the return measurements discussed in this chapter have been pre-tax computations—that is, the financial impact of federal, state, and local income tax laws has not been taken into consideration in any way. There are three reasons why real estate economic models generally adopt a pre-tax bias.

- Most real estate projects are owned by so-called *pass-through tax entities*—that is, entities that do not directly pay any taxes, but rather pass on all tax attributes and consequences to its equity owners.[23]

- The tax consequences of a real estate investment may vary widely from investor to investor due to the individual tax profile of each investor. It is, therefore, virtually impossible to create an economic model of general applicability that accurately measures and compares the after-tax return produced from a real estate investment.

- The tax laws governing the development and ownership of real estate change so rapidly as to make the formulation of any enduring after-tax economic model extremely difficult. Examples of major tax legislation passed during the period of

---

[23] *See infra* Chapter 7, pages 216–219 for a further discussion of the tax treatment of "pass-through entities."

the author's practice of law are the Tax Reform Act of 1976, The Economic Recovery Tax Act of 1981, The Deficit Reduction Act of 1984, The Tax Reform Act of 1986, and the Growth and Tax Relief and Reconciliation Act of 2001. Each of these acts significantly altered the way that real estate investments are treated for federal income tax purposes. If the current administration is to be believed, investors can expect drastic changes (albeit of an unknown content) in the way their real estate investments are taxed in the future.

Although the tax consequences of investing in real estate may not be susceptible to inclusion in any tight economic model, those consequences nonetheless significantly impact the overall economic benefits of a particular taxpayer's investment in real estate. The provisions of the Internal Revenue Code governing depreciation deductions, tax credits, passive losses, like-kind exchanges, and capital gains are of particular import to the real estate investor. While these and other tax law provisions can impact a real estate investor's financial returns, they currently are seldom the driving force behind an investor's decision whether it will or will not invest in a particular project. Whether that circumstance continues under the current administration is anybody's guess.

VII.   COMPARABLE INVESTMENTS

Developers develop commercial real estate projects and institutional investors invest in commercial real estate projects for one simple and very obvious reason—to make money. As such, commercial real estate is what one prominent real estate expert has referred to as an "investable asset."[24] As stated many times in this chapter, an investor puts its money into a commercial real estate project with the expectation of receiving both (1) current income on a periodic basis (represented by the project's annual NOI and the investor's annual before tax cash flow), and (2) a big payday when the project is sold for a price in excess of its original cost (represented by the project's residual value).

When courting investors, the developer and its lawyer must recognize that there are many "investable assets" other than commercial real estate. The following are the five primary asset classes that attract the attention of institutional investors:[25]

---

[24] *See* GELTNER, *supra* note 22, at 135.

[25] Professor Geltner list four "investable" asset classes in his book—cash, stocks, bonds, and real estate. *See id.* at 135–136. I have chosen to add commodities as a fifth asset class. I considered adding closely-held start-up businesses as yet another "investable asset," but decided not to (as did Professor Geltner) for the reason that venture capitalists who invest in start-ups seldom invest in the other listed asset classes. *See id.* at 135, note 13.

- Cash (Treasury notes, money market accounts, certificates of deposit, and other cash equivalents);

- Stocks;

- Bonds;

- Commodities (gold, oil, wheat, etc.); and

- Real estate.

The real estate developer's task is to persuade the institutional investor that at least a portion of the investor's portfolio should be invested in the developer's real estate project. In order to do so, the developer must be prepared not only to convince the investor that the developer's project is a superior investment compared to other real estate projects, but also to persuade the investor that the developer's project merits the investor's investment when compared with all other "investable" asset classes.

An institutional investor looks at many factors when determining how to invest its available capital. The investor's ultimate goal is to maximize the ***risk-adjusted return*** of its portfolio. An investor determines its "risk-adjusted return" by attempting to infuse in its financial return calculations discount factors that take into consideration the variance in risk among the panoply of available investable assets.[26] In doing so, the institutional investor focuses on the following questions when determining whether to invest dollars in cash, stocks, bonds, commodities, or the developer's real estate project:[27]

- What is the projected current income generated from each investment?

- What is the projected growth in value of each investment?

- What are the tax consequences of the investor's receipt of cash distributions from each investment?

- What is the risk associated with the investor's receipt of the projected income and value growth of each investment?

- What investment makes the most sense for the investor given the make-up of the investor's existing portfolio (for example, is its portfolio under-invested in stocks or over-invested in real estate)?

The answer to each of these questions is a decided "it depends"—both when the return/risk parameters of each asset class are viewed on an historical basis and when those parameters are viewed on a date certain. By way of

---

[26] *See* KOLBE, *supra* note 6, at 301–313, and 518; and BRUEGGEMAN, *supra* note 8, at 384–414.

[27] *See* GELTNER, *supra* note 22, at 135–145; and Thomas F. Kaufman, *Understanding Real Estate Economics,* in ALI-CLE MODERN REAL ESTATE TRANSACTIONS, Course No. SY006 1031, 1033–1034, and 1053 (August 2016).

example, I submit that the ranking of the desirability of the following investments would likely differ if the investment decision were being made in 2000, 2009, or 2017:

- Stock in Microsoft;

- Bond issued by the City of Chicago;

- Money market account at Deutsche Bank;

- Gold;

- Warehouse building in Columbus, Ohio 100% leased to Macy's.

All the developer needs to do is convince an institutional investor that the developer's Columbus, Ohio warehouse building produces risk-adjusted returns that fit squarely within the investor's then existing investment profile. To achieve that objective, the developer needs to (1) take into consideration the impact the time value of money has on the financial returns produced by the developer's project, and (2) produce a thoughtful economic model that justifies the wisdom of the investor's investment in the developer's project. Those two topics are addressed in the final two sections of this chapter.

VIII.   TIME VALUE OF MONEY

Dr. Mike Miles, a noted real estate finance expert, once described the fundamentals of real estate investment in the following simple, but sage way:

> When comparing alternatives for investment, investors are motivated by two preferences:
>
> *MORE IS BETTER THAN LESS; AND*
> *SOONER IS BETTER THAN LATER.*[28]

Dr. Miles provided the following gloss on the two simple axioms set forth above.

> When comparing alternative investments that carry comparable risk and require an equal capital investment, investors prefer the alternative that will produce the most total income from operations and resale; hence more is better than less. And among alternatives for investment with comparable risk and equal total income, investors prefer the option that will produce income more quickly; hence, sooner is better than later.[29]

This chapter has thus far focused on the magnitude of economic returns, measured both from the perspective of the project as a whole (the

---

[28] MILES, *supra* note 1, at 83 (emphasis added).

[29] *Id.*

concepts of net operating income, residual value, and return on total costs) and from the separate perspectives of the construction lender (return on debt) and the investor (return on equity). The magnitude of the cash flows is what Dr. Miles was referring to when he made his "more is better than less" statement.

This chapter has also discussed how the element of project risk affects the investment decisions and return expectations of the parties. Implicit in Dr. Miles' quoted statement is the proposition that, if the magnitude and timing of the receipt of cash flows from two investment alternatives are comparable, then the investor will select the alternative that has the least risk. In this context, risk is defined in terms of the relative predictability of the investor's actual receipt of the projected cash flows from the project. Once an investor begins to question the likelihood that a project will produce cash flow in the projected magnitude and at the projected times, then its choice is either to decline the investment opportunity as being too risky, or to demand that its projected return from the investment be increased to reward it for its acceptance of increased project risk.

One consideration that has not yet been factored into this chapter's discussion of project economics is the impact that the timing of the projected cash flows has on (1) the value of a real estate project, and (2) the investor's economic return from its investment in that project. The remainder of this chapter is devoted to a review of the implications to the investor of the *time value of money*.

Dr. Miles' statement that "sooner is better than later" is the essence of the time value of money concept. As explained by Dr. Miles, "three major concepts drive the notion that a dollar received today is more valuable than a dollar received in the future: (1) opportunity cost, (2) inflation, and (3) risk."[30]

- *Opportunity cost* is the "foregone opportunity to earn interest on funds committed to other investments."[31] In other words, if a particular investment calls for a deferral of the investor's receipt of a payment, then that investor is deprived for the period of the deferral of the ability to invest the amount of that payment in an interest-bearing account or another investment vehicle.

- *Inflation* is an economic concept with which everyone is fairly familiar. Inflation is generally defined as an increase in prices that results in a decline in purchasing power. In the context of the valuation of real estate, inflation simply means that if a payment is to be received in the future, then its value in today's dollars is reduced by the percentage of inflation

---

[30] *Id.*

[31] KOLBE, *supra* note 6, at 514

that occurs through the period ending with the future payment date.

- **Risk** is the concept that acknowledges the chance that a future payment may not be received at the projected time or in the projected amount.

All three of these factors must be taken into account when determining how much less valuable a future payment is when compared to a current payment in a like amount (the so-called **present value** of the future payment). The **discounted cash flow model** is a real estate valuation methodology that is designed to take all these time value of money concepts into consideration.

IX. REAL ESTATE VALUATION METHODOLOGIES[32]

There are four principal methodologies that developers, lenders, and investors use to evaluate and compare real estate development projects— (1) the discounted cash flow model, (2) the internal rate of return model, (3) the capitalization rate model, and (4) the payback period model. The pros and cons of each of those valuation methodologies are discussed below.

A. DISCOUNTED CASH FLOW

The discounted cash flow model (**DCF**) is "[a]n investment evaluation technique that incorporates adjustments for both volume and timing of anticipated future cash flows and is generally accepted as the most desirable approach to evaluating opportunities."[33] The DCF model requires the financial analyst to undertake each of the following tasks.

- First, all future revenues and expenses of the real estate project must be *FORECASTED* with as much accuracy and foresight as possible. It is common for the forecasting period to be at least ten years in duration, with the end point of that forecasting period being the projected sale of the project.

- Once the financial forecast is completed, all of the forecasted revenue and expense items are then *DISCOUNTED* (or reduced) to determine their present value under the time value of money concepts discussed above.

1. Forecasting of Future Cash Flows

The forecasting of future cash flows is a very time-consuming and painstaking process. In effect, the DCF method requires the analyst to

---

[32] For an excellent discussion of the various valuation methodologies used to analyze real estate investments, *see generally* Kaufman, *supra* note 27, at 1038–1050.

[33] *See* KOLBE, *supra* note 6, at 504.

predict in great detail both the amount and the timing of each monthly item of income and expense generated from a project over a period of years. The end product of the financial analyst's forecasting efforts is a set of projected cash inflows and outflows that is known in the real estate industry as the *pro forma*.

In preparing the project pro forma, the financial analyst must make a number of assumptions concerning future occurrences, for example:

- The timing and degree to which the building will be leased to rent-paying tenants;

- The rents that will be achieved on the building's lease-up;

- The developer's costs of operating the project once it is leased (for example, utility costs, real estate taxes, insurance premiums, etc.);

- The level of inflation that will occur in both rents and operating costs;

- The costs that the developer will have to incur to ready each tenant's space for occupancy;

- The likelihood that a tenant will default in the payment of its rent;

- The prospects that a tenant will renew its lease;

- The length of time that it will take the developer to re-lease the space and the added costs that the developer will need to incur if a tenant opts not to renew its lease;

- The financial terms of a permanent loan on the project;

- The projected cost of maintaining and repairing the building in future periods; and

- The purchase price at which the project will ultimately be sold.[34]

This is an extremely arduous task that requires the participation of a financial analyst who is both experienced in the real estate industry generally and intimately acquainted with the financial and legal details associated with the specific project in question. Aspiring real estate development lawyers should be forewarned that the developer often calls upon its lawyer to review and bless the analyst's assumptions that relate to the various economic rights, obligations, and liabilities spelled out in the leases and other legal documents governing the project's operations. So a shout out to the aspiring real estate development lawyer—get ready to learn and contribute.

---

[34] *See* Kaufman, *supra* note 27, at 1048–1049.

2. Selection of Discount Rate

Once the financial forecast is completed, the financial analyst must then select an appropriate rate at which to discount all of the future cash flows (both income and expenses). Determining the appropriate discount rate is a function of the time value of money concepts discussed above—that is, opportunity cost, inflation, and risk. The import of these elements (and, hence, the discount rate used to evaluate a particular project) varies from investor to investor and from project to project. While there are numerous secondary sources that attempt to collect data about discount rates being used in the marketplace at any particular point in time, there is little doubt that the process of selecting a discount rate "is as much an art as it is a science."[35]

An investor's perception of risk is the key determinant in the investor's selection of a discount rate to evaluate a real estate investment opportunity. As the word "perception" indicates, the assignment of a risk variable to a particular project is an inherently subjective task. As part of its risk assessment, the investor needs to take into account a number of factors, expressly including: (1) the product type of the subject real estate project (office building, warehouse, retail center, etc.); (2) the geographic market in which the project is located; (3) the supply and demand curves for comparable properties in the geographic market where the subject project is located; and (4) the degree to which the project is pre-leased to creditworthy tenants. By way of example, an office building in New York City that is 100% pre-leased to Microsoft Corporation for a term of 20 years is likely to command a lower discount rate than a fully speculative 100,000-square-foot office building in Mobile, Alabama.

The ultimate question that the investor must answer when setting a discount rate for a specific real estate development project is—What is the minimum rate of return that the investor requires as a condition to its investment in a particular project? That minimally acceptable rate of return (commonly referred to as a *hurdle rate*) is the discount rate that the investor will use when it runs its DCF model on the subject real estate project. One thing to always remember is that the value assigned to a particular real estate project has an inverse relationship with the discount rate used in the DCF modeling—that is, the *HIGHER THE DISCOUNT RATE, THE LOWER THE VALUE OF THE PROJECT*.

3. Operation of DCF Model

The operation of a discounted cash flow model is best illustrated by reference to a few rudimentary examples.

---

[35] Circo, *supra* note 6, at 9.

Example 3-3: Assume that a real estate project has the following financial characteristics:

- Equity contributions $2,000,000
- Annual cash flows
  - Year 1 $200,000
  - Year 2 $225,000
  - Year 3 $250,000
- Net sale proceeds in Year 4   <u>$3,000,000</u>
- Total cash flows $3,675,000

The project generates a net positive return for its investors (before the application of any time value of money concepts) of $1,675,000 (total cash flows of $3,675,000, less the investors' equity contributions of $2 million).

The next two examples show how the time value of money concepts impact an investor's real financial returns.

Example 3-4: Assume that a discount rate of 10% is determined to be a fair reflection of the opportunity cost, inflation, and risk associated with a deferral of the cash flows generated from the project that was the subject of Example 3-3. The following table shows the present values of the project's annual cash flows in Years 1–3 and the net proceeds of the sale of the project in Year 4.[36]

Time Period	Actual Cash Flow	Present Value of Cash Flow (@ 10%)
Year 1	$200,000	$181,818
Year 2	$225,000	$189,950
Year 3	$250,000	$187,828
Year 4 Sale	$3,000,000	$2,049,040
Total Cash Flows	$3,675,000	$2,604,636
Less: Equity Contributions	$2,000,000	$2,000,000
Net Positive Cash Flow	$1,675,000	$604,636

---

[36] For the purposes of Examples 3-4 through 3-6, it is assumed that the annual cash flows are received once a year on the last day of the year and that the net proceeds of sale are received on the last day of Year 4 (with the project not producing any other cash flow in Year 4).

The operation of the DCF model shows that the ***net present value*** of the investor's investment in Example 3-4 is $604,636 (the aggregate present value of all of the project's cash flows, less the investors' initial equity contributions of $2 million).

Example 3-5: Assume that the investors' equity contributions ($2 million) and the selected discount rate (10%) are the same as in Example 3-4, but that the cash flows produced from the project are as follows:

Annual cash flows

Year 1	$100,000
Year 2	$150,000
Year 3	$275,000
Net sale proceeds in Year 4	$3,150,000
Total cash flows	$3,675,000

The total cash flows payable to the investors in Example 3-5 are the same as in Example 3-4—that is, $3,675,000. The difference between the cash flows in the two examples is that the cash flows in Example 3-5 are more back-loaded than those assumed in Example 3-4—that is, the net proceeds of sale in Example 3-5 are $150,000 higher than those in Example 3-4, but its annual cash flows in Years 1–3 are $150,000 lower than those produced from the project in Example 3-4.

The implications under a DCF analysis of the back-loading of the cash flows in Example 3-5 are evidenced in the following table.

Time Period	Actual Cash Flow	Present Value of Cash Flow (@ 10%)
Year 1	$100,000	$90,909
Year 2	$150,000	$123,966
Year 3	$275,000	$206,611
Year 4 Sale	$3,150,000	$2,151,492
Total Cash Flows	$3,675,000	$2,571,978
Less: Equity Contributions	$2,000,000	$2,000,000
Net Positive Cash Flow	$1,675,000	$571,978

The net present value of the investors' investment in Example 3-5 is $571,978 (the present value of all of the project's cash flows, less the investors' equity contributions of $2 million). This result is $32,385 less than the net present value of the investor's position under Example 3-4—a differential that exists even though the aggregate cash flows payable to the investors under both examples is $3,675,000. The difference in the net present value numbers produced in the two examples is attributable to the fact that the Example 3-4 project produced cash flows to its investors quicker than did the project illustrated in Example 3-5. Under the time value of money concept represented by Dr. Miles' "sooner is better than later" maxim, a rational investor with limited capital should select the Example 3-4 project for investment over the Example 3-5 project.

The present values of the cash flows in both Examples 3-4 and 3-5 were calculated using the same 10% discount rate—meaning that an investment in the two hypothetical projects was determined to be of equal risk. What would happen if the project in Example 3-4 were determined to be so risky that it merits the use of a discount rate higher than 10%? Example 3-6 shows how the element of risk affects a project's value under a DCF analysis.

Example 3-6: Assume all of the same facts applicable to Example 3-4, with one exception—the investor determines that the location of the project makes its receipt of the projected cash flows much less predictable than was the case with respect to the Example 3-4 project. As a result, the investor determines that the proper discount rate to evaluate its future cash flows is 12% (and not 10% as used in Example 3-4). The impact of this adjustment to the project's discount rate is illustrated in the following table.

Time Period	Actual Cash Flow	Present Value of Cash Flow (@ 12%)
Year 1	$200,000	$178,571
Year 2	$225,000	$179,368
Year 3	$250,000	$177,945
Year 4 Sale	$3,000,000	$1,906,554
Total Cash Flows	$3,675,000	$2,442,438
Less: Equity Contributions	$2,000,000	$2,000,000
Net Positive Cash Flow	$1,675,000	$442,438

The adjustment of the discount rate to reflect greater project risk causes the net present value of the Example 3-6 project to be $162,198 less than that of the Example 3-4 project—despite the fact that both the amount and timing of the cash flows in those two examples are identical. This reduction in the net present value of the Example 3-6 project is solely attributable to the investor's perception of the greater risk inherent in that project.

4. Investor's Use of DCF Results[37]

If the net present value of an investor's investment exceeds zero, then, by definition, an investor with unlimited funds should invest in that project. This proposition flows from the fact that the discount rate presumably used by the investor in running its DCF model is the investor's hurdle rate, which, as noted earlier in this chapter, represents the minimum rate of return that the investor demands as a condition to its investment in the project. Investing in every project that produces a return in excess of its hurdle rate (meaning that the net present value of the investor's investment exceeds zero) should theoretically position an investor to achieve its desired investment returns—unless, of course, the investor selected a discount/hurdle rate that failed to accurately reflect the real risk of investing in the subject project. Similarly, any project that produces a net present value that is less than zero should be rejected out of hand by the investor because, by definition, the returns produced by that project are less than the investor's hurdle rate.

OK, that is enough discussion of what an investor with unlimited funds should theoretically do—because there is no such thing as an investor with unlimited funds (even CALPERS and the Abu Dhabi Investment Authority fall a bit short of that theoretical classification). The real world investor uses DCF modeling to rank the relative attractiveness of each investment opportunity presented to it and then invests in those projects that produce the highest net present values until the amount of the investor's budgeted equity contributions are exhausted. If an investor looking at the projects described in the prior section of this chapter has $4 million to invest in a particular year, its DCF modeling would lead it to conclude that it should invest in the projects described in Examples 3-4 and 3-5, because those projects produce higher net present values ($604,636 and $571,998, respectively) than the project described in Example 3-6 ($442,438).

B. INTERNAL RATE OF RETURN

The end result of a DCF analysis is a net present value number that can then be compared to the investor's original cash outlay to determine

[37] *See generally* Kaufman, *supra* note 27, at 1045–1046.

whether the subject investment generates a return that is greater or less than the investor's minimum hurdle rate for that investment. The DCF analysis does not, however, show the exact percentage rate of return that is generated from an investment alternative. An investor who wants to know the percentage return on equity of a particular investment opportunity must instead use an *internal rate of return* calculation.

An investment's internal rate of return (**IRR**) is the percentage rate at which the present value of a series of future cash flows is exactly equal to the required initial cash investment. An investment that has a positive net present value should have an internal rate of return in excess of the investor's hurdle rate for that investment, while an investment that has a negative net present value should have an IRR below the investor's hurdle rate. Consistent with the above DCF discussion, a project that has an IRR less than the investor's hurdle rate should be rejected, while a project having an IRR in excess of the investor's hurdle rate should theoretically be acceptable to the investor who has unlimited financial resources.

The DCF and IRR calculations usually provide the prospective investor with the same signals as to those projects that are suitable for the investor's equity investment. The primary difference between these two evaluation techniques is that the DCF of a prospective investment is expressed in terms of dollars, while the IRR is expressed in percentage terms. In most situations, a prospective equity investor (particularly an institutional investor) will use both DCF and IRR calculations to determine the acceptability of a particular investment opportunity.[38] I have opted to devote more attention to DCF modeling than the IRR methodology, because (1) my experience tells me that most real estate investors favor DCF over IRR calculations, and (2) many of the same factors that shape DCF modeling also apply to an IRR analysis (for example, the establishment of a hurdle rate based on the investor's evaluation of the risk of investing in a project).

C. CAPITALIZATION RATE

The use of a *capitalization rate* to determine a project's value is another commonly used valuation method. This method determines the value of a project by "capitalizing" (that is, dividing) a stabilized project's NOI by a percentage rate that is used to determine the price payable for the sale of comparable properties. The capitalization rate valuation formula is as follows: project value = stabilized NOI ÷ capitalization rate.

The capitalization rate (or *cap rate*) is intended to represent the percentage return a buyer will demand as a condition to its purchase of a

---

[38] For a comparison of the DCF and IRR methodologies and the usage of those methodologies by members of the real estate industry, *see* Kaufman, *supra* note 27, at 1043–1044, 1047; and KOLBE, *supra* note 6, at 247–258.

particular project. In this respect a cap rate shares many of the same attributes as the "hurdle rate" mentioned earlier in this chapter. The selected cap rate is determined by looking at sales of comparable properties and calculating the ratio between the purchase price paid for each property and its net operating income in the year of sale.

Example 3-7: Assume that the sales of two office projects have the following characteristics:

Office Building A:

- Sales Price = $5,000,000; and
- NOI = $350,000.

Office Building B:

- Sales Price = $6,000,000; and
- NOI = $480,000.

The sale of Office Building A for $5 million produces a cap rate of 7% (NOI of $350,000, divided by the sales price of $5 million), while the sale of Office Building B produces a cap rate of 8% (NOI of $480,000, divided by the sales price of $6million). Under the capitalization rate valuation method, the value of a development project considered comparable to Office Buildings A and B could be determined by dividing the project's stabilized NOI by a capitalization rate of 7.5% (the average of the two capitalization rates produced from the sales of Office Buildings A and B).

The attraction of the cap rate model is its simplicity. While it is not quite to the point of being a "back of the napkin" valuation, it certainly is nowhere near as complex or involved as are the DCF and IRR calculations discussed in the prior sections of this chapter. For this reason, the capitalization rate method is more likely to be used by brokers trying to put a general price tag on a listed property than it is by an equity investor or lender evaluating a project for potential investment. Lenders and investors tend to rely on DCF and IRR valuations for the following three reasons.

- DCF and IRR models require the preparer to make very explicit assumptions about every aspect of a project's future operations. The reasonableness of the assumptions can be evaluated by a lender or investor and then subjected to a sensitivity analysis to determine the impact of changed assumptions on the project's value.

- The cap rate method is premised on the relative stability and equality of a project's NOI from year to year—an assumption that is frequently ill-founded. The DCF and IRR analyses not only expressly allow for variations in a project's annual cash flows, but also discount those cash flows to properly account for the time value of money.

- The cap rate methodology is based on the assumption that it is possible to identify comparable sales of comparable properties. Given the complexity of today's real estate markets, the process of identifying such comparability is extremely difficult and uncertain.

While a capitalization rate approach is seldom used on a stand-alone basis to determine the projected value of a development project, the use of a cap rate to determine the future sales price of the project is a central component of all valuation methodologies. In both a DCF and IRR calculation, a financial analyst must select a capitalization rate to apply to the project's NOI at the time of sale to arrive at a sales price for the project. The cap rate used to compute the project's sale price is commonly referred as an *exit cap rate*. The selection of an exit cap rate is a daunting task for two reasons—(1) the sale of the project is almost always projected to occur many years in the future (typically at least seven and often up to 20 years after the date of the completion of the project's construction), and (2) the use of an inappropriate cap rate can dramatically affect the projected value of a real estate project, because such a high percentage of a project's total cash flows is represented by its ultimate sales price.

D. PAYBACK PERIOD

Another investment calculation that is frequently used in the real estate industry is the *payback period*. This simple calculation looks at how long it takes an investor to receive cash distributions equal to its original equity contribution. By way of example, if an investor makes a $2 million equity contribution to a real estate venture and receives cash distributions of $500,000 from the venture in Years 1 and 2 and $1 million in Year 3, then the payback period for the investor is three years—that is the time it takes the investor to receive cash distributions from the venture equal to its initial $2 million equity contribution.

The payback period calculation is obviously not nearly as instructive when evaluating competing real estate projects as are the DCF and IRR models discussed earlier in this chapter. The payback period does not account for any cash distributions (or losses) occurring in any period after the date on which the investor receives cash equal to its initial equity investment. The payback period calculation also fails to fully take into consideration the concept of the time value of money. Having said that, virtually every real estate developer I have ever met is generally more interested in the payback period for a project than it is the IRR or the NPV of that project. For that reason, most DCF and IRR models I have seen over the years contain a line item that specifically notes the payback period for the investor's equity contribution.

E. DANGERS ASSOCIATED WITH ECONOMIC MODELS

Before leaving the topic of project economics, one quick note should be made about the dangers inherent in preparing and relying on financial models for a proposed development project. All financial models are based on *PROJECTIONS* of a project's financial performance. Projections are nothing more than a developer's guess (hopefully, an educated one) about how a particular project will fare in the future—for example, how much will the project cost to build, when will it lease and at what rents, and what will the economy look like in the years after the finished project is brought online. There are no definitive answers to these questions when the projections are being prepared. The old adage about "garbage in, garbage out" is as applicable to real estate as it is to any other industry. Developers and investors should, therefore, be careful not to place too much stock in a project's initial financial projections.

A practitioner who is well-acquainted with the world of real estate finance offered up the following critique of the role that financial models play in the real estate investment arena.

> Models are important for evaluating real estate and great care should be exercised in creating, reviewing and relying on them. Nevertheless, the best real estate investors do not necessarily have the best models. If the key to real estate was the best models, then the best spreadsheet or model would create the most successful investor and that is clearly not the case. Common sense, single-minded conviction, hard work, intuition and luck are all key elements of a successful real estate investment portfolio.[39]

In the aftermath of the financial crisis of 2008, one particularly jaundiced, real estate observer made much the same point by noting that "[r]eal estate is a good business for B students who work hard, not PhDs with computer models."[40] For what it is worth, I believe that a good real estate development lawyer must possess both the moxie and drive of the exalted developer and the grades and intellect of the disparaged PhD.

X. SUMMARY

After slogging your way through this chapter, you are undoubtedly once again asking "Do I really need to know all of these economic concepts

---

[39] *See* Kaufman, *supra* note 27, at 1035.

[40] *See* URBAN LAND INSTITUTE AND PRICEWATERHOUSECOOPERS, EMERGING TRENDS IN REAL ESTATE 10 (October 2009).

and formulas?" Like it or not, the answer to that question is an unequivocal "yes." Today's loan and equity documents are strewn with definitions of net operating income, present value, internal rates of return, loan-to-value ratio, debt service coverage, and the like. The real estate development lawyer must understand these concepts so that the lawyer can manipulate the variables and assumptions implicit in such definitions in a manner that favors the developer. Entering into negotiations with counsel for a lender or equity investor without a solid understanding of all these economic concepts will produce the same result for the real estate development lawyer that follows from a fellow going to a gunfight with a knife—the fight will be lost in a quick and very spectacular fashion.

CHAPTER 4

THE HEATHROW INTERNATIONAL BUSINESS CENTER: A CASE STUDY

• • •

I. INTRODUCTION

As I started work on the second edition of this book, I gave serious consideration to changing the case study that was used throughout the first edition (the Heathrow International Business Center, circa 1992–2002) to a case study of more recent vintage. I ultimately decided to stick with Heathrow International Business Center as the case study for the second edition for a few reasons:

- The Heathrow International Business Center deal is a perfect platform for a discussion of the ten stages of a real estate development project—and one with which I am intimately familiar due to my work on that deal over a ten-year period;

- The real estate development business and the practice of real estate development law are timeless endeavors in which anything of real substance seldom changes; and

- I am 64 years old and too lazy to rewrite the hundred pages or so of the first edition's rehashing of the Heathrow International Business Center project.

So for all those reasons (both good and bad), let's take a look at the project that serves as the principal case study for the second edition of this book.

II. DESCRIPTION OF PROJECT

The Heathrow International Business Center ("HIBC") is an approximately 400 acre, mixed use, commercial real estate project located off of Interstate Route 4, just north of Orlando, Florida. I was fortunate to be at the center of the development of HIBC throughout the ten-year period covered by this case study. At the time of its sale to Colonial Properties Trust in year 10 (at which time the author's direct involvement in the project largely ceased), the HIBC project included the following components:

Office—15 office buildings containing over 2 million square feet of space;

Hotel—A full service Marriott hotel and a Marriott Courtyard hotel;

Multi-family—Two apartment complexes;

Retail—A neighborhood strip center and a boutique shopping plaza; and

Land—Over 100 acres of undeveloped commercial land.

III. PROJECT'S EARLY HISTORY

HIBC was the brainchild of Jeno Paulucci (of Jeno's Pizza Rolls and Chun-King Foods fame). Paulucci had the dream of developing a high-end, master planned residential and golf community north of Orlando. Paulucci believed (correctly as it turned out, although not in the time frames he originally contemplated) that the golf and residential community should be complemented by a commercial component—hence the creation of HIBC located directly adjacent to the Heathrow golf course and just off of the main north-south highway in Orlando—Interstate Route 4. Paulucci managed to work his way through the State of Florida's complicated zoning and governmental entitlement process and received all of the requisite governmental approvals to kick off development of HIBC.

Paulucci immediately built an elaborate entranceway to the park and oversaw the construction of a Marriott Courtyard Hotel, a neighborhood retail center (grocery store, pharmacy, and local space), and three office buildings.[1] Development of the neighboring golf course and gated residential community was proceeding along smoothly under Jeno's guidance when the Central Florida real estate markets hit the wall. Given the depressed state of the Central Florida real estate economy, a pioneering project such as HIBC was doomed for failure. Jeno became frustrated with the whole HIBC project and decided to exit the Orlando real estate business and take with him whatever still existed of the fortune he had made in the frozen food industry. Once his dalliance with the real estate development world ended, Paulucci went on to found yet another fast food company— Luigino's, Inc., which today sells frozen food under the Michelina brand name.

---

[1] Two of those buildings were speculative office buildings, each of which contained approximately 85,000 square feet of rentable space. The third office building was built by AAA to serve as its new national headquarters. In his self-published biography, *The Power of the Peddler*, Paulucci recounts a story about having to scale a 12-foot high, barbed wire fence at AAA's then corporate headquarters outside of Washington D.C. in order to arrive on time for a meeting with AAA's CEO to make a pitch that AAA should relocate its headquarters to the HIBC site. *See* JENO PAULUCCI, THE POWER OF THE PEDDLER 429–433 (Paulucci International 2006).

Over a period of about seven years, Paulucci was able to extract himself from all entanglements with both the Heathrow residential community and the neighboring HIBC commercial development. His departure was executed through a mixture of sales, foreclosures, and other arrangements with his real estate creditors and partners. Two of those transactions are particularly germane to this case study.

- *HIBC 300 Office Building*—The 300 building was the second office building constructed in HIBC. The development of the 300 building was undertaken by a joint venture between Paulucci and Cabot, Cabot, and Forbes, a prominent Boston-based real estate developer. The Bank of New England provided the construction loan on the 300 building and ended up taking over ownership of that building by way of a deed in lieu of foreclosure. The Bank of New England failed the next year and was taken over by the FDIC. The FDIC immediately began actively marketing for sale all of the Bank of New England's real estate assets, including the HIBC 300 building.[2]

- *Undeveloped HIBC Land*—Paulucci's ownership of the undeveloped HIBC land (then consisting of approximately 350 acres) was subject to a mortgage loan in favor of Chemical Bank. After lengthy work-out negotiations, Paulucci agreed to convey the undeveloped HIBC land to Chemical Bank by way of a deed in lieu of foreclosure. Chemical Bank immediately put the land on the market for sale.

IV. AUTHOR'S HISTORY WITH HIBC

Throughout the ten-year history of this case study, I was Executive Vice President and General Counsel of the Pizzuti Companies ("Pizzuti"), a real estate development company that was headquartered in Columbus, Ohio, and had a satellite office in Orlando, Florida. In Year 1, Pizzuti became aware that the FDIC was planning to put the HIBC 300 building up for sale as part of its attempt to liquidate its ownership of the Bank of New England's real estate portfolio. Through a whole host of fortunate circumstances, Pizzuti was able to circumvent the normal FDIC bidding process and acquire the exclusive right to bid on the purchase of the HIBC

---

[2]   The author had occasion to talk to a loan officer who had handled Bank of New England's construction loan on the HIBC 300 building. The loan officer admitted that neither he, nor anyone else at the bank, had ever visited HIBC. When I asked him why a site inspection had not been scheduled, he replied that he considered such a trip to be unnecessary in light of the fact that the project was "located in downtown Orlando," a location which he and others at the bank felt was a fail-safe market for office development. The fact that the HIBC project was located in a pioneering location about 20 miles north of downtown Orlando was apparently a fact that never reared its ugly head during Bank of New England's underwriting of the construction loan on the HIBC 300 building. Given this type of laissez-faire loan due diligence, there is little wonder why the low quality of its real estate loan portfolio led to the FDIC's seizure of the bank.

300 building. Soon thereafter, Pizzuti closed on its acquisition of the HIBC 300 building and approximately 14 acres of vacant land located immediately adjacent to the 300 building.

As part of its due diligence on the 300 building acquisition, Pizzuti assigned the general manager of its Florida office to conduct interviews with the tenants of the 300 building (which didn't take that long given the building's 45% vacancy rate). During the course of those interviews, one of the tenants (an executive compensation consulting firm known as Newport Partners) passed on to Pizzuti's representative the desire of its principals to become partners in the purchase of the 300 building.

At the time, I was in the process of negotiating the terms of an acquisition loan for the 300 building with Barnett Bank. Because of the high vacancy rate in the building (and hence the lack of an income stream to support its loan), Barnett was insisting that Pizzuti assume personal liability for the repayment of the full loan. When I got the call from our Florida general manager telling me that Newport was interested in becoming a 50% partner in the 300 building acquisition, I somewhat cavalierly told him to pass on to the Newport principals that we would only consider having them as partners if their financial wherewithal was such that Barnett Bank would be willing to have them take over 50% of Pizzuti's personal liability on the acquisition loan (on a several basis). I viewed this as a quick way to get the Newport folks out of our hair, because I thought it was highly unlikely that two executive compensation consultants would have the kind of money to allow Barnett to accept them as guarantors of a 50% several liability position under the acquisition loan. Lo and behold, I received a call later that day from our contact at Barnett Bank asking if I knew the two principals of Newport. They had apparently just deposited $10 million in cash at a Barnett Bank branch office and had given instructions that I be made immediately aware of the deposit. Long story short,[3] Newport became Pizzuti's 50% partner on the 300 building acquisition and would serve as Pizzuti's 50% partner in the development of 11 HIBC office buildings over the next ten years.[4]

The next step in Pizzuti's involvement in HIBC came when Pizzuti received a Request for Proposal ("RFP") from Cincinnati Bell inquiring whether Pizzuti had an interest in submitting a proposal for the development of a 125,000-square-foot office building and a 60,000-square-foot data center in Orlando for Cincinnati Bell's Information Services division ("CBIS"). Pizzuti received the CBIS RFP because Pizzuti owned 14

---

[3] This was one of Ron Pizzuti's favorite phrases and, therefore, may show up frequently in this book.

[4] The two principals of Newport partners would assume a 50% several liability position on the construction loan for each of the 11 office development projects. Several liability (wherein each guarantor is liable for only its designated portion of a loan) stands in sharp contrast to the normal lender practice of requiring each of the loan guarantors to be jointly and severally liable for the repayment of 100% of the loan.

acres of developable acreage located adjacent to the 300 building. Unfortunately for Pizzuti, CBIS also sent its RFP to approximately 20 other developers who owned developable commercial ground in the North Orlando submarket.

Pizzuti's management team viewed the CBIS RFP as an ideal opportunity for Pizzuti (1) to get out from under its ownership of the 14 acres, and (2) to make its mark in the Orlando office market.[5] Unfortunately, after looking at the proposed plans and specifications for the CBIS project, Pizzuti quickly concluded that there was no way that the two CBIS buildings could be configured to fit on Pizzuti's 14-acre site. As the Pizzuti management team desperately tried to figure out an alternative land play that would permit it to respond to the CBIS RFP, yet another fortuitous event occurred that would prove to be pivotal to Pizzuti's development of the HIBC project.

Shortly after its receipt of the CBIS RFP, Pizzuti received a phone call from Chemical Bank asking if Pizzuti had an interest in buying the approximately 350-acre HIBC tract that Chemical had just acquired from Jeno Paulucci by way of a deed in lieu of foreclosure. The convenient juxtaposition of Pizzuti's receipt of the call from Chemical Bank only days after its receipt of the RFP from CBIS was typical of the good fortune that Pizzuti experienced throughout its involvement with the HIBC project. Pizzuti's development department hounded the senior management team unmercifully until Pizzuti's senior management finally agreed to contact Chemical Bank to see if Chemical would agree to sell Pizzuti the 20 or so acres that Pizzuti needed to construct the CBIS office and data center project. Unfortunately, (or, as it later turned out, fortunately), Chemical indicated that it was not willing to sell the HIBC land in bits and pieces and that it would only consider offers for the acquisition of the entire 350 acres. My initial reaction to Chemical's position was "Who the hell is going to be crazy enough to buy 350 acres of undeveloped land located 20 miles north of Orlando at a time when office vacancy rates nationwide and in Orlando are topping out at over 20%?"

Again, long story short, Pizzuti was just that crazy. It put the entirety of the HIBC land under contract at a purchase price of $7.5 million, won the bidding for the CBIS project, and somehow convinced its good friends at Newport to become a partner in the land acquisition and in all future office building projects at HIBC (including the CBIS project). As one principal from Newport said to me when we closed on the acquisition of the HIBC land, "It feels like we just decided to go over Niagara Falls in a barrel." Eight years later, the Pizzuti/Newport partnership had developed over 2 million square feet of office space at HIBC. I presume that Newport

---

[5] Pizzuti had developed two office buildings south of Orlando in the mid-1980's and was determined to significantly expand its presence in the Orlando office market.

still has the wine barrel I sent it following the HIBC land closing and I have one helluva case study for my book on Real Estate Development Law.

V. THE HIBC CASE STUDY

Two important lessons can be gleaned from reading the above history of the HIBC project—(1) the developer who has the initial grand vision for a project seldom is the one who makes the big bucks from that project (say hello to Jeno Paulucci), and (2) as in any other business, success in the real estate development business requires a blend of luck and skill. The foregoing discussion touched upon some of the luck that Pizzuti was blessed to receive during its involvement with the HIBC project. The HIBC project is used as a case study throughout the remainder of this text to examine the skill that the real estate development lawyer must bring to the representation of a developer client.

I selected HIBC as the primary case study for this book for the following reasons.

- First and foremost, HIBC is a "real deal" and not a hypothetical created solely for academic purposes. I am an ardent believer that the best way to learn about a particular practice area is to look at how real lawyers conducted themselves in the face of the challenges presented by real business transactions.

- I was intimately involved in every stage of the HIBC project. I am, therefore, in the unique position of being able to provide answers to the all-important questions of "why" the documents were structured in a particular way and "why" the parties took certain legal and business positions.

- HIBC was a big, complex project, in which the economic stakes of all of the participants were quite high. As a result, intense lawyering was the norm, producing a set of legal documents that, although far from perfect, are the product of ardent negotiations by sophisticated practitioners.

- HIBC is a great case study to examine the ten stages of a real estate development project. The HIBC project involved a little bit of everything from a transactional perspective, which makes it an excellent tool for examining the various trials and tribulations of the real estate development lawyer. Each of the ensuing chapters of this book includes an anecdotal discussion of (1) the legal and business issues faced by Pizzuti at each stage of the development of the HIBC project, and (2) the solutions crafted by Pizzuti's lawyers to respond to those issues.

My hope is that the HIBC case study proves to be as instructive to the reader of this text as it was to me during my ten-year involvement with the project.

CHAPTER 5

STAGE 1: GAINING CONTROL OF THE SITE

▪ ▪ ▪

I. INTRODUCTION

Stage 1 is the starting point for the real estate development lawyer's participation in the real estate development process. In most cases, the first time that the lawyer hears about a project is when the developer calls asking for help in "tying up a site." The story the developer tells its lawyer in this first phone call is almost always the same.

- I have a hot lead on a project and need to eliminate my competition for the project by tying up a site ASAP.

- No, I don't yet know whether the project is feasible. I can't take the time or spend the money to make that decision until I have control of the site.

- I know some of the challenges that lie ahead for the deal, but not all of them.

- I don't want to scare the landowner away, so keep whatever document you put together short and sweet—but make sure I am protected.

- In case I didn't mention it, I told the landowner that we would have something for the landowner to take a look at first thing tomorrow morning.

Once this call is made, the real estate development lawyer is fully immersed in the deal. The documents the lawyer puts together in Stage 1 not only serve as the road map for the project, but also set the tone for the entirety of the deal. In the parlance of the developer, this is the real estate development lawyer's first test to be either a deal maker or a deal killer.

II. BUSINESS OBJECTIVES OF THE PARTIES

The developer's business objective in Stage 1 is clear—it simply wants to tie up the site as quickly and as cheaply as possible. Gaining control of the site provides the developer with an advantage over its competitors as it goes about the process of seeing whether its project is feasible. The developer wants to delay its actual acquisition of the land for as long as possible, so that it has sufficient time to complete its feasibility study and otherwise be in a position to start construction of the project immediately following the land acquisition closing. Delaying the purchase of the development site in such a fashion accomplishes two basic goals of the developer—(1) it lessens the developer's risk that something might happen prior to commencement of construction that will make the project infeasible (that is, in the vernacular of the developer, the project "doesn't work"), and (2) it lowers the developer's overall development costs by eliminating the costs of owning the land (for example, real estate taxes and interest) prior to the land being put into production.

When the developer says it wants to *TIE UP* the land, the developer does not mean that it wants to buy the land right away. In most situations, owning the land is the furthest thing from the developer's mind at this stage of the development process. The developer wants to *CONTROL* the land parcel by securing the exclusive contractual right to buy the parcel if and when the developer ultimately decides to move forward with its development project. Because land is not an income-producing asset, inventorying land separate and apart from an in-process development project is anathema to the typical real estate developer.[1] As one real estate practitioner correctly put it "Land is and should be viewed by developers as a commodity which is consumed in the development process."[2] Contractual control and not fee simple ownership is the developer's goal at this stage #1.

The landowner's business goals are even more simply stated than are the developer's. The free agent, wide receiver in the movie *Jerry Maguire* could have been speaking for every landowner in the world when he issued his now famous incantation to "show me the money."[3] Land sellers come in every form, ranging from the unsophisticated farmer, whose farm just happens to be in the path of development, to the institutional investor who invests millions of dollars to try to find land that will eventually be in that proverbial path of development. Regardless of their level of business sophistication, every land seller wants the same two things—(1) the highest price for the land, and (2) its receipt of the purchase price as quickly as possible and without conditions.

---

[1]   While most developers try to avoid inventorying land, the ownership of land can sometimes prove to be a magnet to help the developer attract new development opportunities. By way of example, Pizzuti would likely not have been on the RFP list for Cincinnati Bell's Orlando project, but for Pizzuti's ownership of an undeveloped 14-acre tract of land in the Heathrow International Business Center—*see infra*, page 91. For this reason, those developers with extremely deep financial pockets occasionally buy large tracts of land that they believe are in the direct line of development in an attempt to gain a competitive advantage over other developers.

[2]   John D. Hastie, *Real Estate Acquisition, Development and Disposition from the Developer's Perspective*, in ALI-ABA COURSE OF STUDY MATERIALS, MODERN REAL ESTATE TRANSACTIONS: PRACTICAL STRATEGIES FOR REAL ESTATE ACQUISITION, DISPOSITION, AND OWNERSHIP, Course No. SS–012, 19 (July 2010).

[3]   JERRY MAGUIRE, directed and written by Cameron Crowe (TriStar Pictures 1996).

It does not take the most ingenious lawyer to figure out that the business objectives of the developer and the landowner are diametrically opposed to each other. The real estate development lawyer's job is to craft a solution that, given the needs and relative bargaining power of the landowner, still serves the developer's legitimate business interests.

HIBC Case Study—Stage 1

Our study of the ten stages of the HIBC project begins when Pizzuti first started thinking about buying the 350-acre tract known as the "Heathrow International Business Center." As noted in Chapter 4 of this book (see pages 83–86), an interesting confluence of events occurred that served to jump start Pizzuti's development of the HIBC project. First, Pizzuti received a letter from Cincinnati Bell Information Services ("CBIS") requesting a proposal from Pizzuti concerning the development of an approximately 125,000-square-foot office building and a 60,000-square-foot data center for CBIS' use in Orlando, Florida. Pizzuti received the CBIS request for proposal, because of its ownership of a 14-acre tract located adjacent to the HIBC office building that it had acquired a couple years earlier. Unfortunately, Pizzuti's development team quickly realized that the CBIS buildings were simply too big to be built on that 14-acre tract. Shortly thereafter, Pizzuti was contacted by Chemical Bank to see whether Pizzuti had any interest in buying the 350-acre HIBC tract that Chemical had just acquired from Jeno Paulucci by way of a deed in lieu of foreclosure.

Pizzuti's receipt of the request for proposal from CBIS and the land sale call from Chemical Bank represent the classic beginning of the first stage of a real estate development project—that is, the developer's identification of an unsatisfied customer need (CBIS' desire to occupy two new buildings in Orlando, Florida) and the developer's formulation of a preliminary plan to satisfy that need (the acquisition of a portion of the HIBC tract to serve as the site for the CBIS buildings). The CBIS project presented a wonderful development opportunity for Pizzuti, because the project had the potential to be extremely profitable and because the project would also serve as a high profile kick-off for Pizzuti's plans to become a major player in the office development market in Central Florida.

There were, however, many hurdles to be cleared before Pizzuti could make a determination that its development of the CBIS project was feasible—not the least of which was the fact that approximately 20 other developers had also received the CBIS request for proposal. Promptly after being contacted by Chemical Bank, Pizzuti dispatched its development team to figure out whether a part of the HIBC acreage could support the CBIS development. Pizzuti's development team targeted an approximately 20-acre parcel in the southeast quadrant of HIBC as being the perfect location for the CBIS project. Pizzuti was confident that tying up the 20-acre HIBC parcel would give it a competitive edge in its efforts to be awarded the CBIS project,

There was, however, one glitch in Pizzuti's grand development plan— Chemical Bank was adamant that it would not entertain any offer to purchase less than the entirety of the 350-acre tract. Chemical's goal was to get the HIBC land off of its books as quickly as possible. It believed that the best alternative for it to accomplish this goal was to sell the entire tract at one time to one buyer. As a result, Chemical was intent on finding a qualified buyer who had the financial wherewithal to pay a fair price for the 350 acres and who could do so quickly without the need for a financing contingency (in other words, a buyer who could just write a check to cover the full price of the land).

It was against this factual backdrop that Pizzuti made its first phone call to its real estate development lawyer—me. The assignment that I was given by Pizzuti's development team was to "tie up the HIBC property ASAP." The dynamics of the ensuing negotiation with Chemical Bank are alluded to throughout this chapter.

III. THE LETTER OF INTENT

After receiving the call from the developer, the real estate development lawyer must first decide whether to use a letter of intent or go straight to a more formal real estate purchase agreement. The letter of intent vs. purchase agreement conundrum has long been and still is a favorite topic for debate among real estate lawyers.[4]

Let me try to put an end to that debate. There are admittedly good legal reasons why a letter of intent should not be used in all cases. However, any lawyer who routinely advises a client to never use a letter of intent has either not practiced real estate development law for very long or not practiced it very successfully. The fact of the matter is that the letter of intent is now a widely-accepted preliminary step in the acquisition and disposition of commercial real estate. Whether lawyers like it or not, their clients (both sellers and buyers) are going to continue to insist on using

---

[4] *See e.g.*, Gregory G. Gosfield, *The Structure and Use of Letters of Intent as Prenegotiation Contracts for Prospective Real Estate Transactions,* 38 REAL PROPERTY, PROBATE AND TRUST JOURNAL 130 (2003); Thomas C. Homburger and James R. Schueller, *Letters of Intent—A Trap for the Unwary,* 37 REAL PROPERTY, PROBATE AND TRUST JOURNAL 509 (2002); Georgette C. Poindexter, *Letters of Intent in Commercial Real Estate,* in ALI-ABA COURSE OF STUDY MATERIALS, MODERN REAL ESTATE TRANSACTIONS: PRACTICAL STRATEGIES FOR REAL ESTATE ACQUISITION, DISPOSITION, AND OWNERSHIP, Course No. SS–012, 61 (July 2010); and David A. Fenley, *Letters of Intent: A Survey of Their Enforceability and Desirability in Real Estate Transactions,* in ACREL PAPERS (April 2002).

letters of intent. The job of the real estate development lawyer is to make sure that the letter of intent achieves its intended goal (and nothing more).

A. WHAT ARE LETTERS OF INTENT AND WHY DO CLIENTS LIKE THEM?

The *letter of intent* goes by a number of names—"term sheet," "deal letter," "written handshake," and, my personal favorite, the "hug."[5] The letter of intent (referred to in the remainder of this chapter by the acronym *LOI*) is generally a two to three-page document that is viewed by both the seller and the buyer as nothing more than a preliminary expression of those key deal points on which they have reached a consensus. While an LOI is customarily signed by both the seller and the buyer, there is seldom an expectation on the part of either the seller or the buyer that the LOI in any way legally binds them to consummate the purchase and sale of the property that is the subject of the LOI.

The above description makes the LOI seem like a rather innocuous, if not wholly useless document. Why then have LOIs become so commonplace in today's commercial real estate industry? The following are the benefits, both actual and perceived, of using an LOI.

- The LOI is a relatively quick and inexpensive way for the buyer and seller to see if they have common ground on the essential deal points (for example, the purchase price, deal contingencies, and the anticipated closing date). The alternative of paying lawyers to prepare and negotiate a complex purchase agreement is distasteful to both the seller and the buyer (if not to their respective counsel).

- For the land seller, the LOI is a useful tool to evaluate the level of interest of potential buyers.

- For the buyer, the LOI is an opportunity to tie up the property while the buyer tries to make a determination of the feasibility of its development project.

- The LOI is a quick way to create *deal momentum*. Deal momentum is the circumstance where the parties feel committed mentally and emotionally to doing a deal even though they are not legally committed to do so. This is the "hug" effect mentioned earlier in this chapter.

- Finally, the LOI serves as the parties' CliffsNotes for the deal. Once an LOI is signed, the lawyers for the buyer and seller

---

[5]   *See* Nina B. Matis and Elliot M. Surkin, *The Hug: "There is Commercial Utility to Allowing Persons to Hug before They Marry." A Discussion of Letters of Intent in Purchase and Sale Transactions,* in ALI-ABA COURSE OF STUDY MATERIALS, MODERN REAL ESTATE TRANSACTIONS: PRACTICAL STRATEGIES FOR REAL ESTATE ACQUISITION, DISPOSITION, AND OWNERSHIP, Course No. SS–012, 89 (July 2010).

are charged with responsibility for writing a book (the purchase agreement) that is consistent with those notes.

B. DANGERS ASSOCIATED WITH THE USE OF A LETTER OF INTENT

Both the seller and the buyer generally view an LOI as a non-binding document. As a result, the parties are sometimes careless in their wording of the LOI. The lack of attention to the content of the LOI can cause unintended consequences if the parties fail to bring the same attention to detail to the LOI that they customarily do to purchase agreements and other documents that they perceive to be binding. The "unintended consequence" of a poorly-drafted LOI is that a judge finds that the LOI is partially or wholly enforceable against the parties. In other words, a document that was initially thought to be non-binding suddenly becomes binding to the detriment of one of the parties to the LOI.

There are two scenarios where the enforceability of an LOI is called into question after the LOI is signed by both the seller and the buyer—(1) the LOI buyer finds a better or cheaper site for its development project, or (2) the LOI seller finds someone who will pay more for its land than the LOI buyer. The result produced under both of these scenarios is the same— one party to the LOI abandons the negotiations in favor of a better opportunity, which causes the jilted party to file a lawsuit arguing that the LOI is a binding legal contract.

As noted in a prior section of this chapter, an LOI is typically only two to three pages long and often contains a statement contemplating the parties' future execution of a lengthier purchase agreement. So how under those circumstances could a judge possibly find that an LOI is a binding legal contract? The legal theories used by judges to turn a seemingly non-binding LOI into a binding contract are summarized below.[6]

- The LOI itself evidences the parties' intentions to be legally bound by its terms, because either (1) the LOI is sufficiently detailed that all the essential terms of the deal are spelled out in the LOI, or (2) the LOI provides a mechanism for a judge to ordain what the missing terms are by saying that the remaining terms will be determined in accordance with "community custom," "commercially reasonable standards," or a similar soft standard.[7]

---

[6] *See* Michael Hamilton, *Purchase and Sale Transactions*, in COMMERCIAL REAL ESTATE TRANSACTIONS HANDBOOK 5–1, 5–3 to 5–7 (Mark A. Senn ed., 4th ed. 2011); Mark A. Senn, *Some Letter of Intent Cases*, in ALI-CLE MODERN REAL ESTATE TRANSACTIONS, Course No. SY006 (August 2016); and Fenley, *supra* note 4.

[7] *See e.g.*, Goren v. Royal Investments Incorporated, 516 N.E.2d 173 (App. Ct. Mass 1987).

- While the words of the LOI do not, standing alone, evidence the parties' intentions to be legally bound, the transaction contemplated by the LOI is nonetheless enforceable under the equitable concepts of part performance or promissory estoppel.[8]

- While the LOI is not binding, the parties to the LOI have an implied obligation to negotiate in good faith to finalize the terms of a definitive purchase agreement.[9]

The lesson to be learned from the case law summarized above is not, as one lawyer stated, that "a letter of intent is an invention of the devil and should be avoided at all costs."[10] The real lesson to be learned from the case law is that the real estate development lawyer should heed the words of wisdom espoused by the adorably insightful Humpty Dumpty, when he gave this great advice to Alice—"When I use a word . . . it means just what I choose it to mean—neither more nor less."[11]

The parties in all the contested cases made the mistake of not clearly articulating their intentions as to whether they were or were not legally bound by the provisions of the LOI. In the cases that have held that an LOI is binding, the parties failed to include in the LOI a clear, unambiguous statement that it was their shared intentions that the provisions of the LOI would not be legally binding on either party. The inclusion of a clause similar to the one below will goes a long way toward assuring the parties that the LOI is not enforceable against either of them.

> This letter of intent is merely an expression of certain preliminary, basic business points discussed by the parties in connection with a potential purchase and sale of the subject property and is not intended in any way to create any obligations of any kind on either of the parties to this letter of intent. The parties will not be bound to each other in any way, unless and until a formal agreement for the purchase and sale of the property is executed by both parties. This provision as to the non-binding nature of this letter of intent supersedes any provisions herein or any past or future actions of the parties to the contrary.[12]

---

8   *See e.g.*, Budget Marketing v. Centronics, 927 F.2d 421 (8th Cir. 1991).

9   *See e.g.*, Copeland v. Baskin Robbins, 96 CA4th 1251 (2002); and Teacher's Insurance and Annuity Association of America v. Tribune Company, 670 F. Supp. 491 (S.D.N.Y. 1987);

10   *See* Steven Volk, *The Letter of Intent*, 16 INSTITUTE ON SECURITIES REGULATION 145 (1985). *See also* Gregory G. Gosfield, *A Primer on Real Estate Options*, 35 REAL PROPERTY, PROBATE AND TRUST JOURNAL 129, 133–134 (2000), where the author states that "Letters of intent are indubitably the devil's work . . . [and] the letters are wolves in sheep's clothing, plastique that can fit any shape and explode with fatal consequences, vipers poised to bite the fool who tries to collar them."

11   *See* LEWIS CARROLL, THROUGH THE LOOKING GLASS: AND WHAT ALICE FOUND THERE 205 (1872).

12   *See* Matis, *supra* note 5, at 95.

Some practitioners have recommended including in an LOI a non-binding statement that specifically disclaims every conceivable legal theory that has been relied upon by the courts to hold that an LOI is enforceable—for example, by expressly saying: that there is no obligation to negotiate in good faith; that the actions of the parties can never be relied on; that the terms of the LOI can be ignored by the parties when negotiating the definitive purchase agreement, etc. In my view, that approach, while legally supportable, only works when both parties to the LOI are sophisticated business entities. If the seller under the LOI is an unsophisticated landowner, then the inclusion in the LOI of a statement that the proposed buyer does not have to act in good faith is virtually a guarantee that the landowner will either not sign the LOI or, at the bare minimum, call the landowner's attorney—a circumstance that defeats the developer's intention to create deal momentum.

Practice Tip #5-1: When and How to Use an LOI

The real estate development lawyer should trust the instincts of the developer as to when the submission of an LOI is an appropriate preliminary step in the land purchase negotiations. Developers have a more refined sensitivity for the dynamics of deal negotiations than do lawyers (even those who have read this book) and, as such, are better equipped than their lawyers to make the decision as to whether a particular merits skipping the LOI stage and moving directly to the preparation of a purchase contract.

Once a decision is made to use a letter of intent, the real estate development lawyer must resist the natural inclination to overlawyer a deal and, instead, prepare a very short and simple LOI. A sample of a skeletal LOI is included as Document #1 in the Document Appendix. An LOI should address only the most essential terms of the proposed land acquisition—(1) a description of the land, (2) the amount of the purchase price and how it will be paid, (3) the allocation of responsibility for the payment of closing costs, (4) the scope of the buyer's contingencies, (5) the scheduled closing date, and, of course, (6) a clear statement of the non-binding nature of the LOI. Keeping the LOI "short and sweet" serves two important purposes: first, it enhances the possibility that the landowner might create the desired "deal momentum" by signing the LOI without first running that document by its lawyer; and second, it significantly reduces the chance that a court might decide that the document is so detailed that the document should be deemed to be binding on the parties to the LOI.

C. PARTIALLY BINDING LETTERS OF INTENT

As stated at the very outset of this chapter, the developer's goal in Stage 1 is to tie up the site so that its competitors cannot steal the developer's business opportunity by buying the targeted land from the landowner. The execution of a non-binding letter of intent, while creating positive deal momentum, does not actually tie up the site (at least not to the extent desired by the developer). Under a true non-binding LOI, the landowner is free to continue to market its land and accept purchase offers from third parties until such time as the developer and the landowner execute a definitive land purchase agreement.

The developer's desire to try to tie up the land under an LOI has led to the creation of a legal document that is often referred to as a "partially binding non-binding letter of intent." This oxymoronic document name simply means that one or more elements of the LOI are binding, while the remainder of the LOI is non-binding. The following are three provisions that a real estate development lawyer often tries to insert into an otherwise non-binding LOI.

- *"No Shopping" Clause*—By placing a ***no-shopping clause*** in an LOI, the real estate development lawyer seeks to create a binding obligation on the landowner to refrain for a specified period of time from entering into or continuing any negotiations or discussions with any party other than the developer concerning the sale of the landowner's land. The no-shopping clause is intended to prevent the landowner from "shopping" the developer's deal to other potential buyers to see if a better deal can be had. The term of the typical no shopping clause begins on the date the LOI is signed by the landowner and expires on the earlier of (1) the date on which the parties execute a fully-binding purchase agreement, or (2) an outside date specified in the LOI (for example, 30 days after the effective date of the LOI).[13]

---

[13] The highest profile case focusing on a no-shopping clause was the dispute that arose between Wells Fargo and Citigroup in the wake of the 2008 financial crisis. On September 29, 2008, Citigroup and Wachovia Corp. entered into a non-binding LOI that contemplated Citigroup's purchase of Wachovia. Citigroup and Wachovia also signed a no-shopping agreement that prohibited Wachovia from talking to any other potential buyers for a period of seven days, during which time the lawyers for Citigroup and Wachovia hoped to finalize a definitive agreement for Citigroup's purchase of Wachovia. During that seven-day period, Wells Fargo & Co. submitted a bid to buy Wachovia for a price that was well in excess of that which was being offered by Citigroup. Long story short, Wachovia was sold to Wells Fargo and Citigroup filed a lawsuit against Wells Fargo and Wachovia asking for $60 billion in damages for a breach of the no-shopping clause. The case was settled in 2010 when Wells Fargo agreed to pay Citigroup $100 million. *See* Abigail Rubenstein, *Wells Fargo to Pay Citi $100M to Settle Wachovia Fight*, LAW360 (November 19, 2010), available at http://www.law360.com/articles/210608/wells-fargo-to-pay-citi-100m-to-settle-wachovia-fight.

- *Obligation to Negotiate in Good Faith*—As one might expect, landowners often reject the developer's attempt to include a binding no shopping clause in the LOI. On occasion, the developer will try to circumvent the landowner's rejection of its no shopping clause by including a provision in the LOI that seeks to impose a binding obligation on the parties "to negotiate the terms of a definitive purchase agreement in good faith and to use reasonable efforts to cause a definitive purchase agreement to be prepared and executed within ___ days after the parties' execution of the letter of intent." By inserting such a provision in the LOI, the developer seeks to gain a quantum of leverage against the landowner if the landowner ends up agreeing to sell the land to someone other than the developer. The real estate development lawyer should, however, be mindful that a mutual obligation to negotiate in good faith can come back to haunt the developer if, for instance, the developer finds a cheaper or better land alternative for its project and, accordingly, seeks to abandon negotiations with the LOI landowner. The insertion of a good faith negotiation clause in an LOI creates a slippery slope for both the seller and the buyer and, as such, should be included in an LOI only with great caution and a full awareness of its potential consequences.

- *Confidentiality Clause*—A developer may also attempt to achieve its objective of precluding the landowner from shopping the deal to other potential buyers by including a clause in the LOI that says that the developer and the landowner must keep the existence and terms of the LOI confidential and may not disclose any facet of the LOI to a third party. If a binding confidentiality clause is included in an LOI and if the landowner stringently follows the terms of the clause, then the developer may be able to partially accomplish its goal of preventing the landowner from sharing the price and other terms of the LOI with competing land buyers. Proving that a landowner has breached a confidentiality clause can, however, be a rather dicey proposition for a developer.

If an attempt is made to insert a binding clause into an otherwise non-binding LOI, it is imperative that the real estate development lawyer make it clear within the four corners of the LOI document what provisions are binding and what provisions are non-binding. If that distinction is not made clear in the LOI, the developer may be exposed to a risk that a court might decide that no provision of the LOI is binding (including the provisions that the developer wants to be binding) or that the entirety of the LOI is binding (including the provisions that the developer does not want to be binding).

Finally, in order for a no-shopping, good faith negotiation, or confidentiality clause to be enforceable against the landowner, the landowner's agreement to abide by the subject clause must be supported by adequate consideration. Developer's counsel should, therefore, be careful to include a recital of adequate consideration in any "binding" clause that counsel opts to include in an LOI (for example, the payment of a nominal sum of cash or a promise on the developer's part to take or refrain from taking a specific action).[14]

IV. PAPERING THE DEAL

The preliminaries are now over and the seller and the buyer are ready to move on to the preparation and execution of a binding land acquisition document. Before beginning an examination of the key provisions of the land acquisition document, this chapter first discusses two topics that are central to the real estate development lawyer's ability to prepare a solid first draft of the acquisition document:

- What questions should the lawyer ask the developer in order to gain a proper understanding of the business deal and the risks associated with that deal; and

- What form of contract should the lawyer select to best evidence the developer's business deal.

A. LEARNING THE BUSINESS DEAL

A real estate development lawyer is not in a position to start drafting the purchase contract until the lawyer thoroughly understands the client's business deal. In this context, the business deal encompasses both (1) the essential business terms of the land acquisition, and (2) the nature, status, and timing of the project that will be developed on the acquired land.

The signed LOI (assuming there is one) provides the real estate development lawyer with the basic business points that define the land acquisition—for example, the property description, purchase price, deal contingencies, and projected closing date. To learn the rest of the business deal, the real estate development lawyer needs to sit down with the developer and ask a series of questions designed to augment the lawyer's understanding of the overall deal. Among the principal questions that the lawyer should ask the developer are the following.

---

[14] *See* John S. Hollyfield, *Letters of Intent (with Sample Clauses),* 25 No. 5 PRACTICAL REAL ESTATE LAWYER 33, 37 (September 2009).

- What is the projected end use of the land (for example, an office building or shopping center)?

- Is the property zoned to permit the developer's projected end use?

- Are all needed utilities, roads, and other infrastructure already extended to the boundaries of the land? If not, who has the responsibility to arrange for the infrastructure extension?

- What are the biggest risks associated with the deal?

- What has to happen for the deal to become a reality (for example, the pre-leasing of all or a portion of the development project, the finalization of the project design, or the bidding out of the project's construction costs)?

- Is the developer willing to close on the acquisition of the land before all aspects of its broader development project have come together?

- What events could cause the project deal to blow up?

- Does the developer need to secure financing for the acquisition of the land and the development of the project? If so, has the developer received a commitment for the required financing?

- Will the developer have any equity partners in the development project?

- Are there any governmental incentives or approvals that are essential components of the business deal?

- What is the status of the site due diligence (soils tests, environmental assessments, etc.)?

- What is the developer's projected time line for the acquisition of the land and the commencement of construction of the project?

This question and answer session serves two valuable purposes—(1) it provides the lawyer with the level of understanding of the overall business deal and its associated risks and challenges that the lawyer needs in order to protect the developer's business interests, and (2) it may bring into focus certain issues that the developer has not previously thought of or resolved.

B. SELECTING THE RIGHT FORM OF CONTRACT

The next question faced by the real estate development lawyer is what form of document should be used to evidence the business deal the lawyer just learned about from meeting with the developer? That question has two parts to it.

- Should the document take the form of a purchase contract or an option?

- Should the lawyer use a "killer" form[15] that is designed to protect the developer from every conceivable risk or should the lawyer use a more user-friendly contract form that seeks to accommodate the legitimate interests of the landowner?

The answer to this two-part question depends upon the complexity of the deal and the sophistication and experience of the landowner.

1.   Purchase Contract vs. Option

A purchase contract establishes an obligation of the buyer to buy the land, subject to the satisfaction of those conditions specifically set forth in the purchase contract. An option, on the other hand, creates a right, but not an obligation, to buy the land that the prospective buyer may exercise unilaterally at any time within the fixed period set forth in the option agreement. Under an option, the buyer must provide consideration for the option that is separate and distinct from the purchase price payable following the exercise of the option. Most commentators believe that the payment of a relatively nominal amount of cash will provide the requisite consideration needed to establish the enforceability of an option.[16]

Based on the definitional difference between an option and a purchase contract, it would at first blush seem obvious that a lawyer representing a buyer/developer should always select an option as the form to use when preparing the first draft of the land acquisition document. After all, what rational person would select "obligations" over "rights"? The reality, however, is that the land acquisition document typically used in the commercial real estate development world is a purchase contract and not an option.

The reasons why a purchase contract is the favored document form for a commercial real estate deal are discussed below.

- Many sophisticated landowners/sellers simply will not agree to use an option agreement. In consideration of its agreement to take its land off the market, a seller wants the buyer to have an obligation to buy and not just the right to buy. If a seller can somehow be convinced to go with the option form,

---

[15] The term "killer" document was originally coined by the New York Bar Association to describe the pro-landlord form of lease that was widely used in the 1980's. *See* JOHN B. WOOD AND ALAN M. DI SCIULLO, NEGOTIATING AND DRAFTING OFFICE LEASES 1–2 and 1–3 (2002).

[16] *See* Gosfield, *Primer on Real Estate Options, supra* note 10, at 141; and Harvey L. Temkin, *Too Much Good Faith in Real Estate Purchase Agreements? Give Me an Option*, 34 UNIVERSITY OF KANSAS LAW REVIEW 43 (1985).

it will likely seek to extract such an exorbitant non-refundable cash consideration for the grant of the option as to render the option untenable from the buyer's perspective.

- The legal distinction between an option and a purchase agreement is one with limited practical difference for either the seller or the buyer. As is discussed in more detail later in this chapter at pages 117–120, the courts have consistently recognized the validity of a purchase contract that sets forth the buyer's determination of the "suitability" or "feasibility" of the land as a condition to the buyer's purchase obligation. From the buyer's perspective (as opposed to that of the buyer's anal-retentive lawyer), there is little significant difference between a broad suitability contingency in a purchase contract and the unilateral right to buy set forth in an option agreement.

- Except for the "option" versus "contingency" language noted in the above paragraph, the provisions of the option agreement and the purchase contract are virtually identical. If an option is used by the development lawyer, it is incumbent upon the lawyer to include in the option agreement all the terms and conditions that will govern the purchase and sale of the land if and when the buyer exercises its purchase option. Those terms and conditions generally are the same under both the purchase contract and the option agreement.

The bottom line is that, in the ideal world, the buyer/developer may be marginally better off going with an option than with a purchase contract. Unfortunately, the real estate development lawyer seldom is afforded the luxury of functioning in the ideal world. For this reason, the remainder of this chapter assumes that the selected form for the land acquisition is the purchase contract and not the option (although as noted above, there really is not that much practical difference between those two forms).

2. Using the "Killer" Form of Purchase Contract

Experienced practitioners are all too familiar with the lawyer who insists on using a "killer purchase contract" form for every transaction. The killer form is the 50-page document that the lawyer (or more likely one of the lawyer's senior partners) has labored over for years. It has ten pages of definitions (mostly arcane legal terms) and an intentionally intricate (albeit, virtually indecipherable) set of cross-references to other internal sections of the document. The killer form seeks to place every marginally conceivable deal risk and responsibility squarely on the shoulders of the seller and to give the buyer the right to do whatever it pleases throughout the acquisition process—usually "in its sole and absolute discretion."

In my view, the killer form is aptly named because the lawyer who insists on its use is more likely to kill the deal than make the deal. The submission of the killer form to the unsophisticated seller so intimidates the seller that making a deal becomes at best difficult and on occasion impossible. Sending a killer form to the sophisticated seller unnecessarily increases the tension and combativeness of the acquisition negotiations, thereby potentially wasting two things that the developer holds most precious—time and money.

As has been said many times in prior chapters, the real estate development lawyer's job is to help the developer achieve its business objectives. At Stage 1, that objective is to tie up the targeted site quickly and in a cost-effective manner. The successful real estate development lawyer should not waste the time of either the developer or the landowner by preparing a purchase contract draft that is commercially unreasonable, overreaching, or unnecessarily complex. To be sure, the development lawyer must adopt a form that protects the lawyer's client from legitimate deal risks. The insecure lawyer too frequently seeks to protect the client by using a killer form that the lawyer has been told will insulate the client from every risk, both real and imagined. This lawyer has likely never taken the time to understand the client's business deal because the lawyer feels sufficiently comforted by the perception that the killer document will serve as a substitute for knowledge of the deal. Unfortunately, once the negotiations start, the insecure lawyer is ill-equipped to rebuff the requested document modifications by seller's counsel for the simple reason that the insecure lawyer does not understand how the acquisition fits into the developer's bigger business deal or what is commercially reasonable under the circumstances. The insecure lawyer's choice at that point is either (1) to risk killing the deal by blindly refusing to change any substantive provision of the contract, or (2) to chance looking stupid in the eyes of the developer by letting the seller's counsel dominate the dialogue throughout the negotiations.

The challenge presented to the real estate development lawyer in Stage 1 is to prepare a purchase contract that appropriately manages the delicate balance between the developer's desire to tie up the property as quickly and as cheaply as possible and the lawyer's responsibility to protect the developer from legitimate project risks. There is no purchase contract form that is appropriate for every occasion or every deal. The real estate development lawyer's job is to match the occasion with the proper form, so that both of the above objectives are achieved.

Practice Tip #5-2: Drafting Rules and Techniques

The purchase contract is the first document that is analyzed in depth in this book. Before embarking on a review of the substantive provisions of a purchase contract, let me digress and take the opportunity to discuss several drafting rules and techniques that have held me in good stead over the years. This is not a book on legal writing and, therefore, I will not talk about clarity, concision, syntax, or punctuation. What I will present are my thoughts on what a real estate development lawyer can do to improve the lawyer's document drafting. The importance of the real estate development lawyer being a skilled draftsman cannot be overstated. Simply put, a lawyer who is not an accomplished draftsman should look for a field of practice other than real estate development law.

Here are ten rules that a real estate development lawyer should follow when preparing a legal document.

- **Think Before You Write**—Before beginning drafting, the lawyer must think through the following points—(1) what are the deal risks faced by the developer and how can those risks best be handled (the so-called "what-if" list referred to in Chapter 2—The Ten Stages of a Real Estate Development Project, at page 30), and (2) what conditions must be satisfied before the developer is prepared to buy the land.

- **Know What Each Provision Means and Why It Is in the Document**—Every provision in a legal document has a consequence. The real estate development lawyer's job is to make sure that the consequence of each contractual provision is consistent with the developer's business interests. This is especially true with respect to the inclusion in a document of so-called "boilerplate" language, such as provisions on "governing law," "assignability," and "notice." Nothing is more embarrassing than having to respond to a question as to why a particular provision is in the contract by saying "I don't know—we just always put it in."

- **Don't Try to Sound Like a Lawyer**—The excessive use of legalese makes a lawyer look pompous, not smart.

- **Use Standard Forms Judiciously**—A standard form can be a very valuable starting point to help the development lawyer identify legal issues and create a structure and format for the drafting of a document. A standard form should not, however, be used as a crutch or held sacrosanct in any way. The document prepared by the lawyer must be tailored to fit the client's business deal. Too many young lawyers make the mistake of trying to make the client's business deal fit within *the standard form rather than taking the proper approach of customizing the document to fit the deal.*

- ***Keep the Document as Short and Simple as Possible—** This point was previously made in the course of the discussion of the killer form of contract. Quite simply, it takes a lot more skill and talent to cover all appropriate issues in a ten-page document than it does in a 50-page document. While clarity should never be sacrificed strictly for the sake of brevity,[17] the thoughtful draftsman should always seek to convey the intended message in as few words as possible.*

- ***Use Defined Terms to Make the Document Easier to Read and Understand—** Most legal documents repeat important concepts and terms multiple times. For example, a purchase contract needs to refer to the property being sold and the person to whom it is being sold on literally dozens of occasions. The use of defined terms to refer to these two concepts ("Property" and "Buyer") can greatly aid both the internal consistency and readability of the purchase contract. The real estate development lawyer must, however, avoid falling prey to the temptation to define every other word in a document. As one practitioner has noted, "overuse of defined terms imparts significance to terms which are not of significance, injects confusion instead of clarity and results in a document which is at best silly and at worst offensive to the reader."[18]*

- ***Avoid Excessive Cross-References—** Each section of an agreement should be understood simply by reading the words contained in that section. Excessive cross-references to other sections of the document can make the document utterly unreadable.*

- ***Always Use Good Grammar—** A lawyer who is respected by other practitioners is given much greater latitude throughout the deal negotiations. Nothing can cause a lawyer to lose the respect of the practicing bar quicker than the lawyer's repeated violation of basic rules of grammar (for example, a lack of parallelism or the use of dangling modifiers).*

- ***Adopt an "Inverted Pyramid" Structure for the Document—** Every legal document needs to be organized in a logical order. I have found that the "inverted pyramid" format works best—that is, including the most important concepts at the beginning of the document and the least important at the*

---

[17] *See* Joshua Stein, A Practical Guide to Real Estate Practice 63 (2001).

[18] Hastie, *supra* note 2, at 14.

end. The relative importance of the various provisions of a document should be evaluated from the perspective of the lawyer's client. Years of experience have taught me that no client actually reads the entire document and, therefore, it is wise to include the provisions of most interest to the client as early in the document as possible.

- ***Don't Ignore the Look of the Document****—As is the case in every business, style sells in the legal profession. Just as a lawyer wearing a $2,000 Armani suit is initially given more credence than is a peer wearing a J.C. Penny design replete with gravy stains, a document that looks crisp and professional is afforded much greater deference than is a document that has never been introduced to the wonders of font manipulation under Microsoft Word.*

V. IDENTIFYING AND MITIGATING RISK

Before drafting the purchase contract, the real estate development lawyer should pause and ask "What could go wrong that would cause the developer to conclude that it no longer wants to acquire the land?" The circumstances that could lead the developer to reach such a conclusion include both those that are specific to the to-be acquired land (***land risks***) and circumstances that relate in a broader sense to the viability of the developer's proposed real estate project (***deal risks***).

A. LAND RISK

Land risk refers to a circumstance where there is something intrinsically wrong with the developer's selected parcel that makes that parcel ill-suited to serve as the site for the developer's development project. The following are examples of typical land risks:

- The site is not zoned to permit construction and use of the project;
- Utilities have not been extended to the site;
- The site soils will not support construction of the project;
- There is no access to the site from a public roadway;
- The site is contaminated with hazardous substances or other environmental contaminants;
- Protected wetlands are present on part of the site; and
- Title to the site is unmarketable or otherwise not suited for the development of the intended project.

B. DEAL RISK

As noted earlier in this chapter, most developers do not want to acquire land unless the land can be promptly commoditized as part of a development project. In other words, even if the developer's selected land parcel is free of all the land risks described in the prior section, a developer typically does not want to buy that parcel unless the developer's development project is also a "go." This is one more reason why it is important that the real estate development lawyer understand the business side of the proposed development project. A land purchase contract that protects the developer only from land risks (and not deal risks) could result in the developer being forced to buy land for which the developer has no present development use—a circumstance that is sure to infuriate even the most mild-mannered of developers (of which there are precious few).

The following are common examples of deal risks that might cause a developer to want to jettison its plans to develop a project on the land.

- The numbers on the developer's project pro forma do not "pencil out;

- The developer cannot secure debt or equity funding for the payment of the project's development costs;

- The developer fails to secure a governmental incentive or approval that is considered central to making the project economics work;

- The developer cannot lease the project within the projected time frames or at the projected rental;

- The developer discovers that it cannot build the project on time and on budget;

- The economy tanks, with the result that there is no appreciable demand for the developer's project;

- A project that is directly competitive with the developer's project is started by another firm, leaving the developer with a significantly diminished class of targeted customers for its project; and

- The developer suffers a major financial loss on another deal and, as a result, no longer has the financial wherewithal to develop the proposed project.

VI. THE PURCHASE CONTRACT

Once the real estate development lawyer has identified the developer's land and deal risks, the lawyer is ready to start drafting the real estate purchase contract. The purchase contract is the road map for the land acquisition. It should show anyone picking up the purchase contract not only where the developer wants to go, but also how and when it proposes to get there and what interim stops it needs to make on the way.

The pages that follow undertake a detailed analysis of each of the key provisions of the land purchase contract. The divergent approaches of the seller and the buyer on the main deal points are highlighted in the course of that analysis. The order in which such provisions are examined is roughly based on the order in which those provisions appear in the Real Estate Purchase Agreement included as Document #2 in the *Document Appendix* (referred to in the remainder of this chapter as the "Form Purchase Agreement"). Parenthetical reference is made in the caption of each of the following provisions to the section of the Form Purchase Agreement where such provision is addressed.

A. IDENTIFICATION OF PARTIES
(Preamble)

The identities of the seller and the buyer are customarily described in the first paragraph of the purchase contract. To ensure enforceability of the various obligations and liabilities set forth in the contract, it is important to accurately identify each party to the contract by using such party's full legal name. If one of the parties is a legal entity of some type (which is usually the case), care should be taken to not only use the right legal name for that entity, but also to identify the party by entity type and the jurisdiction in which it was formed—for example, "a Delaware corporation" or "an Ohio limited liability company." Counsel representing each of the buyer and the seller should also try to gather reliable information as to the financial creditworthiness of the identified party. To the extent the named party is a single purpose entity, with little, if any, net worth, consideration should be given to requiring that either (1) the named party to the purchase contract must be changed to a financially viable entity, or (2) the obligations of the named party must be guaranteed by a financially viable entity. Crafting an elaborate set of obligations and liabilities to be placed on a particular party to a purchase contract is of no avail if that party is an entity without significant assets.

B. EFFECTIVE DATE OF EXECUTION
(Preamble)

Most of the time frames set forth in a purchase contract (for example, the date for delivery of a title insurance commitment and the outside date for the satisfaction of contingencies) are described by using the "effective date" of the parties' execution of the contract as the starting point. The effective date is usually the date on which both the buyer and the seller have executed the purchase contract.

C. DESCRIPTION OF PROPERTY
(§ 1)

The description of the property to be sold must accomplish two things.

- It must describe the land in sufficient detail so that no question exists as to its size, location, or boundaries. This is most often accomplished by referencing the number of acres contained in the land parcel and attaching a legal description of the land as an exhibit to the purchase contract. A legal description is generally prepared by a licensed surveyor and describes the property either by means of (1) a metes and bounds description (a description of the property by reference to the length and compass bearings of each of the perimeter boundaries of the property), or (2) a reference to a subdivision map already filed of record in the local real estate records.

- It must reference all other property rights that, although tangential to the land parcel, are nonetheless required for the legal and beneficial use of the land. These additional property rights include easements, access rights, development rights, tradenames, mineral rights, and all other "appurtenances and privileges" related to the land.[19]

D. DEPOSIT
(§ 2)

There is no legal requirement that the buyer pay a deposit under the purchase contract. In practice, most land acquisitions of any significance provide for the buyer's payment of a so-called **earnest money deposit** to evidence to the seller that the buyer is serious about buying the land. There is no reliable rule of thumb as to the size of the deposit. The seller and buyer weigh in on the issue of the size of the deposit in predictable ways— the seller wants to see as big a deposit as possible, while the buyer wants to keep the deposit at a relatively nominal amount. A common compromise is to provide that the deposit will be paid by the buyer in installments over a stated period of time—for example, one third of the total deposit being payable every 30 days during the buyer's 90-day due diligence period. This

---

[19] "Appurtenances and privileges" is an often-used catchall intended to capture all other property rights and interests associated with a particular land parcel. The term "appurtenance" is defined in The ICSC Dictionary of Shopping Center Terms 5 (3rd ed. 2008) as an "extension, such as an easement or right-of-way, that is outside of the property itself, but is considered to be part of the property and adds to its greater use or enjoyment."

type of arrangement is particularly appealing to a buyer because the buyer is then afforded the opportunity to refrain from making additional deposits if the buyer's due diligence during the prior 30-day period was unsatisfactory.

The provisions of the contract dealing with the payment of the deposit should address all of the following topics.

- *Who Should Hold the Deposit?* The holder of the deposit (commonly referred to in this capacity as the *escrow agent*) should be a title company or another independent third party who is unrelated to either the buyer or the seller. The lawyer for the buyer or the seller should normally not act as the escrow agent. If a dispute arises under the purchase contract, a lawyer acting as escrow agent runs the very real risk of being disqualified from the continuing representation of the lawyer's client because the lawyer holds a deposit that is the object of desire of both the seller and the buyer.[20] The terms under which the third party holds the deposit are usually spelled out in a separate escrow agreement between the escrow agent, the seller, and the buyer.

- *What Form Should the Deposit Take?* The deposit is usually paid in cash. However, in large transactions, it is often more cost-effective for the buyer to post the deposit in the form of an irrevocable standby letter of credit. An irrevocable standby letter of credit is a guaranty by a financial institution (usually a bank) that it will pay the holder of the letter of credit a fixed sum of money upon the holder's presentation to the financial institution of a demand for payment. The issuance of a letter of credit does not constitute a current borrowing by the person requesting such letter and, therefore, does not subject that person to ongoing interest charges on the amount of the letter. However, a fee (typically 1 or 2 % of the maximum amount disbursable under the letter of credit) is payable to the financial institution upon the issuance of the letter of credit.

- *Should the Deposit Be Held in an Interest-Bearing Account?* The answer to this question is almost always "yes," with any interest earned on the deposit accruing to the benefit of the buyer.

---

[20] *See* GREGORY M. STEIN, MORTON P. FISHER, JR. AND GAIL M. STERN, A PRACTICAL GUIDE TO COMMERCIAL REAL ESTATE TRANSACTIONS—FROM CONTRACT TO CLOSING 23–24 (2001); and Andrew L. Herz, Bruce B. May, and Gail Livingston Mills, *When Good Deals Go Bad—Purchase Contracts, Defaults, Waivers and Remedies,* in ACREL PAPERS (October 2004).

- *When Should the Deposit Be Refunded to the Buyer?* The deposit (and any interest earned on the deposit) should be returned to the buyer upon the termination of the buyer's obligation under the purchase contract as a result of either (1) the buyer's failure to satisfy or waive certain conditions specified in the purchase contract, or (2) the seller's default under the purchase contract. The drafter of the purchase contract should take great care to specify the exact circumstances under which the deposit must be returned to the buyer. The buyer typically wants the escrow agent to be required to refund the deposit immediately upon the buyer instructing the escrow agent to do so (usually in writing), while the seller does not want the escrow agent to be empowered or obligated to refund the deposit without first receiving the seller's blessing to do so. A frequently used compromise requires the buyer to send a written refund request to both the escrow agent and the seller, with the escrow agent then being prohibited from paying the deposit to buyer for a stated period of time after its receipt of the refund request. This procedure gives the seller the time and opportunity to take whatever action it believes is appropriate to prevent an improper refund of the deposit.

- *When Should the Deposit Be Paid to the Seller?* The deposit (and any interest earned on the deposit) should be paid to the seller upon the closing of the buyer's purchase of the land, with the buyer receiving a credit on the purchase price in an amount equal to the deposit and accrued interest. The question of whether the deposit is to be paid to the seller upon the buyer's default under the purchase contract is a question that is explored in more detail as part of the discussion later in this chapter of liquidated damages and other contractual remedies.

E. PURCHASE PRICE

(§ 3)

This is the one provision of the purchase contract that it is sure to be read by both the seller and the buyer. The purchase price provision should specifically address the following considerations.

- *Amount*—The purchase price may be stated either as a fixed sum or as a product of a formula. It is very common for a commercial land acquisition to have the purchase price determined by multiplying the number of acres contained in the site by a per-acre price. If the price is calculated in this manner, the parties need to stipulate in the contract who will make the determination of the number of acres contained within the site (usually the surveyor) and, somewhat more controversially, whether that determination will be made on the basis of the land parcel's "gross" or "net" acreage. The seller always wants the purchase price to be determined based on gross acreage. The buyer, on the other hand, generally wants the per-acre price to be applied against only those net acres that it can develop, subtracting out any portion of the land that is burdened by an easement or right-of-way or is otherwise not developable (for example, because it is located in a protected wetlands).

- *Method of Payment*—A stock phrase contained in virtually all purchase contracts is that the purchase price will be "paid in cash at closing." This does not mean that the buyer needs to bring a suitcase full of $20 bills with it to the closing. In this context, "cash" means any method of payment where there is no risk of collection on the payment (as there is with a personal check or credit card). In today's environment, the "cash" payment is almost always made by means of a wire transfer of funds through an electronic system maintained by the Federal Reserve System. The careful lawyer should specify in the purchase contract that the buyer will pay the purchase price by means of a wire transfer to a specific account that is either identified in the purchase contract or designated at a later date by the escrow agent.

- Although not as common as a cash payment, the contract may recite that all or a portion of the purchase price will be "paid" by means of either the seller's provision to the buyer of purchase money financing or the buyer's assumption of an existing mortgage debt on the land.

  o *Purchase money financing* is nothing more than a loan made by the seller to the buyer to pay all or a portion of the purchase price for the land. A purchase money loan is almost always secured by a mortgage on the land. If purchase money financing is involved in a land acquisition, the real estate development lawyer should make sure that the essential terms of such financing are specified in the purchase contract—that is, the principal amount of the loan, the interest rate, the amount and timing of all required debt service payments, and all other important business terms related to the extension of the purchase money financing.

    o   A ***loan assumption*** involves the buyer's agreement to expressly assume the seller's existing mortgage loan. If the buyer is going to assume an existing mortgage loan on the land, the purchase contract should recite that the cash portion of the purchase price payable by the buyer will be credited with an amount equal to the outstanding principal balance of the mortgage debt as of the date of closing, with interest being prorated through the date of closing. The purchase contract should also require the seller to fully comply with the terms of the existing mortgage debt at all times prior to closing and to cooperate with the buyer in its efforts to effect an assumption of the mortgage debt. Finally, the purchase contract should require that the existing mortgage lender certify in writing to the buyer that: (1) the seller is not in default under the mortgage debt; (2) the loan is fully assumable by the buyer, without the payment by buyer of any additional fees or, if any such fees are payable, the amount of such fees and who is required to pay them; and (3) the mortgage debt will, from and after the date of buyer's assumption of such debt, be on the economic and business terms and conditions stated in the lender's certification to the buyer (for example, the interest rate, debt service payments, and maturity date of the assumed loan, and the level of the buyer's personal liability, if any, for the repayment of the assumed loan).

Practice Tip #5-3: Strategies to Mitigate Risk

The real estate development lawyer has three separate strategies to mitigate the developer's land and deal risks prior to the land acquisition closing:

- *The receipt during the developer's due diligence of a certification from a third party expert that the land is free of certain risks;*

- *The receipt of a representation and warranty from the seller that the land is free of certain risks; and*

- *The establishment as a contingency to the buyer's obligation to purchase the land that the land is free from certain risks.*

The ways in which the real estate development lawyer utilizes these risk mitigation methods when drafting the land purchase contract are examined in much more detail in the next section of this chapter.

The chart set forth below illustrates which of the three techniques is available to help the real estate developer address each category of land and deal risk mentioned earlier in this chapter.

Land Risks	Contingency	Certificate During Due Diligence	Representation/ Warranty
Zoning	Yes	Yes	Yes
Utilities	Yes	Yes	Yes
Soils	Yes	Yes	Yes
Road access	Yes	Yes	Yes
Environmental conditions	Yes	Yes	Yes
Wetlands	Yes	Yes	Yes
Title/survey	Yes	Yes	Yes
Deal Risks			
Project economics	Yes	No	No
Debt and equity financing	Yes	No	No
Governmental approvals	Yes	No	No
Project lease-up	Yes	No	No
Construction costs/timing	Yes	No	No
Market conditions	Maybe	No	No
New competition	Maybe	No	No
Developer's financial condition	Maybe	No	No

As the above chart illustrates, the real estate development lawyer can use a "belt and suspenders" approach by simultaneously using all three risk mitigation techniques to ameliorate the developer's land risks. However, the only way the real estate development lawyer can address deal risks is to use a contingency mechanism to provide the developer with an out under the contract should one of those deal risks occur.

This Practice Tip is placed here because the next several pages of this chapter are devoted to an analysis of the three principal provisions of the purchase contract that deal with risk mitigation issues—that is, the provisions on contingencies, representations and warranties, and due diligence certifications. The "cheat sheet" provided by the above table is intended to be a handy reference tool to aid the reader's understanding of how a real estate development lawyer can craft the provisions of the purchase contract to try to protect the developer from the land and deal risks noted above.

F. BUYER CONTINGENCIES
(§ 4)

A *contingency* is defined in *The Real Estate Dictionary* as "the dependence upon a stated event which must occur before a contract is binding."[21] The terms "contingency" and "condition" are used interchangeably by real estate developers to describe the situation where a party's obligation to perform under a purchase contract is dependent upon the occurrence of a specified event or circumstance.

In most situations, it is the buyer who seeks to create contingencies to its contractual obligation to purchase the land. The typical contingency provision states that the buyer has a specified period of time in which to "satisfy or waive" the stated contingency. If the contingency is not satisfied or waived by the buyer within the contingency period, then the buyer has the right to terminate its obligations under the purchase contract and receive a refund of its deposit.

The buyer's contingency clause is the second most hotly negotiated provision found in the purchase contract—right after the provision on the purchase price. When it comes to the issue of a buyer contingency, the interests of the buyer and seller are wildly divergent. The buyer wants as broad a contingency for as long a period as possible. The seller, on the other hand, does not want the buyer's purchase obligation to be contingent upon anything that the seller does not believe it can control (for example, the seller's delivery of good title to the land). If the seller is willing to grant the buyer any contingency to its purchase obligation, then the seller wants the scope of the contingency to be as narrow as possible and the duration of the contingency period to be as short as possible.

Despite the seller's natural distaste for buyer contingencies, clauses setting forth some type of contingency to the buyer's purchase obligation are commonplace in contracts for the purchase and sale of commercial real estate. The primary reason why buyer contingency clauses are found in purchase contracts is that even the seller recognizes that there are certain things about the land that the buyer cannot learn until the buyer is given access to the land to conduct its due diligence—for example, whether the site soils can support construction of the contemplated development project. The knowledgeable seller also knows that a buyer will likely not spend the money necessary to perform its costly due diligence unless the

---

[21] *See* JOHN TALAMO, REAL ESTATE DICTIONARY 50 (7th ed. 2001).

buyer has a legally enforceable contractual right to purchase the property. As a result, the real dynamic of the negotiations over the buyer's contingency clause is not whether such a clause is going to be included in the purchase contract, but rather what that clause is going to look like. In order to gain an appreciation of that dynamic, one must first look at how both the developer/buyer and the landowner/seller view contingency clauses.

1. Developer's Perspective on Contingency Clauses

Ideally, the developer would like the contingency clause to effectively convert the purchase contract into a long-term unilateral option agreement—an "I'll buy if I want to" arrangement. An option agreement effectively eliminates the developer's land and deal risks because the developer does not have an obligation to purchase the land—it merely has the right to purchase the land if it elects to exercise the option. However, as noted earlier in this chapter, most landowners are resistant to taking their land off the market unless the buyer has an obligation to buy the land (a purchase contract) and not just the unilateral right to do so (an option). Moreover, it is black letter law that a pure option must be supported by consideration in order to be enforceable. The confluence of these two factors typically leads to the following conversation between the landowner/seller and the developer/buyer.

Developer—*"I want to get an option to buy your land."*

Landowner—*"No way am I going to give you an option unless you pay big-time nonrefundable money to get it."*

Developer—*"OK, well then let's go with a purchase contract."*

Following this conversation with the landowner, the developer then calls its lawyer and says something to the following effect:

"The #@! landowner won't do an option—so put together something called a purchase contract that will still let me walk away from the deal if I decide I don't want to buy the land."*

2. The Suitability Contingency

The above direction by the developer to its lawyer gives rise to the lawyer's drafting of a contractual contingency clause that attempts to get the developer as close as legally possible to the "I'll buy if I want to" position of a pure option. A *suitability contingency* is a clause that conditions the buyer's obligation to purchase the seller's land on a determination by the buyer that the land is "suitable," "acceptable," or "satisfactory" to the buyer. The following is an example of a suitability contingency (commonly referred to as a *free look*) that the developer's lawyer might include in the first draft of the land purchase contract:

> *Clause 1: Buyer's obligation to purchase the Land is contingent upon Buyer determining within ___ days after the Effective Date that the Land is suitable for Buyer's intended use.*

A particularly bold real estate development lawyer might draft a contingency clause that simply states that:

> *Clause 2: The Buyer may terminate its obligations under this contract at any time for any reason.*

Either of these broadly-worded contingencies would, on its face, seem to allow a buyer to achieve its goal of converting a purchase obligation into an option right. Unfortunately, (at least for the developer) the courts have stepped into the fray to limit the ability of the developer's lawyer to fully convert a purchase contract into an option through the use of a suitability contingency.

This book is about as far removed as possible from the typical "cases and materials" law school textbook that lays out an appellate judicial opinion and then asks questions about the "true meaning" of the opinion. Having said that, a real estate development lawyer does need to know how the courts view suitability contingencies so that the lawyer can advise the developer of the circumstances under which the developer can lawfully exit from a purchase contract if the developer decides it does not want to buy the seller's land.

The following is a summary of how courts have interpreted broad suitability contingency clauses that purport to give the buyer a virtually unrestricted right to back out of a land purchase contract.[22]

- When faced with a clause that says that a buyer's obligations to buy the land is subject to the buyer deciding that the land is "suitable" or "satisfactory," the courts have consistently implied an obligation for the buyer to act in good faith in making its decision whether the land is, in fact, suitable or satisfactory. The courts justify their rulings by saying that, absent the imposition of an implied obligation of good faith, the buyer's obligation to purchase the land would be an illusory promise rendering the entirety of the purchase contract unenforceable.[23]

- A recent decision by the California Supreme Court stands for the proposition that the inclusion of a clause that effectively says that the buyer may terminate the contract in its sole discretion at any time and for any reason converts a purchase

---

[22] For a general discussion of the case law on the enforceability and interpretation of contingency clauses, *see* Herz, *supra* note 20; and Michael O'Flaherty, *Real Estate Contracts from Execution to Closing*, in ACREL PAPERS (October 1999).

[23] *See e.g.*, Mattei v. Hopper, 330 P.2d 625 (California 1958). *See also* O'Flaherty, *supra* note 22, at 1–3.

contract into an option that is unenforceable unless supported by sufficient consideration.[24] The court noted that consideration could come in the form of either (1) a nonrefundable cash payment from the buyer to the seller, or (2) the buyer's performance of an act that conferred a bargained-for benefit upon the seller (for example, pursuing a governmental approval for the required subdivision of the seller's land parcel).[25] The court reserved on whether the buyer's posting of a refundable deposit could constitute sufficient consideration to support buyer's otherwise illusory promise to buy real property.[26]

- Finally, courts have occasionally attempted to narrowly construe the scope of a broad suitability condition. In a Georgia case,[27] the court ruled that a contingency clause that gave the buyer the right to terminate the contract if the buyer determined that the property was not satisfactory for the buyer's use only permitted the buyer to terminate its purchase obligation for a reason related to the "physical condition" of the property (land risks) and not the "economic feasibility" of the buyer's project (deal risks).

Real estate development lawyers have adopted a variety of strategies to deal with the case law summarized above. A few of those strategies are discussed below.

- If the lawyer representing a land buyer opts to go with language like Clause 1, above (that is, conditioning the buyer's purchase obligation on the buyer's determination of the suitability of the land), then the lawyer should counsel the developer that the developer must be diligent in establishing and documenting good faith reasons for its determination not to move forward with the land purchase (for example, inferior site soils, environmental problems, or title objections).[28] The lawyer should also try to include an

---

[24] *See* Steiner v. Thexton, 226 P.3d 359 (Cal. 2010).

[25] *Id.* at 16–17.

[26] *Id.* at 17, note 12.

[27] *See* Sheridan v. Crown Capital Corporation, 554 S.E.2d 296 (Ga. App. Ct.).

[28] It is apparent that a buyer's reliance on a contract exit based on a suitability contingency is stronger if the buyer has done thorough due diligence of the land than if the buyer has not done any due diligence. *See* Sheridan, *supra* note 27, at 299. A secondary question is what is the legal effect of a buyer's election to terminate its purchase obligations for pretextual reasons—that is, for reasons that are not the real reasons affecting the buyer's decision. *See e.g.,* Zygar v. Johnson, 169 Or. App. 638 (2000), in which the buyer reasonably believed that the results of the termite inspection were unsatisfactory and, therefore, was able to get out of a contract to buy a house even though it was submitted that the "real" reason for his terminating the contract was that his fiancé had decided she did not want to live there. *See also* Liuzza v. Panzer, 333 So.2d 689 (La. App. 1976); Barber v. Jacobs, 753 A.2d 430 (Conn. Ct. App. 2000); and Loma Linda University v. District-Realty Title Insurance Corp., 443 F.2d 773 (C.A.D.C. 1971).

"economic feasibility" component in its suitability contingency in an attempt to cover the developer's deal risks as well as its land risks.

- A lawyer representing a land buyer might try to further augment the buyer's flexibility under Clause 1 by stating that the buyer's determination to terminate its obligations under the suitability contingency may be made by the buyer "in its sole and absolute discretion." The intent behind the lawyer's insertion of this modifier in the purchase contract is apparent—the lawyer wants to negate the judicial implication of the buyer's obligation to act in good faith in making a decision to exit from the purchase contract and effectively convert the purchase contract into an "I'll buy if I want to" purchase option. Unfortunately, the case law interpreting the "sole discretion" language in the context of a suitability contingency in a real estate purchase contract fails to support the drafting objective of the buyer's lawyer. Courts generally have either opted (1) to ignore the "sole discretion" language and require the buyer to act reasonably and in good faith in making its determination to terminate the purchase contract, or (2) to expressly recognize the import of the "sole discretion" language by holding that the inclusion of such a clause effectively converts the buyer's obligation into an unenforceable illusory promise.[29] I would also be remiss if I failed to mention the difficulty of getting landowner's counsel to agree to the inclusion of the "sole and absolute discretion" modifier in the suitability contingency of a purchase contract.

- If the lawyer representing a land buyer opts to go with language akin to Clause 2, above (that is, providing that the buyer may terminate for any reason at any time), then it is essential that the lawyer include in the purchase contract a clear statement of the consideration being provided to the seller by the buyer. Some practitioners (particularly those practicing in California) have decided to include the buyer's nonrefundable payment of $500 to $1,000 as a standard component of each purchase contract they draft. Others have chosen to rely on the doctrine of part performance to provide

---

[29] *See* Allen D. Shandron, Inc. v. Cole, 416 P.2d 555 (Ariz. 1966), where the court held that the "use of the word 'discretion' specifically means that the Landlord will not act arbitrarily, unreasonably or capriciously." *See also* Bryant v. City of Atlantic City, 707 A.2d 1072 (N.J. 1998) where the court held that, despite the presence of the modifier "in its sole discretion," a developer still had to act reasonably in making its decision as to whether the costs of an environmental remediation were unreasonable. *But see* Reedy v. Reedy, 264 P.2d 913 (Kan. 1953), where the Kansas court held that the use of the word "discretion" to describe a party's review of a contractual matter effectively made the party's promise illusory and that, in such instance, the court would not imply an obligation of good faith to create an enforceable agreement among the parties.

the requisite consideration by placing a contractual obligation on the buyer (1) to take the lead on applying for a governmental approval or doing something else that will redound to the seller's favor if the transaction fails to close, (2) to provide the seller with copies of all of buyer's due diligence reports if buyer opts to terminate the purchase contract, or (3) to post a refundable deposit under the purchase contract (hoping here that the California courts ultimately decide that this last alternative works).[30]

If the real estate development lawyer understands the law on suitability contingencies and remains mindful of the strategies discussed above, then the lawyer will find that a broad suitability contingency is an invaluable tool to be used in an attempt to minimize the developer's exposure to land and deal risks. When structured in an appropriate manner, a suitability contingency clause can provide the buyer with almost as much contractual flexibility as a pure option, without exposing the buyer to the financial downside of having to pay a significant nonrefundable option fee. However, as is discussed in the ensuing pages of this chapter, whether the real estate development lawyer gets to use the tool of a suitability contingency is almost always a topic of intense negotiation with counsel for the landowner.

3.   Landowner's Perspective on Contingency Clauses

For the purpose of the following discussion, assume that the real estate development lawyer has prepared a draft purchase contract that contains the following contingency clause (*see* § 4 of the Form Purchase Agreement):

> *Buyer's obligation to purchase the Land is contingent upon Buyer determining within 270 days after the Effective Date that (a) the condition of the Land is suitable for Buyer's intended use, and (b) Buyer's proposed development of the Land is economically feasible.*

How will the typical landowner react to this type of contingency clause? If the landowner is represented by competent counsel, the usual reaction will be that the contingency is "too broad" and that the contingency period is "too long."

It is important to remember what the inclusion of a contingency clause means to a landowner. By agreeing to a purchase contract with a buyer contingency, the landowner is effectively agreeing to take its property off the market for the duration of the contingency period, without any assurance that the buyer will actually close on the purchase of the land. It

---

[30] *See* GEORGE LEFCOE, REAL ESTATE TRANSACTIONS, FINANCE, AND DEVELOPMENT (6th ed. 2009), at 90.

is this lost opportunity that counsel representing the landowner attempts to minimize when negotiating the terms of a buyer contingency clause.

As stated earlier in this chapter, many landowners are willing to grant the buyer a limited contingency to permit the buyer to perform its site due diligence to rule out the existence of land risks—for example, soils tests, an environmental assessment, title and survey review, etc. From the perspective of the landowner, the duration of a limited due diligence contingency should be somewhere between 20 and 45 days after the contract's effective date.

A contingency like the one set out at the beginning of this section is intended not just to cover the developer's land risks, but also all of the developer's deal risks (for example, the developer's inability to lease up its project or its failure to obtain acceptable debt and equity financing to fund the project). The landowner's typical first response when presented with a clause that the real estate development lawyer has drafted to attempt to cover the developer's deal risks is to say something to the effect that "Deal risks are your problem not mine."

A typical landowner counter-measure to the type of broad suitability contingency clause referenced at the outset of this section would be a clause similar to the following:

> Buyer's obligation to purchase the Land is contingent upon Buyer determining within 30 days after the Effective Date that the Land is physically capable of supporting Buyer's construction of a four-story 100,000-square-foot office building on the Land.

The above clause is the landowners' way of telling the developer that the developer's proposed suitability contingency clause is "too broad" and "too long."

How do the parties bridge the obvious gap that exists between the developer's 270-day broad suitability contingency that covers both land risks and deal risks and the landowner's 30-day due diligence contingency that covers only a limited subset of the developer's land risks? As is the case in any contractual negotiation, that answer ultimately is tied to the parties' relative negotiating leverage. Is the land an in-fill site that is fully zoned and permitted? If so, the leverage swings in favor of the landowner and its desire to provide developer with nothing more than a short and limited due diligence contingency. If the land is neither zoned, nor permitted, and is in a pioneering development location, then the landowner may be more receptive to accepting a broad suitability contingency because the landowner may believe (rightly so) that the only way for the landowner to receive top dollar for its land is to give the developer ample time and flexibility to bring its development project to fruition. However, even in that circumstance, the landowner is likely to want to specifically limit the scope of the developer's contingency to the achievement of a few very specific objectives—for example, the rezoning of the land to permit commercial development and the extension of utilities to the site.

In summary, the landowner wants to make sure that the buyer is seriously committed to buying the landowner's site and is not just trying to tie up that site for as long as possible in the hope that a spectacular development or resale opportunity fortuitously falls into the buyer's lap like "manna from heaven." The landowner's lawyer is, therefore, given the assignment of negotiating a contingency clause that is as far-removed as possible from the "I'll buy if I want to" form of a pure option that is the developer's goal.

The following are negotiating techniques regularly used by seller's counsel to limit buyer contingency clauses.

- A negotiating tactic commonly used by the landowner's lawyer is to try to get the developer (or its lawyer) to specifically identify those land risks that are the most troubling to the developer. The landowner's counsel then tries to turn the table on the developer by pointing out which of the identified land risks are susceptible of being handled by third party certifications or limited representations from the seller. The landowner's lawyer may grudgingly (but only grudgingly) deal with any remaining land risk that the landowner believes to be legitimate in the context of the proposed land acquisition by drafting contingency language that is limited as to both the scope of the contingency and the period in which the contingency must be satisfied or waived by the buyer.

- Seller's counsel often seeks to limit the scope of the buyer's contingency to those land risks that any person seeking to develop the land for any purpose would encounter—for example, a rezoning of the land from an agricultural to a commercial classification. Contingencies covering deal risks specifically associated with the buyer's proposed project (for example, the receipt of acceptable tenant leases, construction financing, or governmental incentives) are routinely rejected by seller's counsel as being "your problem, not mine."

- If a contingency involves an approval that the developer must secure for the project (for example, a rezoning of the land), seller's counsel may try to place an affirmative obligation on the developer to take whatever interim action is required as a prerequisite for the ultimate granting of such approval. By way of example, seller's counsel might insert a clause saying that the buyer is obligated to submit its request for a rezoning of the property within 30 days after the contract's effective date and that developer's failure to do so will result in an automatic termination of the purchase contract.

- Finally, seller's counsel may require a ***stair-stepping*** of the deposit paid by the developer. Stair-stepping a deposit usually entails either (1) the developer paying additional deposits periodically throughout the contingency period (for example, every 60 days), (2) a portion of the developer's deposit becoming nonrefundable at designated points of the contingency period (this is often referred to as the deposit "going hard"), or (3) a combination of (1) and (2).

The negotiations over the buyer's contingency clause are all about breadth and length, as buyer's counsel tries to structure the contingency clause to protect the developer from all risks (both land and deal risks), while seller's counsel seeks to limit the buyer's contingency clause to only those items that any buyer of the subject land would have to accomplish in order to justify the amount of the purchase price set forth in the purchase contract.

HIBC Case Study—The Buyer's Contingency

Pizzuti wanted a contingency clause that was sufficiently broad and long to address both the normal land and deal risks associated with the purchase of a large commercial tract (remember the HIBC parcel was 350 acres) and the deal risks related to Pizzuti's attempt to land the CBIS build-to-suit project. Chemical Bank, on the other hand, wanted to make sure that (1) it was dealing with a serious and financially capable buyer, and (2) the deal would close as quickly as possible. Chemical Bank, as an experienced seller of real estate, fully appreciated that Pizzuti needed a contingency period to permit it to do its due diligence and otherwise figure out if its development of the HIBC land was feasible. Chemical Bank was, however, adamant that it would not make any contractual representations and warranties about the condition of the land and that Pizzuti would be buying the land in its "as is" condition.

Given all of the above factors, counsel for Pizzuti and Chemical had little difficulty agreeing to a broad contingency clause that gave Pizzuti the right to terminate its contractual obligations if it determined that the land was not "suitable for Buyer's intended purpose." The Pizzuti-Chemical land purchase contract defined "suitability" in the following manner:

Determination of the Property's suitability shall include, but not be limited to, Buyer's consideration of the following matters:

a.   Suitability of soils, access, visibility and other physical characteristics of the Property;

b.   Satisfactory results of environmental test and site investigations regarding the Property;

c.   Availability of permits, licenses, variances and other governmental approvals, including land use and zoning approvals, necessary for Buyer's intended use of the Property; and

d.   Economic and market analysis to determine feasibility of the Property for Buyer's development purposes.

Chemical Bank even went so far as to agree that Pizzuti could make the determination of the suitability of the land "in its sole discretion."

The real negotiation on the HIBC contingency clause was over the length of the contingency period. Pizzuti asked for a 270-day contingency period, which, in its mind, would give it sufficient time (1) to determine the feasibility of its development of the 350-acre HIBC tract, and (2) to secure CBIS' commitment to locate its office building and data center on the HIBC parcel. Chemical Bank initially took the position that the contingency period would be only 30 days. The compromise ultimately agreed to by Pizzuti and Chemical Bank was that the contingency period would be 90 days—a time period that Pizzuti believed would be sufficient to complete its physical due diligence of the HIBC tract, but likely not long enough for it either to fully vet the feasibility of the overall HIBC development project or to lock up the CBIS project.

The final part of the negotiation over the HIBC contingency clause related to Chemical Bank's insistence that Pizzuti evidence the seriousness of its interest in acquiring the HIBC land by posting a sizable earnest money deposit—$750,000. Chemical initially took the position that the entirety of the $750,000 deposit would have to be paid upfront upon contract execution and that 1/3 of that deposit (or $250,000) would become nonrefundable 30 days after contract execution, with another 1/3 becoming nonrefundable 60 days after contract execution. Pizzuti ultimately agreed to pay the $750,000 deposit, but retained the right to pay it in three installments over the first 60 days of the contingency period. More importantly, Pizzuti was also able to get Chemical Bank to agree to keep the contingency clause as a "free look" by making the entirety of the deposit refundable throughout the 90-day contingency period.

The HIBC contingency clause is a nice illustration of how a buyer and a seller can resolve their competing business objectives to make a deal. The points in the contingency clause negotiations that were "won" and "lost" by Pizzuti are noted below.

Won	*Lost*
Broad suitability/feasibility contingency	*90-day contingency period*
Fully refundable deposit	*Purchase on an "as is" basis*
Deposit paid in three installments	*Deposit of $750,000*

---

4. Terminating the Contract at End of Contingency Period

The whole point of a buyer contingency clause is to give the buyer the ability to terminate its obligations under the purchase contract if the stated contingency is not satisfied or waived by the buyer. It is imperative that the purchase contract specifically identify the method to be used by buyer if it elects to terminate its purchase obligation. The land seller generally prefers a provision that states that the buyer will be deemed to have waived its contingency unless the buyer gives seller written notice within the contingency period that the buyer is affirmatively electing to terminate the purchase contract. Conversely, a land buyer favors a provision that presumes that the contingency has not been satisfied or waived (and, hence, that the purchase contract is terminated) unless the buyer provides written notice to the contrary to the seller within the contingency period. The selected presumption should be clearly articulated in the contingency provision of the purchase contract.

G. DUE DILIGENCE
(§ 5)

Due diligence is the investigatory process that a land buyer goes through to determine whether the physical condition of a particular parcel of land is suitable for the buyer's intended use of that parcel. As discussed in the prior section of this chapter, a buyer's successful completion of its site due diligence is frequently a contingency to the buyer's obligation to purchase the land.

The buyer must have access to the land in order to perform its site due diligence. The buyer does not automatically gain such access simply by its execution of a purchase contract. The purchase contract should explicitly state that the buyer and its consultants will have access to the land after contract execution so that the buyer and its consultants may conduct appropriate site tests and inspections. The following is a list of those site tests and inspections that are typically conducted by a land buyer:

- A *title insurance commitment* prepared by a title insurance company that describes the quality of the seller's title to the land and specifically identifies all liens, easements, conditions, and other exceptions to seller's clean title to the land;

- A *survey* prepared by a licensed land surveyor that identifies the dimensions and boundaries of the land and the location of any improvements, easements, roads, and encroachments affecting the land;

- An *environmental assessment* prepared by a qualified environmental engineering firm that identifies any environmental problems detected from an inspection of the site and a review of the appropriate federal and state environmental protection agency files;

- A *soils report* prepared by a qualified soils engineer that confirms that the site soils will support the construction of the buyer's proposed project on the land;

- A *wetlands report* prepared by a qualified wetlands consultant that identifies the location, size, and nature of any protected wetlands located on the land;

- An *access and utility study* prepared by the buyer or a consultant hired by the buyer (sometimes the buyer's general contractor) that confirms that the land has direct access to public roads and that utilities of sufficient size and capacity to service the buyer's proposed project are available to the boundaries of the land; and

- A *zoning report* prepared by the buyer or a land use consultant hired by the buyer that recites the current zoning classification of the land and confirms that the buyer's development plans conform to all requirements imposed by that zoning classification.

A word of caution should be noted about the written reports produced by the buyer's consultants during the due diligence process. As noted earlier in this chapter, the developer seeks to limit its exposure to various land risks by retaining experts to provide it with written certifications that the subject land risks do not exist with respect to the land. The issuers of those certifications (be it, the title insurance company, surveyor, environmental engineer, or another outside consultant) regularly try to subject their certifications to a litany of assumptions, limitations, and qualifications, all of which are intended to essentially render the certifications meaningless. For example, it is common for an environmental engineer's first draft of its certification letter to state that the consultant's liability for any errors or omissions contained in its report is limited to a refund of the amount of the fee paid to the consultant by the land buyer—maybe $10,000 on a land purchase that might contain a purchase price in the millions of dollars. It often falls to the real estate development lawyer to negotiate a form of certification that provides true comfort to the developer. In addition to tightening down the terms of the consultant's certification, the lawyer must also determine whether the consultant has sufficient assets (either personally or through errors and omissions insurance coverage) to reimburse the developer for any loss it incurs as a result of the consultant's report being wrong.

A buyer's due diligence efforts may also be aided by its receipt of permission from the landowner to review any prior third party reports and certifications in the landowner's possession concerning the condition of the land. The landowner is often hesitant to grant the buyer access to such documents based on the landowner's fear that its sharing of such reports and certifications might somehow be construed as constituting a guaranty by the landowner of the completeness and accuracy of the furnished reports and certifications. The landowner is often more amenable to providing the buyer with copies of such reports and certifications if (1) the buyer agrees to a relatively short contingency period, and (2) the purchase contract stipulates that the seller's provision of such reports and certifications to the buyer does not constitute a representation or guaranty by the seller of the completeness or accuracy of the reports and certifications. It must be stressed that the buyer's receipt of copies of the seller's historical reports is not a substitute for the buyer securing new reports from its consultants. The buyer does not have any right to hold the issuer of the old reports liable for any error or omission because of a lack of privity between such issuer and the buyer.

In exchange for its agreement to grant the buyer access to its land and records, the landowner customarily requires the following buyer covenants to be spelled out in the purchase contract:

- The buyer's agreement that it will provide the landowner with reasonable prior notice of its entry onto the property for the conduct of its due diligence tests;

- The buyer's agreement to repair any damage caused by entry onto the land of the buyer or its consultants;

- The buyer's indemnification of the landowner against any loss or liability associated with the conduct of any on-site tests;

- The buyer's acknowledgement that all tests conducted by the buyer and its consultants will be paid for by the buyer; and

- Finally, the buyer's agreement that if its acquisition of the land is not closed due to the exercise of the buyer's right to terminate the purchase contract, then the buyer will provide the landowner with copies of all third party reports and certifications received by the buyer during the course of its due diligence efforts.

The due diligence process is examined in more detail in *Chapter 8—Stage 4: Closing the Land Acquisition,* at pages 317–328.

The fact that the purchase contract recites that the buyer may go on the land to conduct its due diligence does not automatically give the buyer the contractual right to terminate its obligation to purchase the land if the results of the buyer's due diligence are unsatisfactory to the buyer. If it is the buyer's intention that it will not be obligated to purchase the land unless its due diligence is satisfactory (which is almost always the case), then the purchase contract should include a buyer contingency clause that gives the buyer the desired "out" under the purchase contract. That "out" may be covered in the form of either (1) a specific statement that the buyer's purchase obligation is contingent upon the buyer's satisfactory completion of its due diligence, or (2) a broad suitability contingency of the type discussed earlier in this chapter that subsumes the concept of the satisfactoriness of the buyer's due diligence. Savvy counsel to the landowner will try to limit the scope of the buyer's by limiting the scope of the due diligence covered by the contingency (for example, only an environmental assessment) and by then imposing an objective standard for the permitted due diligence (for example, the buyer's receipt of an environmental engineer's certification that there is no evidence of "recognized environmental conditions" affecting the land).

H. REPRESENTATIONS AND WARRANTIES

(§ 6)

The seller representation and warranty is the third and final weapon available to the real estate development lawyer to mitigate the developer's exposure to the land risks associated with a land acquisition. A *representation* is a statement of a current fact to induce reliance by the other party to the contract, while a *warranty* is a promise that a statement of fact is or will be true.[31] An example of a seller representation is "seller represents that there are no hazardous materials on the Land." A seller warranty on the same topic would read as follows—"seller warrants that there are no hazardous materials on the Land and that there will be no hazardous materials on the land on the closing date." Most purchase contracts require the seller to make a statement concerning a particular

---

[31] *See* GREGORY STEIN, *supra* note 20, at 26; and TINA L. STARK, DRAFTING CONTRACTS: HOW AND WHY LAWYERS DO WHAT THEY DO 12–13 (2007)

fact both as of the date on which the contract was executed (a representation) and as of the closing date (a warranty). For this reason, the terms "representation" and "warranty" are usually lumped together and treated interchangeably in the purchase contract. For the sake of simplicity, the term "representations" is used throughout the remainder of this chapter as a short-hand reference to include both representations and warranties (*see*, however, pages 135–139 for a discussion of the different remedies that are available to a buyer for the seller's breach of a representation versus its breach of a warranty).

Any substantive discussion of seller representations must first start with the principle of ***caveat emptor***—"let the buyer beware." The doctrine of caveat emptor remains generally applicable to the sale of commercial real property (although significant inroads on that principle have been made in the context of the purchase and sale of residential real property).[32] In its simplest terms, the doctrine of caveat emptor stands for the dual proposition that (1) a seller has no obligation to disclose to the buyer any defects or other problems related to the condition of the real property being sold to the buyer, and (2) the buyer has no inherent legal right to sue the seller if the condition of the real property purchased by the buyer ultimately proves to be at odds with the buyer's expectations.

While the doctrine of caveat emptor does not require a commercial land seller to make any disclosures about the condition of the land, that doctrine does not permit the seller to lie or make an affirmative misrepresentation about the land. A buyer of commercial real estate may, therefore, partially negate the application of the doctrine of caveat emptor by including in the purchase contract specific seller representations concerning the seller's status and authority and the condition and character of its land. A related purpose served by the buyer's inclusion of representations in the land purchase contract is to try to compel the honest seller (is there any other kind) to disclose land risks that the buyer can then assess to determine whether the buyer wants to move forward with the purchase of the land.[33]

1.   Seller's Perspective on Representations and Warranties

Landowners are quick to embrace the doctrine of caveat emptor. As stated at the outset of this chapter, the business objective of the landowner is to sell its land for the highest price, as quickly as possible, and without

---

[32] *See* Hamilton, *supra* note 6, at 5–14 through 5–17; GERALD KORNGOLD AND PAUL GOLDSTEIN, REAL ESTATE TRANSACTIONS, CASES AND MATERIALS ON LAND TRANSFER, DEVELOPMENT AND FINANCE 206–211 (4th ed. 2002); and Kathleen McNamara Tomcho, *Commercial Real Estate Buyer Beware: Sellers May Have the Right to Remain Silent*, 70 SOUTHERN CALIFORNIA LAW REVIEW 1571 (1997).

[33] *See* Edward A. Peterson, *The Effective Use of Representations and Warranties in Commercial Real Estate Contracts*, in ACREL PAPERS (October 1999); and Billie J. Ellis and Douglas A. Yeager, *Practical Implications of a Seller's Representations and Warranties in a Highly Competitive Commercial Real Estate Transaction*, in ACREL PAPERS 68.

conditions. In addition, the land seller wants to make sure that, once the land sale is closed, the seller has no further liability or obligation relative to the sold land.

The landowner's love affair with the doctrine of caveat emptor is evidenced by the inclusion in the standard seller form of purchase contract of a provision similar to the following:

> *EXCEPT AS OTHERWISE EXPRESSLY PROVIDED IN THIS CONTRACT, BUYER ACKNOWLEDGES THAT IT HAS EXAMINED THE PROPERTY AND IS BUYING THE PROPERTY "AS IS", WITHOUT WARRANTY OR REPRESENTATION OF ANY KIND WHATSOEVER, EXPRESS OR IMPLIED, INCLUDING, WITHOUT LIMITATION, ANY IMPLIED WARRANTY OF FITNESS OF THE PROPERTY FOR A PARTICULAR PURPOSE, WHETHER BY SELLER OR BY AN AGENT, BROKER, EMPLOYEE OR OTHER REPRESENTATIVE OF SELLER. ALL UNDERSTANDINGS AND AGREEMENTS HERETOFORE BETWEEN THE PARTIES ARE HEREBY MERGED IN THIS CONTRACT, WHICH ALONE SHALL FULLY AND COMPLETELY EXPRESS THE PARTIES' AGREEMENT.*

> *BUYER ACKNOWLEDGES THAT IT HAS RECEIVED AN ADEQUATE OPPORTUNITY TO INSPECT THE PROPERTY AND TO MAKE SUCH LEGAL, FACTUAL AND OTHER INQUIRIES AND INVESTIGATIONS AS BUYER DEEMS APPROPRIATE WITH RESPECT TO THE PROPERTY. BUYER HEREBY WAIVES, RELEASES AND DISCHARGES ANY CLAIMS THAT IT HAS OR MAY HAVE AGAINST SELLER WITH RESPECT TO ANY CONDITION ON OR ABOUT THE PROPERTY OR ANY OTHER STATE OF FACTS WHICH EXISTS WITH RESPECT TO THE PROPERTY. BUYER FURTHER ACKNOWLEDGES AND AGREES THAT THERE SHALL BE NO ADJUSTMENTS IN THE PURCHASE PRICE FOR ANY PHYSICAL, FUNCTIONAL, ECONOMIC OR ENVIRONMENTAL CONDITION RELATING TO THE PROPERTY.*

The above language (taken directly from the purchase contract entered into by Pizzuti and Chemical Bank for the HIBC land acquisition, replete with all of its wonderful references to "heretofore," "hereby," and "herein") is commonly referred to as an ***as is clause***. An "as is" clause is basically the landowner's homage to the doctrine of caveat emptor.

The sophisticated land seller often starts its negotiations with a buyer by taking the position that the buyer must purchase the land (1) without any contingencies, and (2) subject to an "as is" clause of the type noted above. The land seller is seldom able to successfully defend both of these positions against the entreaties of the land buyer. A seller who is steadfast in its refusal to make any substantive representations usually has to give the land buyer a broad suitability contingency so that the buyer can conduct on-site due diligence to gain a full understanding of the condition and character of the land. Conversely, if the land seller's primary negotiating objective is to severely limit the scope and duration of the buyer's contingency, then the seller may find that the best way for the seller to accomplish that objective is to provide the buyer with a complete set of seller representations.

To the extent the land seller is willing to include certain representations in the purchase contract, the seller's lawyer will try to limit both the number and scope of the included representations. The seller's lawyer will also likely object to the inclusion in the purchase contract of any representation that speaks in absolute terms about the condition or character of the land. The seller does not want to be in a position of insuring or guarantying that any aspect of the land is consistent with the buyer's expectations. The seller's lawyer, therefore, often insists that any representation be couched in terms of the "seller's knowledge" of the subject matter of the representation.

The following are the operative issues that should be considered when attaching a knowledge qualifier to a seller representation.[34]

- Does the seller's knowledge extend not only to information that it actually knows, but also to information that it reasonably should know?

- Is the seller under a good faith obligation to make inquiry or investigation concerning the subject matter of the representation?

- In the context of a representation being made by an entity, is the knowledge imputed to the named entity that of all its current and former employees, officers, directors, and consultants or just a limited subset of that group.

Because state courts differ in their interpretation of knowledge qualifiers, most practitioners now seek to include in the purchase contract an express definition of what is meant by the term "seller's knowledge."[35]

2.   Buyer's Perspective on Representations and Warranties

The seller representation is a device that the real estate development lawyer uses to try to limit the developer's land risks. The development lawyer's counterpoint to the landowner's "as is" clause is the *full*

---

[34]   *See* Kevin L. Shepherd, *Top 10 "Gotchas" in Comprehensive Contracts of Sale*, 17 No. 5 Practical Real Estate Lawyer 17, 19 (2001); and Peterson, *supra* note 33, at 14.

[35]   *See e.g.*, Peterson, *supra* note 33, at 30–31; and Ellis *supra* note 33, at 63–64. *See also* Hamilton, *supra* note 6, at 5–65 and 5–66, for an example of a definition of "seller's knowledge."

warranty sale, where the seller is not only asked to make representations on the complete litany of the developer's potential land risks, but is also asked to provide the buyer with the following "full disclosure" representation:

> *The Seller has fully and accurately disclosed to the Buyer in writing all material facts and circumstances relating to the transaction that is the subject of this Agreement and the ownership, operation, condition, and character of the Land.*

The real estate development lawyer's dream world consists of a purchase contract that includes both a set of full warranty sale representations and a broadly stated suitability contingency. In reality, the real estate development lawyer successfully achieves that level of contractual Nirvana just about as often as seller's counsel gets a buyer to agree to an "as is" sale without any contingencies.

The land risks that are intended to be covered by a full warranty sale fall into two distinct categories:

- *Category 1*—Land risks that *CAN* be resolved by the developer's receipt of clean certifications from third party consultants during its site due diligence; and

- *Category 2*—Land risks that *CANNOT* be resolved as part of the developer's due diligence efforts.

Representations covering the first category of land risks are intended to provide the land buyer with back-up support for the conclusions reached by its consultants during the due diligence process. In legal parlance, this is a classic "belt and suspenders" tactic, where the buyer seeks protection against a particular land risk from two separate sources—the third party certifications of its consultants and the representations made in the purchase contract by the seller.

The receipt of seller representations on category 1 land risks is generally viewed by the buyer as a luxury and not a necessity. If the purchase contract gives the buyer a right to terminate its obligations if the results of the buyer's due diligence are unsatisfactory, then the buyer can safely entertain the notion of dropping from the purchase contract those seller representations that are solely intended to address category 1 land risks.

Assume for the moment that the purchase contract includes a broad suitability contingency that provides the buyer with a contractual out if it determines that the land is not suitable for its intended use. In that circumstance, the real estate development lawyer's attention should be primarily focused on how the lawyer can structure the seller's representations to deal with category 2 land risks—that is, those site-specific risks that cannot be resolved as part of the developer's due diligence. The following are examples of facts or circumstances that fall into that second risk category:

- Notices received by the seller from a governmental agency concerning a condition or circumstance that could have an adverse effect on the utility of the land for the buyer's project (for example, a notice of a proposed condemnation or a notice of a violation of a local zoning ordinance);

- Circumstances or conditions known solely by the seller (and not the general public) that could impact the usability of the land for buyer's project (for example, the seller's knowledge of a threatened lawsuit affecting the land); and

- The seller's unrecorded grant to a third party of a legal or equitable interest in the land.

The one common thread running through all the above examples of category 2 land risks is that the seller has knowledge of a land risk that is not readily discoverable by the buyer through a physical inspection of the land or a review of the public real estate records. Under the doctrine of caveat emptor, the landowner has no common law obligation to disclose its knowledge of those land risks to the prospective buyer. The only strategy available to the buyer to protect itself against the category 2 land risk is to include representations in the purchase contract that are intended to flush out the seller's knowledge of those risks.

There is one additional land risk that the buyer can cover only by the inclusion in the purchase contract of appropriate seller representations—that is, the risk that the seller does not have the requisite status or authority to sell the land to the buyer. The real estate development lawyer should, therefore, be sure to include in the purchase contract specific seller representations confirming that:

- The seller is not required to obtain any third party approval as a condition precedent to its sale of the land to the buyer;

- There are no pending or threatened lawsuits, bankruptcy proceedings, or governmental orders that could adversely affect the seller's authority to sell the land to the buyer; and

- If the seller is an entity, that entity is in good standing in the state of its formation and the state in which the land is located and the person executing the purchase contract is duly authorized to act on the seller's behalf.

3. "As Is" vs. Full Warranty Sale—A Common Compromise

Counsel for the seller and buyer are usually able to carve out a mutually acceptable middle ground between the two extremes of an absolute "as is" sale (the seller's preference) and a full warranty sale (the buyer's preference). Seller's counsel is typically willing to provide a limited set of seller representations addressing (1) those category 1 land risks that are peculiarly within the realm of the seller's knowledge and, hence, cannot be eliminated by the buyer's receipt of third party certifications, and (2) risks associated with the seller's status and authority to sell the land, which again involve matters that are known only to the seller and are not accessible in any way by the buyer. Similarly, buyer's counsel is usually amenable to limiting the scope of at least some of the representations to the "seller's knowledge."

Resolving these largely non-controversial matters still leaves much to be negotiated between the parties concerning the scope of the seller's representations. As part of the customary dance between counsel for the developer and the landowner on the topic of seller representations, the real estate development lawyer pushes for the inclusion in the purchase contract of a laundry list of representations[36] that are designed: to force the seller to disclose everything it knows about the land; and to provide the buyer with added "belt and suspenders" comfort on a variety of matters related to the condition and character of the land. The landowner's counsel then counters by: trying to limit the seller's representations to those matters mentioned in the preceding paragraph that are solely within the province of the landowner's knowledge; and seeking to define the landowner's knowledge as the actual knowledge, without investigation or inquiry, of a very limited number of individuals.

The outcome of the parties' negotiations on the seller's representations is greatly influenced by what they agreed to on the subject of the buyer's contingency—with the number and scope of the seller's representations having an inverse relationship with the breadth and duration of the buyer's contingency. The parties' haggling over the seller representations effectively comes down to an exercise in the allocation of risk—that is, how much risk is each party willing to assume under the land purchase contract in order to get the deal done.

4.   Effective Date of Representations

Most purchase contracts provide that the seller's representations are deemed to be made both as of the date of the parties' execution of the contract and as of the date of the land acquisition closing. A provision of this type effectively burdens the seller with the risk that something happens between the date of the execution of the contract and the date of closing to cause a once true representation to become false. The

---

[36] For an extremely inclusive laundry list of seller representations, *see* Peter Aitelli, *Agreement for Purchase and Sale of Equity Interests in Real Property*, in ALI-CLE MODERN REAL ESTATE TRANSACTIONS, Course No. SY006 87, 115–119 (August 2016). *See also* Hamilton, *supra* note 6, at 5–17, 5–18 and 5–58 through 5–65, for an interesting ranking (from the least to the most controversial) of the representations and warranties customarily requested by the buyer.

implications of this type of provision on the remedies that are available to the buyer to deal with the seller's breach of a representation are discussed later in this chapter.

5. Survival of Representations

Under the common law doctrine of merger, a seller's representations are deemed to have merged into the deed delivered to the buyer at closing and, as such, do not support any post-closing legal action that the buyer might otherwise want to bring against the seller for a breach of a representation.[37] The effective disappearance of the seller's representations after closing rarely, if ever, is consistent with the buyer's intentions.

As such, it is the real estate development lawyer's job to make sure that the purchase contract contains a *survival clause* that recites that the seller's representations (as well as any other seller covenant that is not fully performed prior to closing) survive the closing. The length of the survival period is a subject of negotiation, with the outside survival date being the statute of limitations applicable to any action on the breached representation. Land buyers customarily ask for a survival period of at least two years, while sellers seek to limit the survival period to 12 months or less.

The purchase contract should also recite what actions must be taken by the buyer during the agreed-upon survival period in order to keep alive its legal action for a breach of a representation. The options range from simply sending the seller a written notice alleging a breach to actually filing a lawsuit on or before the outside date of the survival period.

6. Remedies for a Breach of a Representation and Warranty

The preceding discussion intentionally lumped together a seller's representations and warranties under the singular umbrella of "representations." The topic of what happens if the statements made by the seller in the purchase contract prove to be false requires a re-introduction of the distinction between a seller's representation and a seller's warranty.

a. Common Law Remedies

At common law, the remedies for a seller's breach of a representation are different from the remedies available for a seller's breach of a warranty. The common law remedy for a misrepresentation (a statement of fact that was false when made by the seller) is rescission and restitution (unless the misrepresentation was fraudulent, in which event damages, including

---

[37] *See* Lawrence Berger, *Merger by Deed—What Provisions of a Contract for Sale of Land Survive the Closing*, 21 REAL ESTATE LAW JOURNAL 22 (Summer 1992); and Peterson, *supra* note 33, at 14–15.

punitive damages, are available in most jurisdictions). The common law remedy for a seller's breach of a warranty (a breach of seller's promise that a statement of fact is or will be true at a future date) is a damages action.[38]

If a purchase contract were to speak solely in terms of a "seller's representations" (to the exclusion of any "seller warranties"), then the buyer's remedies for a seller's misrepresentation would generally be limited to rescinding its purchases obligations and suing for restitution to recover the out-of-pocket expenses the buyer incurred in relying on the seller's representation. Similarly, if a purchase contract were to speak solely in terms of a "seller's warranties" (to the exclusion of any "seller representations"), then the buyer's remedy for a seller's breach of warranty would generally be limited to suing the seller for damages.

This distinction in available remedies has very little real world impact on a real estate development lawyer because the overwhelming majority of real estate purchase contracts (certainly those prepared by a thoughtful real estate development lawyer) require the seller to make both a representation and a warranty as to each statement of fact addressed in the land purchase contract. By requiring the seller to make both a representation and a warranty on each factual matter, the real estate development lawyer effectively reserves a full slate of remedies for the developer should the landowner's factual statements made in the purchase contract later prove to be false. If a lawyer representing the buyer receives a draft contract from seller's counsel that just references "seller's representations," the buyer's lawyer should be quick to insist that the words "and warranties" be added to the purchase contract (regardless whether seller's counsel is being admirably sneaky or just plain careless).

b.   Pre-Closing and Post-Closing Breaches

If a buyer discovers before closing that a seller's representation and warranty is false, then the buyer may institute a legal action to terminate its purchase obligation, receive a refund of its earnest money deposit, and sue the seller for restitution or damages. In practice, the buyer customarily places a price tag on the breached representation and warranty and tries to negotiate a reduction in the purchase price for the land.

The remedy typically relied on by a buyer to redress a breach of a seller representation and warranty that is discovered after the date of closing is a damages action. A seller who is concerned that it might be nickeled and dimed to death with post-closing allegations of breached representations and warranties should consider inserting in the purchase contract a threshold of materiality that a breached representation and warranty must satisfy before an action may be instituted against the seller. By way of example, a seller might negotiate a provision that says that no action may

---

[38]   *See* Stark, *supra* note 31, at 14–16.

be brought against the seller for the breach of any representation and warranty unless the aggregate money damages that would be owed to the buyer as a result of such breach exceeds $50,000.

c.   *Breach Caused by Post-Execution Occurrence*

As noted earlier in this chapter, it is commonplace for representations and warranties to be deemed remade as of the date of closing. What remedy should be available to the buyer if a seller representation and warranty that was true when made on the date of the execution of the purchase contract turns out to be false as of the date of closing? By way of example, assume that the purchase contract contained the following seller representation—"There are no hazardous materials or toxic substances located on the Land." What should be the buyer's remedy if an unrelated third party dumps toxic waste on the land after the effective date of the contract, but before the closing? What if the seller told the third party that it was OK to dump the toxic waste on the land?

Common sense dictates that the seller should be liable for a post-effective date breach of the above representation only if it intentionally did something during the contract period that caused the representation to become false—for example, giving its approval to the dumping of the waste on the land. The remedy section for the breach of a representation usually addresses this scenario by specifically stating that:

> *Seller will not be deemed to be in default under this Agreement if any fact or circumstance occurs after the Effective Date that renders any of Seller's representations and warranties false, so long as such fact or circumstance is not within the reasonable control of Seller; provided, however, that the occurrence of such fact or circumstance will nonetheless permit Buyer to terminate its obligations to perform under this Agreement as a result of the failure to satisfy the condition precedent that all of Seller's representations and warranties must be true as of the date of closing.*

The proviso in the above clause is needed because the buyer does not want to be obligated to purchase contaminated land, regardless whether the dumping of the toxic waste on the site was the fault of the seller or that of a third party.

d.   *Anti-Sandbagging Clause*

Land sellers often attempt to insert in the land purchase contract what is commonly referred to as an ***anti-sandbagging clause***. This clause, which originated in the M&A world, is intended to preclude a buyer who learns of a seller's breach of a representation and warranty *BEFORE* the buyer acquires title to the land from filing a legal action against the seller for that breach *AFTER* the date of the buyer's acquisition of the land. The following is an example of an anti-sandbagging clause.

> *If Buyer acquires the Property with knowledge of an untrue or incorrect representation or warranty, then upon the closing Buyer shall be deemed to have fully and unconditionally waived and released any and all claims, actions and causes of action whatsoever with respect to such untrue or incorrect representation or warranty.*[39]

Seller's counsel's rationale for the inclusion of an anti-sandbagging clause in a purchase contract is that it simply is not "fair" for the buyer to be able to sue the seller after the date of closing for a breach that the buyer did not find sufficiently material to cause it to back out of its obligation to purchase the land. While this reasoning might gain a level of traction in the M&A world, my experience is that a land buyer's lawyer is typically successful in resisting the inclusion of an anti-sandbagging clause in the purchase contract by suggesting that "the problem goes away if the seller does not lie."

e. Creation of Contingencies in Lieu of Representations and Warranties

Some sellers are extremely wary of being held personally liable for the breach of a representation and warranty—particularly if the buyer has sufficient leverage to require the seller to make a laundry list of absolute representations and warranties that are not subject to any knowledge or materiality modifiers. Faced with such a dilemma, the seller's lawyer often acquiesces to the inclusion in the purchase contract of the buyer's requested list of absolute representations and warranties, but then counters that the buyer's sole remedy for the seller's breach of a representation and warranty is rescission of the purchase contract. By adopting this negotiating tactic, the seller's lawyer effectively converts what on their face look like representations and warranties into buyer contingencies.

f. Credit Support for Seller's Representations and Warranties

The effectiveness of a buyer's remedy for the seller's breach of a representation is, of course, worthless if the seller has no assets at the time that the buyer files its damages action—a circumstance that is quite common in today's marketplace where most sellers are single purpose entities that disburse all of the sales proceeds immediately following the closing. A buyer can protect the viability of its damages remedy by either (1) insisting that a creditworthy entity guaranty the accuracy of the seller's

---

[39] Hamilton, *supra* note 6, at 5–66.

representations and warranties, or (2) holding back payment of a portion of the purchase price for a period of time after the closing to make sure that funds are available to cover any losses incurred by the buyer as a result of a breach that is discovered post-closing.

Practice Tip #5-4: Mitigating Land and Deal Risks

A real estate development lawyer's most important job when drafting and negotiating the land purchase contract is to craft language that mitigates the developer's exposure to land and deal risks that might cause the developer to decide that it does not want to acquire the seller's land parcel. As noted in the prior section of this chapter, a real estate development lawyer has three primary tools to attempt to minimize the developer's land and deal risks.

- *Due Diligence Certifications. The developer's receipt of written certifications from third party experts during the developer's due diligence is a great way for the developer to insulate itself against those land risks that are susceptible of being discovered by a physical inspection of the land or a review of public records—for example, environmental contamination, bad soils, wetlands, improper zoning, and unmarketable title.*

- *Seller Representations and Warranties. The inclusion in the purchase contract of seller representations and warranties is used by developer's counsel for two purposes (1) to buttress the accuracy of the written certifications received by the developer during its due diligence process (the "belts and suspenders" tactic), and (2) to cover those land risks that are not susceptible of being discovered during the developer's due diligence process (for example, circumstances or conditions related to the condition of the land that are known only by the landowner or the landowner's lack of status or authority to sell the land to the developer).*

- *Buyer Contingency. The buyer contingency is the real estate development lawyer's most important risk mitigation weapon because, unlike the two strategies mentioned above, the buyer contingency can be used to address not only the developer's land risks, but also the developer's deal risks.*

The negotiations over the real estate development lawyer's efforts to use these three strategies to lessen the developer's land and deal risks must be conducted in a holistic fashion—meaning that what the real estate development lawyer gets when negotiating one of the strategies has a direct impact on what the lawyer needs or gets when negotiating the other two strategies. The following are a few obvious illustrations of the effect that a negotiating result on one of the three strategies should have on the real estate development lawyer's negotiating posture on the other strategies.

- *Buyer gets a broad and long suitability contingency → Buyer's need for a full set of seller representations and warranties on discoverable land risks is lessened.*

- *Buyer gets a full set of seller representations and warranties from a creditworthy seller → Buyer's need for a long due diligence period and a broad suitability contingency is lessened.*

- *Buyer gets no representations and warranties (an "as is" deal) → Buyer's need for a long due diligence period and a broad suitability contingency is heightened.*

- *Buyer gets a short and limited contingency (30 days to determine that there are no environmental or soils problems) → Buyer's need for a broad set of absolute representations and warranties is heightened.*

I.   TITLE AND SURVEY ISSUES
(§ 7)

This section tackles the topic of what a purchase contract should say about the state of the land title to be conveyed to the buyer at closing. The details of the real estate development lawyer's review of the land title are discussed in *Chapter 8—Stage 4: Closing the Land Acquisition.*

1.   Quality of Title to Be Conveyed to the Buyer

The purchase contract should clearly recite the quality of the title to the land that the seller is obligated to convey to the buyer at the land acquisition closing. The following is a commonly-used statement of the requisite quality of title:

Seller will convey to Buyer marketable, fee simple title to the Land, free and clear of all liens and encumbrances other than the Permitted Exceptions.

The quoted provision establishes a two-pronged standard for the quality of the land title to be conveyed to the buyer.

- First, title to the land must be "marketable." **Marketable title** is a base-line concept that is intended to describe a generic state of title that is legally presumed to be acceptable to all owners of real estate. Title to real estate is generally said to be marketable if it permits the owner to possess, use, and dispose of the subject property, without any unreasonable legal impediment.[40] Most jurisdictions have promulgated standards for determining whether title to a parcel is marketable.[41] It is important to keep in mind that title can be marketable, even though it is subject to certain liens, easements, restrictions, and other exceptions to title.

- Second, title to the land must be free of all liens and encumbrances other than *permitted exceptions*. This requirement is intended to describe the state of title that is required by a particular buyer and is a step up from the base-line concept of marketable title. As is discussed later in this section, the defined term "permitted exceptions" is generally intended to encompass only those liens, easements, restrictions, and other exceptions to a perfectly clean title that the buyer determines will not unreasonably interfere with its ownership and use of the land.

2.   Delivery of Title Commitment

Purchase contracts governing the purchase and sale of commercial real estate almost universally provide that the quality of the title being conveyed to the buyer must be evidenced by a *title insurance policy*. A title insurance policy is a contract in which a title insurance company indemnifies an owner of real estate against any loss that an owner may suffer due to the quality of the owner's title being other than that specified in the title insurance policy.[42] A one-time insurance premium is paid to the title insurance company coincident with the closing of the buyer's acquisition of the land and the insurance company's issuance of its title insurance policy.

The first step in the process of insuring a buyer's title to land is the issuance by the title insurer of a preliminary *title insurance commitment*. The title commitment is the insurer's promise to issue a title insurance policy to the buyer at the land acquisition closing. The title commitment sets forth a legal description of the land and then lists as exceptions to the insurer's promised insurance coverage every lien, encumbrance, restriction, condition, easement, and other adverse interest disclosed during the course of the insurer's review of the public real estate records applicable to the land.

---

[40] *See* LEFCOE, *supra* note 30, at 127–128.

[41] *See e.g.*, Ohio Title Standards, https://www.ohiobar.org/ForLawyers/MemberResources/LegalResources/Pages/StaticPage-101.aspx.

[42] *See* Shannon J. Skinner, A Practical Guide to Title Review, in ALI-ABA Course of Study MATERIALS, MODERN REAL ESTATE TRANSACTIONS, Course No. SL–004, 361, 363 (July 2005).

The purchase contract should address the following issues relative to the title commitment.

- *Who Has the Responsibility for Causing the Title Commitment to Be Issued?* This responsibility generally falls on the seller.

- *When Must the Title Commitment Be Delivered to the Buyer?* Purchase contracts typically require that a title commitment be delivered to the buyer somewhere between 10–30 days after the date of the parties' execution of the contract.

- *Who Gets to Select the Title Insurance Company?* For obvious reasons, the identity of the title insurance company is usually selected by the party who is contractually responsible to pay the title insurance premiums at closing. While the issue of who pays the title premiums is always subject to negotiation, local custom often dictates whether the seller or the buyer is required to pay those costs.

- *What Is the Insured Amount of the Title Insurance Policy?* The insured amount represents the maximum amount that the title insurer will ever have to pay to its insured.[43] The purchase contract should recite that the insured amount is equal to the purchase price.

- *What Type of Title Insurance Policy Will Be Issued?* Most sophisticated buyers want to make sure that the policy that will be issued to it at closing is on a form sanctioned by the American Land Title Association ("ALTA").

3.   Furnishing of Survey

A survey is a visual depiction of the boundaries of the land. It shows the acreage contained within the land parcel and the specific legal description of the parcel (usually called out either by means of a subdivision map or a metes and bounds description).

The provision of a survey to the buyer should be a requirement of every commercial land purchase contract. While a title commitment identifies all exceptions to a parcel's title, a survey is needed to identify the location of such exceptions in relation to the land's boundary lines. A survey is also the vehicle used by the real estate development lawyer to determine where each physical improvement related to the parcel is located—for example, the location of utility lines and public roads. The title commitment excludes from its coverage any "matters which would be revealed by an accurate

---

[43]   *See* id., at 365.

survey of the property."[44] It is, therefore, essential that the survey be provided to the title insurance company, so that this exception to its insurance coverage can be deleted from the final title insurance policy to be issued to the buyer at the closing of the land acquisition.

The purchase contract should address the following matters related to the preparation of the survey of the land.[45]

- ***Who Has the Responsibility for Causing the Survey to Be Prepared and Issued to the Buyer?*** There is no widely-accepted custom concerning who has the responsibility for ordering the survey for the land. The purchase contract should simply identify whether the buyer or seller is assigned that responsibility.

- ***When Must the Survey Be Delivered to the Buyer?*** The time period for the delivery of the survey to the buyer is usually similar to the time period for the delivery of the title commitment—that is, typically around 10–30 days after contract execution. It is, however, key that the period for the buyer's review of title matters not start until it has in its hands both the title commitment and the survey.

- ***Who Gets to Select the Surveyor?*** As is the case with the title commitment, the party responsible for paying for the survey usually gets to determine the identity of the surveyor. The assignment of responsibility for paying the surveyor's fees is open to negotiation between the parties.

- ***What Type of Survey Should Be Required?*** As is discussed in more detail in *Chapter 8—Stage 4: Closing the Land Acquisition*, at pages 321–322, there are many different types of land surveys. In order to make sure that the title insurer is able to remove the preprinted survey exception from Schedule B of the final title policy, the purchase contract should recite that the survey to be furnished to the buyer (and the title company) should be an ALTA survey that complies with the Minimum Standard Detail Requirements for ALTA/NSPS Land Title Surveys.[46]

- ***What Should Be Included in the Surveyor's Certification?*** Unlike a title commitment, a survey is not, in

---

[44] *See* Schedule B to the ALTA OWNER'S TITLE INSURANCE POLICY (2006).

[45] For a general discussion of the role that a survey plays in the land acquisition process, *see* Shannon J. Skinner, *A Practical Guide to Survey Review*, in ALI-ABA COURSE OF STUDY MATERIALS, MODERN REAL ESTATE TRANSACTIONS, Course No. SL–004, 385 (July 2005).

[46] *See* AMERICAN LAND TITLE ASSOCIATION AND NATIONAL SOCIETY OF PROFESSIONAL SURVEYORS, MINIMUM STANDARD DETAIL REQUIREMENTS FOR ALTA/NSPS LAND TITLE SURVEYS (2016).

and of itself, a contract of insurance or indemnification, but rather simply a depiction of certain matters related to the boundaries and configuration of the land. In an attempt to establish a right of action in the buyer for any mistakes in the survey, it is advisable to recite in the purchase contract that the surveyor must certify, at a minimum, that the survey was prepared in accordance with the *Minimum Standard Detail Requirements for ALTA/NSPS Land Title Survey*. The real estate development lawyer should also consult with the developer's prospective construction lender to see if the lender has any additional certifications that it wants included in the survey.

4. Review of Title Commitment and Survey

The purchase contract should specifically address (a) the time period within which the buyer must notify the seller of any objections it has to anything contained in the title commitment or the survey, and (b) the standard for determining the title and survey objections that the buyer is permitted to lodge under the purchase contract.

a. Title Review Period

It is crucial that the real estate development lawyer review the title commitment and survey together. The development lawyer should, therefore, make sure that the purchase contract specifically states that the period for the buyer's review of the title commitment and survey does not begin until *BOTH* the title commitment and the survey have been received by the buyer. The length of the title review period is a matter of negotiation between the parties, but usually runs anywhere from ten to 30 days after the buyer's receipt of the last of the survey and the title commitment. The purchase contract should recite that, in order for a title objection to be effective, a written notice specifying the objection must be delivered to the seller within the title review period. Any title exception that is not addressed in a written objection notice delivered within the stated review period is conclusively presumed to be acceptable to the buyer (and, as such, considered a **permitted exception**. The well-represented seller should want to make sure that the title review period must, in all events, terminate no later than the outside date for the satisfaction of the buyer's non-title contingencies under the purchase contract.

b. Standard for Title Review

The articulation of the standard that governs the buyer's review of the title commitment and survey is one aspect of the title provisions on which the buyer and seller frequently disagree. The seller's primary fear is that an overly broad title review standard can effectively give the buyer an unintended out under the contract by allowing the buyer to object to a title exception that cannot readily be cured by the seller (for example, the location of a utility easement). As one might expect, the "unintended out" is precisely what the real estate development lawyer has in mind when it comes to defining the title review standard in the purchase contract. The relative intransigence of counsel for the seller and buyer on the scope of the title review standard is, of course, significantly lessened to the extent the purchase contract already has in place a broad suitability contingency in buyer's favor (so long as the title review period does not extend beyond the outside date for the satisfaction or waiver of the suitability contingency).

The argument between the seller and buyer over the title review standard is usually centered on the definition of those title exceptions that are considered "permitted exceptions" under the purchase contract. In this context, permitted exceptions are those title matters that may be included as exceptions in both the deed conveying title to the land to buyer at closing and in the final title insurance policy issued by the title insurance company. The following are three definitions of permitted exceptions that are sometimes found in purchase contracts. They are listed in order of preference from the seller's perspective:

- Exceptions other than those existing as of the date of the parties' execution of the purchase contract (with the existing exceptions usually being identified in an exhibit attached to the purchase contract);

- Exceptions that, in the buyer's judgment, will not adversely affect its intended use of the land; and

- Exceptions to which the buyer does not specifically object in a notice delivered to seller prior to the expiration of buyer's title review period.

If the seller and the buyer are each represented by experienced counsel, the negotiations are usually focused on crafting a mutually satisfactory compromise between the first and second alternatives noted above (unless the purchase contract contains a broad suitability contingency, in which case it is common for the parties to opt for the third alternative). One category of title exception that should never be treated as a permitted exception is a mortgage or other monetary lien against the land that can be satisfied by the payment of an ascertainable sum of money.

5. Curing of Title Defects

Once a prospective buyer has delivered its title objections to the seller, the question that next arises is whether the seller is obligated to cure those objections, regardless of the cost or effort that must be expended to effect such a cure. Curing a title objection simply means taking whatever action is required to terminate a lien, encumbrance, restriction, or other exception to title.

The only category of title objections that the purchase contract should, in all instances, require the seller to cure are those mortgages or other monetary liens that can be cured by the payment of an ascertainable sum of money (so-called *monetary liens*). Purchase contracts typically give a buyer the right to remedy any failure by the seller to cure a monetary lien by paying off such lien at closing and then offsetting the full amount of that payment against the cash portion of the purchase price payable by the buyer at closing.

Most purchase contracts do not obligate a seller to cure title defects other than monetary liens. Depending on the title defect in question, a seller may not be able to cure the defect or may only be able to do so by paying an exorbitant sum of money. Given these uncertainties, it is quite common for purchase contracts to give the seller an option (rather than an obligation) to cure the buyer's title objections. If the seller fails to cure the buyer's legitimate title objections within the curative period specified in the purchase contract, then the buyer is customarily given the option either (1) to waive the title objection and proceed to closing, or (2) to terminate the purchase contract and receive a refund of its earnest money deposit. A middle ground frequently seen in purchase contracts is the creation of an obligation on the seller to use "commercially reasonable efforts" to cure the buyer's title objections. Some purchase contracts even go so far as to try to define "commercially reasonable efforts" by requiring the seller to expend up to a specified amount of money in an attempt to cure the buyer's title objections.

Before leaving the topic of the curing of title defects, mention should be made of the seller's practice of getting the title insurance company to "affirmatively insure over" certain title defects. Financially strong sellers are frequently able to secure the title company's commitment to delete a title exception from the title insurance policy, even though the title exception in question has not actually been cured. A seller can sometimes achieve this result by supplying the title company with a guaranty that the seller will reimburse the title company for the amount of any insurance payment that the title company ultimately has to pay to the buyer with respect to the title defect in question. At first blush, this arrangement seems as if it should be perfectly acceptable to the buyer, because the buyer is receiving a clean title policy that contains the title insurance company's agreement to indemnify the buyer against any losses it might suffer due the existence of the subject title defect. However, the reality is that the next buyer of the insured property may not be able to get its title company to similarly insure over the uncured title defect. Additionally, the loss of the buyer's opportunity to sell the property may not be a loss that is covered by the title company's affirmative insurance commitment. In view of this uncertainty, buyer's counsel should be hesitant to accept a title policy that affirmatively insures over any title defect.

6.   Issuance of the Final Title Insurance Policy

Most purchase contracts contain language contemplating that the final title insurance policy will be issued to buyer at the closing. The reality is, however, that the actual issuance of the final owner's policy usually lags the closing and the insurer's receipt of its full title insurance premium by a period of one or two weeks (as is the case with virtually all other insurance policies). The careful real estate development lawyer should address this reality by including in the list of the documents to be delivered to buyer at closing an instrument that both (a) confirms the fact that all conditions to the title insurance company's obligation to issue a title insurance policy have been satisfied, and (b) clearly delineates all of the title exceptions that will be included in the final title insurance policy. These requirements can be evidenced in the form of either a pro forma title insurance policy or a marked-up copy of the title commitment.

J.   CLOSING ISSUES
(§§ 8, 9 and 10)

In the vernacular of the real estate lawyer, the ***closing*** refers to the consummation of all of the transactions contemplated in the land purchase contract, including, most significantly, the buyer's payment of the purchase price to the seller and the seller's execution and delivery of the deed and other documents vesting title to the land in buyer. A well-drafted purchase contract should address six elements of the closing process:

- The conditions to the parties' respective obligations to close the transaction;
- The scheduled date of closing;
- The documents and other items required to be delivered by the parties at closing;
- The allocation of responsibility for the payment of the costs of closing the transaction;
- The income and expense prorations and related purchase price adjustments required to be made at closing; and
- The style of the closing.

1.   Conditions to Closing (§ 8)

The purchase contract should contain a separate section that lists the parties' respective conditions to closing (for example, the buyer's conditions that all the seller's representations and warranties must remain true as of the date of closing and that the buyer must have satisfied or waived all the buyer's contractual contingencies). The inclusion of such a provision helps manage the expectations of the buyer and the seller by providing each of them with a central repository to which they can refer to identify those legal and business matters that must be addressed before the transaction can close.

2. Date of Closing (§ 9)

The purchase contract should recite the outside date by which the closing of the land acquisition must occur. The outside closing date may be described by reference to a certain number of days after the occurrence of a contractual milestone (for example, the effective date of the contract execution or the date of the satisfaction of all closing conditions) or a fixed date in time (for example, December 31, 2017). The setting of an outside closing date is important for a couple reasons:

- First, it establishes the parties' expectations concerning the time frame within which the land acquisition will be consummated; and

- Second, it establishes the date on which a non-performing party will be deemed to be in default for its failure to fully perform all of its obligations under the purchase contract

In addition, the normative rule is that possession and all other benefits and burdens of ownership pass to the buyer on the date of the closing of the land acquisition.

3. Closing Deliverables (§§ 10(a)–(g))

The purchase contract should specifically list in one section all of the documents and other materials that each of the buyer and the seller is responsible for executing and delivering at the closing (the so-called "closing deliverables"). The real estate development lawyer should be able to identify the vast majority of those documents at the time of the initial drafting of the purchase contract based on the lawyer's prior experience in closing real estate transactions. It is nonetheless customary for the drafter of the purchase contract to create a little wiggle room for the parties by inserting contractual language that confirms that "each party will execute and deliver at closing such other documents as are reasonably requested by the other party to further evidence or effect the purchase and sale of the Land in the manner contemplated in this Agreement."

4. Payment of Closing Costs (§ 10(h))

In addition to the buyer's payment of the purchase price, there are a number of other costs that are typically paid at closing. The purchase contract becomes a much more readable and user friendly document if it contains a separate subsection that calls out all such costs and stipulates who has the responsibility for paying them at closing. The following are examples of costs that are customarily paid at closing:

- Fees that are payable to state and local governments with respect to the conveyance of real property (transfer taxes or conveyance fees) and the recording of legal documents in the public real estate records (recording costs);

- Commissions payable to any brokers involved in the land acquisition;

- The premium and other costs that are payable to the title insurance company in connection with the title insurance company's issuance of the owner's title insurance policy; and

- The fees payable to the surveyor for its furnishing of the survey.

Local custom usually influences which of the above costs are paid by the seller and which are paid by the buyer. However, assignment of responsibility for the payment of these costs is always subject to the negotiation of the parties. As such, the responsibility for the payment of known closing costs (such as those noted above) should always be specifically assigned in the purchase contract.

5.   Closing Prorations and Adjustments (§ 10(i))

In determining the amount of the cash paid to the seller at closing, an adjustment to the purchase price needs to be made to deduct the principal amount of any purchase money financing being provided by the seller or the principal amount of any existing mortgage loan that is being assumed by the buyer. No such deduction need be made for any new loan obtained by buyer to fund its acquisition of the land, because, from the seller's perspective, cash is cash regardless whether it is being paid by the buyer or by the buyer's lender.

The cash portion of the purchase price payable by the buyer at closing also needs to be adjusted to deal with those periodic payment obligations that cover a period of time both before and after the date of closing. Examples of such periodic obligations are:

- Real estate taxes;

- Ground lease rentals;

- Interest on any existing mortgage loan being assumed by the buyer;

- Owner's association dues and assessments; and

- Utility charges (for example, water and sewer costs) when the utility provider will not agree to create separate bills for the periods before and after closing.

The norm in handling these periodic costs is to apportion such costs between the seller and the buyer based on the respective portions of such costs that are attributable to the periods pre- and post-closing, with the seller being liable for the portion of such costs that are attributable to the period on or before the closing date and the buyer being liable for the portion of such costs that are attributable to the period after the closing date. By way of example, if real estate taxes are paid annually and if the land acquisition closing occurs on the 100th day of the year, then an appropriate apportionment of the real estate tax bill for the year of closing would result in the seller being responsible for 100/365 of the tax bill and the buyer being responsible for 265/365 of such bill. If the seller has already paid a periodic cost (meaning that the cost was "paid in advance"), then the buyer's prorated share of such cost should increase the amount of cash that the buyer is required to pay to the seller at closing. Conversely, if the periodic cost will have to be paid by the buyer after the closing date (meaning the cost is "paid in arrears"), then the amount of buyer's cash payment at closing should be decreased by an amount equal to the seller's prorated share of such cost.

The vagaries associated with the levying of real estate taxes by local taxing authorities create a number of issues that should be addressed in the purchase contract. In many jurisdictions, real estate taxes are imposed and become a lien on real estate at the beginning of the calendar year, even though such taxes are not due and payable until later in such calendar year (or, in some extreme cases, in the succeeding calendar year). In some locales, the actual amount of the real estate taxes payable by a landowner is not established until well after the date of the initial tax imposition against the land. Indeed, in some jurisdictions, the amount of the real estate taxes payable with respect to a particular parcel can be revised upwards or downwards months after the date of such parcel's sale.[47]

The confluence of all of these circumstances often creates a scenario where, at the time of their execution of the purchase contract, the buyer and seller are unable to determine the exact amount of the real estate taxes to be apportioned between them at closing. The purchase contract should address this possibility by specifically stating that the closing apportionment of real estate taxes will be done either on the basis of (1) the

---

[47] *See e.g.*, OHIO REVISED CODE §§ 5715.19 (2016). Under Ohio law, a complaint can be filed to revise a parcel's real estate taxes a full 15 months after the initial assessment of such taxes even if an intervening sale of such parcel has occurred. Indeed, it has become common practice in Ohio for lawyers representing local school boards (whose funding is largely dependent upon real estate tax collections) to file complaints seeking to have the real estate taxes increased for any large commercial property that is sold during the 15-month period for a purchase price that exceeds the amount of the existing valuation of the property for real estate tax purposes.

most currently available real estate tax information (frequently the taxes for the prior taxable year), or (2) the parties' best estimate of what the taxes will ultimately prove to be for the taxable year in question. The lawyer for the landowner customarily seeks to have the real estate tax apportionment calculated on the basis of the most current tax information and to have the resulting apportionment be final and conclusive on the parties regardless whether the actual real estate taxes are subsequently adjusted by fiat of the taxing authorities. Counsel for the buyer, on the other hand, wants either to have the taxes prorated on the basis of a multiple of the prior year's taxes (for example, 110% of the prior year figures) or to subject the apportionment of such taxes to a post-closing adjustment if the actual real estate taxes prove to be higher than those used for the apportionment calculation at closing.

6.   Style of Closing (§ 9)

When I first started practicing law almost 40 years ago, the word "closing" brought forth a vision of a large conference room (usually smoke-filled) in which representatives of the seller and the buyer and their respective lawyers gathered to hammer out the final details of the land acquisition and sign all those documents called for in the purchase contract. This type of all-hands gathering of lawyers and clients is often referred to as a *New York style closing*. Alas, in today's impersonal, electronic age, New York style closings are few and far between—even in New York.

Virtually all commercial real estate transactions are now closed via an *escrow closing*.[48] In an escrow closing, the parties do not get together at one time in one place for the purpose of signing documents. Instead, each party executes whatever documents it needs to sign at a time and place of its choosing prior to the scheduled closing date and then forwards the executed documents to the title insurance company or another independent third party (with such party commonly being referred to as the *escrow agent*). The buyer deposits into the escrow agent's trust account (usually via an electronic wire transfer of same-day funds) whatever cash is required to close the deal. Counsel for each of the buyer and the seller then send detailed written instructions (*escrow instructions*) to the escrow agent, specifying the circumstances under which the escrow agent is authorized and directed (1) to release the documents from escrow, (2) to forward the appropriate purchase price payment to the seller, (3) to disburse funds to discharge all land liens and pay all closing costs, (4) to record the deed conveying title to the land to the buyer, and (5) to take whatever other actions are required to consummate the land acquisition in the manner contemplated in the purchase contract.

---

[48] In keeping with the geographical theme, escrow closings are sometimes referred to as "California style closings." *See* LEFCOE, *supra* note 30, at 314.

Some purchase contracts go into excruciating detail describing the precise manner in which the escrow closing must be structured and implemented. My experience has been that playing out the closing mechanism in all its glory (or lack thereof) in the purchase contract detracts from the real issues at hand and is generally just a waste of time and words. If the parties intend to close the land acquisition in escrow (and they almost always do), the purchase contract should simply identify who will serve as the escrow agent and leave the details of the escrow closing for the lawyers to address in detailed escrow instructions prepared by them just prior to closing when all of the salient factors to be incorporated into such instructions are better known by the parties. The lawyers will occasionally seek to shortcut the whole matter by opting to establish a New York style closing as the default rule in the purchase contract, with the full knowledge that the lawyers will later work out a mutually satisfactory escrow arrangement so that they can spare their clients (and themselves) the agony of ever having to sit across the table from each other and exchange closing-day pleasantries.

Finally, it should be noted that, in the not too distant future, most land acquisitions will likely be closed electronically (a so-called **eClosing**). The eClosing is fast becoming the default mechanism to close residential real estate transactions. The lack of uniformity in the transaction documents for commercial real estate transactions has thus far forestalled the use of the eClosing in the commercial world. It is, however, only a matter of time until electronic platforms are successfully created to handle commercial land acquisitions.[49]

K. DEFAULTS AND REMEDIES
(§ 11)

The purchase contract should contain specific provisions that (1) define when a party is deemed to be in default in the performance of its obligations under the purchase contract, and (2) specify the remedies available to the other party upon the occurrence of a default.

1. Event of Default

Most land purchase contracts condition the occurrence of an event of default on:

- The receipt by the defaulting party of a written notice from the non-defaulting party describing the exact nature of the alleged default; and

---

[49] *See generally* Josias N. Dewey and Gavin Williams, *The Commercial Paperless Closing: How Close Is It,* THE REAL ESTATE FINANCE JOURNAL 82 (Spring 2012).

- The defaulting party's failure to cure such default within a stated period of time following its receipt of the written notice.

The requirement for prior written notice and an opportunity to cure is usually something that is desirable from both the seller's and the buyer's perspectives. Depending on the nature of the alleged default, the applicable cure period commonly ranges from ten to 30 days after receipt of the written notice alleging the existence of the default.

2.   Remedies

Absent a provision in the purchase contract to the contrary, each of the buyer and the seller has the following remedies available to it upon the occurrence of an event of default by the other party to the purchase contract:

- Rescission;
- Damages; and
- Specific performance.[50]

An in-depth analysis of the case law discussing the nature and scope of these three remedies is clearly beyond the scope of this chapter. However, the point needs to be made that it is incumbent upon the real estate development lawyer to understand how the courts in the lawyer's jurisdiction have interpreted each of these remedies, so that the lawyer can properly advise the developer about both (1) the risks faced by the developer if it defaults in the performance of its contractual obligations, and (2) the ways in which the developer can protect itself against the risk of a default by the seller.

3.   Contractual Limitation of Remedies

The courts have made it clear that the parties to a real estate purchase contract can limit their legal remedies by including in the purchase contract a clear and unequivocal statement of their intentions to do so.[51] The following are examples of contractual limitations on remedies often seen in land purchase contracts.

- *Limitations on the Seller's Remedies:*
  o   Remedies limited to retention of earnest money deposit as liquidated damages (see discussion of liquidated damages in the next section of this chapter); and
  o   Specific performance eliminated as an available remedy.

---

[50] *See* Herz, *supra* note 20, at 12–14; and Lefcoe, *supra* note 30, at 157–166.
[51] *See* Herz, *supra* note 20, at 12–14.

- *Limitations on the Buyer's Remedies:*
    o   Remedies limited to liquidated damages, with the amount of the liquidated damages being equal to a fixed percentage of the purchase price;

    o   Remedy for the seller's breach of a representation and warranty limited to buyer's termination of the contract and receipt of a refund of its earnest money deposit, so long as such breach is attributable to the occurrence after the date of the contract execution of an event that is not within the seller's control; and

    o   Action for damages eliminated as an available remedy, except in the instance of a willful failure to perform by seller, in which event the buyer may pursue recovery of the out-of-pocket costs incurred by the buyer in connection with its due diligence efforts.

The topic of contractual remedies is one area of the purchase contract where lawyers commonly make the mistake of "failing to see the forest for the trees." Lawyers often fall in love with the intricacy of their prose in describing the parties' available remedies, without stepping back to consider whether a party's financial standing effectively negates the utility of the stated contractual remedies. A lawyer representing the buyer of a property from a financially-troubled seller should, if possible, require a guaranty of the seller's obligations by a well-healed affiliate of the seller and, in all events, ardently resist any attempt by the seller's counsel to eliminate specific performance as a remedy available to the buyer. The lawyer representing the seller of property to a newly-formed entity should take one or both of the following approaches to protect the seller's interests—(1) secure a guaranty of the buyer's obligations from an entity having a substantial net worth, or (2) insist upon the posting of a sizable earnest money deposit and the inclusion in the contract of a provision that makes it clear that the deposit may be retained by the seller in the event of a default by the buyer.

4.   Liquidated Damages

Liquidated damage clauses are common in land purchase contracts. A liquidated damage clause is simply "a contract provision by which the parties agree in advance to the amount of damages payable on a breach."[52] While occasionally used to redress seller's breaches, liquidated damage clauses are far more often utilized as the seller's remedy for the buyer's failure to perform under the land purchase contract. The typical seller liquidated damage clause calls for the posting by the buyer of a significant earnest money deposit and for the receipt by the seller of the entirety of

---

[52]   *See* LEFCOE, *supra* note 30, at 159.

that deposit as liquidated damages in the event of a contractual default by the buyer.

The following are reasons why a liquidated damage clause is an attractive method to redress a buyer's default.

- The typical liquidated damage clause is designed to protect the seller from the credit risk of contracting to sell its land to a newly-formed single purpose entity. By requiring the buyer to pay a significant deposit into escrow, the seller gains the comfort of knowing that money is available to cover its losses if the buyer fails to perform.

- A liquidated damage clause allows both the buyer and the seller to avoid the pain and cost associated with protracted litigation.

- Finally, under a liquidated damage clause, both parties know the exact consequences of the buyer failing to perform its obligation to purchase the land. This level of predictability stands in sharp contrast to the uncertainty associated with the pursuit of other legal remedies.

It is relatively settled law that an enforceable liquidated damage clause must satisfy both of the following requirements:[53]

- The liquidated sum must be a reasonable forecast of the financial loss caused by the breach;[54] and

- The harm caused by the breach must be difficult to estimate accurately.[55]

---

[53] *See* Frank C. Dunbar, Jr., Drafting *the Liquidated Damage Clause—When and How*, 20 OHIO STATE LAW JOURNAL 221 (1959). An emerging trend in the case law on liquidated damages is to ignore the traditional two-pronged legal test noted above and, instead, to focus on the relative bargaining power of the seller and the buyer. That trend is illustrated by Uzan v. 845 UN Limited Partnership, 778 N.Y.S.2d 171 (2004), in which the illustrious Donald Trump (pre-2016 presidential election) triumphed one more time by getting the New York Supreme Court to agree to enforce a liquidated damage clause that resulted in two Turkish billionaires forfeiting an $8 million earnest money deposit (25% of the $32 million purchase price for two penthouse apartments in Manhattan). In that case, it was held that a liquidated damage clause (at least in the factual context of the purchase of luxury condominium units) is enforceable absent a showing of "disparity of bargaining power or of duress, fraud, illegality, or mutual mistake." *See id.* at 178.

[54] The courts are divided on the issue of whether the liquidated sum must be a reasonable approximation of damages both at the time the contract was executed and at the time of default. *See* GRANT S. NELSON, DALE A. WHITMAN, ANN M. BURKHART, AND R. WILSON FREYERMUTH, REAL ESTATE TRANSFER, FINANCE, AND DEVELOPMENT, CASES AND MATERIALS 62–64 (8th ed. 2009).

[55] The courts have almost uniformly determined that the harm caused by the breach of a real estate sales contract is difficult to estimate. *See* Jeffrey B. Coopersmith, *Refocusing Liquidated Damage Law for Real Estate Contracts: Return to the Historical Roots of the Penalty Doctrine,* 39 EMORY L. J. 267 (1990), where the author persuasively notes that "the market for real property often fluctuates across relatively short time frames, making any pre-estimate rather meaningless." *Id.* at 286.

The typical liquidated damage clause attempts to react to these two requirements in the following manner:

> *Seller is entitled to receive the entire amount of the Deposit as full and complete liquidated damages to redress a default by Buyer in the performance of Buyer's obligations under this Agreement; it being expressly acknowledged by Seller and Buyer that Seller's damages in the event of a default by Buyer would be difficult to ascertain and that the receipt of the Deposit constitutes a reasonable liquidation of such damages and is not intended as a penalty.*

5. Exclusivity of Liquidated Damages Remedy

One interesting question concerning the liquidated damage clause is, Does such a clause need to be the sole and exclusive remedy of the seller? Is a liquidated damage clause enforceable if the purchase contract purports to preserve the seller's right to pursue (a) an action for specific performance against the buyer, (b) an action for damages, or (c) both (a) and (b)? The majority rule is that the inclusion of a liquidated damages clause in a purchase contract precludes the seller from pursuing an action for damages, even if the purchase contract purports to give the seller that option.[56] However, somewhat surprisingly (at least to this author), the rule is just the opposite as it relates to the remedy of specific performance. There the majority rule is that, unless otherwise clearly stated to the contrary in the purchase contract, the presence in a purchase contract of a liquidated damages clause does not serve as a legal bar to the seller's pursuit of an action for the specific performance of its contract.[57]

The parties to a real estate purchase contract should not leave to chance the issue of whether liquidated damages is the exclusive remedy of the seller. A clear, unequivocal statement in the purchase contract that liquidated damages are the seller's "sole and exclusive remedy to redress a default by the buyer" and that the seller "waives all other remedies,

---

[56] *See* Catholic Charities of Archdiocese of Chicago v. Thorpe, 741 N.E.2d 651 (Ill. App. 2000) in which the court noted that a clause purporting to give the seller a choice between retaining a deposit as liquidated damages or instituting a damages action against the buyer is unenforceable because it is nothing more than an attempt by the seller "to have his cake and eat it too." *See also* Phoenix Capital, Inc. v. Dowell, 2007 WL 5765720 (Colo. Dist. Ct. 2007); and Linda A. Francis, Annotation, *Provision in Land Contract for Liquidated Damages upon Default of Purchaser as Affecting Right of Vendor to Maintain Action for Damages for Breach of Contract,* 39 A.L.R. 5th 33 (1996).

[57] *See* LEFCOE, *supra* note 30, at 160–161. *But see* Hatcher v. Panama City Nursing Center, Inc., 461 So.2d 288 (Fla. Dist. Ct. App. 1985), where the court held that the presence of a liquidated damages clause in a purchase contract precluded a seller from pursuing a specific performance action even though the contract did not specifically state that specific performance was unavailable to redress a buyer default. *See also* Coopersmith, *supra* note 55, at 302, where the author comments that "[i]f the seller has the choice of either . . . liquidated damages or suing for specific performance, the concept of liquidated damages as a form of risk allocation is destroyed. Upon a breach by the buyer, the seller would simply elect the more lucrative alternative."

including the remedy of specific performance" puts an end to any uncertainty concerning the seller's remedial options. Absent such a clause, the seller might be able to "have its cake and eat it too"—a situation that a buyer will always find to be intolerable.

HIBC Case Study—Remedies

Chemical Bank was initially adamant that Pizzuti's sole remedy for Chemical's default under the HIBC purchase contract should be specific performance. Chemical Bank wanted no part of a damages action that might expose it to an extraordinarily high level of damages based on an argument that the fair market value of the HIBC land far exceeded the purchase price being paid by Pizzuti. The only inroad that Pizzuti was able to make on this point was to get counsel for Chemical to agree that, in the event of a "willful refusal to close" by Chemical, Pizzuti could supplement its specific performance action with a damages action, so long as the amount of the collectible damages was capped at the sum of Pizzuti's "direct out-of-pocket expenses to unaffiliated third parties incurred by Buyer in reliance on this Contract." The remedies clause ultimately agreed to by Chemical and Pizzuti is representative of the type of clause a seller should insist on when it has the fear that appraisers might differ wildly on how to value a large parcel of land that is being sold in bulk to one buyer (versus piecemeal to a number of different purchasers).

Conversely, Chemical sought to "have its cake and eat it too" when it came to its remedies for a default by Pizzuti. The Contract for Sale and Purchase of Real Estate provides that Chemical had the choice to either (a) retain the deposit as liquidated damages, or (b) "pursue all of its legal and equitable remedies against Buyer, including an action for specific performance." Based on the Hatcher *case cited and described in note 57, this clause was probably unenforceable when entered into by Chemical and Pizzuti—although I profess to not have heard of the* Hatcher *case at the time.*

Pizzuti's position on the seller remedies clause was fairly typical for a buyer of commercial land. Pizzuti took the position that it was not worth getting into a long negotiation with Chemical on the seller remedies, so long as Pizzuti was given a broad contingency that permitted it to terminate its purchase obligation if it decided the project was not feasible for some reason. The Contract for Sale of Purchase and Real Estate specified that the closing would take place a mere 27 days after the expiration of Pizzuti's contingency period. Pizzuti believed that if it felt comfortable enough to waive its feasibility contingency at the end of the 90-day review period, the likelihood was that nothing would occur in the subsequent 27 days to change its mind about closing on the acquisition of the HIBC land. Refraining from arguing about Chemical's remedies also permitted me to claim the high ground in the negotiations by asserting that I did not care about Chemical's remedies because Pizzuti would never default on a deal. Such moral high ground is more easily attained when a broad suitability contingency, such as the one set out in the Pizzuti-Chemical purchase contract, gives the buyer a relatively easy out under the purchase contract.

L. RISK OF LOSS
(§ 12)

What happens if a serious flood damages the land or a governmental authority commences an eminent domain proceeding against the land after the date of the parties' execution of the purchase contract, but before the actual land acquisition closing? Does the risk of such a loss fall on the buyer or the seller?

Under the principle of equitable conversion, the risk of loss due to the occurrence during the contract period of a flood, eminent domain proceeding, or another casualty falls on the buyer. An Ohio court summarized the rule of equitable conversion as follows:

> The rule underlying the doctrine of equitable conversion is that a contract to sell real property vests the equitable ownership of the property in the purchaser; and thus, where there is any loss by a destruction of the property through casualty during the pendency of the contract (neither party being guilty of causing the destruction) such loss must be borne by the purchaser.[58]

Simply stated, the rule of equitable conversion means that the buyer remains obligated to purchase the land at the price set forth in the purchase contract, even though, due to the interim occurrence of the casualty, the land no longer has the same value to the buyer as it did when the purchase contract was executed.

There is a strong minority position that the doctrine of equitable conversion has no application to the purchase and sale of land if the prospective buyer of the land has neither taken possession, nor actually acquired legal title to the land.[59] The Uniform Vendors and Purchasers Risk Act codifies the minority rule.[60]

The careful real estate development lawyer should take pains to negate the potential impact of the doctrine of equitable conversion by making it clear in the purchase contract that the risk of loss remains with

---

[58]   Sanford v. Breidenbach, 173 N.E.2d 702, 707 (Ohio App. 1960).

[59]   *See* NELSON, *supra* note 54. at 94–95.

[60]   *See* LEFCOE, *supra* note 30, at 122–123.

the seller until closing. The Form Purchase Agreement contains the following clause:

> The risk of loss to the Property from the occurrence of a casualty or a taking by any public authority under the power or right of eminent domain (or by the threat of such a taking) will be borne by Seller until the closing of Buyer's purchase of the Property.

The purchase contract should button up this point by specifically stating that the buyer has the right to terminate the purchase contract if a property loss occurs during the contract period. Quite often the seller tries to limit the buyer's termination option by introducing a materiality concept that effectively provides that the buyer remains obligated to purchase the land if the occurrence of the subject casualty or taking has no significant impact on the value of the land. The materiality of the loss can be described in a variety of ways—for example, a loss of at least $100,000 or a taking of at least 20% of the land's acreage. If the contract remains in place following the occurrence of a casualty or taking (either due to the immaterial nature of the resulting loss or the buyer's election not to exercise its termination option), then the seller should be obligated by the purchase contract to assign to the buyer all insurance claims, condemnation awards, and other potential recoveries related to the casualty or taking.

M. BROKERAGE COMMISSIONS

(§ 13)

There is generally no requirement that a brokerage agreement be recorded in the chain of title to a land parcel in order for the broker to be entitled to a commission on the sale of such parcel. Indeed, in some jurisdictions, the doctrine of promissory estoppel supplies the broker with the ability to enforce its alleged right to a sale commission even if no written agreement of any kind was ever entered into by the broker and a party to the sales transaction.[61] Given these two facts, it is not at all uncommon for a broker to unexpectedly show up at closing (or even worse after the closing) with an outstretched hand asking for a commission.

In order to safeguard against the unexpected commission claim, counsel for the buyer and the seller should include in the purchase contract a mutual representation and warranty confirming that neither party has taken any action or entered into any agreement that could result in a brokerage commission, finder's fee, or similar charge being owed with respect to the sale of the land to the buyer. To the extent either the seller or the buyer has an agreement to pay a commission to a third party, the

---

[61] *See* Orlando Lucero, *The Brokerage Agreements—What You Don't Know Can Hurt You*, 20 No. 2 PRACTICAL REAL ESTATE LAWYER 39, 40 (March 2004).

commitment of that party to pay the commission in full on or before the date of closing should be clearly spelled out in the purchase contract.

Finally, each party should indemnify the other against any liability for any commission claimed in breach of its "no commission" representation and warranty. This is yet another area where lawyers are well-advised to inquire into the creditworthiness of the party making the representation and warranty.

N. OPERATION OF THE PROPERTY DURING THE CONTRACT PERIOD
(§ 14)

The real estate development lawyer should try to insert in the purchase contract a clear statement limiting the seller's ability to take any action with respect to the land after contract execution that could adversely affect the value or utility of the land to the buyer. A clause such as that set forth in § 13 of the Form Purchase Agreement seeks to protect the buyer from the seller taking any of the following actions during the pendency of the purchase contract:

- Granting any easements, licenses, or other contract rights or property interests with respect to the land that could survive the buyer's purchase of the land;

- Performing any excavation or construction activities on the land or taking any other action that could affect the natural condition of the land as it existed on the date of the execution of the purchase contract; or

- Seeking a rezoning or other change in any governmental rule or approval applicable to the land.

A seller often takes the position that it should have the right to take any of the above actions, without the buyer's consent, at any time prior to the date on which the buyer has waived all of the contingencies to the buyer's obligation to purchase the property. If such a provision is agreed to by the buyer (in most cases it should not be), the real estate development lawyer should insert in the purchase contract a specific requirement that the developer be given prompt written notice of the seller's taking of any such action, so that the buyer will have ample time to terminate the contract prior to the expiration of the contingency period if the buyer determines that the seller's action has made the buyer's project infeasible.

During the contract period, the developer is often busy trying to get governmental agencies, utility companies, and other third parties to agree to take an affirmative action with respect to the land. By way of example, the developer may be trying to rezone the land to permit its proposed development project or to get the local water company to agree to pay for the extension of water lines to the boundaries of the land. It is often difficult for the developer to make any headway in its negotiations over these types of land changes unless the seller is willing to cooperate in at least a minimal fashion in the developer's efforts to secure the desired project approvals. It is, therefore, recommended that the real estate development lawyer include in the purchase agreement a requirement that the seller and its representatives cooperate in good faith with the buyer's efforts to effect a change in the condition or character of the land. A thoughtful lawyer for the seller will, however, want to make sure that the seller's obligations are limited in the following two respects:

- The seller will not be required to incur any out-of-pocket expense in connection with its cooperation with the buyer's efforts; and

- The seller will not be obligated to consent to buyer's taking of any action that would legally bind the seller or its land prior to the buyer's closing on the acquisition of the land.

O. BOILERPLATE PROVISIONS
(§§ 15–24)

We now come to one of my least favorite topics of all time—the so-called **boilerplate** provisions included in the purchase contract. Merriam-Webster's Collegiate Dictionary defines "boilerplate" as "standardized, formulaic, or hackneyed language."[62] To many lawyers (particularly young lawyers), boilerplate clauses are those standard provisions that are stuck in the back of every agreement "just because they always are." The consensus is that, although nobody ever takes the time to understand or even read the boilerplate provisions, some wise old lawyer years ago determined that the provisions were essential to an agreement and that excising those provisions from a document could have extremely disastrous consequences. Boilerplate provisions are, therefore, viewed as the quintessential "cover your ass" clauses.

I am here to tell you that there is no such thing as a boilerplate clause—at least if that term is used to describe a provision that the lawyer does not have to understand, but one that should be included in every agreement a lawyer drafts. One of the most embarrassing experiences I ever had as a young lawyer was when one of my senior partners began his review of a draft document that I had worked on all night by turning to the last page of the document and asking me what the "Complete Agreement" provision meant and why I had included it in my draft. I assure you that

---

[62] *See* MERRIAM-WEBSTER'S COLLEGIATE DICTIONARY 165 (10th ed. 2001).

the senior partner was less than impressed with my response that "I just thought I was supposed to include that boilerplate in every document."

The lesson to be learned from the above story is that the real estate development lawyer should never include a clause in purchase contract without having a legitimate reason for doing so. Before discussing those clauses that, although often referred to as boilerplate, nonetheless should be included in most purchase contracts, let me throw out an example of the danger of using the same old boilerplate language in every document. One of the standard provisions contained at the back of many contracts is the following clause.

> *The rights and remedies of the parties to this Agreement are cumulative and are not in lieu of, but are in addition to, any other rights or remedies that the parties may have at law or equity.*

This certainly sounds like the kind of nice, safe clause that should be included in every contract. What would happen, however, if this nice, safe clause were to be included in a purchase contract that contained a provision purporting to establish liquidated damages as the seller's sole and exclusive remedy for the buyer's default under the purchase contract?

OK, it is now time for me to get off my high horse and mention several clauses that I believe should be included at the end of most purchase contracts. Please, however, indulge my sensitivities and let me call them "miscellaneous" and not "boilerplate" provisions. The clauses discussed below are set forth in their entirety at the end of the Form Purchase Agreement.

- *Assignment of Agreement (§ 15)*—This clause negates the common law rule that all contracts are freely assignable, unless otherwise stated in the contract.[63] In most (but not all) situations, the buyer and the seller share the view that the other party to the purchase contract should not be able to assign its rights or obligations under the contract to any other person without first obtaining the consent of the other contracting party. By way of example, the seller generally wants to prohibit the buyer from having any right to assign the buyer's rights under the purchase contract because otherwise a buyer who obtains a contractual right to purchase land at a favorable price could "flip" its contract rights to a third party and make a profit without ever having to acquire the land. It is, however, important that both sides to the transaction consider whether any exceptions to the general rule should be set forth in the purchase contract—for example, the exception contained in the Form Purchase

---

[63]   *See* TINA L. STARK, NEGOTIATING AND DRAFTING CONTRACT BOILERPLATE 31 (2003).

Agreement for the buyer's assignment of its interest in the purchase contract to its affiliates.

- **_Governing Law (§ 16)_**—This provision should be included in the miscellaneous provisions to remind the lawyer to give thought to whether any portion of the purchase contract should be construed in accordance with the laws of a state other than the state in which the land is located. By way of example, if the property is located in Florida, but both the seller and the buyer are headquartered in Ohio, it might be appropriate to provide that any disputes over the purchase contract are determined under Ohio law.

- **_Counterparts (§ 17)_**—This provision is intended to permit a document to become effective as soon as each party has signed a purchase contract and sent it to the other party. It does not, however, require that both the seller and the buyer sign the same document. The use of counterparts regularly saves the parties a full day in making the document effective—the day that it would take for one party to send its signed document to the other party so that both signatures could be affixed to the same document.

- **_Attorney's Fees (§ 18)_**—This clause should be included in those jurisdictions that permit the prevailing party in a lawsuit to recover its legal fees—particularly if attorney's fees can only be recovered in the jurisdiction if the contract expressly sanctions such a recovery. The Form Purchase Contract is the form I used for transactions in Florida, where prevailing party legal fees are recoverable.[64]

- **_Entire Agreement (§ 19)_**—This clause is intended to negate the effect of any prior letters of intent or other written documents entered into by the buyer and the seller and to make it clear that the purchase contract may only be amended by a document signed by both such parties.

- **_Reasonableness of Consent (§ 20)_**—I consistently include this clause in my documents. I find that requiring both parties to act reasonably gives me access to the higher ground in negotiations, without putting my client at any particular disadvantage—in part because my clients are always reasonable and in part because the law often implies a duty for a party to a purchase contract to act reasonably. While this clause fits my style and that of my clients, I assure you that the majority of today's practicing lawyers would never

---

[64] *See e.g.*, Moritz v. Hoyt Enterprises, Inc., 604 So.2d 807 (Fla. 1992).

countenance the inclusion of this clause in their package of "boilerplate" provisions.

- *Notices (§ 21)*—It is important to specify in the purchase contract how each notice called for in the contract must be sent and when the notice is deemed to be effective. The notices called out in the purchase contract normally have a significant legal impact on the purchase and sale transaction (for example, the buyer's notice terminating the contract or identifying its title objections). In a nod to today's electronic age, the Form Purchase Agreement expands the customary forms of contract notices to expressly include email.

- *Date for Performance (§ 22)*—It is common for purchase contracts to call out the time for a party's performance of a particular obligation by reference to a stated number of days after a fixed date—for example, the obligation to deliver the title commitment within 20 days after the date of the parties' execution of the purchase contract. Lawyers often find it to be a useful and pleasant shortcut to include a provision in the purchase contract saying that if any time period ends on a weekend or holiday, then the time period is automatically pushed back to the next business day.

- *Confidentiality (§ 23)*—I have found that most of my developer clients prefer to keep their potential land acquisitions a secret until they are ready to go to the press with a full-blown story about their planned projects. Including a confidentiality clause in the purchase contract is intended (and sometimes even works) to prevent the seller from stealing the developer's thunder by prematurely going public about the proposed land sale.

- *Defined Terms (§ 24)*—Except in the most complex agreements, I prefer to define terms when they are first used in the text of the document. I find that this approach enhances the flow and readability of the purchase contract. Having said that, I do like to list all of the defined terms in one place with appropriate section cross-references so that a reader can go to one central place for guidance in figuring out the meaning of a defined term.

The above is not intended to be an exhaustive list of every miscellaneous clause to be included in a purchase contract. Nor is it intended as a directive that every purchase contract should include the listed clauses. The only absolute associated with these types of miscellaneous clauses is that the real estate development lawyer absolutely must include only those clauses that are appropriate to serve the developer's business objective.

Practice Tip #5-5: Contract Negotiations

Lawyers often seek to elevate the nature of what they do on a daily basis by characterizing contract negotiations as an "art form." While I certainly accept the fact that there is not a lot of "science" to negotiating a contract, referring to a lawyer as an "artist" seems to me to be a bit of misdirected hyperbole. Likening contract negotiations to a game of chess is a much more apt analogy. Strategy and consistency are the hallmarks of a good negotiator, not creativity and spontaneity.

The following are some guidelines that can help make a real estate development lawyer a more successful negotiator.

- ***Control the Drafting of the Document.*** *Preparing the initial draft of the purchase contract presents the real estate development lawyer with an opportunity to set the agenda for the negotiations and to incorporate contractual language that is responsive to the developer's business interests. Assuming responsibility for subsequent redrafts of the purchase contract also allows the real estate development lawyer to both dictate the pace of the negotiations and craft the negotiated changes in a manner that is most favorable to the developer.*

- ***Understand and Take Advantage of Your Negotiating Leverage.*** *In the context of a real estate deal, "leverage" simply means that a party has the upper hand on a subject of the negotiations. Negotiations are all about understanding the relative leverage of the parties on each negotiating topic. The real estate development lawyer must decipher which party has the leverage on each particular point. In order to make that determination, the real estate development lawyer must understand (1) the competing business positions and objectives of the buyer and the seller, and (2) the strengths and weaknesses of opposing counsel. By way of example, if a landowner is desperate to sell its land so that it can pay off the creditors of its separate operating business, then the real estate development lawyer should be in a unique position to structure a deal that is highly beneficial to the developer.*

- ***Be a Consequential Thinker.*** *Before taking a position in any negotiation, the lawyer must anticipate how the other side will react to that position. Much like a good chess player, the real estate development lawyer must think several steps ahead* *to avoid being hemmed into a negotiating strategy that effectively "checkmates" the developer's business interests. For instance, a real estate development lawyer needs to be careful that insisting on a full slate of seller representations and warranties does not result in the seller refusing to provide the buyer with a broad suitability contingency clause (which is likely more important to the developer).*

- ***Adopt Your Own Negotiating Style and Stick with It.*** *Just as the real estate development lawyer needs to understand the strengths and weaknesses of opposing counsel, so must the real estate development lawyer understand and accept the lawyer's own negotiating strengths and weaknesses. Over the years, I learned that I tend to grow tired and lose focus during lengthy meandering negotiations conducted over the phone or in person. As a result, I always try to articulate my position (and minimize the wisdom of the other side's position) in written communication with the other side so that our in-person or telephonic negotiations can be more focused and shorter in duration. The lesson to be learned is that there is more than one way to successfully conduct a negotiation and the lawyer who most often succeeds is the one who frames the negotiations to highlight the lawyer's personal strengths and expose the weaknesses of opposing counsel.*

- ***Don't Take Unreasonable Positions.*** *There is nothing that damages a lawyer's reputation more quickly than constantly taking unreasonable positions. A lawyer who adopts extreme positions on behalf of a client without any real rationale for doing so the very real risk of earning the worst of all possible reputations in the real estate bar—that of being a deal killer.*

- ***Get What You Need.*** *A good negotiator knows what the client NEEDS to move forward with a deal and focuses on making sure the client's needs are adequately served in the contract documents. Only after the lawyer serves the client's needs is the lawyer free to negotiate for the client's WANTS. Indeed, Mick Jagger and Keith Richards could have been writing about the real estate development business when they penned* *the following lyric (even though their more likely inspiration was sex, drugs, and rock and roll).*

YOU CAN'T ALWAYS GET WHAT YOU WANT,

BUT IF YOU TRY SOMETIME,

YOU JUST MIGHT FIND,

YOU GET WHAT YOU NEED." [65]

VII. SUMMARY

This chapter began with the statement that Stage 1 of the real estate development process is the real estate development lawyer's first opportunity to exhibit the skills and inclination of a "deal maker." The efforts of the real estate development lawyer at this first stage are focused on helping the developer achieve two basic objectives:

- Tying up the identified site as quickly and as cheaply as possible; and

- Doing so in a fashion that minimizes the developer's exposure to land and deal risks.

The developer's goal of tying up the site can be achieved in a variety of ways—by using a preliminary letter of intent or by going straight to a binding purchase document (be it a purchase contract or an option). While there are legitimate legal risks associated with the use of a letter of intent, the commercial reality is that the use of a letter has become a commonly accepted first step in the developer's attempt to gain legal control of land. The real estate development lawyer must, therefore, learn how to utilize the letter of intent format in a way that serves the developer's interests, without creating any unexpected and unwanted legal obligations for the developer.

A significant part of this chapter was devoted to a discussion of how a real estate development lawyer can use the land purchase contract as a vehicle to protect the developer from the risk that something occurs after the purchase contract is executed, but before the developer closes on the land acquisition, that causes the developer to decide not to buy the land. The developer's risk comes in two basic forms—(1) land risk involving a circumstance that is specific to the subject site (for example the presence on the site of environmental contaminants), and (2) deal risk involving a circumstance that has nothing to do with the site itself, but that relates in a broader fashion to the feasibility of the developer's overall development project (for example, a fall-off in tenant demand for the project because of

---

[65] ROLLING STONES, YOU CAN'T ALWAYS GET WHAT YOU WANT (Abkco Music, Inc. 1964).

the kick-off of a nearby competitive project or a sudden, unexpected downturn in the real estate economy). The real estate development lawyer's efforts to minimize the developer's exposure to both of these categories of risk revolve around the lawyer's artful use of buyer contingencies, due diligence certifications, and seller representations and warranties.

As stated at the outset of this chapter, the land purchase contract serves as the road map for the real estate development project. The real estate development lawyer's job is to produce a purchase contract that, like any good road map, gets the developer where it wants to go.

CHAPTER 6

STAGE 2: SECURING GOVERNMENTAL APPROVALS AND INCENTIVES

■ ■ ■

I. INTRODUCTION

The real estate development business is a heavily regulated industry in which the involvement of the public sector often is the determining factor in a project's success or failure. When I first started practicing law almost 40 years ago, the government's participation in the development process was typically limited to the issuance of zoning letters, building permits, and other administrative clearances. In today's real estate industry, federal, state, and local governments are proactive players at every stage of the development process, ranging from the initial visioning of the project to its ultimate funding, construction. and operation.

The focus of this chapter is on how the government can provide incentives to aid the development of a private real estate project. Those incentives are examined from the perspectives of both the developer who asks for help and the government that then needs to decide whether the developer's project merits such help. The chapter concludes by straying into an area that is quite unique for this text—that is, those issues of public policy that affect (or at least should affect) the government's decision to provide aid to a private development project.

The following are a few additional clarifying comments about the context and scope of this chapter.

- The term "government" is used in this chapter as an all-inclusive shorthand reference to all levels of government, including federal, state, county, city, village, and township governments, and to all of the constituent agencies and offices at each such governmental level.

- This chapter has as its focus government assistance provided to a private development project. As such, no attempt is made to discuss development projects undertaken directly by the government or by a quasi-governmental agency where the ultimate driver for the project is different from the seeking of bottom-line profits that is the focus of this book (for example, an urban redevelopment agency established by a municipality to spearhead the redevelopment of a distressed area of the city).

- This chapter does not make reference to the Heathrow International Business Center project that serves as a focal point for the examination of the other nine stages of a real estate development project. The HIBC case study is not a good platform for the discussion of Stage 2 because the key governmental approvals secured for the HIBC project (and there were plenty of them) were all linked to the peculiarities of the State of Florida's growth management rules—none of which have any particular application to the practice of real estate development law in jurisdictions other than Florida

II. DEVELOPER'S BUSINESS OBJECTIVE

Prior to closing on its acquisition of the land, the developer wants to make sure that it has received all those governmental approvals that the developer considers to be essential conditions precedent to a kick-off of the development project. Those approvals generally fall into one of two categories:

- Approvals that are required to permit the project to be constructed in accordance with the developer's development plan (commonly referred to in the real estate industry as *entitlements*); and

- Approvals that are required to make the project economics work or otherwise make the project feasible (better known as *incentives*).

The threshold question for the developer during Stage 2 is what governmental approvals are "essential" to its decision to move forward with the project. In an ideal risk-free world, the developer would have received final and irrevocable governmental approvals for all components of the project before the developer is required to commit to purchase the land on which the project is to be constructed (including a full-blown building permit authorizing the developer to prosecute and complete construction of the entirety of the project). However, commercial real estate developers are seldom afforded the luxury of operating in a risk-free environment. Developers routinely make judgments that certain approvals are so insignificant, ministerial in nature, or otherwise free of political controversy that their receipt can be deferred until after the project land is purchased. All other approvals (be they related to entitlements or incentives) fall into the "essential" category and are the focus of the developer's efforts during Stage 2 of the development process.

III. ENTITLEMENT VS. INCENTIVE

While entitlements and incentives both fit within the definition of those essential approvals that a developer should secure prior to the onset of its commitment to purchase the project land, the two categories of approvals are markedly different. An ***entitlement*** approval is issued when the government determines that a proposed real estate project satisfies a set of governmental rules that are applicable to all similarly situated projects. The developer is legally required to secure the entitlement approval before it can proceed with the construction of the project.

The following are examples of entitlement approvals that are frequently viewed by the developer as being essential to its decision to commit to purchase the project land:

- A rezoning required for the developer's use of the project in a particular manner;

- A development plan approval where the government has discretion to disapprove the design or layout of the proposed project;

- An environmental or wetlands clearance required as a condition precedent to the start of construction on the project site; and

- The grant of development rights that are consistent with state-wide growth management rules.

The government's primary power in the area of entitlements is its limited right to say *"NO."* The developer's receipt of an entitlement approval simply means that it can proceed to build its project—it does not mean that it should do so. The grant of an entitlement makes the project possible, but not necessarily feasible.

An ***incentive*** approval is in many ways the flip side of the entitlement coin. There is no legal imperative for the developer to request the grant of an incentive, nor is there typically any set of fixed governmental rules to determine whether the incentive should be granted to a particular project. The government's primary power in the area of incentives is the government's authority to favor a particular project by saying *"YES"* to the grant of a benefit to that project that is not shared in common with similarly situated projects. The developer's receipt of an incentive approval does not mean that it can build its project, but it often goes a long way toward answering the question of whether it should do so. The grant of an incentive makes the project feasible, but not necessarily possible.

There is not much instructive guidance that can be given in this chapter about the developer's efforts to receive an entitlement approval, other than—(1) the developer needs to get those entitlement approvals that the developer believes are essential to the project before the developer buys the project land and kicks off construction of the project, and (2) the developer must employ all appropriate measures to ensure that its proposed development plan complies with the governmental rules that govern the grant of the subject entitlement. I have now exhausted my advice on the topic of entitlements, so the remainder of this chapter is devoted to the topic of primary interest during Stage 2 of a development project—that is, the developer's enhancement of its project's feasibility through its receipt of governmental incentives.

IV. WHY DOES THE DEVELOPER WANT (OR NEED) INCENTIVES?

The wildly popular book *Freakonomics* contains the following passage that nicely encapsulates the developer's quest for governmental incentives:

> Economics is, at root, the study of incentives: how people get what they want, or need, especially when other people want or need the same thing.[1]

For the commercial real estate developer, the receipt of governmental incentives can satisfy one (and sometimes both) of the following wants and needs:

- Give the developer's project a competitive advantage over similar projects that do not receive the incentive; or

- Make feasible a project that would not be so, *BUT FOR* the receipt of the incentive.

The developer's quest to secured a governmental incentive to distinguish its project from those of its competitors is illustrated by looking at two identical suburban office buildings located within close proximity of each other. The only difference between the two buildings is that the municipality in which Building A is located has agreed to abate all real estate taxes on the building for a period of ten years (producing a $200,000 annual cost savings), while the municipality in which Building B is located is unwilling to grant any tax abatement for Building B. Solely due to the existence of the tax abatement, the owner of Building A can lower its rents by $200,000 per year and still achieve the same annual return on costs that flows to the owner of Building B—a clear competitive advantage that will result in tenants flocking to Building A (and away from Building B).

The developer's desire to receive a governmental incentive to make an otherwise infeasible project feasible is particularly pertinent for urban development projects. The cost of developing a project in an urban setting is typically much higher than the cost of doing so in the suburbs (for a whole

---

[1]   STEVEN D. LEVITT AND STEPHEN J. DUBNER, FREAKONOMICS 16 (2005).

host of reasons, including higher land costs, outdated infrastructure, environmental problems, and constrained work sites). The receipt of incentives is, therefore, frequently needed to level the playing field between a downtown project and a competing project constructed in the suburbs.

The following is a list of the four principal ways in which the competitive posture and feasibility of developer's project can be benefited by the receipt of governmental incentives:

- *Lower the developer's cost of capital* through the provision of low-interest loans, grants, or other financial subsidies;

- *Reduce the project's development costs* through direct government funding of land acquisition or infrastructure costs or the use of tax increment financing or other creative financing tools to fund a portion of the project's development costs;

- *Increase the project's net operating income* by providing tax and financial incentives to attract new tenants, reduce the project's operating costs, or increase the project's revenues; and

- *Eliminate barriers to entry for the project* by streamlining the approval and permitting process, using the government's eminent domain powers to assist the developer in its land assemblage, constructing infrastructure to enhance the marketability and functionality of the project site, or assisting the developer in its clean-up of environmentally contaminated sites.

The specific incentive techniques that are available to help the developer achieve these four objectives are discussed in more detail later in this chapter.

V. WHY IS THE GOVERNMENT WILLING TO PROVIDE INCENTIVES?

It is easy to understand why a developer is happy to receive governmental incentives for its project. But why does the government want to provide incentives to a developer? What possible public interest is served by the government's provision of aid to a private development project? Is the provision of incentives favoring a single developer over its competitors really a valid exercise of the government's powers?

The reason why governments put together incentive packages to aid the development of a private project can be understood by again referring to a quote from *Freakonomics*.

An incentive is simply a means of urging people to do more of a good thing and less of a bad thing.[2]

By providing incentives to a private developer, the government hopes to cause the developer to "do a good thing" by developing a project of a type and in a location desired by the government (and not "do a bad thing" by developing a project of a type or in a location that is not favored by the government). It is this simple concept that has provoked virtually every political subdivision in the United States, from large states like California to the smallest of townships in Maine, to staff an office of economic development to craft incentives to encourage private development within its boundaries.

But why does the government care whether a particular type of a project is developed within its geographic borders? There are both economic and social policy justifications for a government's decision to try to direct the course of real estate development in its jurisdiction.

A. ECONOMIC REASONS

The primary purpose of government is to provide for the health, education, welfare, and safety of its citizens. Government serves that purpose by operating schools, staffing police and fire departments, and offering a variety of services intended to foster the well-being of those living within its boundaries. Performing those tasks costs money that must be funded out of the government's revenues (largely generated from taxes and fees imposed on the general populace). Over the last few decades, it has become the job of the government's economic development officer to figure out inventive ways to increase the government's revenue base, without the government having to impose additional taxes on its citizens. It is this goal of increasing government revenues that has given rise to the offering of governmental incentives to spur the development of private real estate projects.

The development of the right real estate project can augment the government's revenues in a variety of ways. The most obvious source of additional revenue is the property taxes that will be imposed on the new project's value. Even more important are the additional property taxes that will be generated from surrounding properties if (and it's a big "if") the developer's project has the desired dual effect of (1) increasing the value of surrounding properties, and (2) serving as a catalyst for the development of new projects inside the government's borders.[3]

Property taxes are not the only source of additional revenue that a government hopes to generate by offering incentives to a private real estate

---

[2]   LEVITT, *supra* note 1, at 17.

[3]   *See* Theodore J. Novak, *Magnet Public/Private Projects: Does the Pull Really Work,* in ACREL PAPERS (Fall 2002).

project. It is the government's objective when structuring its incentive package to encourage (and sometimes actually require) the creation of new jobs—jobs for the construction workers employed by the developer's contractor, jobs for the occupants of the developer's project (be it an office building, retail center, or warehouse), and jobs for the occupants of all of the new development projects that are hopefully spawned by the construction of the incentivized project. The creation of new jobs produces two results that are equally important to the government—(1) it increases the government's income and sales tax revenues (because the more money people make, the more they spend on both commodities and taxes), and (2) it produces a content citizenry that may be inclined to cast their votes to keep the existing officeholders in power.

The one point made obvious by the above discussion is that the government's goal of enhancing its revenue base is only achieved if the incentivized project actually has the intended effect of spurring additional development and increasing property values in the surrounding neighborhood. The dynamics and magnitude of the *BET* that government makes when it identifies a project as a candidate to trigger additional development is discussed in more detail later in this chapter.

B. SOCIAL POLICY REASONS

Governments also use incentives to promote social policy agendas. As noted in the previously-quoted excerpt from *Freakonomics*, governments create incentives to urge developers to "do more of a good thing and less of a bad thing."[4]

The following are some of the "good things" that governments have encouraged developers to do by offering incentives:

- Rebuild blighted areas;

- Clean up and redevelop environmentally contaminated sites;

- Use "green" and other sustainable building practices;

- Construct affordable housing;

- Dedicate parkland and other public space;

- Preserve and renovate historic structures;

- Design projects consistent with a particular zoning model;

- Build downtown (and not in suburbs or exurbs); and

- Invest in low-income communities.

In all of the above cases, the government offers up something that the developer wants (for example, financial subsidies, tax abatements, or

---

4   *See* LEVITT *supra* note 1, at 17.

increased project density) in exchange for the developer behaving in a governmentally-prescribed way.[5]

VI. TYPES OF GOVERNMENTAL INCENTIVES

The incentives that are available to a government to assist a private development project fall into four general categories:

- Financial incentives;
- Tax incentives;
- Regulatory assistance; and
- Development assistance.

It should be noted that the particulars of the various governmental incentives discussed in this chapter vary widely by jurisdiction. This chapter does not analyze any specific state statute or local ordinance, but rather discusses governmental approvals and incentives in general terms in an attempt to highlight the principal issues that a real estate development lawyer must address in the jurisdiction in which the lawyer practices.

Practice Tip #6-1: Incentives Are a Really Big Deal

In 2012, the New York Times printed a series on economic development incentives offered to private entities by federal, state, and local governments in the Unites States.[6] Here are two eye-popping statistics from that article:

- *Combined federal, state, and local incentives—$170 billion per year; and*

- *Combined state and local incentives—$80 billion per year.*

While I certainly cannot vouchsafe for the accuracy of the statistics cited in the New York Times article, there is no denying that the grant of governmental incentives has become a big business in the 21st century. Even if one accepts the lower-end estimate of state and local incentives as being

------

[5] The government could, of course, better advance its policy agenda if it were to mandate that developers act in the prescribed fashion (rather than simply encouraging them to do so through the use of incentives). The policy debate over the use of mandates versus incentives is an interesting one that is discussed at length in the following articles—Denise J. Lewis, Thomas J. Coyne and Dwight H. Merriam, *Tax and Other Inducements for the Development of Real Estate— "Carrots and Sticks: How Governments Cajole and Bludgeon Developers into Submission,"* in ACREL PAPERS 1 (Fall 2006); and Carl J. Circo, *Using Mandates and Incentives to Promote Sustainable Construction and Green Building Projects in the Private Sector: A Call for More State Land Use Policy Initiatives,* 112 PENN STATE LAW REVIEW 731 (2008).

[6] *See* Louise Story, *As Companies Seek Tax Deals, Governments Pay High Price,* NEW YORK TIMES, December 1, 2012, available online at http://www.nytimes.com/2012/12/02/us/how-local-taxpayers-bankroll-corporations.html?pagewanted=all&_r=0.

ONLY $50 billion per year,[7] *the magnitude of the governmental incentives handed out to the private sector each year is ample testament to the importance that the public sector now plays in the financing of private enterprises.*

VII.   FINANCIAL INCENTIVES

There are a wide variety of financial incentives that a government can offer to a developer of a private real estate project. The purpose of all such financial incentives is to improve the developer's project economics by lowering the project's development costs.

The precise nature and scope of the financial incentives that are available for use by a particular governmental entity are typically defined in enabling legislation adopted by such entity. Because the specifics of such financial incentives vary substantially by jurisdiction, it is impractical to list in this text all of the financial incentives available at each level of federal, state, and local government. It can, however, be stated that those financial incentives generally fall in one of the following three buckets:

- ***Direct grants and subsidies***, where the government makes a direct payment or property contribution either to the developer or to one of the developer's vendors;

- ***Low-cost financing***, where the government provides debt to the developer at below-market pricing and terms;[8] and

- ***Tax increment financing***, where the government uses the enhanced revenues generated from the new project to fund a portion of the project's development costs.

Depending on the size and complexity of the project, a developer of a single project might receive several financial incentives from different

---

[7]   *See* Brian Chappatta, *Paying for Jobs: Tax Breaks and Bidding Wars*, February 11, 2015, at https://www.bloomberg.com/quicktake/paying-for-jobs; Carl Davis, *Tax Incentives: Costly for States, Drag on the Nation*, INSTITUTE ON TAXATION AND ECONOMIC POLICY, August 12, 2013; and Alan Peters and Peter Fisher, *The Failures of Economic Development Incentives*, JOURNAL OF THE AMERICAN PLANNING ASSOCIATION, Vol. 70, No. 1 Winter 2004.

[8]   Two common ways that a governmental entity provides low-cost financing for the benefit of a private project are through (1) its issuance of tax-exempt bonds (either backed by the full faith and credit of the governmental entity issuing the bonds or by the revenue created from the new project), and (2) its creation of a special assessment district where the cost of public infrastructure required by the incentivized project is funded by the assessment of taxes and fees against all property owners that benefit from construction of such infrastructure. The specifics of both of these financing techniques are beyond both the scope of this chapter. Those interested in learning more about these governmental financing alternatives are referred to the following resources—Novak, *supra* note 3, at 5–6; J. Murphy McMillan III, William S. Mendenhall and James A. Richardson, *Use of Public Incentive Finance in Commercial Real Estate Developments: A Developer's Perspective*, REAL ESTATE FINANCE JOURNAL 10 (Summer 2007); URBAN LAND INSTITUTE, INFO PACKET NO. 308, INFRASTRUCTURE FINANCING (February 2006); and CHARLES LONG, FINANCE FOR REAL ESTATE DEVELOPMENT 176–177 (Urban Land Institute 2011).

governmental entities. By way of example, the developer of an industrial park might receive the benefit of a state grant to pay for the cost of needed road improvements, a low-interest bond financing sponsored by the county to cover the cost of extending sewer and water lines to the project, and a tax increment financing agreement from the city to fund the developer's site-wide infrastructure costs. The result of the developer's receipt of such financial incentives is that its lower cost structure gives the developer's project a competitive advantage over other nearby industrial parks.

A. TAX INCREMENT FINANCING

Tax increment financing is an incentive tool that has become immensely popular in recent years. Given the prevalence of its use and the significance of the benefit it can bestow on the private developer, the topic of tax increment financing (a *TIF*) deserves special mention in this chapter.

A TIF is a financing device that uses the *incremental taxes* (typically real estate taxes, but occasionally sales and other business taxes) derived from a new real estate project to pay for a portion of the project's development costs. The incremental taxes consist of the additional future taxes imposed on the project over and above the taxes attributable to the pre-development value of the project (usually the "land only" value of the project site).[9] In other words, the incremental taxes are those taxes that would not be payable *BUT FOR* the development of the new project.

In a TIF arrangement, the project owner pays its annual real estate taxes on the full value of the completed project (and not just the pre-existing land only value of the project site). The incremental piece of those taxes (commonly referred to as the *increment*) is then diverted from the government's normal pool of tax revenues and specifically used to repay the TIF-financed project costs.

The following example illustrates how a TIF works.

Example 6-1: Assume that Developer plans to construct an office building in Downtown. In order for its cost structure to be competitive with other Downtown office buildings, Developer believes that it needs to reduce its development costs by $5 million (which, conveniently for this illustration, is the exact amount of the infrastructure costs that Developer needs to incur for the project's road and utility improvements). The existing value of the

---

[9]   The calculation of the taxes attributable to the pre-development value of the project is not as clear-cut as it might seem. The principal issue that the negotiators of a TIF must address is what happens if the applicable tax rate increases during the term of the TIF, either as a result of a specific vote of the electorate or an automatic adjustment for inflation. Should the additional taxes produced from the tax rate increase (including those related to the pre-development value of the project) be included in the tax increment? The answer to that question is the product of the specific language of the applicable TIF statute and the negotiating skills of the lawyers for the developer and the government.

land on which Developer's office building will be constructed is $1 million. This land only value currently produces an annual real estate tax bill of $25,000. Developer estimates that the value of its new project at completion will be $28 million. At that number, the completed project would generate an annual real estate tax liability of $700,000.

Based on the above facts, Downtown could create a TIF to fund $5 million of Developer's infrastructure costs. The annual tax increment of $675,000 (the projected annual tax bill on the completed project of $700,000, minus the existing land only tax bill of $25,000) would be captured and used by Downtown to pay off the $5 million of infrastructure costs financed under the TIF (plus interest calculated at whatever level is sanctioned under the TIF statute applicable to Downtown). Assuming that the interest rate on the TIF is 5.5% and that the actual annual tax increment matches Developer's pre-development estimate of $675,000, the $5 million TIF amount would be fully repaid in approximately ten years.

The tax dollars produced from Developer's project during each year of the ten-year term of the TIF would be used in the following fashion— (1) $675,000 to repay the TIF costs; and (2) $25,000 to fund the government's general operating costs (schools, police and fire, etc.). Upon the repayment of all of the TIF costs, the entirety of the tax payment (including the increment of $675,000) would then revert back into the government's coffers to pay its general operating costs.

Example 6-1 begs one very important question—who bears the risk that the actual tax increment is not sufficient to pay off the TIF-financed costs? Does the developer bear that risk or is the governmental entity that provided the TIF at risk for the unreimbursed TIF costs? The answer to that question depends, at least in part, on whether the TIF is structured as a *pay as you go TIF* or as a *bonded TIF*.

- *Pay as You Go TIF*—With this type of TIF, the developer is responsible for the upfront payment of the full amount of the TIF costs ($5 million in the Example 6-1) and is then reimbursed for that payment by its receipt of the actual tax increment over the term of the TIF. Under the pay as you go arrangement, the developer bears the full risk that the tax increment actually produced from the project is less than initially projected (and, hence, not big enough to fully reimburse the developer for its earlier payment of the TIF costs).

- *Bonded TIF*—Developers frequently ask the government to structure its TIF as a bonded arrangement. Under a bonded TIF, the government uses its borrowing power to issue bonds[10] in an amount equal to the TIF costs. The TIF provider pays the proceeds of the bond sale to the developer to cover the full amount of the developer's TIF-covered costs. The government provider then uses the tax increment actually paid by the project owner during the TIF term to retire the principal and interest due on the bonds. A typical unvarnished bonded TIF serves two primary developer objectives—(1) it places the risk that the actual tax increment is insufficient to pay the TIF costs on the government, and (2) it relieves the developer of the liquidity burden of having to make an upfront payment equal to the TIF-covered costs. In an attempt to shift the risk of a lower than projected increment back to the developer, many governmental entities insist that the developer personally guaranty or collateralize all or a portion of the shortfall between the TIF costs and the actual increment.

B. TIF LEGAL ISSUES

A TIF is a statutory creation. While the overwhelming majority of states have statutes in place authorizing a local government's use of a TIF,[11] the provisions of those statutes vary widely. It is, therefore, essential for a real estate practitioner to master the intricacies of the practitioner's state's TIF statute before entering into negotiations with a governmental entity concerning that entity's provision of a TIF for the benefit of the practitioner's client.

The following are the principal issues that are presented under state TIF statutes.

- *What governmental entities can use a TIF?* Is a TIF a tool that can be used by all state or local governmental entities (state, county, municipal, village, and township governments, as well as instrumentalities and agencies of such governmental units) or only by a limited subset of such entities?

---

[10] The government can fund the TIF costs by its issuance of either general obligation bonds or revenue bonds. General obligation bonds are backed by the full faith and credit of the issuing governmental entity and, hence, can be issued at a very low interest rate. Revenue bonds are backed by the revenues created from the incentivized project and are not supported by the full faith and credit of the government. Therefore, the interest rate on revenue bonds is normally slightly higher than that payable on general obligation bonds (but is still below that typically charged by banks and other construction lenders). *See* Novak, *supra* note 3, at 3; MIKE E. MILES, GAYLE L. BERENS AND MARC A. WEISS, REAL ESTATE DEVELOPMENT: PRINCIPLES AND PROCESS 259 (3rd ed. 2000); and LONG, *supra* note 8, at 174–177.

[11] *See* George Lefcoe, *Competing for the Next Hundred Million Americans: The Uses and Abuses of Tax Increment Financing*, 43 URBAN LAWYER 427, 436 (2011).

- *What types of projects are eligible for a TIF?* Here the question is whether the use of a TIF is limited to certain types of projects—for example, only non-residential properties or only those properties to which the public has access (for example, a performing arts center or stadium).

- *What conditions warrant the use of a TIF?* All states require the presence of a public purpose for the diversion of tax revenues to pay for the development costs of a private project. The issue is whether that public purpose is satisfied simply by the developer and the governmental entity agreeing and stipulating that the construction of the project will promote *economic development* (that is, the potential creation of new jobs and further development in the vicinity of the incentivized project) or whether a more restrictive definition of public purpose is imposed—for example, the remediation of blight. The resolution of this issue largely determines whether a TIF can be used for a suburban greenfield project or whether it is only available for development in higher density urban areas. In addition, several state statutes require a specific government finding that the development of the incentivized project would not occur *BUT FOR* the government's creation of the TIF.[12]

- *What costs are eligible for funding under a TIF?* TIFs have traditionally been used to fund the costs of constructing public infrastructure, such as sewer and water lines and public roadways. However, the statutes of many states have in recent years been interpreted to permit a much more expansive view of the development costs that can be funded under a TIF.[13] Costs that are frequently permitted to be funded under a TIF now include not only roadway, utility, and other infrastructure costs, but also the costs of acquiring the project land, cleaning up environmental contamination, demolishing existing site improvements, and, in some circumstances, even the cost of financing the construction of new buildings, such as parking garages. Ultimately the precise wording of a particular state's statute (supplemented by the creative interpretation of that statutory language by

---

[12] *See* Richard Ward, *To TIF or Not to TIF: Debating the Issues*, DEVELOPMENT STRATEGIES REVIEW 1, 2 (Summer 2000), reprinted in URBAN LAND INSTITUTE, INFO PACKET NO. 357, TAX INCREMENT FINANCING (February 2006).

[13] *See* Novak, *supra* note 3 at 3; and Ward, *supra* note 13, at 3. *Also see e.g.,* JG St. Louis West Limited Liability Company v. City of Des Peres, 41 S.W.3d 513 (Mo. App. Ct.), where a Missouri court upheld the use of a TIF to finance the costs of constructing a parking garage to serve a retail center.

real estate lawyers) provides the answer to the question of what costs are eligible for TIF funding.

- ***What are the geographical boundaries of the TIF district?*** Some states provide the government with broad authority to establish the boundaries of the TIF district beyond the site on which the construction of the funded improvements are being erected (on the theory that those improvements will provide a direct or indirect benefit to surrounding properties). Setting the boundaries of the TIF district beyond those of the specific incentivized project creates a larger increment that can then be used to fund more development costs over a quicker period of time (good for the developer). The downside from the government's perspective of creating a larger than required TIF district is that the increment created from new development in areas surrounding the incentivized project is diverted to the repayment of the TIF costs and is not available to fund the government's general operating costs.

- ***What is the maximum term of a TIF?*** Some jurisdictions place a cap on the length of the term for the repayment of the TIF-covered costs—for example, Ohio's TIF statute provides for a maximum TIF term of 30 years.[14] Most developers prefer to push the term out as far as possible in an effort to maximize the amount of the development costs that can be covered under the TIF (an approach that runs counter to the government's desire for a quick payback of the TIF-funded costs).

- ***What percentage of the tax increment can be used to repay the TIF costs?*** Some governments seek during their negotiations with developers to limit the percentage of the tax increment that can be used to repay the TIF costs—for example, 50% of the increment. Doing so means that the remaining 50% of the increment is immediately available to pay the government's general operating costs.

- ***Is the consent of the school district or any other taxing district required prior to the adoption of a TIF?*** As noted at the outset of this section, the effect of a TIF is to divert the tax increment generated by the incentivized project away from school districts, police and fire departments, and other taxing districts that get their funding from the government's general operating revenues. In order to protect the interests of such taxing districts, some state statutes specifically

---

[14] *See* OHIO REVISED CODE § 5709.40(C)(4) (2016).

require that a TIF cannot become operative unless all or a portion of those taxing districts consent to the creation of the TIF. By way of example, Ohio's statute provides that the school district's consent is required if the term of the TIF is greater than ten years or the percentage of the diverted tax increment is more than 75%.[15]

The answers to all of the above questions are provided in each state's TIF-enabling statute. The negotiating teams representing the developer and the government need to structure the terms of a TIF in a manner that both complies with the statutory constraints and serves the respective interests of the developer and the government.

C. TIF POLICY ISSUES

The use of TIFs to encourage private development has been the source of an ongoing public policy debate.[16] TIF proponents argue that a TIF is an ideal governmental incentive because it encourages economic development without negatively impacting the government's operating revenues. They point out that the tax increment that is used to finance the TIF costs would not have existed *BUT FOR* the developer's construction of its new project—which, in turn, would not have been kicked off *BUT FOR* the incentives provided to the project by the sponsoring governmental entity. In other words, the use of a TIF does not cost the government anything at all during the TIF term and provides the government with (1) the use of the tax increment on the TIF project once the term of the TIF expires, and (2) the unfettered use both during and after the TIF term of the additional tax revenues created from the increased property values and additional development spawned in the surrounding area by the incentivized project. To TIF supporters, the use of a TIF is a perfect example of a government "making a development pay for itself."[17]

TIF opponents argue that a TIF is nothing more than a convenient way for government officials to allocate tax revenues away from schools and other taxing districts to the benefit of politically well-connected developers—and to do so without having to obtain the consent of the electorate. These opponents discount the "but for" argument of the TIF proponents by asserting that, in almost all instances, the developer would

---

[15] *See* OHIO REVISED CODE § 5709.40(B) (2016).

[16] *See generally* Lefcoe, *supra* note 11; DAPHNE A. KENYON, ADAM H. LANGLEY, AND BETHANY P. PAQUIN, RETHINKING PROPERTY TAX INCENTIVES FOR BUSINESS 34–38 (Lincoln Institute of Land Policy 2012); Alyson Tomme, *Tax Increment Financing: Public Use or Private Abuse,* 90 MINNESOTA LAW REVIEW 213 (2005); and Richard F. Dye and David F. Merriman, *Tax Increment Financing: A Tool for Local Economic Development,* 18 LAND LINES 2 (Lincoln Institute of Land Policy 2006)

[17] *See* MILES, *supra* note 10, at 259.

have moved forward with the project with or without the TIF.[18] In their view, a TIF permits private developers to improve the bottom line profitability of their projects by getting the government to fund project development costs that are strictly private in nature and serve no valid public purpose. While TIF opponents may not object to the use of a TIF to finance the construction of roads and sewer lines that serve the public at large, they object strenuously to the use of a TIF for the benefit of a private development project. TIF opponents also point out that the existence of a TIF has the potential of creating a deficit in the government's operating revenues if the government has to provide additional services and facilities for the occupants of the TIF project (something that is often a very real prospect). Because the increment from the TIF project is not available to pay for the additional services and facilities provided to the TIF project, the government could find itself in the politically unenviable position of having to increase taxes to deal with the additional demands placed upon it by the occupants of the incentivized real estate project.

In recent years, the public policy debate over the pros and cons of TIFs has spilled over into the courts. Taxpayers have filed numerous lawsuits seeking to restrain the government's use of TIFs to support private development projects.[19] Local taxing districts are also beginning to get into the act by resorting to the courts to try to prevent municipalities from creating TIFs that have the effect of diverting revenues away from such taxing districts.[20] While no judicial decision has come down to date that significantly impedes the government's latitude to assist private development projects through the use of tax increment financing, practitioners are well-advised to diligently monitor judicial developments on this topic in the years to come.

VIII.   TAX INCENTIVES

The grant of tax incentives is probably the technique most commonly used by the government to encourage the construction of a private development project. While tax incentives take many forms, they all share the attribute of reducing the tax burden of either the owner of the incentivized project or the tenants of that project. Taxes that are typically

---

[18] *See* Dye, *supra* note 16, at 2); KENYON, *supra* note 16, at 36–37; and Lefcoe, *supra* note 11, at 460–463.

[19] *See* Novak, *supra* note 3, at 3; and Lefcoe, *supra* note 11, at 462 One very high profile project that was the subject of taxpayer litigation contesting the use of a TIF was the Florida Marlins stadium project in Miami. The Florida Supreme Court in *Braman v. Miami-Dade County*, 18 So.3d 1259 (2009), affirmed a lower court's decision upholding the use of a TIF to fund a portion of the costs of developing the Florida Marlins new stadium complex in Miami.

[20] *See* David Stokes, *Counties, Not Municipalities Should Decide TIFs*, 6 SHOW-ME INSTITUTE No. 8 (March 24, 2010), available online at http://showmeinstitute.org/blog/corporate-welfare/counties-not-municipalities-should-determine-tifs.

the subject of governmental incentive packages include real estate taxes, income taxes (at the federal, state, and local levels), and sales taxes.

Tax incentives afford the developer of a private development project the opportunity to enhance its net operating income and, hence, the ultimate value of its project. A reduction in the real estate taxes that a developer must pay on its newly-developed project boosts the developer's NOI by reducing its operating expenses. A government-sponsored reduction in the income and sales taxes payable by tenants of a particular project not only makes the developer's project more attractive to prospective tenants, but also potentially clears the way for the developer to charge premium rents to those tenants who decide to relocate to the developer's new project.

There are three basic categories of tax incentives that can be used to benefit the development of a private real estate project. The tax incentive categories are listed in the order of developer preference—from the most to the least desirable. The developer's preference is based largely on time value of money considerations, with the abatement creating the best time-valued benefit to the developer (because the developer never has to pay the tax) and the rebate providing the least time-valued benefit (because the developer has to pay the taxes before it is entitled to an eventual refund and, therefore, the developer loses the use of the funds for a period of time).

- *Tax abatement*—An abatement reduces (or wholly eliminates) a taxpayer's tax liability for a fixed period of time. An example of a typical tax abatement that a government might use to incentivize a private development project is the abatement for ten years of 100% of the real estate taxes that would otherwise be assessed on improvements constructed on the project site. An abatement can be issued either on a single project site or offered on a blanket basis for all projects constructed within a designated geographical area (for example, a community reinvestment area or an enterprise zone). Care must be taken to make sure that the grant of an abatement does not defeat the purpose of other governmental incentives provided for a particular development project. For example, a real estate tax abatement typically should not be given to a project that is the subject of a TIF because an abatement reduces the amount of the tax increment available to be captured to finance the TIF-funded costs.

- *Tax credit*—This incentive provides the taxpayer with a credit that it can apply as an offset against its existing tax liability. Examples of tax credits used to incentivize private real estate projects are the federal income tax credits included in the Internal Revenue Code for costs incurred by a taxpayer in connection with the rehabilitation of a certified historic structure or the development of a commercial real estate project in a low-income community (see *Practice Tip #6-2: The New Markets Tax Credit*, at pages 186–189). A taxpayer is ordinarily not entitled to receive any direct payment from the IRS if the amount of the taxpayer's credit exceeds its tax liability for the current tax period. Unused credits are, however, frequently permitted to be carried forward to offset the taxpayer's tax liability in future tax periods.

- *Tax rebate*—A rebate is a governmental refund of taxes previously paid by a taxpayer. A rebate can be used with respect to any kind of tax, including sales and income taxes. In recent years, it has become commonplace for municipalities to try to entice a user to relocate to a particular project by offering the user a full or partial rebate of all income taxes paid to the municipality by the user's employees during a designated period of time. By way of example, the City of Columbus has adopted a policy that rebates payroll taxes to companies that agree to relocate to office space in downtown Columbus from anywhere outside of the city limits. The amount of the rebate is tied to the length of a company's commitment to its new space and the number of new jobs created by its move.[21]

The result of the government's use of any of these incentives is the same—the developer's net operating income is increased and the government's tax revenues are decreased.

Practice Tip #6-2: The New Markets Tax Credit

In 2000, the United States Congress enacted the New Markets Tax Credit as § 45D of the Internal Revenue Code. The **New Markets Tax Credit (NMTC)** is intended to incentivize developers, lenders, and investors to pour dollars into commercial real estate projects located in low-income communities. During the period from 2001 through 2014 (the most current data available), the NMTC generated approximately $26 billion in direct capital investments in commercial estate projects located in qualifying economically distressed communities and supported the development of almost 165 million square feet of commercial real estate

---

[21] *See* https://www.columbus.gov/development/economic-development/Downtown-Business-Incentives/ (last visited on January 28, 2017).

space.[22] The NMTC was recently extended through December 31, 2019, and bills are pending in Congress that would make the NMTC a permanent part of the U.S. tax law.[23]

The success of the NMTC is surpassed only by the complexity of its governing provisions. Section 45D is replete with acronymic defined terms such as LIC (Low-Income Community), CDE (Community Development Entity), QEI (Qualified Equity Investment), QALICB (Qualified Active Low-Income Community Business), and QLICI (Qualified Low-Income Community Investment). The complexity of the § 45D framework has produced a new cottage industry of lawyers specializing in NMTC transactions (a welcome result because a full command of the NMTC intricacies is beyond the capabilities of most practicing real estate development lawyers).

The essence of the NMTC is the grant to a private investor (most often a bank or other financial institution) of a federal tax credit for its investment in a commercial real estate project located in a low-income community. For the purpose of the NMTC, a "low-income community" is defined as a population census tract where either (1) the poverty rate is at least 20%, or (2) the median family income does not exceed 80% of the median income of the broader state or metropolitan area in which the tract is located. In exchange for making an equity investment in a project in a low-income community, the investor gets a federal tax credit equal to 39% of the amount of its equity investment. The 39% tax credit is spread over seven years, with the investor receiving a credit of 5% of its investment in each of years one through three and 6% of its investment in each of years four through 7.

The following is an illustration of the most basic structure of a commercial real estate project seeking NMTCs.

Equity Investors
↓
Community Development Entity
↓
Qualified Active Low-Income Community Business

Here is generally how the above structure functions.

- *The real estate developer comes up with an idea for a commercial real estate project located in a qualified low-*

[22] *See* U.S. DEPARTMENT OF THE TREASURY, COMMUNITY DEVELOPMENT FINANCIAL INSTITUTIONS FUND, NEW MARKETS TAX CREDIT PUBLIC DATE RELEASE: 2003–2014 SUMMARY REPORT 3 (September 2, 2016); and U.S. DEPARTMENT OF TREASURY, COMMUNITY DEVELOPMENT FINANCIAL INSTITUTIONS FUND, COMMUNITY REVITALIZATION BY REWARDING PRIVATE INVESTMENT, https://www.cdfifund.gov/Documents/NMTC%20Fact%20Sheet_Jan2016v2.pdf.

[23] *See* The New Markets Tax Credit Extension Act of 2015, S. 591 and H.R. 855. 114th Congress (2015).

*income community (a QLIC)—Note: residential projects are
not qualified investments under the NMTC.*

- *The developer then submits a written application to an entity
  (a Community Development Entity or CDE) whose primary
  mission is to provide investment capital for projects located in
  a low-income community. A CDE must be certified by the
  affiliate of the U.S. Treasury Department that is charged with
  the administration of the NMTC program (the Community
  Development Institutions Fund or the CDFI Fund). CDEs are
  typically national non-profit organizations, state and local
  governmental economic development authorities, or affiliates
  of banks (Bank of America, Wells Fargo Bank, and PNC Bank
  are examples of private banking institutions that have set up
  CDEs).*[24]

- *The developer, acting in conjunction with the CDE, then
  canvasses the market to identify financial institutions that
  might be willing to invest capital in the developer's project in
  exchange for the receipt of a 39% NMTC.*

- *The CDE then submits a formal request to the CDFI Fund to
  receive an NMTC allocation (that is, tax credits that can be
  passed on to each equity investor who agrees to provide equity
  capital to the project in exchange for its receipt of the 39%
  NMTC).*

- *If the CDFI Fund approves the CDE's request for an NMTC
  allocation, the developer then forms the private entity that will
  own the real estate project (the Qualified Active Low-Income
  Business or QALICB). The developer and its non-NMTC
  equity investors are typically the principals in the QALIB.*

- *Once all the requisite approvals are received, the equity
  investors fund their equity investments to the CDE, which, in
  turn, disburses those funds to the developer's QALIB as a loan.
  The project then proceeds much like any other private real
  estate development project.*

- *At the end of the seven-year period during which the equity
  investor receives it NMTCs, the NMTC transaction is
  unwound so that the CDE no longer owns any interest in the
  developer's QALIB and the loan made to the QALIB by the*

---

[24] *See* NEW MARKETS TAX CREDIT COALITION, THE NEW MARKETS TAX CREDIT PROGRESS
REPORT 2016 8 (June 2016); and Janice E. Hetland, Thomas C. Huston, and Kathryn C. Murphy,
New Markets Tax Credits (A QALCIB Is Not an Australian Marsupial), in ACREL PAPERS, Tab
10, 4 (Fall 2011).

> *CDE is either refinanced or passed up in whole or in part to the equity investors.*

The above discussion is an overly simplistic description of the structure and operation of an NMTC transaction. One of the primary complicating factors involved in an NMTC transaction is the equity investor's desire to increase the return attributable to its receipt of NMTCs by borrowing a portion of the funds that it contributes as equity to the CDE middleman (with an equity contribution of those funds being a prerequisite to the investor's entitlement to NMTCs). By way of example, if the equity investor has $4 million in available cash that it is willing to commit as equity to the project, the investor will receive an NMTC of $1.56 million (the $4 million equity contribution, multiplied by 39%). If, however, the equity investor borrows another $6 million through a so-called "leverage loan" from a third party (who could be an affiliate of the equity investor, the developer, or an independent lender) and then contributes $10 million (its initial equity investment of $4 million, plus the leverage loan of $6 million) to the CDE, then the equity investor would be entitled to an NMTC of $3.9 million (the $10 million deemed equity contribution, multiplied by 39%). For this reason, virtually all NMTC investments are now structured with a "leverage loan." The real trick is finding a willing leverage lender (a community fund or a bank seeking to satisfy its Community Reinvestment Act requirements)[25] and then structuring the leverage loan to permit the loan to be retired in some fashion at the end of the seven-year NMTC grant period. Complexity abounds when structuring a leveraged NMTC transaction, as do the legal fees payable to the tax experts commissioned to put the deal together.[26]

There is little doubt that structuring an NMTC deal is both time-consuming and expensive. Having said that, the NMTC model can sometimes provide a real estate developer with a needed tool to fund a gap in its project funding by effectively selling tax credits to financial institutions interested in investing in low-income communities.

IX. REGULATORY ASSISTANCE

As noted at the outset of this chapter, there are a wide variety of governmentally-imposed rules that a developer must comply with when constructing a real estate project. Local zoning laws restrict the manner in

---

[25] *See* The Community Reinvestment Act, 12 U.S.C. 2901 (1977). *See also* NEW MARKETS TAX CREDIT COALITION, *supra* note 24, at 12.

[26] For a more detailed discussion of the operation of the New Markets Tax Credit, *see generally* Hetland, *supra* note 24; Denise J. Lewis, *Financing the Challenging Project: Using Ne Markets Tax Credits,* 29 No. 1 PRACTICAL REAL ESTATE LAWYER 9 (January 2013); and John G. Cameron and Christina K. McDonald, *Real Estate Development in 2012: Tax Credits and Government Grants Can Make Your Project Happen,* 28 No. 2 PRACTICAL REAL ESTATE LAWYER 25 (March 2012).

which a project can be used and the dimensions and components of the improvements that can be constructed on the project site. State and federal laws govern the timing and scope of the remediation of environmental contamination found on a particular site. State building codes impose constraints on materials and practices used during the construction of project improvements. State and local authorities impose fees and establish timelines for the developer's application for and receipt of building permits and other development approvals.

Complying with these and other governmental rules has the effect of costing the developer both time and money. One way that a governmental entity can provide meaningful assistance to a private real estate project is by loosening the strictures that a developer must follow during the course of its development efforts. The following are three examples of techniques frequently utilized by governmental entities to help private development projects make their way through the maze of governmental regulation.

- *Zoning and Building Code Variances*—Oftentimes, the most beneficial contribution that a government can make to a private development project is the grant of a variance permitting the developer to avoid a particularly troublesome governmental rule. By way of example, a municipality's decision to reduce the number of parking spaces required in a project or to permit construction of improvements within ten feet (instead of 20 feet) of the site's side boundary line could make the difference between a project being economically feasible or infeasible.

- *Streamlined Approval Process*—To the developer, time really is money. In recognition of that fact, many governmental entities have begun to promise developers relaxed submission requirements and expedited development approvals. One example of a government streamlining its approval process to benefit a private developer is found in the actions taken by the City of Chicago during its efforts in 2000 to convince Boeing to relocate its corporate headquarters from Seattle to Chicago. Chicago agreed to provide Boeing with a single governmental point of contact that was then given the authority to orchestrate and expedite the grant of all required permits from all the governmental agencies having jurisdiction over the Boeing project. The end result of this "single point of contact" arrangement was that Boeing was able to significantly lessen the prospect of government-caused delays in getting its project completed.[27]

---

[27] *See* Novak, *supra* note 3, at 6.

- ***Waiver/Reduction of Development and Building Permit
  Fees***—One way in which the government has sought to
  reduce its financial deficits is by significantly increasing the
  level of development and building permit fees it charges for
  the construction of a new project in its jurisdiction. In some
  states, governmentally-imposed fees represent a significant
  line item cost for a developer. A full or partial waiver of those
  fees can, therefore, be a very meaningful benefit to a
  developer.

The next two sections examine regulatory assistance techniques that
can have a dramatic impact on the developer's bottom line economics.

A. INCENTIVE ZONING

An interesting phenomenon of recent vintage has been the rise of
incentive zoning as a vehicle to cause developers to design and construct
their projects in a certain way. Incentive zoning consists of a local
government providing a bonus to a developer in exchange for the developer
agreeing to do something that the government believes is desirable.[28] The
primary bonus handed out by local governments is the right of the
developer to increase the density of its project—that is, the number of
square feet in "for lease" projects or the number of units in "for sale"
projects. In the idiom of the developer, increased density equates to
increased project profits. If a developer is allowed to increase the quantity
of its revenue-producing product (and that is what density is all about)
without any concomitant increase in its land, infrastructure, or soft costs,
then the developer's projected net operating income from the project is
augmented by an amount equal to the increased net revenues produced by
the bonus density, less the actual cost of the developer's compliance with
the government's incentive zoning program.

Governments also sometimes agree to provide developer bonuses in
the form of a reduction in development fees or a waiver of a construction
requirement otherwise mandated in the government's zoning and building
codes (for example, lowering the number of parking spaces the developer is
required to provide for the project). The adoption of green building
practices, the dedication of land for parks, the inclusion of affordable
housing, and the contribution of public art are other types of private
developer conduct that are often encouraged under incentive zoning
programs.[29]

---

[28] *See supra* note 5 for a list of articles addressing the difference between government
mandating that developers act in a certain way versus government incentivizing developers to do
so.

[29] *See e.g.*, Richard F. Klawiter, *Inclusionary Zoning: How to Make a Good Social Policy
Better and More Fair*, THE REAL ESTATE FINANCE JOURNAL 33 (Fall/Winter 2015); Claude Green,
Getting Inclusionary Zoning Right, Urban Land 78 (July/August 2016); Roger Schwenke, *Green
Building Regulations: The Mandatory, The Voluntary and Some Incentives*, in ACREL PAPERS 325

B. BROWNFIELD REDEVELOPMENT

One of the more difficult challenges facing governments in the 21st century is the task of revitalizing areas of their communities that flourished in the past as industrial sites, but are now vacant as a result of a decline in the U.S. manufacturing sector. A high percentage of these vacant properties (commonly referred to as *brownfield* sites) have at least a moderate level of environmental contamination. The "brownfield" tag is given to "real property, the expansion, redevelopment, or reuse of which may be complicated by the presence or potential presence of a hazardous substance, pollutant or contaminant."[30] Brownfield sites occupy a position somewhere between those properties with no environmental problems whatsoever (so-called *greenfield* sites) and those properties that are so severely contaminated that they "present an imminent and substantial endangerment to health or the environment."[31]

Developers were historically hesitant to buy and develop brownfield sites, because of the uncertain application to such sites of federal and state environmental laws. In the late 1970's and early 1980's, the federal government (and most state governments) adopted expansive legislation intended to give government the authority to impose liability on a broad array of persons to clean up severely contaminated properties. Unfortunately, laws such as the Resource Conservation and Recovery Act ("RCRA"),[32] the Comprehensive Environmental Response, Compensation, and Liability Act ("CERCLA"),[33] and state laws patterned after those two pieces of federal legislation snared within the scope of their liability and clean-up provisions all properties having any level of environmental contamination (and not just those properties that were so severely contaminated as to present a real risk to human health). Developers legitimately feared that, despite the relatively moderate level of contamination present on most brownfield sites, they might be required under applicable environmental laws to immediately convert brownfields into greenfields by removing all vestiges of hazardous substances from those sites. The potential cost associated with such wholesale remediation efforts made it too risky for developers to commit to redevelop brownfield sites, no matter how well located or configured those sites were.

In an effort to encourage the redevelopment of brownfield sites (and, hence, the expansion of the government's revenue base), virtually every state has now enacted legislation and designed programs intended to eliminate (or at least reduce) the barriers to the redevelopment of

---

(Fall 2009); Yuanshu Deng and Jared Eigerman, *Non-Federal Green Building Incentives*, REAL ESTATE FINANCE JOURNAL 54 (Spring 2010).

[30]   42 U.S.C. § 9601(39)(B) (2016).

[31]   42 U.S.C. § 6991 (2016).

[32]   *See* 42 U.S.C. § 6901 *et seq.* (2016).

[33]   *See* 42 U.S.C. § 9601 *et seq.* (2016).

brownfield sites. The state brownfield initiatives are generally referred to as *voluntary action programs* or *VAPs*. The following are common elements of state voluntary action programs.[34]

- *Limited Clean-Up Standards*—An essential component of each state program is the development of limited clean-up standards that do not require brownfield developers to remove all hazardous substances from the affected site. The state programs adopt risk-based approaches intended to limit the population's exposure to dangerous environmental conditions without imposing on the developer the unrealistic obligation to return the site to a fully pristine condition. By way of example, a developer might be relieved of an obligation to remove mildly contaminated soils from a site if the developer stipulates that all areas containing such contaminated soils will be capped with a concrete pad (either as part of the main building pad or a parking lot), thereby effectively eliminating any real risk that anyone will ever be exposed to the contaminated soils. Development practices of this genre are commonly referred to as *institutional controls* and go a long way to reducing the cost of redeveloping brownfield sites.

- *Covenants Not to Sue*—Most states have regulations in place authorizing the state's environmental officer to issue a covenant not to sue to a developer who completes a voluntary clean-up of a brownfield site in accordance with the limited clean-up standards mentioned under the prior heading. The developer's receipt of a covenant not to sue has the effect of insulating it from any further liability to the state with respect to the environmental condition of the site.

- *Expedited Governmental Review*—The VAPs of most states have implemented shortened regulatory timelines for the state environmental agency's review and approval of a developer-sponsored remediation plan, thereby mitigating the risk to the developer that an interminable governmental review process effectively kills its development project (under the old, but still true, adage that "time kills all deals").

---

[34] *See generally* ENVIRONMENTAL ASPECTS OF REAL ESTATE AND COMMERCIAL TRANSACTIONS: FROM BROWNFIELDS TO GREEN BUILDINGS 253–292 *(*James B. Witkin ed., 4th ed. 2011); Amy Edwards, *Brownfields Redevelopment Initiatives*, 19 No. 2 PRACTICAL REAL ESTATE LAWYER 47 (March 2003); Wendy E. Wagner, *Chapter 2: Overview of Federal and State Law Governing Brownfield Cleanups*, in BROWNFIELDS—A COMPREHENSIVE GUIDE TO REDEVELOPING CONTAMINATED PROPERTY (Todd S. Davis ed., 2002); and ENVIRONMENTAL PROTECTION AGENCY, STATE BROWNFIELDS AND VOLUNTARY RESPONSE PROGRAMS: AN UPDATE FROM THE STATES, Publication Number: EPA–560–R–09–522 (November 2009).

- *Financial and Tax Incentives*—Many states go the extra
  step of providing financial and tax incentives designed to
  encourage the redevelopment of brownfield sites. By way of
  example, a state could provide (1) a project-specific grant to
  fund a portion of the developer's costs of cleaning up a select
  brownfield site, and (2) a tax abatement to a brownfield
  project that qualifies for the government's issuance of a
  covenant not to sue.

The United States Congress has also sought to encourage the
development of brownfield sites by the passage of legislation such as the
Small Business Liability Relief and Brownfields Revitalization Act of 2001
(the "Revitalization Act").[35] The Revitalization Act provides funding to
assist state and local governments in the administration of their voluntary
action programs and grants relief from liability under CERCLA for persons
buying and then cleaning up brownfield sites in compliance with a state's
VAP.

All of the state and federal efforts mentioned above are intended to
permit a brownfield site to be developed in a cheaper and liability-free
manner. The conversion of vacant, environmentally-troubled sites into
vital redevelopment projects can have a dramatic impact on the revenue
bases of the affected governmental subdivisions.

X. DEVELOPMENT ASSISTANCE

The final category of incentives that a government can provide to
support a private real estate project is development assistance. There are
two principal sources of development assistance that a private developer
might want to consider seeking from a governmental entity.

- *Construction of Public Infrastructure*—The feasibility of
  certain development projects is inextricably tied to the
  addition   or   enhancement   of   public   infrastructure
  improvements that serve the project. By way of example, the
  development of a retail center in the suburbs may not work
  unless the state and federal governments agree to fund and
  construct a new freeway interchange that feeds into the retail
  site. Similarly, a downtown residential complex may not be
  feasible unless oversized sewer lines are extended to the
  boundary of the project site or a stoplight with right and left
  turn lanes is installed at the intersection of the two roads
  bordering the site. The government can assist such a

---

[35] *See* PUBLIC LAW NO. 107–118, 115 STAT. 2356 (codified as amended in scattered sections of
42 U.S.C. §§ 9601 *et seq.* (2016)).

development project by agreeing to design and construct the requisite infrastructure improvements at its cost.

- *Eminent Domain*—A developer's grand plans are often stymied by its inability to assemble all the land required for the subject development project. Land assemblage problems are particularly prevalent in the context of an urban redevelopment project where the land targeted as the site for the project might be owned by numerous property owners (and not just one person as is the case in many greenfield projects). One or two recalcitrant or unreachable property owners can thwart an otherwise promising real estate project. The government's exercise of its eminent domain powers can be a useful solution of last resort for the developer's land assemblage problems.

Federal, state, and local governments generally have the right to acquire private property without the property owner's consent, so long as the government acquires the property for a valid "public use" and pays the property owner "just compensation" for such acquisition.[36] While the issue of what constitutes "just compensation" is itself an interesting and complex topic,[37] it is the "public use" issue that is most germane to the question whether a government can exercise its eminent domain powers to aid a private development project. The U.S. Supreme Court's decision in *Kelo v. City of New London*[38] tackled that issue head on and, in doing so, framed a public policy debate that will rage on for years to come concerning the legitimacy of the government's use of its powers to encourage the development of a private real estate project.[39] Many of the issues raised by the Supreme Court in *Kelo* (particularly the issue of whether "economic development" standing alone is a sufficient public purpose to support a

---

[36] The takings clause of the Fifth Amendment to the United States Constitution creates these two conditions to the government's exercise of its eminent domain powers. *See* U.S. CONSTITUTION Amendment V. The constitutions of most states have provisions like the takings clause found in the U.S. Constitution.

[37] *See e.g.* Jack R. Sperber, *Just Compensation and the Valuation Concepts You Need to Know to Measure It*, in ALI-ABA COURSE OF STUDY MATERIALS, CONDEMNATION 101: HOW TO PREPARE AND PRESENT AN EMINENT DOMAIN CASE, Course #SP–007, 1 (January 2009).

[38] 545 U.S. 469 (2005).

[39] For a further discussion of the *Kelo* case and the judicial and legislative reactions to that decision, *see* Daniel B. Kelly, *Supreme Court Economics Review Symposium on Post-Kelo Reform: Pretextual Takings: Of Private Developers, Local Governments and Impermissible Favoritism*, 17 SUPREME COURT ECONOMIC REVIEW 173 (2009); Amy Brigham Boulris and Annette Lopez, *2007–2008 Update on Judicial Reactions to Kelo,* in ALI-ABA COURSE OF STUDY MATERIALS, EMINENT DOMAIN AND LAND VALUATION LITIGATION, Course #SP–006, 63 (January 2009); Ross F. Moskowitz and Joan H. Kim, *Eminent Domain: The Taking of Private Property for Public Use— An Examination of Recent New York State Decisions in Light of Kelo v. City of New London*, REAL ESTATE FINANCE JOURNAL 82 (Spring 2010); Steven J. Eagle and Lauren A. Perotti, *Coping with Kelo: A Potpourri of Legislative and Judicial Responses,* 42 REAL PROPERTY, PROBATE AND TRUST JOURNAL 799 (Winter 2008); and Andrew P. Morriss, *Supreme Court Economic Review Symposium on Post-Kelo Reform: Symbol or Substance? An Empirical Assessment of State Responses to Kelo,* 17 SUPREME COURT ECONOMIC REVIEW 237 (2009).

government action that benefits a private project) are discussed in the next section of this chapter on *Public Policy Issues.*

XI. PUBLIC POLICY ISSUES

This chapter has now addressed two of the three questions that always characterize any discussion of Stage 2 of a real estate development project—(1) why does a private development project need governmental incentives (and why does the government want to make those incentives available to the developer), and (2) what can the government do to aid the private development project? A much tougher question to answer is *SHOULD* the government provide incentives to a private development project? Answering that question requires a closer examination of the various public policy issues that a government must weigh each time a developer asks the government for help

A. THE GOVERNMENT'S BET

Before venturing into the thorny entanglement of public policy issues, it is important to first focus on the nature of the *BET* that the government makes each time it decides to provide incentives to a private development project. As noted earlier in this chapter, a government lends its support to a private development project to grow the government's revenue base and advance the government's social policy agenda. The use of incentives to serve these goals creates the following two-pronged dilemma for the government:

- In the short-term, the government's decision to provide incentives to a private project either (1) depletes the government's existing revenue base (if it uses existing revenues to provide grants or other financial subsidies to the incentivized project), or (2) defers the government's access to the new revenues generated from the private project (if it uses tax abatements or a TIF to incentivize the private project); and

- The byproduct of the government's use of incentives to serve its social policy objectives is frequently an increase in the project's development costs—a circumstance that almost always causes the developer to return to the well and ask for more financial and tax giveaways, which, in turn, further depletes the government's existing revenue base.

In other words, by using incentives to serve its long-term objectives, the government inevitably worsens its short-term revenue position.

When it provides public incentives to a private development project, the government is effectively betting that the incentivized project is a long-term success and that the existence of that project creates new jobs, increases property values, and spurs additional development in the surrounding neighborhood. If those things do not occur, then the government loses its bet, with the end result being that the government's coffers are less full than when it first decided to sponsor the incentivized project. The importance of the government making the right bet is highlighted by the fact that it is estimated that state and local governments expend between $50–80 billion annually in an effort to stimulate economic development.[40]

One economist has characterized the government's bet in the following manner.

> The issue isn't whether economic development incentives can work; empirical evidence suggests they can. The issues are whether benefits of incentives outweigh costs, and how benefits and costs are affected by local conditions and incentive design.[41]

Although the economist's statement is both thoughtful and succinct, I prefer to think about the government's bet in much less academic terms. As one who greatly enjoys sitting down at a blackjack table in Vegas, I view the decision of a government to give incentives to a private development project as being a bit like doubling down on an eleven—it produces a wonderful result if your next card has a picture on it, but it will likely cost you twice as much money if the next card is a deuce. The economic development officer's challenge is to figure out what the next card turned over by the dealer will be—a deuce or a jack.

In keeping with the blackjack analogy, I would be remiss if I didn't point out that there is nothing that forces the economic development officer to sit down at the betting table in the first place. Government can avoid making its bet if it "just says no" when it is asked to provide incentives to a private development project. The downside of that approach is, of course, that the government may lose the opportunity to enhance its long-term revenue base by helping a private developer kick off a project that ultimately proves to be wildly successful for both the developer and the government. The upside of "just saying no" is that another developer may come along at some point down the road with an idea for a better project and, even better yet, one that does not require the government's provision of any incentives.

The public policy discussion that follows examines the context in which the economic development officer makes the judgment whether to play,

---

[40] *See supra* notes 6 and 7 and accompanying text.

[41] Timothy J. Bartik, *Eight Issues for Policy Toward Economic Development Incentives,* W.E. UPJOHN INSTITUTE FOR EMPLOYMENT RESEARCH (1996). Mr. Bartik's paper was published by the Minneapolis Federal Reserve for a conference held in Washington D.C. on May 21–22, 1996, on the topic of *The Economic War among the States.*

fold, or hit when a developer asks the government to provide governmental assistance to a private development project.

B. PUBLIC PURPOSE

The first policy question that the economic development officer must answer when weighing the use of governmental incentives to aid a private development project is, Does the provision of incentives serve a valid public purpose? In answering that question, the economic development officer (with a little help from the ever friendly real estate development lawyer) needs to consult three different sources—(1) the statute that creates the incentive, (2) case law interpreting the public purpose doctrine, and (3) the one most often ignored by lawyers, the body politic. If any one of those sources provides a "no" answer to the proffered question, the economic development officer should reject the notion of providing incentives to the private development project.

1. Statutory Definition

Most statutory and constitutional provisions authorizing the use of a governmental incentive establish the existence of a public purpose as a precondition to the government's provision of such incentive. The lawyers representing both the developer and the government must begin their respective analyses of the public purpose issue with a close examination of the definition of and context in which such term is used in the enabling statutory or constitutional provision. By way of example, if the operative state statute provides that the only public purpose supporting the creation of a TIF is the remediation of blight, it then becomes the lawyers' jobs to divine whether the private development project being proposed by the developer satisfies the blight remediation test.

2. Judicial Interpretation

There is a rich body of case law interpreting the doctrine of public purpose in the context of a governmental incentives designed to aid private projects.[42] The most renown and controversial case addressing the public

---

[42] *See e.g.*, Maready v. City of Winston-Salem, 467 S.E.2d 615 (N.C. 1996) (finding a valid public purpose for the provision of approximately $13.2 million in governmental incentives for businesses agreeing to locate in Winston-Salem, North Carolina); Blinson v. State, 651 S.E.2d 268 (N.C. App. 2007) (upholding the existence of a valid public purpose for the government's provision of approximately $242 million in incentives to induce Dell, Inc. to build a facility in North Carolina); Poe v. Hillsborough County, 695 So.2d 672 (Fla. 1997) (confirming the existence of a public purpose to support the government's issuance of approximately $180 million in bonds to finance the construction of a stadium for the Tampa Bay Buccaneers). For a general discussion of the evolution of the public purpose doctrine, *see* Anne C. Choe, *Recent Development: Blinson v. State and the Continued Erosion of the Public Purpose Doctrine in North Carolina*, 87 NORTH CAROLINA LAW REVIEW 644 (2009); Thaddeus Pitney, *Loans, and Takings, and Buildings—Oh My: A Necessary Difference between Public Purpose and Public Use in Economic Development*, 56 SYRACUSE LAW REVIEW 321 (2006);and Gregory W. Fox, *Note, Public Finance and the West Side Stadium: The Future of Stadium Subsidies in New York*, 71 BROOKLYN LAW REVIEW 477 (2005).

purpose doctrine is the United States Supreme Court's 2005 decision in
Kelo v. City of New London.[43] In *Kelo,* Justice Stevens affirmed that the
City of New London's economic development objectives (new jobs and
increased tax revenue) constituted a sufficient public purpose to support
the City's exercise of its eminent domain powers to benefit a private
development project.[44] Justice Stevens' opinion triggered a populist
outrage in many parts of the country and served as the predicate for Justice
O'Connor's now famous assertion in her dissenting opinion that under the
majority opinion in *Kelo* "Nothing is to prevent the State from replacing
any Motel 6 with a Ritz Carlton, any home with a shopping mall, or any
farm with a factory."[45]

In the years following the issuance of the *Kelo* decision, the
legislatures of several states attempted to re-define "public purpose" in in
a much more restrictive fashion than was presented by the legislation that
was the subject of the City of New London's exercise of its eminent domain
powers—for example, by imposing a requirement that the only reason that
a government may exercise its eminent domain powers is to remediate
"blight," with blight being very specifically and narrowly defined to exclude
economic development. A few court cases have interpreted "public purpose"
in a more constrained fashion than did Justice Stevens in *Kelo*.[46] Having
said that, the Supreme Court's decision in *Kelo* remains the law of the land
and continues to serve as instructive precedent for the interpretation of the
doctrine of "public purpose."

There is a common theme running throughout *Kelo* and most of the
other case law on the public purpose doctrine—specifically, that the courts
are extremely hesitant to overturn a legislative finding that the provision
of a public incentive to a private project is supported by a valid public
purpose. This is especially true in the case law examining the scope of the
"public purpose" doctrine in the context of a government's use of its
incentive powers other than eminent domain. Many commentators have
adopted the position that the public purpose doctrine should be construed
more strictly in the context of a governmental taking than it should in the
context of the provision of other governmental incentives (principally
because of the more direct involvement of private property rights in the
eminent domain arena).[47] Whether the judiciary's extreme deference to
legislative findings of public purpose will continue in the post-*Kelo* legal

---

[43] 545 U.S. 469 (2005).

[44] *Id.* at 484–486.

[45] *See id.* at 503.

[46] *See e.g.,* Norwood v. Horney, 110 Ohio St.3d 353 (2006). *See also* the discussion of post-*Kelo* case law in Boulris, *supra* note 39; and Moskowitz, *supra* note 39.

[47] *See* Pitney, *supra* note 42, at 330–332; and Audrey G. McFarlane, *Local Economic Development Incentives in an Era of Globalization: The Exploitation of Decentralization and Mobility,* 35 URBAN LAWYER 305, 312–313 (2003).

and political environments is a question that will likely play out in the courts over the next decade.

The bottom line is that the case law on the public purpose topic is sufficiently nuanced and varied by jurisdiction that a lawyer spending time structuring and negotiating incentive packages has no choice but to stay well-versed on the decisions rendered by the courts of the state in which the lawyer practices. After mastering those judicial nuances, the real estate development lawyer must then be prepared to "spin" that law in a manner that favors the developer in its quest to receive governmental incentives for its private development project.

3.   Political Decision

The most important definition of public purpose is found not in the language of an enabling statute or the text of an appellate court decision, but rather in the constantly evolving opinions of the true gatekeepers of governmental incentive packages—the mayors, city council members, county commissioners, township trustees, economic development officers, and other government officials who are asked on a daily basis to make an evaluation as to whether a particular private development project merits the receipt of a governmental incentive. There is, unfortunately no guidebook to provide a real estate development lawyer with the specifics of this political definition of public purpose. The political definition of public purpose changes daily (and sometimes hourly) based on the sentiments of the electorate and the perceptions of such sentiments by the government's elected and appointed officials. An incentive package that is meticulously crafted by the developer's lawyer to comply with the public purpose parameters specified by applicable statutory and case law is nonetheless doomed for rejection if the developer is unable to convince four of seven township trustees to vote for it. No truer words were ever spoken than when a city council member commented to me in the middle of a heated discussion that "public purpose is what I say it is."

Practice Tip #6-3: Hiring Political Clout

The grant of governmental incentives is, at its essence, a political process. In almost every instance, a developer's receipt of an incentive is dependent upon a discretionary legislative or regulatory determination being made that the developer's project is worthy of assistance from the public sector. That determination is part legal are the tests set forth in the enabling statute satisfied), but even more political. When casting a vote for or against the grant of an incentive, a government official tasked with that responsibility must answer two basic questions—(1) is the grant of the incentive good public policy, and (2) will the grant of the incentive poll favorably with the official's voting constituency? The real estate development lawyer's job is to persuade the government official that the answer to both those questions is "yes."

It has been my experience that a real estate development lawyer is often well-advised to retain outside counsel to help a developer secure the sought-after incentives. This is especially true when the development project is located outside of the lawyer's primary practice jurisdiction. In hiring outside counsel, the development lawyer should look for someone who knows local politics and has personal access to those government officials who will be making the ultimate determination on the grant of the incentives to assist the developer's project. While hiring such political clout is important, the real estate development lawyer must make sure to retain someone the lawyer is comfortable with becoming the public face for the developer during the course of the incentive negotiations. Hiring the mayor's best drinking buddy will not work unless that person also has the talent and style to do the job in a manner commensurate with the developer's overall approach to the real estate development business. Stated differently, it is crucial that outside incentive counsel be retained not just for who he knows, but also for what he knows.

C. THE "BUT FOR" TEST

It is common for a developer to approach its state and local economic development officers with a simple proposition—that is, the government needs to provide a laundry list of incentives to support the developer's private project or the project will never be built. When braced with such a comment, the economic development officers (and, ultimately, the members of the legislative and regulatory bodies that must cast their votes for or against the incentive grant) must decide whether the project satisfies or fails the political **but for test**. Is the developer correct in saying that the development will not occur *BUT FOR* the provision of governmental incentives or is the developer bluffing to further feather its already plush nest? Ultimately, the success of the government's bet on the project is dependent on how accurately it answers the "but for" test.

If the economic development officer decides to call the developer's bluff based on a belief that the project will proceed with or without incentives and the developer then pulls the plug on the project, the development officer probably should start looking for another job. However, the officer's tenure as a civil servant will also be called into question if officer gives into the developer's demands and further depletes the government's coffers, only to subsequently learn that the project was destined to go full speed ahead with or without the assistance of the state and local governments.

It is a commonly accepted notion that government should not provide incentives to a project if the project would have been developed without the incentives.[48] A recent study issued by the Ohio Department of Development sums up this point by in the following fashion.

> [N]ot all development requires direct public assistance, and public assistance is not an entitlement. Incentives should be concentrated on encouraging those projects that would not go forward in our state without incentives.[49]

However, as noted in a report presented to the Federal Reserve Bank of Atlanta, "it is impossible to know what might have happened without incentives."[50] In order to realistically assess whether a project would have occurred without public support, government officials need to get inside the developer's head by receiving, reviewing, and analyzing all of the financial, demographic, marketing, and other development information that the developer took into account when making its decision concerning the feasibility of the proposed project. Obvious questions abound as to both the completeness and accuracy of the information provided to the government by the developer and the government's capability of reviewing that information to make a well-reasoned decision of the project's feasibility. Therefore, while government must always confront the "but for" test when deciding whether it will aid a private development project, the application of that test is inherently much more ad hoc and political in nature than it is empirical.

A trending thought among economists is that the governments are not applying the "but for" test in an appropriate manner. A study conducted by the Institute on Taxation and Economic Policy concluded that:

> Based on the "consensus" estimates in the academic literature about the responsiveness of business decisions to taxes, as many as 9 out of 10 hiring and investment decisions subsidized with tax incentives would have occurred even if the incentive did not exist."[51]

---

[48] *See* Lefcoe, *supra* note 11, at 33– 36; Kenyon, *supra* note 16, at 46–49; and CHICAGO METROPOLITAN AGENCY FOR PLANNING, ECONOMIC DEVELOPMENT INCENTIVES 3 (June 2009).

[49] *See* OHIO DEPARTMENT OF DEVELOPMENT, OHIO ECONOMIC DEVELOPMENT INCENTIVE STUDY 41 (May 2009).

[50] *See* Jessica LeVeen Farr, *Attracting Economic Development—At What Cost?* 15 No. 3 PARTNERS IN COMMUNITY AND ECONOMIC DEVELOPMENT 1 (December 22, 2005). *See also* Timothy J. Bartik and Richard D. Bingham, *Can Economic Development Programs Be Evaluated,* DILEMMAS OF URBAN ECONOMIC DEVELOPMENT, 246, 250 (Richard D. Bingham and Robert Miers eds., 1997).

[51] *See* Carl Davis, INSTITUTE ON TAXATION AND ECONOMIC POLICY, TAX INCENTIVES: COSTLY FOR STATES, DRAG ON THE NATION 1 (August 12, 2013); Peters, *supra* note 7, at 32; Peter Fisher, SELLING SNAKE OIL TO THE STATES, JOINT REPORT BY GOOD JOBS FIRST AND IOWA POLICY PROJECT (November 2012), available at http://www.goodjobsfirst.org/snakeoiltothestates; and Timothy J. Bartik, *Who Benefits from State and Local Economic Policies*, W.E. Upjohn Institute (1991).

Whether this trend in economic theory gains traction in the years to come remains an open issue. It is, however, a virtual certainty that governments granting incentives to aid private development projects will soon begin to require developers to provide detailed data to support the developer's assertion that the aided project cannot move forward *BUT FOR* the receipt of the requested governmental incentives.

D. THE ZERO-SUM GAME

On the public policy front, the ***zero-sum game*** is a close relative to the "but for" test. As noted under the previous heading, the "but for" test requires governmental officials to determine whether a developer's project would happen with or without the provision of governmental incentives. The zero-sum game comes into play when the question is not whether the developer's project will happen (the but for test), but rather whether it will happen in jurisdiction A or jurisdiction B? The zero-sum game is played when the developer successfully pits one jurisdiction against another in a crusade to maximize the amount of incentives the developer receives for the project.[52] The bidding war that breaks out when jurisdictions compete for a project may be pejoratively characterized as an "economic race to the bottom" as jurisdictions unnecessarily give away their tax bases by engaging in incentive competitions with other jurisdictions.

The "zero-sum" nomenclature refers to the fact that the larger economy (be it global, federal, state, or local) is not affected one way or the other by the developer's decision where to locate its project. If the developer selects jurisdiction A over jurisdiction B, the gains flowing to jurisdiction A are directly and equally offset by the losses flowing to jurisdiction B.[53] In the zero-sum game, the developer wins, the larger economy loses (or at best breaks even), and jurisdictions A and B are the recipients of offsetting gains and losses.

The public policy issue presented by the zero-sum game is whether a legitimate public purpose is served by a governmental entity's provision of incentives to cause a developer to choose one jurisdiction over another as the location for its project. Should a political subdivision be required to think about the greater good that would best be served if no incentives were provided to the developer, thereby maximizing the tax revenues generated

---

[52] *See e.g.*, Farr, *supra* note 50, at 2. *But see* Bartik, *supra* note 41, at 3–4, for a presentation of the opposing view that "competition should bid business taxes down to equal the marginal cost of providing businesses with public services, . . . minus the marginal social benefit the businesses provide by creating jobs. Such a business tax system is economically efficient."

[53] One writer has noted that what results from interstate competition for a particular business or project is "at best, not job creation but job relocation from one area in the Unites States to another." *See* Peter D. Enrich, *Business Tax Incentives: A Status Report,* 34 URBAN LAWYER 415, 416 (2002). *See also* Davis, *supra* note 7, at 2; Emily Badger, *Should We Ban States and Cities from Offering Big Tax Breaks for Jobs*, WASHINGTON POST (September 15, 2014), https://www.washingtonpost.com/news/wonk/wp/2014/09/15/should-we-ban-states-and-cities-from-offering-big-tax-breaks-for-jobs/; and Kenyon, *supra* note 16, at 27.

from the project and forcing the developer to make a location decision on the merits and not on the artifice of a jurisdiction's incentive package? Or is it legitimate for a governmental political subdivision to fashion whatever incentives are required to cause a developer to select its community over a neighboring community?

Numerous scholarly articles have been written about the relative policy merits of permitting political subdivisions to compete for private development projects through the offering of incentives.[54] Most of those articles take the position that the zero-sum game is detrimental to the economy as a whole and that legislation should be adopted that prevents states and local jurisdictions from offering incentives designed to cause a business to relocate to another state or locale.[55] However, as long as tax revenues are generated and spent at the local level, it seems likely that governmental entities will continue to play the zero-sum game.[56]

E. EFFICACY OF INCENTIVES

The final public policy question that must be addressed by government officials is whether governmental incentives really work. Governmental incentives work only if (1) the revenues generated from the incentivized project are greater than the government's cost of providing the incentives, and (2) the project would not have been developed but for the grant of the incentives.

A fair amount of analysis and self-examination has occurred in recent years concerning the efficacy of the use of governmental incentives. A 2009 study commissioned by the Chicago Metropolitan Agency for Planning concluded that "on balance, the available research on the effectiveness and impacts of economic development incentives yields mixed results."[57] Recent reports examining the governmental incentive programs offered in

---

[54] *See* literature summary discussed in CHICAGO METROPOLITAN AGENCY FOR PLANNING, *supra* note 48, at 32–36. *See also* Bartik, *supra* note 41; and McFarlane, *supra* note 47.

[55] *See* Melvin L. Burnstein and Arthur J. Rolnick, *Congress Should End the Economic War Among the States,* 96 STATE TAX NOTES 125–44 (June 27, 1996) for a discussion of the perceived need for Congress to pass federal legislation prohibiting states from competing with one another to retain and attract businesses through the provision of tax and other financial incentives. Also, taxpayer lawsuits have been filed in the last several years seeking to use the Commerce Clause of the United States Constitution to invalidate a state's use of tax incentives to convince a business to locate within its borders. *See e.g.*, DaimlerChrysler Corp. v. Cuno, 547 U.S. 332 (2006), *vacating and remanding in part* 386 F.3d 738 (6th Cir. 2004); Olson v. State, 742 N.W.2d 681 (Minn. Ct. App. 2007); and Blinson v. State, 651 S.E.2d 268 (N.C. App. 2007). Those cases have all been decided in the government's favor. *See generally*, Morgan L. Holcomb and Nicholas Allen Smith, *Community Efforts to Attract and Retain Corporations: Legal and Policy Implications of State and Local Tax Incentives and Eminent Domain: The Post-Cuno Litigation Landscape*, 58 CASE WESTERN RESERVE LAW REVIEW 1157 (Summer 2008).

[56] One of the most glaring examples of the dangers involved in acquiescing to the zero-sum game is the incentive battle waged in recent years by the two Kansas Cities—one in Kansas and one in Missouri. *See The New Border War,* THE ECONOMIST (March 22, 2014).

[57] CHICAGO METROPOLITAN AGENCY FOR PLANNING, *supra* note 48, at 18.

Michigan and Ohio have reached similar, inconclusive conclusions.[58] On the other hand, two recent studies published by national think tanks share the conclusions that:

> Unfortunately, despite the enormous expenditures being made on these programs, the evidence suggests that tax incentives are of little benefit to the states and localities that offer them, and that they are actually a drag on national economic growth.[59]

The essential question that must be addressed by government officials is whether the incentives provided by the government truly impact developer and user conduct. Does a developer decide to proceed with a particular project in a particular location as a direct result of its receipt of governmental incentives or are the provided governmental incentives just a way for the developer to increase its NOI and otherwise enhance the value of its project? Does a prospective tenant or buyer decide to lease or buy space in a project because of its receipt of incentives or are those incentives truly incidental to its space decision and, as such, just a pot sweetener?

The answers to these questions depend, in large part, on the identity of the responder. Most government officials take the position that "incentives remain one of the only tools available to localities attempting to create jobs and enhance their revenue streams."[60] Legal scholars and representatives of taxpayer groups tend to conclude that "they don't work— no business executive worth his salt will make a location decision based on state . . . incentives."[61] Economists tend to equivocate (imagine that) by pointing out that the "upshot . . . is that on this most basic question of all— whether incentives induce significant new investment or jobs—we simply do not know the answer."[62] Finally the intended recipient of the governmental incentive (a developer or user) characteristically responds by saying "they work for me."

My four decades of experience in the private sector tells me that incentives do work—sometimes. There are good projects that create jobs, add to the government's revenue base, and advance socially important

---

[58] *See* OHIO DEPARTMENT OF DEVELOPMENT, *supra* note 49; and Anderson Economic Group LLC, MICHIGAN'S BUSINESS TAX INCENTIVES (2009).

[59] Davis, *supra* note 7, at 1. *See also* Kenyon, *supra* note 16, at 59.

[60] CHICAGO METROPOLITAN AGENCY FOR PLANNING, *supra* note 48, at 3.

[61] David Brunori, *The Politics of State Taxation: Helping States to Hurt Themselves,* STATE TAX NOTES 752 (June 6, 2005).

[62] Peters, *supra* note 7, 27 (2004). In defense of economists generally (and Messrs. Peters and Fisher specifically), it should be noted that there is a growing consensus among economists that "there are very good reasons—theoretical, empirical and practical—to believe that economic development incentives have little or no impact on firm location and investment decisions." *See id.* There is also a developing consensus that, while incentives "rarely tip the location choice . . . across different regions . . . [they] do contribute somewhat to interregional business location decisions." CHICAGO METROPOLITAN AGENCY FOR PLANNING, *supra* note 48, at 32. *See also* Kenyon, *supra* note 16, at 26–29.

goals that would simply not be feasible without the receipt of governmental incentives. I rather fancy the accuracy of the following quote by Greg LeRoy of Good Jobs First.

> An incentive is for something that should happen, but isn't happening, that won't happen unless . . . [the government] gets involved: bringing a grocery store to a food desert, helping an ex-con get a job, cleaning up a brownfield. If you spend money to do these things, those are worthy incentives, not subsidies, windfalls or giveaways.[63]

There are, however, also plenty of projects that do not serve any of the government's economic, social, or political objectives, but that nonetheless receive governmental incentives simply because that is the way business is done in the 21st century. It is the government's job to examine the existing facts and circumstances surrounding a development project to ferret out which incentives work and when those incentives are needed to encourage a private development project.

F.   REMEDIES FOR FAILED INCENTIVES

A related issue is what happens if the benefits produced from the use of governmental incentives do not materialize in the intended manner—for example, the project doesn't produce the 500 new jobs heralded by the developer or the developer delays its construction of the affordable housing units that were central to its receipt of a density bonus? The trend in recent years is to clearly articulate in a development agreement signed by the developer and the government the specific actions that must be taken by the developer to establish its entitlement to and continued retention of the benefit of the governmental incentives. By way of example, the development agreement could recite that the project's payroll tax rebate is contingent upon the project producing 500 new jobs and the developer completing its affordable housing units within three years from the date of the parties' execution of the development agreement.

The key from the government's perspective is that the development agreement must contain effective governmental remedies for the developer's failure to meet the conditions recited in the agreement. The following are examples of remedies that can be used to protect the interests of the government if the developer fails to comply with the conditions and obligations placed upon it under the terms of the applicable development agreement:

- A denial of a governmental certificate of occupancy for the project;

---

[63]   Badger, *supra* note 53, at 5.

- An automatic suspension of the continued operation of the incentive; or

- A required repayment by the developer of the economic benefit of the incentive (commonly referred to as a *clawback*).

The above protections are intended to allocate to the developer the risk that the project fails to generate the intended governmental benefit due to the developer's failure to perform. The same protections are not, however, typically afforded the government if the project fails to produce the anticipated benefit, because of a dislocation in the market or another cause beyond the developer's control (including an initial misreading of the market dynamics by the government).

G. PROPOSED INCENTIVE REFORM

In recent years, there has been a clamor by economists and legal theorists for the adoption at every level of government (federal, state, and local) of legislative and regulatory reforms to governmental incentive programs.[64] Examples of the proposals made by the reform proponents are (1) the establishment of regional cooperation pacts and revenue-sharing arrangements to eliminate inter-jurisdiction competition for the same project, and (2) the passage of legislation at the federal level to preclude states from granting incentives to lure businesses to relocate from another state (a so-called "anti-poaching" statute). The issue of the advisability and feasibility of these and other reforms being bandied about in academia is well beyond the scope of this chapter and, most certainly, the competency of the author.

What I can say with confidence is that any reform of the governmental incentive process must confront the following four realities:

- Developers will take the incentives offered to them even if they do not need them;

- One jurisdiction's grant of an incentive puts pressure on other jurisdictions to follow suit—the so-called "incentive race";

- Politicians like to pick winners and losers (and take credit for the winners); and

- Nobody wants the governmental incentive process to be transparent (other than economists, professors, and taxpayers).

---

[64] *See e.g.,* McFarlane, *supra* note 47, at 315; Kenyon, *supra* note 16, at 52–61; and Davis, *supra* note 7, at 3–4.

XII. THE PERILS OF A PUBLIC-PRIVATE PARTNERSHIP

The focus of this chapter has thus far been on the benefits produced for both the private and public sectors by the government's provision of incentives to encourage the development of a private real estate project. When all the stars align properly, the collaborative efforts of a private developer and the government (a so-called *public-private partnership* or a *PPP*) can produce wonderful results for both the public and private sectors—witness such high profile PPP projects as Faneuil Hall Marketplace in Boston, the Inner Harbor redevelopment in Baltimore, and the Arena District project in Columbus, Ohio. There is, however, a definite downside to the creation of a PPP from the perspectives of both the developer and the government.

From the government's perspective, the negatives associated with the creation of a PPP are mostly political in nature. A governmental entity that is interested in supporting development within its borders has little choice but to collaborate with the private sector—for the simple reason that government does not possess the expertise, experience, or staffing needed to pull off a complicated real estate development project. The necessity underlying its participation in a PPP does not, however, insulate the government from the cries of the general public that the government has sold out to rich developers and is not looking out for the best interests of its citizenry. If a PPP with a private developer fails, the result is often the one thing that both appointed and elected government officials fear most—the incumbent party's loss at the next election.

Participation in a PPP also has a decided downside for the private developer. A developer who is used to controlling its own destiny and being able to respond quickly to market changes and development challenges will find its collaboration with the public sector to be frustrating and sometimes excruciatingly painful. The following are a few negatives associated with a developer's participation in a PPP.

- *Loss of Development Control*—An inevitable consequence of a developer's request for governmental incentives is the developer's loss of a level of control over the design, construction, and operation of its development project. A governmental entity providing economic and development support for a private project typically demands a role in the development process (in much the same way that a private equity investor demands a presence at the table when it provides funding for a private development project). From the developer's perspective, the participation of the public sector in the development process is particularly rankling for two reasons—(1) development is a dynamic and often chaotic process that is a bit like the making of sausage—in other words, a process that, by definition, does not stand up well to public scrutiny, and (2) most developers believe that government officials are clueless when it comes to the reality of project economics and private real estate markets.

- *Protracted Development Schedules*—Negotiating and approving a PPP is an exacting and complex process that often takes an inordinate amount of the developer's time and energy. As a result, a PPP project takes much longer to plan and complete than does the typical private development project—a circumstance that can call into question the overall profitability of the project.

- *Increased Project Costs*—PPP projects customarily cost more than wholly private development projects for two reasons—(1) the often extraordinary legal and other transactional costs associated with the negotiation and approval of the governmental incentive package, and (2) the direct costs of complying with those governmentally-mandated construction practices that are frequently part and parcel of a PPP-supported project—for example, the adoption of "green" building practices or the compliance with local prevailing wage rules.

The confluence of these three circumstances means that it is much tougher for a developer of a PPP project to properly respond to market conditions and complete the project on budget and on time—all hallmarks of a successful real estate project. For these reasons, most private developers are hesitant to effect a PPP unless doing so is necessary to make the project feasible.

Practice Tip #6-4: Preparing the Developer for a PPP

If a developer decides to embark on the path of developing its project as a PPP (despite the above warnings about the downside of doing so), the real estate development lawyer should counsel the developer to abide by the following rules.

- *Make sure the public partner is capable of doing the deal—As is the case when selecting a private sector partner, it is essential that the developer make a realistic assessment as to whether its putative public partner has the requisite expertise, financial standing, and political command to deliver on its promise to provide incentives and other governmental support for the developer's project.*

- ***Protect the pro forma at all costs***—*The developer should not be bashful about the level of financial return it needs to receive from the project. While it certainly does not want to openly flaunt the projected profitability of a PPP project, the developer must also resist the public sector's attempt to get the developer to agree to concessions that negatively impact the project's NOI.*

- ***Sell the "big picture" and the "moment"***—*When seeking to secure public incentives for its project, the developer needs to refine its sales pitch to cater to the tastes of the intended public audience. That audience is unlikely to be swayed by details concerning the quality of the project's construction or the efficiency of the project's cost structure. The public wants to know three things—(1) how many jobs the project might create (note the use of the word "might"), (2) how many dollars the project might (there's that word again) add to the government's revenue base, and (3) how the project will positively impact the city's landscape (lots of pretty pictures required for this one). In selling its public audience on the benefits of its project, the developer should stick with big picture talking points and avoid putting too much detail into the public domain concerning the developer's development plan. Finally, the developer must sell the "moment"—that is, what the proposed project can do for the government right now (wholly ignoring how the site might be developed by someone else in the future).*

- ***Always count your votes***—*Obtaining the requisite governmental approvals and incentives for a private development project is, at its essence, a political process. It is all about getting a majority of the ordinary people serving on city council, the county commission, or township board of trustees to vote for the developer's project. Every action taken by the developer and its legal team during the incentive negotiation process must be directed to getting and keeping the votes needed to secure passage of the developer's incentive package.*

XIII. SUMMARY

The government is an active player in the development of every commercial real estate project. Regardless whether the government's participation is limited to it serving as a gatekeeper in the issuance of those approvals required for the commencement and prosecution of project construction or as a more full-bodied provider of governmental incentives, it is incumbent upon the real estate development lawyer to appreciate the business, legal, and political considerations that surround the government's participation in the development process. As such, this important second stage of a real estate development project requires the lawyer to be part legal technician and part political advisor.

I want to end this chapter with one concluding thought about the role that governmental incentives play in the development of private real estate projects. While legal scholars and economists continue to debate the issue of whether the government should provide incentives to aid private development projects, the fact of the matter is that such incentives are more prevalent in today's marketplace than they have ever been. Indeed, the receipt of governmental incentives is fast becoming the "new normal" for the real estate development industry. The successful real estate lawyer of the future must not only be comfortable counseling the developer about representations, warranties, and title defects, but also about TIFs, abatements, and incentive zoning.

CHAPTER 7

STAGE 3: FORMING AND CAPITALIZING THE PROJECT ENTITY

∎ ∎ ∎

I. INTRODUCTION

I recently ran across the following quote from a seasoned real estate lawyer:

> Contrary to what some attorneys might believe, very few attorneys make money for a client; the reverse is ordinarily true. It is more probable that an attorney will lose money for a client by being untimely or so complicating a factor as to render the transaction uneconomical.[1]

Stage 3 of the real estate development process presents the real estate development lawyer with an opportunity to disprove the accuracy of this quote (which I nonetheless believe to be generally true). When it comes to structuring the entity that owns the project, a real estate development lawyer who is well-versed in tax, corporate, finance, and partnership law can add real value to the developer's project.

This chapter first looks at those tax and non-tax factors that serve as the guideposts for the lawyer in designing the ownership and capital structure that best serves the developer's business objectives. It then moves on to an examination of the "bewildering array of ownership entity choices"[2] and how the selection of the appropriate entity is influenced by the investment goals and business objectives of the providers of the capital that is needed to kick off the developer's project. The chapter concludes with a detailed discussion of the myriad of economic, operational, and tax issues that must be taken into consideration by the real estate development lawyer when drafting the documents that govern the formation and conduct of the owning entity and the relationship between the developer and its outside equity investors. Particular attention is paid to the seminal issue present at Stage 3—that is, how are the financial results produced by

---

[1]   *See* John D. Hastie, *Real Estate Acquisition, Development and Disposition from the Developer's Perspective*, in ALI-ABA COURSE OF STUDY MATERIALS, MODERN REAL ESTATE TRANSACTIONS: PRACTICAL STRATEGIES FOR REAL ESTATE ACQUISITION, DISPOSITION AND OWNERSHIP, Course No. SS–012, 1, 54 (July 2010).

[2]   *See* PHILLIP T. KOLBE AND GAYLON E. GREER, INVESTMENT ANALYSIS FOR REAL ESTATE DECISIONS 196 (7th ed. 2009).

the development project allocated between the developer and the outside equity investor.

It should be noted that it is not unusual for the developer to provide all the capital initially required to develop a commercial real estate project. However, for instructional purposes, this chapter proceeds on the assumption that most of the capital needed to fund the development project is provided by one or more outside equity investors, with the remainder of the required capital being provided by the developer. Where the context permits, references to the "owners" or "investors" include both the developer and its outside equity investors. As was the case in earlier chapters of this book, the terms "equity" and "capital" are used interchangeably to refer to the cash or other property contributed to the project by the developer and the outside equity investors.

II. BUSINESS OBJECTIVES SERVED BY THE CHOICE OF ENTITY

There are three business objectives that must be taken into consideration when selecting the optimal structure for the entity that will own the developer's real estate project. Those three objectives are discussed below.

A. AVOIDANCE OF DOUBLE TAXATION

In most situations, the positive cash flow produced from a real estate project is distributed to the beneficial owners of that project no less frequently than annually. It should always be the goal of the person designing the ownership entity structure to avoid subjecting the project's income to taxation both when earned by the project entity and then again when the cash flow associated with that income is distributed to the project's beneficial owners. Subjecting the same income stream to this type of *double taxation* reduces the amount of cash that can be pocketed by the developer and its investors by increasing the tax dollars paid to the federal, state, and local tax authorities.

The negative impact that double taxation has on the investors' economic returns is illustrated in the following simple example.

Example 7-1: Assume that Project X generates the following annual returns from its rental operations:

- Net cash flow from operations—$500,000; and

- Taxable income—$400,000.[3]

---

[3] The taxable income and cash flow generated by a real estate project are produced under separate calculations that factor in, among other items, (1) non-cash deductions from taxable income such as depreciation, and (2) non-deductible expenditures from cash flow, such as debt principal payments and capital expenditures.

Assume further that the investors in Project X are two individuals who have agreed that all available cash flow from the project will be distributed to them at the end of each calendar year. Finally, assume that the investors in Project X are both in the 39.6% tax bracket for federal income tax purposes.[4]

If Project X is subject to only one level of taxation (imposed at the individual investor level), then the annual *after-tax return* to the investors from their investment in Project X is $341,600, computed as follows:

Net cash flow from project operations	$500,000
Less: Federal income tax paid by investors	
(Taxable income of $400,000 × 39.6% tax rate)	($158,400)
After-tax return to investors	**$341,600**

If, however, the project is subjected to two levels of tax on its earnings (once at the entity level at the maximum marginal corporate tax rate of 35%[5] and then again at the investor level at the current maximum dividend tax rate of 20%)[6], then the annual after-tax return to the investors is reduced to $288,000, computed as follows:

Net cash flow from project operations	$500,000
Less: Federal income tax paid by entity	
(Taxable income of $400,000 × 35% tax rate)	($140,000)
Cash flow available for distribution to investors	$360,000
Less: Federal income tax paid by investors	
(Dividend income of $360,000 × 20% tax rate)	($72,000)
After-tax return to investors	**$288,000**

Under the above example, the imposition of a second level of tax at the entity level results in $53,600 of project cash flow being taken away from

---

[4] As of the date of the writing of this chapter, the 39.6% rate is the maximum marginal tax rate imposed on ordinary income earned by an individual taxpayer. *See* I.R.C. § 1(i)(3). Most real estate investors also pay an additional 3.8% net investment income tax on the income generated by their investment in commercial real estate projects. *See* I.R.C. § 1411. For the sake of simplicity, an investor's net investment income tax liability is not taken into consideration in Example 7-1.

[5] *See* I.R.C. § 11(b).

[6] *See* I.R.C. § 1(h)(11).

the investors and placed in the coffers of the IRS—a result that is anathema to all taxpayers, but particularly so to real estate investors.

Practice Tip #7-1 that follows this section makes the point that the real estate development lawyer achieves the avoidance of double taxation objective by making sure that the entity that owns the developer's real estate project is taxed as a "partnership" for federal income tax purposes. Prior to 1996, practitioners were required to engage in a complicated analysis based on state law considerations to determine whether an entity could legitimately be treated as a partnership for federal income tax purposes (and, thus, avoid the double taxation of a real estate project's income stream). The IRS' adoption in 1996 of the self-styled "check the box regulations" has greatly simplified the analysis of whether an entity is properly classified as a partnership for tax purposes.[7] Under the check the box regulations, most unincorporated businesses (expressly including limited liability companies, general partnerships, and limited partnerships) are automatically classified as "partnerships" for federal income tax purposes unless an entity expressly elects to be taxed as a C corporation by "checking the box" to be excluded from the operation of the Subchapter K of the Internal Revenue Code. As a result, avoiding double taxation is now a readily achievable administrative task for the well-informed real estate development lawyer.

Practice Tip #7-1: Pass-Through Tax Entities

Example 7-1 illustrates how subjecting the income stream of a real estate project to double taxation has the effect of "robbing Peter to pay Paul," with Peter being the poor real estate owner and Paul being the monolithic force known as the Internal Revenue Service. The real estate development lawyer's job is to design an entity structure that eliminates a second tax imposed at the entity level.

The need to avoid subjecting the project's income to two levels of tax leads the real estate development lawyer into the confounding world of partnership taxation under Subchapter K of the Internal Revenue Code.[8] If the goal of subjecting the real estate project's income to a single level of tax is to be achieved, the entity selected to hold title to the project must be taxed as a "partnership. For this purpose, a "partnership" means all those business entities that are taxed under Subchapter K of the Code and includes general partnerships, limited partnerships, and limited liability companies. Corporations (both C and S corporations) are the principal non-partnership tax entities.

---

[7]   *See* Treas. Reg. § 301.7701–1.
[8]   *See* I.R.C. §§ 701–777.

Before focusing on what it means for an entity to be taxed as a partnership, it is advisable to take note of how Judge Raum of the United States Tax Court characterized the workings of Subchapter K.

The distressingly complex and confusing nature of the provisions of subchapter K present a formidable obstacle to the comprehension of these provisions without the expenditure of a disproportionate amount of time and effort even by one who is sophisticated in tax matters with many years of experience in the tax field. . . . Surely, a statute has not achieved "simplicity" when its complex provisions may confidently be dealt with by at most only a comparatively small number of specialists who have been initiated into its mysteries.[9]

Given Judge Raum's cautionary note about Subchapter K, it would seem senseless to try to summarily describe the fundamental principles of partnership taxation. Unfortunately, I have no choice but to try to do so. This is, after all, a treatise on real estate development law and not on partnership taxation. Therefore, I do not have the luxury (or undoubtedly the competence) to explore the complexities of Subchapter K in a multi-volume text as did Messrs. McKee, Nelson, and Whitmire in their landmark book FEDERAL TAXATION OF PARTNERSHIPS AND PARTNERS.[10] Having said that, the principles of partnership taxation are so fundamental to the practice of the real estate development lawyer that I am left at this juncture with the unenviable option of trying in 1,000 words or less to give the reader an overall sense of what it means to be taxed as a partnership.

The following is a quick bullet point summary of the basics of partnership taxation under Subchapter K of the Code. All references in the following summary to "partnerships" and "partners" include all entities subject to Subchapter K and all equity participants in those entities.

- *A partnership is not a taxable entity. As such, a partnership does not pay any federal income tax, thereby achieving the investors' objective of avoiding the double taxation of the income stream associated with a real estate project*

- *All partnership's items of taxable income and loss are "passed through" to its partners (hence, the characterization of an entity taxed as a partnership under Subchapter K as **a pass-through entity**).*

---

[9]   David A. Foxman, 41 TC 535, 551, note 9 (1964).

[10]   *See* WILLIAM S. MCKEE, WILLIAM F. NELSON, AND ROBERT L. WHITMIRE, FEDERAL TAXATION OF PARTNERSHIPS AND PARTNERS (4th ed. 2007). I heartily recommend the McKee book to all those wanting to understand both the intricacies of Subchapter K and the logic on which it was constructed. During my almost 40 years of practice, I have relied on the McKee treatise more than any other resource material.

- *Each partner reports its share of the partnership's income and loss on the partner's separate income tax return. The federal income tax payable on the income and loss generated by the partnership's activities is, therefore, calculated based on the personal tax situation of each partner (including the marginal tax rate applicable to such partner).*

- *The amount, character, and timing of the income and loss passed through to the partners is, however, determined at the partnership level.[11] The partnership (and not any individual partner) is responsible for adopting the accounting method, taxable year, and other tax elections that are necessary to determine the amount and character of the income or loss to be passed through to the partners.*

- *Each partner's share of the partnership's income and loss is determined based upon the allocation provisions contained in the partnership agreement.[12]*

- *A partner may not deduct its share of partnership losses to the extent such losses exceed the partner's basis in its partnership interest.[13] For this purpose, a partner's initial basis in its partnership interest is generally equal to the amount of cash and the fair market value of property contributed by it to the partnership, plus its share of partnership liabilities.[14] The basis of the partner's partnership interest is thereafter adjusted to reflect the partner's share of the partnership's income and loss, any contributions made to or distributions received from the partnership, and any changes in the amount of the partnership's liabilities.*

- *Contributions made to the partnership by a partner (whether in cash or in-kind) are generally made tax-free.[15]*

---

[11] The reason why such items are determined at the entity level has been characterized as "necessary to avoid the administrative nightmare that would result if each partner had to calculate her own share of partnership income using her own accounting method, taxable year, method of depreciation, etc." *See* L. CUNNINGHAM AND N. CUNNINGHAM, THE LOGIC OF SUBCHAPTER K: A CONCEPTUAL GUIDE TO THE TAXATION OF PARTNERSHIPS 8 (3rd ed. 2006).

[12] Under the Treasury Regulations promulgated under Section 704(b) of the Internal Revenue Code, the tax allocation provisions of the partnership agreement will be respected for federal income tax purposes so long as those provisions either have "substantial economic effect" or are otherwise in accordance with the "partners' interests in the partnership." *See* Treas. Reg. § 1–704-1(b), (1) and (3). The rules governing the allocation of items of taxable income and loss among the equity participants in a pass-through tax entity are extremely complex and clearly beyond the scope of this chapter. For an excellent discussion of those tax rules, *see* McKEE, *supra* note 10, at ¶ 11.02; and Gary E. Fluhrer and Robert G. Gottlieb, *Until the Tax Lawyer Arrives: Understanding Tax Provisions in LLC Agreements,* in ACREL PAPERS 595 (March 2004).

[13] *See* I.R.C. § 704(d).

[14] A partner's share of the partnership's liabilities are determined in accordance with a complex set of rules set forth in Treas. Reg. §§ 1.752–1, 2, and 3.

[15] *See* I.R.C. § 721(a).

- *Distributions made to the partner (whether in cash or in-kind) are tax-free, except to the extent the amount of such distributions exceed the partner's basis in its partnership interest.*[16]

- *Although the partnership is not a taxable entity, it is required to file an informational tax return (IRS Form 1065) with the IRS reporting all items of income, gain, loss, deduction, and credit generated from the partnership's activities. The partnership is also required to provide each partner with a statement (Schedule K–1) of the partner's share of such partnership tax items.*

The above is a quick summary of the more salient tax considerations that a real estate development lawyer must take into consideration during Stage 3 of the real estate development process (designed to stay within the self-imposed "1,000 words or less" regimen).

B. LIMITED LIABILITY

One way a real estate development lawyer can mitigate the risk associated with an investor's investment in real estate (thereby enhancing the attractiveness of the investment) is to devise an ownership structure that limits the investor's liability to the amount of the capital the investor contributes to the project. The worst-case scenario for a real estate investor is that it not only loses the capital it contributed to the project, but also exposes its personal assets (for example, cash, cars, planes, and artwork) to the claims of a failed project's creditors. The entity structure ultimately put into place by the real estate development lawyer must insulate the investors from personal liability for the debts of the project.

C. INVESTMENT AND OPERATIONAL FLEXIBILITY

If there is one word that a lawyer should always keep in mind when representing a real estate developer, it is "flexibility." The development business is extremely dynamic in nature and is conducted by a particularly mercurial class of individuals. For this reason, the real estate development lawyer must imbue the project documents with as much flexibility as possible to permit the developer to quickly change course to deal with unexpected occurrences. Nowhere during the development process is this axiom more applicable than when the real estate development lawyer is tasked with the assignment of crafting an ownership structure that is both (1) attractive to potential equity investors who yearn for predictability and

---

[16] *See* I.R.C. § 731(a)(1).

certainty, and (2) acceptable to the developer who almost always has a total aversion to being pinned down in any way

When seeking to attract outside equity investors to its development project, the developer wants its lawyer to design an ownership structure that affords the developer two distinct types of contractual flexibility.

- *Investment Flexibility*—The developer needs to have the flexibility to allocate tax and financial attributes associated with the project in whatever manner is required to meet the unique business objectives and financial return parameters of the developer and its outside equity investors.

- *Operational Flexibility*—The developer also wants the flexibility to devise an entity governance scheme that grants the investors a level of dominion over major project decisions (for example, a sale or refinancing of the project) without unduly restricting the developer's freedom to manage the project's day-to-day operations in a manner that the developer deems appropriate to maximize the project's overall success.

The investment and operational wants and needs of equity investors vary widely from project to project. The real estate development lawyer must be vigilant to choose an entity form that provides the developer with the flexibility the developer needs in its pursuit of acceptable outside equity investors.

III. ENTITY CHOICES

As mentioned at the outset of this chapter, the real estate development lawyer has a "bewildering array of ownership entity choices"[17] to consider when selecting the appropriate form of entity to own the real estate project.

The advantages and disadvantages of each ownership entity choice are highlighted in the ensuing sections by examining how each entity fares in achieving the three business objectives noted at the inception of this chapter—that is, (1) the avoidance of double taxation, (2) the existence of limited liability, and (3) the creation of investment and operational flexibility.

A. TENANTS IN COMMON

Tenancy in common is defined in THE REAL ESTATE DICTIONARY as "an undivided ownership interest in real estate by two or more persons."[18] When two or more persons hold title to a real estate project as tenants in common, the deed conveying title to them must specify the percentage

---

[17] *See* KOLBE, *supra* note 2.

[18] *See* JOHN TALAMO, THE REAL ESTATE DICTIONARY 187 (7th ed. 2001).

ownership interest of each of them (with the presumption that, unless otherwise stated, each of the named tenants in common owns an equal percentage interest in the property).[19] Each tenant in common has a direct ownership interest in the real property (as contrasted to a situation where an entity holds title to the real estate and the individual owns an interest only in the entity and not directly in the real estate).

- *Avoidance of Double Taxation*—There is no double taxation of the taxable income of a project held as tenants in common. Each individual tenant in common reports its proportionate share of the project's income and expense items directly on its individual tax return.

- *Limited Liability*—Each tenant in common is personally liable for its proportionate share of any debt or expense related to the co-owned real estate project (for example, a mortgage loan or real estate taxes).[20] For this reason, commercial real estate development projects are rarely, if ever, titled in the names of tenants in common.

- *Investment and Operational Flexibility*—The lack of investment and operational flexibility is another reason why tenancy in common arrangements are seldom selected as an ownership entity for real estate development projects. The general rule is that all decisions made with respect to a tenancy in common project must be made with the consent of all the tenants in common. While this rule may be modified in certain circumstances by the agreement of the parties, it is questionable whether that rule can be changed to any significant degree without causing the tenancy in common arrangement to be treated as a partnership for both state law and federal income tax purposes.[21] Moreover, a tenancy in common arrangement does not afford the developer the ability to allocate financial or tax attributes of the project in any way other than in strict accordance with the specific percentage ownership interests of the individual tenants in common. This lack of investment flexibility makes the tenancy in common format a difficult vehicle to use when trying to raise outside equity to fund a project's development costs. Finally, one of the hallmarks of a tenancy in common structure is the reserved right of each tenant in common to

---

[19] *See* 20 AMERICAN JURISPRUDENCE 2d, *Cotenancy and Joint Ownership* § 116 (2016).

[20] *See* GEORGE LEFCOE, REAL ESTATE TRANSACTIONS, FINANCE, AND DEVELOPMENT 675 (6th ed. 2009); and NORTON L. STEUBEN, REAL ESTATE PLANNING, CASES, MATERIALS, QUESTIONS AND COMMENTARY 8 (4th ed. 2006).

[21] *See* Stefan F. Tucker, *The Importance of Choice of Entity in the World of Planning for Entrepreneurs and Particularly Real Estate Entrepreneurs,* in ALI-CLE MODERN REAL ESTATE TRANSACTIONS, Course No. SY006, 539, 553–554 (August 2016).

petition the courts to partition or sell the co-tenancy property. A right of partition is the antithesis of the level of contractual flexibility that the real estate development lawyer strives to achieve in selecting an entity to hold title to the developer's real estate project.

B. C CORPORATION

Title to a real estate project may be held by a corporation in which the developer and the outside equity investors are the shareholders. Most corporations are taxable under Subchapter C of the Internal Revenue Code[22] and, therefore, are commonly referred to as *C corporations*.

- *Avoidance of Double Taxation*—A C corporation is a separate taxable entity. As such, the income stream of a real estate project held by a C corporation is subject to double taxation—first when the income is earned by the corporate titleholder and second when a distribution of the related cash flow is made to the shareholders. In addition, tax deductions and losses generated from the real estate project (including depreciation deductions) cannot be passed through to the shareholders of a C corporation, but rather may be used only to offset the positive taxable income of the C corporation (which may not exist if the sole asset of the C corporation is the real estate project). For these reasons, commercial real estate projects are seldom owned by C corporations (unless the project is built solely for the use and occupancy of the corporation).

- *Limited Liability*—The one advantage of a C corporation is that its shareholders are not personally liable for the corporation's debts and claims. As such, an investor's liability on a real estate project titled in the name of a C corporation is limited to the amount of the investor's capital contribution to the corporation.

- *Investment and Operational Flexibility*—Corporate governance issues are covered by the corporate statute of the state where the corporation is incorporated. The specificity of such statutory provisions places an inherent limitation on the operational flexibility available under the C corporation ownership option. The C corporation format also significantly restricts the creativity of the parties with respect to the allocation of financial and tax attributes associated with the ownership and operation of a real estate project. A minimal level of investment flexibility can be achieved using multiple

---

[22] *See* I.R.C. §§ 301–395.

classes of stock and the issuance of corporate debt instruments.

C. S CORPORATION

An *S corporation* is a corporation that elects to be taxed for federal income tax purposes under Subchapter S of the Internal Revenue Code[23] (and not Subchapter C). Subchapter S of the Internal Revenue Code was adopted by Congress to achieve a modicum of tax neutrality between the taxation of partners and Subchapter S shareholders.[24] However, significant differences persist in the tax treatment afforded to partnerships and S corporations that weigh heavily against the use of an S corporation to hold title to a real estate development project.

- *Avoidance of Double Taxation*—Generally, an S corporation is not treated as a separate taxpayer for federal income tax purposes. A single layer of tax is imposed at the shareholder level on the income generated from a real estate project owned by the S corporation. There are, however, a couple exceptions to this general rule that negate the wisdom of using an S corporation as the ownership entity for a real estate project.[25]

    o   First, unlike the tax treatment afforded to an equity participant in a partnership or limited liability company, a shareholder of an S corporation cannot increase the tax basis of the shareholder's stock to take into consideration the shareholder's percentage interest in the S corporation's entity-level debt. The S shareholder's right to receive tax-free cash distributions and deduct entity-generated losses is limited to the tax basis of the shareholder's stock in the S corporation. The fact that the tax basis of a partner's or LLC member's equity interest (but not that of an S shareholder's stock) includes its allocable share of the entity's debt means that the ability of a partner or LLC member to receive tax-free cash distributions and deduct entity tax losses is much greater than the ability of the S shareholder to do so. This distinction is particularly important as it relates to the distribution to the equity holders of the proceeds of a refinancing where the amount of the new debt exceeds the amount of the refinanced debt (a situation that is common in the real estate development business). In a

---

[23]   *See* I.R.C. §§ 1361–1379.

[24]   *See* MCKEE, *supra* note 10, at ¶ 2.02[3].

[25]   *See generally* Tucker, *supra* note 21 at 557–575.

partnership or limited liability company context, the distribution of the excess refinancing proceeds is almost always tax-free to a partner or limited liability company member because the tax basis of its equity interest includes its allocable share of the entity's debt. Because the S corporation shareholder is not able to include any portion of the corporation's debt in the basis of the shareholder's stock, the distribution of refinancing proceeds by a S corporation is much more likely to trigger taxable gain at the equity holder level than is a distribution of refinancing proceeds by a partnership or limited liability company.

o   Second, Subchapter S imposes an entity level tax on the distribution of appreciated property to its shareholders.[26] Entities taxed as partnerships under Subchapter K (which includes general and limited partnerships and limited liability companies) are not subject to separate entity tax upon the distribution to its equity owners of appreciated property.

- *Limited Liability*—An S corporation shareholder has the same limited liability as a C corporation shareholder (which is a good thing).

- *Investment and Operational Flexibility*—The investment and operational flexibility afforded by the S corporation format is even less than that which exists for a C corporation. Unlike a C corporation, an S corporation can only have 100 shareholders, all of whom must either be individuals, estates, or qualifying trusts.[27] As such, the use of an S corporation denies the developer access to its most important source of seed capital for its project—that is, life insurance companies, pension funds, venture capital firms, foreign nationals, and other non-individual taxpayers. Subchapter S also expressly provides that an S corporation may only have one class of stock.[28] The "once class of stock" restriction effectively means that all allocations and distributions made by the S corporation to its shareholders must be made in direct proportion to the shareholders' respective ownership interests in the S corporation's stock. These statutory restrictions on the capital structure of an S corporation effectively prevent the S corporation from attaining anywhere

---

[26] *See* I.R.C. § 311(b).

[27] *See* I.R.C. § 1361(b)(1)(A) and (B).

[28] *See* I.R.C. § 1361(b)(1)(D).

near the level of investment and operational flexibility afforded regular C corporations, let alone that available in the partnership and LLC formats.

The lack of investment and operational flexibility, when coupled with the negative tax attributes of the S corporation noted earlier in this section, have caused the authors of the pre-eminent treatise on partnership taxation to comment that "there is rarely a reason to create a corporation with the intention of electing to be taxed under Subchapter S."[29]

D. GENERAL PARTNERSHIP

A *general partnership* is an unincorporated organization in which two or more persons agree to share profits and losses associated with the conduct of a business or investment activity.[30] The conduct and activities of a general partnership are governed by state statutes that are patterned after the Uniform Partnership Act. A general partnership is taxed under Subchapter K unless an affirmative election to be taxed as a C corporation is filed with the IRS.[31]

- *Avoidance of Double Taxation*—A general partnership is treated as a pass-through entity for federal income tax purposes. As such, there is no federal income tax imposed at the partnership level. All items of income and expense generated by the general partnership are passed through to and reported on the personal tax returns of its partners. The income stream generated from a real estate project held by a general partnership is, therefore, subject to a single layer of tax.

- *Limited Liability*—In a general partnership, each general partner is personally liable for all partnership debts and claims.[32] The fact that each partner's separate individual assets are potentially at risk if the real estate project proves to be unsuccessful generally makes a general partnership a poor choice for an entity to hold title to a real estate development project.[33]

- *Investment and Operational Flexibility*—The Uniform Partnership Act provides for a series of default rules that, unless otherwise provided in the partnership agreement, determine how the partnership's profits and losses must be split and how the partnership must conduct its affairs and

---

29 *See* MCKEE, *supra* note 10 at § 2.02[3].

30 *See* UNIFORM PARTNERSHIP ACT § 102(11) (1997, last amended 2013).

31 *See* TREAS. REG. § 301.7701–3(c).

32 *See* UNIFORM PARTNERSHIP ACT (1997, last amended 2013) § 306.

33 *But see infra Practice Tip7-2: LLPs and LLLPs*, pages 229–230.

activities.[34] By way of example, absent a provision to the contrary in the partnership agreement, the Uniform Partnership Act provides that (1) all partnership profits and losses are shared equally by its partners,[35] and (2) each partner has "equal rights in the management and conduct of the partnership business."[36] These default rules can, however, be modified by a written partnership agreement, thereby giving the partnership ample operational flexibility with respect to the manner in which the partnership's financial profits and losses are split and the way in which the partnership's business is managed and operated. In addition, Subchapter K of the Internal Revenue Code permits the partners to allocate items of taxable income and expense among themselves in any fashion they see fit (including in a manner different from the way they share the partnership's underlying financial profits and losses), as long as such allocation has "substantial economic effect"—that is, it substantially affects the value of the partners' partnership interests independent of tax consequences.[37] A general partnership, therefore, is engrained with as much investment and operational flexibility as any tax pass-through entity (including a limited partnership or a limited liability company) and much more than the tenancy in common or corporate ownership arrangements discussed previously in this chapter.

E. LIMITED PARTNERSHIP

A *limited partnership* differs from a general partnership primarily because it affords potential limited liability status to a group of investors referred to as *limited partners*. Limited partnerships are also treated as pass-through entities for federal income tax purposes under Subchapter K. Until the advent of the limited liability company in the early 1990's, the combined features of limited liability and treatment as a pass-through entity for tax purposes made the limited partnership the favored ownership entity for commercial real estate projects.

- *Avoidance of Double Taxation*—A limited partnership is taxed for federal income tax purposes in the same manner as a general partnership. Therefore, vesting title to a real estate

---

[34] *See* UNIFORM PARTNERSHIP ACT § 105(b) (1997, last amended 2013).

[35] *See* UNIFORM PARTNERSHIP ACT § 401(a) (1997, last amended 2013).

[36] *See* UNIFORM PARTNERSHIP ACT § 401(h) (1997, last amended 2013).

[37] *See* I.R.C. § 704(b) and Treas. Reg. 1.704–1(b). For an extended discussion of the tax allocation rules of Subchapter K, *see* MCKEE, *supra* note 10, at Chapter 11, *Determining the Partners' Distributive Shares*; and Mark Stone, *Partnership Allocations—Getting It Drafted Simple, But Right*, 21 TAX MANAGEMENT REAL ESTATE JOURNAL 206 (July 6, 2005).

project in a limited partnership avoids the imposition of any double tax on the project's income stream.

- *Limited Liability*—The most recent version of the Uniform Limited Partnership Act provides "a corporate-like liability shield for limited partners, protecting them against the debts, obligations and other liabilities of the limited partnership— i.e., against vicarious liability for the obligations of the entity," even if the limited partner participates in the management and control of the limited partnership.[38] A limited partnership must, however, by statute, have at least one general partner who is generally liable for all of the entity's debts and claims.[39] A common gamut employed during the limited partnership's heyday in the 1970's and 1980's was to make the sole general partner of the partnership a shell corporation without any significant assets, thereby effectively giving limited partnerships the same limited liability status as corporations. This approach was the subject of a great deal of litigation as the IRS sought to have such limited partnerships taxed as corporations (and not as pass-through entities)[40] and creditors sought to pierce the corporate veil and collect damages against the limited partners of the partnership and the shareholders of the corporate general partner. As noted earlier in this chapter, the IRS' adoption of the check-the-box regulations has now rendered moot the issue of whether a thinly-capitalized corporate general partner might cause a limited partnership to be taxed as a corporation. However, the use of a minimally capitalized shell entity as the sole general partner of a limited partnership still creates the theoretical risk under state law that the limited partners or the equity owners of the shell entity might be held personally liable for the debts and claims of the limited partnership.[41] This theoretical risk marginally

---

[38] *See* COMMENT TO UNIFORM LIMITED PARTNERSHIP ACT § 303(a) (2001, last amended 2013). Prior versions of the Uniform Limited Partnership Act subjected a limited partner to a potential loss of its limited liability if it participated in the control of the business. Limited partnerships formed in states that have not adopted the Uniform Limited Partnership Act (2001) may, therefore, not be able to provide a complete liability shield for its limited partners.

[39] *See* UNIFORM LIMITED PARTNERSHIP ACT § 404(a) (2001, last amended 2013).

[40] *See* MCKEE, *supra* note 10, at ¶ 3.02

[41] *See* Norton L. Steuben, *Choice of Entity for Real Estate after Check the Box and the Entity Explosion*, 37 REAL PROPERTY, PROBATE AND TRUST JOURNAL 54, 80 (Spring 2002), where the author notes that the theories underlying the IRS' attack on thinly capitalized corporate general partners "might be resurrected and applied to impose sham or thin treatment on limited partnerships having corporate general partners possibly resulting in the limited partners having general liability or the partnership failing to comply with RULPA and, therefore, not being treated as a limited partnership."

detracts from the attractiveness of the limited partnership as an entity to hold title to a real estate development project.

- *Investment and Operational Flexibility*—The investment flexibility of a limited partnership is as complete as it is in a general partnership. In those states that have enacted the 2001 version of the Uniform Limited Partnership Act (with its absolute liability shield for all limited partners), the operational flexibility of a limited partnership is effectively the same as that of a general partnership. However, in all other jurisdictions, the prohibition on a limited partner's participation in the control of the business is a factor that limits the operational flexibility of a limited partnership and, hence, weighs against the selection of a limited partnership as an owner of a real estate development project.

F. LIMITED LIABILITY COMPANY

A *limited liability company* (*LLC*) is a relatively recent statutory creation. The first LLC statute was adopted by the Wyoming legislature in 1977. Today all 50 states, plus the District of Columbia, have statutes in place that permit the creation of a limited liability company.[42] The LLC is an entity that seeks to take the best of both the corporate and partnership worlds by combining the limited liability status of corporations with the pass-through tax status and operational and investment flexibility of partnerships. An LLC has quickly become the entity of choice for real estate developers.

- *Avoidance of Double Taxation*—An LLC is automatically taxed as a partnership for federal income tax purposes unless its members make an affirmative election to be taxed as a C corporation under the check-the-box regulations. As such, no federal income tax is imposed at the LLC level.

- *Limited Liability Status*—The liability of a member in a LLC is akin to that of a shareholder in a corporation. The LLC member's personal assets are immune from attack by the creditors of the LLC even if the member directly participates in the management and control of the LLC's business.[43]

- *Investment and Operational Flexibility*—An LLC has the same operational and investment flexibility as does a general partnership. There are effectively no limits on how the LLC's business operations are managed. Indeed, the members of an LLC may elect to delegate to a non-member manager all or

[42] *See* LARRY E. RIBSTEIN AND ROBERT R. KEATINGE, RIBSTEIN AND KEATINGE ON LIMITED LIABILITY COMPANIES Appendix A (2nd ed. 2010).

[43] *See* REVISED UNIFORM LIMITED LIABILITY COMPANY ACT, § 304 (2006, last amended 2013).

any part of the authority to manage the LLC's activities.[44] The members of an LLC also have the same flexibility as do the partners in general and limited partnerships to allocate the entity's financial and tax attributes in whatever fashion they deem appropriate.

Practice Tip #7-2: LLPs and LLLPs

*The prior discussion of entity choice gave a nod to limited liability companies and corporations over general and limited partnerships on the issue of the limited liability of a real estate project's investors. The traditional models of general and limited partnerships place vicarious liability on each named general partner for all partnership's debts and claims and, therefore, fall short of the full liability shield offered up to the project's investors by the corporate and LLC entity formats. However, in recent years the advantage held on the limited liability guideline by corporations and LLCs has been called into question by the introduction of two new entities—the **limited liability partnership (LLP)** and the **limited liability limited partnership (LLLP)**.*

The most recent versions of the Uniform Partnership Act and the Uniform Limited Partnership Act both set out a procedure for a partnership to elect limited liability status for all named general partners.[45] Both a general partnership formed under the UPA and a limited partnership formed under the ULPA may now wipe out the vicarious liability of all general partners by making a simple filing with the secretary of state's office. The advent of the LLP and LLLP means that the achievement of limited liability for the project's investors "is no longer a determinant factor in the choice of business form."[46] The real estate development lawyer can theoretically achieve the goal of eliminating the vicarious liability of the project's investors by choosing an LLC, an S or C corporation, or an LLP or LLLP.

There are a couple caveats that need to be mentioned with respect to the ability of an LLP or an LLLP to produce the desired limited liability status.

- *LLLPs are authorized in only 20 states.[47] Even if a lawyer practices in a state that sanctions LLLPs, the use of an LLLP*

---

[44] *See* REVISED UNIFORM LIMITED LIABILITY COMPANY ACT, § 407(c)(6) (2006, last amended 2013).

[45] *See* UNIFORM PARTNERSHIP ACT § 901(1997, last amended 2013); and UNIFORM LIMITED PARTNERSHIP ACT § 102(9) (2001, last amended 2013).

[46] *See* RIBSTEIN, *supra* note 42, AT § 2.7.

[47] *See* UNIFORM LIMITED PARTNERSHIP ACT, *Legislative Fact Sheet*, available at http://www.uniformlaws.org/LegislativeFactSheet.aspx?title=Limited%20Partnership%20Act%20(2001)%20(Last%20Amended%202013) (last visited on February 2, 2017).

> *may create problems if the entity also does business in a state where LLLPs are not recognized.*

- *Some states limit the use of LLPs to professional service businesses, such as law firms or accounting firms.*[48]

Given these two important caveats, the real estate development lawyer should continue to lean toward the use of an LLC to achieve limited liability for the project investors—at least until there is wider acceptance and uniformity among all the pertinent state statutes governing LLPs and LLLPs.

1. LLC as Entity of Choice for Developers

It is clearer today than at any time in recent history that there is one entity that should almost always be chosen to own a real estate development project—an LLC.[49] As the chart set forth below reveals, the LLC does not possess any of the negative characteristics that are associated with the other potential entity choices. For example, unlike a tenancy in common arrangement, the LLC does not expose its members to any personal liability for the project's debts or claims, nor does it require the unanimous consent of its members to a sale, lease, or mortgage of the project. An LLC does not have the general liability concerns of a general partnership, nor does it have the double taxation problems associated with a C corporation. An LLC is superior to an S corporation both because of the S corporation's lack of operational and investment flexibility and because of the previously-discussed ways in which the S corporation's tax treatment falls short of a full pass-through of its tax attributes to the shareholders. Even the once favored limited partnership format fails to measure up against the LLC due to (1) the requirement that there be at least one entity (the general partner) that has general liability for the entity's debts and claims, and (2) to a lesser extent, the rule still followed in a number of jurisdictions that a limited partner may not participate in the control of the business without risking the loss of its limited liability.

---

[48] *See* Ribstein, *supra* note 42, at § 2.7.

[49] *See generally* L. Andrew Immerman and Ethan D. Millar, *Why Not Form a Business as an LLC?*, 19 No. 3 PRACTICAL TAX LAWYER 21 (Spring 2005); Elliot M. Surkin, John E. Blyth, Gary E. Fluhrer, Kenneth M. Jacobson, Robert A. Nix II and James A. Winkler, *The LLC Vehicle—Is There Ever a Reason Not to Use It?*, in ACREL PAPERS (April 2000),; and James A. Winkler and Gary E. Fluhrer, *Limited Liability Companies—Management Structures and Selected Issues in Using LLCs*, in ACREL PAPERS (October 2000); and LEFCOE, *supra* note 20, at 663.

Entity Type	Single Level of Taxation	Limited Liability	Investment/Operational Flexibility
Tenants in Common	Yes	No	No
C Corporation	No	Yes	Limited
S Corporation	Limited	Yes	Limited
General Partnership	Yes	No	Yes
Limited Partnership	Yes	Limited	Limited
Limited Liability Company	Yes	Yes	Yes

The above chart shows that the LLC is the only entity that fully satisfies all three of the business objectives noted at the outset of this chapter—that is, (1) the avoidance of double taxation of the income stream generated from the operation of the real estate project, (2) the limitation of the equity participant's personal liability for project debts and claims, and (3) the creation of sufficient operational and investment flexibility to permit the developer and its outside equity investors to structure their business deal in whatever fashion best suits their needs.

2. Use of an Entity Other than an LLC

As stated above, the LLC is almost always the ownership entity of choice for closely-held real estate development projects. Indeed, when six seasoned lawyers were asked to prepare a paper for the American College of Real Estate Lawyers on the traditional "choice of entity" topic, they ended up entitling their article *The LLC Vehicle—Is There Ever a Reason Not to Use It?*[50] The answer they provided to that question was "We came to believe that many of the instances where the ownership vehicle in a closely-held real estate deal was an entity other than an LLC resulted from habit or conservatism (resistance to change) of either the lawyer or the client and not from careful analysis."[51]

---

[50] *See* Surkin, *The LLC Vehicle*, *supra* note 49.

[51] *Id.* at 2.

There are three instances where a real estate development lawyer might want to consider having an entity other than an LLC hold title to a development project.

- ***Publicly-Held Property***—If the developer desires to raise capital by accessing the public markets, an LLC format is not the most desirable entity choice. Most publicly-held real estate in the United States is owned by ***real estate investment trusts (REITs)***. REITs are creatures of the federal income tax laws and may be organized as either a corporation or unincorporated trust or association for state law purposes. A REIT must have at least 100 shareholders. A REIT is not subject to an entity-level tax, if it satisfies a series of complex tests, including the requirement that the REIT distribute at least 90% of its qualifying income each year to its shareholders.[52] As of the end of 2016, there were 224 REITs that had an aggregate equity market capitalization value of approximately $1.019 trillion.[53]

- ***State Tax Law Barriers***—There are a handful of states that subject LLCs to an entity-level state income or franchise tax.[54] The instances of double taxation for state tax purposes are often anomalies resulting from the existing state tax laws not yet being revised to take cognizance of the LLC entity form. Nonetheless, in those states where the LLC is afforded unfavorable state tax treatment, the real estate development lawyer should consider using a limited partnership or another entity type to hold title to the developer's real estate project.

- ***Deal-Specific Investor Concern***—A real estate deal is occasionally structured to appeal to a particular investor who, for a reason peculiar to the investor's status or investment objectives, may not want to become a member in an LLC.

The limited exceptions noted above make up the universe of the 1% of occasions on which the rational developer decides not to use an LLC to hold title to a privately-held commercial real estate project. The focus of the

---

[52] *See generally* LEFCOE, *supra* note 20, at 683–688; DAVID C. LING AND WAYNE R. ARCHER, REAL ESTATE PRINCIPLES: A VALUE APPROACH 473–478 (3rd ed. 2010); and Robert G. Gottlieb, *How REITS Are Different from Other Real Estate Investors*, 31 PRACTICAL REAL ESTATE LAWYER No. 1 49 (January 2015).

[53] *See* NAREIT US REIT INDUSTRY EQUITY MARKET CAP, available online at https://www. reit.com/data-research/data/us-reit-industry-equity-market-cap (last visited on February 2, 2017). The topic of REITs and other publicly-held real estate ownership vehicles is beyond the scope of this book. However, it is important to recognize the enormity of the role that REITs serve in the development and ownership of commercial real estate projects.

[54] *See* Surkin, *supra* note 49, at 4–7; and ROBERT KEATINGE AND ANN E. CONWAY, KEATINGE AND CONWAY ON CHOICE OF BUSINESS ENTITY: SELECTING FORM AND STRUCTURES FOR A CLOSELY-HELD BUSINESS, Appendix 16A (2016).

remainder of this chapter is on the 99% of occasions when the entity of choice is the LLC.

———————

Practice Tip #7-3: The Single Member LLC

One additional advantage of the LLC format is the ability to have an LLC owned by a single member.[55] This contrasts markedly with either a general or a limited partnership in which there must be two partners in a validly formed entity.

*The **single member LLC (SMLLC)** is commonly used by a real estate developer to hold title to each of its real estate projects in a separate, discrete ownership vehicle. This ownership structure is like a corporation's formation of a series of wholly-owned subsidiaries in a holding company structure.*

The advantages of forming an SMLLC as a subsidiary of another LLC are as follows.

- *The assets of the parent LLC (including its ownership of other SMLLCs) are not at risk to satisfy the claims and debts of an SMLLC.*

- *Under the partnership tax rules of Subchapter K of the Internal Revenue Code, the SMLLC is wholly ignored for federal income tax purposes, with the result that a separate informational tax return does not have to be filed by the SMLLC.[56] An SMLLC that is disregarded for federal income tax purposes is commonly referred to as a **disregarded tax entity**.*

- *The existence of the SMLLC conforms to the typical requirement of a lender that any project on which it is making a secured loan must be owned by a separate entity (commonly referred to by lenders as a **single purpose** or **bankruptcy remote entity**), to preclude the possibility that the entity owning the real estate project might be forced into bankruptcy for reasons having to do with financial problems not directly associated with the project that secures the lender's loan.[57]*

———————

---

[55] *See* UNIFORM LIMITED LIABILITY COMPANY ACT § 201(d) (2006, last amended 2013).

[56] *See* Treas. Reg. § 301–7701–3(a).

[57] The 2009 bankruptcy of General Growth Properties has cast doubt upon the effectiveness of the lender's typical requirement that a real estate project be held in a bankruptcy remote entity. *See* Samantha J. Rothman, *Lessons from General Growth Properties: The Future Of The Special Purpose Entity*, 17 No. 1 FORDHAM JOURNAL OF CORPORATE AND FINANCIAL LAW 227 (2012).

IV. SOURCES OF PROJECT EQUITY

Approximately 70–90% of the development costs of a typical real estate project are funded through a construction loan secured by the developer from a bank or another commercial lending source. This leaves 10–30% of a project's development costs to be funded through capital contributions made by the equity owners of the real estate project.

A project's capital may be provided by (1) the developer, (2) outside equity investors, or (3) most typically, a combination of (1) and (2). For the following discussion, it is assumed that the needed capital is being provided by a combination of the developer and its outside equity investors.

Historically, the developer's cadre of outside equity investors fell into the category of the developer's "family and friends"—that is, the developer's extended family, country club buddies, doctor, dentist, and a host of other people personally acquainted with the developer. This category of investor is usually willing to take a fair amount of entrepreneurial risk on a real estate investment, in large part due to the investor's personal familiarity with and confidence in the developer.

Institutional investors, such as life insurance companies and pension funds, have historically been hesitant to assume the level of risk attendant to an investment of seed capital on the front-end of a development project. Institutional investors were fully content to invest only in mature, stabilized real estate projects that were fully leased and producing predictable income streams. The reticence of the institutional investment community to invest in development projects has eroded due to the saturation of the investment market for stabilized real estate projects and the never-ending quest of the institutional investor to increase the yield from its real estate investments. As alluded to in Chapter 3 of this text, one way for an investor to increase its investment yield is to increase its tolerance for project risk.

Thus, the commercial real estate developer now has two available sources of outside equity investment—(1) family and friends, and (2) institutional investors. The risk tolerance and financial return expectations of these two groups are, however, markedly different. The differing perspectives of these two investor groups are highlighted where appropriate in the discussion that follows concerning the key provisions of an LLC operating agreement.

HIBC Case Study—Two Very Different Equity Sources

Pizzuti relied on two very different equity sources during its development of the HIBC project. At the inception of the HIBC project, the principals of Newport Partners, an executive compensation consultant headquartered in Orlando, Florida, served as Pizzuti's outside equity investor. The Newport principals fit squarely within the "family and friends" category of investors discussed in the previous section of this chapter. They were rich entrepreneurs who were looking for a way to diversify their investments and increase the yield on their portfolios. They wanted to invest in the HIBC project due to their perception that Pizzuti was an accomplished developer with a proven track record of producing above-market returns on its development projects. As one of the Newport principals mentioned to me repeatedly during the Pizzuti-Newport relationship, "We are comfortable investing with you as long as we know that you are putting your own money into the deals and are assuming the same investment risk that we are." It was this fundamental premise that served as the genesis for the following unusual equity deal struck by Pizzuti and Newport.

- *Pizzuti and Newport formed a general partnership to own and operate each office project in which they were co-investors. The general partnership vehicle was selected for two reasons— (1) an LLC was not yet a viable entity choice in the State of Florida,[58] and (2) Pizzuti wanted Newport to be generally liable for all project debts and liabilities (a proposition that would have been rejected out of hand by an institutional investor).*

- *Pizzuti and Newport each provided 50% of the equity capital required for each office project.*

- *The principals of Newport agreed to personally guaranty (on a several basis) 50% of each construction loan obtained by a Pizzuti-Newport general partnership (something that would have been absolutely beyond the pale for any institutional investor).*

This unique capital structure was used for ten office projects developed by the Pizzuti-Newport team in the HIBC office park and another 12 warehouse and office projects developed by them in Central Ohio.

Pizzuti eventually decided to pursue a more traditional equity arrangement for the funding of its existing portfolio and its future development efforts. Pizzuti formed a new equity venture with Nationwide Realty Investors, Ltd. ("NRI"). NRI was the real estate arm of Nationwide Insurance Company, a large institutional investor headquartered in Columbus. The new venture entity (known as "Pizzuti Properties LLC") ultimately acquired all the HIBC office projects (plus the entirety of Pizzuti's

---

[58] Florida imposed an entity-level state income tax on LLCs until 1998. In addition, the Florida limited liability statute that was in effect in the early and mid-1990s was perceived as being both overly complex and not sufficiently flexible. *See* Gregory J. Marks, *New Florida Limited Liability Company Act*, GREENBERG TRAURIG ALERT (June 1999).

portfolio of industrial properties scattered throughout the Midwest). Pizzuti and NRI agreed that all Pizzuti's future development projects would be owned by Pizzuti Properties LLC and that NRI would provide 90% and Pizzuti would provide10% of the equity required to fund the new projects. Pizzuti was required to provide all personal guaranties required by any construction lender for a new project.

The deal struck between Pizzuti and NRI typifies the distinction customarily drawn in institutional equity deals between the developer as the "service partner" and the investor as the "money partner." It was Pizzuti's job to identify new development opportunities and then use its personal resources to bring the project to fruition. NRI's job was to provide most of the money needed to fund the projects.

The specifics of Pizzuti's relationship with these two very different equity sources is examined in more detail in the remaining pages of this chapter.

Practice Tip #7-4: Three New Equity Sources

In the years following the Great Recession of 2008, developers struggled to find equity investors to help fund development projects. Traditional equity sources (families and friends and institutional investors) either exited the market altogether or were interested in investing only in fully-stabilized trophy projects located in the Big 6 U.S. markets (New York, San Francisco, Washington D.C., Boston, Los Angeles, and Chicago). Creative (and desperate) developers seized upon the following three alternative equity sources to fund their proposed development projects.

- ***Crowdfunding** is a product of the internet age. In its essence, crowdfunding is the "online syndication of investments to a group of investors who did not have access (whether through regulatory burdens, high investment minimums or other reasons) to such investments in the past."[59] In the typical crowdfunding deal, a digital investment platform like Realty Mogul, CrowdStreet, or Fundrise offers a data base of wealthy accredited investors the opportunity to invest online in institutional-grade real estate projects. One real estate commentator recently described crowdfunding in the following manner:*

  > *By financing development and acquisitions over the internet, real estate investment is opened to a broader*

---

[59] *See* Bjorn Hall, *Real Estate Crowdfunding 2.0—Solving Key Issues,* in ACREL PAPERS Tab 3 (Fall 2015).

group of investors, many of whom have never had access before. They include software engineers at Google, product managers at Facebook and Yahoo, and finance folks at Amazon. These investors now have a way to invest in real estate that they are comfortable with—the internet.[60]

While crowdfunding is still in its infancy in the real estate equity marketplace, it is reported that $2.5 billion of equity was raised on crowdfunding platforms in 2015 alone.[61] *To date, crowdfunding has been used primarily for relatively small real estate projects. Time will tell if the prediction that crowdfunding is the "Uberization of finance" comes true in the coming years.*[62]

- *EB–5 is an immigration program that grants a residency visa to a foreign investor who invests a minimum of $500,000 in a real estate project that creates a statutorily-required number of jobs. Almost $2 billion of EB–5 capital was raised in 2014, a large portion of which was provided by Chinese nationals. The most prominent EB–5-funded project to date is Related Companies' Hudson Yard project in New York City where the developer raised almost $600 million in EB–5 funds.*[63]

An interesting question about EB–5 is how will the program fare during the presidential administration of new President Donald J. Trump? During his presidential campaign, then candidate Trump railed about two topics that form the centerpiece of EB–5—specifically U.S. policy on immigration visas and the U.S. relationship with China. He famously made the following comment about China—"They've taken our jobs, they've taken our money, they've taken everything."[64] *Given those kind of comments, it would seem unlikely that EB–5 would find a friend in President Trump—at least, that is, until word broke in 2016 that the 50 story Trump Bay Street apartment project being developed in Jersey City by*

---

[60] MIKE E. MILES, LAURENCE M. NETHERTON, AND ADRIENNE SCHMITZ, REAL ESTATE DEVELOPMENT: PRINCIPLES AND PROCESS 194 (5th ed. 2015).

[61] *See* Patrick J. Kiger, *The Staying Power of Crowdfunding in Real Estate*, 75 URBAN LAND MAGAZINE 37, 38 (May/June 2016).

[62] *Id.* at 37.

[63] *See* Susan J. Booth, *EB–5 Capital in Real Estate Transactions: The Fundamentals*, THE REAL ESTATE FINANCE JOURNAL 11, 22 (Fall/Winter 2015). *See also* S.H. Spencer Compton and Diane Schottenstein, *EB–5: The Intersection of Real Estate and Immigration*, 30 No. 4 PRACTICAL REAL ESTATE LAWYER 5 (July 2014); and Andrew J. Weiner and Frederick L. Klein, *Foreign Investment in U.S. Real Estate—Now More than Ever*, in ACREL PAPERS, Tab 10 (Fall 2016).

[64] Jesse Drucker, *Trump Tower Funded by Rich Chinese Who Invest Cash for Visas*, BLOOMBERG NEWS, available at https://visawolf.com/mr-trump-eb-5-foreign-investment-visas-are-working-for-america/ (March 6, 2016).

Jared Kushner, President Trump's son-in-law, supposedly raised more than $50 million from EB–5 investments, with most of the capital being supplied by Chinese investors.[65] *As infamously noted by Al Pacino's character in the Godfather, "It's not personal. It's strictly business."*[66] *In the case of the EB–5 program, it is also just business—and business appears to be booming.*

- *A **portfolio joint venture** is an equity arrangement between a developer and an outside equity investor that goes beyond the parties striking a deal for their co-investment in a single project and, instead, extends to their establishment of a complex set of upfront parameters for their joint investment in a portfolio of new development projects. The deal struck by Pizzuti and Nationwide Realty Investors (see HIBC Case Study—Two Very Different Equity Sources, at pages 234–236) was an early example of a portfolio joint venture.*

The portfolio joint venture structure emerged from the confluence of two related circumstances—(1) the institutional investor's continuing chase for higher yields and predictable deal flow, and (2) the developer's need for a readily available source of equity funding for its development plans. In a portfolio joint venture, a developer and an outside equity investor agree in writing in advance that that they will jointly develop and co-invest in all real estate projects that meet certain pre-defined criteria—for example, all office projects developed in a particular suburban office park, such as HIBC. The developer and the investor also agree to the financial and business terms that will govern their co-investment in all projects developed under the umbrella of the portfolio JV, including: the amounts and types of their respective capital contributions to each project; the manner in which each project's profits and losses will be split between them; and the terms that will govern the joint venture's decision-making and management control. As stated by one practitioner "A [portfolio] joint venture is not just 'a' deal. Rather, . . . [it] contemplates a continuing relationship and, as it were, a 'marriage' of sorts between two organizations."[67] *As is the case*

[65] *See* Drucker, *supra* note 64; *Mr. Trump: EB–5 Foreign Investment Visas Are Working for America*, VISAWOLF (July 15, 2015), available online at https://visawolf.com/mr-trump-eb-5-foreign-investment-visas-are-working-for-america/; and *5 Reasons the EB–5 Program Will Still Thrive under Trump*, JUWAI (January 20, 2017), available online at https://list.juwai.com/news/2017/01/5-reasons-the-eb-5-program-will-still-thrive-under-trump.

[66] THE GODFATHER (Paramount Pictures 1972).

[67] *See* Josh Kamin, John Mallinson, and Vytas Petrulis, The Programmatic Real Estate Venture, 31 No. 3 PRACTICAL REAL ESTATE LAWYER 53, 54 (May 2015).

in any "marriage," the participants in a portfolio joint venture must confront head on in the initial formation document how exclusive their relationship will be, how they will deal with conflicts, and when and how they can split up—extremely vexing issues in both life and the real estate business.

The future of these three new equity sources is intriguing but uncertain. What is certain is that real estate developers will test the viability of these and other new equity sources in their never-ending search for funding for their real estate development projects.

V. THE LLC OPERATING AGREEMENT

The document that governs the relationship of the owners of an LLC and the operation of the LLC's business is called an ***operating agreement***. The owners of an LLC are called ***members*** and their equity interests are referred to as ***membership interests***.

A sample Operating Agreement for a Delaware LLC is included in the *Document Appendix* as Document #3 (the "Form Operating Agreement"). The Form Operating Agreement is based on the Delaware Limited Liability Company Act[68] because Delaware is the jurisdiction of choice for most practitioners when forming an LLC. Perhaps the most attractive feature of the Delaware LLC Act is its whole-hearted embracing of the principle of contractual flexibility. The Delaware LLC Act recites that "It is the policy of this chapter to give the maximum effect to the principle of freedom of contract and to the enforceability of limited liability company agreements."[69] In effect, the Delaware Act creates a blank slate for the parties to craft the terms of a business deal that are acceptable to them.

The remainder of this chapter focuses on an analysis of the following key provisions of an LLC operating agreement:

- The provisions that describe the nature and scope of the members' obligations to make capital contributions to the LLC—Article 2 of the Form Operating Agreement;

- The provisions that govern the manner and order of priority in which the LLC's cash flow is distributed to its members—Article 3 of the Form Operating Agreement; and

- The provisions that delineate who is responsible for the management of the LLC's business and what limitations, if any, are placed on that person's management authority—Article 5 of the Form Operating Agreement.

---

[68] *See* DEL. CODE ANN., title 6, chapter 18 (West 2016).

[69] DEL. CODE ANN., title 6, § 18–1101(b) (West 2016).

The typical LLC operating agreement contains numerous provisions other than the three articles highlighted above. By way of example, the Form Operating Agreement has separate articles addressing: the requirements for the initial organization of the LLC (Article 1); the allocation of items of taxable income and loss among the members (Article 4); the handling of the LLC's accounting and fiscal affairs (Article 6); the placement of restrictions on the transferability of the LLC membership interests (Article 7); and the procedures attendant to the dissolution and liquidation of the LLC's business (Article 9). These provisions are, for the most part, covered by a specific set of statutory or regulatory rules. For example, most of the provisions contained in Articles 1, 6, 7, and 9 of the Form Operating Agreement are either a confirmation of the default rules set forth in the Delaware Limited Liability Company Act or a specific divergence from those default rules. Additionally, the essence of the provisions of Article 4 of the Form Operating Agreement (those relating to the allocation of items of taxable income and loss among the members for federal income tax purposes) is governed by the highly complex rules set forth in the Treasury Regulations promulgated under Section 704(b) of the Internal Revenue Code. While it is essential that the real estate development lawyer master these statutory and regulatory doctrines to effectively represent the developer, a detailed discussion of those highly technical rules is simply beyond the scope of this chapter. While certainly important, these provisions tend to be more technical than substantive in nature and are seldom the subject of much controversy in the negotiations between the developer and its outside equity investor.

Because the stated mission of this book is to examine the principal issues that a real estate development lawyer encounters when representing a developer, the choice has been made to focus just on those provisions of the operating agreement that are most often the subject of extended negotiations between the real estate development lawyer and counsel for the outside equity investor. The reader is, however, urged to carefully read through the other sections of the Form Operating Agreement to gain a sense of the legal and business issues underlying those sections.[70]

The three key provisions of the LLC operating agreement (that is, the provisions relating to the LLC's capital structure, its cash distribution scheme, and its management plan) are examined from the perspective of both the developer and the outside equity investor. The Form Operating Agreement serves as the template for the discussion of those three

---

[70] For an excellent discussion of such "other" provisions, *see* Kenneth M. Jacobson, *Sweating the Details: Issue and Negotiation Point Checklist for Limited Liability Company Operating Agreement Matters Pertaining to Capital Contributions, Management Structures and Decision-Making, Distributions, Exit Strategies and Indemnification*, in ACREL PAPERS 102 (March 2004); and Gary E. Fluhrer, Jan K. Gruben, Kenneth M. Jacobson, Lewis R. Kaster, Keith E. Osber, Joel M. Reck and Jonathon Rivin, *Multi-party Limited Liability Company Operating Agreement*, in ACREL PAPERS 133 (March 2004).

provisions. The section of the Form Operating Agreement where the provision under discussion can be found is identified in a parenthetical reference in the caption heading.

VI. CAPITALIZATION OF THE LLC
(Article 2)

Article 2 of the Form Operating Agreement covers the topic that is the central reason why the developer and its investors come together in the first instance—money. This article addresses two fundamental questions— (1) how is the LLC initially capitalized, and (2) under what circumstances will additional capital be contributed to the LLC by its members?

A. INITIAL CAPITAL CONTRIBUTIONS
(§ 2.1)

An LLC is initially capitalized through cash, property, and services contributed to the LLC by the developer and its outside equity investors (referred to collectively in the remainder of this chapter as the "members"). The legal and business issues related to each of these capital contributions are addressed separately in the next several sections of this chapter.

1. Cash Contributions

In the typical real estate development deal, the members contribute cash to the LLC in an amount equal to the project's total development costs, minus the principal amount of the project's construction loan. The section of the operating agreement that covers the members' cash capital contributions needs to address the following three considerations:

- The amount of the cash contribution to be made by each member;
- The timing for the making of such cash contributions; and
- Any conditions precedent to a member's obligation to fund its cash contribution.

An outside equity investor generally insists that the developer make a significant equity contribution to the real estate venture. The equity investor wants to make sure that the developer has a financial stake in making the project a success for all its investors. This financial stake is colloquially referred to as the developer's *skin in the game*. The amount of the developer's co-investment is typically in the 10–20% range, but varies depending on the nature of the deal and the relative liquidity of the developer.

The developer generally wants to receive the equity investor's cash contribution without condition and as soon as possible—preferably coincident with the members' execution of the operating agreement. The outside equity investor, on the other hand, often seeks to have its obligation to fund its cash contribution made expressly contingent upon the occurrence of an event that confirms that the project is a "real deal"—for example, the closing of the construction loan or the obtaining of an essential governmental approval. In all events, the lawyer representing the outside investor should require the developer to fund its cash contribution coincident with the outside investor's funding of its contribution

2. Tax Consequences of Cash Contributions

A member's cash capital contribution to an LLC is tax-free to both the member and the LLC under Section 721 of the Internal Revenue Code.[71] The federal income tax basis of a member's LLC membership interest is initially equal to the amount of the member's cash capital contribution to the LLC.[72]

3. Property Contributions

While the capital contribution of the outside equity investor almost always take the form of cash (that is, after all, the one thing the equity investor has that the developer most wants), the developer frequently contributes property to the LLC (either as its sole capital contribution or in addition to its cash contribution). The following are the two most common property interests contributed to the capital of an LLC by a developer:

- The land on which the project will be constructed (if the land is already owned by the developer); and

- Intangible personal property related to the project—for example, the developer's contractual rights under the land purchase contract, architectural plans and specifications, and building permits and other governmental approvals.

If the developer plans to make a property contribution to an LLC, the operating agreement should address the following considerations.

- *Agreed-Upon Fair Market Value of Property Contribution*—Under financial accounting principles, the contributor of property is deemed to have made a capital contribution to the LLC in an amount equal to the fair market value of the property as of the date of its contribution. Because the determination of the fair market value of

---

[71] *See* I.R.C. § 721(a).
[72] *See* I.R.C. § 722.

contributed property has a direct impact on the computation of the members' respective distributive shares of the LLC's profits and losses, the topic of the agreed-upon fair market value of the contributed property is often the subject of intense negotiations. The agreed-upon value of the developer's property contribution should be clearly spelled out in the operating agreement to preempt any future attempt by either the developer or the other member to renegotiate the fair market value of the contributed property. If the members decide that the property contribution has no discernible fair market value (as is often the case when the developer's property contributions consists of contractual and development rights related to the project), then the members should be equally assiduous in reflecting in the operating agreement their agreement that the contributed rights have a $0 value.

- *LLC's Assumption of Liabilities*—The developer wants to make sure that the LLC assumes all liabilities and obligations of the developer with respect to the contributed property—for example, any mortgage loan that encumbers the contributed land or any contractual obligation placed on the developer under the land purchase contract. An indemnification from the LLC with respect to such liabilities and obligations is customarily included in the operating agreement.

- *Representations and Warranties*—To the extent land is being contributed to the LLC, the developer should expect the outside equity investors to insist that the developer make representations and warranties to the LLC similar to those customarily contained in a land purchase contract. If the property contribution consists of contractual and development rights associated with the LLC's proposed project, the representations and warranties are usually limited to an affirmation that the developer has the ability to transfer those rights to the LLC and that no default exists under the transferred rights. The outside equity investor typically also asks for the inclusion in the operating agreement of a right to reduce any cash distributions owed to the developer by the amount of any damages incurred by the LLC due to the developer's breach of its representations and warranties.

4. Tax Consequences of Property Contributions

A contribution of property to an LLC in exchange for the contributor's receipt of an LLC membership interest is generally a tax-free event at both the LLC and property contributor level.[73] Exceptions to this general rule may apply if (1) the contributor receives cash in return for its contribution of property to the LLC, or (2) the contributor is relieved of liabilities in excess of its tax basis in the contributed property. The tax rules governing these two scenarios are extremely complex.[74] A lawyer representing a developer who either receives cash or is relived of a liability as the result of its contribution of property to an LLC should consult those tax rules to determine their applicability to the developer's property contribution.

The initial tax basis of the property contributor's membership interest is equal to the tax basis of the contributed property in the contributors' hands immediately prior to such contribution.[75] The tax basis of the contributed property in the hands of the LLC is similarly deemed to be equal to the adjusted tax basis of that property in the hands of the property contributor immediately prior to its contribution to the LLC.[76] These tax rules stand in sharp contrast to financial accounting principles that state that the property contributor's capital account must be credited with an amount equal to the agreed-upon fair market value of the contributed property. There is, therefore, a disparity between the value of the contributed property on the LLC's books and the LLC's tax basis in such property. The difference between the value and the tax basis of the property on the date of its contribution to the LLC is referred to as a ***book/tax disparity***. Under § 704(c) of the Code, any taxable gain realized by the LLC on its ultimate sale of the contributed property must first be allocated to the property contributor in an amount equal to such book/tax disparity.[77]

The operation of this tax rule is illustrated by the following example.

Example 7-2: Developer contributes land to ABC LLC. The contributed land has an agreed fair market value of $1 million. Developer's tax basis in the land on the date of its contribution to ABC LLC is $800,000. Investor makes a cash contribution to ABC LLC of $3 million. Developer and Investor agree to split all profits and losses generated by the activities of ABC in the same 75–25% ratio that characterizes the respective values of their capital contributions to ABC. The land is later sold by ABC for $1 million, triggering a taxable gain of $200,000 (the $1 million purchase price, less ABC's adjusted tax basis in the land of $800,000).

---

[73] *See* I.R.C. § 721(a).

[74] *See generally* MCKEE, *supra* note 10, at § 4.01[1][a].

[75] *See* I.R.C. § 722.

[76] *See* I.R.C. § 723.

[77] *See* I.R.C. § 704(c).

Under Section 704(c) of the Code, the entire $200,000 gain realized by ABC LLC must be allocated to Developer and reported on its federal income tax return. If the land had been sold for $1.2 million (thereby triggering a taxable gain of $400,000), the first $200,000 of such gain would have been allocated to Developer (equal to the book/tax disparity created at the time of the land contribution), with the remaining $200,000 of gain being allocated 75% to Investor and 25% to Developer.

5. Service Contributions

The developer is often granted an LLC membership interest in consideration of its past efforts in putting the deal together (for example, putting the land under contract, getting the property rezoned, and attracting tenants to the project) and its agreement to continue to work in the future to bring the project to a successful conclusion. The equity interest given to the developer in consideration of its provision of services to the LLC is usually in addition to the equity interest received by the developer in exchange for its contribution of cash or property to the LLC. By way of example, the developer might receive (1) a 25% membership interest in exchange for its cash contribution of 25% of the LLC's total required capital, plus (2) an additional 15% membership interest in consideration of its provision of past and future services to the LLC.

There are two types of membership interests that can be granted to a developer in exchange for its contribution of services to the LLC—a *capital interest* and a *profits interest*. A capital interest entitles the developer to an immediate share of the value of all then existing LLC assets. In contrast, a profits interest only entitles the developer to a share of the profits that are attributable either to the LLC's future operations or a future appreciation in the value of the LLC's assets.

The following simple example highlights the difference between these two interests.

Example 7-3: Assume that ABC LLC's sole asset is a parcel of land purchased by ABC for $1 million on the date of ABC's formation. Assume further that Investor contributes cash of $1 million to fund ABC's land acquisition and that Developer makes no cash or property contribution whatsoever. Investor is given a 70% interest in the LLC and Developer receives a 30% LLC interest. Finally, assume that ABC sells its land one year later for $1.5 million.

If Developer's membership interest is characterized as a capital interest, then the proceeds of the land sale would be distributed to the members as follows:

- Developer—$450,000

- Investor—$1,050,000

If, on the other hand, the developer's membership interest is treated as a profits interest, then the proceeds of the land sale would be distributed to the members as follows:

- Developer—$150,000

- Investor—$1,350,000

The difference between the two types of interests is that a capital interest gives Developer a 30% interest in all $1.5 million of the land sale proceeds (including both the portion of such proceeds attributable to the initial land value of $1 million and the portion attributable to the land appreciation of $500,000), while a profits interest restricts Developer's share of the land sales proceeds to 30% of the land appreciation of $500,000.

6. Tax Consequences of Service Contributions

For the last 40+ years, legal scholars and practitioners have engaged in a vigorous debate as to whether the grant of an equity interest in exchange for a contribution of services should result in the recognition of current taxable income to the service provider.[78] The putative treatment of the receipt of a profits interest as a taxable event is, of course a developer's worst nightmare—the developer is required to pay income taxes on its receipt of an equity interest *BEFORE* the developer has received any cash benefit from its ownership of that interest. While the courts and legal commentators long ago agreed that the grant of a capital interest to a service provider should be a taxable event, no such consensus existed until recently on the issue of whether a service provider's receipt of a profits interest should be taxable.

In 1993, the IRS finally provided a level of certainty on the issue of the tax consequences of a taxpayer's receipt of a profits interest in exchange for services. In Revenue Procedure 93–27, the IRS stated that it will generally not treat a partner's receipt of a profits interest as a taxable event.[79] The IRS defined a profits interest as being any interest other than a capital interest. It then described a capital interest as "an interest that

---

[78] The debate started in 1971 when the Tax Court held that the receipt of a profits interest was taxable to a service partner. *See* Sol Diamond v. Commissioner, 56 T.C. 530 (1971), *aff'd* 492 F.2d 286 (7th Cir. 1974). For a discussion of subsequent court decisions addressing the tax consequences of the grant of a profits interest to a service partner, *see* MCKEE, *supra* note 10, at § 5.02.

[79] *See* Revenue Procedure 93–27, 1993–2 C.B. 343, § 4.01. Revenue Procedure 93–27 states that its pronouncements do not apply to the receipt of a profits interest if—(1) the profits interests relates to a "substantially certain and predictable stream of income from high quality debt securities or a high-quality net lease", (2), within two years of receipt, the partner disposes of the profits interest, or (3) the profits interest is a limited partnership interest in a "publicly traded limited partnership." *See id.* at § 4.02.

would give the holder a share of the proceeds if the partnership's assets were sold at fair market value and then the proceeds were distributed in complete liquidation of the partnership. This determination is generally made at the time of the receipt of the partnership interest."[80]

In May of 2005, the IRS issued Proposed Regulations that also sought to deal with the tax consequences of a service provider's receipt of an equity interest from a pass-through tax entity.[81] The Proposed Regulations start out by rejecting the notion embraced by Revenue Procedure 93–27 that a person's receipt of a profits interest in exchange for the performance of services is not a taxable event. Rather the Proposed Regulations expressly state that capital and profits interests (collectively referred to in the Proposed Regulations as "compensatory partnership interests") will be treated in a like manner for federal income tax purposes, with the recipient of either such interest being deemed to have received taxable income in an amount equal to the excess of the fair market value of such interest over the amount paid for such interest by the service provider.[82]

At first blush, the Proposed Regulations seem to be a drastic departure from the tax treatment afforded to a member's receipt of a profits interest under Revenue Procedure 93–27. Fortunately, however, the IRS simultaneously released an IRS Notice[83] that, when read together with the Proposed Regulations, creates a safe harbor that effectively provides the same tax result for the recipient of a profits interest as that currently mandated under Revenue Procedure 93–27.[84]

The Proposed Regulations state that the fair market value of a compensatory partnership interest is deemed to be equal to its "liquidation value." In IRS Notice 2005–43, the IRS defines "liquidation value" in a manner that is virtually identical to the definition given to a "capital interest" in Revenue Procedure 93–27. Specifically, IRS Notice 2005–43 states that:

> Liquidation value . . . means the amount of cash that the recipient of the Compensatory Partnership Interest would receive if, immediately after the transfer, the partnership sold all of its assets (including goodwill, going concern value, and any other

---

[80] *Id.* at § 2.01. The reference in Revenue Procedure 93–27 and other IRS pronouncements to a "partnership interest" includes a membership interest in a limited liability company that is taxed as a partnership under Subchapter K of the Internal Revenue Code.

[81] *See* Prop. Treas. Reg. §§ 1.721–1(b)(1) and 1.83–3(e) (2005).

[82] *See* MCKEE, *supra* note 10, at § 5.02[8].

[83] *See* IRS Notice 2005–43, 2005–1 C.B. 1221 (May 24, 2005).

[84] The safe harbor established for profits interest under IRS Notice 2005–43 is only available to those entities that affirmatively elect to be covered by its provisions. The procedures to be followed in making such election are specified in the IRS notice and specifically include the insertion in an LLC's operating agreement of a provision authorizing and validating the LLC's safe harbor election. *See id.* at § 3.03(2). Section 6.3 of the Form Operating Agreement contains such a safe harbor election (based on the premise the Proposed Regulations will become final in their current form).

intangibles associated with the partnership's operations) for cash equal to the fair market value of those assets and then liquidated.[85]

As discussed in the previous section of this chapter, a profits interest does not give a member the right to receive any cash upon a liquidation of the LLC immediately following the member's receipt of its membership interest. Under the Proposed Regulations and IRS Notice 2005–43, a profits interest, by definition, has a $0 liquidation value. Therefore, while the member's receipt of the profits interest may be a taxable event within the meaning of the Proposed Regulations, no tax is payable as a result of the member's receipt of that profits interest because the profits interest has no discernible liquidation value when received by the service member.

A member's receipt of a capital interest, however, clearly produces taxable income for that member under the Proposed Regulations and IRS Notice 2005–43. A recipient of a capital interest gains an immediate share in the value of the entity's existing assets. If the entity were to sell its assets and liquidate immediately following the issuance of a capital interest to one of its members, that member would be entitled to a share of the liquidation proceeds—with that share being deemed to be the "liquidation value" of the member's capital interest under IRS Notice 2005–43. Under the rules set forth in the Proposed Regulations, the recipient of the capital interest would be deemed to have taxable income in the year of its receipt of such interest in an amount equal to the interest's liquidation value (measured by the member's percentage capital interest, multiplied by the fair market value of the LLC's assets as of the date of the member's receipt of its capital interest).

If final regulations are adopted that are wholly consistent with the Proposed Regulations (as supplemented by IRS Notice 2005–43), then Revenue Procedure 93–27 will automatically become obsolete.[86] The Proposed Regulations are currently in the comment stage and, as of the date of the writing of this chapter, no date has been publicly projected for the issuance of final Regulations.[87]

There are two general propositions that are clear under whichever tax regime is ultimately in force (that is, either Revenue Procedure 93–27 or the Proposed Regulations):

- The receipt of a profits interest in exchange for the performance of services will not result in the recognition of

---

[85] See IRS Notice 2005–43, supra note 83, at § 4.02.

[86] See IRS Notice 2005–43, supra note 83, at § 7.

[87] According to Professor McKee, "a representative of the U.S. Treasury Department has stated publicly that they are waiting to see what happens with the carried interest legislation proposed in early 2009 before acting to finalize the 2005 Proposed Regulations." See MCKEE, supra note 10, at § 5.02[8]. See infra pages 281–285, for a discussion of the proposed carried interest legislation.

any taxable income by the recipient of that profits interest; and

- The receipt of a capital interest in exchange for the performance of services will result in the recipient's recognition of taxable income in an amount equal to recipient's share of the liquidation value of the entity's assets, less the amount of any cash or other property contributed by it to the entity.

The practitioner should, however, be mindful that, if the Proposed Regulations become effective, the rules that will govern the qualification of a profits interest for tax-free treatment will be considerably more complex and administratively exacting than is the case under current tax practice.

7. The Importance of Profits Interests

So why the big fuss about a profits interest? The answer lies in the fact that the developer's receipt of a profits interest in exchange for its provision of services to the LLC is the most commonly used method to financially reward the developer for its efforts in putting the real estate deal together. Key employees of the developer are also frequently given profits interests to reward them for their past performance and to incentivize them to perform in the future in a manner intended to maximize the profitability of the LLC's real estate project. Truth be told, the author would likely never have had the luxury of writing this book if he had not been a "key employee" recipient of a profits interest in the Pizzuti-Nationwide Realty Investors joint venture.

The existence of a generous profits interest is often the linchpin of the economics supporting a developer's decision to move forward with a project. A profits interest affords the developer and its senior staff with the opportunity to reap significant financial rewards, without having to take any commensurate capital risk. The fact that a profits interest can be doled out in an extremely tax efficient manner is an added reason why the grant of a profits interest is an indispensable component of most equity deals struck between the developer and its outside equity investor.

The developer's receipt of a profits interest can have a dramatic impact on the cash distributions received by the developer and its equity investors from the development project. The profits interest topic is, therefore, a focal point of the negotiations that take place between the developer and the outside equity investors. The foregoing discussion examined the nature and tax consequences of a profits interest. The dollars and cents negotiation over the developer's receipt of a profits interest is discussed in much more detail in the section of this chapter dealing with cash distributions—see pages 257–280.

HIBC Case Study—Profits Interests

The equity deal struck in by *The Pizzuti Companies* (the developer) and *Nationwide Realty Investors, Ltd.* (its outside equity investor) stands as an excellent example of how the grant of profits interests can be structured to benefit the developer and its key employees. The operating agreement for the Pizzuti-Nationwide LLC stated that profits generated from new development projects would be split as follows:

Nationwide	55%
Pizzuti	30%
Key Pizzuti Employees	15%

While Pizzuti and its key employees were granted an aggregate profit split of 45%, they were only obligated to contribute 10% of the required capital (10% by Pizzuti and 0% by the key employees). The 35% incremental profit share (referred to by real estate investment bankers as a "promoted interest" or "promote") was granted to Pizzuti and its employees in exchange for their performance of services for the benefit of the LLC. Nationwide was willing to grant the 35% promoted interest to the developer and its employees for two reasons:

- The promote would only kick in after Nationwide had first received a 10% preferred return on its capital contributions (the concept of preferred returns is discussed later in this chapter at pages 267–271); and

- The promote would incentivize Pizzuti and it senior executives to do everything within their power to make the new projects a success—thereby producing a true win-win for all the equity participants.

Because the promoted interests were properly structured as profits interests in accordance with the guidelines laid out in Revenue Procedure 93–27, the grant of the 35% promote was effected in a tax-free manner.

The Pizzuti-Nationwide equity structure was markedly different from the arrangement that Pizzuti had struck with its prior equity investor— Newport Partners. The equity deal that Pizzuti negotiated with Newport did not provide for the grant of ANY profits interests to either Pizzuti or its employees. The profits generated from their jointly-owned projects were split in the same 50–50 ratio that governed their respective obligations to contribute capital to the entities that owned such projects. The absence of any promote was directly attributable to Newport's willingness to serve as a general partner of each project entity and to personally guaranty 50% of all construction debt. The trade-off for Newport's agreement to reduce Pizzuti's overall project risk was the concomitant reduction in Pizzuti's overall *financial return from the project (manifested in the elimination of any disproportionate profits interest in Pizzuti's favor). While Pizzuti deemed this to be an acceptable trade-off during the early years of its work on the HIBC project (when the risk associated with that project was at its peak), it was the absence of a profits interest for itself and its key employees that drove Pizzuti to later replace Newport with Nationwide as its principal outside equity provider for the HIBC project.*

B. ADDITIONAL CAPITAL CONTRIBUTIONS
(§ 2.2)

The discussion thus far in this section has focused on the capital contributed by the members at the inception of the LLC's formation. The next topic to be addressed is the post-formation capitalization of an LLC in the form of additional capital contributions made by the members. Many of the principles and concepts addressed in the initial capitalization section have equal applicability to the topic of additional capital contributions. For example, additional capital contributions can take the form of cash or property contributions and the tax consequences of such additional contributions are the same as those discussed earlier with respect to the initial capitalization of the LLC.

Additional capital contributions involve the funding of those project costs that were not sufficiently foreseeable on the date of the LLC's formation to be included in the company's initial capital budget. Unforeseeable project costs generally fall into one of two categories:

- Costs attributable to an unexpected expansion or change in the LLC's business; or

- Costs attributable to project cost overruns or operating deficits.

The category in which a project cost falls goes a long way toward determining whether such cost will be funded through additional capital contributions made to the LLC by its members.

1. Optional vs. Mandatory Contributions

The first question that must be answered is whether a member is obligated to make an additional capital contribution to the LLC and, if so, under what circumstances does that obligation exist? The answer to that question is clear as it relates to the first category of costs referenced above—that is, those costs that are triggered by an unexpected expansion or change in the LLC's business. A member will rarely, if ever, agree in advance to be obligated to make an additional contribution to fund the payment of a cost in that category. Indeed, in most negotiated deals, whoever is managing the LLC will likely be prohibited from expanding or changing the nature of the LLC's business unless the manager first obtains the consent of all the members of the LLC.

The funding of costs attributable to project cost overruns or operating deficits raises an entirely different and more difficult set of questions. The following are two classic examples of this second category of project costs:

- Debt service payments that were not included in the project budget either due to (a) an unexpected increase in the floating rate of interest on the project's construction debt, or (b) a slower than anticipated lease-up of the project, thereby postponing the budgeted onset of rental income to cover the debt service payments (producing an "operating deficit"); and

- Construction costs incurred to address adverse soils conditions or another project condition that was unknown at the time of the formation of the LLC (producing a "cost overrun").

The developer typically tries to hedge the LLC's financial risk by including in the project's initial capitalization budget a contingency reserve or other miscellaneous account to deal with the funding of cost overruns and operating deficits. However, despite such preventive measures, cost overruns and operating deficits occur on a regular basis on real estate development projects. If left unfunded, cost overruns and operating deficits can delay the timely completion of the project, cause a payment default on the LLC's loan, or, in the most extreme of situations, lead to the construction lender's foreclosure of the project. The question, therefore, becomes not whether, but how to fund cost overruns and operating deficits.

The members' customary first option for the funding of cost overruns and operating deficits is debt—either an increase in the amount of the project's existing mortgage loan or a new loan. However, debt may not be available in sufficient amounts to fund the payment of the cost overruns and operating deficits or may be available only on prohibitive economic and business terms. In recognition of this fact, the members of an LLC usually include in the LLC operating agreement a provision that deals in some fashion with the members' making of additional capital contributions to fund the payment of cost overruns and operating deficits. As might be expected, the views of the developer and the outside equity investor on how those provisions should be crafted are quite divergent.

2. Investor's Perspective on Additional Contributions

The outside equity investor's posture on additional capital contributions is influenced by its belief that cost overruns and operating deficits are invariably the fault of the developer. After all, didn't the developer market the project to the investor by selling itself as a real estate development expert, who was eminently qualified to complete and operate the project on time and on budget?

Given this mind set (which is, at least to some extent, logically justifiable), it should not be surprising that the equity investor's typical starting point in negotiations about additional capital contributions is that:

- The investor will have no obligation whatsoever to make any additional capital contributions to the LLC;

- Any cost overrun or operating deficit will first be covered by reducing the amount of any development, management, leasing, or other fees payable to the developer;

- The developer will be required to make additional capital contributions to cover 100% of the balance of any other cost overruns or operating deficits; and

- Any additional capital contributions made by the developer will be subordinate to the investor's capital position (meaning that such additional capital will only be repaid to the developer after the investor has received a full return "of" its initial capital and maybe even a minimum stated percentage of a return "on" its invested capital.

By adopting this stance, the outside equity investor is effectively asking the developer to guaranty the accuracy of the project budgets on which the LLC's initial capitalization was based.

3. Developer's Perspective on Additional Contributions

The developer's view of operating deficits and cost overruns is colored by its pragmatic world view that "stuff happens." In the developer's mind, a project budget is not a financial guaranty, but rather simply a reasonable estimate of the costs, income, and expenses related to the development and operation of a real estate project. The developer's counter to the investor's assertion that the developer should be responsible for the funding of cost overruns and operating deficits is to state in very plain (and sometimes profane) language that real estate development is not an exact science and that the developer cannot control all of the variables that impact the financial performance of a commercial real estate project.

With these thoughts in mind, the real estate development lawyer's first draft of the additional capital contribution section of the operating agreement customarily has the following flavor:

- The developer will have a unilateral, unconditional right to call for the members to make additional capital contributions to fund any project cost overrun or operating deficit; and

- The members' funding of such additional capital contributions will be made in the same ratio and with the same relative priority as the funding of their initial capital contributions to the LLC.

A particularly cheeky developer might take this position one step further by asserting that the outside equity investors should be responsible for funding 100% of the cost overruns and operating deficits, without any financial participation whatsoever by the developer.

4. Possible Compromises

While the developer and its equity investor may differ on who should be responsible for funding cost overruns and operating deficits, they share the objective of wanting to make sure that those overruns and deficits are ultimately funded—because they know that if the overruns and deficits are not funded, the project's commercial viability may be threatened. The following is a list of compromise provisions that are often used to bridge the parties' differences on the additional capital contribution subject.

- The members can agree to a limited number of cost and expense categories that will be subject to mandatory additional capital contributions—for example: debt service costs; costs set forth in an approved operating budget; real estate taxes and other operating expenses that, if not timely paid, could produce significant adverse legal consequences to the LLC; and any other costs or expenses that are not within the reasonable control of the developer.

- The members can stipulate that certain types of cost overruns and operating deficits must be funded by the developer—for example, those overruns and deficits that are caused by the developer's negligence or misconduct.

- The members can agree to place a cap on the amount of the additional capital contributions that a member is obligated to make to the LLC; or

- The members can agree to afford a priority return status to certain additional capital contributions—for example, by imposing a requirement that any additional capital contributions made by the outside equity investor must be repaid in full, with interest, before any cash distributions are made to the developer.

Each of the suggested compromise provisions may be used separately or in conjunction with one or more of the other provisions. By way of example, § 2.2 of the Form Operating Agreement adopts a hybrid approach by limiting each member's mandatory capital contribution obligation to the

funding of those costs that are incurred for an "approved purpose"—
generally meaning any cost that is consistent with a budget previously
approved by the members.

5. Remedies for Failure to Contribute Additional Capital (§ 2.3)

The Operating Agreement should identify the remedies that are
available to the LLC and the non-defaulting members to redress a
member's failure to make a mandatory additional capital contribution. The
following is a menu of contractual rights and prohibitions that are
commonly included in an operating agreement to remedy a member's
failure to make a required additional capital contribution to an LLC:[88]

- The right of a non-defaulting member to make up the
  shortfall in the defaulting member's additional capital
  funding, either in the form of an additional capital
  contribution to the LLC or a loan to the defaulting member
  (with the non-defaulting member receiving an exalted
  priority return status on the amount of its shortfall funding,
  with interest accruing on such funding at a healthy rate);

- The loss by the defaulting member of certain rights granted
  to it in the LLC operating agreement—for example, the right
  to vote on proposed LLC actions, or the right to trigger a buy-
  sell provision;

- The grant to the LLC of the right to offset the amount of a
  defaulted additional capital contribution obligation against
  any cash or property distributions otherwise due to the
  defaulting member under the terms of the operating
  agreement;

- The grant of an option to the non-defaulting members to buy
  the membership interest of the defaulting member at a
  discounted price (sometimes called a *haircut*);

- If the defaulting member is the developer, the loss of the
  developer's promoted profit interest and the termination of
  all service agreements between the LLC and the developer
  and its affiliates;

- A so-called *squeeze-down* right, pursuant to which the non-
  defaulting member may elect to cause the LLC to recalculate
  the ratios in which the members share in the LLC's profits
  and losses. A squeeze-down provision usually seeks to punish

---

[88] *See* Demetri Datch, *Drafting Capital Call Remedies for Real Estate Partnerships*, 29
PRACTICAL REAL ESTATE LAWYER No. 5 5 (September 2013; and Michael H. Glazer, *The Money
Partner's Reaction to the Global Recession of 2009: Recent Changes in Key Real Estate Joint Venture
Terms*, in ACREL PAPERS 308, 315 (Fall 2013).

the defaulting member for its failure to fund its share of the required additional capital by reducing the defaulting member's future financial sharing ratio below its share of the total capital contributed to the LLC. By way of example, a squeeze-down provision might state that the defaulting member's future participating percentage will be equal to 50% of the ratio that the defaulting member's total funded capital contributions bears to the total funded capital contributions of all the members.[89] If the defaulting member is the manager or managing member of the LLC, then the application of a squeeze-down provision also customarily results in the defaulting member's loss of all of its management authority.

The listed alternatives may be used separately or in conjunction with each other and are in addition to the normal remedies triggered by any contractual default—for example, damages, specific performance, and rescission.

One consideration that a lawyer representing the developer must keep in mind when negotiating remedy provisions is that, in most instances, the outside equity investor has greater financial strength and liquidity than does the developer. As such, the careful real estate development lawyer should resist an attempt to give the outside equity investor a right make a unilateral call for additional capital to the disadvantage of the developer. This advice is particularly crucial if the operating agreement contains provisions (for example, a squeeze-down or loss of management) that would permit the outside equity investors to significantly reduce or wholly eliminate the developer's interest in the project if the developer is unwilling or unable to satisfy the investor's capital call.

VII.   CASH DISTRIBUTIONS
(Article 3)

The cash distribution sections of the operating agreement are the one set of provisions that are sure to be read (over and over again) by the developer and the outside equity investor. These provisions address the two topics that hold the most interest for the members—how the cash flow created by the development project is split among the members and when that cash flow is paid to them? As emphasized repeatedly earlier in this book, a real estate development project's value is ultimately determined based upon the amount and timing of the cash flows generated from that project. Article 3 of the Form Operating Agreement spells out the manner

---

[89] *See e.g.*, Fluhrer, Multi-party Limited Liability Company Operating Agreement, *supra* note 70, at § 4.3.

in which each member participates in the project's cash flow and, hence, in the overall value of the development project.

It is important to take note of the difference between a project's ***cash flow*** and its ***profit and loss***. Profit and loss is an accounting and tax concept that measures the overall economic profitability (or lack thereof) of the LLC's business activities. Cash flow is the amount of cash that is available to be distributed to the LLC's members after deducting from the LLC's gross cash revenues all cash expenditures made by the LLC over a stated period (monthly, quarterly, or annually). Over the entirety of the LLC's existence, the profits and losses incurred by the LCC should equal the LLC's cash flow during such entire period (less the amount of cash flow consisting of a return of the members' capital contributions to the LLC). There can, however, be significant timing differences between the amount of the LLC's profits and its cash flow during an interim period of the LLC's existence. By way of example, the members of an LLC could opt to use a portion of the cash generated in a period to purchase an adjacent tract of land for future development—a decision that would decrease the LLC's cash flow, without decreasing the LLC's profits for such period. The attention of the members is generally focused on the timing and amount of the cash distributions they receive from the LLC and not on the more ethereal tax and accounting concept of profit and loss.

A.   CATEGORIES OF CASH FLOW

There are two basic categories of cash flow that an LLC derives from its ownership and operation of a real estate development project:

- Cash flow attributable to the LLC's day-to-day conduct of its rental and development operations (***operating cash flow***); and

- Cash flow attributable to the occurrence of certain capital transactions, such as the sale of all or a part of the project, the refinancing of project debt, a condemnation or casualty related to the project, or the occurrence of another event outside the realm of the LLC's regular business activities (***capital proceeds*** or ***extraordinary cash flow***).

Cash flow is separated into these two separate categories because the members often want to distribute operating cash flow and capital proceeds in different ways. If the members opt to distribute operating cash flow and capital proceeds in the same way (for example, in proportion to their respective capital contributions to the LLC), there is no need to create two categories of cash flow in the operating agreement and both such categories can be included under a single umbrella definition of "cash flow."

Exhibit A to the Form Operating Agreement contains the following definitions of the two cash flow categories.

"Capital Proceeds" means the gross cash receipts of the Company produced from the occurrence of a Capital Event,[90] reduced by the sum of the following: (a) all cash expenditures paid in connection with the Capital Event, including, without limitation, any brokerage commissions or fees paid to any party; (b) the repayment of the principal and any accrued and unpaid interest on any debt being refinanced or retired as part of the Capital Event; and (c) such cash reserves as Developer may decide to establish, with the consent of the Investor, to cover future occurrences and contingencies.

"Operating Cash Flow" means, with respect to each Fiscal Quarter of the Company, the sum of the gross cash receipts of the Company from any source other than Capital Proceeds, plus the amount of any previously-established, but unused cash reserves, reduced by the sum of the following items paid by the Company: (a) all principal and interest payments and all other sums paid on or with respect to any indebtedness; (b) all operating expenses incurred incident to the operation of the Project; (c) all capital expenditures incurred incident to the construction, repair, or replacement of the Project; (d) such cash reserves as Developer may from time to time decide to establish, with the consent of the Investor, to cover future occurrences and contingencies; and (e) all other cash expenditures made by the Company related to the ownership, operation, or management of the Project and the Company's business (other than any expenditure made in connection with the occurrence of a Capital Event).

Note that there is a reduction in both definitions for a *cash reserve* established by the developer (in this case, with the investor's consent). A "cash reserve" is a deposit made by the LLC into a "rainy day" bank account. Cash reserves are usually created for one of two reasons—either as (1) a general reserve to hedge the LLC's exposure to unknown and unforeseeable contingencies, or (2) a specific reserve to deal with a reasonably foreseeable future occurrence that could result in the LLC not having sufficient cash on hand to pay its expenses (such as a tenant moving out of the project). A natural tension exists on the topic of cash reserves between the developer (who is generally loath to set up any reserves) and its outside equity investors (who regularly push for the establishment of significant cash reserves). The developer tends, by nature, to be more optimistic than the typical conservative equity investor who sees financial catastrophe lurking around every corner. This inherent difference in

---

[90] A "Capital Event" generally refers to a sale or refinancing of a project or the occurrence of another event outside of the course of the LLC's normal business activities (for example, a condemnation or casualty that produces cash proceeds to the LLC. *See e.g., infra Document Appendix*, Form Operating Agreement, Exhibit A, Definitions, ¶ 15 at page 675.

approach is amplified by the fact that the outside equity investor is often entitled to receive its cash distributions from the LLC before the developer receives its cash distributions. As such, the establishment of a cash reserve hits the developer in the pocketbook well before it affects the outside investor. A carefully crafted operating agreement should specifically address which of the members has the authority to establish a cash reserve and what, if any, limitations are placed on that authority.

B. SCHEMES FOR THE DISTRIBUTION OF CASH FLOW

The previous section focused on the calculation of the amount of cash flow that is available for distribution to the LLC's members. The next question that the real estate development lawyer must address is how that cash flow is to be divided among the members of the LLC. In answering that question, the first place to look are the default rules contained in the applicable state LLC statute. By way of example, the Delaware Act provides that:

> Distribution of cash or other assets of a limited liability company shall be allocated among the members . . . in the manner provided in the limited liability company agreement. If the limited liability company agreement does not so provide, distributions shall be made on the basis of the agreed value (as stated in the records of the limited liability company) of the contributions made by each member to the extent they have been received by the limited liability company and have not been returned.[91]

The default rule, therefore, is that all cash flow is to be distributed to the members in proportion to the respective amounts of their capital contributions (the so-called *capital split*). Outside equity investors are typically more than happy to follow the default rule because doing so means that the investor receives a percentage of the LLC's cash flow that is commensurate with its capital split (which, in the typical situation is much higher than the developer's capital split).

The default rule is not viewed with the same level of acceptance by the developer who has contributed its *sweat equity* (that is, past and future services) to making the project successful. The developer wants the project's positive cash flow to be split not in accordance with the members' capital splits, but rather in accordance with a percentage split that is more favorable to the developer—the so-called *profit split*.

We are now at the precipice of the main event of the negotiation between the developer and its outside equity investor—that is, should the project's cash flow be distributed in accordance with the capital splits that favor the equity investor or the profit splits that favor the developer. As

---

[91] *See* DEL. CODE ANN., Title 6, § 18–504 (West 2016).

noted earlier in this chapter, the developer is usually able to convince its equity investor of the general wisdom of disbursing the LLC's positive cash flow based on the members' profits splits and not their capital splits. The interests of the developer and the investor are generally aligned on this conceptual point. The developer believes that disbursing cash flow based on profit splits is a deserved *REWARD* for the developer's efforts in making the project successful. On the flip side of the coin, the investor acquiesces in the developer's assertion that cash flow should be disbursed per the members' profit splits, because the investor wants to provide the developer with an *INCENTIVE* to work as hard as possible to maximize the project's profitability. Where the developer and the equity investor disagree is on the magnitude of the reward/incentive. The developer believes in its heart of hearts that it deserves a mammoth reward for its disproportionate contribution to the project's success. The investor wants the developer's incentive to be just enough to make the developer work a little harder— and then only after the investor has already made a decent profit on its investment.

The remainder of this discussion assumes that the preliminary negotiation between the developer and the equity investor produced a handshake agreement that cash contributions to the LLC will be made 75% by the outside equity investor and 25% by the developer (the members' *capital splits*), while the LLC's "profits" will be split 50–50 (the members' *profit splits*). With the conclusion of this preliminary negotiation, the developer and the equity investor are ready to get down and dirty and start arguing about what each of them means when it talks about the LLC's "profits." How that discussion goes will determine how much of the LLC's cash flow is distributed per the members' profits splits and how much ends up being distributed per the members' capital splits. The verbal sparring between the developer and the investor on this topic inevitably revolves around the magnitude and timing of the payment of the developer's "promote" versus that of the investor's "preferred return." The import of those two all-important terms of art is the focus of the next several pages of this text.[92]

---

[92] The cash distribution topic not only serves as the bedrock of the deal struck by the developer and the equity investor, but it also stands as the most intricate and complex part of the negotiations conducted by the respective counsel for the developer and its outside equity investors—witness the approximately 40 pages of text devoted to cash distributions in this book. I have opted not to insert footnote after footnote in those 40 pages citing to authorities supporting the analyses and strategies I offer up on the cash distribution topic. Instead, I recommend that a reader who wants to dig even deeper into the cash distribution schemes used in real estate joint ventures check out the following practitioner-authored articles that I find particularly insightful on the cash distribution topic—*see generally* STEVENS A. CAREY, REAL ESTATE VENTURES: FORMULATING AND INTERPRETING PROMOTE HURDLES AND DISTRIBUTION SPLITS (2016); Scott A. Lindquist, *A Real Estate Lawyer's Guide to Equity Investment (with Forms*, 25 No. 2 PRACTICAL REAL ESTATE LAWYER 41 (March 2009); Dean C. Pappas, Steven A. Waters, Vicki R. Harding, Gary E. Fluhrer, and Robert G. Gottlieb, *The Changing World of Real Estate Equity Investment*, in ACREL PAPERS 45 (Spring 2008); ROBERT L. WHITMIRE, WILLIAM F. NELSON, WILLIAM S. MCKEE, MARK A. KULLER, SANDRA W. HALLMARK, AND JOE GARCIA JR., STRUCTURING AND DRAFTING

1.   Cash Distribution Example

The negotiation that takes place between the developer and its equity investors about the developer's promote and the investor's preferred return is really all about math—specifically, how much of the project's cash flow gets paid to the developer and how much gets paid to the investor. The following example serves as the platform for the discussion that follows in the remainder of this section about the LLC's cash distribution scheme.

Example 7-4: Assume that Developer and Investor have agreed that Developer will contribute 25% of the LLC's required equity and get 50% of the LLC's profits and that Investor will contribute 75% of the required equity and get 50% of the LLC's profits (the "handshake agreement" referred to in the prior section of this chapter). To flesh out the math behind the parties' competing definitions of "profit," let's make the following assumptions:

- Cash capital contributions = $2 million:
  - o   Developer—$500,000 (25% capital split); and
  - o   Investor—$1.5 million (75% capital split).
- Project debt—$8 million (borrowed from local bank).
- LLC buys building for $10 million.
- LLC operates the building for two years producing:
  - o   Year 1 operating cash flow of $1 million; and
  - o   Year 2 operating cash flow of $1.2 million.
- LLC sells the project in Year 3 for $12 million producing capital proceeds of $4 million ($12 million sales price, less repayment of project debt of $8 million).
- Aggregate cash flow available for distribution to Developer and Investor = $6.2 million.
  - o   Operating cash flow = $2.2 million
    - o   Year 1 = $1 million; and
    - o   Year 2 = $1.2 million;
  - o   Capital proceeds = $4 million.

OK, the "math" question that counsel for Developer and Investor must answer when drafting the cash distribution section of the LLC's operating

PARTNERSHIP AGREEMENTS (INCLUDING LLC AGREEMENTS) §§ 5.03–5.05 (3rd ed. 2003); Dale Ann Reis, Deborah Levinson, and Stanford Presant, *Opportunistic Investing and Private Equity Funds*, 6 WHARTON REAL ESTATE REVIEW 39 (Spring 2002); Gary E. Fluhrer, Jan K. Gruben, Kenneth M. Jacobson, Lewis R. Kaster, Keith E. Osber, Joel M. Reck and Jonathon Rivin, *Multi-party Limited Liability Company Operating Agreement*, in ACREL PAPERS 133 (March 2004); and Glazer, *supra* note 88.

agreement is, How much of the $6.2 million of aggregate cash flow goes to Developer and how much of that cash flow goes to Investor?

The answer to that question brings us back to two concepts discussed in *Chapter 3—What the Real Estate Lawyer Needs to Know About Project Economics*—specifically the members' return *OF* capital versus the return *ON* capital. In Example 7-4, $2 million of the LLC's aggregate cash flow consists of a return *OF* the capital originally contributed to the LLC by Developer and Investor, and $4.2 million of the LLC's aggregate cash flow is the return *ON* the member's contributed capital. The new math question that counsel must resolve is, Should the $2 million return of capital be distributed in the same fashion as the $4.2 million return on capital or should the two cash flow components be distributed to the members under separate cash distribution schemes?

2. Distribution of Return *OF* Capital

The first question that needs to be addressed is, How should the return of capital component of an LLC's cash flow (the $2 million in Example 7-4) be disbursed to the LLC's members—that is, in accordance with the members' capital splits or their profit splits? The short answer to that question is that the $2 million return of capital should be paid per the members' capital splits—specifically 25% ($500,000) to Developer and 75% ($1.5 million) to Investor. The rationale for that answer is provided by (1) the tax rules on the treatment of capital interests vs. profits interests, and (2) the dictates of logic.

Let's start with the tax rationale. Revenue Procedure 93–27 and IRS Notice 2005–43 discussed earlier in this chapter[93] stand for the proposition that the developer's receipt of a share of the LLC's positive cash flow that is disproportionate to the developer's capital split is not a taxable event unless the interest received by the developer is a "capital interest." A capital interest is defined as an interest that would result in the developer receiving a cash distribution greater than its cash capital contribution if the LLC were to be hypothetically liquidated immediately after developer's receipt of its membership interest.

Under those tax rules, the developer in Example 7-4 would not recognize taxable income from its receipt of its membership interest unless the developer's cash take from a hypothetical immediate liquidation of the LLC exceeds the developer's $500,000 cash capital contribution to the LLC. If the LLC in Example 7-4 were to distribute the return on capital component of its cash flow ($2 million) in accordance with the negotiated profit splits (50-50), then Developer would be entitled to receive cash liquidation proceeds of $1 million—$500,000 more than the amount of Developer's cash contribution to the LLC. Under Revenue Procedure 93–

---

[93] *See supra Tax Consequences of Service Contributions*, pages 246–249.

27 and IRS Notice 2005–43, the LLC's decision to distribute its liquidation proceeds per the members' profits splits would result in Developer recognizing taxable income on day one of $500,000—a definite downer seeing that Developer does not actually receive any cash from a hypothetical liquidation of the LLC.

If, however, the LLC were to adopt a cash distribution scheme that mandates the distribution of return of capital component of its cash flow per the members' capital splits (75-25), Developer's cash distribution from a hypothetical liquidation of the LLC would only be $500,000—the exact amount of Developer's cash contribution to the LLC. Under Revenue Procedure 93–27 and IRS Notice 2005–43, Developer's hypothetical receipt of liquidation proceeds equal to Developer's cash contribution to the LLC means that Developer's membership interest is a "profits interest" that does not result in the recognition of any taxable income by Developer.

The oxymoronic conclusions under the tax rules are as follows:

- Developer does not recognize any taxable income if the LLC's operating agreement states that the return of capital piece of the LLC's cash flow must be distributed per the members' capital splits (because that means that Developer has received a profits interest); and

- Developer does recognize taxable income if the LLC's operating agreement states that the return of capital piece of the LLC's cash flow must be distributed per the members' profit splits (because that means that Developer has received a capital interest).

The bottom line under the current tax rules is that a developer should insist that the LLC's operating agreement recite that the members' contributed capital must be returned to them in proportion to the members' capital splits (75-25 in Example 7-4).

As noted at the outset of this section, the distribution of the LLC's return of capital component of its cash flow per the members' capital splits is also supported by the dictates of logic. This point is best illustrated by another example.

Example 7-5: Assume all of the same facts as in Example 7-4, except that:

- The LLC operates the building in Years 1 and 2 at a breakeven point—meaning that no operating cash flow is generated during those years.

- The LLC sells the building in Year 3 for $10 million—the exact price that it paid for the building in Year 1.

Under these facts, the aggregate cash flow available to be distributed to Developer and Investor is just $2 million (the $10 million sales price of the building in Year 3, less the $8 million project debt). In effect, the LLC has not generated any potential return *ON* capital because the LLC's total cash flow is equal to the members' original contributed capital—in other words, the LLC has not produced any profit from its ownership and operation of the project. Therefore, the entirety of the LLC's cash flow over the three-year period squarely falls in the return *OF* capital category.

The issue raised by Example 7-5 is, Are there any circumstances under which Investor would be willing to have the LLC's $2 million of cash flow distributed to the members other than per their capital splits? Logic dictates that the answer to that question is a clear and unequivocal "no." The rational Investor would insist that it receive full repayment of its invested capital of $1.5 million because the project did not generate any profit. Even an irrational Investor would understand that a distribution of the $2 million per the members' profit splits would result in a breakeven project producing a profit for Developer (its receipt of a distribution of capital proceeds of $1 million, compared to its cash contribution of $500,000) and a loss for Investor (its receipt of a distribution of capital proceeds of $1 million, compared to its cash contribution of $1.5 million)—obviously an untenable result for Investor.

Having established that the return of capital component of an LLC's cash flow should be distributed to the members in accordance with their capital splits, the next questions are—

- Will the return of the outside equity investor's capital contributions be required before any return of capital is made to the developer?

- Will the return of the outside equity investor's capital contributions be required before any distributions are made with respect to the developer's profits interest?

The answers to these questions vary depending on the relative negotiating leverage of the parties. That negotiating leverage tilts in favor of the outside equity investor if the project has a high risk quotient and if the outside equity investor agrees to provide virtually all of the required capital. For example, a venture capitalist investing in a high-risk, high-growth start-up business customarily structures its venture capital investment so that it receives a full return of its capital contributions, plus a minimum return *ON* that capital (frequently measured by an internal rate of return calculation) before the service partner is entitled to participate in any cash distributions. In the venture capital context, the economic interest of the service partner is commonly referred to as a ***carried interest*** because it is "carried" by the service partner without any financial benefit until the venture capitalist has received all of its money back, plus a negotiated level of return on that money. It is important to note that, in the context of a venture capital deal, the service provider seldom makes any significant cash contribution to the venture.

Because the real estate development business is far less risky than the typical start-up business targeted by venture capitalists and because the real estate developer usually makes a significant capital contribution to the deal, the developer is frequently able to negotiate return of capital provisions that fall well short of the pure carried interest arrangement discussed above. The real estate development lawyer's success in crafting distribution provisions that provide "no" answers to both of the questions posed at the beginning of this section is dependent upon how much capital the developer has committed to the deal and the level of risk associated with its proposed project (with the lawyer's chance for success being better the greater the developer's capital and the lower the project risk). The issue of the relative timing of the developer's and the investor's receipts of cash flow distributions from the LLC is discussed in more detail later in this section (see pages 273–277).

3. Distribution of Return *ON* Capital

Now that the issue of how the return *OF* capital component of the LLC's cash flow component should be distributed to the members has been settled (per their respective capital splits), the issue next becomes how should the return *ON* capital component of the LLC's cash flow be shared between the developer and its outside equity investors. The return *ON* capital piece of an LLC's cash flow represents the profit produced by the LLC over and above the return of the members' invested capital. This profit component is equal to the total cash flow available for distribution to the LLC's members over the life of the LLC, minus the capital contributed by the members to the LLC. In Example 7-4, the profit component was stipulated as being $4.2 million, consisting of (1) $2.2 million of operating cash flow in Years 1 and 2, plus (2) the $2 million of capital proceeds from the sale of the LLC's project that is available for distribution to the members after the retirement of the project debt and the return of the members' capital contributions.

Remember that in Example 7-4, Developer and Investor reached conceptual agreement that the LLC's "profits" would be split 50% to Developer and 50% to Investor, even though Developer only contributed 25% of the total capital required by the LLC. Developer's receipt of a disproportionate share of the LLC's profits is its reward/incentive for the sweat equity Developer contributes to the LLC.

The answer to the question of how the portion of the LLC's cash flow that represents the entity's "profit" should be distributed to Developer and Investor seems obvious—that cash flow should be distributed to Developer and Investor in proportion to their 50-50 profit splits. Both Developer and

Investor in Example 7-4 would undoubtedly agree on that point. Where they disagree is on is the magnitude of the LLC's "profit."

Developer's take is that the LLC's "profit" in Example 7-4 is $4.2 million and that Developer and Investor should each receive a cash distribution of $2.1 million. Investor's perspective is that the LLC's true "profit" is something less than $4.2 million and that it is only that lesser amount that should be split 50-50 by the Developer and Investor, with the remainder of the $4.2 million being split 75% to Investor and 25% to Developer (that is, per their capital splits). The differing perspectives of Developer and Investor on the math of the profit splits are founded on two important concepts—the developer's *promote* and the investor's *preferred return*.

C. DEVELOPER'S PROMOTE

The leading expert on the topic of the developer's promote is Stevens A. Carey, a California transactional lawyer. Carey defines the developer's promote as follows:

> A promote . . . is a share of profit distributions given to an operating partner that is not attributable to the operating partner's capital contributions. It is a contingent payment that is generally intended to incentivize and reward good performance and to compensate for value creation when that value is established by cash profits received by a partnership.[94]

Stated somewhat differently, the developer's promote is the portion of the developer's profits split that exceeds the developer's capital split. In Example 7-4, Developer received a 25% promote (its profits split of 50%, minus its capital split of 25%) in recognition of Developer's contribution of its past and future services to the LLC.

The negotiations over the developer's promote focus on two basic questions.

- What is the percentage interest of the developer's promote?

- What is the amount of the profit against which the developer's promote percentage is applied?

The answer to the first question is a simple matter of negotiating leverage with the developer arguing for a high percentage, the investor arguing for a low percentage, and the promote percentage typically being set somewhere between the two proffered extremes. The agreed-upon promote percentage serves as the multiplier for the calculation of the amount of the developer's promote.

---

[94] CAREY, *supra* note 92, at 6 (2016).

The art of the negotiation over the developer's promote centers on the second question posited above—that is, what is the amount of the "profit" against which the promote percentage is multiplied. The developer's answer to that question is that the profit amount is equal to the entity's total cash flow, less the members' contributed capital. In Example 7-4, Developer would take the position that the profit amount is $4.2 million.

Counsel to the outside equity investor argues that the true amount of the LLC's profit must be reduced by subtracting from the entity's total cash flow not only the investor's return *OF* its contributed capital, but also a minimally acceptable return *ON* that contributed capital (the "preferred return" that is the subject of the next section of this chapter). Reducing the amount of the LLC's profit to take into consideration the investor's preferred return has the obvious, intended effect of reducing the value of the developer's promote.

D. PREFERRED RETURN

Counsel for the outside equity investor invariably insists that the investor must receive a minimum cash return on its capital contributions before the developer gets to receive any distributions attributable to its promote. This minimum cash return is commonly referred to as a *preferred return*. There are several subsets of questions related to the setting of the preferred return.

- *Is the payment of the preferred return guaranteed by the LLC or the developer?* In Chapter 3, it was noted that the primary difference between debt and equity is that there is no fixed obligation to repay the capital contributed to the LLC by a member or to pay any return on that contributed capital. As a general rule, the only source for the repayment of a member's capital contribution (including the payment of any return on such contribution) is the cash flow generated by the LLC's business activities. If there is no cash flow, then no payments are due to the equity investor. While it is not unheard of for a developer to agree to guaranty the payment of a minimal preferred return to the equity investor for a limited period of time (for example, the first two years of the LLC's existence), the real estate development lawyer should agree to the inclusion of such a guaranty only in those very rare instances where such a guaranty is absolutely essential to the developer's ability to secure the funding commitment of an equity investor.

- *What is the amount of the preferred return?* Historically, the rate of the annual preferred return rate on real estate development deals has run somewhere between 8 and 12% of the contributed capital. The preferred return rate can also be tied to a financial index or stated in terms of an internal rate of return. The setting of the preferred return rate is, in large measure, dependent upon the parties' perception of the risk of the subject real estate investment, with the preferred return rate being higher for riskier projects.

- ***Is the preferred return cumulative?*** The LLC's obligation to make a preferred return payment to its investors is conditioned upon the LLC having sufficient cash on hand to make those payments. The question, therefore, becomes, What if the LLC does not have enough cash available in a particular period to pay the investors the full amount of the stipulated preferred return? Does the shortfall carry over to the next period, thereby increasing the amount of the preferred return to be paid to the investors in the subsequent period? In most situations, the outside equity investor carries the day in its insistence that the preferred return be calculated on a cumulative basis, with the end result that any shortfalls in the payment of the required preferred return carry over to the next calculation period.

- ***Is the preferred return calculated on a compounded basis? If so, how frequently is it compounded?*** The compounding of the preferred return simply means that any unpaid preferred return is added to the base amount against which the preferred return is calculated. The frequency of the compounding of any unpaid preferred return commonly falls somewhere between monthly and annually, although a particularly aggressive capital provider might be able to get the concept of daily compounding incorporated into the documents. The good news for the real estate developer is that it usually stands a better chance of successfully eliminating the compounding feature from the investor's preferred return than it does the cumulative feature of that return.

- ***When does the accrual of the preferred return begin?*** The preferred return customarily begins accruing on the date that the capital is first contributed to the LLC. However, it is not unheard of for an operating agreement to recite that the investors' preferred return does not begin to accrue until after the real estate project is completed and ready to be occupied by tenants. The theory posited by the real estate development lawyer in this attempt to defer the beginning date for the accrual of the preferred return is that a real estate project cannot produce any cash to pay the investor a return on its capital until the project is capable of being occupied by rent paying tenants. The countervailing point made by counsel for the equity investor is that the investor is simply not in a business of providing its capital to anyone on an interest-free basis—and that includes capital invested during the construction period of a commercial real estate project.

The real estate development lawyer's goal in negotiating all of the above preferred return issues is quite simple—the lawyer wants to do everything possible to reduce the aggregate amount of the investor's preferred return. The lawyer can accomplish this goal not only by simplistically negotiating down the percentage of the investor's preferred return, but also by vigorously negotiating positions that favor the developer on the cumulative and compounded nature of the investor's preferred return and the date on which the calculation of the investor's return first begins to accrue.

The negotiation of the issues related to the developer's promote and the investor's preferred return is fought with competing contractual language, but it really is all about the math. The developer's goal is to maximize the amount of the project cash flow that is distributed according to the members' profit splits (50-50 in Example 7-4). The developer accomplishes that goal by limiting the amount of the preferred return distributions that are required to be made to the investor, because each preferred return distribution reduces on a dollar-for-dollar basis the amount of the "profit" that is left to be paid to the developer per the promoted profit splits.

The following example illustrates the impact that differing levels of the investor's preferred return has on the value of the developer's promote.

Example 7-6: Assume the following facts:

- Members' capital contributions:
  o Investor = $5 million; and
  o Developer = $0.
- Operating cash flow:
  o Year 1 = $100,000; and
  o Year 2 = $1.2 million.
- Cash flow splits after payment of preferred return:
  o Investor = 50%; and
  o Developer = 50%.

The following chart illustrates the relative cash distributions received by Investor and Developer under the following three preferred return scenarios:

- **Scenario #1**—No preferred return (producing $0 preferred return to Investor);

- **Scenario #2**—8% non-cumulative, simple preferred return (producing $500,000 preferred return to Investor); and

- **Scenario #3**—10% cumulative, compounded monthly preferred return (producing $990,000 preferred return to Investor).

Preferred Return Scenarios	*Investor's Split*	*Developer's Split*
Scenario #1	$650,000 (50%)	$650,000 (50%)
Scenario #2	$900,000 (69%)	$400,000 (31%)
Scenario #3	$1,145,000 (88%)	$155,000 (12%)

Example 7-6 validates the simple notion that the higher the investor's preferred return, the lower the value of the developer's promote. The effect of increasing the investor's preferred return is to decrease the portion of the LLC's cash flow that is distributed according to the members' profit splits and increasing the portion of the LLC's cash flow that is distributed according to the members' capital splits—a bad situation for the developer all the way around.

There are a few other issues related to the investor's preferred return that can impact the cash distributions made to the investor and the developer.

- ***Who is entitled to a preferred return?*** In Example 7-4, Developer contributed 25% of the required LLC capital and Investor contributed the remaining 75%. Is Developer entitled to a preferred return on its contributed capital or is the preferred return payable only on the Investor's capital? In the typical joint venture arrangement, preferred return is calculated on the capital of all the members, including the developer' capital. If a real estate development lawyer acquiesces to an investor only preferred return, then the product of that misguided concession is that the value of the developer's promote is further eroded, because a portion of the profit component of the LLC's cash flow equal to the investor's preferred return is distributed 100% to the investor (and not just per the members' capital splits).

- ***Is a preferred return payable out of both operating cash flow and capital proceeds?*** As noted at the outset of this section, there are two principal categories of cash flow—operating cash flow generated by the LLC's day-to-day rental operations, and capital proceeds produced by a sale, refinancing, or other capital event related to the LLC's real estate project. LLC operating agreements almost always require that the members' unreturned capital contributions *AND* any unpaid preferred return must be paid to the members before any portion of the LLC's capital proceeds are paid out based upon the promoted profit splits. The majority of real estate ventures also extend the priority given to preferred return payments (but not always unreturned capital—see pages 272–273) to the distribution of operating cash flow.

- ***Can there be more than one preferred return hurdle?*** It is increasingly becoming the norm for the payment of the developer's promote to be subjected to more than one preferred return hurdle.[95] By way of example, an LLC operating agreement could provide that cash flow will be distributed 75-25 until the investor has achieved a preferred return of 8%, then 65-35 until the investor has received a preferred return of 12%, and then 50-50 thereafter.

E. STRUCTURING THE CASH DISTRIBUTION PROVISIONS

The discussion in this section has thus far discussed the three basic categories of cash distributions that are typically present in a sophisticated real estate venture—specifically, (1) return of capital, (2) preferred return, and (3) promote distributions. The point has been made that the members of an LLC often draw a distinction between two types of cash flow—that is operating cash flow versus capital proceeds. It is now time to meld all these concepts into a coherent set of provisions that govern the manner and order of priority of all cash distributions made to the members of an LLC.

1. Priority of Different Categories of Cash Flow

Let's start with the low hanging fruit. As noted in the prior section of this chapter, virtually every LLC operating agreement contains provisions that require capital proceeds to be distributed as follows:

---

[95] *See* CAREY, *supra* note 92, at 7.

- First to return the members' unreturned capital contributions;

- Second to pay the members' unpaid preferred returns; and

- Third to pay the members any remaining capital proceeds per the promoted profit splits.

This distribution structure is driven by two factors—(1) the tax requirement that priority must be given to the return of the member's contributed capital in order for the developer to avoid recognizing taxable income upon its receipt of its promoted profits interest, and (2) the fact that capital proceeds are typically payable upon the sale of the LLC's real estate project when the members can make a final reckoning of the venture's profitability (or lack thereof).

The provisions governing operating cash flow distributions are not susceptible to characterization with the same level of universality as are the capital proceeds distribution provisions. There are no fixed tax drivers that compel operating cash flow to be distributed in a particular way. Further confounding the issue is the circumstance that the LLC members seldom know at the time an operating cash flow payment is scheduled to be distributed to the members whether their investments will ultimately be wildly or mildly profitable or not profitable at all. The developer and the outside equity investors are, therefore, free to structure the operating cash flow distributions in any fashion they deem appropriate.

The primary determinants of the structure of an LLC's operating cash flow distribution provisions are (1) the equity investor's perception of the risk associated with its investments in the LLC, and (2) the magnitude of the developer's capital contribution to the LLC. If the investor believes that the developer's project is extremely risky and if the investor contributes 95–100% of the project's required capital, then the investor might insist that operating cash flow be distributed in the same manner as capital proceeds—that is:

- First to return the members' unreturned capital contributions;

- Second to pay the members' unpaid preferred returns; and

- Third to pay the members any remaining operating cash flow per the promoted profit splits.

This is the structure commonly used when a venture capital fund invests in a start-up business. The structure is uncommon, but not rare, in the context of real estate ventures.

A typical real estate venture of middling risk where the developer makes a significant capital contribution (10% and up) more typically produces the operating cash flow distribution provisions along the following lines (note the elimination of the return of capital requirement):

- First to pay the members' unpaid preferred returns; and

- Second to pay the members any remaining operating cash flow per the promoted profit splits.

Finally, a relatively risk-free real estate venture (an office building in Manhattan that is 100% leased to Microsoft) where the developer makes a significant capital contribution might skip both the return of capital and preferred return hurdles and provide that all operating cash flow will immediately be disbursed in accordance with the members' promoted profit splits (because the members are comfortable with the ultimate profitability of a project that produces positive operating cash flow).

2.   Relative Priorities of Developer and Investor

The next question that counsel for the developer and the investor need to answer is whether the developer and the investor will be treated on equal footing as it relates to each cash distribution category—that is, the return of capital, the payment of preferred return, and the payment of the promoted profit splits. In structuring the distribution priorities, counsel has two basic choices:

- A *pari passu* distribution where the respective rights of the developer and investor to participate in a particular cash distribution category called out in the LLC's operating agreement are placed on "equal footing" (which is what "*pari passu*" means in Latin); and

- A *waterfall* distribution where one of the members has a superior right to participate in a cash distribution category.

When drafting the cash distributions of an LLC operating agreement, counsel must decide at each cash distribution level (that is, the payment of the members' respective returns of capital, preferred returns, and promoted profit splits for both operating cash flow and capital proceeds) whether the relative priority of the developer and the outside equity investor should be *pari passu* or subject to a waterfall. Here are representative examples of *pari passu* and waterfall provisions for the distribution of capital proceeds to return the members' contributed capital:

- *Pari Passu*—First 80% to Investor and 20% to Developer until each of Investor and Developer has received a full return of its contributed capital.

- *Waterfall*—

    o   First to Investor until Investor has received a full return of its contributed capital; and

o   Second to Developer until Developer has received a full
        return of its contributed capital.

The cash impact of the *pari passu* vs. waterfall distributions is felt
when the LLC does not have enough cash flow to fully pay a distribution
category to both the investor and developer. By way of example, assume
that the LLC has capital proceeds of $1 million and that the investor
contributed capital of $1 million and the developer contributed capital of
$250,000. Under the *pari passu* clause, the LLC would pay capital proceeds
of $800,000 to the investor and $200,000 to the developer. Under the
waterfall format, the entire $1 million of capital proceeds would be paid to
the investor and the developer would not get any cash whatsoever.

As noted earlier, the *pari passu* versus waterfall issue must be
resolved for each type and each level of the LLC's cash flow that is available
for distribution to the developer and its outside equity investors.
Specifically, counsel for the developer and counsel for the investor must
articulate in the four corners of the operating agreement's cash distribution
provisions the relative priorities of the developer versus the investor (that
is, equal footing under a *pari passu* arrangement or a subordinate position
for the developer under a waterfall arrangement) as to the return of capital,
preferred return, and promote for each operating cash flow and capital
proceeds distribution. As a result, it is not uncommon for the cash
distribution article of an LLC operating agreement to be several pages
long—especially if the members opt to include multiple preferred return
hurdles and promoted profit splits.

3.   Holdbacks, Lookbacks, and Clawbacks

Before concluding the discussion of the cash distribution provisions of
an LLC operating agreement, a quick note should be made of a danger that
arises if the LLC operating agreement sanctions the distribution of a
portion of the LLC's operating cash flow to the developer in accordance with
the developer's promoted profits interest—which, as noted in the prior
section of this chapter, is fairly typical in all but the most risky of real
estate ventures. The following example illustrates the unintended business
consequence that can result if the LLC's operating agreement provides that
the developer is entitled to receive its share of operating cash flow based
upon its promoted profits interest and not its lower capital split.

Example 7-7: Assume that ABC LLC is formed to buy an office
building and that the purchase price of the building is $5 million,
all of which is paid through capital contributions from ABC's
members. The members agree that Investor will supply 75% of the
required capital ($3.75 million) and that Developer will provide
the remaining 25% ($1.25 million). The members' handshake
agreement is that they will split all profits 50–50. Because the
members have read this chapter, they know that Developer

cannot be given more than a 25% interest in the existing value of
the office building ($5 million), unless Developer is willing to
recognize taxable income coincident with its receipt of a
membership interest in ABC (which it clearly does not want to do).
As such, the members agree that, while operating cash flow will
be split 50–50, capital proceeds will first be used to return the
members' capital contributions, with the remaining capital
proceeds then being split in accordance with the agreed-upon 50–
50 profit sharing ratio.

All goes well for ABC's business during the first two operating
years. The financial results for those two years are as follows:

Year 1:	LLC's operating cash flow	$450,000
	Developer's 50% share	$225,000
	Investor's 50% share	$225,000
Year 2:	LLC's operating cash flow	$550,000
	Developer's 50% share	$275,000
	Investor's 50% share	$275,000

At the beginning of Year 3, the office building's anchor tenant goes
bankrupt and ABC is forced to sell the office building for $4
million—$1 million less than it paid for the same building two
years previously. Per their agreement, the sales proceeds are split
between the members in accordance with their capital interests
(that is, 75% to Investor and 25% to Developer).

Year 3:	LLC's capital proceeds	$4,000,000
	Developer's 25% share	$1,000,000
	Investor's 75% share	$3,000,000

The following recap shows how Developer and Investor fared on their
respective investments in ABC.

Developer's Cash Flow:

Year 1 operating cash flow	$225,000
Year 2 operating cash flow	$275,000
Year 3 capital proceeds	$1,000,000
Total cash distributions	$1,500,000
Less: Initial capital contribution	$1,000,000
Net Investment Profit	**$500,000**

Investor's Cash Flow:

Year 1 operating cash flow	$225,000
Year 2 operating cash flow	$275,000
Year 3 capital proceeds	$3,000,000
Total cash distributions	$3,500,000
Less: Initial capital contribution	$4,000,000
Net Investment Loss	**($500,000)**

The above example shows what can happen under a fairly typical cash distribution scheme when early project profits are followed by subsequent project losses. The LLC basically broke even on its investment in the office building (putting aside for a second everything the reader learned in Chapter 3 about the time value of money). The LLC generated operating cash flow of $1 million in Years 1 and 2 and then was forced to sell its only asset in Year 3 at a loss of $1 million. One would think that the parties' handshake agreement that they would share any profits 50–50 should result in neither of them making any money on its investment—because the LLC failed to earn an overall profit. However, as the above example illustrates, the operation of ABC's cash distribution scheme actually resulted in Developer making $500,000 on its investment, while Investor lost $500,000.

While Developer probably thinks that its lawyer did a helluva job in drafting the cash distribution provisions of ABC's operating agreement, the end result is clearly inconsistent with the original tenor of the business deal struck by Developer and Investor. There are a few ways that the members could have fixed this problem.

- The members could have established a cash reserve (a *holdback*) from operating cash flow to partially hedge the risk of a future downturn in the project's overall financial condition. In Example 7-7, the establishment of a holdback of $500,000 out of the $1 million of aggregate operating cash flow distributions made in Years 1 and 2 would have cut the inappropriate shifting of cash to Developer from $500,000 to $375,000.

- The members could have agreed to a *lookback* provision that would have allowed the LLC to deduct from Developer's share of the capital proceeds the $250,000 of operating cash flow distributed to the developer in Years 1 and 2 with respect to its 25% promoted profits interest.

- The members could have agreed to a *clawback* provision that would have permitted Investor to institute a legal action against Developer (or a creditworthy affiliate of Developer) to recover the $500,000 of excess distributions received by the Developer.

4. Distribution Provisions of the Form Operating Agreement (§§ 3.1–3.3)

The distribution provisions of the Form Operating Agreement are fairly typical for a real estate development LLC. Those provisions prescribe the following simple schemes for the distribution of the LLC's operating cash flow and capital proceeds in the context of a deal struck by a developer and its equity investor where their capital splits are 75-25 in the investor's favor and their profit splits are 50-50.

- ### Distribution of Operating Cash Flow:
  o First, 25% to the developer and 75% to the investor, until each member has received the full amount of its unpaid preferred return (calculated at a cumulative compounded rate of 10%); and

  o The remainder 50% to the developer and 50% to the investor.

- ### Distribution of Capital Proceeds:
  o First, 25% to the developer and 75% to the investor until each member has received a full return of its capital contributions;

    o   Second, 25% to the developer and 75% to the investor until each member has received a full return of its unpaid preferred return; and

    o   The remainder 50% to the developer and 50% to the investor.

The cash distribution provisions of the Form Operating Agreement are to some extent pro-developer. The Form Operating Agreement does not authorize the establishment of any investor-mandated holdback, look-back, or clawback. Moreover, the Form Operating Agreement provides that the developer and the investor are given the same priority on a *pari passu* basis in the LLC's distribution of all return of capital, preferred return, and promote distributions.

5.   Timing of Cash Distributions

The default rule set forth in the Delaware Act calls for the making of distributions on the withdrawal of a member or on the dissolution of the LLC.[96] This default rule seldom works for either the developer or its outside equity investors and, therefore, is usually overridden by specific provisions of the operating agreement.

Distributions of operating cash flow are typically required to be made no less frequently than annually. Many investors push to have operating cash flow distributed on a quarterly or monthly basis. Capital proceeds are generally distributed coincident with the occurrence of the capital event giving rise to the capital proceeds (for example, the sale of the project or the refinancing of the project debt). With respect to the distribution of both operating cash flow and capital proceeds, the drafter of the operating agreement should specify that the distributions must be made within a specified number of days after the end of the selected fiscal period or the occurrence of the capital event, as the case may be. The selected period should be sufficiently long to permit the LLC's financial officers ample time to make an accurate calculation of the amount of the cash flow that is available for distribution to the members.

6.   Take Home Points on Cash Distributions

The following are the key points to remember about the cash distribution provisions of a typical LLC operating agreement where the developer and the investor agree to give the developer a promote—that is, an interest in the LLC's profits that is disproportionate to the developer's share of the LLC's contributed capital.

- The members' capital contributions should be returned per the members' capital splits.

---

[96] *See* DEL. CODE ANN., Title 6, § 18–601 (West 2016).

- The LLC's "profit" (meaning the excess of the LLC's total cash flow over the members' contributed capital) may be distributed in any way the members determine.

- The developer wants 100% of the LLC's profit to be distributed per the members' profit splits.

- The investor wants a portion of the LLC's profit to be distributed as preferred return per the members' capital splits.

- The higher the preferred return paid to the investor, the lower the value of the developer's promote (because there is then less cash flow available to be distributed per the promoted profit splits).

- Although cash distributions are all about "math," that math is determined by the words the lawyers use when drafting the LLC's operating agreement—so please draft wisely.

HIBC Case Study—Cash Distributions

The cash distribution provisions of the Pizzuti-Newport general partnership agreement stated that all cash flow would be distributed 50% to Pizzuti and 50% to Newport. Pizzuti did not receive any promoted profits interest as part of its relationship with Newport. As a result, there was simply no need to address any of the complexities discussed in the prior section.

The distribution provisions of the Pizzuti-Nationwide operating agreement, on the other hand, were quite complex. Promoted profits interests were granted to both Pizzuti and a separate LLC formed by Pizzuti's key employees (thankfully including the author). The specifics of these promoted interests are discussed in the prior section of this chapter captioned "HIBC Case Study—Profits Interests" (see pages 250–251). The existence of the promoted interests necessitated the inclusion in the Pizzuti-Nationwide operating agreement of provisions on (1) the accrual and payment of a preferred return to the equity investors, and (2) the separate calculation of operating cash flow and capital proceeds. The basics of those provisions were in most respects comparable to the pro-developer provisions of the Form Operating Agreement summarized in the previous section of this chapter.

Most of the complexity found in the distribution provisions of the Pizzuti-Nationwide operating agreement was attributable to the fact that the new entity was formed to own: (a) more than 20 existing real estate projects; (b) an unlimited number of real estate projects to be newly developed under the ownership umbrella of the newly formed entity; and (c) a real estate operating company that was responsible for developing, leasing, and managing all of Pizzuti's and Nationwide's jointly-owned real estate projects. Pizzuti and Nationwide negotiated different financial sharing ratios and conditions for each of the three classes of properties owned by the new Pizzuti-Nationwide entity. For example, the preferred return on the existing properties was set at 9.5%, while the preferred return for newly developed properties was pegged at 10% (illustrating the point made earlier in this chapter that the setting of the preferred return rate is linked to the perceived risk of the subject real estate investment). The promoted interests granted to Pizzuti and its employees also differed by property class—for example, an aggregate 35% promote for the operating company and the newly-developed projects versus a 5% promote on the existing properties.

The disparate treatment afforded each of these three property classes required that the cash flow attributable to the activities of each of those classes be separately calculated. The issue that consumed an inordinate amount of time during the drafting and negotiation of the Pizzuti-Nationwide operating agreement was how the calculation of one category of cash flow should impact the calculation of cash flow for another property category. There were two specific questions that counsel for Pizzuti and Nationwide spent hours discussing (sometimes in civil tones).

- Should a loss realized on the sale of one property impact the distribution of capital proceeds on the later sale of another property?

- Should the positive operating cash flow produced from one property category (for example, the existing properties) be used to subsidize the payment of the preferred return payable on another property category (for example, the newly-developed properties)?

Pizzuti argued passionately that each cash flow category should be calculated and distributed on a totally free-standing basis and that the level of capital proceeds produced on the sale or refinancing of one property should never be taken into consideration when determining the proper distribution of capital proceeds attributable to another property. Why was Pizzuti so adamant in its position? If you were representing Nationwide, what grounds would you have postulated to support your position that both of the above questions should be answered in the affirmative? FYI—sadly, Pizzuti lost the argument on both of these points.

F. THE "CARRIED INTEREST" TAX CONTROVERSY

As noted in an earlier section of this chapter, the developer's receipt of a profits interest that is disproportionate to its share of the LLC's contributed capital (the developer's promote) is not subject to tax at the time the interest is received because that interest does not entitle the developer to any share of the liquidation value of the LLC's existing assets.[97] The rules of Subchapter K of the Internal Revenue Code further provide that an LLC's taxable income and loss are passed through to its members, with the character of such items in the hands of the members being determined at the partnership level.[98] As such, a sale of a commercial real estate project that produces a long-term capital gain at the LLC level is treated as a long-term capital gain on the tax returns of the LLC's constituent members. Under current federal tax law, long-term capital gains are taxed at a maximum rate of 20%, while ordinary compensation income is subjected to a maximum tax rate of 39.6%.[99]

The convergence of the above-described tax rules results in an extremely favorable treatment for the developer's promote. The following example illustrates the effect that these rules have upon the after-tax return earned by a developer from its receipt of a promoted profits interest.

Example 7-8: Assume Developer makes a capital contribution to ABC LLC of $500,000 (representing 25% of the total capital contributed to ABC by all its members). ABC uses the contributed capital from all its members to purchase land at an initial cost of $2 million. Developer receives a 50% profits interest in ABC that consists of its 25% capital interest and a promoted profits interest of 25% (which was properly structured to avoid Developer's current recognition of taxable income). Two years later, ABC sells the land for $4 million, producing a long-term capital gain of $2 million. Immediately following the sale, ABC distributes the $4 million in land sales proceeds to its members, with Developer receiving a total distribution of $1.5 million (its invested capital of $500,000, plus its 50% share of the $2 million profit generated on ABC's sale of the land).

The after-tax profit generated from Developer's investment in ABC is quite impressive—a net return to Developer's bottom line of $800,000.

---

[97] *See supra* pages 246–249.

[98] *See* I.R.C. § 702(b).

[99] *See* I.R.C. §§ 1(h) and (i). These rates do not include the additional tax surcharge of 3.8% imposed on net investment income under I.R.C. § 1411.

Developer's Cash Distribution on Sale of Land	$1,500,000
Less: Developer's Capital Contribution to ABC	$500,000
Less: Developer's Income Tax Payment	
(Developer's 50% Share of $2 million capital gain × 20% capital gains rate)	$200,000
Developer's Net After-Tax Return	**$800,000**

The results produced in Example 7-8 stand as a testament to (1) the financial importance of a developer's receipt of a promote (the developer's 25% promote produced an additional pre-tax distribution to Developer of $500,000—that is, the 25% promote × the $2 million land profit), and (2) the beneficial tax treatment afforded to a developer's receipt of a distribution attributable to the occurrence of a project sale at the entity level. If Developer's entire share of the gain produced on the sale of ABC's land had been taxed at the 39.6% rate applicable to ordinary compensation income (instead of the advantaged capital gains rate of 20%), Developer's net after-tax return from its investment in ABC would have been decreased by $196,000 (its 50% share of the $2 million gain produced on the sale of the land × the 19.6% differential between the tax rates payable on capital gains vs. ordinary income).

The favorable tax treatment imparted to a developer's receipt of a promoted profits interest is being threatened by proposed legislation first introduced in Congress in 2007 (and re-introduced in a variety of forms since that date). Earlier that year, Blackstone Group, a leading private equity firm that was in the process of going public, filed reports with the SEC indicating that Steven Schwarzman, Blackstone's CEO, had earned approximately $400 million in 2006—most of which was apparently produced from profits interests held by Mr. Schwarzman in a variety of ventures and, therefore, was taxed at the then maximum capital gains rate of 15%. The disclosure of the tax benefits achieved by Schwarzman's use of what in private equity and hedge fund circles is called a "carried interest" (a promote in the vernacular of the real estate investor) triggered a public outcry that led Representative Sander Levin to introduce H.R. 2834 in an attempt to better serve tax fairness by subjecting all income produced under a carried interest to taxation as ordinary compensation income (and not, under any circumstances, as capital gain).[100] Versions of H.R. 2834 have been reintroduced in Congress repeatedly over the last several years.

---

[100] *See* H.R. 2834, 110th Congress (2007).

The most recent version of the proposed legislation is titled the Carried Interest Fairness Act.[101]

The Carried Interest Fairness Act covers profits interests (referred to in the proposed legislation as "investment services partnership interests") related to the investment, purchase, sale, management, or financing of "specified assets." For this purpose, the "specified assets" covered by the proposed legislation expressly include not just securities, commodities, and other interests generally dealt with by the targeted hedge fund managers and private equity firms, but also "real estate held for rental or investment."[102]

The proposed legislation holds both good news and bad news for real estate developers and investors:

- ***The Good News***—The pending bills would confirm the tax treatment of capital and profits interests referred to earlier in this chapter (that is, the current recognition of income on the receipt of a capital interest, but not a profits interest);[103] and

- ***The Bad News***—The proposed legislation would require all income produced under an "investment services partnership interest" to be taxed as ordinary compensation income—and specifically not as a capital gain. This mandated ordinary income treatment expressly includes any gain produced on the sale of an entity's assets or an investor's sale of its equity interest in such entity. The "not so bad" news is that the Carried Interest Fairness Act makes an exception for a "qualified capital interest," which is generally defined as the portion of a person's equity interest that is granted in consideration of the person's contribution of cash or property to a pass-through entity. As such the passage of the Carried Interest Fairness Act would impact only the promoted portion of the equity interest granted to a real estate developer and not the portion of such interest that was directly proportionate to the developer's capital split.[104]

If legislation is passed that is consistent with the Carried Interest Fairness Act, then Developer's tax charge under the facts of Example 7-8 would increase by $98,000—producing a 12% reduction in Developer's net after-tax return from its investment in ABC. Developer's additional tax obligation is calculated as follows—the percentage of Developer's promoted profits interest (25%) × ABC's land sale gain ($2 million) × the increase in

---

[101] *See* S. 1686, 114th Congress (2015–2016); and H.R. 2889, 114th Congress (2015–2016).

[102] *See id.* at § 3.

[103] *See id.* at § 2.

[104] *See id.* at § 3.

the tax rate applicable to the sale under the proposed legislation (19.6%). The imposition of this additional tax liability would decrease Developer's net, after-tax return from $800,000 to $704,000. Please note that under the "qualified capital interest" exception found in the Carried Interest Fairness Act, Developer's 25% share of ABC's land sale gain that was attributable to Developer's capital split (granted in recognition of Developer's capital contribution to ABC of $500,000) is still afforded capital gain treatment and taxed at a 20% rate.

The argument proffered in support of the Carried Interest Fairness Act is that the financial benefit received by a taxpayer under a carried interest or promote is, in essence, nothing more than compensation received by the holder of that interest in exchange for the holder's performance of services for the entity. The proponents of the approach adopted in the Carried Interest Fairness Act assert that rich developers and hedge fund managers should not be "paying lower tax rates than their secretaries or the janitor that cleans up the building."[105] Supporters of the Carried Interest Fairness Act also point out that added tax revenues are desperately needed to help reduce the federal deficit.

The proposed legislation on carried interests has been met with fierce opposition from both private equity firms and real estate industry groups. Steven Schwarzman, the CEO of Blackstone Group, whose 2006 receipt of millions of dollars of carried interest benefits prompted the introduction of the carried interest legislation, somewhat wildly stated that President Obama's prior support for the carried interest legislation "is like when Hitler invaded Poland."[106]

The essence of the argument proffered by opponents of the proposed carried interest legislation is twofold—(1) a carried interest subjects the holder of that interest to the same type of entrepreneurial risk that characterizes a taxpayer's investment in stocks, bonds, and other investment assets that are afforded capital gain treatment, and (2) subjecting carried interests to taxation as ordinary income will severely retard economic growth in the financial and commercial real estate sectors of the U.S. economy.

As of the date of this writing, it is uncertain whether legislation will ultimately be passed subjecting carried interests to ordinary income taxation or whether that legislation will extend to commercial real estate investments. The resolution of that issue likely depends less on principles

---

[105] *See* Jann S. Wenner, *Obama Fights Back: The Rolling Stone Interview*, ROLLING STONE, October 15, 2010 (quote from President Obama).

[106] *See* Jonathon Alter, *A "Fat Cat" Strikes Back*, NEWSWEEK, August 15, 2010.

of "tax fairness" than on the comparative strength of the lobbyists hired by the proponents and opponents of the proposed legislation.[107]

Equally uncertain is what impact the passage of the Carried Interest Fairness Act would have on the commercial real estate industry. Stated differently, will changing the manner in which promotes are taxed actually cause developers to refrain from kicking off a development project or will it just add a different flavor to the economic negotiations between the developer and its outside equity investors? My experience tells me that the latter conclusion is closer to the truth than the former. The developer is likely to ask for a higher percentage promote or another increase in its overall share of the entity's cash flow (for example, increased development and property management fees) to offset the higher tax that the developer will have to pay on the financial fruits of that promote. The equity investor is likely to say "no" to that request. The negotiation that follows will focus on whose "ox is gored" by the diversion of a portion of the project profits to the IRS' coffers—the developer, its equity investor, or, more likely, both of them. In the interests of full disclosure, I should note that my retirement from the active practice of real estate development law was greatly supported by my receipt of promotes on projects such as HIBC.

VIII. MANAGEMENT OF THE LLC
(Article 5)

The LLC ownership format provides its members with a high degree of flexibility to select a management structure that best suits the members' needs. The Delaware LLC Act provides that an LLC can be managed by either: (1) its members (a ***member-managed LLC***); or (2) a manager chosen in the manner provided in the operating agreement (a ***manager-managed LLC***). The default rule established in the Delaware LLC Act states that:

> Unless otherwise provided in a limited liability company agreement, the management of a limited liability company shall be vested in its members in proportion to the then current percentage or other interest of members in the profits of the limited liability company owned by all of the members, the decision of members owning more than 50 percent of the said percentage or other interest in the profits controlling.[108]

---

[107] *See* Chester W. Grudzinski, Jr., *How Carried Interest Legislation Could Change Real Estate Investing*, REAL ESTATE TAXATION (Third Quarter 2012); Aviva Aron-Dine, *An Analysis of the "Carried Interest" Controversy*, CENTER ON BUDGET AND POLICY PRIORITIES (July 31, 2007), available online at http://www.cbpp.org/7–31–07tax.pdf; and Scott Greenberg, *The Carried Interest Debate is Mostly Overblown*, TAX FOUNDATION, available online at http://taxfoundation.org/blog/carried-interest-debate-mostly-overblown.

[108] DEL. CODE ANN., Title 6, § 18–402 (West 2016).

As is the case with most of the Delaware Act's default rules, the members are free to dispense with this member-managed default rule and adopt another management structure for the LLC. The operating agreement should expressly recite whether the LLC is member-managed or manager-managed.

A. MEMBER-MANAGED LLC

A member-managed LLC is an LLC in which all control over the management of the LLC's business is vested in its members. In its purest form, a member-managed LLC functions much like a general partnership, with each member having the right to approve all LLC decisions and each member having the unfettered right to bind the LLC by its actions. At the other end of the management spectrum would be a member-managed LLC in which the members appoint a managing member and delegate to such managing member plenary authority to make all decisions and to take all actions in the name and on behalf of the LLC. This type of an arrangement is akin to a limited partnership in which the general partner is given full authority to manage the business of the limited partnership.

In most cases, the management structure of a member-managed LLC falls somewhere between these two extremes. In the context of a member-managed LLC formed by a developer and one outside equity investor to own and operate a single real estate development project, the developer is usually appointed as the managing member of the LLC. The reason that the developer (and not the investor) is typically designated as the managing member is driven not by legal reasons (there is no legal impediment to the outside equity investor being appointed as the managing member), but rather by the fact that most investors do not have the time or the expertise to manage the day-to-day affairs of a local real estate venture. In its capacity as the managing member, the developer is given fairly broad authority to take most actions in the name and on behalf of the LLC. The developer's authority is however, typically limited by the requirement that the developer must obtain the equity investor's consent before taking certain *major decisions*.

A hybrid of the member-managed structure that has become quite popular in recent years is a corporate-like structure, whereby the members delegate most of their rights and powers to manage and control the business and affairs of the LLC to a board of directors comprised of individuals selected by the members to represent their respective interests. Those equity investors who are accustomed to interacting with corporate boards of directors often feel more comfortable with such a corporate-like structure. The use of a quasi-corporate structure also proves useful in an LLC in which there are multiple outside investors who have varying voting interests and approval rights.[109] However, in the context of a single asset deal between a developer and one outside investor, the formalities associated with a corporate-like management structure usually prove to be unproductive and overly cumbersome.

B. MANAGER-MANAGED LLC

A manager-managed LLC is an LLC in which the management and control of the business and affairs of the LLC is centralized in one or more managers. A *manager* of an LLC may, but need not be, a member of the LLC.[110] A manager (regardless whether it is also a member) is not liable for any debt, obligation, or liability of the LLC solely by reason of acting as the manager of the LLC.[111]

Once the members decide to appoint a manager to manage and control the business and affairs of the LLC, the members must next determine the scope of the manager's authority. This is the same issue that the members of a member-managed LLC face following the designation of one of its members to serve as a managing member of the LLC. The customary approach is to give the manager the full power to take all actions on behalf of the LLC, except for those specifically-designated major decisions for which the manager must first obtain the consent of the members.

C. THE SELECTION OF A MANAGEMENT STRUCTURE

Developers often prefer a manager-managed LLC structure for two reasons.

- Under the LLC statutes of certain states, a non-managing member of a member-managed LLC is given apparent authority to execute documents and take other actions that bind the LLC. A member's apparent authority to bind the LLC can largely be eliminated by implementing a manager-managed LLC structure.[112]

- The developer frequently conducts its development business in an entity separate from the entity in which it opts to hold title to its real estate portfolio. In that circumstance, all of the personnel, technology, and other management tools required to manage the LLC's business and affairs are housed in a non-member entity. For this reason, the developer may want to select a manager-managed format and have its operating

---

[109] The Delaware LLC Act provides that an operating agreement may provide for classes, groups, and series of members, all of whom have different voting rights. *See* DEL. CODE ANN. §§ 18–215 and 18–302 (West 2016). *See also* Phillip D. Weller, *Series LLCs*, in ALI-CLE MODERN REAL ESTATE TRANSACTIONS, Course No. SY006, 853 (August 2016).

[110] *See* DEL. CODE ANN. § 18–403 (West 2016).

[111] *See* DEL. CODE ANN. § 18–303 (West 2016).

[112] *See* RIBSTEIN, *supra* note 42, at § 2.4.

company named as the non-member manager of the LLC, while the developer's investment company serves as a member of the LLC.

Conversely, there are a couple reasons why the outside equity investor might want the LLC to adopt a member-managed structure.

- A member-managed format is generally considered more conducive to the establishment of a quasi-corporate structure, where management oversight is provided by a board of directors appointed by the members. Large equity investors, such as insurance companies and pension funds, who are accustomed to dealing with corporate bodies often prefer a member-managed format in which the members delegate their management authority to a board of directors.

- A member-managed structure is also the structure of choice if the outside equity investor reserves the authority to take certain affirmative actions to bind the LLC. By way of example, an equity investor might want to both control the LLC's board of directors and reserve the right to take the lead in negotiations for the sale of the LLC's property (see the discussion of *The Prudential Case Study—Investor Dominance* that follows this section).

The choice between a member-managed LLC and a manager-managed LLC frequently comes down to the relative negotiating strength of the developer and the outside equity investor, with the developer preferring a manager-managed arrangement and the equity investor favoring a member-managed structure. Each of those structures is, however, sufficiently flexible that the developer and the equity investor can achieve their business objectives under whichever management structure is ultimately selected.

The discussion in the remainder of this section focuses on the management issues faced by the members in the context of the development of a single real estate project by an LLC that is owned by the developer and one outside equity investor. For the purposes of that discussion, it is assumed that the developer serves as either the manager or managing member of the LLC and that the members have opted not to form a board of directors to oversee the developer's activities.

Before embarking on a discussion of the management provisions that should be addressed in the operating agreement for a traditional real estate development venture, this chapter takes a slight detour by introducing a new case study involving a less traditional development style.

The Prudential Case Study—Investor Dominance

This chapter has thus far focused on the usual circumstance where a developer and an equity investor of relatively equal bargaining strength elect to blend their particular talents (the developer's development expertise and the investor's cash resources) to jointly develop a real estate project. In such a circumstance, the developer is typically given broad control over the management of the LLC, with the investor's role being limited to its exercise of a veto right over certain major decisions. As the following case study illustrates, the equity investor is not always content to assume such a passive role in the management of the LLC's business.

Pizzuti had long wanted to expand its warehouse development business into the greater Chicagoland market. However, because of its lack of familiarity with the dynamics and players in the Chicagoland market (one of the top three warehouse markets in the United States), Pizzuti was hesitant to take on the level of risk that it assumed when it acquired the HIBC land.

In the same time frame, The Prudential Insurance Company of America was trying to devise ways to enhance the financial yield of its vast real estate portfolio. Prudential had historically centered its real estate investment efforts on the purchase of fully-leased real estate projects. By doing so, Prudential effectively insulated itself from two of the most pervasive real estate risks—namely that (1) the development of the project is not completed on budget and on time, and (2) the project is not leased within the time frame and at the rental rates identified in the project's financial projections. The trade-off for so limiting its risk was its acceptance of a lower rate of return on its investment dollars. Prudential decided that the only way for it to increase its investment return was for it to change its investment style and accept more risk.

It was against the backdrop of these changes in their normal risk profiles that Pizzuti and Prudential struck an interesting deal to jointly participate in the development of a warehouse project in Joliet, Illinois. The essential terms of that deal are outlined below.

- Pizzuti would develop a warehouse project in accordance with plans and specifications and a development budget pre-approved by Prudential. The development cost budget would include a development fee to Pizzuti of 4% of the project's total costs.

- Upon completion of the project's construction, Pizzuti and Prudential would form a Delaware LLC to acquire the completed project from Pizzuti. The purchase price for the LLC's acquisition of the warehouse project would be equal to *the lesser of the pre-approved cost budget or the actual project development costs.*

- *The purchase price would be funded by cash capital contributions made to the LLC by its members in the following percentages—95% by Prudential and 5% by Pizzuti.*

- *Upon the LLC's acquisition of the warehouse project, the LLC's operating cash flow would be split in accordance with the members' capital contribution percentages (that is, the 95–5 ratio mentioned above), until such time as the members had received a preferred return on their capital contributions of 9.75%, at which time further operating cash flow distributions would be split 70% to Prudential and 30% to Pizzuti. Capital proceeds would be paid 95% to Prudential and 5% to Pizzuti, until each of them had received cash distributions sufficient to fully return its capital contributions and preferred return and provide it with an internal rate of return on its investment of 12.5%. Thereafter, the economic split would shift to 70% for Prudential and 30% for Pizzuti. The effect of this arrangement was to provide Pizzuti with a 25% promote (after Prudential's receipt of the specified priority distributions).*

- *Any funds needed by the LLC over and above the cash contributions funded coincident with the formation of the LLC would be provided through additional capital contributions made 70% by Prudential and 30% by Pizzuti (that is, per the members' profit splits).*

From Pizzuti's perspective, the above-described deal structure (commonly referred to as a "pre-sale") afforded it with a relatively risk-free opportunity to get is feet wet in the Chicago warehouse market. Pizzuti's only required financial commitment to the project was the 5% capital contribution that it was required to fund on the date of the LLC's acquisition of the Joliet warehouse project. The amount of Pizzuti's capital contribution was only slightly more than the 4% development fee it was entitled to receive under the pre-approved development cost budget. Therefore if the deal went poorly, Pizzuti's principal risk was the loss of its development fee. If the deal proved to be successful, Pizzuti would profit nicely from its 25% promoted interest in the LLC.

The primary benefit to Prudential of the pre-sale structure was that it provided Prudential with the potential to garner a higher than normal return on its investment dollars by acquiring a completed project not at the project's retail price (which was Prudential's typical method of operation), but at the project's cost. In order to position itself to achieve the higher return, Prudential had to do something that it was not accustomed to doing—that is, subject its investment to the risk that the project would not produce the desired rental stream due to the project's failure to lease up at the expected rental rates and within the expected time frame. Prudential attempted to deal with this unaccustomed risk by negotiating a string of very advantageous provisions in its operating agreement with Pizzuti.

Prudential held the upper hand in its negotiations with Pizzuti, because Prudential was willing to fund 95% of the project's development costs and limit Pizzuti's downside risk on the project. Prudential opted to use its dominant negotiating leveraged to fashion management provisions that placed it in a position to actively control the management of the business and affairs of the LLC. The Prudential-Pizzuti operating agreement contained the following provisions:

- The LLC adopted a member-managed structure;

- A five member executive committee was appointed to exercise control over all aspects of the LLC's business and affairs, with Prudential having the right to appoint three of the executive committee members;

- Prudential reserved the unilateral right to call for additional capital contributions to be made to the LLC by its members (including Pizzuti) per the members' profit splits (a particularly bold move by Prudential) and further reserved the right to "squeeze down" Pizzuti's profits interest to virtually nothing if Pizzuti failed to fund its 30% share of the capital call;

- Prudential reserved the unilateral right to sell the project; and

- Prudential reserved the unilateral right to refinance the project's debt.

The Prudential-Pizzuti operating agreement was a stark example of an investor using its negotiating leverage to secure two characteristics that are uniquely available under the LLC ownership format—(a) investor control over the management of the LLC's business, and (b) limited liability.

So whatever came of this investor-dominated real estate development project? Unfortunately, the Joliet warehouse project failed to generate the level of rents initially projected for the project. The following was the end result of the project's dismal lease-up.

- Prudential used its control of the executive committee to replace Pizzuti as the property manager and leasing representative for the project.

- Prudential made a call for additional capital and, following Pizzuti's refusal to fund the call, exercised its squeeze-down right to effectively eliminate Pizzuti's ongoing percentage interest in the project's cash flow (which was non-existent).

- *Prudential exercised its right to put the project on the market for sale. There were, however, no takers for the building.*

- *Prudential and Pizzuti terminated their relationship when Pizzuti withdrew from the LLC and transferred all of its remaining interest in the Joliet project to Prudential.*

- *Prudential later sold the Joliet project back to Pizzuti when, unbeknownst to Prudential, Pizzuti found a tenant to lease the entirety of the Joliet building. Prudential ended up suffering a small loss on its investment in the Joliet project, while Pizzuti squeezed out a small gain.*

The Joliet project is an excellent illustration of the indisputable principle that it is better to invest in a good project on mediocre terms than it is to invest in a bad project on great terms. While the legal provisions inserted into the Prudential-Pizzuti operating agreement gave Prudential its desired management control, that control was not enough to overcome the fact that the Joliet building was simply a bad real estate project—yet another reminder of the subordinate role that the lawyer plays in the real estate development process.

D. MANAGEMENT PROVISIONS OF AN OPERATING AGREEMENT

The following is a discussion of the key provisions of the management section of the operating agreement. Where appropriate, a parenthetical reference is made to the section of the Form Operating Agreement where such provision is addressed. Unless otherwise specifically stated, all references in the following discussion to the "manager" have equal applicability to both the manager of a manager-managed LLC and the managing member of a member-managed LLC.

1. Grant of Management Authority to Manager (§ 5.1)

The operating agreement should contain an express grant to the manager of the authority to manage and control the business and affairs of the LLC. There are two basic methods to accomplish that objective:

- The inclusion in the operating agreement of a simple statement that the manger has the full and exclusive right, power, and authority to manage and control the business and affairs of the LLC and to take all actions that an LLC is authorized to take under the applicable state LLC statute; or

- The recital in the operating agreement of a laundry list of the general powers granted to the manager.

Regardless which drafting method is adopted, the grant of management authority should make specific cross-reference to any limitations on the manager's management authority.[113]

2. Limitations on Manager's Authority—Major Decisions (§ 5.2)

This provision is one of the most hotly negotiated provisions of the entire operating agreement. The real estate development lawyer wants the list of limitations on the developer's management authority to be short and specific. Counsel for the investor typically prefers to use the terms "long" and "general" to characterize the list of limitations on the manager's authority.

The general theory behind this section of the operating agreement is that there are certain decisions that are so significant to the LLC's business that those decisions should not be made without the consent of all the members. While the developer and the investor almost always disagree on the identity and scope of the major decisions, they generally are in agreement that there are certain decisions that should be made jointly by both members. By way of example, one area of common consensus between the members is that the manager should not be able to admit a new member to the LLC without first obtaining the consent of the other member.

The major decisions clause of the operating agreement is intended to give the outside equity investor a veto right over certain actions that the developer proposes to take on behalf of the LLC. The outside investor is typically not empowered under this section to either (1) to take any independent affirmative action on behalf of the LLC, or (2) compel the manager to act in any prescribed manner (although equity investors successfully made some incursions on these points in the aftermath of the Great Recession of 2008).[114] Unless otherwise expressly stated elsewhere in the LLC's operating agreement, all the investor can do is say "no" to a proposal presented to it by the manager.

What then are LLC decisions that an investor might try to include within the definition of those major decisions that require its prior consent? The following are examples of certain decisions that arguably fall into that category:[115]

---

[113] Section 5.1 of the Form Operating Agreement adopts the first of these drafting methods— see *infra* at page 662. For an example of a management provision employing the second drafting method, *see* Pappas, *supra* note 92, at 65–67.

[114] *See* Glazer *supra* note 88, at 318–319.

[115] For other sample listings of "major decisions," *see* Pappas, *supra* note 92, at 68–73; Jacobson, *supra* note 70, at 116–117; and Lindquist, *supra* note 92, at 59–62.

- The sale of the LLC's real estate project;

- The obtaining of a mortgage loan secured by the LLC's assets;

- The entering into of any contract for the construction or design of the LLC's project;

- The acquisition of a significant new asset;

- The admission of a new member to the LLC;

- The selection or replacement of the project's leasing agent or property manager;

- The filing of a bankruptcy for the LLC;

- The execution of an amendment to the operating agreement;

- The implementation of a material change in the nature of the LLC's business;

- The merger or consolidation of the LLC with another entity;

- The institution or settlement of a lawsuit in which the LLC is a named party;

- The taking of any action that would cause the LLC's dissolution and termination;

- The hiring of an affiliate of the manager to perform services for the LLC;

- The filing of any tax election that would result in the LLC being taxed as a corporation;

- The determination of the types and levels of insurance coverage to be maintained by the LLC;

- The execution of a significant lease of space in the LLC's project;

- The incurring of any significant unbudgeted expenditure;

- The approval of annual operating and capital budgets;

- The demolition or significant alteration of the LLC's real estate project;

- The distribution of any cash or assets to any member or affiliate of any member in a manner that is not expressly prescribed by the terms of the operating agreement;

- The grant of the LLC's guaranty of any third party debt;

- The execution of an agreement with any governmental authority that would significantly alter the project's zoning or other governmental entitlements;

- The establishment of a cash reserve;

- The compromise of a significant claim held by or asserted against the LLC;

- The retention of legal counsel or an accountant;

- The issuance of a press release to any media outlet;

- The taking of any action that would violate the terms of the operating agreement or make it impossible for the LLC to conduct its business; and

- The taking of any other action that is outside of the ordinary course of the LLC's business.

The above sampling is neither an exhaustive list of those decisions that the investor should try to include within the category of major decisions, nor a representative list of those decisions that the developer might be willing to accept in that category. The identity and scope of such major decisions varies depending on both the nature of the LLC's business and the relative negotiating leverage of the developer and the equity investor.

The repeated use in the above list of the adjective "significant" is meant to serve as a reminder that, even if the members can agree that a particular matter should be treated as a major decision, the precise scope of such item is sure to be the subject of intense negotiations between the lawyers representing the developer and the equity investor. To better illustrate this point, take a look at typical developer and investor versions of the definition of a major decision involving the LLC's execution of a "significant" lease.

- *Investor Version*—"The execution of any lease of more than 5,000 square feet of rentable space."

- *Developer Version*—"The execution of any lease of more than 100,000 square feet of rentable space if the average annual net effective rent generated during the first five years of the lease term is less than $15 per rentable square foot."

This example highlights the nature of the negotiations that regularly occur between the real estate development lawyer and the attorney representing the outside investor. The real estate development lawyer wants to subject the developer's actions to oversight by the outside investor only if it is a "really big deal" and then only if that "really big deal" adversely affects the LLC's projected economics. Counsel for the investor obviously wants the investor's approval to be required for a much broader spectrum of transactions and circumstances.

The conflicting perspectives of the developer and the investor on the composition of an LLC's "major decisions" are driven by their differing views of the importance of their respective contributions to the success of a real estate project. The developer is absolutely convinced that its development expertise is what is going to make the project successful and that the investor is nothing more than a glorified lender. The investor on the other hand believes that its balance sheet and financial acumen take primacy in determining the fate of the real estate project and that the developer is just a hired hand charged with the ministerial task of constructing and managing building. The real estate development lawyers' challenge is to structure management provisions that preserve the right of the investor to participate in decisions that directly impact the profitability of the investor's investment in the LLC, without unduly restricting the developer's flexibility to respond to market conditions in a manner designed to enhance the value of the LLC's real estate project.

Practice Tip #7-5: Drafting Limitations on the Manager's Authority

When representing a real estate developer, I always tried to incorporate the following three points into the provisions of the operating agreement that purported to limit my client's management authority:

- *An exclusion for any action that is either required by law (for example, the payment of real estate taxes) or required by the terms of any agreement previously approved by the investor (for example, the construction of tenant improvements as required by an approved lease);*

- *An exclusion for any action taken by the manager that is consistent with leasing guidelines and cost budgets approved by the investor at the outset of the project; and*

- *The use of dollar amounts or another objective measurement standard to determine whether a particular decision is sufficiently "significant" to justify its inclusion within the definition of those major decisions that require the consent of the outside investor—for example, the right of the manager to settle a lawsuit for less than $100,000, to buy land containing less than five acres, or to incur any cost that does not result in the actual project development costs being more than 5% over the budgeted project development costs.*

Including these kind of provisions in the operating agreement greatly enhances the flexibility of the developer to manage the ordinary day-to-day activities of the LLC, without interference from the outside investor. Examples of the use of this technique are found in § 5.2 of the Form Operating Agreement.

3.   Manager's Duties (§ 5.3)

It is advisable from the perspectives of both members to itemize in the operating agreement any specific duties that are assigned to the manager. A specific itemization of those duties goes a long way toward clarifying the understanding of both the developer and the investor as to exactly what is expected of the developer when acting in its capacity as the manager of the LLC. By way of example, if the manager is expected to put together annual operating budgets for the LLC, then the operating agreement should specify both the required content and the timing for the delivery of such budgets. Examples of other specific duties to be performed by the manager are set forth in § 5.3 of the Form Operating Agreement.

4.   Manager's Compensation (§ 5.4)

The fees that are to be paid to the manager should be specifically recited in the operating agreement. In the context of a real estate development deal, the following is a representative list of fees that are potentially payable to a manager:

- A development fee to compensate the manager for services provided in connection with the overall development of the LLC's real estate project—customarily stated as a percentage of total development costs (typically, anywhere from 3 to 10% of such costs);

- A property management fee to compensate the manager for services provided in connection with the oversight of the project's operations following completion of construction, including the collection of rent, maintenance of the project, and preparation of operating budgets—customarily stated either as a fixed sum or as a percentage of project's total rentals (typically anywhere from 2 to 6% of such rentals);

- A leasing fee to compensate the manager for services provided in connection with the leasing of the project—customarily stated as a percentage of the total rents payable under the leases (typically, anywhere from 3 to 10% of such rents); and

- A construction management fee to compensate the manager for services provided in connection with either the initial construction of the project or the later construction of tenant improvements—customarily stated as a percentage of construction costs (typically anywhere from 3 to 10% of such costs).

If any of the above services are to be provided by an affiliate of the manager (which is often the case), then the LLC and such affiliate should enter into a separate services agreement that describes the scope of the services to be provided to the LLC and the amount of the fees to be paid to the affiliate.

The outside investor obviously wants to limit the amount of the fees paid to the manager. One of the most common gripes heard from an investor is that the developer is trying to "fee up" the deal. "Feeing up the deal" is investor jargon for the developer charging fees to the LLC in an amount in excess of those fees that would be charged by an independent third party for the provision of comparable services. If the investor's lawyer is in a particularly aggressive mood, the lawyer may also argue that any fees payable to the developer or its affiliates should be wholly eliminated or at least set at below market rates, because the developer is already receiving a promoted profits interest to compensate it for its contribution of services to the LLC. Whether any credence is given to this argument is dependent upon the size and scope of the developer's promote. For example, the investor's point may be well taken if the developer is contributing only one percent of the LLC's capital in return for a 50% promote in a fully pre-leased project that has little risk of failure. However, in the typical development deal, the investor is usually willing to acknowledge that the developer is entitled to both a promote to reward it for its entrepreneurial risk and market rate fees to help cover its overhead and compensate it for the services it provides to the LLC.

5. Removal of the Manager[116]

The equity investor frequently seeks to reserve a right to revoke the developer's authority to manage the LLC's business if the developer is failing to achieve the promised financial results for the project, either due to its malfeasance, misfeasance, nonfeasance, or simply the vagaries of the marketplace.[117] The investor can achieve its objective of terminating the developer's management control by either (1) reserving the right to appoint itself as the new manager of the LLC, or (2) removing the developer as the manager of the LLC and substituting a third party as the new manager of the entity.

The developer, of course, strongly resists any attempt by the investor to wrest away the developer's control of the management of the LLC's business. As noted in earlier sections of this chapter, the developer's primary economic interest in a real estate venture is typically represented

---

[116] The reader will note that the Form Operating Agreement is totally silent on the issue of the removal of the manager. I simply could not bring myself to include a removal provision in the Form Operating Agreement, which, except for this point, is a fairly balanced, unbiased document.

[117] *See generally* Lloyd G. Kepple, *The Delicate Dance: Negotiating the Right to Remove the Managing Member in a Real Estate Joint Venture*, in ACREL PAPERS 269 (Fall 2013); Glazer, *supra* note 88, at 319; and Pappas, *supra* note 92, at 61–62.

by its receipt of a promoted profits interest in the LLC. The developer views its retention of control over the management of the LLC's business as the best way for it to preserve and maximize the value of its promote.

A real estate development lawyer will find it difficult to resist the investor's request for the right to remove the developer as the manager of the LLC "for cause"—at least as long as a "for cause" removal is limited to the developer's fraud, criminality, bankruptcy, or willful misconduct. Investor's counsel is also frequently successful in arguing that the investor should have the right to terminate the developer's management authority if the developer defaults on its obligation to contribute additional capital to the LLC.

In recent years, equity investors ravaged by the effects of the Great Recession of 2008 have aggressively sought to broaden the scope of the events that permit the investor to terminate the developer's management authority to include, among others, the following triggers:[118]

- The departure of key executives from the developer's employ; and

- The LLC's failure to produce positive cash flow at a targeted level (regardless of the cause underlying that failure).

A lawyer for the investor who seeks to add these type of "non-bad act" circumstances to the permitted triggers for the termination of the developer's management authority should be prepared to engage in a long, arduous, and often unfruitful negotiating session with counsel for the developer.

Counsel for the investor also frequently tries to impose an economic penalty against the developer if the investor exercises a contractual right to remove the developer as the manager of the LLC. That economic penalty is usually couched in terms of a reduction or elimination of the developer's promote, because the investor realizes that it may have to offer a similar promote to entice a third party to take over the developer's role as the manager of the LLC. The developer's loss of the right to receive ongoing property management, leasing, and construction management fees from the LLC is another potential penalty that can be imposed by the investor. Finally, the equity investor may seek to establish the removal of the developer as the LLC's manager as a trigger for the investor's exercise of a right to buy out the developer's membership interest in the LLC.

6.   Dealing with Affiliates (§ 5.5)

The Delaware LLC Act establishes the following default rule for a manager's or member's self-dealing with the LLC:

---

[118] *See* Kepple, *supra* note 117, at 276–278.

Except as provided in a limited liability company agreement, a member or manager may lend money to, borrow money from, act as a surety, guarantor or endorser for, guarantee 1 or more obligations of, provide collateral for, and transact other business with, a limited liability company and, subject to other applicable law, has the same rights and obligations with respect to any such matter as a person who is not a member or manager.[119]

This provision of the Delaware LLC Act is representative of the LLC statutes of most states in its statement that a manager or a member is free to negotiate any type of self-dealing arrangement with the LLC and, in doing so, put its self-interest above that of the LLC and the other members.

Despite (or, more accurately, because of) this broad statutory blessing of self-dealing, most operating agreements include a general prohibition against the manager entering into any agreement with any of its affiliates, unless such agreement is first approved by the investor. This prohibition is intended to preclude the manager from hiring an unqualified affiliate to perform services or provide materials to the LLC or agreeing to pay an affiliate of the manager an above market fee for its services or materials. The real estate development lawyer should make sure that any affiliate agreements that the developer intends to sign are excluded from the general prohibition set forth in this section. Investor's counsel frequently seeks to have a clause inserted into the operating agreement that recites that the investor (and not the manager) has the right to administer and enforce any affiliate contract on the LLC's behalf (see § 5.5 of the Form Operating Agreement, at page 665).

The Form Operating Agreement adopts a less restrictive approach to the developer's engagement of affiliates to provide services to the LLC. Instead of prohibiting any affiliate contract that is not pre-approved by the outside investor, § 5.5 of the Form Operating Agreement authorizes the developer to enter into any agreement with an affiliate as long as the terms and conditions of such agreements are "comparable to those that would govern the provision by an independent third party in an arm's length transaction of comparable services and materials in the locale in which the Project is located."

7. Other Business Ventures (§ 5.6)

Both the developer and its equity investor may have interests in other ventures that are competitive with the LLC's business. For example, it would not be unusual for an office developer to own more than one office building in the same office park and for the developer to have different equity investors for each such building. Similarly, the equity investor may

---

[119] DEL. CODE ANN., Title 6, § 18–107 (West 2016).

have investments in any number of competing projects in the same submarket in which the LLC's project is located.

A member's ownership of an interest in a business venture that is competitive with the LLC's project creates an obvious conflict of interest for that member. The legal questions are (1) does the existence of such a conflict of interest constitute a breach of the fiduciary duty owed by a member to the other members of the LLC, and (2) if so, can the members expressly waive such fiduciary duty in the LLC's operating agreement?

The answer to these two legal questions is a qualified "yes." Most jurisdictions expressly recognize that a member owes a duty of loyalty to the LLC and the other members to not engage in self-dealing that runs counter to the LLC's interests (although a few state statutes, such as Delaware's, do not expressly recognize the duty of loyalty). Similarly, most jurisdictions permit the duty of loyalty to be modified or abrogated by specific provisions of LLC's operating agreement (although a few state statutes parrot the language of the Uniform Limited Liability Company Act that recites that an operating agreement may "restrict or eliminate the duty to refrain from competing with the company" only if it is not "manifestly unreasonable" to do so).[120]

The bottom line is that if the members want to permit member conduct that is competitive with the LLC's business, it is essential that a well-crafted clause blessing such competitive activities be inserted into the operating agreement. An example of such a clause is set forth in § 5.6 of the Form Operating Agreement (see page 665).

There are circumstances that warrant a carve-out from the "freedom to compete" provision of the operating agreement. For example, an investor in a grocery-anchored neighborhood shopping center might want to prohibit the developer from developing another grocery-anchored center (presumably with another grocer) in the immediate vicinity of the LLC's project. Conversely, the developer of a suburban office building might want to preclude its equity investor from being the primary funding source for the development of a competitive office project in the same sub-market where the developer's project is located. To the extent a member wants to limit another member's competitive activities, it should include a specific non-competition covenant in the operating agreement.

8.   Deadlocks and Buy-Sell Provisions (§ 5.11)

Most operating agreements put in place a management structure that requires the consent of all or a super-majority of the members to the making of certain major decisions. In drafting the operating agreement, a key question that the real estate development lawyer must ask is, What

---

[120] For a thorough discussion of the law on an LLC's waiver of the duty of loyalty, *see* RIBSTEIN, *supra* note 42, at §§ 9.3 and 9.4 and Appendices 9–5, 9–6, and 9–7.

happens if the members cannot reach agreement on a major decision? The point at which the parties agree to disagree is commonly referred to in operating agreements as a "deadlock" or an "impasse".

At the beginning of a business deal, the members are usually totally in sync on all matters related to the LLC's real estate development project. Talking about the potential for future disagreements is a real downer that both parties would prefer to skip. It is, however, a topic that the real estate development lawyer must force the developer to confront. The occurrence of a deadlock can be a death knell for even the most successful of real estate projects unless the parties have taken the time to construct a pre-determined plan to deal with the consequences of the deadlock.[121]

Once agreement is reached on the list of those major decisions that require the members' mutual consent, the real estate development lawyer must take the time to sit down and ask the "what if they can't agree" question as it relates to each of the major decisions. The lawyer must then devise and incorporate into the operating agreement two separate strategies to deal with each potential deadlock situation:

- One strategy that is designed to permit the conduct of the LLC's business to continue in an orderly fashion while the members try to work out their differences (the "interim strategy"); and

- A second strategy that addresses how the parties can terminate their relationship (hopefully in an amicable and profitable fashion) if they are ultimately unable to resolve their disagreements (the "exit strategy").

The following example shows why it is important for the members to incorporate mutually acceptable interim and exit strategies into the operating agreement.

Example 7-9: Developer and Investor form ABC LLC to develop an office building in Columbus. Eighty percent of ABC's development costs are financed under a construction loan obtained from Buckeye Bank. The construction loan has a term of three years and is personally guaranteed by Developer.

The office building is 100% leased at above pro forma rents to a AAA-credit tenant. At the beginning of ABC's third year of operations, Developer requests Investor's approval to refinance the construction loan with a permanent nonrecourse loan from

---

[121] *See generally* Alvin Katz, *Exiting the Real Estate Venture*, in ACREL PAPERS 151 (Fall 2011); Elliot M. Surkin, *How Do I Get Out of Here? A Discussion of Exit Strategies in Closely-held Real Estate LLCs*, in ALI-ABA COURSE OF STUDY MATERIALS, MODERN REAL ESTATE TRANSACTIONS, Course No. SP–002, 1241 (August 2008); Stevens A. Carey, *Buy/Sell Provisions in Real Estate Joint Venture Agreements*, 39 REAL PROPERTY, PROBATE AND TRUST JOURNAL 651 (2004); and Pappas, *supra* note 92, at 61.

Heartland Insurance Company. The refinancing with Heartland will (1) lock in a high level of operating cash flow for the members of ABC, (2) let Developer get off the hook on its guaranty to Buckeye Bank, and (3) produce refinancing proceeds sufficient to pay off the Buckeye Bank loan and provide a partial return of capital to ABC's members.

Investor refuses to consent to the Heartland financing because it wants to realize all of its investment profit "right now" by selling the building. In an effort to force the Developer to agree to sell the building, Investor also refuses to approve Developer's operating budget for the office building. The construction loan, which is personally guaranteed by Developer, is scheduled to mature in nine months. Developer calls his lawyer in a panic and asks— "What do I do now?"

The easy way out would be for Developer to accede to Investor's demands and sell the building. A building sale would pay off the loan, retire Developer's guaranty, and probably produce a nice payday for both Developer and Investor. But Developer doesn't pay its lawyer to show it the easy way out of a dilemma. Developer still wants to hold onto the building by doing the refinancing with Heartland and it tells its lawyer to figure out a way to "get it done."

Hopefully, the operating agreement prepared by the developer's lawyer incorporated interim and exit strategies of the type found in §§ 5.8 and 5.11 of the Form Operating Agreement (see pages 665–666). The three strategies contained in the Form Operating Agreement that could help a developer achieve its business objective are described below.

- *Cooling-Off Period*—Section 5.11 of the Form Operating Agreement provides that promptly following an investor's refusal to consent to a developer's refinancing proposal, the developer and the investor are required to meet and negotiate in good faith for a period of up to 30 days to try to resolve their differences. This 30-day cooling off period is intended to provide the developer with an opportunity to try to convince the investor of the wisdom of the developer's ways.[122]

- *Budget Approval Carryover*—An LLC cannot stop paying its bills just because an investor refuses to approve a developer's operating budget for the upcoming year. Section

---

[122] Some operating agreements go so far as to include a provision requiring the parties to submit their disagreement to mandatory mediation. I am not the biggest fan of mediation and, therefore, did not include such a requirement in the Form Operating Agreement. My apologies on this point to Nancy Rogers, the former dean of the Moritz College of Law, who created one of the leading alternative dispute resolution programs in the country during the term of her leadership at Moritz.

5.8 of the Form Operating Agreement addresses this point by providing that the developer is authorized to act in accordance with the budget approved for the prior year, adjusted to reflect (1) any actual increases in the amount of **uncontrollable expenses**, such as debt service, real estate taxes, utilities, insurance premiums, and the like, and (2) increases in all other line item expenses to reflect any upward movement during the prior year in the Consumer Price Index. While not perfect, this type of budget carryover provision lets a developer attempt to conduct business as usual while it attempts to resolve its business dispute with an equity investor.

- *Push-Pull Buy-Sell*—The above two provisions are examples of interim strategies intended to permit an LLC to continue to conduct its business while the members see if they can work out their differences. Section 5.11 of the Form Operating Agreement is an example of an exit strategy that can be triggered if the members cannot resolve their disagreements. The exit strategy set forth in the Form Operating Agreement is commonly referred to as a *push-pull buy-sell* provision. Its purpose is to provide deadlocked members with a mechanism they can use to go their separate ways, with one member acquiring the LLC's assets and the other member liquidating its membership interest.

A push-pull buy-sell is triggered when one member notifies the other member of the price at which it is willing to either buy the other member's interest or sell its interest to the other member. The member receiving the buy-sell notice has the option of either selling its interest or buying out the other member at the price stated in the initial buy-sell notice. The "push-pull" nature of this buy-sell is intended to enhance the fairness of the buy-out by letting one member set the buy-out price, while the other member gets to decide whether it will be a buyer or a seller at the designated price. The theory underlying the push-pull buy-sell is that the member who sends the buy-sell notice will be reluctant to lowball its buy-out price because it fears that the other member will turn around and opt to purchase its membership interest at the lowball number.

The following points should be noted about the buy-sell provision contained in § 5.11 of the Form Operating Agreement.

- o The buy-sell can only be triggered after the occurrence of a deadlock. A deadlock is deemed to occur only if the parties are unable to resolve their differences over a proposed major decision during the 30-day cooling-off period mentioned earlier in this section.

- o The buy-sell cannot be exercised at any time during the first three years of the LLC's existence (regardless whether a deadlock occurs during that three-year period). This so-called *lock-out period* is designed to provide time to permit the developer to complete construction and fully lease the project without any disruption caused by a disgruntled investor.

- o The buy-sell provision contained in the Form Operating Agreement can only be opened up by the developer. The buy-sell provisions are applicable following the occurrence of a deadlock and the developer controls whether a deadlock exists. If the investor disapproves a major decision proposal presented to it by the developer, then the developer has the choice either (1) to withdraw the proposal (in which event no deadlock exists), or (2) to notify the investor that a deadlock has occurred and that the buy-sell may be exercised by either member. The developer's ability to control the availability of the buy-sell is intended to provide the developer with a tool to help it overcome the timing and liquidity problems described in the next paragraph.

- In most real estate development LLCs, the investor is financially stronger than the developer and almost always much more liquid. The investor is, therefore, usually in a much better position than the developer to make a "buy" election under the push-pull buy-sell. The developer is seldom capable of simply writing a check out of its available cash resources to buy out the interest of the malcontent investor. The developer needs time to arrange debt or equity financing for a purchase of the investor's membership interest. The Form Operating Agreement gives the developer a minimum of 210 days after its receipt of a buy-sell notice from the investor in which to put together the requisite funding to purchase the investor's LLC interest (180 days in which to respond to the buy-sell notice and another 30 days in which to close on the purchase following its notice to the investor that it will be a "buyer" on the transaction). The investor's lawyer wants to shorten this time period to effectively force the developer to be a seller under the push-pull, buy-sell. As noted in the prior bulleted paragraph, the developer's ability to control when the buy-sell first becomes available for exercise gives it another tactical weapon to try to buy the time needed to find the requisite funding to purchase the investor's membership interest.

• Finally, in many situations the warring members are so concerned about the inherent uncertainties associated with the exercise of the push-pull provision (will I be a buyer or a seller and should I lowball the purchase price) that they end up hammering out a negotiated settlement of their disagreements. This *in terrorem* effect of the push-pull buy-sell is why it is often labeled a **Russian roulette** provision. The question whether there really is a bullet in the chamber serves as a very real incentive for the parties to sit down at the negotiating table to structure a mutually acceptable resolution of their differences. As such, the threat of the use of the buy-sell is frequently more effective than the actual exercise of that provision.

There are many other mechanisms that can be employed to provide the members with an exit strategy.[123] Two of the most commonly used alternative exit strategy methods are:

• A *forced sale*, where a member has the right to force the LLC to market its project for sale to third parties; and

• A *drag along*, where a member has the rights to sell its membership interest to a third party and to compel the other member to sell its membership interest to the third party purchaser on the same terms.[124]

A variation commonly used under both the forced sale and drag along methods is to provide the other member a limited preemptive right to purchase the LLC's assets (in the case of a forced sale) or the member's equity interest (in the case of a drag along) at either a predetermined strike price or at the price offered by the third party purchaser.[125] Both the forced sale and the drag along arrangement can work to achieve the members' objectives of terminating their venture relationship. For my money, however, neither method is as reliable or effective as the push-pull, buy-sell provision.

---

[123] For a discussion of other exit strategies, *see generally* Katz, *supra* note 121; Lindquist, *supra* note 92, at 51–56; Surkin, *How Do I Get out of Here*, *supra* note 121; Carey, *supra* note 121; and Pappas, *supra* note 92, at 61.

[124] A corollary to a drag along clause is the tag along clause, where a member has the right to have its membership interest included in the sale of the other member's membership interest to a third party.

[125] *See* Katz, *supra* note 121, at 163–166.

HIBC Case Study—The Value of a Push-Pull Buy-Sell

The Pizzuti-Newport general partnership agreement contained a classic example of a push-pull buy-sell provision. The buy-sell was only exercisable upon the declaration of a deadlock between the partners. Pizzuti and Newport jointly owned nine office projects in the HIBC office park and another 10 office and warehouse projects in various locations in Ohio. All of those properties were owned by general partnerships whose activities were governed by partnership agreements containing push-pull buy-sell provisions.

Pizzuti eventually decided that it was time for it to tap into a more substantial equity source than Newport in order to permit Pizzuti to expand its development business throughout the eastern half of the United States. Pizzuti had also become disenchanted with the cost of Newport's capital. As noted earlier in this chapter, Newport's capital was given the exact same return and priority as was Pizzuti's—that is, Pizzuti was not receiving any promote under its arrangement with Newport.

For these reasons, Pizzuti approached Newport to discuss Pizzuti's desire to find a new capital partner. The proposal that Pizzuti presented to Newport was that Newport would have the right to continue to invest in Pizzuti's development deals, but that it would have to do so under the same financial return parameters agreed to by the new capital partner. Newport indicated that, while it was not thrilled with the concept, it would be willing to look at any equity proposal that Pizzuti was ultimately able to negotiate with an institutional equity investor.

Pizzuti ultimately struck an equity deal with Nationwide Realty Investors, Ltd. that called for Nationwide to invest in all of the existing Pizzuti-Newport deals and provide the lion's share of the capital needed for Pizzuti's future development projects. The deal initially struck by Pizzuti and Nationwide contemplated that Newport would (1) contribute its interests in the existing portfolio to the new venture, and (2) have the right to invest in new deals on the same basic terms as Nationwide (albeit at a much smaller level). After several contentious meetings with Pizzuti representatives, Newport balked and told Pizzuti that it was not willing to participate in the Nationwide equity deal. Newport's refusal put the entirety of the Nationwide deal in jeopardy because Newport's contribution of its interests in the existing portfolio to the new Pizzuti-Nationwide entity was a condition precedent to Nationwide doing the deal.

Pizzuti's relationship with Newport quickly soured following Newport's refusal to participate in the new venture with Nationwide. Pizzuti felt that it was absolutely essential to the long-term health of its development business that the deal with Nationwide be consummated. As a result, Pizzuti met with Nationwide and received its agreement to buy out all of Newport's interests in the combined Pizzuti-Newport portfolio. Newport, however, refused to sell its interests to Nationwide.

Pizzuti was, therefore, left between the proverbial rock and a hard place. Its relationship with Newport had disintegrated to the point that there was no realistic prospect of going back to a "business as usual" posture and doing co-investment development deals with Newport. Moreover, Nationwide was adamant that it would not fund Pizzuti's new development deals unless Nationwide also received the sweetener of an interest in the stabilized and highly profitable real estate portfolio that Pizzuti co-owned with Newport. A classic deadlock situation existed that cried out for the implementation of an exit strategy for the Pizzuti-Newport relationship. Pizzuti found that exit strategy in the push-pull buy-sell provisions contained in all of the Pizzuti-Newport general partnership agreements.

Shortly after the breakdown in the Newport negotiations, Pizzuti delivered 19 separate buy-sell notices to Newport. Each buy-sell notice set forth a purchase price for the Pizzuti-Newport project that was equal to the price that Nationwide had indicated it was willing to pay for the project. In delivering the buy-sell notices, Pizzuti was gambling that (1) Newport did not have the required liquidity to effect a buy-out of Pizzuti's interests in all 19 projects, and (2) Newport's previously-stated disinterest in taking on the management of a real estate project would deter it from becoming a buyer of some (but not all) of Pizzuti's partnership interests. This was a significant gamble by Pizzuti, but one that it felt that it had no choice but to take.

Long story, short, the delivery of the buy-sell notices to Newport had the desired effect. Newport returned to the negotiating table and an agreement was ultimately reached for Nationwide's buy-out of Newport's entire interest in the Pizzuti-Newport portfolio. Newport received a nice bit of cash and Pizzuti gained the freedom to close its equity deal with Nationwide.

The Newport story highlights the importance of incorporating an exit strategy into the entity documents. If the Newport general partnership agreements had not contained push-pull buy-sells, Pizzuti would have had zero leverage in its efforts to force Newport to go along with the Nationwide deal—something that Pizzuti correctly believed was a necessary next step in the progression of its business model. Pizzuti would have been forced to try to strike a deal with Nationwide or another equity provider for the funding of its new pipeline deals without being able to throw in the deal sweetener of the grant to the equity provider of an interest in an existing real estate portfolio. The end result would have been an equity deal that was far less favorable to Pizzuti than was the combined deal that it ultimately struck with Nationwide.

IX. SUMMARY

I started off this chapter by noting that Stage 3 is a step in the real estate development process where a real estate development lawyer who brings to bear a thorough understanding of tax and legal principles and superior negotiating and drafting skills can add real value to a developer's project by helping the developer attract cheap, efficient, and undemanding capital for its development project. The rest of the chapter detailed the diametrically opposed perspectives of the developer and its outside equity investors on a number of important fronts, including the members' obligations to make additional capital contributions to the LLC, the manner in which the LLC's cash profits are distributed to its members, and the allocation of control over the management of the LLC's business operations. During Stage 3, the real estate development lawyer has the enormous responsibility of crafting solutions that advance the developer's cause on these and many other substantive fronts.

However, the lawyer's challenge at Stage 3 is as much one of style and process as it is of substance. The "elephant in the room" during the negotiation of each of the substantive points mentioned in this chapter is that the end goal of the negotiations is the creation of a long-standing business relationship between the developer and the outside equity investor. If the lawyers do their jobs during Stage 3, their respective clients will become "partners" in the everyday sense of that word. A lawyer who hammers away in an adversarial fashion on each of the substantive points highlighted in this chapter could permanently damage the members' future relationship or, even worse, kill that relationship before it is ever created. A true professional understands this unique Stage 3 dynamic and strives with the utmost level of civility to work through the competing perspectives of the developer and the equity investor by crafting solutions that serve the valid business concerns of both parties.

CHAPTER 8

STAGE 4: CLOSING THE LAND ACQUISITION

■ ■ ■

I. INTRODUCTION

Stage 4 is the point in the real estate development process where the proverbial "rubber meets the road" for the developer. The developer has made the determination that its development project is feasible and that the time is at hand to buy the land and kick off its construction efforts. It is the real estate development lawyer's job to make sure that all of the various land and deal risks identified in the purchase contract are either eliminated or otherwise dealt with in a manner that is acceptable to the developer. Once that portion of the job is done, the lawyer next turns to the task of doing that which is necessary to close the land acquisition as quickly and professionally as possible.

The following are the general topics that are addressed as part of the discussion of Stage 4 of the development process:

- The identification of the players involved in the process of closing the land acquisition;

- The preparation of the checklist that serves as the lawyer's guidebook throughout the closing process;

- The completion of the due diligence process, including the review of title, survey, environmental, and land use matters;

- The negotiation of any amendments to the land purchase contract that are required to remedy problems discovered during the buyer's due diligence;

- The preparation of those closing documents that are required to evidence and consummate the developer's acquisition of the land, including the deed, entity authority documents, seller's affidavits, and the closing statement;

- The allocation and apportionment of the economics of the closing process, including the making of appropriate closing prorations and the payment of applicable closing costs; and

- The orchestration of the moving parts that make up a real estate closing.

For the purpose of simplifying the analysis of the real estate development lawyer's activities in Stage 4, it is assumed that the buyer is using its own cash to purchase the land and is not obtaining outside debt or equity funding. It is further assumed that the developer has made a positive determination that the development project planned for the land is economically feasible and that the developer is ready to waive its purchase contract contingencies, buy the land, and begin construction of its project as soon as its lawyer advises that it is time to do so.

II. WHAT IS A CLOSING?

The term *closing* is used by lawyers and businesspersons to refer to the event that represents the final consummation of a legal transaction. In the context of a land acquisition, the closing occurs when title to the land is formally conveyed from the seller to the buyer and the buyer pays the purchase price to the seller.

The land purchase contract signed by the buyer and the seller typically goes into great detail specifying (1) the conditions that must be satisfied prior to closing, and (2) when and how the closing will be effected. In that sense, the purchase contract represents the road map to be followed by the buyer and the seller in their quests to reach their final destination points— for the seller, the receipt of the negotiated purchase price, and, for the buyer, the acquisition of legal title to the land so that it can start construction of its real estate project.

While a "closing" technically refers to the specific moment in time when title to the land is conveyed to the buyer in exchange for buyer's payment of the purchase price to the seller, that term is commonly used by practitioners to also include all those preliminary actions that must be taken by the buyer and the seller to arrive at their final destination points. The closing is, therefore, both an event and a process. In order to gain the reputation of being a good "closer" (a highly sought after moniker in the legal business), a lawyer must learn how to master both the closing process and the ultimate closing event. One experienced real estate practitioner notes that "commercial real estate closings require management skills and techniques much like those you would need to produce a Broadway show, build a building or invade a small country."[1]

III. THE PLAYERS

The closing process involves the participation of many players beyond the buyer and the seller. The identity and role served by each of those players is discussed below.

---

[1]   *See* Joshua Stein, *Preparing for the Commercial Real Estate Closing (Part 1)*, 15 No. 4 PRACTICAL REAL ESTATE LAWYER 1 (July 1999).

- *Buyer's Counsel*—The lawyer for the buyer plays the leading role in closing the buyer's acquisition of the land. Buyer's counsel customarily assumes primary responsibility for preparing and monitoring the closing checklist that includes not only those tasks that must be performed prior to and at the actual land acquisition closing, but also those additional tasks related to the raising of debt and equity to fund the broader set of project development costs. In this capacity, buyer's counsel serves as the director of the Broadway play that is the land acquisition closing.

- *Local Counsel for Buyer*—The buyer should consider hiring local counsel in one of two situations—(1) the buyer's customary counsel does not regularly practice in the jurisdiction where the land is located, or (2) the nature of the subject land acquisition requires the hiring of a legal expert in a field that is outside of the core competency of buyer's counsel (for example, zoning or environmental law).

- *Seller's Counsel*—The land seller has a singular goal at Stage 4—give me the money. The seller's limited goal usually produces a relatively minor role for its counsel in the land acquisition closing. In the typical land sale, the role of the seller's lawyer is confined to preparing the conveyance documents and arranging for the execution and delivery of those documents by the seller at closing.

- *Title Insurance Company*—The title insurance company is the deep pocketed expert that is responsible for insuring the quality of the title to the land that is being conveyed to buyer. The selection of the title company is a matter that should be addressed in the land purchase contract.

- *Surveyor*—The surveyor is responsible for visiting the land and producing a precise drawing that shows the location of the land's boundaries and any improvements, easements, or other conditions affecting the title or use of the land.

- *Escrow Agent*—The escrow agent is a neutral third party (frequently the title insurance company) who is assigned the task of holding the earnest money deposit posted by the buyer and helping the buyer and seller close the land acquisition. Best practices discourage either seller's counsel or buyer's counsel from agreeing to serve as the escrow agent. Absent a specific agreement to the contrary, a lawyer who both represents a party to the land purchase contract and acts as the escrow agent will likely be disqualified from continuing to represent a party to the purchase contract (be it the seller or the buyer) if a dispute arises between the seller and the buyer under the purchase contract. The escrow agent is also routinely assigned the task of holding and disbursing the legal documents signed by the seller and buyer in advance of the actual land closing. The conditions governing the escrow agent's handling of the earnest money deposit and closing documents are typically spelled out in written escrow instructions prepared by buyer's or seller's counsel (or both of them).

- *Real Estate Brokers*—Most commercial land is sold with the involvement of a licensed real estate broker hired by the seller (the *listing broker*) and often with the cooperation of a licensed broker retained to represent the interests of the buyer (the *cooperating broker*). The brokers are typically commissioned salespersons who only get paid if the transaction actually closes. While many real estate brokers are extremely knowledgeable real estate professionals, the nature of their "if come" compensation arrangements tends to color their judgment as to the wisdom of closing a particular transaction. It has been my experience that a broker rarely says "no" and almost always says "yes" when asked whether a land purchase makes sense for the buyer. The buyer is, therefore, usually well-advised to rely on the brokers to help the buyer find a suitable tract of land for its development project, but not to advise the buyer as to the propriety of the purchase.

- *Environmental Engineer*—Virtually every purchase of commercial land is dependent upon the buyer's receipt of a report from an environmental engineer confirming that no hazardous substances are present on the land. The environmental engineer is typically hired and compensated by the buyer.

- *Wetlands Consultant*—The buyer should retain the services of a wetlands consultant to provide buyer with a delineation of the location of any protected wetlands located on the parcel of land that is the subject of buyer's land purchase contract. The environmental engineer often is capable of also serving as the buyer's wetlands consultant.

- *Other Site Consultants*—Depending on the location and configuration of the land and the nature of the buyer's planned development project, the buyer may also want to retain other independent consultants to provide buyer with advice as to whether the land is suitable for the buyer's intended use. The following are a few subjects on which the buyer might want to receive the advice of an independent site consultant—(1) the availability of adequate access and utilities to the site, (2) the ability of the site's soils to support the buyer's planned improvement, (3) the compliance of the land (and the buyer's intended use of the land) with applicable zoning and land use laws.

It falls to the real estate development lawyer (the "buyer's counsel" at this Stage 4) to coordinate the activities of the above players to make sure that the developer/buyer has all the information it needs to decide whether to purchase the seller's land. One interesting aspect of the land closing process is that, once the buyer decides to move forward with the acquisition, all the players share the same objective of making the closing happen as quickly and efficiently as possible. As the director of the closing "play," the real estate development lawyer has the ultimate responsibility for reigning in the enthusiasm of the players to ensure that the closing occurs only when and as appropriate to protect the developer's legitimate interests.

IV. THE CLOSING CHECKLIST

The first thing that the real estate development lawyer should do after the execution of the purchase contract is to prepare a closing checklist. The checklist should recite all those tasks that must be performed and all those conditions that must be satisfied prior to the closing of the land acquisition. The tasks to be addressed on any useful closing checklist include not just legal matters that must be performed by lawyers (for example, the preparation of a deed or a bill of sale), but also logistical matters that are the province of non-lawyers (for example, the issuance of an environmental report or the funding of the earnest money deposit).[2]

Once completed, the closing checklist endures as the script to be followed by all the players participating in the closing process. It is the real estate development lawyer's responsibility not only to prepare the first draft of the closing checklist, but also to constantly monitor the players' progress in accomplishing the listed tasks (and, when appropriate, to supplement and modify the description of those tasks). The march toward the land acquisition closing is a constantly evolving process and the closing checklist maintained by the real estate development lawyer must keep pace with every twist and turn that occurs during the course of the purchase and sale transaction.

---

[2] *See generally* Andy Jacobson, *An Updated and Expanded Narrative Real Estate Acquisition Due Diligence Checklist*, 31 No. 6 PRACTICAL REAL ESTATE LAWYER 15, 21–30 (November 2015); and Dorothea W. Dickerman, *Navigating Commercial Real Estate Closings (Part 1)*, 26 No. 2 PRACTICAL REAL ESTATE LAWYER 45, 54–55 (March 2010).

The closing checklist should recite all those tasks that must be performed in order for the buyer and seller to close the land acquisition. Those tasks can be broken down into the following three components:

- Due diligence;

- Third party approvals; and

- Legal documents.

The closing checklist must list not only what has to be done, but also who has to do it and when it must be done. If the closing checklist is going to be useful closing tool, the checklist must (1) allocate performance responsibility to the person best suited to perform each listed task, and (2) set a target date for the completion of that task that is consistent with the requirements of the purchase contract and the dictates of the parties' business objectives.

Practice Tip #8-1: How to Prepare a Closing Checklist

The drivers for the preparation of the closing checklist are (1) the applicable provisions of the land purchase contract, and (2) those business considerations that are germane to the development business, generally, and to the developer's proposed project, specifically. The starting place for the lawyer's preparation of a closing checklist is the purchase contract executed by the developer and the land seller. A well-crafted purchase contract should provide even the novice lawyer with a clear road map to complete the majority of the "what," "who," and "when" columns of the closing checklist. By way of example, the closing checklist should specifically recite the dates on which the buyer is required to post the earnest money deposit, deliver its title objections to the seller, and waive the buyer's contractual contingencies.

The remaining items in the closing checklist must be fleshed out through a combination of the lawyer's past deal experience and the developer's project-specific business objectives. The inexperienced lawyer should consult closing checklists prepared by other lawyers or standard checklists reproduced in practitioner-authored literature[3] to highlight those tasks that need to be achieved in similar transactions. The only way to unearth the developer's project-specific checklist items is for the lawyer to sit down with representatives of the developer to review the project and ask the developer pointed questions about what must happen to make the project a reality.

---

[3]   *See e.g.,* Jacobson, *supra* note 2; Dickerman, *supra* note 2; and GREGORY M. STEIN, MORTON P. FISHER, JR., AND GAIL M. STERN, A PRACTICAL GUIDE TO COMMERCIAL REAL ESTATE TRANSACTIONS: FROM HANDSHAKE TO CLOSING 358 (2nd ed., 2009).

The following are a few tips about how to prepare a closing checklist that is both user-friendly and user-productive:

- *Organize the listed tasks in chronological order according to their targeted completion dates;*

- *Include specific contact information for each person assigned responsibility for the performance of any closing task (name, email address, and telephone number);*

- *Include cross-references to sections of the purchase contract that discuss each checklist item;*

- *Keep the checklist as short as possible by not replicating the entirety of the purchase contract or restating the painfully obvious;*

- *Prepare and maintain two checklists—one master checklist that can be circulated to the seller and all the other players and one more detailed version that is for the buyer's "eyes only" (due to the inclusion of deal-sensitive buyer considerations);*

- *Circulate the master checklist to the players in the closing process (including opposing counsel) to keep them advised as to the parties' progress toward closing; and*

- *Find the most anal person in your office (if it's not you) and assign that person the job of monitoring and updating the closing checklist on a regular basis. One practitioner embraces this bit of advice by asking and answering the following question, "Why do clients use lawyers for closings? Answer: Lawyers are diligent, obsessive and careful."[4]*

A closing checklist that is thorough and succinct when first prepared and regularly reviewed and updated should be the real estate development lawyer's bible throughout the duration of Stage 4 of a real estate development project.

V. DUE DILIGENCE

Due diligence involves the gathering and analysis of information that permits the buyer to decide whether it wants to purchase the land. For the purposes of the following discussion of the due diligence process, two baseline assumptions are made concerning the purchase contract entered into by the seller and the buyer—(1) the contract expressly gives the buyer and its representatives a right to enter onto the seller's land for the purpose of inspecting and performing tests on the land (see § 5 of the Standard

---

[4]   Joshua Stein, *Closings: Step by Step,* 45 No. 7 PRACTICAL REAL ESTATE LAWYER 77, at 79.

Form of Purchase Agreement at pages 640–641), and (2) the contract contains a broad suitability contingency that affords the buyer the right to terminate the contract if it makes a determination that the land is not suitable for buyer's intended use (see § 4 of the Standard Form of Purchase Agreement at page 640). It is also assumed that the buyer has concluded that the development project it has planned for the land is economically feasible—so the only issue that remains is whether the land is physically and legally suitable for the buyer's planned project.

The due diligence process is focused on resolving the issue of the suitability of the land for buyer's intended use. In an effort to resolve that issue, the buyer and its counsel must undertake the following due diligence tasks:

- A review of the status of the title to the land;

- An examination of a survey of the boundaries, improvements, and attributes affecting the land;

- An assessment of the environmental condition of the land;

- An evaluation of the presence of any protected wetlands on the land;

- An inspection of the physical condition of the land; and

- An analysis of the land's compliance with zoning and land use regulations.

The real estate development lawyer's job is to coordinate the performance of these due diligence tasks (as well as any others that are necessitated by the peculiar nature of the land or the proposed project) so that the buyer can make a well-reasoned and timely decision concerning the suitability of the land for the buyer's project. To the extent possible, the real estate development lawyer should visit the site as soon as possible during the closing process (or better yet prior to the execution of the purchase contract) to become better acquainted with the possible due diligence issues associated with the subject land parcel.

A. TITLE INSURANCE

The first step in the title review process is the issuance of a title insurance commitment by a title insurance company selected in accordance with the applicable provisions of the purchase contract. A title insurance commitment is an agreement by the title insurance company to issue a title insurance policy at the closing of the land acquisition, subject to those terms, conditions, exceptions, and limitations specifically set forth in the title commitment.[5] The purchase contract customarily provides the buyer

---

[5]   *See generally* Shannon J. Skinner, *A Practical Guide to Title Review (With Checklist)*, in ALI-ABA COURSE OF STUDY MATERIALS, MODERN REAL ESTATE TRANSACTIONS, Course No. SN–001, 377 (July 2007); and John C. Murray, supplemented by Deborah Yahner and Jim Gosdin,

and its counsel a limited period of time to review the title commitment and convey the buyer's title objections to the seller. It then falls to the seller to either cure the buyer's title objections or take the risk that the buyer may elect to terminate its obligation to buy the land if the seller fails to cure all the buyer's title objections.

Buyer's counsel should first confirm that the commitment correctly recites the facts surrounding the proposed transaction—specifically the name of the proposed insured (the legal entity that will take title to the property at closing), the insured amount of the title insurance policy (almost always the purchase price being paid for the land), the nature of the estate being conveyed to the buyer (typically fee simple), and the legal description of the land (which must match the legal description of the land provided on the survey described in the next section of this chapter). All of these factual items are covered in Schedule A of the title insurance policy.

Once the accuracy of the facts set forth in Schedule A are verified, buyer's counsel must next turn to the heart of the title review—Schedule B of the commitment. Schedule B–1 recites the requirements that must be satisfied as conditions precedent to the title insurance company's obligation to issue an owner's title insurance policy to the buyer (for example, the seller's execution and delivery of a deed and the discharge of a mortgage on the land). Schedule B–2 lists all those exceptions to the title insurance company's insurance of absolutely clean title to the land. The **Schedule B–2 title exceptions** fall into two categories—(1) general exceptions that are applicable to all properties (the "standard preprinted exceptions"), and (2) the specific exceptions applicable to the parcel of land that is the subject of the title commitment (the "special exceptions").

The three standard preprinted exceptions typically set forth in Schedule B–2 of a standard ALTA owner's policy are exceptions for the following matters that do not appear of record in the public real estate files maintained by the jurisdiction in which the land is situated:

- Rights of parties in possession of the land;

- Encroachments, boundary disputes, easements, and other matters that an accurate survey of the land would disclose; and

- Mechanics and other construction-related liens.

Buyer's counsel can usually arrange for the title company to agree to delete these standard preprinted exceptions from the title insurance policy by providing the title company with an acceptable current survey of the land and an affidavit executed by the land seller certifying that there are

---

Title Insurance in Commercial Real Estate Transactions, in COMMERCIAL REAL ESTATE TRANSACTIONS HANDBOOK, Chapter 7 (Mark A. Senn ed., 4th ed. 2011); and GREGORY STEIN, *supra* note 3, at §§ 3.23–3.24.

no liens, conditions, easements, or other exceptions to title other than those specifically recorded in the public real estate records.

The special exceptions listed in Schedule B–2 of the commitment are those mortgages, liens, encumbrances, conditions, easements, restrictions, taxes, lawsuits, and other matters affecting the title to the land that appear of public record. Buyer's counsel should insist on receiving legible copies of the complete legal documents that evidence the Schedule B–2 special exceptions. Buyer's counsel should closely review those documents to determine whether any of the listed special exceptions could adversely affect the buyer's use of the land for its proposed development project.

Mortgages, delinquent real estate taxes, and other recorded liens that are susceptible of being discharged by the payment of money (so-called **monetary liens**) should be objected to by buyer's counsel (with the end result that the title commitment will require that they be paid off at or prior to closing in accordance with the requirements of Schedule A of the title commitment). The following are examples of reasons why buyer's counsel might object to other special exceptions listed in Schedule B–2:

- A utility easement runs through the middle of the proposed building pad for the buyer's planned structure;

- Recorded **covenants, conditions, and restrictions** (**CCRs**) restrict the use of the land in a fashion that is inconsistent with the buyer's proposed use;

- A **reciprocal easement agreement** (**REA**) requires the owner of the land to make an unacceptable financial contribution to the construction and maintenance of an infrastructure improvement that benefits both the land and an adjoining parcel;

- A recorded covenant requires the approval of a third party as a condition to the seller's sale of the land; or

- A lease gives a third party the right to extract subsurface minerals located beneath the land.

Once buyer's lawyer determines which, if any, of the special exceptions listed in the title commitment are objectionable to the buyer, the lawyer should then send written notice of such title objections to both the seller and the title insurance company, making sure that the notice is delivered within the time period specified in the purchase contract. Negotiations will then ensue among counsel for the seller, buyer, and title company in an effort to produce a modified set of title exceptions that are achievable by the seller and the title company and acceptable to the buyer.

Depending on the jurisdiction where the property is located, buyer's counsel may also be able to obtain endorsements to the title commitment and policy that provide the buyer with expanded protection against potential title defects. By way of example, in most states, a title company can issue endorsements confirming that the buyer's proposed use of the land complies with applicable zoning laws and that the land has access to a public roadway. The availability, scope, and cost of such endorsements vary widely by jurisdiction. When considering obtaining any such title endorsement, buyer's counsel must engage in a detailed cost-benefit analysis to determine whether the added benefit of getting a particular title endorsement (which is often minimal) outweighs the cost of paying for it (which can be astronomical).

B. SURVEY

A *survey* is a visual depiction of the location, boundaries, and size of a tract of land that is produced by a surveyor physically visiting the site and taking field measurements related to the land.[6] The survey often represents the only opportunity that buyer's counsel has to "see" the land prior to closing.

There are two basic types of surveys—(1) a *boundary survey* that simply identifies the boundary lines of a particular tract, and (2) an *as-built survey* that goes a step further by identifying all improvements and other legal attributes affecting the tract. An as-built survey is considerably more costly and usually takes more time to complete than a boundary survey.

The most common form of as-built survey is an *ALTA survey* that is prepared in accordance with surveying standards jointly promulgated by American Land Title Association and the National Society of Professional Engineers. In addition to showing the location of all boundary lines and improvements located on the land, an ALTA survey also locates adjacent infrastructure improvements, driveways, and means of access and shows all easements and other locatable title matters of record affecting the land. If requested by the party ordering the survey, an ALTA survey can also show: any portion of the land located within a flood zone; the acreage contained within the land's boundaries; the location of building setback lines mandated by applicable zoning codes; the location and number of spaces contained within any parking area; and the location of utility lines existing on or serving the land.[7] The provision of an ALTA survey is a

---

[6]   *See generally* Shannon J. Skinner and Gary R. Kent, *Surveys,* in COMMERCIAL REAL ESTATE TRANSACTIONS HANDBOOK, Chapter 6 (Mark A. Senn ed., 4th ed. 2011).

[7]   All of these items (and more) are listed as "optional survey responsibilities and specifications" in Table A of the MINIMUM STANDARD DETAIL REQUIREMENTS FOR ALTA/NSPS LAND TITLE SURVEYS, as adopted by AMERICAN LAND TITLE ASSOCIATION AND NATIONAL SOCIETY OF PROFESSIONAL ENGINEERS (2016). *See also* Peter Aitelli, *Survey Says: Plotting Your Way Through the New 2016 Minimum Standard Detail Requirements for ALTA Surveys,* ACREL NOTES (June 2016).

standard requirement in most sophisticated commercial real estate transactions.

Upon receipt of the survey (which for the purposes of this chapter is assumed to be an ALTA survey), buyer's counsel should first compare it to the title insurance commitment to make sure that the legal description included in the commitment matches that shown on the survey. Buyer's counsel should next physically locate on the survey all those easements and other special title exceptions listed in Schedule B–2 of the title commitment that are capable of being plotted on a survey. Once those two tasks are completed, buyer's counsel should conduct a qualitative review of the survey in an effort to answer the following questions.[8]

- Does the acreage and configuration of the land conform to the buyer's expectations when it entered into the purchase contract?

- Do any of the improvements located on the land encroach upon the boundaries of adjoining properties (or vice versa)?

- Is the location of any existing easement, building setback line, improvement, etc. in any way inconsistent or otherwise at odds with the buyer's development plans for the land?

- Are easements or publicly-dedicated rights-of-way in place to provide utility and vehicular access to the boundaries of the tract?

- Are the requisite utility lines and roadways located within the aforementioned easement or right-of-way areas?

- Does the survey show that any portion of the land is located in a flood plain?

Any title objections produced by buyer's counsel's review of the ALTA survey should be incorporated into the buyer's counsel's title objection notice sent to the title company and the seller's counsel.

Buyer's counsel should also make sure that the survey is signed by a surveyor licensed to do business in the jurisdiction in which the land is located and that the survey is dated after the date of the parties' execution of the purchase contract. An ALTA survey should also include the surveyor's certification that the survey was performed in accordance with the Minimum Standard Detail Requirements for ALTA/NSPS Land Title Surveys.

---

[8] *See* Everett S. Ward, *Legal Due Diligence Issues in Real Estate Purchase Transactions*, REAL ESTATE FINANCE JOURNAL 9, Appendix 2 (Spring 2007), for a sample checklist for the review of a survey.

C. ENVIRONMENTAL ASSESSMENT

The buyer should not waive its purchase contract contingency unless it has received written confirmation from a qualified environmental engineer that there are no "recognized environmental conditions" affecting the land.[9] The receipt of such an environmental assessment is the best way for the buyer to insulate itself from risk under environmental laws such as the Comprehensive Response, Compensation and Liability Act[10] that seek to impose strict liability on landowners for environmental problems unless the landowner has made "all appropriate inquiry into the previous ownership and use of the property consistent with good commercial or customary practice."[11]

The report typically furnished to the buyer by an environmental engineer in the context of a land acquisition is a so-called *phase one environmental assessment*. In preparing a Phase One assessment, the environmental engineer reviews public records and engages in a routine walk-through of the land in an effort to determine if there is any indication of any existing or historical environmental problem on the land. If the environmental engineer identifies any potential environmental problems, it will then recommend that a more rigorous environmental investigation be conducted that may include the taking of core samples and the testing of ground water. The results produced by such an additional round of testing are then summarized in what is commonly referred to as a *phase two environmental assessment*.

Because the performance of a phase one assessment (and certainly any follow-up phase two assessment) can take a long time to complete, it is imperative that the buyer order its environmental assessment as early as possible following the full execution of the purchase contract If the environmental engineer does not provide the buyer with written assurance in the form of either a phase one or phase two report that there are no recognized environmental conditions associated with the land, then the buyer would be well-advised to promptly send written notice to the seller terminating the buyer's obligation to purchase the land.[12]

---

[9]   ASTM E-1527–13, STANDARD PRACTICE FOR ENVIRONMENTAL SITE ASSESSMENTS; PHASE I ENVIRONMENTAL SITE ASSESSMENT PROCESS, § 1.1.1 (2013). *See generally* Larry Schnapf, *ASTM Publishes New Phase 1 Standard—But Will It Matter?*, 30 No. 2 PRACTICAL REAL ESTATE LAWYER 5 (March 2014); Jack Fersco and Robert A. Stout, Jr., *Environmental Issues in Commercial Real Estate Sales and Leases*, in COMMERCIAL REAL ESTATE TRANSACTIONS HANDBOOK, Chapter 12 (Mark A. Senn ed., 4th ed. 2014); and ENVIRONMENTAL ASPECTS OF REAL ESTATE AND COMMERCIAL TRANSACTIONS: FROM BROWNFIELDS TO GREEN BUILDINGS (James B. Witkin ed., 4th ed. 2011)

[10]   *See* 42 U.S.C. §§ 9601–9675 (2016).

[11]   *Id.* at § 9601(35)(A) and (B).

[12]   For a discussion of the impact on commercial real estate transactions of the issuance of environmental insurance policies to mitigate a land buyer's environmental risks, *see* Michele Schroeder, *Environmental Insurance and the Real Estate Transaction*, in ACREL PAPERS Tab 3 (Fall 2012).

D. OTHER TESTS OF PHYSICAL CONDITION OF LAND

The buyer may also want to receive written confirmation from qualified experts that the physical condition of the land is conducive to the development project that the buyer has planned for the land. By way of example, the buyer might commission a geotechnical engineer to test the quality, composition, and compactness of the site soils to verify that the soils will support the type and intensity of the improvements that the buyer intends to construct on the land. The buyer might also want to receive an engineer's written analysis confirming that the site is served by utilities and roadways that are adequate to service the buyer's proposed development project. Land buyers also now routinely seek written assurances from independent third parties that no portion of the land is located within a protected wetland, flood zone, or other specially-protected district and that there are no endangered animals or plants present on any part of the land. The receipt of these written assurances gives the buyer additional comfort that it will not incur the additional cost and time delay that could be triggered by the presence of these negative conditions on the land.

E. LAND USE MATTERS

Land use considerations are the last piece to the buyer's due diligence puzzle. The buyer must verify during its due diligence process that the property is zoned to permit the improvement and use of the land in a manner consistent with the buyer's development plan. This inquiry goes well beyond just confirming that the property is zoned for commercial use (as opposed to strictly residential or agricultural use). The buyer must also receive comfort that the specific uses it has planned for the site (for example, a three-story office building and two free-standing casual restaurants) and the location, design, composition, and density of its proposed project improvements are all sanctioned under the applicable zoning code. Provisions of the zoning code mandating standards for parking, signage, and building setback lines and imposing impact and other development fees are of particular concern for the buyer/developer. Additional land use issues are created by statute in those states that have adopted state-wide growth management systems and in CCRs put in place by prior landowners to regulate the nature, scope, and intensity of the use of the land in question.

The requisite solace sought by the buyer on these and similar land use due diligence matters can be provided in a number of different ways. First, on certain matters, the buyer may be able to get an affirmative statement from a governmental entity confirming the validity of the buyer's plans for the site. Although a helpful part of the buyer's site due diligence, the receipt of such a governmental clearance letter has limited legal utility. One practitioner urged lawyers who make the mistake of relying solely on short-form government clearance letters to "remember (i) there is no estoppel against governmental entities in the exercise of their normal duties, and (ii) the phone number of your malpractice carrier."[13]

Additional comfort on a land use due diligence topic might be provided by the title company's issuance of a zoning endorsement or another form of affirmative insurance. Finally, the buyer can request a certification from a land use consultant or a legal opinion from special counsel on a particularly difficult or vexing land use issue. Ultimately, however, responsibility for performing the land use due diligence falls upon the real estate development lawyer who must exercise prudence in identifying the land use issues of most concern to the buyer and then figuring out the most effective and cost-efficient way to resolve those issues to the buyer's satisfaction.

F. CONCLUSION OF DUE DILIGENCE

It is essential that the buyer and its counsel secure all requisite due diligence reports as soon as possible and, in all events, prior to the expiration of the buyer's contingency period. Each due diligence report should be signed by an authorized representative of the provider of the report. The real estate development lawyer should closely review each due diligence report to make sure that the qualifications and limitations contained in the report "do not swallow the rule." By way of example, it is not unusual for an environmental assessment to purport to limit the environmental engineer's liability for an inaccurate report to the five figure fee paid to the engineer by the land buyer—a circumstance that is not particularly helpful if the land buyer has bought a multi-million dollar environmentally contaminated parcel in reliance on the engineer's report.

Once all the due diligence reports are in hand, the buyer and its counsel should jointly evaluate whether their combined due diligence efforts justify the buyer waiving its contingency and proceeding to close on its purchase of the land. Assuming that the answer to that question is "yes," buyer's counsel should promptly prepare and send to the land seller and its counsel a formal written notice waiving the buyer's contingency and scheduling a closing date in accordance with the terms of the purchase contract. If the answer is a "no", buyer's counsel should either send the seller a written notice terminating the purchase contract or seek to negotiate an amendment to the purchase contract that extends the buyer's contingency period or otherwise solves its due diligence objections.

---

[13] James W. Theobald, *Land Use Due Diligence Considerations for Transactional Attorneys,* in ACREL PAPERS 85, 91 (Spring 2004).

G. PAPERING DEAL CHANGES

As the date of the expiration of the buyer's contingency draws near, the developer and its lawyer need to caucus to decide which of the following three options the developer should elect—(1) terminate the deal by sending a written termination notice to the land seller, (2) move forward to close the deal "as is," or (3) negotiate changes to the deal outlined in the executed land purchase contract. It is my experience that it is more usual than not for the buyer in a commercial land deal to go with alternative (3) to try to restructure a deal that better serves the developer's overall business objectives.

There are many drivers that could cause the developer to want to change the terms of the land acquisition contemplated in the original land purchase contract. The developer may have uncovered an adverse land condition during its site due diligence that needs to be remediated by the seller. The developer's rethinking of the feasibility of its proposed development project might also cause the developer to want to change the terms of the original land acquisition deal. Finally, the developer might just want to take a shot at bettering its project economics by trying to negotiate a reduction in the purchase price of the land.

Whatever motivates the developer to want to change the deal initially struck with the land owner, the key point for the developer and its lawyer to keep in mind is that the optimal time for them to negotiate and document a deal change is just prior to the expiration of the buyer's suitability contingency under the land contract. That is the time when the developer has the leverage to tell the land seller "I will waive my contingency and close on the purchase of the land, but only if you agree to the following deal changes."

If the developer convinces the land seller to change the deal (either by reducing the land purchase price or by placing an affirmative obligation on the seller to remedy a land defect), then the real estate development lawyer must draft an amendment to the land purchase contract and get the seller and the buyer to sign that amendment before the expiration of the buyer's contractual contingency. If the land seller refuses to go along with the developer's requested deal changes, then the developer faces the same decision that it did before it asked for the changes—either close the deal on the terms set forth in the original land purchase contract or back out of the deal by sending a termination notice to the land seller.

HIBC Case Study—Assembling the Due Diligence Team

The land purchase contract governing The Pizzuti Companies' purchase of the 350-acre HIBC tract gave Pizzuti only 90 days in which to perform its due diligence and make a determination whether to waive its suitability contingency and proceed to close on its purchase of the tract. Pizzuti's chore of completing its due diligence on such a sprawling tract in only three short months was made even more daunting by the facts that (1) title to the HIBC tract was extremely complicated, with more than 50 special exceptions appearing in Schedule B of the title commitment, including more than 30 roadway and utility easements and a 40+-page set of convoluted CCRs, (2) part of the land was located in and subject to the jurisdiction of the municipality of Lake Mary, while the remainder of the land was subject to the jurisdiction of Seminole County, and (3) Pizzuti had limited experience developing property in the State of Florida and zero experience doing so in Seminole County and the City of Lake Mary. Pizzuti's challenge, therefore, was to try to figure out how to complete its due diligence on the HIBC land in only 90 days (an incredibly exacting proposition in and of itself) without having a tried and true development team in place to lead its due diligence efforts.

The first call I made following the execution of the HIBC land purchase contract was to Jim Seay, an Orlando lawyer with whom I had worked on a couple prior occasions.[14] I quickly explained to him the challenge that Pizzuti was facing and asked whether he would be willing to head up our due diligence efforts. Fortunately for me and the Pizzuti organization, Jim Seay was not only incredibly competent, but also extremely well-connected in the Orlando real estate market. Within a matter of hours, Jim was able to put together a due diligence team that included all of the best third party experts in the Orlando market, all of whom had prior experience in working on the HIBC tract. As a result, the Pizzuti organization was able to successfully complete its due diligence within the 90-day period (with hours to spare) and proceed to close on the purchase of a 350-acre tract of land that would dramatically improve its business prospects for years to come.

There are two important points that should be taken from the above discussion. First, sometimes the single best thing that a practicing lawyer can do on a transaction is to hire special counsel who has the expertise and local contacts needed to get the job done. While doing so may be a bit of a blow to the lawyer's ego ("there is actually somebody out there who is better suited to do the job than I am"), it is essential that the real estate development lawyer acknowledge the need for help. Second, when putting together the team to conduct the buyer's due diligence, the lawyer's objective should always be to hire the best available consultants (even if they are not the cheapest). The long-term benefit of being advised by the best people in their respective fields far outweighs the short-term savings that might be

---

[14]   When the HIBC land acquisition was pending, Jim Seay was practicing with the Orlando-based firm of Maguire, Voorhis & Wells (later merged into Holland & Knight). To this day, Jim remains one of the best lawyers that I have ever known and, I am proud to say, is also a great friend.

achieved by hiring a less qualified person (who just happens to be related to the boss).

VI. THIRD PARTY APPROVALS

Another task involved in the closing process is the identification and receipt from third parties of all those approvals that are required for the buyer to consummate its acquisition of the land. The required third party approvals fall into two categories—(1) those governmental approvals that the buyer considers to be essential conditions precedent to a kick-off of its development project, and (2) those public and private approvals that are required to permit the seller and the buyer to close the land acquisition in the manner contemplated in the purchase contract. Examples of those categories of approvals are set forth below.

- ***Essential Governmental Approvals Required for the Kick-off of the Buyer's Project:***

  o   A rezoning to change the permitted use of the land:

  o   The approval of tax and financial incentives for the buyer's development project;

  o   The approval of the buyer's development plan; or

  o   The issuance of a clearance letter from the Army Corps of Engineers approving the developer's plan to disturb protected wetlands.

- ***Public and Private Approvals Required for the Closing of the Buyer's Land Acquisition:***

  o   A governmental approval permitting a subdivision of the land from a larger tax parcel owned by the land seller;

  o   The consent of a board, partner, or shareholder to the sale of the land by the seller or the purchase of the land by the buyer;

  o   The consent of a lender to the buyer's assumption of the seller's existing mortgage loan; or

  o   The approval of the sale by adjoining property owners under a reciprocal easement agreement or covenants, conditions, and restrictions.

The real estate development lawyer should meet with the developer as early in the process as possible to identify all those third party approvals that (1) are important to the overall transaction, and (2) vest significant discretion in the third party to grant or withhold its approval. Ideally, all the required approvals are identified prior to the execution of the purchase contract so that buyer's counsel can structure the contract to provide ample time for the buyer to obtain the approvals prior to the required waiver of its purchase contract contingencies. To the extent that the need for a certain approval is unearthed after the execution of the contract, buyer's counsel may have no choice but to go back to the seller on bended knee asking to amend the purchase contract to make the buyer's receipt of the missed third party approval an additional condition to the buyer's obligation to purchase the land.

VII. LEGAL DOCUMENTS

The final part of the closing process that needs to be addressed in the closing checklist relates to the identification of those legal documents that must be prepared, negotiated, executed, and delivered to close the land acquisition in accordance with the terms of the purchase agreement. The closing checklist should not only list each required legal document, but also make it clear who has the responsibility for drafting each document and when the document needs to be drafted, executed, and delivered.

It is important for the parties to try to reach agreement on the form and content of all the legal documents prior to the outside date for the buyer's waiver of its contractual contingencies. The parties to the land contract can accomplish this objective by either attaching forms of all required legal documents as exhibits to the executed purchase contract or requiring that drafts of the legal documents be prepared and approved prior to the expiration of the buyer's contingency period. The one legal document that tends to be in play right up until the actual funding of the purchase price is the closing statement. It is, therefore, advisable for the lawyers to include as much detail as possible in the purchase contract concerning the manner in which the various financial calculations, prorations, and adjustments must be made in the final closing statement executed at closing.

A. DEED

The deed is the document that conveys legal title to the land from the seller to the buyer. There are three basic types of deeds—a general warranty deed, a limited warranty deed, and a quitclaim deed. All three deeds accomplish the same objective of conveying title to the land to the buyer. The difference in the three deed forms relates to the warranty made by the seller concerning the state of title to the land that it is conveying to the buyer

In a ***general warranty deed***, the seller warrants that it is conveying good title to the land to the named buyer and that the buyer may bring a cause of action against the seller if the title is defective, regardless whether the title defect arose during or prior to the seller's ownership of the land. In a *limited warranty deed*, the seller's title warranty only extends to defects caused by an act or omission of the seller during the period of its ownership of the land (and specifically not to any defects caused by the seller's predecessors-in-title). Finally, a *quitclaim deed* contains no warranty of title whatsoever, but just purports to convey to the buyer whatever interests the seller owned at the time of its execution and delivery of the quitclaim deed.

From the above description, it is apparent that a seller would prefer to use a quitclaim deed, while a buyer would opt in favor of using a general warranty deed. In actual practice, the deed choice in a land sale usually comes down to either a general warranty deed or a limited warranty deed and depends on the custom of the locale in which the land is located and the relative bargaining strength of the seller and the buyer. It is important to keep in mind, however, that a title warranty (be it a general or limited warranty) is only as good as the credit standing of the seller making the warranty. In today's marketplace where most commercial real estate is owned by single purpose entities having little or no net worth, the buyer's most effective recourse for title defects is against the title insurance company that issued the title insurance policy on the land. As a result, the negotiations between the buyer and the seller over the form of the deed to be used in a particular transaction are usually quite short-lived and relatively insignificant.

B. BILL OF SALE

The deed is intended to convey a real property interest to the buyer. If the buyer is also acquiring personal property (for example, a shed, tractor, or landscaping supplies located on the land), then the seller must execute and deliver at closing a *bill of sale* transferring the seller's rights to such personal property to the buyer. If the deal specified in the purchase contract contemplates the transfer to the buyer of various contractual rights or intangible property (for example, a farm lease, development rights, or a trade name), then the bill of sale should also provide for the assignment to the buyer of those contract rights and intangible property.

C. CLOSING AFFIDAVITS

In the typical land acquisition closing, the seller is required to execute three affidavits—(1) a *title affidavit* certifying the absence of any off-record title matters to both the buyer and the title company (required to permit the title insurance company to delete the standard preprinted exceptions from the owner's title insurance policy), (2) a *FIRPTA affidavit*, confirming that the seller is not a "foreign person" subject to the withholding of taxes under the Foreign Investment in Real Property Tax

Act,[15] and (3) a **bring-down certificate** that confirms that the representations and warranties made by the seller in the purchase contract remain true as of the date of the closing.

D. ENTITY AUTHORITY DOCUMENTS

To the extent either the seller or the buyer is an entity, the list of closing documents should also include (1) a **certificate of good standing** affirming that the entity exists and is in good standing under the laws of the state in which the entity was formed and, if different, under the laws of the state in which the land is located, and (2) a **resolution** certified by an authorized officer of the entity confirming that all requisite action has been taken by the entity to authorize its participation in the purchase and sale transaction and that the person who is signing the closing documents on behalf of the entity is duly authorized to do so. A legal opinion provided by the entity's lawyer is frequently required to further confirm that the entity exists and is authorized to close the deal.

E. APPROVED TITLE INSURANCE DOCUMENTS

An essential component of the closing process is the production of a written document that embodies the parties' agreement concerning the precise form and content of the title insurance policy that the title company is obligated to issue to the buyer at closing (including the deletion of any Schedule B title exceptions and the issuance of any requested endorsements). The title company typically satisfies this requirement by either drafting a pro forma title insurance policy or marking up the title commitment to indicate exactly what the title policy will look like when issued. The title company then indicates on either the pro forma policy or the marked-up commitment that the title company will be obligated to issue the title insurance policy upon the closing of the subject transaction and the payment of the title company's insurance premiums.

F. CLOSING STATEMENT

The **closing statement** is the document that shows how much money the buyer needs to pay to close the land acquisition and to whom that money is to be disbursed. Too many lawyers make the egregious mistake of focusing on the purely "legal" documents (like the deed and entity resolutions) and leaving the preparation and review of the closing statement to the principals of the buyer and the seller and their respective financial analysts and accountants. The lawyer who fails to give due regard to the admonition to "follow the money" does so at the lawyer's own peril— and to the potential financial detriment of the lawyer's client who may have to pay more or receive less than it should.

---

[15] *See* I.R.C. § 1445.

A well-drafted purchase contract provides counsel for the buyer and the seller with an instruction manual to determine the exact amount of the buyer's cash payment at closing and the manner in which that cash payment must be distributed to the seller and other participants in the closing process. If the purchase contract fails to clearly describe how the money should be handled at closing, then the parties will be faced with the prospect of having to enter into fresh negotiations at the closing table that could, in turn, threaten the viability of the entire purchase and sale transaction. Careless lawyers will, on occasion, take a short-cut by seeking to leave the financial closing calculations to "community custom"—a singularly bad idea because there is no such thing as "community custom" in commercial real estate transactions.

The first line of any closing statement is the purchase price being paid for the land by the buyer. The stated purchase price establishes the threshold for the calculation of both the net amount of cash required to be funded at closing by the buyer and the net sales proceeds payable to the seller. The buyer's net funding obligation is reduced by the amount of its previously-paid earnest money deposits, while the seller's share of the net sales proceeds is reduced by the pay-off balance of any mortgage loan that encumbers the land. The loan pay-off should be addressed in a letter provided by the lender to the seller and the escrow agent that indicates (1) the balance of the outstanding principal and interest due under the loan as of the projected closing date, and (2) the amount of the per diem interest carry that must be added to the amount of the loan pay-off if the loan is not fully repaid on the projected closing date. The pay-off letter also usually contains the lender's commitment that the lender will take all requisite actions to discharge its recorded mortgage on the land promptly after its receipt of the loan pay-off balance.

The next step in the lawyer's preparation of the closing statement is the allocation of responsibility between the seller and the buyer for the payment of those third party costs that are payable at closing. Third party costs regularly paid at the land acquisition closing include the following:

- Title insurance premiums (payable to the title company);

- Surveying fees (payable to the surveyor);

- Real estate commissions (payable to the licensed real estate brokers involved in the transaction);

- Transfer taxes, documentary stamps, conveyance fees, and recording fees (payable to the local governmental agency charged with administering and maintaining the public real estate records); and

- Legal fees (payable to counsel for the buyer and the seller, respectively).

The allocation of responsibility for paying these closing costs is a matter of negotiation between the seller and the buyer and should be clearly specified in the executed purchase contract. Closing costs assigned to the buyer increase the net cash payable by the buyer at closing, while closing costs assigned to the seller decrease the seller's share of the net sales proceeds.

The final closing statement entries are those relating to closing adjustments that must be made to the purchase price to reflect the proration of real estate taxes and other periodic payment obligations that cover a period of time both before and after the date of closing. If the seller has pre-paid such an obligation, then the amount of the cash payable by the buyer and the net proceeds payable to the seller at closing are each typically increased by an amount equal to the portion of such prepayment that is attributable to the period after the date of closing. Conversely, if such an obligation remains unpaid at closing, then the amount of the cash payable by the buyer and the net proceeds payable to the seller at closing are typically each decreased by an amount equal to the portion of the outstanding obligation that is attributable to the period prior to the date of closing.

Once completed, the closing statement should set forth a figure for the "net cash payable by buyer at closing." That figure should equal the sum of (1) the closing costs payable by seller and buyer at closing, and (2) the "net sales proceeds payable to seller at closing." The format of the closing statement is a matter of individual preference. Some lawyers use the HUD–1 settlement statement created by the Department of Housing and Urban Development for use on residential transactions. I always found the HUD–1 form to be inadequate for most commercial real estate transactions and instead preferred to use a more extensive form of closing statement that incorporated a detailed schedule of all cash disbursements made at closing and a series of notes explaining the support for and method of calculation of the various closing costs, prorations, and adjustments set forth in the closing statement. A sample Closing Statement applicable to the sale of the HIBC land by The Pizzuti Companies is included as Document #4 in the *Document Appendix,* at pages 679–683.

Practice Tip #8-2: Getting Paid at Closing

I have always been amazed at how infrequently legal fees appear as a line item on a closing statement. For some reason, lawyers representing both the buyer and the seller are often hesitant to include their fees as costs that must be paid out of the proceeds of the closing. I have never figured out if those lawyers are bashful or just plain embarrassed about the amount of their bills. I do know, however, that real estate brokers, title insurance companies, surveyors, and other players in the closing process rarely share the lawyers' reluctance to get paid at closing. Indeed, my experience has been that those other players actually seem quite proud to submit their bills and get paid at closing.

My own personal view is that the fees of both buyer's and seller's counsel should regularly appear on the closing statement and be paid at closing. A client wants to be able to quantify its all-in costs of the transaction and deserves to know what its legal bill is going to be at the same time as it learns of its other transactional costs. From the lawyer's perspective, it is fitting that the person who has labored the most to close the transaction gets to walk away from the closing with a check in hand. I have also found over the years that there is no better time to get paid than when your client is in the midst of celebrating the closing of a transaction.

HIBC Case Study—Negotiating the Closing Numbers

The $7.5 million purchase price for the HIBC land was established very early in the negotiations between Pizzuti and the land seller—indeed, I seem to clearly remember the words "take it or leave it" being muttered by the Chemical Bank loan officer assigned responsibility for negotiating the land sale. In an attempt to save negotiating face, I decided to take a crack at easing Pizzuti's financial burden by getting Chemical Bank to agree to a few concessions concerning the manner in which responsibility for various closing costs would be allocated between the seller and the buyer.

The first draft of the land purchase contract (prepared, of course, by Chemical Bank's counsel) sought to place the obligation on Pizzuti to pay all closing costs other than the seller's legal fees and the 7% real estate commission that Chemical had agreed to pay to its listing broker. Based less on my negotiating prowess than on the fact that I had already acceded to Chemical's insistence on a purchase price of $7.5 million, I was able to win a few small victories in the negotiation over the allocation of responsibility for the payment of closing costs. Specifically, Chemical Bank agreed that it would pay one-half of the title insurance premiums payable to the title company and one-half of the documentary stamps payable to Seminole County (an aggregate savings for Pizzuti of approximately $50,000).

The biggest financial concession I was able to secure cost Chemical nothing, but benefitted Pizzuti to the tune of $150,000. As noted earlier, Chemical had previously agreed with its listing broker that it would pay a real estate commission of 7% of the purchase price upon a closing of the sale of the HIBC land. Based on a $7.5 million purchase price, this meant that Chemical was on the hook for the payment of a real estate commission of $525,000. Because The Pizzuti Companies owned a licensed real estate *brokerage firm in Orlando (creatively named "Pizzuti Realty"), I asked Chemical to recognize Pizzuti Realty as a cooperating broker on the HIBC land sale and pay Pizzuti Realty a commission of 2% of the purchase price ($150,000). Because the terms of its commission agreement with the listing broker expressly permitted Chemical to deduct the amount of any cooperating broker commission from the commission otherwise payable to the listing broker, Chemical was relatively quick to agree to my request to divert a portion of the committed real estate commission to Pizzuti Realty. The end result was that The Pizzuti Companies' out-of-pocket funding at closing was reduced by $150,000, while Chemical's share of the net sales proceeds was unaffected.*

The bottom line impact of the closing cost negotiations was that Pizzuti saved approximately $200,000 (at least when compared to the positions put forth in Chemical's first draft of the purchase contract). I actually felt pretty good about that—at least until my boss reminded me that the agreed-upon purchase price of $7.5 million was $300,000 higher than the maximum price that he wanted to pay for the HIBC land.

VIII. THE ACTUAL CLOSING

The actual closing is the point in time where all of the closing preliminaries have been concluded and the buyer is prepared to pay its money and receive title to the land. In the "olden days" when I first started practicing law, the next step would be for the lawyers to negotiate where the closing would be held ("your place or mine") and, once that was decided, to notify their respective client representatives to book their flights and hotel rooms and be prepared to spend a couple of days cloistered away in a conference room drinking coffee, eating deli sandwiches, and watching the lawyers compile closing documents, haggle over the remaining open issues, and generally act lawyerly.

While a full sit-down closing of the type described above is certainly "interesting" (describing it as "fun" would be a bit of an overstatement), clients and lawyers have come to realize that, in most instances, it is an extremely inefficient way to close a real estate deal. The norm in today's fast-paced commercial world is for the transaction to be by way of an **escrow closing** (instead of a **New York style closing** where everybody gathers around the table and eats those deli sandwiches). In an escrow closing, the buyer and seller stay put at their respective places of business and the lawyers use overnight couriers to deliver the signed closing documents to the local escrow agent who is handling the closing—a much more efficient style of closing that benefits all concerned (except for the owner of the local deli who would otherwise be supplying all of the sandwiches for the closing).

The logistics of conducting an escrow closing (viewed principally from the perspective of counsel for the buyer) are described below.

- *Document Execution*—The lawyer's first step is to get the client to sign all those closing documents that require its execution. The lawyer should make sure that all blanks in the documents are completed, all exhibits are attached, and all execution formalities are properly followed (for example, the proper notarizing or witnessing of any documents that are to be recorded in the local real estate records). The executed originals of the closing documents should then be sent to the escrow agent via overnight courier, along with the written escrow instructions described in the next paragraph.

- *Escrow Instructions*—Counsel for the buyer and the seller (acting separately or jointly) prepare and deliver to the escrow agent detailed written *escrow instructions* setting forth the conditions under which the escrow agent is to hold, disburse, and, ultimately, record the signed closing documents (as well as the funds wired to the escrow agent by the buyer under the next paragraph of this section). Escrow instructions prepared by buyer's counsel typically address the following topics—(1) a listing of those documents and funds being delivered to the escrow agent by the buyer, (2) a recital of the specific conditions that must be satisfied before the escrow agent is authorized to disburse the escrowed documents and funds (for example, the receipt of all requisite signed documents from the seller, the title insurance company's delivery to buyer's counsel of a letter indicating that it is prepared to issue a title insurance policy to buyer in the exact form of the marked-up title commitment or pro forma title policy, and the escrow agent's receipt of a signed letter from buyer's counsel specifically authorizing the escrow agent to "break escrow"), (3) a statement specifying what the escrow agent is to do once it is authorized to break escrow—that is, disburse the buyer's wired funds in accordance with the closing statement signed by representatives of the buyer and seller, record the deed and any other specifically-designated documents in the public real estate records of the jurisdiction in which the land is located, and distribute copies of the recorded documents and executed originals of all other documents to buyer and seller in accordance with a document disbursement schedule appended to the escrow instructions, and (4) a statement of what the escrow agent should do if all of the escrow conditions have not been satisfied by a specified outside date (usually send all the signed documents back to buyer's counsel and wire the buyer's funds back to the buyer's bank account).

- *Wiring of Funds*—Upon receipt of a copy of the escrow instructions signed by the escrow agent, counsel for the buyer should then arrange for the buyer to send the money required to close the land acquisition to the escrow agent's designated bank account. The buyer's payment is typically sent directly to the escrow agent's account by means of a wire transfer of same day funds through an electronic system maintained by the Federal Reserve. The escrow instructions sent to the escrow agent by buyer's counsel (or a supplemental set of written instructions) should specify the manner in which the buyer's funds should be invested during the pendency of the escrow (for example, in a liquid, interest-bearing account).

- *Giving the "Green Light"*—Once all the conditions specified in the escrow instructions have been satisfied, the lawyers representing the buyer and the seller will give the "green light" (either in writing or over the phone) to the escrow agent to release the documents and funds from escrow and disburse them in the manner specified in the escrow instructions.

- *Closing the Escrow*—Once it gets the green light from buyer's and seller's counsel, the escrow agent will then close the escrow by recording the deed, disbursing the escrowed funds, and distributing the remaining documents as instructed in the escrow instructions.

Once the deed is recorded and the funds are disbursed, it is time for: the seller to celebrate; the buyer to get to work developing its real estate project on the acquired land; and the lawyers to do it all over again on behalf of other clients.

HIBC Case Study—A Hybrid Closing

The closing of the HIBC land purchase was a hybrid between a New York-style sit-down closing and a California-style escrow closing. The closing was structured as an escrow closing, with all the business principals staying at home and all the closing documents and funds being placed in escrow with the escrow agent pursuant to carefully drawn escrow instructions prepared by counsel for the seller and the buyer. However, unlike a pure escrow closing, all the lawyers representing the seller and the buyer (including yours truly) gathered around the table in the escrow agent's offices in Orlando to compile the documents, haggle over the remaining open issues, and, yes, consume plenty of coffee and deli sandwiches.

Over the years, I have developed a strong preference for conducting commercial real estate closings in a style similar to the hybrid arrangement employed for the HIBC land purchase. While an escrow closing is infinitely more efficient than an all-hands sit-down closing, there is still something very comforting about being physically present to make sure that it really is the right time for the actual closing to occur.

Practice Tip #8-3: The "Paperless Closing"

The typical closing of a commercial real estate transaction involves reams of paper stacked to the ceiling on a conference room table. We are, however, now living in a digital age where no one (other than commercial real estate lawyers and law school professors) still revere "paper files."

The eClosing has already become a staple of the residential mortgage lending industry. With the adoption in a majority of the states of the Uniform Real Property Electronic Recording Act and the Uniform Electronic Transaction Act and the passage at the federal level of the Electronic Signatures in Global and National Commerce Act, the stage is set for the advent of the electronic "paperless closing" for commercial real estate transactions.[16] The only two obstacles to electronic closings of commercial real estate transactions are (1) the lack of uniformity in commercial real estate documentation, and (2) the stubborn reluctance of the practicing real estate bar to fully embrace the digital age. It is, however, just a matter of time before the cost efficiencies derived from the eClosing surmount those two obstacles.

IX. POST-CLOSING MATTERS

A lawyer's natural temptation once a transaction closes is to put the land acquisition file aside and immediately move on to the next deal. It is important, however, that the lawyer take a few minutes (after finishing off the celebratory libations) to address a variety of post-closing matters.

It is not unusual for a closing to occur despite the existence of a few minor loose-ends that must be addressed by the parties—for example, notifying an owner's association of the identity of the new landowner or splitting a pending bill for the property that was discovered at the last moment. Before putting the file away for good, the lawyers should document all the loose ends in a brief letter agreement and establish responsibility and a timeline for taking care of those matters (and maybe

---

[16] *See* UNIFORM REAL PROPERTY ELECTRONIC RECORDING ACT (2004, last revised 2005); UNIFORM ELECTRONIC TRANSACTIONS ACT (1999); and ELECTRONIC SIGNATURES IN GLOBAL AND NATIONAL COMMERCE ACT, Pub. L. No. 106–229 (2000). *See also* Josias N. Dewey and Gavin Williams, *The Commercial Paperless Closing: How Close Is It?*, THE REAL ESTATE FINANCE JOURNAL 82 (Spring 2012).

escrow some of the closing proceeds until all the loose ends are successfully tied up).

Buyer's counsel also needs to attend to the following three post-closing items—(1) the preparation and distribution to the buyer of a ***closing bible*** that includes copies of all of the pertinent legal documents related to the land acquisition (now typically done electronically), (2) the calendaring of any pertinent post-closing dates (for example, the outside date for the reproration of real estate taxes or the filing of a claim for the breach of a representation or warranty), and (3) the receipt from the title company of a final title insurance policy for the land. Once those items are handled, buyer's counsel can comfortably move on the next transaction.

X. SUMMARY

Stage 4 requires the real estate development lawyer to be prepared, organized, diligent, and, quite frankly, anal. While preparing a closing checklist and working out the logistics of a land acquisition closing may not be the most intellectually stimulating of tasks, there is a wonderful dual reward awaiting the real estate development lawyer who successfully manages the process that is the closing of the land acquisition—the self-satisfaction of knowing that the lawyer is a deal closer (and not a deal killer) and, of course, the closing dinner with the client at the local steakhouse (if the lawyer is willing to pay).

CHAPTER 9

STAGE 5: OBTAINING
CONSTRUCTION FINANCING

■ ■ ■

I. INTRODUCTION

A developer typically funds approximately 70–90% of its development costs by obtaining a construction loan from a commercial bank or other financing source. The remaining development costs are paid with equity contributions made to the development entity by either the developer or its investors.

Let's start with a quick review of why the developer wants (or, more accurately, needs) to fund the majority of its development costs with dollars borrowed from a construction lender—the use of so-called "other peoples' money" or "OPM." There are three basic reasons supporting a developer's use of OPM (referred to in more elite academic circles as *leverage*).

- Leverage permits the developer to diversify its real estate investments by funding 10–30% of the development costs in several deals, rather than 100% of those costs in just one project. This diversification lowers the developer's real estate risk by permitting it to spread that risk over several different projects. This approach is similar to a stock investor purchasing a mutual fund versus putting the entirety of its investment in a single stock.

- Leverage can be used to increase or "juice" the developer's return on equity. This is true because construction lenders ordinarily require a lower percentage return on their loan dollars than equity investors require on their equity contributions (largely because of the greater risk borne by the equity investor).

- Finally, most developers just flat out *NEED* to obtain a construction loan to get their projects done. Real estate is an incredibly capital-intensive business requiring the long-term investment of significant dollars. A typical suburban office building may easily cost $20 million or more, with the building owner being required to keep its investment intact for a period of upward of five to ten years. Moreover, few developers develop only one project at a time. Indeed, the diversification principle mentioned at the outset of this section frequently results in a developer having a number of projects in its development pipeline at the same time. The need for leverage can be illustrated by looking at an office developer who has five projects being developed in the same 12-month period at an aggregate cost of more than $100 million—a situation that is far from atypical in the development world. How many people do you know who can personally write a check for $100 million without using other peoples' money?

Given the above considerations, it is easy to see why the securing of a construction loan is a key element of most real estate development projects.

Large national developers often finance their real estate projects not with traditional construction loans, but rather through the use of lines of credit provided by a consortium of financial institutions. These lines of credit are intended to provide the developers with flexible financing for the concurrent acquisition and development of multiple projects. Although acquisition and development lines of credit present unique legal issues (for example, cross-default and financial covenant issues), the negotiation of those lines of credit centers on many of the same issues that characterize the negotiation of the single asset construction loan that is the focus of this chapter.

This chapter begins with an examination of the many ways in which a construction loan is different from the conventional mortgage loan with which most people are familiar. It then moves on to a quick discussion of the business objectives of both the construction lender and the borrower and the typical way in which most construction loans are structured and papered. The remainder of the chapter is devoted to an in-depth analysis of the unique risks faced by a construction lender and the various techniques that the lender uses to help mitigate those risks—and, of course, the developer's "pushback" on each of those risk mitigation techniques. All of these topics are discussed against the backdrop of two similar (but, in many ways, starkly different) suburban office projects developed in Orlando, Florida by my former employer—one being an 87,000-square-foot building designed for occupancy by a single tenant and the other being a 75,000-square-foot speculative multi-tenant building.

II. THE UNIQUE NATURE OF A CONSTRUCTION LOAN

The typical home buyer finances approximately 80% of the price of buying a personal residence by getting a residential mortgage loan from a local bank or savings and loan association. In return for the lender providing loan dollars to cover the majority of the purchase price of the home, the borrower commits to repay the loan over a term of 30 years, with the amount of the borrower's monthly principal and interest payments being fixed in a manner set forth in the loan documents. If the borrower fails to keep current on the required monthly loan payments, then the lender's principal recourse is to foreclose on the mortgage and take over ownership of the residence (at least until it finds someone who will buy the residence back from the lender).

In the commercial real estate context, the second cousin of the residential mortgage loan is a financing structure commonly referred to as a ***permanent loan***. The permanent lender (typically an insurance company, pension fund, or other financial institution) makes a loan to permit a borrower either to pay a significant portion of the price of acquiring a completed commercial real estate project or to refinance an existing loan on the project. The borrower agrees to use the net operating income produced from its operation of the commercial property to make monthly payments of principal and interest to repay the loan over a fixed period of years (typically a term of more like seven to ten years than the 30-year term commonly seen in residential mortgage loans). The permanent lender's principal remedy for the borrower's failure to make its monthly mortgage payments is to foreclose on the mortgage and take over ownership and operation of the commercial project that was pledged as collateral to secure the borrower's repayment obligation.

A construction loan is vastly different from a conventional permanent loan. The only characteristic that is common to both a construction loan and a conventional permanent loan is that the lender takes a mortgage on the underlying real estate in order to provide it with a level of security in case the borrower fails to repay its loan. This is not a book on mortgage financing, so this chapter does not address either the fundamentals associated with a borrower's pledging of real estate collateral to secure its loan or the manner in which the priority of those having competing claims to the underlying real estate is determined.[1] Suffice it to say that many of the same legal principles related to the grant of the mortgage and the determination of the mortgage's priority are common to both construction loans and conventional permanent loans.

That is, however, where the similarity between a construction loan and a conventional permanent loan ends. The following is a list of the fundamental differences between a construction loan and a conventional permanent loan. Those differences, which are highlighted in a somewhat

---

[1]   There are a number of excellent law school texts devoted to the topic of mortgage financing. *See, e.g.*, STEVEN W. BENDER, CELESTE M. HAMMOND, MICHAEL T. MADISON AND ROBERT M. ZINMAN, MODERN REAL ESTATE FINANCE AND LAND TRANSFER: A TRANSACTIONAL APPROACH (4th ed. 2008); AND GRANT S. NELSON, DALE A. WHITMAN, ANN M. BURKHART AND R. WILSON FREYERMUTH, REAL ESTATE TRANSFER, FINANCE, AND DEVELOPMENT: CASES AND MATERIALS (8th ed. 2009).

cursory and conclusory fashion below, are examined in greater detail later in this chapter as part of the discussion of the unique risks faced by the construction lender and the techniques that are available to help mitigate its exposure to those risks.

A. NATURE OF UNDERLYING COLLATERAL

The most fundamental and consequential difference between a construction loan and a conventional permanent loan revolves around the nature of the real estate collateral that secures the borrower's obligation to repay its loan. In the case of a conventional permanent loan, the permanent lender holds a mortgage on real property having a defined income stream and, hence, a readily realizable value. In the context of a construction loan, the value of the lender's collateral is tied to the completion and leasing of the project for which the construction loan proceeds are being disbursed. In a very real sense, therefore, the construction loan proceeds are being used to *CREATE* the value of the lender's underlying collateral.

Another way to think about the difference between a construction loan and a conventional real estate loan is to imagine that one bank (akin to the construction lender) is asked to make a loan of $5 million to Jasper Johns[2] to fund the costs associated with Mr. Johns' painting of a new mural on the side of a building in downtown Chicago, while another financial institution (similar to the permanent lender) is asked to make a loan of $5 million to permit an art enthusiast to buy an existing Jasper Johns painting. In the first instance, there is no existing value in the "to be created" work of art, while in the second situation, the collateral is an actual painting that has a readily determinable financial value in the art world. The bank that makes the "creative" loan to Jasper Johns will have its loan adequately collateralized only if Johns actually paints the proposed mural *AND* that mural is enthusiastically embraced by the modern art community. It is, therefore, absolutely essential from the perspective of the "creative" lender that Johns use the loan proceeds to fund the costs of completing his new masterpiece. The same state of affairs exists for the real estate construction lender who wants to make sure that its loan proceeds are used by the developer to construct and lease a commercial real estate project in accordance with the developer's project schematics and financial pro forma. As is discussed in later sections of this chapter, it is this evolving creative nature of the construction lender's collateral that is the primary driver for most of the provisions of the lender's construction loan agreement.

---

[2]   Jasper Johns is one of the most successful, living American artists. Two of his best known works are "The Flag" and "Savarin Cans," both of which are prime examples of the American Pop Art movement. Please accept my apology for the blasphemous comparison of the work of Jasper Johns to a suburban office building. Comparing the two "creative" scenarios is simply my clumsy attempt to clarify the difference between a construction loan and a permanent loan and is not intended in any way to diminish the artistry of Mr. Johns.

B. BASIS OF LOAN UNDERWRITING

When a lender is asked to make a conventional permanent loan on a commercial real estate project, the primary focus of its analysis of the wisdom of making the loan (commonly referred to as the **underwriting** of the loan) is the project's existing income stream. Is the project leased and on what terms? What is the amount of the project's annual net operating income? Are there any foreseeable circumstances that could cause the project's revenues to decrease or its expenses to increase in the future?

A construction lender, on the other hand, is not afforded the luxury of underwriting a construction loan based on historical data. While the permanent lender gets to inspect a completed facility and look at historical financial information, the construction lender is forced to make an up or down decision on a proposed construction loan based solely on the developer's *PROJECTIONS* as to both the physical appearance and the financial performance of the imagined project. As a result, the focus of the construction lender's attention when underwriting a loan is not only on the relative merits of the proposed development project (for example, are the projected construction costs reasonable and can space in the project be leased at the projected rents), but also on the capability and financial wherewithal of the borrower and its development team (for example, can this development team complete and lease the project in the proposed manner). The end result is that a construction loan is inherently part real estate loan and part personal loan.

C. DISBURSEMENT OF LOAN PROCEEDS

The principal amount of a conventional permanent loan is fully disbursed at closing to allow the borrower to either purchase an existing project or refinance the debt that then encumbers the project. Conversely, the principal amount of a construction loan is disbursed incrementally over time when and as the project's development costs are incurred. A construction loan for a typical office building might involve ten to 15 separate monthly disbursements of loan proceeds, while a regional mall project could easily require the construction lender to make three times that number of monthly disbursements.

There are two reasons why a construction loan is not disbursed in a lump sum at closing. First, the periodic disbursement of the construction loan proceeds helps the borrower reduce the interest it pays on the construction loan (because it does not have to pay interest on the undisbursed portion of the construction loan). Second, if the construction lender were to disburse the entire principal amount of the construction loan at closing, then the lender would be exposed to an even greater risk that the borrower might use those proceeds for a reason other than the completion of the proposed real estate project (and, hence, the creation of the value of the lender's loan collateral). Both of these topics are discussed in more detail later in this chapter.

D. LENGTH OF LOAN TERM

A typical term for a permanent mortgage loan is anywhere from five to 15 years. The permanent lender has the ability to make a loan having a term of that length because it is dealing with a completed asset that has a proven financial track record and a relatively predictable financial future.

The customary term of a construction loan is much shorter than that of a permanent loan—12 to 36 *MONTHS* as opposed to five to 15 *YEARS*. The shorter duration of the construction loan term is primarily attributable to the uncertain future value of the "to be constructed" project and the lender's concomitant desire to get its loan repaid as soon as construction of the project is completed.

E. IDENTITY OF LENDER

Construction loans are, for the most part, the province of commercial banks. As noted earlier in this section, a construction loan is part real estate loan and part personal loan. A commercial bank is much more apt than a life insurance company or pension fund to have the local knowledge, experience, and personal relationships required to properly underwrite and administer such a combination loan. In addition, commercial banks naturally gravitate to the shorter terms of construction loans due to their need to maintain liquidity to meet the more immediate cash needs of their retail customers.

Permanent loans, on the other hand, are made based upon an evaluation of the physical and financial components of an existing real estate asset and, as such, do not require the same level of local knowledge or hands-on administration that a construction loan does. As a result, permanent loans are typically made not by commercial banks, but rather by financial institutions, such as life insurance companies and pension funds, that tend to have a longer-term investment perspective.

F. CALCULATION OF INTEREST RATE

The norm in the permanent loan market is for interest to be set at a fixed annual percentage (for example 7%) for the entire duration of the loan term. Fixed pricing works in the permanent loan arena because the permanent lender disburses the entire principal amount of its loan in a lump sum on a date that is in close proximity to the date on which it accesses the funds it uses to make that loan disbursement. As a result, the permanent lender is in a position to quantify and fix upfront both its cost of funds and the interest rate it charges to its borrower. A permanent lender's cost of funds is determined by reference to the comparative levels of its cash inflows (for example, from insurance premiums or pension contributions) and its cash outflows (for example, for the payment of death or pension benefits). A permanent lender's cost of funds is generally more stable than that of a commercial bank due to the long-term nature of the permanent lender's business model. The permanent lender's profit on the permanent loan transaction (assuming that the loan is kept current and is paid in full at maturity) is equal to the excess of the permanent loan's fixed interest rate over the lender's cost of funds as of the date of the permanent loan closing.[3]

The principal amount of the construction loan is disbursed not in a lump sum at closing, but rather incrementally over the 12 to 36 month term of the construction loan. Because its loan disbursements are spread over a lengthy period of time, the construction lender (unlike the permanent lender) is not in a position to determine its cost of funds and fix its interest rate at the time of the initial construction loan closing. By way of example, assume that the construction lender's cost of funds (a blend of the interest rate that the bank has to pay on its customers' deposits and the interest rate at which the bank borrows funds from other financial institutions) as of the date of the initial construction loan closing is 4% and that the construction lender would be happy to receive a profit on the construction loan of 3% of the loan balance. If the lender's cost of funds remains constant throughout the full term of the construction loan, then the lender could achieve its desired loan profit by fixing the borrower's interest rate at 7% (the lender's cost of funds of 4%, plus its desired profit spread of 3%). But what happens if the construction lender's cost of funds increases to 6% after it has disbursed only 25% of the total proceeds available under the construction loan? If the lender fixes its interest rate at 7% at the time of the construction loan closing, then the subsequent increase in its cost of funds would result in the lender's profit margin on the loan being reduced by an amount equal to 2% of the 75% portion of the loan proceeds remaining to be disbursed after the cost of funds increase—a result that would certainly not be acceptable to the construction lender.

For the above reason, construction loans typically provide for a variable or *floating interest rate* that is adjusted during the loan term to reflect changes in a specified financial index. The *prime rate* and the London Interbank Offered Rate (*LIBOR*) are the two financial indices most commonly used by construction lenders to set their floating interest rates.

The "prime rate" is the interest rate charged on loans made by a financial institution to its most creditworthy customers. The specific prime rate used as the benchmark for the setting of the interest rate on a construction loan is routinely expressed in terms of either (i) the prime rate announced by the subject construction lender, (ii) the prime rate published

---

[3] *See generally* DAVID M. GELTNER, NORMAN G. MILLER, JIM CLAYTON AND PIET EICHOLTZ, COMMERCIAL REAL ESTATE ANALYSIS AND INVESTMENTS 389–390 (2nd ed. 2007).

by a national bank other than the construction lender (for example, Bank of America), or (iii) the prime rate referenced in a national publication (for example, the Wall Street Journal).

LIBOR is a daily reference rate based on the interest rate at which banks borrow unsecured funds from other banks in the London wholesale money market (or interbank market). Because LIBOR is based on the borrowing rates afforded to other banks (and not a bank's commercial customers, as is the case with the prime rate), LIBOR is almost always lower than the prime rate. As such, the spreads quoted on LIBOR are historically higher than those quoted on the prime rate—for example, LIBOR plus 3% versus the prime rate plus 1%.

By tying its floating interest rate to the variable performance of a financial index like the prime rate or LIBOR, the construction lender is able to protect the amount of its potential construction loan profit from an unanticipated increase in the lender's cost of funds that occurs during the term of the construction loan. The following is a common example of how the construction loan documents might describe the variable rate of interest charged under the construction loan—"the Lender's Prime Rate in effect from time to time, plus 1%, with any change in the rate of interest due to a change in the Prime Rate being effective on the date such change is announced by the Lender."

It should be noted that the numerical interest rate charged on construction loans is customarily higher than the numerical interest charged by permanent lenders. Why do you suppose that is the case? Does the phrase "the greater, the risk, the greater the reward" mean anything to you?

G. IMPOSITION OF LOAN FEES

Construction and permanent lenders both charge upfront loan fees to all but their best customers (who frequently have enough negotiating leverage to get those fees waived). Loan fees are typically expressed in terms of a percentage of the principal amount of the loan—for example, a fee of 1% (also referred as either a *point* or *100 basis points*) on a $10 million permanent loan means that the borrower has to pay a $100,000 upfront fee to the lender. These upfront fees are in addition to the borrower's required interest payments and are typically referred to as "origination," "commitment," or "loan processing" fees. The fees are imposed to achieve one or both of the following lender objectives—(i) the reimbursement of the lender's cost of making the loan, and (ii) the augmentation of the lender's profit on the loan transaction.

Construction lenders typically charge higher upfront fees on their loans than do permanent lenders. The construction lender's imposition of such higher fees is justified (at least in the construction lender's mind) by the facts that (1) a construction loan is inherently more risky than a permanent loan, and (2) the post-closing administration of a construction loan is much more labor-intensive than that of a permanent loan.

H. BORROWER'S RECOURSE ON LOAN

Most permanent loans are ***nonrecourse*** to the borrower.[4] What this means is that the borrower has no personal liability for the repayment of the permanent loan. The permanent lender's sole remedy for a loan default is to foreclose on its mortgage and take over ownership and operation of the underlying real estate project. The permanent lender is in a position to grant this concession to its borrower because the project which serves as collateral for the loan presumably has a predictable stream of income that the lender can look to as a reliable source for the loan's repayment.

The construction loan borrower is seldom in a position to demand (or even reasonably request) the inclusion in the construction loan of a nonrecourse provision. Indeed, the norm is for the construction loan to be fully recourse to both the named borrower (typically a single purpose entity with little, if any net worth) and another creditworthy entity under a personal guaranty. The reason behind the construction lender's insistence that its loan be fully recourse is quite simple—the construction lender's collateral is an amorphous "to be created" asset that is producing no current revenue and, hence, has no existing value. The requirement that somebody with a relatively deep pocket be personally liable for the repayment of the construction loan is one way for the construction lender to hedge its bet on the ultimate successful completion and lease-up of the development project.

I.   VALUE OF FORECLOSURE REMEDY

Both construction and permanent lenders reserve the right to foreclose on the borrower's mortgage if the borrower defaults under the loan. The value of that foreclosure remedy is, however, markedly different for the construction lender versus the permanent lender.

When the permanent lender forecloses on its permanent loan mortgage, it inherits full control and ownership of a completed project that presumably has an existing income stream (although maybe not at the level that was present when the loan was initially made). What does the construction lender get when it forecloses on its construction loan mortgage? The answer to that question is "not much." A partially constructed development project has little, if any, existing value and is frequently worth less than the principal amount of the construction loan.

---

[4]   It has become common in the last several years for permanent loans to include exceptions to the general nonrecourse rule. Those exceptions are commonly called "nonrecourse carveouts" and are discussed *infra* in *Chapter 12—Selecting an Exit Strategy*, at pages 603–605.

The only thing that the construction lender gains from foreclosing on its mortgage is the right to complete construction of the project and then try to lease it to rent-paying tenants—a right that is more in the nature of a daunting challenge than it is any positive current benefit to the construction lender. It is for this reason that the typical construction loan is not only secured by a mortgage on the underlying real estate, but also further secured by a personal guaranty posted by a creditworthy affiliate of the borrower.

J.   FUNDING OF DEBT SERVICE PAYMENTS

As is the case with residential mortgage loans, permanent loans require the borrower to make monthly principal and interest payments in an amount designed to pay off the loan at maturity. The permanent loan borrower uses the net operating income generated by its commercial real estate project to fund these debt service payments. Unlike a residential mortgage loan, most permanent loans provide for a final *balloon payment* to be made at the maturity of the loan, with that final payment being significantly greater than the installment of principal and interest payable during each month of the permanent loan term. An oversized final payment is required because the periodic principal and interest payments due under a construction loan are typically computed based on a 15–30-year amortization schedule, while the term of the permanent loan is usually only five to 15 years.

A construction loan project does not have any net operating income that the borrower can use to fund the debt service payments owed on the construction loan. In recognition of this fact, debt service payable under a construction loan is traditionally "interest only"—meaning that the borrower is not required to make any payments of principal during the term of the construction loan. But if the development project is not producing any income stream whatsoever (which is usually the case during at least the first 12 months or so of the construction loan term), where does the borrower get the funds to make its interest payments? The answer is quite simple—it borrows them from the construction lender. As a result, most construction loan budgets contain a line item expense for the payment of the borrower's construction period interest. The fact that the borrower typically pays its interest carry with borrowed funds is further underscored by a provision routinely included in construction loan documents that expressly grants the construction lender the right to make payments to its own account to pay the borrower's construction interest (see for example, § 6.1(f) of the Form Construction Loan Agreement set out as Document #5 of the *Document Appendix,* at page 704).

III. BUSINESS OBJECTIVES OF BORROWER AND LENDER

The following is a summary of the business objectives of the lender and the borrower during the construction financing stage of the development process.

A. BORROWER/DEVELOPER

The following are the four main business objectives of the developer/borrower during Stage 5.

- *Cheap Debt*—The developer wants the interest rate and any loan fees payable by the developer under the construction loan to be as low as possible. All other things being equal, a construction loan that bears interest at 1 point over LIBOR is obviously more advantageous to the borrower than a construction loan that bears interest at 2 points over LIBOR.

- *Ready Access to Loan Disbursements*—The developer wants to receive construction loan disbursements when and as needed to pay the developer's bills. The developer does not want the construction loan documents to present any obstacles or impediments to its ability to promptly receive disbursements of loan proceeds in the exact amount required to pay its contractors, consultants, and itself. The reference to payments "to itself" specifically includes disbursements of loan proceeds to pay the developer (1) its development fee, and (2) the unrealized profit on the land it contributes to the venture. The competing perspectives of the borrower and the lender on the wisdom of using loan proceeds to pay the development fee and land profit is examined in some detail later in this chapter at pages 392–395.

- *Preferential Use of Debt*—The developer strives to fund as many of its development costs as possible (including soft costs and fees payable to the developer) with debt and defer the use of its equity contributions until as late in the process as possible. Because the relative return required by equity investors (including a self-funding developer) is typically higher than the cost of the construction debt, the use of debt dollars on a "first in" basis effectively reduces the developer's overall project costs and leaves more profit to be divided among the developer and its equity investors. Deferred equity contributions of the type described in this paragraph are commonly referred to as *back-end equity*. *Front-end equity* is equity contributed before the funding of the construction loan proceeds. As noted later in this chapter at pages 377–379, the adoption at the federal level of the Basel III Rule has now largely eviscerated any hope that the developer has to convince its construction lender to sanction a back-end equity contribution scheme.

- ***Limitation of Personal Liability***—The developer wants to limit its personal liability on the construction loan in any way possible. In this respect, it is the developer's goal to make the construction loan more a real estate loan than a personal loan.

The developer is not always in a position to perfectly achieve these objectives. By way of example, the developer seldom gets its wish to back-end its equity contributions or limit its personal recourse on the construction loan. Counsel to the developer must nonetheless be fully cognizant of the developer's business objectives in order to massage the construction loan documents to achieve those objectives to the maximum extent possible.

B. CONSTRUCTION LENDER

The construction lender has one fundamental business objective—to maximize the positive ***spread*** between its cost of funds and the payments it receives from the borrower. It is this spread that represents the construction lender's profit on the transaction. The construction lender makes money when it receives a deposit from a customer to purchase a CD earning 2% and then turns around and makes a construction loan to one of its developer customers at an interest rate of 7%.

A bank's profit on a construction loan transaction is dependent not only on the interest rate at which it prices the construction loan (which is obviously always higher than its cost of funds), but just as importantly on the construction loan being paid off in its entirety at maturity. It does not take a mathematical genius to figure out that a construction loan with a theoretical spread of 5% will not produce a profit to the lender if the borrower cannot repay the loan at maturity and the lender ends up having to sell the loan at 60 cents on the dollar.

C. SHARED BUSINESS OBJECTIVES

There is a natural tension between the business objectives of the construction lender and the borrower. The remainder of this chapter is devoted to an analysis of those strategies and techniques that are available to the parties to try to bridge the gap between their competing business objectives. One important consideration to keep in mind is that the construction lender and the borrower share one very important business objective—achieving the completion of the development project in accordance with the developer's initial projections and leasing plan. One prominent practitioner underscored this point in a very interesting and telling fashion by noting that "the construction lender's lawyer should always remember the admonition of the typical developer/borrower that once the lender has advanced the first million dollars the construction lender and the borrower are partners."[5]

HIBC Case Study—The Tale of Two Construction Loans

Shortly after its acquisition of the 350-acre HIBC land, Pizzuti commissioned its architects to begin the design of two new HIBC office buildings, each of which would contain approximately 75,000 square feet of rentable space. At the same time, Pizzuti began an intense marketing blitz to identify and secure office tenants for the two proposed buildings. Pizzuti's marketing efforts turned up a number of tenant prospects, the hottest of which was HTE, Inc., a software development firm that was interested in leasing somewhere around 70–90,000 square feet of space in the north Orlando submarket. While HTE's business seemed to be booming, its balance sheet was not—its net worth was just barely into eight figures.

In addition to HTE, Pizzuti's leasing agents turned up a long list of other tenants who were interested in relocating their businesses to HIBC. A consistent refrain heard from those prospective tenants was that, while they were definitely intrigued by the possibility of moving to HIBC, they could not view the alternative as being "real" unless and until they saw a new HIBC building under construction. None of the prospective tenants (other than HTE) was willing to enter into lease negotiations based on artist renderings of what the new office buildings would look like.

Based on that feedback from its leasing agents, Pizzuti took the following steps—

- *It immediately instructed its architects and leasing agents to work directly with HTE to come up with a design and ten-year lease structure for a building to be 100% occupied by HTE. The building ultimately designed for HTE contained approximately 87,000 square feet of rentable space.*

- *It also announced that it would immediately begin construction of a 75,000-square-foot speculative or "spec" office building to be known as the "500 Building." The "spec building" parlance meant that Pizzuti was committed to*

---

5   Phillip D. Weller, *Fundamentals of Construction Lending*, in ALI-ABA COURSE OF STUDY MATERIALS, MODERN REAL ESTATE TRANSACTIONS: PRACTICAL STRATEGIES FOR REAL ESTATE ACQUISITION, DISPOSITION, AND OWNERSHIP, Course No. SS–012, 1470, 1478 (July 2010).

beginning construction of the 500 Building even though it had not secured leasing commitments from any tenants.

Pizzuti's next task was to identify banks who might be interested in providing construction financing for both the HTE building and the 500 Building. Two lenders expressed a preliminary interest in providing construction loans for both buildings—Barnett Bank (now part of Bank of America) and First Union National Bank (now part of Wells Fargo Bank). Pizzuti immediately submitted the following construction loan proposals to both Barnett and First Union.

Proposed Loan Terms	HTE Building	500 Building
Total Development Costs	$10 million	$10 million
Loan Amount	$9 million (90% of costs)	$8 million (80% of costs)
Loan Term	24 months, with one 12-month extension option	36 months with one 24-month extension option
Interest Rate	LIBOR plus 1%	LIBOR plus 1.5%
Commitment Fee	Waived	1%
Equity Requirement	$1 million of back-end equity	$2 million of front-end equity
Credit Enhancement	Completion and payment guaranties from a creditworthy affiliate of developer	Completion and payment guaranties from a creditworthy affiliate of developer
Required Date of Completion	12 months after loan closing	12 months after loan closing

The substance of Pizzuti's construction loan negotiations with Barnett and First Union are addressed later in this chapter as part of the examination of the risk mitigation techniques commonly used by construction lenders to advance and protect their business objectives. Until then, let me give the reader the main story lines (HTE's less than stellar credit and the whole "spec building thing") and the ultimate punch line (First Union made construction loans on both the HTE and 500 Buildings, as well as six other office buildings ultimately developed by Pizzuti at HIBC).

Practice Tip #9-1: The Basel III Rule

The Great Recession of 2008 crippled the U.S. and global economies and put many private banks on the brink of extinction. The so-called **Basel III rule** *issued by The Federal Reserve Board, the Office of the Comptroller of the Currency, and the Federal Deposit Insurance Corporation in July 2013 is designed to discourage the risky loan practices followed by U.S. banks prior to the onset of the recession is 2008.*[6]

The hallmark of the Basel III rule for the construction lending industry is the introduction of the concept of the **high-volatility commercial real estate loan (an HVCRE loan).** *Under lending rules that were in force prior to the adoption of Basel III, a bank making a commercial real estate construction loan was required to hold capital reserves equal to 8% of the principal balance of the construction loan. Under Basel III, a bank is required to have capital reserves of 12% (150% of the prior requirement) if the bank makes a "high-volatility commercial real estate loan." This more vigorous capital reserve requirement for HVCRE loans is certain to have a deleterious effect on the construction lending practices of U.S. banks—at least as viewed from the perspective of the borrower/developer.*

So what is this monstrous thing called a "high-volatility commercial real estate loan"? Basically any construction loan made by a bank to finance the construction of a commercial real estate project will fall under the dreaded HVCRE loan category unless the construction loan meets all the following tests throughout the term of the construction loan:

- *The loan's loan-to-value ratio must be 80% or less;*

- *The borrower must make equity contributions to the project of at least 15% of the project's "as completed" value (and not the lower "cost" number);*

- *All the borrower's equity contributions must be in the form of cash, unencumbered readily marketable assets, or out-of-pocket project expenses;*

- *All the borrower's required equity contributions must be contributed to the project before the funding of any construction loan proceeds; and*

---

[6] *See Final Basel III Regulatory Capital and Market Risk Rule*, 78 FED. REG. 62018 (October 11, 2013). *See generally* Sarah V.J. Spyksma, *Real Estate Finance in the Era of Basel III*, in ACREL PAPERS Tab 4 (Fall 2015); Thomas A. Hauser, *Debt Markets—Dead, Delayed or Dynamic: Current Factors Influencing Real Estate Finance*, in ACREL PAPERS Tab 2 (Fall 2016); and Joseph Rubin, Stephen Giczewski, and Matt Olsen, *New Rules Under Basel III Likely to Impact Commercial Real Estate,* URBAN LAND MAGAZINE (September 16, 2013), available online at http://urban land.uli.org/capital-markets/new-rules-under-basel-iii-likely-to-affect-commercial-real-estate/.

- *All the borrower's required equity contributions must remain invested in the project until the construction loan is paid off in full through a sale or refinancing.*

The exact import of the Basel III rule remains to be fleshed out. By way of example, it is unclear whether (1) the borrower can use the proceeds of unsecured loans or the appreciated land value to satisfy its equity requirement, or (2) the borrower can distribute excess positive cash flow to its equity participants prior to the pay-off of the construction loan. In April 2015, the government issued responses to a set of "frequently asked questions" that seemed to raise more questions than it provided answers.[7]

While the precise scope of the Basel III rules are not yet known, there are a few clear conclusions that can be drawn at this point:

- *Banks are going to be extremely hesitant to make construction loans that fall under the category of high-volatility commercial real estate loans;*

- *Those banks that decide to make a construction loan despite its HVCRE label will do so only if they receive an above-market return on that loan; and*

- *As a result, developers will need to either:*

  - *Give up their hopes of securing a construction loan featuring a high LTV and back-end equity;*

  - *Be willing to pay the price for the privilege of getting an HVCRE loan; or*

  - *Find a lending source that is not governed by the Basel III rules (for example, a private equity fund or a mortgage REIT).[8]*

IV. DOCUMENTING THE CONSTRUCTION LOAN

Before launching into a discussion of the unique risks attendant to the making of a construction loan, it first makes sense to set the platform for that discussion by talking about the documents used to paper a construction loan. The general categories of loan documents and the constituent components of those document categories are set forth below.

A. COMMITMENT LETTER

The **commitment letter** serves a purpose comparable to that served by the letter of intent in the land acquisition stage of the development process. It sets forth the principal terms on which the construction loan

---

[7]   *See* Spyksma, *supra* note 6, at 4–7.

[8]   *See id.* at 8; and Rubin, *supra* note 6, at 2–3.

will be made and creates the platform for counsel's later drafting and negotiation of the loan documents that will be executed by the borrower and the lender at the closing of the construction loan. In most situations, the commitment letter is executed somewhere between 20 to 180 days in advance of the construction loan closing.

The commitment letter prepared by lender's counsel customarily addresses the following topics:

- **Loan amount** (including any overriding limitations on the loan amount based on lender-imposed requirements, such as loan-to-value, loan-to-cost, debt service coverage, and debt yield tests);

- **Loan term** (including the length of the initial term and the conditions to the exercise of any extension option);

- **Interest rate** (including a description of the financial index on which the rate will be calculated and a provision addressing the manner in which adjustments will be made to the floating rate);

- **Payment obligations** (including the due dates for all of the borrower's payment obligations and whether the loan will be interest only—the norm—or require principal amortization—usually only applicable during an extension of the construction loan term);

- **Equity requirements** (including both the amount of the borrower's required equity contributions and when those contributions must be made—that is, before or after the lender's disbursement of the proceeds of the construction loan);

- **Fees and reimbursable costs** (including the amount of any origination, commitment or loan processing fees and the identification of all costs to be paid/reimbursed by borrower— for example, the lender's legal fees, title insurance premiums, survey costs, environmental charges, etc.);

- **Guaranties** (including the general terms of any completion or payment guaranties and the identity of the guarantor);

- **Conditions to closing and loan funding** (including any pre-leasing threshold and a listing of all required closing deliverables, such as soils tests, title policy, survey, environmental assessment, construction and design contracts, insurance policies, etc.);

- **Loan disbursement procedures** (including the timing of the disbursements, the documentation that must be submitted in support of any requested disbursement, and the approval process applicable to each submitted draw request);

- *Identification of collateral* (including a first mortgage, conditional assignment of leases, collateral assignment of construction and design contracts, payment and performance bonds, letters of credit, etc.); and

- *Closing date and procedures* (including the outside date for the loan closing and a listing of all those documents that must be executed and delivered at closing).

The commitment letter is usually signed by both the lender and the borrower. However, as is the case with the land purchase letter of intent, the commitment may or may not be binding on the parties. Even if the lender and the borrower evidence their agreement to be bound by the specific provisions of the commitment letter, both sides to the transaction (particularly the lender) regularly seek to reserve a high level of discretion to back out of the deal based on a change in market conditions or the occurrence of other events outside of the skin of the commitment letter— for example, the disapproval of the deal by the lender's loan committee or the borrower's receipt of a more competitive loan offer from another construction lender. The construction lender invariably attempts to impose an obligation on the borrower to pay the lender's fees and costs even if the loan does not close for a reason expressly sanctioned in the body of the commitment letter.

B. EVIDENCE OF INDEBTEDNESS

The borrower's obligation to repay the principal and interest due under the construction loan is evidenced by the borrower's execution of a *promissory note*. The promissory note is the document that sets forth the maximum loan amount, the maturity date of the loan, the borrower's interest rate, and the amount and timing of the periodic debt service payments due under the construction loan.

C. COLLATERAL DOCUMENTS

The primary collateral document used in both conventional permanent loans and construction loans is a *mortgage* or *deed of trust*, pursuant to which the borrower grants the lender a first priority lien on the borrower's real estate project. Other collateral documents frequently used to secure the borrower's obligations under a construction loan are:

- *An assignment of leases* under which the borrower assigns to the construction lender the right to receive rents and enforce the performance of the tenants under all project leases;

- *A collateral assignment of all construction and design contracts* that authorizes the lender to take over the borrower's position under these contracts and complete the project in the event of a default by the borrower;

- *UCC financing statements* that, when filed in the required state and local offices, perfects the lender's security interest in any fixtures and personal property associated with the project;

- *A completion guaranty* under which a creditworthy entity affiliated with the borrower agrees to do whatever is necessary to complete the project in accordance with the agreed-upon plans and specifications and construction schedule; and

- *A payment guaranty* under which a creditworthy entity affiliated with the borrower agrees to guaranty the borrower's payment obligations under the construction loan documents.

D. CONSTRUCTION LOAN AGREEMENT

The *construction loan agreement* is the document that sets the construction loan apart from a conventional permanent loan. As is discussed in great detail in the ensuing sections of this chapter, the construction lender faces a series of unique risks when it makes a construction loan—many of which revolve around the earlier-discussed phenomenon that the loan proceeds disbursed under the construction loan are used to CREATE the value of the lender's loan collateral.

One practicing lawyer described the challenges faced by counsel for the borrower and the lender in drafting and negotiating the construction loan documents in the following way:

> Construction loans are one of the most difficult kinds of loan for a lender and a borrower to negotiate, document and carry out to conclusion. There are many reasons for this phenomenon. Construction projects are subject to change, delays, cost overruns and unanticipated events. The construction loan documentation must be structured so as to anticipate the unforeseen.[9]

A sample construction loan agreement is contained in the *Documents Appendix* as Document #5 at pages 685–707. The provisions of a construction loan agreement are the dominant focus of the rest of this chapter.

---

[9] Susan G. Talley, *Selected Issues in Construction Lending*, in ALI-ABA COURSE OF STUDY MATERIALS, COMMERCIAL REAL ESTATE FINANCING: STRATEGIES FOR CHANGING MARKETS AND UNCERTAIN TIMES, Course No. SP-008, 125, 127 (January 2009).

V. UNIQUE RISKS FACED BY THE CONSTRUCTION LENDER

The construction lender must confront and navigate its way through a series of risks that are not presented in the context of a conventional permanent loan. These unique risks are all driven by two fundamental considerations—(1) the construction lender is forced to conduct its loan underwriting on the basis of the developer's *PROJECTIONS* of what the project is going to look like and how it will perform financially (and not based on an inspection of an existing real estate asset or an analysis of in-place leases and other historical financial data), and (2) the proceeds of the construction loan will be used to *CREATE* the value of the collateral for that loan.

The following are five unique risks faced by the construction lender:

- The project is not completed on time;

- The actual completed cost of the project is greater than its budgeted cost;

- The actual value of the completed project is less than its projected value;

- The borrower uses the construction loan proceeds for a purpose other than the completion of the project; and

- A lien filed by a third party after the date of the loan closing gains priority over the construction lender's mortgage.

The possible causes and consequences of each of these risk scenarios are discussed below.

A. COMPLETION RISK

The nature and consequences of the completion risk faced by the construction lender are best illustrated by reference to the two HIBC development projects that are serving as the case study for this chapter—the 500 and HTE buildings. Each building was projected to cost $10 million and to be completed within 12 months. The following are examples of how completion risk could play out in the context of these two projects.

- ***Non-Completion Risk***—Construction of the 500 Building is permanently halted six months into the construction period after the borrower has taken down $4 million in loan proceeds (40% of the overall projected costs of the 500 project).

- ***Late Completion Risk***—Construction of the HTE project is completed nine months later than anticipated (and six months after the date of HTE's scheduled occupancy of the building).

The onset of non-completion and late completion risks can be triggered by any number of events and circumstances, including those described below.

- *Execution Risk*—This is the risk that the developer fails to execute on its construction schedule for some reason, including—

  o   An overly optimistic construction schedule (frequently triggered by the developer's motivation to meet a completion deadline established by a third party—for example, HTE's targeted occupancy date);

  o   The general contractor's incompetency;

  o   The developer's failure to timely secure all essential governmental permits and approvals (for example, a rezoning of the site or the issuance of a building permit to begin work on the project); or

  o   The developer's failure to conduct appropriate site due diligence, with the result that adverse environmental, soils, or other site-related conditions present insurmountable obstacles to the developer's completion of the project in accordance with its construction schedule.

- *Financial Risk*—This is the risk that the developer runs out of money and cannot fund its required equity contributions. The financial position of a well-heeled developer can quickly deteriorate after the construction loan closing for any number of reasons, including: a sudden drop in the stock market; a severe loss suffered by the developer on another real estate project; a falling out between the developer and one of its principal equity investors; or a drunken (and unlucky) weekend in Las Vegas. Regardless of the reason for the developer's financial straits, the bottom line is that construction of the project cannot go forward if the developer does not have the funds to pay its share of the project's development costs.

- *Unforeseen Risk*—This is the risk that lawyers are referring to when they use the fancy legal term *force majeure*—that is, the risk of the occurrence of an event that is beyond the developer's anticipation or control, but that nonetheless delays or prevents the construction of the developer's project. Examples of typical *force majeure* events are a fire, hurricane, or strike.

So what are the consequences of the occurrence of the above risks? That question can be answered by reflecting once again on the two HIBC case studies introduced at the beginning of this section.

- *Non-Completion of 500 Building*—In this scenario, the value of the collateral for the construction lender's loan is never created because construction of the building is never finished. The value of a half-finished building is almost always less than its cost. As a result, what the construction lender hoped would be a real estate loan supported by valuable collateral turns into a personal loan where the construction lender's only viable alternative is a legal action against the borrower/guarantor under the loan.

- *Late Completion of HTE Building*—At first blush, it would seem that the construction lender is in a much better position on its HTE loan than on the 500 Building loan. After all, the lender has a first mortgage on a finished office building in a first-class business park. But is there any true value to that finished office building? What if the developer's lease with HTE includes a clause permitting HTE to terminate its lease if the building is not completed by its targeted occupancy date? From a construction lender's perspective, there are few things worse than being left with a mortgage on a single tenant building that does not have a tenant. This is especially true where the building's design has been tailored to meet the particular needs and eccentricities of the putative tenant and, hence, is not usable by other prospective tenants unless the lender is willing to incur the additional costs needed to retrofit the building.

B. RISK OF COST OVERRUNS

What if the cost of completing construction of the 500 Building ends up being $12 million (instead of the projected $10 million)? The specter of project cost overruns is not only the most common risk faced by a construction lender, but also one of the most significant.

A cost overrun on a development project can be attributable to the occurrence of both foreseeable and unforeseeable events. The following are common examples of events that can trigger a project cost overrun:

- An incomplete listing in the developer's project budget of those development costs that must be incurred to complete construction of the project;

- An inaccurate construction cost estimate provided by the developer's general contractor;

- A change in the nature or scope of the construction project due to either (1) the developer's perception that a change is necessary to respond to an evolving market condition (for example, a perceived need for an office building to have an on-site fitness center), or (2) a prospective tenant's operational needs (for example, a tenant's decision that it needs a computer server room);

- The occurrence of a *force majeure* event; or

- An unanticipated spike in the project's interest carry costs due to either (1) an increase in the financial index specified in the construction loan documents (for example, LIBOR or the prime rate), (2) a longer than anticipated lease-up period (which has the effect of decreasing the revenue stream that would otherwise be used to pay the construction loan interest), or (3) the developer's front-loading of its development costs (which would increase the daily average of the outstanding principal balance during the construction loan term and, hence, the amount of the borrower's overall interest expense).

From the construction lender's perspective, the existence of a cost overrun is not overly consequential if the developer steps up and funds the excess costs out of its own pocket. But what happens if the developer is either unable or unwilling to pay the amount of the project cost overruns? Under that scenario, the construction lender is faced with two bad choices:

- It can refuse to provide the additional loan dollars needed to fund the cost overruns, in which event construction of the project will likely never be completed (thereby converting a cost overrun risk into the non-completion risk mentioned under the prior heading of this section); or

- It can agree to provide the additional loan dollars to fund the cost overruns, in which event the lender's cushion between the amount of the construction loan and the ultimate value of the completed project will be significantly reduced.

Regardless which course of action the lender opts to pursue to deal with a cost overrun, the impact on the net value of its collateral under the construction loan is the same—the net value of its collateral position decreases.

C. RISK OF INSUFFICIENT PROJECT VALUE

For the purposes of looking at the next risk faced by a construction lender, assume that construction of the 500 Building is completed on-time and on-budget (meaning that the construction lender has successfully managed to avoid both the completion and cost overrun risks). But what happens if the fair market value of the completed 500 Building project (originally projected by the developer to be $12 million) turns out to be $9 million—or $1 million less than the cost of constructing the 500 Building?

The following are some of the more common causes that can trigger a decline in a building's value upon completion.

- A failure of the project to lease up in accordance with the developer's initial projections (for example, a lease-up that is slower than projected or at lower rental rates than projected);

- A change in general market conditions (for example, the advent of an across-the-board reduction in the pricing of commercial real estate due to a credit crunch of the type experienced in the U.S. during the Great Recession of 2008); or

- The occurrence of an event that adversely affects the position of the building in the marketplace (for example, the construction of a newer, bigger, and better office building two blocks down the road from the project being financed under the construction loan).

The typical sources for the repayment of a construction loan (the lender's "exit strategy") are either (1) the outright sale of the project to a third party buyer, or (2) the refinancing of the construction loan with a conventional permanent loan. A marked decline in the completed value of a project calls into question the efficacy of both of these exit strategies.

The 500 Building case study illustrates how a decline in the actual value of a completed project can eviscerate the construction lender's hope for an exit under its construction loan. First, assume that the loan-to-value ratio prevailing in the permanent loan market as of the date the construction lender committed to make a construction loan on the 500 Building is 66%—meaning that a permanent lender would be willing to make an $8 million permanent loan on the 500 Building (an amount that would be sufficient to fully retire the construction loan) if the value of the 500 Building at completion is at least $12 million. If, as assumed in the prior hypothetical, the value of the completed 500 Building is only $9 million, then the permanent loan market would only support a loan on that building of $6 million—the $9 million value multiplied by the loan-to-value ratio of 66%. That state of affairs leaves a funding gap of $2 million between the outstanding principal balance of the construction loan ($8 million) and the maximum principal amount that can be obtained under a permanent loan ($6 million)—a gap that largely takes away the refinancing exit strategy customarily afforded the construction lender by the permanent loan market.

The decision tree created by the above fact situation is as follows:

- If the developer has a deep pocket, the developer can refinance the construction loan with a $6 million permanent loan and pay off the remaining $2 million balance with its personal funds (something that would make the construction lender happy, but would certainly not please the developer); or

- If the developer does not have a deep pocket, the developer's options are limited to the following—

    o   It can try to sell the project for a price sufficient to pay off the $8 million construction loan; or

    o   If it cannot sell the project for at least $8 million, then the developer can ask the construction lender to either—

        - Extend the maturity of the construction loan to give the developer time to increase the project's value (the so-called "extend and pretend" tactic), or

        - Agree to take up to a $2 million loss on the construction loan (often referred to as a *haircut*).

It is this last branch of the decision tree that the construction lender wants to avoid at all costs.

D. RISK OF MISAPPLICATION OF FUNDS

The next construction loan risk can be illustrated by assuming that the construction lender fully disburses the $9 million loan amount under the HTE construction loan only to subsequently discover that the developer applied a mere $6 million of the loan proceeds to the payment of development costs on the HTE project. The first question that comes to mind is how could that possibly happen?

The answer to that question lies in the manner in which the principal amount of a construction loan is disbursed to the borrower. Under a conventional permanent loan, the lender customarily disburses 100% of the loan amount at closing. The permanent lender funds the portion of the permanent loan that is required to pay off any existing mortgage loans directly to the holders of those loans, with the remaining proceeds then being deposited to the borrower's account. By making a lump sum payment directly to the account of the existing lien holders, the permanent lender controls its risk that the borrower absconds with the funds and fails to pay off the existing project loans (which is the permanent lender's only real concern about the borrower's use of the proceeds of the permanent loan).

Unlike a conventional permanent loan, the principal amount of a construction loan is disbursed incrementally over a period of many months.

As a result, the construction lender cannot realistically protect itself against the risk of a misapplication of funds by dictating on a one-time only basis that the loan proceeds must be disbursed in a lump sum to a party or parties designated by the lender.

What would cause a developer to misuse the loan proceeds in the manner described above? The simplest answer to that question is the three-headed monster of avarice, greed, and evil. In other words, the developer sees the construction loan process as a convenient way to feed its gambling, drug, or sex addictions.

A more common cause of a developer's misappropriation of construction loan proceeds is not evil, but desperation. Real estate development is a very capital-intensive business and one where cash flow is unpredictable. Absent any restrictions on its conduct, a developer might be tempted to take construction loan proceeds from one project to try to stem a cash flow problem it is experiencing on another project. The well-intentioned developer would, of course, fully expect to repatriate the proceeds to the lender's construction project as soon as the developer resolves its temporary cash flow problems on the other project.

So what happens to the construction lender if the developer's temporary cash flow problems become permanent? In that situation, the proceeds of the loan that were intended to be used to create the value of the lender's loan collateral are forever diverted for another purpose. The developer's misapplication of the construction loan proceeds leaves the construction lender with the exact dilemma it faces when the project experiences a cost overrun—the lender either provides the additional loan dollars needed to complete the project or it accepts the prospect that it will be forced to take a sizable loss on the construction loan transaction.

E. RISK OF INTERVENING LIENS

The primary source of a construction lender's security for the borrower's repayment of the construction loan is the mortgage that is recorded against the borrower's real estate project. The goal of the construction lender in requiring the execution, delivery, and recordation of that mortgage is to establish in the lender's favor a first priority lien on the project that secures the developer's obligation to repay the full amount of the construction loan.

This seemingly simple goal is potentially undercut by the manner in which the loan proceeds are disbursed under a construction loan. As previously discussed, disbursements under a construction loan may be made months and, in some cases, years after the date of the recordation of the construction lender's mortgage. The extended time frame for the making of disbursements under a construction loan gives rise to the possibility that a third party might file a lien against the underlying real estate project *AFTER* the date of the recordation of the construction lender's mortgage, but *BEFORE* the date on which the loan proceeds are fully disbursed by the construction lender. The issue that confronts the construction lender is whether the lender's first mortgage position extends to all disbursements made under the construction loan (because the construction loan mortgage was recorded prior to the recording of the third party's lien) or just to those disbursements made prior to the recording of the third party lien.

The import of this issue is best understood by looking at a timeline involving the loan disbursements made pursuant to one of our case study construction loans. Assume that the timeline for the 500 Building construction loan plays out as follows.

- *June 1*—A mortgage securing a construction loan of $8 million is recorded in the real estate records of Seminole County, Florida.

- *June 2 through December 31*—The construction lender makes periodic disbursements of loan proceeds totaling $6 million.

- *January 1*—A third party files a lien against the project for $2 million.

- *January 2 through April 30*—The construction lender disburses the remaining $2 million of loan proceeds to the borrower.

- *June 1*—The third party lien holder forecloses on its lien and the real estate project is sold at a sheriff's sale for $8 million.

Under this hypothetical timeline, the question is, Who gets the proceeds of the sheriff's sale? Is the construction lender entitled to all $8million or just the $6 million that was distributed prior to the date of the filing of the third party lien, with the remaining $2 million going to the intervening lien holder? If the third party's lien is given priority over construction loan disbursements made after the January 1 lien filing date, then the construction lender's collateral position under its construction loan is adversely affected to the tune of $2 million.

Fortunately (at least for the construction lender), most states have statutes on the books that confirm the priority of all advances made under a construction loan over liens that are perfected after the date of the recording of the construction loan mortgage. Those statutes expressly provide that a construction loan mortgage (variously referred to in statutes as a *future advance* or *open-end mortgage*) has priority over all subsequently recorded liens to the full extent of all amounts secured by the mortgage regardless whether the disbursements are made before or after the date of the perfection of the intervening lien.[10] Liens that take on a subordinate position under these state statutes include subsequent mortgages, judgment liens, and vendor liens.

There is, however, one type of intervening lien that is afforded special protection under the statutes and case law of many states—the **mechanics' lien**. A mechanics' lien is a right created by statute whereby a person who works on or provides materials to a real estate project can file a lien against that project if that person is not paid in full for its efforts. The genesis for the adoption of mechanics' lien statutes was the principle that "those whose work or materials go into an improvement to real estate should be permitted, in fairness, to satisfy their unpaid bills out of that real estate."[11]

Mechanics' lien law varies widely from state to state as to both the content of the statute creating the mechanics' lien and the judicial gloss placed on the statute by local courts. That variance is particularly noteworthy on the primary topic that attracts the construction lender's attention—that is, can a mechanics' lien ever gain priority over a construction mortgage filed of public record before the filing of the mechanics' lien?[12]

Before attempting to answer the construction lender's priority question, a practitioner must first become thoroughly acquainted with the particulars of the mechanics' lien statute of the state where the underlying real estate project is located. The practitioner's first point of inquiry is to determine the date on which the applicable state statute says a mechanics' lien is deemed to have attached to the owner's real estate project. The "attachment date" (referred to in some jurisdictions as the "effective date" or "priority date") of a mechanics' lien is the date that is used to determine the relative priorities of the mechanics' lien and the construction mortgage. If the mechanics' lien's attachment date pre-dates the date of the recordation of the construction mortgage, then the mechanics' lien is usually treated as having full priority over the construction mortgage.

Most liens (including construction mortgages) are deemed to have attached as of the date on which the lien is first filed in the real estate records of the county in which the real estate is located. If this rule were to be applied to mechanics' liens, the comparative priority of a mechanics' lien

---

[10] *See* BENDER, *supra* note 1, at 317; and Harold E. Leidner, *An Overview of Mechanics' Liens and Future Advance Mortgages*, 3 PRACTICAL REAL ESTATE LAWYER 39, 42 (1987).

[11] NELSON, *supra* note 1, at 1007.

[12] There are a host of other legal issues related to the validity of a mechanics' lien—for example, who can file a mechanics' lien, when and where the lien must be filed, what form the filing must take, etc. Those issues are beyond the scope of this chapter, which is intentionally limited to a discussion of the comparative priorities of a mechanics' lien and construction loan mortgage. For a more detailed discussion of the law of mechanics' liens, *see* GEORGE LEFCOE, REAL ESTATE TRANSACTIONS, FINANCE, AND DEVELOPMENT Chapter 26 (6th ed. 2009); and NELSON, *supra* note 1, at 1006–1025.

and a construction mortgage would almost always be determined in favor of the construction mortgage (because a mechanics' lien is typically filed months after the recording of the construction mortgage and the start of construction on the mortgaged site). Unfortunately for the construction lender, only a handful of state statutes provide that a mechanics' lien attaches as of the date on which the mechanics' lien is filed of public record.

In a majority of states, the attachment date of a mechanics' lien relates back to the date of the "commencement of work" on the project.[13] There are two important components to the "commencement of work" test.

- First, the commencement date is the first date that *ANYBODY* performs any work on the site. It does not refer just to work performed by a particular lien claimant. Therefore, if excavation of the site first began on January 1, 2017, then the effective date of a roofer's mechanics lien is January 1, 2017—even if the roofer did not perform any work on the project until October 1, 2017.

- Second, state law is far from consistent as what constitutes "commencement of work." A standard commonly used by state courts to determine when work has commenced is that the work must be sufficiently "conspicuous and substantial" to be apparent to all observers that improvements are being constructed on the site. The courts have not, however, been able to articulate with any clarity what specific improvements satisfy that "conspicuous and substantial" standard.[14]

The above rule can wreak havoc on the priority of the construction lender's mortgage. Many developers routinely start site work on a project before the construction loan is closed and the construction lender's mortgage is recorded. If that work is later found to constitute a "commencement of work" under the applicable state statute, then the construction lender could find itself in a position where the lien of its mortgage is subordinate to all subsequently-filed mechanics liens.

The measures that a construction lender can take to protect itself against a loss of priority for its mortgage in those jurisdictions that follow

---

[13] *See* LEFCOE, *supra* note 12, at 572. The jurisdictions that do not follow the "visible commencement of work" rule define the effective date for a mechanics lien in a wide variety of ways. Some states take the position that the effective date of a mechanics lien is the date on which the mechanic lien claimant first performed work at the site. Other states establish the effective date as the date on which the owner/developer first files a notice of commencement in the public real estate records. There are also a handful of jurisdictions that say that the priority date of a mechanics lien is the date on which the lien is first filed in the public real estate records. *See* NELSON, *supra* note 1, at 1010.

[14] *See* BENDER, *supra* note 1, at 308; LEFCOE, *supra* note 12, at 572; and David A. Schmudde, *What You Should Know about Construction Financing*, 20 No. 2 PRACTICAL REAL ESTATE LAWYER 51, 55 (September 2004).

the "commencement of work" rule is reviewed at length later in this chapter (see pages 425–427). Suffice it to say at this point that a lender working in those jurisdictions should be extremely hesitant to permit any work to be done on the site before its construction mortgage is recorded.

The construction lender cannot, however, solve all of its mechanics' lien problems simply by recording its construction mortgage prior to the start of any work on the mortgaged property. In many jurisdictions, the courts have extended the construction mortgage loan's priority over subsequently-filed mechanics liens only to an *obligatory advance* that the construction lender is contractually required to make under the applicable provisions of the loan documents. If the construction lender is not contractually obligated to make a future advance, then any loan advance made by the construction lender after its receipt of notice of the existence of an intervening mechanics lien is categorized as an *optional advance* and held to be subordinate to the mechanics' lien.[15]

The implication to the construction lender of the optional versus obligatory advance dichotomy is illustrated by referring back to the prior example where the 500 Building construction lender has disbursed $6 million of its construction loan when it receives notice that a subcontractor on the project has filed a $2 million mechanics lien against the underlying real estate. The construction lender is motivated to continue to make loan disbursements under its construction loan because if it fails to do so the project will not be completed—and, as discussed previously, the lender will then face the prospect of suffering a loss on its construction loan due to the meager value attributed to a partially-completed development project. However, if the construction lender is not contractually obligated to make the future loan advances, the lender's security for the disbursement of the last $2 million of loan proceeds might be subordinate to the subcontractor's $2 million mechanics lien. If that is the case, the relative priorities of the construction lender and the mechanics lien claimant in the borrower's real estate project take on the look of what one author has called an "Oreo cookie."[16] The construction lender has a first priority position in the real property collateral for $6 million (the amount of the loan disbursed before its receipt of notice of the intervening mechanics lien) and a third priority position in that collateral for another $2 million (the amount of the loan disbursed after its receipt of notice of the intervening mechanics lien). Sandwiched between the construction lender's first and third priority positions is the mechanics' lien claimant's second priority position of $2 million—the cream filling between the construction lender's two cookies.

In those jurisdictions that recognize a distinction between obligatory and optional advances, the operative issue for the construction lender

---

[15] *See generally* Leidner, *supra* note 10, at 42; NELSON, *supra* note 1, at 1016–1025; and BENDER, *supra* note 1, at 308–323.

[16] *See* NELSON, *supra* note 1, at 1017.

becomes, When is a future advance obligatory and when is it optional? A resolution of that issue becomes particularly problematic given the fact that most construction loan agreements contain numerous conditions to the construction lender's obligation to disburse proceeds under the loan— for example, the continuing accuracy of borrower representations and warranties, the borrower's submission of documentation evidencing its compliance with the approved project budget, and the absence of a borrower default under the construction loan documents.

Several states have sought to add clarity to that issue by amending their mechanics' lien statutes to specifically sanction conditions that do not cause a loan advance to be considered optional.[17] Other states have enacted statutes that abolish the obligatory vs. optional advance distinction and make it clear that all disbursements made under a construction loan have priority over a mechanics' lien as long as the construction loan mortgage is recorded prior to the attachment date of the mechanics' lien.[18] A lawyer representing a construction lender must determine whether the jurisdiction where the land is situated recognizes the distinction between an obligatory and an optional advance and, if so, what provisions need to be inserted into the construction loan documents to preserve the priority of the construction loan mortgage to the maximum permissible extent.

VI. THE CONSTRUCTION LENDER'S RISK MITIGATION TECHNIQUES

The point has now been repeatedly and emphatically made that a construction lender faces a myriad of unique risks when it makes a construction loan on a commercial real estate project. The remainder of this chapter is devoted to an examination of the ways in which the construction lender can seek to mitigate its exposure to those risks.

In developing its risk mitigation strategy, the construction lender's primary objective is to do that which is necessary to hasten and enhance its profitable exit from the loan. The construction lender's exit strategy is inextricably tied to the willingness of institutional investors to provide the capital necessary to pay off the construction loan either through a purchase of the completed real estate project or a refinancing of the construction loan. The construction lender must, therefore, structure and price its construction loan with an eye toward the needs and desires of the institutional investor community. Moreover, if the project is going to

---

[17] *See* LEFCOE, *supra* note 12, at 585. By way of example, Ohio's open end mortgage statute contains the following language—"a holder of a mortgage is 'obligated' to make an advance if such holder . . . has a contractual commitment to do so, even though the making of such advance may be conditioned upon the . . . occurrence or existence, or the failure to occur or exist, of any event of fact." OHIO REV. CODE ANN. § 5301.232(E)(4) (West 2016).

[18] *See* LEFCOE, *supra* note 12, at 584. THE RESTATEMENT (THIRD) OF PROPERTY (MORTGAGES) § 2.3 (2016) also adopts this approach.

attract the interest of institutional investors, the construction lender must do everything within its limited powers to ensure that (1) the project is completed within the time and cost parameters set forth in the developer's initial development projections, (2) the project is completed lien-free and in accordance with the approved plans and specifications, and (3) the completed project has a value consistent with the value assigned to the project as part of the construction lender's original underwriting of its construction loan.

The discussion that follows separately examines the lender's attempt to protect itself from each of the five categories of construction loan risk mentioned in the previous section of this chapter. The template for that discussion includes—(1) a description of the techniques available to the lender to deal with the cited risk, (2) a cross-reference to the section of the Form Construction Loan Agreement that seeks to implement the discussed technique, (3) a brief overview of the way in which each of the noted risks was handled in the context of the two HIBC construction loans that are the subject of the case study being utilized throughout this chapter, and (4) typical borrower "pushbacks" to the lender's proposed use of its risk mitigation techniques. A "pushback" is industry jargon to describe one party's response to a proposal made by the other party to a negotiation. I have opted to use the slang term in this chapter because it is wonderfully descriptive of what actually occurs during the course of a negotiation—where one party pushes and the other party "pushes back."

A. DEALING WITH COMPLETION RISK

The construction lender has a host of ways in which it can seek to insulate itself from the risk that the real estate project is not completed—either at all or not on time. The range of the lender's risk mitigation methods is described below.

1. Project Due Diligence (§§ 2.2 and 3.2)

The first thing that a construction lender must do to protect itself against completion risk is to undertake a thorough due diligence of the developer's proposed project. The purpose of the lender's due diligence is to validate both the general feasibility of the proposed project and the specific construction schedule proffered by the developer in its loan request.

The construction lender's due diligence efforts can be separated into two distinct undertakings. First the construction lender typically retains its own consultant (an architect or engineer) to conduct an independent review of the borrower's plans and specifications and construction schedule. The consultant's job is to answer the following questions.

- Has the developer missed anything that would prevent the project from being completed within the projected time period—for example, an unscheduled requirement that a water line be extended to the project's boundaries from an off-site location?

- Is the developer's proposed construction schedule reasonable—for example, does it permit sufficient time to complete all of the required construction tasks before the onset of winter weather conditions?

The construction lender seeks to further protect itself from completion risk by inserting in the commitment letter and the construction loan agreement a requirement that, as a condition to lender's obligation to close and fund the construction loan, the borrower must furnish the lender with a variety of third party certifications and approvals concerning the suitability and readiness of the project site for development. The following are examples of certifications and approvals customarily required by a construction lender:

- A title insurance commitment confirming the quality of the borrower's title to the land on which the project will be constructed and insuring the first priority position of the lender's construction mortgage;

- A survey showing the boundaries of the borrower's land and further indicating that there are no encroachments or other physical impediments to the borrower's proposed development;

- An environmental site assessment certifying that there are no adverse environmental conditions existing on the site that could prevent or delay the borrower's development efforts or subject the borrower or lender to any liability for the cost of remediating such conditions;

- A wetlands report stating that there are no protected wetlands on the site;

- A soils report saying that the soils on the site are of a sufficient type and level of compaction to support the proposed improvements;

- Letters from local utility companies stating that all requisite utilities are available to service the borrower's real estate project;

- A zoning letter provided by the local zoning authority affirming that the property is zoned to permit the construction and intended use of the proposed project; and

- All building permits and other governmental approvals required for the construction and use of the proposed improvements.[19]

A construction lender typically also wants to reserve the right to approve both (1) the identity of the firms providing the third party certifications, and (2) the form and content of the furnished certifications and approvals. Quite predictably, the lender also requires that the borrower pick up the cost of providing all of the required certifications and approvals (which typically runs well into five figures).

Borrower's Pushback: The borrower is seldom in a position to resist the construction lender's insistence on the above due diligence requirements. Instead, the borrower focuses its negotiating efforts on trying to get the lender's blessing that the required certifications may be provided by consultants previously hired by the borrower. By prevailing on this point, the borrower controls the process (presumably its consultants will not give the lender any unnecessary bad news) and limits its costs (by not having to reimburse the lender for duplicate due diligence reports from a second set of independent consultants). My experience has been that most lenders will accede to such a request by the borrower as long as (1) the borrower's consultants are firms with proven track records, and (2) the consultants provide separate written certifications addressed directly to the lender in a format approved by the lender.

2. Conditions to Loan Advances (§§ 3.1, 4.1, 5.1 and 5.2)

The construction lender conditions its obligation to make the initial disbursement of loan proceeds (a *loan advance)* upon its receipt of all the certifications and approvals referred to in the preceding section. The lender also requires the borrower to make a series of representations and warranties that are intended to further protect the lender against the risk that the project is not completed on time. The lender then completes the loop by conditioning its obligation to make any loan advance (either the initial advance or any subsequent advance) upon the continuing accuracy of the borrower's representations and warranties at the time of each advance. The borrower representations and warranties repeat the substance of the affirmations addressed in the above-described third party certifications (for example, the soils are suitable for construction, there are no hazardous substances on the site, etc.) and further attempt to elicit from the borrower generalized, broadly phrased statements concerning the project construction schedule (for example, the borrower has obtained all

---

[19] For an overview of the lender's due diligence process, *see* David A. Weissmann, *The Construction Lending Process (With Forms)*, 24 No. 2 PRACTICAL REAL ESTATE LAWYER 39 (March 2008).

approvals required for the timely completion of the project in accordance with the plans and specifications).

The construction loan agreement typically includes the following prototypical borrower covenant concerning the borrower's adherence to its projected construction schedule:

> *Borrower will: (a) commence construction of the Improvements no later than 30 days after the Effective Date of this Agreement; (b) cause the construction to be prosecuted with diligence and continuity in a good and workmanlike manner in accordance with the Approved Plans; and (c) will complete construction of the Improvements on or before the Completion Deadline.*

Borrower's ongoing compliance with this covenant is then expressly stated to be a condition to the construction lender's obligation to continue disbursing proceeds under the loan.

Borrower's Pushback: In the ideal world, the borrower has in hand prior to the loan closing all the certifications and approvals required for it to move forward with the construction of the improvements. A borrower living in that ideal world is not troubled by provisions of a construction loan agreement that condition the lender's obligation to make loan advances on (1) the lender's receipt and approval of all requisite certifications and approvals, and (2) the borrower's compliance with all of the representations, warranties, and covenants contained in the construction loan agreement.

Unfortunately, commercial real estate developers seldom reside in such an ideal world. This is especially true on so-called "fast-track" construction projects, where the developer has little choice but to start construction of its project well before it has finalized the construction plans and specifications or received all of the requisite project approvals and certifications. The HTE case study is an example of such a fast track project. In order to get HTE to sign its lease, Pizzuti had to agree that it would have the building completed and ready for HTE's occupancy by no later 270 days after the date of the execution of the lease. Pizzuti knew that the only way that it could meet that targeted occupancy date was to begin construction before all the construction schedule niceties had been put to bed.

A borrower like Pizzuti on the HTE project has no choice but to ask the lender to agree to disburse a portion of the construction loan proceeds before all of the required certifications and approvals are obtained. While a construction lender is usually hesitant to grant the borrower such a concession, a lender such as First Union on the HTE project needs to balance the resulting increase in its completion risk against the risk that the project value will dissipate (or perhaps totally disappear) if construction of the project does not proceed on a fast-track schedule.

3. Underwriting of Development Team (§§ 3.2(f)–(h) and (k))

An aspect of a construction loan that distinguishes it from a conventional permanent loan is the construction lender's need to analyze and underwrite not only the real estate project that serves as collateral for its loan, but also the competency and creditworthiness of the borrower and its development team. The construction lender's due diligence on the development team is especially pertinent to the construction lender's attempt to limit its exposure to completion risk.

The focus of the construction lender's underwriting of the development team is initially on the developer. The developer is responsible for overseeing and coordinating the efforts of all the players in the development process, including architects, engineers, contractors, leasing brokers, and, yes, even lawyers. Before committing to a construction loan, the lender must get affirmative answers to the following questions about the developer's capabilities:

- Does the developer have the requisite experience and expertise to pull off the proposed development project;

- Does the developer have a reputation for honesty and professionalism; and

- Does the developer have enough money to get the job done?

The development process seldom proceeds without at least a few bumps in the road. The construction lender should be extremely focused on whether the developer has the talent, background, inclination, experience, and financial staying power to overcome those bumps and still complete the project on schedule.

Once the lender gets comfortable with the developer, the next step in its loan underwriting is a review of the construction, design, and marketing team put together by the developer to work on the project. The construction lender demands that it have the right to approve both the identity of the project architect and general contractor and the form and content of their respective contracts with the borrower. Depending on the nature and complexity of the project, the lender may also require approval rights for certain major subcontracts. The focal point of the lender's review of the resumes of the development team is on whether the team members have a proven track record for timely completing projects comparable to the project for which the lender is providing the bulk of the development funding. The relative financial strength of the general contractor is also a major subject of the lender's underwriting analysis—particularly if the developer's balance sheet is suspect.

The final bit of personal underwriting done by the construction lender relates to the named borrower under the construction loan. The construction lender may insist that the borrower be a single purpose entity that is formed solely for the purpose of holding title to the project that is the subject of the lender's construction loan. The lender's reason for wanting a single purpose entity as the borrower is the lender's belief that such an entity is more "bankruptcy remote" than an entity that has ownership interests in a variety of assets and businesses. A **bankruptcy remote entity** is an entity that has little risk of becoming embroiled in a bankruptcy proceeding for any reason that is not directly related to the financial success of the real estate project on which the construction lender holds a first mortgage.[20]

Borrower's Pushback: This is the one aspect of the lender-borrower relationship where there really is no pushback from the developer. The borrower is in a full-throttle sales mode as it tries to convince the construction lender that the developer and its entire development team are eminently well-qualified to shepherd the project to completion. Golf with the lender's loan officer and members of its credit committee is the norm at this stage of the construction loan process. The only part of the sales process that is the least bit partisan is the developer's enticing promise that, if the lender cooperates on the pricing and structuring of the subject construction loan, the developer will provide the lender with plenty of additional loan business in the future.

4. Front-End Equity

One of the construction lender's biggest fears when underwriting a construction loan is that the developer loses interest in completing its development project. The developer may realize after the fact that its vision for the project is inaccurate or that the project simply missed its mark in some fashion. The lender wants to make sure that, in such instances, the developer has the proper incentive to direct all of its attention and skills to righting the ship and making the project a success.

One of the best ways for the construction lender to keep the developer interested in the project is to require the developer to make its entire equity contribution (the 10–30% of the development costs not funded through the construction loan) *BEFORE* the lender is required to make any

---

[20] For a discussion of the "bankruptcy remote" borrower, *see generally* Robert A. Thompson and Brian D. Smith, *Negotiating Loan Transactions*, in COMMERCIAL REAL ESTATE TRANSACTIONS, 9–134 (Mark A. Senn ed., 4th ed. 2016). It should be noted that the "bankruptcy remote" nature of a single purpose entity has been called into question by a decision handed down in May, 2009, by the Bankruptcy Court for the Southern District of New York in the General Growth Properties, Inc. bankruptcy proceeding. *See In re General Growth Properties, Inc.*, 412 B.R. 122 (Bankr. S.D.N.Y. 2010). In that proceeding, the Bankruptcy Court approved the upstreaming to the parent corporation's cash management account of rents produced from properties held by separate single purpose entities. By effectively overriding the separateness of the single purpose entities from their corporate parent, the Bankruptcy Court's order has raised concerns within the practicing bar about the efficacy of bankruptcy remote entities. *But see* Malcolm K. Montgomery, Robert J. Sein, and Christian Rudolff, *Top 10 Lessons from the Recession for Commercial Real Estate Lenders*, 27 THE REAL ESTATE FINANCE JOURNAL 5, 9 (Fall 2011).

disbursement of construction loan proceeds. This *front-end equity* is often referred to by construction lenders as the developer's "skin in the game."

The alternative funding mechanism favored by all developers is ***back-end equity,*** where the developer is required to use its equity to fund development costs only after the construction lender has fully disbursed the entirety of the construction loan amount. It is easy to fathom how a developer with a back-end equity requirement might be sorely tempted to divert its attention away from a project that the developer thinks is a loser to a project where the developer has a larger, more direct financial interest at stake—even though it is at that precise juncture that the lender most wants the developer to focus all of its energy on turning the loser project into a winner. For this reason, most construction lenders have historically been extremely loath to grant their borrowers the luxury of back-end equity funding. The death knell for back-end equity effectively occurred in 2013 when the Federal Reserve Board, the Comptroller of the Currency, and the Federal Deposit Insurance Corporation adopted the Basel III Rule that treats a loan with back-end equity as a risky outlier that requires the lender to significantly increase its capital reserves (see *Practice Tip #9-1: The Basel III Rule*, at pages 355–356).

Construction lenders often attempt to further focus the developer's attention on the project at hand by taking the position that the developer's front-end equity may only be used to fund the project's hard costs—that is, those construction costs that are directly tied to the construction of actual physical improvements on the developer's land. This "hard cost only" funding limitation is imposed by the lender to prevent the borrower from applying its equity contributions to defray two categories of costs that the lender views as "phantom equity"—(1) development, leasing, and other fees payable to the developer and its affiliates, and (2) the appreciation in the value of the contributed land over its initial cost. The construction lender wants the developer's "skin in the game" to consist of real cash and not items that redound to the developer's favor.

Borrower's Pushback: Prior to the federal government's issuance of the Basel III Rule, developers argued mightily in favor of permitting their equity to come in only after the full funding of the construction loan proceeds. Back-end equity generally improves the developer's return on equity by permitting the developer to use less costly loan dollars to fund the project's development costs in advance of the developer's use of the more costly equity dollars (see *Chapter 3—What the Real Estate Lawyer Needs to Know About Project Economics*, at page 60). After Basel III, a developer has little chance of convincing a construction lender to make a loan that sanctions back-end equity.

The negotiating table is also slanted in favor of the lender's position that borrower's upfront equity may only be used to pay hard costs. The best that most borrowers can hope to achieve on this issue is the receipt of lender's acknowledgement that the developer's fees and its land profit are legitimate project costs that may be paid with the proceeds of the construction loan—but only after all of the borrower's required equity contributions have first been used to pay project hard costs.

5. Completion Guaranty

The construction loan agreement customarily contains a provision requiring the borrower to complete construction of the project by a fixed outside date. However, the borrower is typically a shell entity that has no assets other than the project under development. For this reason, the construction lender routinely insists that the borrower also furnish the lender with a *completion guaranty* from a creditworthy affiliate of the borrower.

A completion guaranty is a promise by the guarantor that it will do whatever is necessary to complete construction of the project in accordance with the approved plans and specifications and by the outside completion date specified in the construction loan agreement. A well-drafted completion guaranty makes it clear that, although the completion guarantor may not be obligated to repay the construction loan, it is obligated to pay whatever costs are needed to finish construction of the project. This obligation specifically includes the obligation to fund additional equity contributions if the construction loan has been fully disbursed prior to project completion.

A completion guaranty should not be viewed by the construction lender as a panacea for its completion risk. In the first instance, a completion guaranty (like any other guaranty) is often difficult to enforce. Moreover if the borrower has defaulted on its completion obligation, it is likely that its affiliated completion guarantor may do the same thing. This is especially true in those jurisdictions in which the measure of damages for the breach of a completion guaranty is limited to the incremental value that would have been added to the lender's security if the project had been completed (and not the full cost of completing the project). If the cost of completing the project exceeds the incremental value that would inure to the lender's benefit from completion of the improvements (which is typically the case on a troubled project), the completion guarantor has a clear motivation not to abide by the express terms of its completion guaranty.[21]

The real purpose of the completion guaranty is not to insure the construction lender that the project is completed as required under the construction loan agreement, but rather to keep the attention of a person

---

[21] *See generally* Patricia J. Frobes, *Completion Guarantees and Carry Guarantees*, in ALI-ABA COURSE OF STUDY MATERIALS, REAL ESTATE FINANCING DOCUMENTATION: STRATEGIES FOR CHANGING TIMES, Course No. SL–007, 139, 140–142 (January 2006).

related to the borrower who hopefully has a deep pocket. The other negative associated with a completion guaranty is that, if the guarantor's supposed deep pocket has a hole in it, the completion guaranty is not worth the paper it is written on.

Borrower's Pushback: If the borrower is a single purpose entity, borrower's counsel has little choice but to accept the construction lender's requirement for the furnishing of a completion guaranty by an affiliate of the borrower. The issue typically is not whether a completion guaranty is furnished, but who provides it, with the borrower preferring to offer up a lesser credit in the developer's constellation and the lender insisting that the completion guaranty be provided by the deepest of deep pockets in developer's organizational structure.

6.   Payment and Performance Bonds

One of the construction lender's best protections against completion risk is the borrower's selection (and the lender's approval) of an experienced general contractor who has both the financial strength and industry knowledge to timely complete construction of the borrower's proposed project. But what if the general contractor selected by the borrower fails for whatever reason to finish the job? Is there anything the construction lender could have required as part of the construction loan closing to mitigate the risk of a default by the general contractor?

The answer that counsel for the construction lender frequently trots out to the above question is the *payment and performance bond*. Under a payment and performance bond, a surety company agrees to guaranty that construction of the project is completed in accordance with the terms of the general contractor's contract and that all persons owed money under such contract for the performance of work or the provision of materials to the project are paid. In exchange for the surety's issuance of such guaranties, the purchaser pays the surety an upfront fee that is ordinarily equal to a percentage of the total price of the bonded construction contract. The amount of the surety's fee is directly tied to its perception of the degree to which it is at risk that the general contractor does not complete its performance under the construction contract. If the surety perceives that the risk is too great (generally because of the general contractor's lack of financial standing), it will refuse to issue payment and performance bonds—regardless of the amount of its promised fee.

Borrower's Pushback: Borrower's counsel's immediate reaction when it sees a requirement for the posting of payment and performance bonds in a construction loan agreement is to hit the delete button for the entire section. From the borrower's perspective, payment and performance bonds are guilty of two cardinal sins in the development business—(1) they increase the borrower's project costs, and, even worse, (2) they do not add any real value to the project from anyone's perspective (other than the surety company that collects its fee for issuing the bonds).

The gist of the borrower's problem with payment and performance bonds is that a surety company will usually only issue its bonds if the general contractor is so financially strong as to make the existence of the bonds wholly meaningless. It is analogous to Bill Gates guarantying that Warren Buffet will not go bankrupt. Moreover, the fine print of the payment and performance bonds creates a plethora of defenses to any attempt by the bondholder to enforce the terms of the bonds against the surety.[22]

A borrower can frequently negotiate a waiver of the requirement that it obtain payment and performance bonds—unless the borrower's general contractor has a low net worth, in which case, the lender will legitimately stand firm on its requirement that the project be bonded. Unfortunately, if the relative financial strength of the general contractor scares the construction lender, it is a safe bet that the surety company will refuse to issue payment and performance bonds for the project. The lesson to be learned from this charade is that if the borrower wants to secure a construction loan for its proposed project, it should select a financially-strong general contractor.

7. Collateral Assignment of Construction and Design Contracts (§ 3.2(*l*))

The "worst day ever" for a construction lender is when it is left with no option other than to foreclose on its mortgage on an uncompleted development project. The value of a partially-completed commercial real estate project is often less than the outstanding principal balance of the construction loan. If the foreclosing construction lender has any hope of getting its loan fully repaid, it needs to complete construction of the project.

The best path for the construction lender to follow to complete construction of the project is to retain the borrower's development team to finish the job they started (assuming that the team was not the cause of the project's failure). The construction lender's fear is that the project architect and the general contractor will refuse to continue work on the project or will agree to do so only if they are able to extract exorbitant additional fees from the construction lender. The construction lender counters this fear by inserting in the construction loan agreement a requirement that the borrower collaterally assign to the construction lender all the borrower's right, title, and interests in its contracts with the architect, general contractor, and other essential design and construction professionals. Most construction lenders also require the borrower to collaterally assign to them all governmental approvals, building permits,

---

[22] *See* Weissmann, *supra* note 19, at 47; and LEFCOE, *supra* note 12, at 512.

construction bonds, and other intangibles and contract rights that the lender needs to complete the project. The foreclosing construction lender then stands in the shoes of the borrower in its efforts to compel the borrower's development team to complete construction of the project.

Construction and design contracts regularly contain provisions prohibiting a party from assigning its interest in the contract without first obtaining the consent of the other party. A standard provision of an architect's contract is that the ownership of the plans and specifications remains in the architect, with the owner being given a license to use those plans and specifications in connection with the construction of the designed project. In order to avoid being stymied by either of these contractual provisions following the foreclosure of its construction mortgage, the prudent construction lender conditions its obligation to close and fund the construction loan upon its receipt of (1) the written consent of the architect and general contractor to the borrower's collateral assignment of its construction and design contracts (including the architect's affirmation that the lender has the right to use the project plans and specifications), and (2) the acknowledgements of the architect and general contractor that they will remain obligated to perform under their respective contracts following the construction lender's foreclosure of its construction mortgage.

Borrower's Pushback: To use an old Texas political saying, borrowers "really don't have much of a dog in that fight." While there are a number of issues that trigger intense negotiations between the construction lender and the architect/general contractor concerning the form and content of the aforementioned acknowledgement and consent,[23] the borrower's sole concern is that the architect and contractor provide the lender with something that makes the lender happy enough to close and fund the loan.

8.   Retainage (§§ 2.1 and 4.2)

It is in the best interests of both the borrower and the construction lender to create a strong incentive for the general contractor and its subcontractors to fully complete their work and remedy all defective construction conditions. A common way to accomplish that objective is for the construction lender to withhold from its loan advance a portion of the payment that would otherwise be payable to the general contractor. The withheld amounts (commonly referred to as *retainage*) are released by the lender only after the project is completed. Retainage characteristically falls somewhere between five to ten percent of each of the contractor's requested construction payments (commonly referred to in the construction industry as "draw requests"). The exact amount of the retainage varies depending on the nature of the work, the creditworthiness of the contractor, and the

---

[23]   *See* Alfred G. Kyle, *Commercial Real Estate Construction Lending (With Forms) (Part 3)*, 22 No. 4 PRACTICAL REAL ESTATE LAWYER 7, 9–10 (July 2006).

percentage of completion of the project. The general contractor should withhold a like amount of retainage from each payment it owes to its subcontractors, thereby giving each of those parties an incentive to remain on call to do whatever follow-up work is necessary to complete the project.

Borrower's Pushback: It is the responsibility of borrower's counsel to make sure that the retainage provisions of the construction loan agreement are fully consistent with those set forth in the borrower's construction contract with the general contractor. The borrower will not be pleased if the construction loan agreement recites that the construction lender will withhold 10% of each construction draw, while the general contractor's contract sets the applicable retainage percentage at 5%—because the borrower will have to temporarily fund the differential out of its own funds until the lender disburses the retainage on final completion.

The borrower frequently requests that (1) the retainage percentage only apply to the first 50% of the work, and (2) the retainage applicable to certain discrete portions of the work be fully released upon the completion of that portion of the work (for example, the completion of all site work by an excavation contractor). The construction lender is usually inclined to work with the borrower to make these changes as long as the lender does not perceive the requested changes as unduly impairing the objective of getting the project completed on schedule.

9.   Builder's Risk Insurance (§ 3.2(e))

One aspect of the lender's completion risk that has not yet been addressed is the risk that a natural occurrence beyond the control of the borrower's development team causes construction of the project to be halted or delayed. What happens if a tornado rips off the roof of a warehouse in the middle of construction or a fire destroys all of a building's interior improvements? Dealing with such natural risks is particularly important on a single tenant build-to-suit project, such as the HTE building, where a delay in completing construction may call into question the tenant's obligation to take occupancy and begin paying rent on the facility.

Construction lenders deal with this category of risk by requiring either the borrower or the general contractor (or sometimes both of them) to obtain insurance coverage commonly referred to as *builder's risk insurance* that insures the owner against damage caused to a development project by fire, wind, explosion, lightning, hail, and other causes beyond the parties' control.[24] The premium for obtaining builder's risk insurance is yet another development cost that must be included in borrower's overall project budget, either as a direct cost or as a cost

---

[24] *See generally* James T. Lobb and Brittany Griffin Smith, *Builder's Risk Insurance and Other Special Coverages that the Owner and Lender Need on a Construction Project*, in ACREL PAPERS, Tab 9 (Fall 2015).

subsumed in the general contractor's price for the project. The insured amount of a builder's risk policy is customarily capped at the value of the completed project.

Borrower's Pushback: The borrower acknowledges the need for a builder's risk policy. Its only issue is keeping the cost of obtaining that coverage as low as possible. The premiums payable for builder's risk insurance are based on a number of variables, including the nature and cost of the insured project and the volume of business done with the insurer by the insured (be it the general contractor or the owner). Those pricing considerations sometimes dictate that the general contractor obtain the builder's risk policy, while at other times weigh in favor of the borrower doing so.

HIBC Case Study—Dealing with Completion Risk

First Union National Bank was the construction lender on both the HTE and 500 projects. The selection of First Union over Barnett Bank was the result of two factors—(1) First Union's determination to gain a foothold in the Orlando market, and (2) Pizzuti's desire to establish a "go to" construction lender for all its HIBC projects.

First Union was an aggressive bank headquartered in Charlotte, North Carolina. The bank had targeted Orlando as a growth market in which it wanted to significantly expand its construction lending business. It dispatched one of its young aggressive loan officers (for the purposes of this case study, he is known as "Abe") to try to originate construction loan business from the Orlando real estate development community. Abe's style was a bit too flashy (and pushy) for the staid good old boy developers who at that time still dominated the Orlando market. As a result, First Union was not making much of a mark in Orlando until Abe ran into the troops from Pizzuti who were also viewed in the Orlando community as outsiders and a bit too aggressive and trendy for their own good. The burgeoning relationship between Pizzuti and First Union was also helped along by the fact that Abe and his counterparts at Pizzuti shared a passion for three things—creative real estate deals, golf, and beer.

At the same time that First Union was attempting to expand its Orlando business base, Pizzuti was trying to figure out how to best deal with the massive development project that was HIBC. Pizzuti concluded that if it was going to be able to develop office projects at HIBC with optimal velocity, it needed to put together a development team that would work on the entirety of the project. In Pizzuti's view, a major player on its development team needed to be a construction lender that was both capable of doing multiple deals in the same location and willing to issue loan commitments with a fair amount of alacrity and consistency. It did not take long for Pizzuti to realize that Barnett Bank (the then dominant construction lender in Orlando) was not a viable candidate to become the construction lender on the Pizzuti team. Barnett was leery of taking on too much construction loan exposure in one business park and was also well-known for its ponderous, lengthy, and overly cumbersome underwriting process—something that was a clear turn-off for an aggressive and impatient developer like Pizzuti.

Abe and First Union were smitten with Pizzuti's pitch that it was looking for one lender to do the HTE and 500 Building loans and Pizzuti's dangling carrot that "there will be plenty more where these came from." The coupling of Pizzuti and First Union was a marriage made in heaven between two aggressive real estate outsiders, each of whom wanted to make a big splash in the Orlando market. It certainly did not hurt that First Union (unlike Barnett) was willing to make a land development loan to help Pizzuti fund the cost of extending roads, utility lines, and other infrastructure throughout the undeveloped portions of the HIBC tract.

Having established how and why First Union agreed to make construction loans on the HTE and 500 Building projects, the discussion next turns to how First Union and Pizzuti dealt with the lender's completion risk on the two projects. Pizzuti made two strategic decisions on the front-side of its negotiations with First Union that paved the way for a relatively quick and easy negotiation on the completion risk pushbacks described earlier in this chapter.

First, Pizzuti selected Brasfield & Gorrie, a construction company headquartered in Birmingham, Alabama, to serve as its general contractor on both projects. Although a bit of an outsider to the Orlando market (a status it shared with both Pizzuti and First Union), Brasfield had two attributes that greatly appealed to First Union—(1) it had a lot of money, and (2) it had a wonderful reputation for both competency and timeliness in its construction of projects throughout the Southeast.

The second decision Pizzuti made that helped get First Union comfortable with its completion risk on the two buildings was its decision to offer up a completion guaranty on both projects from Pizzuti Equities Inc., a company that had a sizable net worth. The combined financial strengths of Brasfield and Pizzuti Equities gave First Union a great deal of comfort that the projects would be completed in a timely fashion.

So what did Pizzuti ask for in exchange for its agreement to select a financially strong general contractor and provide a completion guaranty from an equally strong entity? First and foremost, it asked for (and received) First Union's commitment to provide construction loans on both projects— one being a build-to-suit with the single tenant having OK but not great credit and the other being a 100% speculative project—something that was far from the norm in the Orlando lending market. It also received First

Union's continuing commitment (more of a "handshake" than an actual contractual commitment) that it would work with Pizzuti on a restructuring and expansion of its existing HIBC land development loan.

On the specific topic of the lender's completion risk, Pizzuti asked for the following lender concessions:

- The back-ending of the $1 million of equity required for the HTE project (even Pizzuti was not so bold as to request a back-ending of equity on the speculative 500 Building);

- A waiver of the payment and performance bond requirement;

- The elimination of the 10% retainage requirement once the project was 50% complete;

- A loosening of the loan advance conditions on the HTE project to permit $2 million to be disbursed prior to the receipt of all the project certifications and approvals required in the construction loan agreement (including the final development plan approval from Seminole County and the issuance of a building permit for the 87,000-square-foot office building); and

- The setting of completion deadlines for both projects as the date that was 12 months after the construction loan closing (which, as to the HTE project, was approximately three months after HTE's targeted occupancy date).

So how did Pizzuti fare on its requests? Actually, it did pretty well. First Union agreed to back-end 50% of the equity required on the HTE project. It granted all of Pizzuti's other requests, with the exception that First Union insisted that the completion deadline on the HTE loan coincide with the targeted commencement date specified in the HTE lease. First Union did, however, agree to extend that completion deadline for the same force majeure delays specifically sanctioned in the HTE lease. All in all, not a bad day's work for Pizzuti's overworked and underpaid general counsel.

There is one final footnote on the "marriage made in heaven" between First Union and Pizzuti. The First Union-Pizzuti "marriage" ended in divorce a few years after the closing of the HTE and 500 Building loans. The cause of that divorce was twofold—(1) Abe moved on to bigger and better things and was replaced by a loan officer whose approach to the construction lending business was too conservative and slow-moving for Pizzuti's tastes, and (2) the economy picked up in a very noticeable fashion creating a whole new set of construction loan "dance partners" for the HIBC development.

B. DEALING WITH THE RISK OF COST OVERRUNS

The next risk that the construction lender must protect itself against is the risk that the project costs more than originally projected. The result of that risk becoming reality is that either the project cannot be completed or the net value of the lender's collateral is compromised by the amount of the cost overrun. Some of the same techniques discussed with respect to the lender's completion risk are equally applicable to help insulate the lender from the risk of cost overruns—for example, the required provision of a completion guaranty and payment and performance bonds and the underwriting of the competency and financial strength of the borrower's development team. There are, however, a number of new tools that the construction lender can use to deal with the risk of project cost overruns.

1. Approval and Enforcement of Project Budget (§§ 2.1, 2.2 and 3.2(*o*))

The construction lender begins its efforts to combat the risk of a cost overrun by instructing its financial analysts and consultants to closely review the borrower's proposed development budget (including the general contractor's detailed construction budget) to validate the accuracy and completeness of the various line item expenses noted in the budget. Do the developer's proposed costs square with the normative unit pricing that the lender has seen on similar projects? Does the budget include all those costs that must be incurred if the project is going to be completed in accordance with the approved plans and specifications and project schedule? Are the budgeted construction and design costs consistent with the fees and costs listed in the borrower's design and construction contracts?

Once the lender has approved a development budget for the project, it is essential that the approved budget thereafter serve as the benchmark for determining the amount of all future disbursements made under the construction loan. The lender accomplishes this goal by attaching a copy of the approved budget as an exhibit to its construction loan agreement and then including provisions in the construction loan agreement specifying that (1) the budget cannot be changed without the lender's consent, (2) all disbursements requested by borrower under the construction loan must be specifically linked to a particular line item in the approved budget and (3) unless otherwise expressly approved by the lender, the aggregate of all disbursements for a particular line item cost may not exceed the amount specified for that line item in the approved budget.

Borrower's Pushback: There is nothing that drives a borrower crazier than to have its construction lender try to change the borrower's development budget. Borrowers are not generally known for their deference to or respect for the financial and development expertise of their lenders. Moreover, the borrower clearly understands the lender's end game when the lender attempts to increase the borrower's development costs (by the way, it never goes the other way). I have never known a lender to couple its insistence on an increase in the borrower's development costs with a related offer to increase the loan amount on a dollar-for-dollar basis. Rather, virtually every lender-sponsored increase in the amount of the approved development costs triggers a like increase in the amount of the borrower's required equity contribution.

The borrower often voices one additional objection to the lender's demand that the construction budget serve as the bible for the making of all construction loan disbursements. It is the borrower's reasoned judgment that the lender's proper point of inquiry should be the borrower's aggregate development costs and not each line item cost. Stated differently, the borrower takes the position that it should be able to fund a cost overrun in one line item with the cost savings achieved in another line item. The borrower, of course, seeks to employ a rather expansive definition of "cost savings" to effectively include any excess in a budgeted line item cost over the amount of that line item cost that has already been disbursed under the construction loan. Taken to its logical conclusion, the import of the borrower's expansive definition of "cost savings" is that a cost overrun can never exist until late in the construction process (because the borrower always has a theoretical cost savings until all of the construction loan proceeds have been disbursed). Experienced lender's counsel will counter the borrower's position by asserting that a cost savings is achieved on a particular line item only when all work associated with that line item has been completed—for example, only if 100% of the site work has been completed at a cost that is less than the projected site work cost set forth in the approved budget.

2. Contingency Reserve

The construction lender's concern when making a construction loan is that something bad happens that causes the project to cost more than originally anticipated—regardless whether that "bad thing" is triggered by an act or omission of the borrower or the occurrence of an event or circumstance that is outside of the borrower's control. The knee jerk reaction of many lenders to the specter that "something bad might happen" is to require the borrower to include in its construction budget a new line item for the funding of a *contingency reserve*.

Depending on the nature of the project and the persistence of the lender, a contingency reserve may run anywhere from one to ten percent of the project's total development costs. The lender views the insertion of a contingency reserve in the development budget as its hedge against "something bad happening" that could adversely affect the value of its collateral for the construction loan.

Borrower's Pushback: To quote Ronald Reagan in his 1980 presidential debate with Jimmy Carter, "there you go again." The borrower once again knows that a consequence of the lender's insistence on the establishment of a contingency reserve is an increase in the borrower's equity requirement in an amount equal to the dollar amount of the contingency reserve. As a result, the borrower mightily resists the creation of a contingency reserve by saying things like—"the prospect for cost overruns are already covered by the completion guaranty," "the general contractor has a contingency reserve in its construction contract" (assuming that is true), and "my numbers are solid so there's no need to include any additional cushion." A savvy borrower often includes a small contingency reserve in its initial development budget in an effort to assuage the lender's concern over the prospect of cost overruns. The amount of the borrower's proposed contingency reserve is merely intended as "eye candy" to lend its budgeting processes an air of fairness and legitimacy and is seldom of a magnitude sufficient to give the lender any real comfort on the cost overrun issue.

3.   Limitation on Change Orders (§ 5.2(k))

Cost overruns may also occur due to a change or addition made to the project's plans and specifications (commonly referred to in the real estate industry as *change orders*). Change orders can be as simple as replacing carpet tiles in the building lobby with marble or as complex as adding a structured parking garage in lieu of a surface parking lot. Similarly a change order can be sponsored by either the contractor (to correct an error or deficiency in the existing plans and specifications), the developer (to respond to an evolving market condition by adding a health club or upgrading building finishes), or a tenant of the project (to better serve the tenant's use of the leased space by adding a computer server room).

The construction lender has a natural and quite legitimate aversion to change orders. When it signs the construction loan agreement, the construction lender is agreeing to finance construction of a project whose nature, scope, dimension, and cost are specifically defined by plans and specifications approved by the lender. A change order can negatively impact the lender's collateral position under the construction loan by either (1) reducing the value of the completed project (for example, by means of a change order that downgrades the quality of the building's interior and exterior finishes), or (2) increasing the project's total development costs (for example, by means of a change order that upgrades the quality of the building finishes).

The construction lender's preferred way to deal with the change order risk is to say that the plans and specifications are inviolate and cannot be changed in any way without the lender's prior written consent. By taking this extreme approach, the lender puts itself firmly in control of the project that will ultimately be built with its loan proceeds.

Borrower's Pushback: A recurring theme in the borrower's negotiations with the construction lender is the borrower's need to reserve flexibility to do that which the borrower believes is needed to optimize the project's value by responding in an appropriate fashion to market conditions or the desires of prospective tenants. The borrower also wants to maintain the right to make minor changes to the plans and specifications to keep the project on schedule and on budget (for example, changing the light fixtures in the building lobby because the originally selected light fixtures are on back order).

The borrower's desire for construction and design flexibility runs directly counter to the lender's desire to retain control over the development process by prohibiting all change orders that are not expressly sanctioned by the lender. A compromise often requested by the borrower (and commonly granted by the lender) involves the establishment of a materiality standard to identify those change orders that require the lender's prior consent. The materiality standard can be stated either numerically (any change order that causes a change of more than $X in the project's development costs) or descriptively (any change order that significantly alters the structural components or exterior aesthetics of the improvements or could result in the borrower not being able to complete construction of the improvements by the completion deadline). The borrower's goal in crafting the materiality standard is to maximize its development flexibility, while the lender's goal is to preserve its control over the development process. There is, obviously, a fair amount of negotiating room between these two extremes.

4. Receipt of a Fixed Construction Price from General Contractor

The largest single line item in any development budget is the general contractor's price for constructing the improvements. As a result, one of the construction lender's greatest concerns is that the general contractor's actual construction price ends up being greater than the construction price identified in the approved development budget.

The price component of a construction contract can be described in a variety of ways. Two of the most common pricing alternatives are—

- *Stipulated Sum*—that is, a fixed price, regardless of the amount of the contractor's actual construction costs; or

- *Cost of the Work Plus a Fee*—that is, the contractor's actual construction costs, plus a contractor fee equal to a stated percentage of the actual costs.

Given a choice, the construction lender always prefers a stipulated sum contract. A stipulated sum contract largely eliminates any prospect of a cost overrun in the general contractor's pricing (at least if the general contractor has a solid balance sheet). The cost plus a fee arrangement is especially troublesome for a construction lender because it invites a significant negative variance between the budgeted construction price and the actual price paid to the general contractor. It is, therefore, common for the construction loan agreement to contain a requirement that the agreement between the borrower and the general contractor must include a stipulated sum construction price in an amount that is no greater than the amount of the hard costs of construction set forth in the approved project budget.

Borrower's Pushback: Why would the borrower have a problem with the lender's insistence on a stipulated sum construction price? Is not the interest of the borrower also served by putting into place a pricing mechanism that effectively eliminates the prospect of a construction cost overrun? The answer to those questions is "yes, but. . . ."

The "but" part of this answer is tied to the borrower's perception of the following two realities of the construction industry—

- A general contractor seldom agrees to a stipulated sum price unless it first has the opportunity to formally bid out the final plans and specifications to a pool of subcontractors to fix its costs on the project; and

- The universal reaction of a contractor that is asked to provide fixed pricing is to hedge its position by increasing its construction price over the price that it realistically believes would be produced under a cost plus a fee pricing arrangement.

Given these commercial realities, the developer argues that the lender's insistence on a stipulated sum construction contract will cost the developer money and will effectively eliminate the developer's ability to land a deal such as the HTE project where the need to fast track construction does not lend itself to a time-consuming formal bid process.

A middle ground between the two pricing extremes that appeals to both the construction lender and the borrower is a ***guaranteed maximum price***. In a guaranteed maximum price contract, the contractor is paid for its cost of work plus a fee, up to but not exceeding a fixed aggregate number. It is, therefore, a hybrid of the cost plus and stipulated sum pricing models.

The setting of a guaranteed maximum price is more art than science and involves intense negotiations between the developer and its selected general contractor. The developer's goal is to secure a guaranteed maximum price that fits within the financial parameters set forth in its development budget. The general contractor's objective is to provide a guaranteed maximum price that is low enough for it to get the job, but high enough to give it a cushion if construction costs unexpectedly spike after the construction contract is signed. The guaranteed maximum price established for a project where the construction plans and specifications are in their formative stage (such as the HTE project) is, therefore, almost always higher than the maximum price set for a comparable project with a well-developed set of plans and specifications (like the 500 Building).

The construction lender is usually fine with a guaranteed maximum price contract as long as the guaranteed maximum price is the number inserted into the approved budget as the developer's hard costs of construction. The benefit to the borrower of a guaranteed maximum price arrangement is that its actual construction costs may prove to be less than the stated maximum price. The cynical borrower (are there any other kind) knows, however, that it is likely that the final construction price will equal the guaranteed maximum price unless the general contractor is economically incentivized to minimize its construction costs. The cynical, but smart, borrower tackles this issue head on by offering to increase the amount of the contractor's fee if the general contractor completes construction of the project for less than the guaranteed maximum price. By way of example, a borrower could agree to share 50% of any cost savings with the general contractor as an additional contractor fee, with the cost savings being equal to the excess of the guaranteed maximum price over the actual costs of construction.

5. Limitations on Funding of Soft Costs

The prior section addressed one of the ways that a construction lender can protect itself against cost overruns related to the hard costs of construction. But how does the lender deal with its obligation to provide loan disbursements to cover soft costs, such as legal fees, development fees, architectural fees, interest carry, the developer's land profit, and leasing commissions?

As stated on countless occasions in this chapter, the construction lender's overriding business objective is to make sure that the borrower's project is completed on time and on budget so that the project can be leased to rent-paying tenants. Soft costs, by definition, do not directly involve the construction of an asset having an enduring value. As such, the construction lender's preferred position on the funding of the borrower's soft costs is typically represented by one or some combination of the following three verbs—"eliminate," "decrease," and "defer."

At the outset, it needs to be acknowledged that there are "soft costs" and then there are "really soft costs." The lender generally does not object to funding those soft costs that are owed to a third party unrelated to the borrower to compensate the third party for its performance of a service that is essential to the creation of the borrower's real estate project—for example, architectural and engineering fees, title insurance premiums, survey costs, brokerage commissions, and even the legal fees of borrower's counsel. While the construction lender intellectually would prefer to defer the funding of those soft costs until after construction of the project is fully completed, the lender usually recognizes that such a deferral is neither practical, nor realistic.

There is another group of soft costs that the lender not only does not object to funding, but actually insists be funded on a special priority basis. These soft costs are the interest carry and loan fees payable to the lender and the fees payable to the lender's consultants—for example, its lawyer, appraiser, and inspecting architect.

That leaves the "really soft costs." These are costs that inure to the benefit of the borrower and its affiliates. The two most glaring examples of "really soft costs" are (1) the development fees paid to the borrower/developer, and (2) the borrower's unrealized profit on the land on which the project is being built.

Development fees are payable to developer in recognition of its past services in putting the deal together and its future services in overseeing the ongoing development of the project. Development fees are usually expressed as a percentage of the project's total development costs—anywhere from two to ten percent depending on the nature of the project. Due to the illiquid nature of commercial real estate assets, many developers rely on the receipt of development fees funded with construction loan proceeds to cover their overhead and other operating expenses.

The construction lender views development fees as being part of the profit that the developer makes from its real estate project. The lender does not want to fund any portion of the developer's profit before a realistic determination can be made that the project's actual cost structure is consistent with the development cost budget. Therefore, the construction lender typically seeks to either wholly *ELIMINATE* its obligation to fund development fees; *DECREASE* the amount of the development fees to be included in the approved development budget; or *DEFER* the date of the funding of the development fees until the project is fully completed.

The lender's view of the borrower's unrealized land profit is frequently even less favorable than its view of development fees. What exactly is the borrower's unrealized land profit? The following example based on the HIBC case study is an illustration of the perspectives of the borrower and the lender on the subject of unrealized land profit.

Example 9-1: Assume that Pizzuti's cost basis in the ten-acre tract underlying the HTE building is $1 million. Assume further that Pizzuti believes that the fair market value of the ten-acre tract is $2.5 million. Pizzuti's proposed development cost budget includes a line item for land of $2.5 million. Pizzuti's intention is to draw down the full $2.5 million land value as part of its initial loan advance under the First Union construction loan.

So how would a construction lender react to the scenario described in the above example? That's right—

- *Choice #1—ELIMINATE* its obligation to fund the unrealized land profit of $1.5 million (the excess of the $2.5 million estimated current value of the land over the land's initial acquisition cost),

- *Choice #2—DECREASE* the value of the land included in the development budget (say to $1.5 million), and

- *Choice #3—DEFER* its funding of loan dollars to pay the land profit until final completion of the development project.

The construction lender frequently combines choices #'s 2 and 3 by decreasing the amount of the land profit included in the development budget and then insisting that funding for the reduced land profit be deferred until the date of the final loan disbursement.

Borrower's Pushback: From the developer's perspective, the issue of the lender's funding of the borrower's "really soft costs" is all about cash flow. The borrower desperately wants to front-load the lender's funding of those costs that ultimately find a home in the developer's pocket. Ideally, the borrower wants the lender to fund 100% of the borrower's development fee and the full fair market value of the borrower's land as part of the initial loan advance made at the construction loan closing. Under the HTE example noted above, that would mean that Pizzuti would receive a cash payment at the construction loan closing of $3 million—a land payment of $2.5 million and a development fee of $500,000 (assuming that Pizzuti's proposed development fee is 5% of its $10 million development cost budget).

So how can a developer possibly justify its receipt of such a sizable cash payment out of the initial loan advance? The developer has three possible (and maybe even plausible) arguments that it can make to support its receipt of the development fee and land profit at the initial loan closing. First, it can, with a totally straight face, contend that it has fully earned its development fee by putting the deal together and getting the tenant to sign its lease. Second, it can point out that it would be well within its rights to sell the land to the borrower at its full fair market value (instead of conveying the land to the newly-formed entity as a capital contribution).[25] Finally, the developer can argue that the issue of the timing of the

---

[25] The reason that a developer generally contributes the land to the borrowing entity is tax-driven. By making a capital contribution of the land to the venture, the developer is able to defer its recognition of a taxable gain on its land profit. *See* I.R.C. § 721(a). *See also supra Chapter 7—Forming and Capitalizing the Project Entity*, at pages 244–245.

disbursement of the "really soft costs" is a matter of little overall consequence to the lender because the construction loan is fully recourse to the borrower and probably is also supported by completion and payment guaranties provided by a creditworthy affiliate of the developer.

When confronted with these compelling arguments, the construction lender either repeats its mantra of "eliminate, decrease, and defer" or tries to find a mutually acceptable middle ground. A solution that often works for both the borrower and the lender is for (1) a portion of the development fee to be funded in the initial loan advance (for example, 50%), with the disbursement of the remainder of the fee to be spread over the construction period in proportion to the project's percentage of completion, and (2) the unrealized land profit to be included in the approved development budget, but its funding deferred until later in the construction period (for example, the date of the borrower's execution of binding leases on a designated percentage of the rentable square footage contained within the project's improvements).

A developer can also tackle the issue of the funding of these "really soft costs" by getting the construction lender to concede that the sum of the unrealized land profit and the developer's development fee counts toward the developer's obligation to contribute front-end equity to its development project. In the HTE example referenced earlier in this section, taking the suggested approach would result in Pizzuti being credited with having made a $3 million front-end equity contribution to the project (the sum of the land value of $2.5 million—including the unrealized land profit of $1.5 million—and the development fee of $500,000). Most lenders resist this developer tactic because it has the effect of reducing the developer's true "skin in the game" to what the lender views as "phantom equity"—that is the portion of the developer's hoped for "profit" from the project represented by the estimated land appreciation and the developer's fees. It is also not clear whether such "phantom equity" can be used to satisfy the developer's front-end equity requirement imposed by the Basel III Final Rule discussed earlier in this chapter at pages 355–356.

6.   Establishment of Generous Interest Reserve

A unique feature of a construction loan is its *floating interest rate*— that is, an interest rate that changes over the term of the construction loan based upon changes in a financial index that is designed to measure the lender's cost of funds. The floating interest rate is intended (1) to protect the lender's profit margin against a post-loan closing increase in its cost of funds, and (2) to permit the borrower to benefit from a post-loan closing decrease in the lender's cost of funds.

Another unique feature of a construction loan is that the interest that accrues under the loan is treated as a development cost and is typically funded through construction loan advances. The reason that construction period interest is funded out of the proceeds of the construction loan is quite simple—the commercial real estate project that is being developed with the aid of the construction loan does not produce any income during the construction period to fund the payment of the construction period interest.

The combination of these two unique features creates a cost overrun risk for the borrower and the construction lender. What happens if inflation significantly drives up the borrower's floating interest rate during the construction loan term, with the result that the borrower's interest carry costs are dramatically higher than originally contemplated in the borrower's development cost budget? By way of illustration, assume that the interest rate identified in the commitment letter is LIBOR plus 2% and that, at the time of the parties' execution of the commitment letter, LIBOR stands at 4%. Based on these facts, the borrower's development budget includes an interest carry cost calculated on the assumption that the interest rate under the construction loan will be 6% throughout the loan term. That assumption produces a projected aggregate interest carry over the 24 month term of a $10 million construction loan of $900,000.[26] If LIBOR suddenly surges from 4% to 6%, the impact on the borrower's interest carry costs can be dramatic—a cost overrun of $300,000 based on the assumptions used in the above illustration.

A cost overrun triggered by an increase in the borrower's floating interest rate creates the same problem for the construction lender as does any other cost overrun—that is, if the borrower is not able to fund the increased interest carry, the lender is left with the dilemma of either advancing additional loan dollars to cover the additional interest (in which event the net value of its collateral position suffers) or putting the progress of the development project on hold until the borrower identifies an alternative funding source to cover its increased carry costs.

Is there anything the construction lender can do to try to protect itself against the prospect of a cost overrun attributable to a jump in the financial index used to price its loan? The prophylactic measure customarily used by construction lenders is to make sure that the interest carry number included in the approved development budget assumes a reasonable increase in the borrower's interest rate during the construction loan term. In the example used earlier in this section, a construction lender trying to protect itself against an interest carry cost overrun might require that the borrower calculate its interest carry costs based on an assumption that the interest rate payable during the loan term will be 7% (rather than the 6%

---

[26] Interest accrues on only the disbursed portion of the construction loan. The borrower's aggregate interest carry costs will, therefore, vary not only based on increases and decreases in the applicable financial index, but also based on the pace at which the borrower draws down its loan advances. The calculation in the text is based on a commonly-used rule of thumb that the average daily balance of a 24 month construction loan (assuming an actual construction period of 12 months) is 75% of the loan's maximum principal amount.

figure produced by utilizing the applicable LIBOR rate as of the date of the construction loan closing).

Borrower's Pushback: As is the case with respect to any lender-sponsored attempt to alter the borrower's proposed development budget, the borrower's primary pushback on the calculation of its interest reserve is grounded in the comparative development expertise and experience of the borrower and the lender—in other words, "I know what I am doing and you don't." This response is particularly predictable given the fact that the borrower is acutely aware that any increase in its interest reserve will more than likely lead to a similar increase in its upfront equity requirement.

It should be noted that the borrower and the construction lender share a desire to avoid a cost overrun triggered by a dramatic increase in the financial index. From the borrower's perspective, the best way to avoid a precipitous increase in its interest carry costs is to get the lender to agree to fix the interest rate for the entirety of the construction loan term—that is, setting the interest rate at a fixed rate of 6% and not LIBOR plus 2%. However, fixing the interest rate exposes the construction lender to the risk that its loan profit could be eroded by an increase in its cost of funds without a concomitant increase in the interest rate being paid by the borrower. This dilemma leads to the discussion in *Practice Tip #9-2* of **interest rate hedges** that are sometimes put in place at the volition of the borrower and sometimes implemented as a lender-imposed condition to the making of a construction loan.

Practice Tip #9-2: Interest Rate Hedges

There are a variety of financial products (more pejoratively referred to as "derivatives") that are designed to provide a hedge against the risk associated with a fluctuation in floating interest rates. The three basic categories of interest rate hedges are (1) an interest rate cap, (2) an interest rate collar, and (3) an interest rate swap.[27] All three of these hedge techniques are intended to protect the borrower against the ravages of an unbudgeted increase in its floating interest rate, while at the same time preserving the integrity of the construction lender's spread between its cost of funds and the interest payable to it by the borrower under the construction loan. Hedge products can be purchased from a variety of financial institutions, including the derivatives department of the bank that makes the construction loan.

---

[27] *See generally* Steven R. Davidson and Eric M. Schiller, *Interest Rate Hedging Products*, in ALI-ABA COURSE OF STUDY MATERIALS, COMMERCIAL REAL ESTATE FINANCING: STRATEGIES FOR CHANGING MARKETS AND UNCERTAIN TIMES, Course No. SP–008, 555 (January 2009); and Gary A. Goodman, Malcolm K. Montgomery, and Jeffrey H. Koppele, *Hedging Your Bet: Interest Rate Hedge Agreements in Real Estate Financings*, in ACREL PAPERS Tab 3 (FALL 2015).

Preliminarily, it should be noted that the interest rate hedges discussed in this Practice Tip are different from a negotiated cap where the construction lender simply agrees in the construction loan documents that the interest rate payable by the borrower will never exceed a fixed maximum rate, regardless of the level of future increases in the applicable financial index. Negotiated caps were fairly common before the prime rate increased by more than 12 points during a two-year period from April 1978 to April 1980. That period of rapidly escalating interest rates resulted in the virtual demise of negotiated caps in construction loan transactions and the concomitant need for the three hedging techniques discussed in this Practice Tip.

*The discussion in this Practice Tip assumes that the borrower purchases an interest rate hedge to cover the full amount of its construction loan. There is no requirement that the borrower limit the principal amount of its interest rate hedge (known as the **notional amount**) in that fashion. A borrower may (and frequently does) purchase an interest rate hedge to cover a broader portfolio of its construction loans. Similarly a borrower could acquire a hedge for just a portion of one construction loan (although borrowers seldom do so due to the high legal fees and other transactional costs associated with the purchase of an interest rate hedge).*

***Interest Rate Cap:** An interest rate cap is essentially what it sounds like—the placing of a cap or a ceiling on the maximum interest rate that the borrower ever has to pay on its construction loan regardless of the level of increases in the base financial index used in the construction loan. By way of example, if the floating interest rate specified in the construction loan documents is LIBOR plus 200 basis points and the borrower buys a 7% interest rate cap (commonly-referred to as the "strike price"), then the maximum level of interest that the borrower ever has to pay is 7% even if LIBOR increases to 6% at some time during the construction loan term. It is important to note, however, that a borrower who buys an interest rate cap still retains the benefit of a decline in the floating interest rate. Therefore, if LIBOR falls from 4% to 3%, the hypothetical borrower's interest rate is decreased to 5% irrespective of its purchase of an interest rate cap.*

It is important to keep in mind that the interest carry payable by the borrower to the construction lender is not directly affected by the borrower's purchase of an interest rate cap. In the above example, if LIBOR goes to 6%, then the borrower remains obligated to pay interest to its construction lender at an 8% rate (LIBOR plus 2%). However, the borrower is also entitled to receive a payment from the provider of the interest cap in an amount equal to the product of (1) the notional amount of the purchased cap, multiplied by (2) the excess of the construction loan interest rate over the strike price of the cap. The end result is that the borrower's net interest carry on its development project is effectively capped at the 7% level, but the construction lender still gets to receive the full economic benefit provided by the floating interest rate feature of the construction loan.

The protection afforded to the borrower by an interest rate cap obviously does not come free. In most situations, the borrower has to pay a sizable upfront fee to the party that is providing the cap—be it an affiliate of the construction lender or an unrelated bank, insurance company, or other financial institution. The size of that fee is directly related to the level of the purchased cap, with the amount of the fee increasing as the strike price decreases. In return for its receipt of the upfront fee, the provider of the interest rate cap agrees to make payments to the borrower if the floating interest rate under the construction loan ever rises above the strike price of the purchased cap.

Interest Rate Collar: An interest rate collar is a variation of the interest rate cap. An interest rate collar places both a ceiling and a floor on the level of the borrower's floating interest rate exposure. By way of example, an interest rate collar might place a ceiling of 8% and a floor of 4% on the floating interest rate that the borrower is obligated to pay during the term of the collar. If the interest rate computed in accordance with the floating rate methodology used in the construction loan exceeds 8%, then the provider of the cap is obligated to make a payment to the borrower in the amount of that excess. Conversely, if the floating interest rate falls below the 4% floor, then the borrower is obligated to make a payment to the collar provider in an amount equal to that difference. If the interest rate floats between the 4% floor and the 8% ceiling, no payments are made under the collar.

As is the case with an interest rate cap, the provider of an interest rate collar typically charges the borrower an upfront fee for the collar. The amount of that fee is generally less than the fee payable for an interest rate cap because the provider of the collar has bargained for its receipt of a portion of the benefit associated with declining interest rates—unlike the situation with an interest rate cap where 100% of the benefit of falling interest rates remains with the borrower.

Because an interest rate collar contemplates the possibility that the borrower may have to make future payments to the collar provider, an issue presented by the collar that is not present with a cap is the credit standing of the borrower. If the borrower's credit is not sufficiently solid, the provider of the collar could insist that the borrower post collateral to secure its future payment obligations. The borrower's financial standing also has a direct bearing on the level of the upfront fee that the borrower has to pay for the collar.

Interest Rate Swap: A swap is the most frequently purchased hedge against fluctuations in floating interest rate indices. In a typical interest rate swap, the borrower agrees to make a fixed interest rate payment to the *provider of the swap and the swap provider agrees to make an interest payment to the borrower based on a floating rate of interest. To illustrate how a swap works, assume that the borrower decides to swap out its floating rate exposure on the entirety of a fully-funded $10 million construction loan where the interest rate on the loan is stated to be a variable rate equal to a spread over LIBOR. Finally, assume that the swap provider is willing to swap out the floating rate interest rate for a fixed rate of 6%.*

Under an interest rate swap, the borrower remains obligated to make its floating interest rate payment to the construction lender throughout the construction loan term. Therefore, under the above example, the borrower would make a monthly interest payment to the construction lender based on the then level of LIBOR regardless of the existence of the swap. The borrower and the swap provider would then make payments to each other depending on whether the borrower is "in the money" or "out of the money" on the swap. If the floating interest rate in a particular month is more than the fixed rate of the swap, then the swap provider would be obligated to make a payment to the borrower who would be considered to be "in the money" on the swap. If, however, the floating rate for the month is less than the swap's fixed rate, then the borrower would be obligated to make a payment to the swap provider and the borrower would be considered to be "out of the money" on the swap.

The following chart illustrates the impact that a move in the floating interest rate has on the operation of the hypothetical interest rate swap mentioned at the outset of this discussion (that is, a swap of a floating interest rate on a fully-funded $10 million construction loan for a fixed rate of 6%).

Floating Interest Rate	Monthly Interest Payment to Construction Lender	Swap Provider's Monthly Payment to Borrower	Borrower's Monthly Payment to Swap Provider	Borrower's Net Monthly Interest Payment
5%	$41,667	None	$8,333	$50,000
6%	$50,000	None	None	$50,000
7%	$58,333	$8,333	None	$50,000

By entering into the swap, the borrower has fixed its net monthly interest payment at $50,000, thereby effectively converting its floating rate construction loan to a 6% fixed rate loan. Under a swap, the borrower protects itself against a dramatic increase in its floating interest rate, but totally surrenders any benefit that it might otherwise receive from a decrease in the applicable financial index.

An interest rate swap can often be obtained without the need for the borrower to make any upfront fee to the swap provider. The absence of an upfront fee causes many borrowers to favor a swap over an interest rate cap or collar (both of which require the payment of a sizable fee to the swap provider).

Summary: *Interest rate hedges are valuable tools for use by eligible borrowers and construction lenders[28] to hedge the risk of a cost overrun occasioned by a rapid rise in the level of the financial index specified in the construction loan documents. There are, however, a host of complex legal and business issues associated with swaps, caps, collars, and other hedge techniques, all of which are beyond the scope of this discussion. Anyone considering the use of an interest rate hedge should consult the sources cited in the footnote for a more detailed examination of those issues.[29]*

7. Loan Balancing Provision (§ 6.1(c))

The *loan balancing provision* is the capstone of a lender's protection against the risk of a project cost overrun. The following is a typical loan balancing provision:

> *If at any time Lender notifies Borrower that, in Lender's sole judgment, the undisbursed balance of the Loan proceeds allocated to any line item in the Project Budget is insufficient to complete and fully pay the remaining Hard or Soft Costs represented by such line item, then Borrower shall promptly deposit with Lender cash in an amount equal to such deficiency. Lender shall have no obligation to make any further Loan advances until it has received the required cash deposit from Borrower.*

Under the above clause, a construction loan will be considered *OUT OF BALANCE* if the lender's projection of the actual cost of fully funding a particular line item expense is more than the amount allotted for such expense in the approved development budget.

From the perspective of a construction lender, the purpose of a loan balancing provision is to permit the lender to suspend its obligation to make loan disbursements if the lender believes that a cost overrun has called into question whether the project can be completed for the budgeted cost. The lender does not want to compound its problems by "throwing good money after bad" on a project whose completion is questionable because of

---

[28] In order to participate in any of the interest rate hedges discussed in this *Practice Tip*, the borrower and the hedge provider must each be an "eligible contract participant"—a term that is generally defined in the Commodity Exchange Act as a party having at least $10 million in total assets—7 U.S.C. § 1a (18) (2016). *See also* Goodman, *supra* note 27, at 3–4.

[29] *See* Davidson, *supra* note 27; and BENDER, *supra* note 1, at 305–306; and Goodman, *supra* note 27.

the existence of a cost overrun.[30] The lender's suspended funding obligation will only be reinstated if and when the borrower provides assurances acceptable to the lender that there are sufficient proceeds (whether debt or equity or a combination of both) to pay all costs needed to complete the project in accordance with the approved plans and specifications.

When structuring its loan balancing provision, the construction lender looks to serve a number of objectives.[31]

- It wants to have the ability to make a determination that the loan is out of balance as early in the construction process as possible based on its projection of future costs. It does not want to have to wait to suspend its funding obligation until there is an actual (as opposed to a projected) cost overrun.

- It wants to preserve the right to make an unrestricted independent determination that the loan is out of balance, without having to receive any validation of its decision from any other party (for example, the project architect or the general contractor).

- It wants to have the right to enforce the balancing remedy as to each separate line item of the approved project budget, without regard to any arguable cost savings in another line item of the budget.

- It wants to retain control over the use of any contingency reserve and the reallocation of any actual verified cost savings in other line items. (Note: The loan balancing provision brings out an interesting dichotomy in the construction lender's thought process. It wants to make a determination that a loan is out of balance based on "projected" costs, while at the same time insisting that any offsetting cost savings must be determined on the basis of "actual" costs.)

- It wants to make it clear that the only acceptable cure for a loan that is out of balance is the borrower's immediate deposit of cash with the construction lender in an amount sufficient to fund the projected cost overrun.

A loan balancing provision structured along the above lines[32] provides the lender with significant protection against the risk of a project cost overrun—at least if the borrower/guarantors have the requisite financial

---

[30] Montgomery, *supra* note 20, at 10.

[31] *See generally* Patricia J. Frobes, *Selected Issues in Secured Construction Lending*, IN ALI-ABA COURSE OF STUDY MATERIALS, REAL ESTATE FINANCING DOCUMENTATION: STRATEGIES FOR CHANGING TIMES, Course No. SL-007,122, 123–125 (January 2006).

[32] For an example of a loan balancing provision that serves all of the lender's listed objectives, *see* Talley, *supra* note 9, at 143–144.

standing and liquidity to put the loan back into balance by committing additional equity to the project. Even if the borrower/guarantors are incapable of putting additional cash into the project, a well-crafted loan balancing provision should give the lender the right to suspend its funding obligation while it seeks out other solutions to the cost overrun.

Borrower's Pushback: Developers view a cost overrun as just one more challenge that must be overcome as part of the dynamics of the development process. Most developers ardently believe that they can figure out a way to deal with an apparent cost overrun, either by shaving costs in other areas of the project or by identifying an unbudgeted revenue source to cover the cost overrun. All the developer asks is that the construction lender continue to provide funding to advance the project toward completion while the developer works on devising an acceptable way to resolve the cost overrun problem.

Given its perspective on the development process, it is not surprising that the borrower finds much to object to in the construction lender's typical loan balancing provision. The following are objections frequently raised by borrower's counsel to the lender's loan balancing provision.

- The loan should be deemed out of balance based only on actual (and not projected) cost overruns.

- The existence of a cost overrun must be validated by a written statement from the project architect or the general contractor (or, at the bare minimum, made by the lender in the exercise of its reasonable judgment).

- The loan balancing remedy should apply only if there is an overrun in the developer's aggregate development costs (and not just in any one line item).

- The borrower should have the unfettered right to use the contingency reserve and projected cost savings in other line items to offset any cost overrun. (Note: The borrower's thought process on the issue of whether and when projected or actual costs should be used in the implementation of the loan balancing provision is just as inconsistent as is the lender's thought process on that topic. The borrower wants the determination that a loan is out of balance to be based on "actual" costs, with any offsetting cost savings being determined on the basis of "projected" costs.)

- If the loan is legitimately determined to be out of balance, the borrower should have the right to cover the cost overruns in a variety of ways, expressly including (1) posting a letter of credit or other collateral to secure its obligation to fund a cost overrun with a back-end equity contribution, and (2) securing secondary financing to fund the cost overrun.

While the differences between the lender and the borrower on the loan balancing provision might seem irreconcilable, the lawyers representing the borrower and the lender are usually able to structure a mutually acceptable compromise. By way of example, most lenders are willing: to agree to act reasonably when making a determination that the loan is out of balance; to give the borrower a degree of flexibility to use cost savings and the contingency reserve to offset a project cost overrun; and to provide the borrower with a reasonable range of alternatives to put the loan back in balance. The construction lender's willingness to make these concessions is, in large measure, driven by the lender's recognition that, even when faced with a potential cost overrun, the lender's best course of action is usually to do that which is necessary to ensure completion of the project.

A related topic that often becomes the subject of intense negotiations between the construction lender and the borrower is the standard prohibition contained in the construction loan documents against the existence of any secondary project financing (that is, any borrowing in addition to the construction loan). If a borrower is concerned about its ability to provide equity to fully fund the gap between the project's overall development costs and the amount of the construction loan (which gap can exist either at the outset of the loan or as a result of the construction lender's exercise of its loan balancing right), the borrower should try to negotiate revisions to the secondary financing prohibition so that the borrower can source additional debt financing to help fund the cost gap. A common source for the funding of that gap is ***mezzanine financing*** where a financial institution provides debt to help a borrower defray its equity requirements in exchange for the borrower's agreement (1) to pay an above-market interest rate to the mezzanine lender (sometimes in the form of a profit participation), and (2) to pledge ownership interests in the borrower as collateral for the mezzanine loan. The placement of mezzanine financing on a real estate project raises a host of very complex issues regarding the construction and mezzanine lenders' respective interests and priorities in the underlying real estate project. Those issues are typically addressed in an intercreditor agreement entered into by the mezzanine and construction lenders. See *Chapter 12—Stages 8–10: Selecting an Exit Strategy,* at pages 613–615 for a further discussion of mezzanine debt.[33]

---

[33] *See also* Kyle, *supra* note 23, at 130–131; Michael Weinberger, *Mezzanine Finance*, in ALI-ABA COURSE OF STUDY MATERIALS, COMMERCIAL REAL ESTATE FINANCING: STRATEGIES FOR CHANGING MARKETS AND UNCERTAIN TIMES, Course No. SP–008, 357 (January 2009); K.C. McDaniel, *Intercreditor Remedies—When and How*, in ALI-ABA COURSE OF STUDY MATERIALS, COMMERCIAL REAL ESTATE FINANCING: STRATEGIES FOR CHANGING MARKETS AND UNCERTAIN TIMES, Course No. SP–008, 1445 (January 2009); Ellen M. Goodwin, *Debt Markets—Dead, Delayed or Dynamic? Developments in Mezzanine and CMBS Finance in 2016, and the Impact of new Regulatory Requirements on the Capital Markets Generally*, in ACREL PAPERS Tab 2 (Fall 2016);

HIBC Case Study—Dealing with the Risk of a Cost Overrun

Reaching agreement on the cost overrun mitigation techniques discussed in this section did not prove to be a particularly challenging endeavor for Pizzuti and First Union. Much of the pressure normally felt by a construction lender to tighten the screws on possible cost overruns was relieved because Pizzuti was able to produce a guaranteed maximum price ("GMP") contract from, its general contractor, Brasfield & Gorrie, on both the HTE and the 500 projects. Brasfield's GMP on both projects included a fairly significant contingency reserve—1.5% of the total construction costs for the HTE project and 1% of such costs for the 500 Building project. Finally, Brasfield's GMP was further backed by a completion guaranty from Pizzuti Equities.

With this anti-cost overrun support in place, Pizzuti was able to get First Union to agree to the following concessions to its standard cost overrun provisions:

- The grant to Pizzuti of the right to make change orders up to a stipulated dollar amount without having to obtain First Union's consent;

- First Union's acknowledgement that Pizzuti could use the contingency reserve and verifiable cost savings in any line item to defray a cost overrun in another line item of the development budget;

- First Union's agreement that it would fund 50% of Pizzuti's development fee in the initial loan advance, with the remainder to be allocated proportionately over the remaining draws based on the percentage of completion of each project; and

- First Union's acceptance of Pizzuti's estimate of the fair market value of the land as the "land cost" included in the approved development budget. Pizzuti was also able to get First Union to agree to treat the full fair market value of the land as a credit against its required equity contribution on both projects.

Thus, by addressing First Union's primary cost overrun concerns by providing the lender with an acceptable GMP contract and a completion guaranty, Pizzuti was able to get significant relief from the more draconian provisions of First Union's standard construction loan provisions on cost

and Marianne Ajemian, *Are Mezzanine Loans Really the Lesser of Two Evils?*, 31 No. 3 PRACTICAL REAL ESTATE LAWYER 35 (May 2015).

overruns. This is an instructive lesson for a new practitioner—if you understand and try to satisfy the legitimate business needs of the other side to a negotiation, you will be well-positioned to negotiate contractual concessions that are essential to your client's achievement of its primary business objectives.

C. DEALING WITH THE RISK OF INSUFFICIENT VALUE ON COMPLETION

The prior two sections addressed the issue of what the construction lender can do to protect itself against the risk that the project is not completed on time or on budget. Once it has dealt with those two issues, the construction lender is faced with yet another significant risk—what happens if the project is completed on time and on budget, but the project's value is less than the value projected by the borrower at the inception of the loan underwriting process?

The diminished value of the underlying real estate collateral is an issue that, in some measure, is faced by all real estate lenders—both construction and permanent lenders. However, the risk is elevated in the context of a construction loan because there is no income stream in place when the construction lender has to make its decision to commit to make a construction loan. Unlike the permanent lender, who only has to worry about a future deterioration in a project's existing income stream, the construction lender must also be concerned with the creation of the value of the project in the first instance. If that value is not created to the extent projected in the lender's initial loan underwriting, the construction lender may be left without a viable exit strategy for the repayment of its construction loan.

The next several sections of this chapter examines the risk mitigation techniques that a construction lender can use to lessen its exposure to this value risk.

1. Credit Enhancement (§§ 3.2(b) and (h), 5.1(d) and 5.3)

The best way for a construction lender to limit its value risk is to shift its primary security for the loan's repayment away from the value of the underlying real estate collateral and toward the balance sheet of the borrower/guarantor. In other words, the construction lender tries to make its construction loan less a real estate loan and more a personal loan. The value risk faced by a construction lender on a $10 million construction loan to build a warehouse in Columbus is very different if the borrower is Warren Buffet versus yours truly. If I am the borrower, the lender has no choice but to pull out all the stops in using the other techniques discussed in this section to mitigate its value risk. If Mr. Buffet is the borrower, the construction lender has the luxury of being somewhat lax on its structuring of the risk mitigation provisions of the construction loan agreement.

The following discussion highlights the two credit enhancement techniques that are most commonly used by a construction lender to lessen its value risk—(1) a payment guaranty, and (2) a letter of credit.

a. *Payment Guaranty*

The norm in today's lending environment is for the borrower to be a single purpose entity with no net worth beyond the value of the project that is the subject of the construction loan. The credit standing behind a construction loan is, therefore, typically provided by an affiliate of the borrower who executes a payment guaranty that unconditionally obligates the guarantor to repay the construction loan.[34]

The construction lender wants to secure a payment guaranty from the most creditworthy person associated with the developer—which typically is the developer's principal equity owner. Once the identity of an acceptable guarantor is determined, the lender next turns its attention to including provisions in the payment guaranty that are designed to buttress the utility and enforceability of that document—for example the inclusion in the payment guaranty document of the following provisions:

- A clause making it clear that the lender need not exhaust its remedies against the borrower or the collateral before pursuing a collection action against the guarantor;

- A statement acknowledging that the construction loan and the underlying collateral documents may be modified or dealt with in any fashion without notice to the guarantor and without affecting the ongoing liability of the guarantor;

- A provision affirming that the guaranty will survive the bankruptcy of the borrower;

- A representation confirming the guarantor's current net worth and a warranty obligating the guarantor to maintain that level of net worth throughout the term of the construction loan; and

- A covenant requiring the guarantor to provide the lender with its current financial statements at least annually throughout the term of the construction loan.

---

[34] The many issues associated with the structuring and enforcement of payment guaranties are beyond the scope of this chapter. For a more detailed discussion of payment guaranties in the context of real estate financing transactions, *see generally* Andrea M. Mattei, *Credit Enhancements in Turbulent Times*, in ALI-ABA COURSE OF STUDY MATERIALS, COMMERCIAL REAL ESTATE FINANCING: STRATEGIES FOR CHANGING MARKETS AND UNCERTAIN TIMES, Course No. SP–008, 663 (January 2009) and Diana C, Liu, *An Annotated Guaranty*, 17 No. 5 PRACTICAL REAL ESTATE LAWYER 45 (September 2001).

Borrower's Pushback: Most borrowers acknowledge that they will not be able to secure construction financing unless they furnish the lender with a payment guaranty from a creditworthy entity. From the borrower's perspective, the principal issue comes down to who has to provide the guaranty—the individual owners of the borrower/developer or, preferably, a lesser credit entity owned and controlled by the individual owners.

A borrower occasionally seeks to place an upper limit on the dollar amount of the guarantor's exposure under its payment guaranty. The following are examples of common guaranty limitations:

- A guaranty of the "top 50% of the loan";[35]

- A guaranty of the "bottom 50% of the loan";[36]

- A several guaranty limited to the guarantor's percentage equity interest in the deal;

- A reduction of the guaranty to 25% of the loan upon the completion of the project; or

- An elimination of the guaranty upon the project achieving a lease-up of more than 90% of its rentable space.

The guarantor's ability to negotiate a limited guaranty is a function of the creditworthiness of the borrowing entity, the lender's perception of the risk associated with the underlying real estate project, and the competitiveness of the construction loan market

b. Letter of Credit

If the borrower is either unable or unwilling to fully satisfy the lender's demand for the provision of a payment guaranty from a creditworthy person, then the construction lender might ask the borrower to further secure the loan by posting a *standby letter of credit* that unconditionally commits the issuer of the letter of credit (typically a bank) to pay the amount of the letter of credit to the construction lender upon the issuer's receipt of a lender demand for payment that says nothing more than "the borrower is in default under the construction loan."[37] The letter of credit is typically for an amount less than the full amount of the construction loan.

---

[35] A guaranty of the "top" 50% of a $10 million loan means that the guarantor protects the lender against the first $5 million of loss. As such, if the borrower forecloses on a project and sells it at a sheriff's sale for $4 million (producing a lender loss of $6 million), the guarantor will be obligated to pay $5 million to the lender (thereby reducing the lender's net loss to $1 million).

[36] A guaranty of the "bottom" 50% of a $10 million loan means that the guarantor protects the lender against the last $5 million of loss. As such, the guarantor will not have any liability to the lender under its payment guaranty, unless the sale of the project at a sheriff's sale produces sales proceeds of less than $5 million. For obvious reasons, construction lenders seldom, if ever, agree to a guaranty of the bottom portion of a loan.

[37] *See generally* LEFCOE, *supra* note 12, at 510; and Mattei, *supra* note 34, at 671–674. A sample irrevocable standby letter of credit is attached to the Mattei article at 679–682.

Borrower's Pushback: The borrower's principal concern with a letter of credit is its cost. The bank issuing the letter of credit usually charges the borrower an annual fee of 1–3% of the letter of credit amount ($40–120,000 per year for a $4 million letter of credit). The letter of credit fee varies based on (1) the amount and duration of the letter of credit, and (2) the financial strength of the person requesting the issuance of the letter of credit (who will also be the person ultimately responsible for the repayment of the letter of credit amount to the issuing financial institution if the construction lender ever draws down on the letter of credit).

One instance where a borrower might want to agree to provide the lender with a letter of credit is where the individual owners of the developer have ample net worth, but do not want to subject themselves to personal liability for the full repayment of the construction loan. In such a circumstance, a borrower may be able to satisfy the lender's credit concerns by buttressing a payment guaranty from a marginally creditworthy entity with the issuance of a letter of credit for a limited portion of the construction loan amount (for example, 10–20% of the loan). This approach, if accepted by the construction lender, would permit the individual owners to reduce their contingent liability on a $10 million construction loan from a full $10 million to $1–2 million (the amount of the guaranty that the owners would be required to provide to the bank issuing the letter of credit)—a result that might justify the borrower's payment of an additional fee of $10–20,000 per year to obtain a letter of credit (based on a fee equal to 1% of the letter of credit amount).

2. Underwriting to the Permanent Loan Market

The construction lender's business model contemplates that a life insurance company, pension fund, or other financial institution will step up to provide the necessary debt or equity dollars to pay off the construction loan once the developer's project is completed and leased. In order to properly position the construction loan for refinancing with a permanent loan, it is essential that the construction lender underwrite its loan based on those lending principles and guidelines that are then prevailing in the permanent loan market. A construction lender that fails to adhere to this simple rule runs the risk of having a bad loan on its books that is not susceptible to being refinanced by a permanent loan. By way of example, if a construction lender makes a loan in a principal amount equal to 90% of a project's total development costs at a time when the permanent loan market is pricing its loans at no more than 70% of project costs, then the construction lender will have rely on the credit of the borrower/guarantor to provide the funds necessary to pay off the portion of the construction loan that cannot be retired with the proceeds of a permanent loan—a scenario that may not be realistic when the construction loan matures.

There are two strategies that a construction lender can adopt to increase the odds that its underwriting of the construction loan squares with the prevailing underwriting practices of the permanent loan market. One such strategy—a "take-out commitment"—operates prospectively, while the other strategy—a "remargining"—works retroactively.

a.   Take-Out Commitment

Until the mid-1980's, the required presence of a permanent loan take-out commitment was a staple of most construction loans. A **take-out commitment** is an agreement by a permanent lender that it will fund a permanent loan to the borrower and fully pay off the construction loan upon the occurrence of certain conditions.

Ideally, the take-out commitment is issued by the permanent lender before the construction loan is closed (or at least before the initial advance of construction loan proceeds). The permanent lender's obligation to "take out" the construction loan can be documented either by a tri-party agreement entered into by the construction and permanent lenders and the borrower or a buy-sell agreement to which just the construction and permanent lenders are parties. The substance of both of these agreements is the same—a recitation of when and under what circumstances the permanent lender is required to close and fund its permanent loan.

The key issue to be addressed in the agreement between the construction and permanent lenders is the scope of the conditions to the permanent lender's take-out commitment. The construction lender wants the conditions to the permanent lender's funding obligation to be as limited as possible and relate solely to the physical condition of the project—that is, the lien-free completion of the project in accordance with the approved plans and specifications. If the conditions to the permanent lender's funding obligation are limited to objectively achievable events, then the existence of a permanent take-out commitment provides the construction lender with its best protection against the risk that the actual value of the completed project is less than that initially projected by the borrower.

The permanent lender, on the other hand, wants the conditions to its funding obligation to be as expansive as possible to provide the permanent lender with a host of outs if something occurs after its issuance of the take-out commitment that causes the permanent lender to change its mind concerning the funding of the permanent loan. The permanent lender wants the funding conditions to extend not just to the completed status of the project, but also to issues that impact the project's income stream—specifically including (1) the lease-up of the project at net rental rates consistent or better than the developer's financial projections, and (2) the absence of any change in prevailing market conditions that would make its funding of the permanent loan inadvisable (for example, a marked increase in capitalization rates used to value commercial real estate projects similar to the developer's project).

The permanent lender's reticence to furnish the construction lender with a condition-free take-out stems from the fact that the permanent lender is being asked to make its loan commitment well in advance of the anticipated permanent loan closing—typically at least 12 months and many times 24–36 months in advance of the closing date. As witnessed by the sudden downturn in the economy in 2008, a lot can happen in 12–36 months to cause a permanent lender to re-think its initial underwriting decision. Following the 2008 disruption of the capital markets, real estate values plummeted and the permanent loan market totally dried up. Given that type of circumstance, it is clear why construction lenders want to rigorously restrict the permanent lender's funding discretion, while the permanent lender wants to instill its take-out commitment with an unending series of contractual escape hatches.

The first sentence in this discussion referenced the fact that take-out commitments were the norm 30–35 years ago. Implicit in that comment is the fact that take-out commitments have lost their luster in recent years. What happened to cause take-out commitments to go out of favor? In addition to the broadening of its take-out conditions, what else can a permanent lender to do to hedge its risk that something untoward occurs between the date of its issuance of the take-out commitment and the anticipated date of the permanent loan closing? The answers to those questions are provided below in the discussion of the *Borrower's Pushback*.

Borrower's Pushback: The borrower shares the construction lender's desire to refinance the construction loan with a permanent loan. Implementing a permanent loan exit strategy permits the borrower to replace a short-term fully recourse debt obligation with a long-term nonrecourse mortgage loan. Having a take-out commitment in hand before starting construction on the project effectively eliminates most of the borrower's risk that something will occur to decrease the borrower's prospects of implementing its permanent loan exit strategy.

So, given the theoretical attractiveness of the permanent loan take-out to both the construction lender and the borrower, why isn't the existence of a binding take-out commitment a required condition of every construction loan? The answer to that question lies in the way in which a permanent lender reacts to a request that it provide a take-out commitment on a development project. When asked to commit to making a permanent loan 12–36 months in advance of the anticipated permanent loan closing date (and, more importantly, before construction of the project has even begun), a cautious permanent lender routinely does three things:

- Sets the permanent loan interest rate at a generous spread over the permanent lender's cost of funds;

- Requires the borrower to pay a sizable non-refundable commitment fee at the time of the permanent lender's issuance of the permanent take-out commitment; and

- Subjects its funding obligation to a plethora of conditions that are designed to convert the loan "commitment" into a loan "option" for the permanent lender, including a broad catch-all condition like the following;

> *As a condition to the initial disbursement of loan proceeds under this Agreement, there shall be no material adverse change in Borrower's financial condition, prospects, profits or operations or the physical condition of the Property.*[38]

From the borrower's perspective, a take-out commitment issued along the lines outlined above is simply not worth the cost of obtaining that commitment. Why, asks the borrower, should I pay an exorbitant upfront commitment fee to obtain an over-priced loan that the permanent lender is only nominally obligated to fund? Moreover, because a take-out commitment is almost always enforceable by the permanent lender (even though it may not be particularly enforceable against the permanent lender), the existence of the take-out effectively precludes the borrower from benefiting from any change in interest rates or market conditions that might otherwise motivate it to look elsewhere for permanent financing.[39]

For all of the above reasons, the existence of a take-out commitment is no longer commonly required as a condition to the funding of a construction loan. One type of project where a take-out commitment is still frequently used is a project that is 100% pre-leased to a credit tenant. In that situation, the borrower may try to increase the amount of its construction loan and decrease its exit strategy risk by securing a take-out commitment from a life company or other institutional investor to either fund a permanent loan or buy the project upon completion. A take-out commitment issued on a project that is fully leased to a creditworthy tenant typically costs less and is subject to a much less expansive set of funding conditions than is a commitment issued on a project that is not blessed with either of those characteristics. In the context of a single tenant project, the construction lender's goal would be to limit the take-out conditions to (1) the lien-free completion of the project in accordance with the approved plans and specifications, and (2) the receipt of an estoppel certificate from the project's sole tenant affirming that the lease is in full force and effect and that the tenant has begun paying rent.

---

[38] *See* Michael Hamilton, *Representing Borrowers in Changing Time*, in ALI-ABA COURSE OF STUDY MATERIALS, COMMERCIAL REAL ESTATE FINANCING: STRATEGIES FOR CHANGING MARKETS AND UNCERTAIN TIMES, Course No. SP–008, 159, 167–168 (January 2009).

[39] *See* Thompson, *supra* note 20, at 9–14.

b. *Remargining the Construction Loan*

A second strategy employed by construction lenders to try to be more responsive to the underwriting guidelines being practiced in the permanent loan market is the inclusion in the construction loan agreement of a ***remargining provision***. A remargining provision obligates the borrower/guarantor to make additional equity contributions to pay down the principal amount of the construction loan to the extent the lender determines that the created value of a development project is less than that projected at the inception of the lender's underwriting for the loan. The following is an example of a fairly standard remargining provision.

> *If at any time during the term of the Loan Lender obtains an appraisal of the Project that shows that the Loan-to-Value Ratio of the Loan is greater than 70%, then Borrower shall immediately make a principal payment to reduce the Loan-to-Value Ratio to 70% or less.*

Under the excerpted remargining provision, a construction lender would have the right to require the borrower to make a $700,000 principal payment on its $7 million construction loan if an appraisal obtained by the lender at the completion of the project shows that the fair market value of the project is $9 million (and not $10 million as initially projected by the borrower). The remargining provision quoted above uses a loan-to-value test to determine whether the borrower needs to pay down the construction loan. Construction lenders also use debt service coverage ratios, debt yield tests, and other income stream measurements as benchmarks for triggering a remargining of the construction loan.

A remargining provision is commonly attached to a provision giving the borrower an option to extend the loan's maturity date for an additional term of two to three years (sometimes referred to as a ***mini-perm loan***). The construction lender frequently conditions the borrower's right to exercise that extension option upon an objective determination being made that the completed project satisfies certain value and income standards—for example, loan-to-value, debt yield, and debt service coverage tests. If the construction loan agreement gives the borrower a right to remargin the loan, then the borrower can preserve its right to exercise its extension option by paying down the principal amount of the construction loan to a level that causes its project to come into compliance with the stated financial conditions.

One point to keep in mind with respect to the remargining technique is that the technique is only as good as the credit and liquidity of the borrower/guarantor. Therefore, while the remargining provision is designed to enhance the lender's exit strategy under the construction loan by retroactively bringing the loan into compliance with the underwriting practices of the permanent loan community, that provision is rendered wholly ineffective if the borrower/guarantor does not have the money required to make the mandated principal payment.

Borrower Pushback: A borrower's initial pushback on the construction lender's inclusion of a remargining provision in the construction loan agreement is to get the lender to delete the entire provision on the grounds that the lender should not the right to change the rules of the game and reduce the amount of the construction loan amount prior to the loan's maturity. If the lender refuses to delete the remargining provision in its entirety, then the borrower's next tactic is to make the remargining provision nothing more than a necessary adjunct to the borrower's mini-perm conversion right.,

Most borrowers accede to the lender's requirement that a remargining provision be included as a condition to the borrower's exercise of its right to convert the construction loan into a mini-perm loan. The devil is, however, in the details when it comes to the substance of the remargining provision. What are the specific financial ratios included in the remargining provision—for example, is the extension of the loan term conditioned on the project satisfying a loan-to-value ratio of 80% or 70%? Is the project's compliance with the mandated financial ratios determined strictly under executed leases or can the borrower factor in projected rentals on vacant space? What other parameters will be used to test the project's compliance with the financial ratios—for example, the identification of a specific capitalization rate for determining the project's value, the recital of the debt amortization period used to determine the project's debt service coverage ratio, etc.?

3.   Control of Project Lease-Up

The value of a commercial real estate project is wholly dependent on the level of the income stream produced from the project's leases. Therefore, one way for the construction lender to protect itself against value risk is to exercise power under the loan documents to cause the borrower to lease its project within the time periods and at the rental rates specified in the borrower's initial financial projections.

The construction lender can exert its control over the lease-up of the project in two distinct ways. First, the lender can establish a pre-leasing requirement as a condition to its obligation to fund advances under the construction loan. The following is a sample clause establishing a pre-leasing requirement:

> *Lender shall not be obligated to make any loan advance until at least ___% of the rentable space contained in the Project has been leased pursuant to written leases approved by Lender.*

The creation of a pre-leasing requirement provides the construction lender with a significant buffer against the risk that the value of the completed project is less than its underwritten value. In the perfect world, the construction lender would condition its obligation to make any loan advances upon the borrower's prior execution of leases at or above pro forma rents for 100% of the rentable space in the project. Under that scenario, the construction lender's value risk would be limited to the risks that (1) the project is not completed at the time required under the executed leases (thereby potentially permitting the tenants to terminate their leasing commitments), and (2) a change or dislocation in the real estate market that leads to a decline in the relative value assigned to the income stream produced under the signed leases (for example, an increase in capitalization rates or the advent of runaway inflation). While most construction lenders do not expect to achieve the perfect world of a 100% pre-leasing condition, the insertion into the construction loan agreement of a lesser pre-leasing requirement (for example, the required pre-leasing of 60% of the rentable space in the project) provides the construction lender with a substantial hedge against the lease-up risk that is at the heart of the lender's value quandary.

The second technique utilized by the construction lender to advance its interest in seeing the project leased in a manner consistent with the developer's initial projections is the lender's reservation of a right to approve all leases of space in the project. The following is an example of such a provision:

> Borrower shall not enter into any lease of space in the Project without first obtaining the written consent of Lender as to both the form and content of such lease. Borrower's breach of the foregoing covenant will constitute an Event of Default that entitles Lender to pursue all remedies available to it at law or in equity to redress the breach, including, without limitation, the right to suspend Lender's obligation to make any further advances under the Loan.

Such a borrower covenant provides the construction lender with added protection against the risk that the borrower leases space in the project for a rent that is less than the rent projected in the developer's approved leasing plan. The construction lender typically further conditions its consent to any lease of space in the project to the tenant's execution of a **subordination, non-disturbance, and attornment agreement (SNDA)** that confirms that the tenant will remain obligated under its lease following the lender's foreclosure of its project mortgage. See *Chapter 11— Stage 7: Negotiating the Project Lease*, at pages 585–587, for a further discussion of the tenant's SNDA obligation.

Borrower's Pushback: The negotiations take a contentious turn when the construction lender seeks to place limitations on the flexibility that the developer feels it needs to lease its project. A pre-leasing requirement particularly rankles a developer who believes (rightly or wrongly) in the old adage of "build it and they will come." It is exceedingly difficult for a developer to get a prospective tenant to sign a lease for space in a building before construction of the building has begun. Tenants tend to be fairly cautious and cynical people who are unwilling to make long-term leasing decisions based on an artist's rendering of a proposed building or a developer's promise that the building will be completed "real soon." A pre-leasing requirement places the developer in a classic Catch 22—it cannot get the prospective tenant to sign a lease until construction has started and it cannot get the construction lender to give it the money it needs to start construction until the lease is signed. A borrower who is forced to accept a pre-leasing requirement will expend considerable negotiating energy in an attempt to place a modest limit on the pre-leasing requirement (for example, the leasing of 20% of the project's rentable space rather than 70% of such space).

A borrower is generally more accepting of the construction lender's insistence that it retain the right to pre-approve any lease signed by the borrower. The borrower, does not, however, want the lender's approval right to deprive the borrower of the discretion that it needs to effectively market its building. The prudent borrower seeks to limit the lender's lease approval rights in a variety of ways, including the following:

- A limitation that the lender has the right to approve only "major leases"—for example, leases of at least 20,000 rentable square feet;

- A provision authorizing the borrower to sign a lease as long as the lease terms are consistent with pre-approved leasing guidelines that specify: a minimum lease term; a maximum tenant improvement allowance; a minimum net rental; and those other business terms that hold particular significance for the construction lender;

- The lender's pre-approval of the borrower's standard lease form and the lender's further agreement that the borrower may make reasonable negotiated modifications to that form as long as the modifications do not materially adversely impair the rental stream created under the lease; and

- A requirement that the lender act reasonably and with dispatch in reviewing any lease requiring its approval under the construction loan documents.

One issue related to the lender's lease approval rights that engenders extensive discussion is the issue of who gets to decide whether a prospective tenant's credit is acceptable, with each of parties predictably taking the position that it should have the final say on that issue. A common compromise is for the construction loan agreement to recite that the lender's approval of the identity of a particular tenant (as opposed to the terms of that tenant's lease) is not required if the prospective tenant meets a minimum net worth standard (for example, a net worth computed in accordance with generally accepted accounting principles of not less than $10 million).

4.   Limitations on Amount of Construction Loan

The most obvious way for a construction lender to limit its value risk is by reducing the amount of the construction loan. A construction loan of $10 million on Project A is by definition more risky than a loan of $8 million on the same project. By the same token, a construction lender makes its money by maximizing the amount of money it loans to borrowers—as long as that money is repaid in full on the maturity of the loan. A construction lender whose risk aversion causes it to unduly limit the amount of its construction loans will discover that it is outbid on project after project by more aggressive construction lenders.

The key for the construction lender is to set its loan amount at a level that gives it reasonable assurance that the loan will be repaid at maturity. The construction lender accomplishes that objective by benchmarking sufficient room between the principal amount of the loan and the anticipated value of the underlying development project.

Construction lenders have devised a series of financial tests to help them create the optimal level of loan cushion. The four most common underwriting techniques used by construction lenders to establish the maximum amount of a construction loan (and, hence, the amount of the lender's loan cushion) are set forth below (see also *Chapter 3—What the Real Estate Development Lawyer Needs to Know About Project Economics*, at pages 49–52).

- *Loan-to-Cost*—Under this test, the loan amount is stated as a percentage of the borrower's total development costs. Loan-to-cost ratios have traditionally hovered in the 70–90% range, although the economic downturn of the late 2000's caused lenders to dramatically drop their loan-to-cost ratios for a period of time. A loan-to-cost ratio of 80% produces a maximum loan amount of $8 million on a project having a total development cost of $10 million.

- *Loan-to-Value*—This test ties the maximum loan amount to a percentage of the projected value of the underlying development project when "stabilized" (that is, when the project is completed and substantially leased). Loan-to-value percentages are normally slightly lower than loan-to-cost ratios based on the theory that a development project should always have a projected value that is well in excess of its cost. A loan-to value ratio of 70% on a project having an anticipated value of $12 million produces a maximum construction loan amount of $8.4 million. The construction lender implements its loan-to-value criterion by conditioning its funding obligation on its receipt of an appraisal from a qualified appraiser showing that the appraised fair market value of the project when stabilized will be equal to or greater than the projected value used by the lender during its underwriting of the construction loan.

- *Debt Service Coverage*—This test establishes the upper boundary of the construction loan amount by requiring that the project's annual anticipated net operating income must comfortably exceed the annual debt service payable under the loan. A debt service coverage ratio of somewhere between 1.1 and 1.3 is fairly typical in the underwriting of construction loans. A debt service coverage of 1.2 means that the project's net operating income must be at least 120% of the debt service payable by the borrower under the construction loan.

- *Debt Yield*—In recent years, the debt yield test has become a popular tool used by lenders in the underwriting of construction loans. Under the debt yield test, the maximum amount of a construction loan is determined by dividing the project's projected annual net operating income by a fixed percentage yield. By way of example, a debt yield percentage of 10% on a project having an anticipated NOI of $1 million produces a maximum loan amount of $10 million.

The specific percentages selected by a construction lender for each of these four tests depends upon the lender's risk profile, its perception of the risk quotient of the subject project, and the conditions then prevailing in the construction financing and permanent loan markets. It is the norm for construction lenders to adopt a lowest common denominator approach by establishing the maximum amount of the construction loan as the lowest figure produced under the tests used by the construction lender in its underwriting of the construction loan.

Borrower Pushback: The typical borrower cares deeply about maximizing the principal amount of its construction loan and cares hardly at all about the lender's need for a loan cushion. A borrower who wants to push the envelope on the outer boundary of the construction loan amount is well-served by (1) establishing a reputation among construction lenders for preparing accurate financial projections, (2) offering up loan guaranties backed by a financially solid guarantor, (3) convincing the construction lender to use an appraiser with whom the developer has an established relationship, and (4) hiring legal counsel who understands the financial tests used by construction lenders and, therefore, is equipped to rebuff any overbearing attempts made in the commitment letter and construction loan agreement to unreasonably limit the amount of the borrower's construction financing.

HIBC Case Study—Dealing with Value Risk

A significant part of the Pizzuti-First Union loan negotiations revolved around First Union's attempts to protect itself against the risk that the HTE and 500 Building projects would not have sufficient value upon completion to facilitate a refinancing of First Union's construction loans. Given the disparate nature of the two projects, the discussion that follows separately examines First Union's attempt to use value risk mitigation techniques for each of the HTE and 500 projects.

__Limitation of Loan Amount:__ The loan proposals submitted by Pizzuti to First Union asked for a 90% loan-to-cost loan for the HTE project and an 80% loan-to-cost loan for the 500 Building. First Union gave its approval to the requested loan amount for the 500 Building, but refused to go along with Pizzuti's request for a 90% loan amount on the HTE project. First Union's position on the HTE loan was largely driven by its concern about HTE's credit (or lack thereof). Long story short, First Union agreed to provide an 85% loan-to-cost loan for the HTE project, subject, however, to a 75% loan-to-value override based on an appraisal to be obtained by First Union. Unfortunately for Pizzuti, the appraisal came in unreasonably low (at least from Pizzuti's perspective) because of the concern over HTE's net worth. The lower than anticipated appraised fair market value for the HTE project resulted in a further reduction of the loan amount to $8.2 million.

__Control of Project Lease-up:__ First Union's approach to the lease-up issue on the HTE project was relatively simple and straightforward. Due to the single tenant nature of that project, First Union required Pizzuti to collaterally assign its interest in the HTE lease to First Union, so that, if necessary, First Union could complete construction of the project and enforce HTE's lease obligations. The construction loan agreement also established the receipt of HTE's signed estoppel certificate and subordination, non-disturbance, and attornment agreement as conditions to the initial loan advance.

First Union's initial approach to the lease-up of the 500 Building was much more rigorous. The first draft of its commitment letter recited that no loan disbursements would be made under the construction loan until at least 60% of the rentable space in the 500 Building was leased pursuant to written leases approved by First Union. The commitment letter purported to give First Union the right to disapprove any lease in its sole discretion. After lengthy negotiations on the point, Pizzuti was able to get First Union to *agree to drop the pre-leasing agreement in its entirety. The bargaining chips Pizzuti played to achieve this result were (1) the financial strength of the parties guarantying repayment of the construction loan, and (2) a marketing report prepared by Pizzuti's leasing broker stating that there was ample pent-up demand for leased space in the north Orlando office market, but that the prospective tenants they had contacted were leery of committing to lease space in a project until they saw a building coming out of the ground. Pizzuti was also able to get First Union to agree to loosen its lease approval rights to exempt any lease with average base rents of at least $19 per square foot and a term of at least five years.*

*   **Permanent Take-out Commitment:** First Union readily acknowledged that a take-out commitment on the 500 building project was infeasible because the 500 building was a purely speculative project with no existing income stream. However, First Union pushed hard to require Pizzuti to obtain a take-out commitment for the HTE construction loan. First Union was concerned about the mediocre credit standing of HTE and felt that the receipt of a take-out commitment from a permanent lender would serve as a needed confirmation of the acceptability of the HTE lease to the permanent loan market. While First Union's position on the HTE take-out condition was eminently logical, Pizzuti was able to eliminate that condition from the loan commitment based on two considerations—(1) the HTE loan was backed by a full payment guaranty from extremely creditworthy persons, and (2) Pizzuti could not get a bankable take-out commitment from a permanent lender on the HTE project (in part because of the permanent loan market's concern with HTE's credit). A "bankable commitment" is a take-out commitment from a permanent lender that the construction lender believes obligates the permanent lender to fund the permanent loan upon the satisfaction of a limited number of objective conditions. A "non-bankable commitment," on the other hand, is a commitment from a permanent lender that is so riddled with subjective conditions as to make the funding of the permanent loan a matter of the permanent lender's inclination and discretion as of the date of the maturity of the construction loan. In the end, First Union had no choice but to back off its requirement for a take-out commitment on the HTE project.*

*   **Loan Remargining/Conversion to Mini-Perm:** In its initial loan submissions, Pizzuti asked for a 12 month extension option on the HTE loan and a 24 month extension option on the 500 Building loan. First Union compromised on these two requests by agreeing to provide an 18 month extension option under each of the construction loans, subject, however, to (1) Pizzuti making fixed monthly principal payments on each loan throughout the extension term, and (2) Pizzuti providing First Union with evidence that the subject building had been completed in accordance with the approved plans and specifications. Neither loan conditioned the exercise of Pizzuti's extension option on the project's satisfaction of any financial*

tests or lease-up standards, nor did either loan contain a remargining provision. Pizzuti's primary goal in negotiating for the extension options was to buy itself time to refinance the underlying construction loans if the permanent loan market was soft when the construction loans matured. Because First Union was comfortable with the credit it had on the two construction loans, it was not as concerned as it normally would have been about pricing its loans to the permanent loan market.

Payment Guaranties: Pizzuti was able to gain the upper hand in its negotiations on the value risk issue by agreeing to furnish First Union with payment guaranties from three very creditworthy persons—Pizzuti Equities (Pizzuti's real estate holding company) and the two principals of Newport Partners (Pizzuti's 50% equity partner in both the 500 Building and HTE projects). Having payment guaranties from guarantors having a combined net worth of just shy of nine figures provided First Union with a great deal of comfort that the loans would be repaid at maturity even if the underlying projects were not as successful as originally projected.

Pizzuti injected a potential point of contention into its negotiations with First Union when it informed First Union that the guaranties of Pizzuti Equities and the two Newport principals had to be 50% several guaranties (and not joint and several guaranties of the full loan amounts as originally anticipated by First Union). What this meant is that Pizzuti Equities guaranty would be limited to 50% of each construction loan and the Newport guaranties would also be limited to 50% of the outstanding construction loan balances.

The several nature of the guaranties was an essential component of the overall equity deal struck by Pizzuti and Newport Partners and, as such, was a non-negotiable point from the borrower's perspective. The implication to First Union of accepting several guaranties was that its credit support on the construction loans would be severely impacted if either Pizzuti Equities or the Newport principals experienced a significant loss of net worth. Although First Union was far from thrilled with the several guaranties, it was nonetheless still comfortable that the net worth and liquidity of each of the guarantors was sufficient on a stand-alone basis to support the repayment of the construction loans.

Practice Tip #9-3: Creating an Entity Guarantor

This is an appropriate spot to pause to highlight a borrowing strategy adopted by many real estate developers. For the bright and accomplished individuals who become successful developers, there is virtually no limit to the wealth they can accumulate. Upper echelon developers love to buy cars, planes, residences, artwork, and other "toys" with the bounty produced by *their successful development projects. They do not, however, want any of those toys to ever be subject to attachment by a lender on a less than successful development project (and every developer has at least one of those).*

Individual developers who want to keep their "toys" from the greedy entreaties of ungrateful lenders are well-advised to create an entity that has sufficient net worth to provide completion and payment guaranties for the developer's construction loans (in lieu of the provision of those guaranties by the individual owners). Adopting such an "entity building" strategy means that the individual developers have to cut back slightly on their purchase of new "toys" and, instead, capitalize an entity with cash and a few profitable real estate projects. The ultimate pay-off for diverting some of the individual's assets into a separate viable entity is the good night's sleep that the individual gets during a downturn in the real estate economy. The goal of getting a good night's sleep was a principal focus of Ron Pizzuti and was met when Pizzuti Equities was capitalized during the 1990's with enough cash and real estate to establish Pizzuti Equities (and not Ron individually) as the loan guarantor on all Pizzuti development projects.

D. DEALING WITH THE RISK OF A MISAPPLICATION OF FUNDS

The next risk that needs to be addressed by the construction lender is the risk that the borrower fails to use the construction loan proceeds to complete the project. The borrower's misapplication of loan proceeds can be triggered by any number of reasons, including greed, temporary cash flow problems, desperation, or carelessness. Regardless of the reason underlying the misapplication, the impact on the lender's position on its construction loan is the same—the value of the project that serves as collateral for the repayment of its loan is either never fully created or is created with a lower net value than originally anticipated by the lender.

The construction lender deals with the misapplication of funds risk by implementing a detailed and tightly supervised process for the review, approval, and funding of the borrower's periodic draw requests. The borrower's **draw requests** are the written requests periodically delivered to the construction lender by the borrower asking the lender to disburse loan proceeds to pay development costs incurred by the borrower during the preceding month. The elements of the construction lender's administration of the borrower's draw requests are described below.

1. Development Budget and Draw Schedule (§§ 3.2(n) and (o))

The construction loan agreement requires the borrower to provide the lender with a detailed development budget and projected draw schedule.

The development budget identifies by line item all of the hard and soft costs that will be incurred in connection with the development of the borrower's commercial real estate project. The draw schedule is the borrower's projection as to the amount of each monthly draw request that the borrower anticipates submitting to the construction lender during the term of the construction loan. Once finalized and approved by the lender, the budget and projected draw schedule become the templates for the submission and funding of all future draw requests.

2. Applications for Payment (§§ 1.1 and 2.1)

Whenever the borrower wants to receive a disbursement of loan proceeds to pay development costs, the borrower must submit an *application for payment* to the lender on a form prescribed in the construction loan agreement. Each application for payment must identify the development costs to be funded by reference to a specific line item contained in the approved development budget. Moreover, the application for payment can only cover costs that have already been incurred by the borrower and incorporated into the project (and not costs that may be incurred in the future).

3. Required Certifications (§ 2.2)

As a condition to its approval of an application for payment, the construction lender requires the borrower, the general contractor, and the project architect to certify that the development costs identified in the application have actually been incurred in the indicated amounts and that the work related to such costs has been incorporated into the borrower's development project. The construction lender then furnishes the lender's inspecting architect with the borrower's application for payment and requires the inspecting architect to visit the project site to verify that the costs referenced in the application have, in fact, been incurred and incorporated into the work. Only after it has received all the above certifications will the construction lender approve and agree to fund the costs covered in the application for payment.

4. Funding of Draw Requests (§§ 2.1, 2.3 and 6.1)

Once it has approved the borrower's draw request and received all the aforementioned certifications, the construction lender will then disburse loan proceeds equal to the costs covered by the draw request, less any retainage required to be withheld from the disbursements per the construction loan agreement. The construction lender (often with the cooperation of a title insurance company) can fund the draw requests in any one of three ways:

- A direct deposit into a checking account designated by the borrower;

- Dual payee checks made out jointly to the borrower and the end recipient of each component of the funded draw request; or

- Checks made payable directly to each intended recipient of a portion of the loan proceeds—for example, directly to the contractor, subcontractor, or material provider.

The methods noted above are listed from the least to the most conservative approach for the lender's disbursement of its loan proceeds. While a construction lender customarily reserves the right in the construction loan agreement to make payments of loan proceeds directly to contractors, subcontractors, and material providers, few lenders actually do so due to a concern that they might subject themselves to lender liability if the project goes awry and the various firms providing work on the project do not get paid.[40]

Borrower's Pushback: The borrower's primary concern about the lender's mandated draw process is that it not be so rigorous and complex as to delay or otherwise negatively impact the borrower's ability to fund the payment of its development costs on a timely basis. Borrower's counsel should consult with the borrower's in-house finance staff to determine whether the logistics of the draw process suggested by lender work for the borrower.

HIBC Case Study—Dealing with the Risk of a Misapplication of Funds

Only one issue of any significance surfaced during Pizzuti's review and negotiation of First Union's standard loan disbursement procedures. The initial draft of First Union's construction loan agreement gave First Union the right at any time during the loan term to make loan disbursements directly to the general contractor, subcontractors, or any other third party performing work or providing services or materials related to the HTE and 500 projects. Pizzuti objected to First Union's reservation of such an unconditional right because Pizzuti wanted to retain the ultimate form of leverage over its general contractor and all other persons involved in the development process—that is, the right to withhold payment to such persons until their performance met Pizzuti's satisfaction. First Union recognized Pizzuti's concern as being legitimate and agreed to condition its right to make direct disbursements to the contractor, subcontractors, and material

---

[40] *See Schmudde, supra* note 14, at 57–58; *Frobes, Selected Issues in Secured Construction Lending, supra* note 31, at 126–127; and *Talley, supra* note 9, at 136–137.

providers upon the prior occurrence of an event of default under the construction loan documents.

E. DEALING WITH THE RISK OF INTERVENING LIENS

The construction lender's security can be significantly impaired if a mechanics' lien gains priority over the lien of the lender's construction mortgage. The ways in which the construction mortgage might become subordinate to a subsequently-filed mechanics' lien were described in detail earlier in this chapter at pages 366–371. As noted in that discussion, the rules governing the perfection and priority of mechanics' liens vary widely from state to state. The differing treatments afforded mechanics' liens in various states make it difficult to be too specific in laying out the techniques that a construction lender can rely on to mitigate its risk of an intervening lien. However, a few general comments may be made concerning what a construction lender can do to try to insulate itself from the risk that its mortgage loses priority to an intervening mechanics' lien.

1. Compliance with State Law (§ 5.1(r))

First and foremost, counsel for the construction lender must master the mechanics' lien statute of the state where the subject real estate project is located and take whatever protective measures are sanctioned in that statute to preserve the priority of the construction mortgage over a subsequently filed mechanics' lien. Depending on the jurisdiction, counsel may need to label the mortgage as an "open-end" or "future advance" mortgage and file a notice of commencement after the date on which the mortgage is first recorded. Counsel also must research the often confusing and frequently inconsistent judicial gloss on the distinction between optional and obligatory loan advances. Finally, the construction lender may need to hold back a certain level of retainage from its loan disbursements or provide statutorily prescribed notices to the project's general contractor. The key is that the construction lender must rigorously comply with the specific mandates of the state's mechanics' lien law.[41]

2. Early Work Prohibition (§§ 5.1(n))

The most common way that a mechanics' lien gains priority over the construction lender's mortgage is if some work on the project is started before the date on which the lender's mortgage is recorded. The surest way for a lender to protect itself against the risk of an intervening mechanics' lien is to prohibit the borrower from starting work on the project prior to the recordation of the construction mortgage. The construction lender

---

[41] *See generally* Weller, *supra* note 5, at 1750; Schmudde, *supra* note 14, at 55; Kyle, *supra* note 23, at 12–13, and Leidner, *supra* note 10, at 44–45.

should require the borrower to sign a **no work affidavit** at the construction loan closing attesting that neither the borrower, nor any contractor, subcontractor, supplier, or material provider has performed any work or provided any materials to the site prior to the closing of the construction loan. The careful lender should also dispatch one of its underlings to the site on the day of the construction loan closing to visually confirm that no work has been started on the project.

3. Lien Waivers (§§ 1.1 and 5.1(i))

Most construction lenders require receipt of written **lien waivers** as a condition to the funding of any construction loan draw. A lien waiver should be signed by each contractor, subcontractor, supplier, and material provider that receives any payment under the funded draw and should specifically state that such person has been fully paid for all work performed on the project and that it waives the right to file a mechanics' lien against the project to the extent of such prior or contemporaneous payments.

4. Title Endorsements (§§ 3.2(c) and 4.1(c))

The construction lender should look to its title insurer to affirmatively insure that the construction mortgage has full priority over any intervening mechanics lien. The title insurer can provide the lender with the desired protection by (1) deleting from the loan policy the standard exception for mechanics' liens, and (2) providing a so-called **date-down endorsement** at the time of each loan disbursement confirming that no mechanics' lien has been filed against the project since the date of the recordation of the construction mortgage.

5. Bonding Off Liens

Most state statutes contain provisions permitting an owner to remove a mechanics' lien against its property by posting a surety bond in the full amount of the perfected mechanics' lien. If the project is located in a state that permits the bonding of mechanics' liens, the construction lender should include a requirement in the construction loan agreement that the borrower post such a bond within a fixed number of days following the filing of a mechanics' lien against the project.

Borrower's Pushback: With one notable exception, the borrower ordinarily has no particular objection to the legal measures employed by the construction lender to protect itself against the risk of an intervening mechanics' lien. The exception relates to the construction lender's attempt to prohibit the borrower from beginning work on its project prior to the recordation of the construction loan mortgage. Developers working on tight construction timelines often have to begin work on the site before all the details of the construction loan closing have been finalized. As a result, borrower's counsel is regularly challenged with devising a scenario that permits the borrower to begin its construction activities before the recordation of the construction mortgage, without exposing the construction lender to any undue risk that its mortgage loses priority to an intervening mechanics lien. The techniques used to achieve those objectives are dependent upon the provisions of the mechanics' lien statute of the state in which the project is located. If counsel for the borrower and the lender assiduously follow those statutory rules, the risk that work done on a site before the construction loan closing causes a subsequently filed lien to gain priority over the lien of the construction lender's mortgage can be eliminated or, at the very least, limited to a lien securing the actual cost of the early work. This limited risk is often dealt with by the borrower (1) covering the early work under a separate contract entered into by the borrower and the person performing that work, (2) obtaining a lien waiver from the person performing the early work, (3) convincing the title company to delete the standard mechanics' lien exception from the lender's loan policy (usually in exchange for the borrower's delivery to the title company of a guaranty from a creditworthy entity covering the cost of the early work), and (4) paying the full cost of the early work out of the initial loan advance made under the construction loan.

Practice Tip #9-4: Upturns and Downturns

During my 40-year career as a real estate practitioner, I have seen my share of real estate cycles—both good and bad. Shortly after I began practicing in 1978, interest rates on real estate mortgages spiked to an unheard of high of 18.5%. In 1981, Ronald Reagan signed into law the Economic Recovery Tax Act that ushered in an onslaught of tax shelters and real estate syndications that was eventually slowed by the passage of the Tax Reform Act of 1986. In the late 1980's the savings and loan crisis blew a mammoth hole in the real estate economy and brought new development to an abrupt halt. The dot.com bubble of the late 1990's drained liquidity from the real estate development business for a period of several years. The incredible go-go years of the early 2000's were brought to a screeching halt by the scariest real estate downturn I have ever experienced—the Great Recession of 2008.[42]

One of the first places that the effect of a downturn in the real estate economy manifests itself is in the pages of a construction loan agreement. Construction lenders desperate to make loans in the years during and after a down cycle (that is, after all, the only way they make money) revamp their

---

[42] Anyone interested in finding out how sub-prime loans, credit default swaps, mortgage securitizations, housing market speculation, and the general divorcing of the principles of risk and reward brought the global economy to the brink of failure should read DOWNS *supra* note 12 (2009).

loan processes and documentation in an attempt to further buttress the lenders' protection from all of the risks discussed in this chapter.

The following are examples of steps that were taken by construction lenders in the aftermath of the Great Recession of 2008 (and are representative of actions taken by lenders following every downturn in the real estate economy in recent memory).[43]

- *Loan amounts were dramatically reduced as the U.S. commercial real estate industry underwent a "massive deleveraging."*[44]

- *Loan-to-cost ratios dropped from 70–90% to 40–60%; loan-to-value ratios fell to 50–60%; required debt service coverage ratios skyrocketed to 1.4 to 1.5; and mandated debt yields hovered around 15–17%.*

- *Construction lenders became much more selective in their identification of developers to whom they would extend construction financing. Loan committees insisted that developers have very deep pockets and established track records of success in the industry.*

- *Pre-leasing requirements become the norm for most development projects. So-called "spec" projects simply were not financeable.*

- *Construction lenders sought to reinstate the pre-1980's requirement of a permanent take-out commitment for individual construction loans.*

- *Back-end equity was eliminated from the lender's vocabulary.*

- *Lenders refused to fund the borrower's "really soft costs" (that is, the developer's fees and unrealized land profit).*

- *Lenders ratcheted up both their underwriting practices and loan due diligence, with the result that closing a construction loan took longer and cost more.*

- *The pricing of interest rate spreads increased significantly as both construction and permanent lenders sought to extract higher returns on their real-estate based loans.*

---

[43] For a discussion of how the real estate finance industry changed in reaction to the Great Recession of 2008, *see* Richard R. Goldberg, *The Future of Real Estate Financing: What to Expect After the Crash,* IN ALI-ABA COURSE OF STUDY MATERIALS, MODERN REAL ESTATE TRANSACTIONS: PRACTICAL STRATEGIES FOR REAL ESTATE ACQUISITION, DISPOSITION, AND OWNERSHIP, Course No. SS–012, 1505 (July 2010); URBAN LAND INSTITUTE AND PRICEWATERHOUSECOOPERS, EMERGING TRENDS IN REAL ESTATE, Chapter 2 (2010); DOWNS, *supra* note 12, at Chapter 9; and Hauser, *supra* note 6, at 2–7.

[44] URBAN LAND INSTITUTE, *supra* note 43, at 5.

- *The length of the typical construction loan agreement went from 20 pages to well over 50 pages.*[45]

As has been the case following every real estate downturn over the last 40 years, the construction lending markets are now starting to loosen and many of the conservative underwriting practices mentioned above are fast fading from reality (although construction loan agreements have not gotten any shorter). The cynical realist in me says it probably will not be all that long before a new generation of construction lenders comes along, forgets the lessons of the past, leaps headfirst onto the bandwagon of "irrational exuberance,"[46] and begins once again to make construction loans at 100% of project costs.

VII.   SUMMARY

Because the construction loan is such an enduring staple of the real estate development business, it behooves all lawyers participating in any fashion in the real estate development process to gain a full understanding of both the unique risks faced by the construction lender and the various strategies at the construction lender's disposal to help shield it from those risks. Once such an understanding of the underlying business and legal principles is achieved, counsel for the borrower and the lender can then have at it in their shared quest to negotiate a financing deal that serves the legitimate business needs of both their respective clients.

---

[45] The Form Construction Loan Agreement set out as Document # 5 in *the Document Appendix* is an example of a pre-2008 loan agreement—and, hence, weighs in at a sleek 21 pages versus the 60–70-page loan agreements now in vogue with many construction lenders.

[46] Any discussion of the credit crisis certainly merits at least one quote from Alan Greenspan. *See* Alan Greenspan, *Remarks at the Annual Dinner and Francis Boyer Lecture of The American Enterprise Institute for Public Policy Research, in Washington, D.C.* (December 5, 1996).

CHAPTER 10

STAGE 6: DESIGNING AND CONSTRUCTING THE PROJECT

∎ ∎ ∎

I. INTRODUCTION

Stage 6 is when the developer's vision for its project is refined and translated first into a specific architectural design and then into a constructed building. One real estate author has described this stage by noting that:

> The developer's role shifts with the move to stage six: he becomes less a promoter and more a manager. Time becomes the critical element of risk. It takes an extremely competent manager to coordinate all the activities that unfold simultaneously during this stage.[1]

This chapter is not intended to be a primer on the drafting of design and construction documents. The specific language to be incorporated into the developer's contracts with its selected design and construction professionals is dependent on the particulars of the developer's project and, as such, is not an appropriate topic for a text of this type. Rather, this chapter attempts to create a base line of knowledge for the practitioner tasked with the responsibility for drafting and negotiating those contracts by first exploring the nature of the construction and design process and then examining the primary contractual issues that the practitioner must address to help a developer convert the developer's theoretical business plan into a bricks and mortar reality.

II. DEVELOPER'S BUSINESS OBJECTIVES

The developer's business objectives during Stage 6 are threefold:

- The articulation of a project design that is both aesthetically and functionally attractive to the developer's customers (including the institutional investor community that will ultimately be called upon to make a debt or equity investment in the project);

---

[1] MIKE E. MILES, LAURENCE M. NETHERTON, AND ADRIENNE SCHMITZ REAL ESTATE DEVELOPMENT: PRINCIPLES AND PROCESS 302 (5th ed. 2015).

- The receipt of satisfactory assurances that the project, as designed, can be built on time and on budget; and

- The construction of the project in accordance with the articulated project design and sound construction practices.

If the developer is to achieve these three objectives, it must: put together a strong team of design and construction professionals; adopt a delivery system that is well-suited for the developer's project; and put in place contracts that are designed to properly incentivize and regulate the conduct of the selected design and construction professionals. The remainder of this chapter is focused on a discussion of these developer responsibilities.

III. THE DESIGN AND CONSTRUCTION PROCESS

A real estate development lawyer cannot properly serve the developer during the sixth stage of a development project unless the lawyer first understands the process involved in designing and constructing a project. The design and construction process involves the developer's expenditure of great sums of money to create a final tangible product that is acceptable to its customers. From start to finish, the process can take anywhere from six months for a simple commercial project to upwards of ten years for a large mixed use project.

The word that most aptly describes the construction process is "dynamic"—that is, a process that is "characterized by continuous change, activity or progress," and that is also "characterized by much activity and vigor."[2] The dynamic nature of the design and construction process is nicely illustrated in the following quote from a 1981 judicial opinion:

> Except in the middle of a battlefield, nowhere must men coordinate the movement of such chaos and with such limited certainty of present facts and future occurrences as in a huge construction project. . . . Even the most painstaking planning frequently turns out to be mere conjecture and accommodation to changes must necessarily be of the rough, quick and *ad hoc* sort, analogous to ever-changing commands of the battlefield.[3]

The dynamic nature of the design and construction process produces an environment that is more conducive than any other stage of a development project to the generation of disputes among the various participants in that process. It is the job of the real estate development lawyer to fashion contract documents that have as their core objective the

---

[2] *See* THE FREE DICTIONARY (2017), at http://www.thefreedictionary.com.

[3] *See* Blake Construction Co. v. C.J. Coakley Co., 431 A.2d 569, 575 (D.C. App. 1981), quoted in Stanley P. Sklar, *Drafting and Negotiating Construction Contracts*, in DRAFTING AND NEGOTIATING TOMORROW'S CONSTRUCTION CONTRACTS TODAY 31, 35 (Stanley P. Sklar Chair, 2009).

avoidance of unnecessary construction disputes—a job that requires the lawyer to fully understand both developer's business objectives and the inherently risky nature of the design and construction process.

The design and construction process consists of three phases—(1) the planning phase, (2) the design phase, and (3) the construction phase. During the planning phase, the developer determines the location and general nature, size, and scope of its proposed project (for example, a four story Class A office building in Orlando, Florida). This is the work that the developer must complete early on in the development process (and certainly before it waives its purchase contract contingencies). For the purposes of the discussion in this chapter, it is assumed that the developer has successfully concluded the planning phase and is ready to embark on the design and construction phases of the process.

A. DESIGN PHASE

At the inception of the design phase, the developer provides the architect with the developer's requirements for the contemplated development project. Those requirements (commonly referred to in the real estate industry as the developer's ***programmatic requirements*** or ***program***) include: the specific location of the project land; the type and size of the project (for example, a four-story speculative office building); the developer's construction budget and schedule for the project; any aesthetic factors that the developer wants to see incorporated into the project (for example a glass curtain wall exterior or a two-story, interior atrium); any performance requirements that the developer has for the project (for example, an HVAC system that complies with a specific industry standard); the developer's marketing strategy for the building (for example, the targeting of mostly full-floor tenants); and any other considerations that the developer wants to see incorporated into the architect's final design package.

With the details of the developer's program in hand, the architect then assumes responsibility for preparing plans and specifications that specifically delineate all aesthetic and functional components of the design of the project. Following its initial meeting with the developer, the architect prepares general design drawings and guidelines (known as ***schematic drawings***) for the developer's review, including a site plan, building elevations, outline specifications, floor plans, and exterior renderings. Once the schematic drawings are approved by the developer, the architect then moves on to the preparation of more detailed drawings (***design development drawings***) that incorporate all the approved aspects of the schematic drawings and add new detail concerning the building's architectural design and the specifics of the building's structural, mechanical, and electrical systems.

The final stage of the design phase involves the architect's preparation of final plans that then serve as the blueprint for the actual construction of the project by the general contractor selected by the developer. The final plans prepared by the architect include all of the following components:

- A site plan showing the precise footprint of the building and all driveways, parking lots, and other exterior common areas serving the building;

- Civil engineering drawings detailing all site work required for the project (including utility work);

- Architectural drawings indicating the precise look of all exterior and interior improvements, including floor plans for each floor of the building and exterior building elevations;

- Engineering drawings depicting the specific location and nature of all structural, mechanical, electrical, plumbing, and fire protection systems associated with the project;

- Landscaping plans displaying all plantings and other landscaping of the site; and

- Detailed narrative specifications identifying the methods to be followed in constructing the project and the type, quality, and quantity of all materials to be incorporated into the project. The project specifications can be further broken down into the following three categories: (1) design specifications that state "precise measurements, tolerances, materials, construction methods, sequences, quality control, inspection requirements, and other information";[4] (2) performance specifications setting forth the performance standards that must be satisfied in the completed building (for example, those relating to the building's HVAC system); and (3) purchase specifications that specifically identify by product name materials required to be used in constructing the building.[5]

B. CONSTRUCTION PHASE

During the construction phase, the general contractor selected by the developer takes over and builds the project in accordance with the approved final plans. The construction phase (which, for the typical commercial real estate project, lasts between six to 18 months) begins when a shovel is first placed in the dirt and ends when the building is fully

---

[4] JUSTIN SWEET, LEGAL ASPECTS OF ARCHITECTURE, ENGINEERING AND THE CONSTRUCTION PROCESS § 19.01(d) (1994)

[5] See generally JOHN C. CAMERON, JR., A PRACTITIONER'S GUIDE TO CONSTRUCTION LAW at 9–6 (2000 with 2009 Cumulative Supplement).

completed and all required certificates of occupancy and other governmental approvals are received to permit the developer to use the project for its intended purpose. The general contractor's job is to orchestrate the activities of a variety of trades (excavators, steelworkers, plumbers, roofers, electricians, drywallers, carpet installers, etc.) to make sure that the project is completed on time, on budget, and in strict accordance with the quality and aesthetic parameters established by the developer. The challenges faced by the general contractor and the developer during the construction phase are fleshed out in later sections of this chapter.

C. FAST-TRACK CONSTRUCTION

It is important to keep in mind that the three phases of the construction process (that is, planning, design, and construction) occur in neat sequential order in only the rarest of commercial real estate projects. The norm in today's fast-paced real estate industry is for there to be at least some overlap in each of the three phases. The compression of the construction process in this manner is frequently referred to as *fast-track construction*, which, in essence, means that construction of a portion of the project is commenced before the planning and design of the entirety of the project is completed. By way of example, the general contractor might be given the go-ahead to begin excavation of the site before the developer and the architect have reached final agreement on the exterior appearance of the developer's proposed building or the capacity and design of the building's HVAC system. Fast tracking construction makes the construction process even more dynamic and, hence, significantly more risky for every participant in that process.

IV. PLAYERS IN THE DESIGN AND CONSTRUCTION PROCESS

The most vital ingredient of a successful construction process is the developer's selection of the right people to serve on its design and construction team. The developer needs to not only choose highly qualified professionals to serve on its team, but to also make sure that all the chosen professionals work together in a cooperative and collaborative fashion for the benefit of the project as a whole. The real estate development lawyer's mission is to craft contract documents that encourage the various players in the construction process to function as a team and not as isolated adversaries.

The complexity of the construction process is driven, in large measure, by the sheer number of the players who make indispensable contributions to the design and construction of a commercial real estate project. The identity of those players is summarized below.

- *Architect*—The architect is the licensed professional who is principally responsible for the design of the project. The architect's duties extend not just to the aesthetics of the project (does it look pretty), but also to its functionality (does it work for the developer's customers).

- *Engineers*—While the architect serves as the lead professional on all aspects of the project's design, a significant portion of the design work is typically farmed out by the architect to engineers who focus on the design and performance of the project's systems and infrastructure. By way of example, the architect may retain a civil engineer to design the utilities and other site improvements serving the project; a mechanical and electrical engineer to design the building's HVAC and electrical systems; and a structural engineer to design the structural components of the building. The required engineering services are typically provided either by members of the architect's in-house staff or by independent engineering firms hired by the architect as subcontractors.

- *General Contractor*—The general contractor is the person who is responsible for constructing the project in accordance with the plans and specifications prepared by the architect and engineers. It falls to the general contractor to schedule and coordinate the activities of all firms providing construction services or materials for the project.

- *Subcontractors*—The general contractor typically subcontracts components of the work to specialized trade contractors (for example, site excavators, steel erectors, plumbers, electricians, drywallers, carpenters, painters, and HVAC installers).

- *Suppliers*—The general contractor also enters into contractual arrangements with a variety of suppliers to acquire materials for incorporation into the building being constructed on the project site. By way of example, the general contractor may assume direct responsibility for buying all cabinetry and floor covering that is then furnished to those subcontractors who are assigned the jobs of installing those materials in the building.

- *Government*—Federal, state, and local governments play a very important role in regulating the manner in which a commercial project is designed and constructed. The two pieces of federal legislation that most directly affect the construction process are The Americans with Disabilities Act[6] (governing required means of access for persons with disabilities) and The Occupational Safety and Health Act[7] (setting forth standards for workers' safety and health on jobsites). State building codes provide standards governing the practices and materials used in connection with the construction of commercial projects, and local zoning and building codes regulate matters of design (for example, building height, setback lines, and required parking areas) and set forth the requirements that must be met for the issuance of a building permit and a certificate of occupancy for a project.

- *Construction Lender*—The construction lender is the person who provides the funds required to pay a majority of the costs of designing and constructing the developer's project. The construction lender imposes on the developer a separate set of requirements concerning the design and construction of the project. Principal among such requirements is the lender's insistence that no construction loan proceeds will be disbursed until such time as an independent architect or engineer hired by the lender has visited the jobsite to confirm that the construction work that is the subject of the developer's loan disbursement request has, in fact, been completed.

- *Developer*—As the person with the most at stake on any construction project, the developer must exercise extreme vigilance in the oversight of all aspects of the project design and construction and the orchestration of the activities of all the players involved in that endeavor. It is essential that all substantive aspects of the design and construction process be subject to the developer's final approval.

- *Real Estate Development Lawyer*—The real estate development lawyer's primary job during Stage 6 is the preparation and negotiation of design and construction documents that empower the developer to oversee the construction process and require and incentivize the various players in that process to perform their services in a collaborative fashion that is consistent with the developer's business needs. Unfortunately, the developer all too often fails to involve its lawyer in those contract negotiations and, instead, opts to execute construction and design documents

---

6   *See* 42 U.S.C. §§ 12101–12213 (2016).

7   *See* 29 U.S.C. §§ 651–678 (2016).

prepared by opposing counsel based on the theory that the documents are "standard forms that everyone uses." In that case, the role of the real estate development lawyer is reduced to fighting battles with the general contractor and architect over disputes that could have been avoided if the real estate development lawyer had been given the opportunity to craft the contract documents in the first instance.

Practice Tip #10-1: Learning the Construction Process

My biggest regret about my years in practice is that I never understood the construction process as well as I should have. While I forced myself to learn all that I could about the development business (including a decent "walking around" knowledge of project economics), I did not apply the same effort to acquaint myself with the intricacies involved in the design and construction of a commercial building. As a result, I found myself acting during Stage 6 as more of a legal technician than a well-rounded advisor and counselor. I knew my way around the standard design and construction documents and felt comfortable dealing with the key "legal issues" that typically surfaced during negotiations with counsel for the general contractor and architect. However, my limited knowledge of the design and construction disciplines often put me at a disadvantage in those negotiations and forced me to interrupt the flow of the discussions by making the hapless statement that "I will have to get back to you on that point after I check with my construction folks." I had, in other words, forgotten the mantra set forth in the first chapter of this book—if you want to succeed as a real estate development lawyer, you first need to understand the real estate development business.

The following practitioner-authored quote further illustrates my mistake—

"The best fisherman in the world will not fare well in unfamiliar waters. Likewise, the best attorney in the world cannot provide sufficient counsel with respect to the construction process if he is unfamiliar with it."[8]

My advice to aspiring real estate lawyers is to do everything within their power to learn about the construction and design process (advice which I took to heart only in the last couple years of my practice career). Here are some tips on how the young (or not so young) lawyer can go about doing just that:

---

[8]   Phillip E. Beck, *Construction Contracts*, in COMMERCIAL REAL ESTATE TRANSACTIONS HANDBOOK, Chapter 4, at 4–9 (Mark A. Senn ed., 4th ed. 2011).

- *Visit the jobsite (and experience the pleasure of putting on a hard hat);*

- *Buy an architect or general contractor lunch to talk about business;*

- *Read whatever you can get your hands on describing the design and construction process;*

- *Attend job meetings where the general contractor, architect, and other professionals talk about the progress of the construction project; and*

- *Ask questions of the developer and anyone else involved in the construction process.*

One bit of final advice—make it clear to your client that you are doing all of these things "off the clock." Your reward will be that you become a better lawyer—and, by the way, get more business as a result.

V. SELECTING THE DESIGN AND CONSTRUCTION TEAM

There are two ways to select members of the developer's design and construction team—bidding and negotiation. In a bidding arrangement, the developer sends its program requirements to a select group of qualified professionals and asks each of them to submit its best bid for the project. The "bid" generally consists of the bidder's proposed price and schedule for the performance of the programmed work and, if the subject of the bid is design work, preliminary design drawings and specifications. Once the developer receives all of the submitted bids, it selects the bidder's proposal that the developer believes is best suited for the project. In the context of general contractors' bids, the developer usually accepts the lowest bid or, if the bidders have not been sufficiently pre-qualified, the "lowest responsible bid."[9] The selected bidder is then formally hired to perform the job on terms and conditions that are consistent with the developer's program requirements and the bidder's submitted bid.

A bid arrangement is normally used by a developer to select its general contractor when the project design is fully complete and the developer is in a position to deliver final construction plans to the general contractors on its bid list. In such a situation, the developer hopes that the competition spawned by the bid process will produce the lowest possible price for the construction work. The bidding process is also frequently used by the

---

[9]   *See* CAMERON, *supra* note 5, at 8–7.

general contractor to select subcontractors and suppliers for certain components of the construction job.

As alluded to above, the bid process only works if the design of the work being bid out is fully complete (or very nearly so). If the design is incomplete, a bid recipient will be unable to determine with the desired precision how long it will take to complete the work and what it will cost it to do so. As a result, the bidder will not be in a position to "sharpen its pencil" on its bid and will either refuse to bid on the project or will submit a high-ball bid that is replete with assumptions, qualifications, limitations, and contingencies.

Selecting a design or construction professional through negotiation means exactly what it sounds like—the developer selects a firm that it believes has the financial wherewithal and technical expertise and experience to do the job and then sits down with the selected firm to see if the parties can reach a mutually acceptable arrangement for the performance of the work. The architect and other design professionals are customarily selected by negotiation, as are general contractors, subcontractors and suppliers when the design of the work has not yet been completed.

There are many reasons why a developer might opt to select its general contractor by negotiation even if the project design is complete. Foremost among those reasons is that the developer may have an established working relationship with a general contractor that it believes is ideally suited to perform the work because of the general contractor's financial strength and its expertise and experience in developing similar projects. The developer may also want to involve the selected general contractor in discussions with the architect concerning the design of the project and in sales presentations to potential users of space in the developed project. Finally, the developer may need to fast-track the construction process and cannot afford to take the extra time required to wade its way through the cumbersome and time-consuming bid process.

The trend in recent years is for a private developer to select its design and construction team by means of negotiation and not a bidding process. For that reason, the discussion in the remainder of this chapter assumes that the developer has opted to select its team through a process of individualized negotiations.

VI. PROJECT DELIVERY SYSTEMS

Once the members of the design and construction team are selected by the developer, the next question that arises is what contract structure should be utilized to establish the responsibilities and authorities of the three prime players in the construction process—that is the developer, architect, and general contractor. The method for assigning responsibility and authority to those three players is referred to in the construction industry as a ***project delivery system***.

There are three basic categories of project delivery systems— (1) ***design-bid-build***, (2) ***construction management***, and (3) ***design-build***. The definition and respective advantages and disadvantages to the developer of each of these project delivery systems are discussed below.[10]

A. DESIGN-BID-BUILD

The ***design-bid-build*** delivery system is also referred to as the "traditional delivery method." The "traditional" designation is assigned to the design-bid-build system because it reflects the historical norm of the developer assigning responsibility for the design function to the architect under one contract and the responsibility for the construction function to the general contractor under a separate contract. In the design-bid-build arrangement, the design and construction functions are performed sequentially, with the project design being finalized before the construction contract is awarded or the construction work is started. The completed plans and specifications prepared by the architect are used by the developer to define the scope of work specified in the contract awarded by the developer to the general contractor.

The tripartite contractual arrangement evidenced by the design-bid-build system is described graphically in the following diagram.

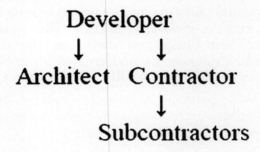

In the design-bid-build system, the developer enters into two separate contracts—one with the architect for the performance of the project design and one with the general contractor for the performance of the project construction. There is no direct contractual relationship between the architect and the general contractor, nor is there any privity of contract

---

[10] For a detailed discussion of the advantages and disadvantages of the different project delivery methods, *see generally* CAMERON, *supra* note 5, at 8–14 through 8–71 of 2009 Supplement; Stanley P. Sklar, *An Overview of Architect and Construction Contracts*, in ALI-ABA COURSE OF STUDY MATERIALS, MODERN REAL ESTATE TRANSACTIONS, Course #SM–002, 2–5 (July 2006); Beck, *supra* note 8 at 4–9 through 4–22; and Robert A. Rubin and Linda M. Thomas-Mobley, *Delivery Systems*, in FUNDAMENTALS OF CONSTRUCTION LAW, Chapter 6 (Carina Y. Enhada, Cheri Turnage Gatlin and Fred D. Wilshusen eds., 2001).

between the developer and the subcontractors (all of whom report directly to the general contractor).

The following are the principal advantages and disadvantages of the design-bid-build system.

Advantages

- The existence of two separate contracts creates a natural check and balance between the authority of the architect and that of the general contractor.

- The design-bid-build method can produce certainty and lower construction costs (assuming that the general contractor's contract is awarded on the basis of final plans prepared by the architect).

- The segregation of the design and construction functions and the performance of those functions in a neat sequential order lend predictability to the construction process, which, in turn, reduces the developer's risk.

- The general contractor has full responsibility and liability for the performance (or non-performance) of all the subcontractors and suppliers.

Disadvantages

- The segregation of the design and construction functions into two contractual "silos" creates a natural tension between the architect and the general contractor. This tension inhibits productive communications between the design and construction professionals and creates an environment in which there is an increased potential for disputes.

- The design-bid-build method does not lend itself to fast-track construction where the design and construction phases of the project overlap to a significant extent.

- The sequencing of the design and construction phases can cause a protracted construction schedule.

- The insertion of the general contractor as a contractual buffer between the developer and the subcontractors can result in higher construction costs because of the additional administrative costs and profit mark-up charged to the project by the general contractor.

B. CONSTRUCTION MANAGEMENT

A second project delivery system is construction management. In a "pure" construction management system (frequently referred to as *construction management—agency* or *CMa*),[11] the developer adds a fourth player to the design and construction process by hiring an independent construction manager to provide the developer with advice concerning the design and construction of the project. The construction manager (usually a construction professional, but occasionally an architect or engineer) is typically hired by the developer prior to the completion of the project design. The construction manager serves as an agent of the owner in: reviewing the architect's proposed design; developing an overall budget for the project; obtaining and negotiating project bids; and supervising the general contractor's performance of its construction work.

The following diagram illustrates the interrelationship of the four parties under the CMa system.

Developer → Construction Manager
↓   **↓**
Architect Contractor
↓
Subcontractors

The construction manager in a CMa arrangement has no contractual relationship with either the architect or the general contractor, but simply serves as an advisor to the developer in the developer's oversight of the functions performed by the architect and the general contractor.

A variation of the pure construction management system described above is the *construction management at risk* or *CM@r*. In the construction management at risk system, the construction manager serves in two capacities—as (1) the owner's advisor during the planning and design phases of the construction process, and (2) the general contractor during the construction phase. The arrangement of the players in a CM@r system is diagrammed in the following manner.

---

[11] *See generally* Rubin *supra* note 10, at 182; and CAMERON *supra* note 5, at 8–50 through 8–94 of the 2009 Supplement.

Developer
↓   ↓
Architect   Construction Manager
↓
Subcontractors

The CM@r arrangement is similar in all respects but one to the design-bid-build method described in the prior section of this chapter. The one difference between the design-bid-build system and CM@r is that in the CM@r method, the construction manager provides advisory services to the developer during the planning and design phases of the construction process. Once those phases of the process are completed, the construction manager sheds its advisory role and assumes direct contractual responsibility for the prosecution of the construction work. The continuity of the construction manager's efforts throughout the entirety of the construction process (including the planning and design phases) has made the CM@R method a more popular delivery system choice for developers than the pure construction management-agency method.

Advantages

- The primary advantage of the CMa arrangement is that it provides a developer that does not have in-house capabilities with an effective means of managing the activities of the architect and the general contractor throughout the construction process.

- In addition to the advantages summarized previously with respect to the design-bid-build method, the CM@r method provides the developer with the added benefit of its receipt of advice from an independent professional during the planning and design phases of the construction process.

Disadvantages

- The disadvantage of the CMa method is that the additional fee payable to the construction manager increases the developer's total project costs.

- Unlike the design-bid-build method, there is a notable lack of case law interpreting the role that a construction manager serves during the construction process.[12]

---

[12] *See* CAMERON, *supra* note 5, at 8–57 of the 2009 Supplement.

- Because the CM@r method is largely indistinguishable from the design-bid-build method, the disadvantages of that construction management system are similar to those applicable to the design-bid-build methodology.

C. DESIGN-BUILD

Over the last 30 years, the ***design-build*** delivery system has become a very popular choice of developers. Under the design-build system, the design and construction functions are combined and delegated to a single entity known as the ***design-builder***. The developer enters into a single contract with the design-builder who contractually agrees to be responsible for both the design of the project and its ultimate construction. The design-builder is typically a general contractor who hires the necessary design professionals either as part of its in-house staff or as subcontractors. The design-builder can also be an architect or a joint venture entity created for the project by a general contractor and an architect.[13]

The following is a diagrammatic depiction of the relationship of the parties in a typical design-build arrangement.

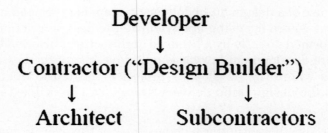

Advantages

- The developer has a single point of contact and responsibility for all aspects of the design and construction of its project. As such, the developer does not have to waste time trying to figure out whether a particular construction defect or delay was caused by the architect or the general contractor (both of whom are quite expert at pointing the finger at the other when a problem arises).

- Because the construction and design professionals are working together as a team (and not as separate functional silos), there is a greater potential to reduce project costs (through value engineering) and expedite project completion

---

[13] *See* Harvey W. Berman, *Understanding Project Delivery Methods,* 15 No. 2 PRACTICAL REAL ESTATE LAWYER 4 (March 1999).

(by overlapping the design and construction phases in a fast-track approach to the construction process).

- The design-build method has been shown to significantly reduce the number of disputes between and claims filed by members of the construction and design teams.[14]

Disadvantages

- The principal disadvantage of the design-build system is that it eliminates the checks and balances provided by the separation of the design and construction functions into separate contracts. In non-design-build structures, the architect's primary allegiance is to the developer. Reversing that arrangement by having the architect be responsible to the general contractor creates a developer fear that "the fox would be guarding the hen house" and that construction and design problems might be "swept under the rug."[15]

- The developer's contact with the architect (and hence its control over the design process) is limited in a design-build structure.

- The use of a design build delivery system is restricted in some states where licensing laws require the design function to be performed directly by a licensed architectural firm.[16] The real estate development lawyer should investigate the laws of the state where the developer's project is located to make sure that the design build delivery system can be utilized in that state.

- There is a potential for a cheapening of the overall quality of the project because all design and construction decisions are being made jointly by the design-builder. This potential for a reduction in the project's overall quality standards is heightened in those instances where the developer fails to provide the design-builder with detailed program requirements for its project.

D. HYBRID DELIVERY SYSTEMS

There are countless hybrid delivery systems that mix and match various elements of the three principal categories of delivery systems discussed above. Two hybrid systems that have gained some traction in the

---

[14] *See* Beck, *supra* note 8, at 4–18.

[15] Beck, *supra* note 8, at 4–18.

[16] *See* CAMERON, *supra* note 5, at 8–99 of 2009 Supplement.

construction industry in the last several years are (1) the multiple prime contractor method,[17] and (2) the integrated project delivery method.[18]

1.   Multiple Prime Contractor

Under the *multiple prime contractor method*, the owner enters into contracts with the architect and each of the prime trade contractors involved in the construction of the project. In this arrangement, there is no general contractor assigned with the task of coordinating the activities of the various trade contractors and suppliers. The owner effectively plays the role of the general contractor and, as such, is directly responsible for the scheduling, oversight, and payment of all the players in the construction process. The multiple prime contractor method provides the owner with the maximum control over the construction process and further permits it to fast-track the construction process by entering into contracts for components of the project (for example, excavation and site work) before the project design is completed. The multiple prime system also reduces the developer's overall project costs by eliminating the developer's obligation to pay a general contractor's fee and overhead. The obvious disadvantage of the multiple prime structure is that it places an incredible burden on the developer to assume responsibility for managing all aspects of the construction process. A developer can lessen the impact of that burden by hiring a construction manager-agent to help it coordinate the construction efforts of the trade contractors and suppliers.

2.   Integrated Project Delivery

The *integrated project delivery method* is a relatively new and quite revolutionary theory of project delivery that stresses the collaboration of the developer, general contractor, and architect throughout all phases of the construction process. Integrated project delivery is described by one industry group as "a project delivery approach that integrates people, systems, business structures and practices into a process that collaboratively harnesses the talents and insights of all participants to reduce waste and optimize efficiency through all phases of design, fabrication and construction."[19] Wow—that is quite a mouthful, isn't it?

---

[17] *See generally*, Berman, *supra* note 13, at 8; and Beck, *supra* note 8, at 4–12.

[18] *See generally* Howard W. Ashcraft, Jr., *Negotiating an Integrated Project Delivery Agreement*, in DRAFTING AND NEGOTIATING TOMORROW'S CONSTRUCTION CONTRACTS TODAY 353 (Stanley P. Sklar chair 2009); and Patrick J. O'Connor, *Integrated Project Delivery: Collaboration Through New Contract Forms*, in DRAFTING AND NEGOTIATING TOMORROW'S CONSTRUCTION CONTRACTS TODAY, 31, 35 (Stanley P. Sklar Chair, 2009); and George J. Meyer and Lauren Catoe, *Integrated Project Delivery: And Now for Something Completely Different*, in ACREL PAPERS Tab 13 (Fall 2015).

[19] *See* AIA CALIFORNIA COUNCIL, INTEGRATED PROJECT DELIVERY, available online at http://www.aiacc.org/integrated-project-delivery/.

Characteristics of the integrated project delivery system include the following:[20]

- The involvement of all three of the key players (that is, the developer, general contractor, and architect) at all time during the planning, design, and construction phases of the construction process;

- The collaborative design of the project to meet agreed-upon performance requirements and budgetary constraints;

- The joint management of the project by consensus of the developer, general contractor, and architect;

- The establishment of a targeted project cost determined through the collaborative efforts of all three players;

- The establishment of compensation incentives for each of the three players that are designed to reward and, where appropriate, punish the players based upon the financial outcome of the project; and

- A waiver or limitation of the liability of the three participants to each other with respect to their respective project performances.

The integrated project delivery system is a largely untested theory that is intended to use emerging technologies and collaborative delivery models in an effort to reduce project costs, eliminate construction delays, and minimize construction disputes. While the integrated project delivery system may have a positive application for certain types of projects (primarily public projects, such as schools, hospitals, and the like), the ceding of developer control that is a key component of the system makes its utility for private development projects highly suspect.

E. SELECTING A DELIVERY SYSTEM

So how does a developer decide which project delivery system it should use for its project? The developer must first understand that just as there is no one set of clothes that fits every person, there is no one delivery system that is the best choice for all commercial real estate projects. The selection of the right delivery system for a particular project depends on the nature of the project and the business objectives and capabilities of the developer.

The following schematic lists a number of common project/developer attributes and then indicates which of the three primary project delivery system is best suited to deal with that attribute (with the following short-hand references being used to describe the project delivery system

---

[20] *See generally* Ashcraft, *supra* note 18, at 372–390; and Meyer, *supra* note 18, at 1–2.

alternatives: DBB = design-bid-build; CMa = construction management agency; CM@r = construction management at risk; and DB = design-build).

- The aesthetics of the project are important and novel → DBB or CMa.

- The project design has been used by the developer on prior projects in other locales → DB.

- The developer has an experienced in-house design and construction staff → DBB or DB.

- The developer has limited in-house design or construction capabilities → DB or CM@r.

- The project needs to be fast-tracked → DB.

- The developer has plenty of time to complete design and bid out the work → DBB.

- The developer wants to secure pricing at the lowest possible number → DBB.

- The project's programmatic requirements are well-defined by the developer → DB or DBB.

- The project's program requirements are not well-defined → DBB or CMa.

- The developer is a "control freak" → DBB.

When selecting a project delivery system, the developer must identify and prioritize all of its design and construction goals for the subject project and then determine which project delivery system will best enable it to meet those goals in a timely and cost-effective manner.

VII. DESIGN AND CONSTRUCTION CONTRACTS

Once the developer (with the advice and counsel of its lawyer) has selected the appropriate delivery system, the lawyer must set about the task of drafting and negotiating design and construction contracts for the project. The remainder of this chapter focuses on the key legal issues that the real estate development lawyer must take into consideration when preparing those contracts.

A. CONTRACT FORMS

Stage 6 is unique in that most design and construction contracts drafted by the real estate development lawyer make use of pre-printed standard forms published by trade associations representing either the architect or the general contractor. The American Institute of Architects (AIA), the Associated General Contractors of America (AGC) and the Engineers Joint Contract Documents Committee (EJCDC) have all produced a series of contract forms designed for each of the basic project delivery systems described in the preceding section of this chapter. The Design Build Institute of America (DBIA) has published a series of standard form contracts for use on design-build projects. Finally, in 2007, a group of 24 construction industry associations representing designers, owners, general contractors, subcontractors, and sureties joined together to create a new alternative set of standard contract forms called the ConsensusDOCS.[21]

The contract documents promulgated by the AIA remain the contract forms most commonly used during Stage 6 of a development project (although the ConsensusDOCS have gained a strong following since their introduction in 2007). The AIA set of forms consist of two separate documents—(1) the specific agreement between the owner and the general contractor or architect, and (2) the general rules governing the construction process (referred to in the AIA documents as "general conditions."

All the standard forms prepared by the noted industry groups attempt both to set forth the specific business deal struck by the parties and to establish a general set of rules governing the assignment and allocation of rights, responsibilities and liabilities among the owner, the architect, the general contractor, and subcontractors. The standard forms are extremely thorough in describing the relationship between the players in the construction process and, hence, serve as an excellent starting point for the real estate development lawyer's preparation of design and construction contracts for its client's project.

The real estate development lawyer must, however, keep in mind that the standard contract forms published by the AIA, AGC, EJCDC, DBIA, and other industry groups all have a decided bias in favor of the player represented by the author of those documents—which, in all instances, is someone other than the developer. As one practicing lawyer accurately noted, "from the developer's perspective, there are three things which must be understood about printed forms of design and construction contracts: (a) they are not fair; (b) they are not adequate; and (c) they generally do not reflect the agreement between the parties."[22] It is, therefore, imperative that the real estate development lawyer read every single word of the proffered standard forms and then revise them to better protect the developer and reflect the deal struck with the other players in the construction process.

Alternatively, the real estate development lawyer could prepare original construction and design documents tailored to meet the needs of

---

[21] *See* ConsensusDOCS Construction Contracts (2007), available at http://www.consensus docs.org/catalog; and Beck, *supra* note 8, at 4.37 through 4.46.1.

[22] John D. Hastie, *Architectural and Construction Contracts: The Developer's Perspective*, in ALI-ABA COURSE OF STUDY MATERIALS, MODERN REAL ESTATE TRANSACTIONS, Course #SB-08 2 (August1996).

the developer and the subject project. For a host of reasons (primarily a lack of opportunity, time, and expertise), the real estate development lawyer rarely wins the "battle of the forms" with a general contractor or an architect and, therefore, is forced to deal with the maze of the standard pre-printed forms created by the construction and design industries.

The discussion in the remainder of this chapter does not deal with any specific set of industry-sponsored contract forms because those forms are so complex as to render any examination of their specific provisions well beyond the scope of this chapter. Moreover, those standard forms are in a constant state of revision and, therefore, any analysis of their specific provisions would be outdated almost as soon as it was written. The limited purpose of this chapter is to highlight those key legal issues that a real estate development lawyer needs to think about during the course of the lawyer's negotiation of design and construction contracts—all of which are equally applicable to each of the project delivery systems discussed in the preceding section of this chapter. Those of you interested in learning the specific ins and outs of revising the AIA, AGC, EJCDC, DBIA, and ConsensusDOCS forms should consult the excellent articles on that topic noted in the accompanying footnote.[23]

Practice Tip #10-2: Drafting Design and Construction Contracts

The first tip I will offer up about the drafting of design and construction contracts is that the real estate development lawyer's first job is to convince the developer that it really is a good idea for the lawyer to review the contracts BEFORE the developer executes them. Developers for some unfathomable reason often fail to involve their lawyers in the negotiation of the design and construction contracts, preferring instead to delegate that task to internal non-lawyer staff members. Design and construction contracts are highly complex legal documents that can directly impact the success or failure of the developer's project. The real estate development lawyer's participation in the preparation, review, and negotiation of those documents is every bit as warranted as is the lawyer's involvement in

---

[23] *See e.g.,* CAMERON, *supra* note 5, at Chapters 6, 8 and 10; Mark C. Friedlander, *Drafting an Effective Design Agreement Using the 2007 AIA Documents: A Practical Guide to New and Controversial Issues in AIA B101—2007*, in DRAFTING AND NEGOTIATING TOMORROW'S CONSTRUCTION CONTRACTS TODAY 107 (Stanley P. Sklar chair, 2009); Steve G.M. Stein and Ronald O. Wietecha, *A Comparison of ConsensusDOCS and AIA Form Construction Contract Agreements*, in DRAFTING AND NEGOTIATING TOMORROW'S CONSTRUCTION CONTRACTS TODAY 207 (Stanley P. Sklar chair, 2009); DANIEL S. BRENNAN, MICHAEL J. HANAHAN, JENNIFER A. NIELSEN AND I. SPANGLER III, THE CONSTRUCTION CONTRACTS BOOK: HOW TO FIND COMMON GROUND IN NEGOTIATING DESIGN AND CONSTRUCTION CLAUSES (2d ed. 2008); and Lynn R. Axelroth, *There Must Be Some Way Out of Here: The Ten Top Issues in Negotiating AIA Form Contracts*, in ACREL PAPERS 21 (Spring 2005).

preparing the land purchase contract, the LLC operating agreement, or the project lease.

The following are four additional tips related to the drafting of design and construction contracts.

- *Put the developer in control of the process. The developer is the person who has by far the most entrepreneurial risk during Stage 6. For that reason, it is imperative that the developer must be the final arbiter of all decisions made during the design and construction process. Most of the preprinted design and construction contracts published by the AIA and other trade groups purport to delegate significant decision-making authority to either the architect or the general contractor. Those provisions must be excised from the developer's contracts and replaced with provisions that cement the developer's position as the "king of the hill" throughout Stage 6. As one seasoned real estate practitioner correctly observed "It is supercilious to suggest that the developer who is responsible for paying the design and construction costs and satisfying the ultimate requirements of end users should have little or no voice in the implementation of the construction contract."[24]*

- *Make sure all the contracts are internally consistent. It is common for there to be a number of contract documents executed in connection with the design and construction of the developer's project (including loan documents evidencing the developer's construction loan). It is important that all these documents treat the same topic in the same way. By way of example, if the developer's loan agreement with its construction lender requires the sign-off of the architect on any draw request submitted to the lender for payment, then the developer's contracts with the architect and general contractor should contain a similar requirement.*

- *Don't overreach in an effort to protect the developer. The Stage 6 contracts establish the relationships among the various members of the design and construction team, all of whom must work together to produce a successful development project. Each such contract "resembles a marriage contract more than a sales transaction or real estate deal."[25] One practitioner provided the following sage advice on how to approach a negotiation of those "marriage contracts"—"If the process of negotiating the design and construction documents*

---

[24] Hastie, *supra* note 22, at 4.
[25] Beck, *supra* note 8, at 4–9.

is undertaken with a patently adversarial attitude, the confrontations which exist during the negotiation phase might well infect the project throughout its duration and provide impetus for the architect or general contractor to 'get even' during the course of producing the project.'[26] *The real estate development lawyer must resist the natural urge to protect the developer at all costs and, instead, remember that the developer is best served by the production of legal documents that foster cooperation (and not conflict) among the players in the construction process.*

- *Follow the guiding principle that "risk and responsibility should follow control." The focus of design and construction contracts is the assignment of responsibility for the performance of a particular task and the allocation of liability should that responsibility not be performed in the contemplated manner. While the contracting parties are generally free to assign responsibility and allocate risk in whatever fashion they deem appropriate, the inclusion of contract provisions that assign risk or responsibility for the performance of a particular task to a party who is not in control of such performance can be counter-productive and lead to the generation of unnecessary disputes among the players in the construction process.*[27]

B. KEY LEGAL ISSUES IN DESIGN CONTRACT

This section addresses some of the key legal issues that arise during the course of the real estate development lawyer's negotiation of the design contract with the project architect.[28] The noted issues exist regardless which project delivery system is selected by the developer for its project.

---

[26]   Hastie, *supra* note 22, at 2.

[27]   Provisions that seek to assign risk and responsibility to a party who has little, if any, power to control or influence an outcome are commonly referred to as "killer clauses." *See* Beck, *supra* note 8, at 4–56 through 4–58, for an analysis of killer clauses. As Mr. Beck notes in the cited article, "*Generally speaking*, a court will give effect to a contract provision placing an inordinate amount of risk on one party even though the result may appear to be 'unfair' or 'unreasonable.' As with most rules, however, there are exceptions; and in this area of the law, the exceptions sometimes seem to swallow the rule." *Id.* at 4–58.

[28]   For a more thorough discussion of the issues that flow out of the negotiation of the design contract, *see generally* CAMERON, *supra* note 5, at *Chapter 5, Preparing a Design Services Agreement*; and Thomas M. Keranen, *The Design Professional*, IN FUNDAMENTALS OF CONSTRUCTION LAW 49 (Carina Y. Enhada, Cheri Turnage Gatlin and Fed D. Wilshusen, eds. 2001).

1. Scope of Services

The first issue that the real estate developer must resolve is exactly what services the architect is required to perform for the project. There are two prongs to the scope of services issue—(1) what is the project that the architect is supposed to design, and (2) what specific services and documents is the architect required to furnish in connection with the project design?

With respect to the first prong, it is incumbent upon the developer to provide the architect with program requirements for the project that set out in as much detail as reasonably practicable the developer's vision for the project. That vision includes the location, type, and size of the proposed project (for example, a 100,000-square-foot office building on a specific ten-acre site in Orlando, Florida), as well as any aesthetic considerations, performance requirements, and budgetary constraints identified by the developer as part of its definition of the design of the project. The developer's provision of a detailed set of program requirements enables the architect to get the project design right on its first try, thereby avoiding the delays and added costs triggered by the architect later having to redesign the project due to a misunderstanding between the developer and the architect about the nature and scope of the project.

The architect's contract should also detail the specific services that the architect is required to perform in connection with its work on the developer's project. The following are samples of questions that should be raised and resolved by the real estate development lawyer with respect to this second prong of the scope of services issue.[29]

- Will the architect be required to prepare schematic design, design development, and construction drawings for the project (or just a limited subset of those categories of drawings)?

- Will the architect be required to provide the developer with **as-built drawings** at the completion of the project that reflect any modifications made to the agreed-upon construction drawings prior to completion of the project's construction?

- Will the architect serve in the role of an **inspecting architect** during the project's construction phase (that is, the person assigned responsibility for making regular jobsite visits to confirm that the progress of construction conforms to the final plans and that the general contractor's draw requests relate to work actually completed on the project)?

---

[29] *See generally* Carl J. Circo, *Building a Better Construction and Design Contract*, 46 No. 2 PRACTICAL LAWYER 2 (July 2000).

- What role, if any, will the architect have in communicating with the general contractor and resolving any disputes between the owner and the general contractor concerning the compliance of the general contractor's work with the final plans?[30]

- Will the architect be required to attend periodic job meetings with representatives of the developer and general contractor throughout the construction process?

- Will the architect be required to appear at public meetings (for example, hearings before a planning and zoning board or a neighborhood commission) to help the developer secure any required approvals for the project?

- Will any specific individuals be required to work on the project on the architect's behalf?

The lawyer's objective should be to prepare a scope of work for the architect that describes in sufficient detail all those services that the architect is required to perform during the design and construction phases. A skimpy or overly general scope of services provision provides the architect with grounds to argue that a particular service requested by the developer is an additional service for which the architect is entitled to additional compensation—a result that is extremely distasteful to the developer.

2. Time for Performance

The design contract should include a timeline that lists the outside date by which the architect is required to perform each component of its design services (for example, the delivery of schematic design drawings within 30 days after contract execution and the delivery of design development drawings within 45 days after the developer's approval of the schematic design). The failure to provide time requirements for the architect's performance of its design services can result in a delayed construction start, which, in turn, can jeopardize the success and profitability of the developer's project.

3. Compensation

There are a number of ways in which the architect may be compensated for its provision of design services. The most common compensation methods are: (1) a fixed fee; (2) a flexible fee based on the

---

[30] The 2007 version of the AIA's standard form documents generally provide that (a) the owner should endeavor to run all of its communications with the contractor through the architect, and (b) the architect will be the initial arbiter of all owner-contractor disputes unless the parties agree to designate some other person to serve as the "Initial Decision Maker." *See* Friedlander, *supra* note 23, at 125 and 131. Both of these provisions are unacceptable to most developers.

number of hours billed to the project and the hourly rates of the design professionals working on the project design; and (3) a fee equal to a stated percentage of the overall project costs While a fixed architectural fee is attractive to the developer because of its certainty, most architects resist the imposition of a fixed fee arrangement unless the owner's program requirements and the architect's scope of services are both tightly defined. By the same token, basing the architect's fee on a percentage of the overall project costs is often unacceptable to the developer because going that route provides the architect with an incentive to design a more costly than necessary project. As a result, most architect contracts adopt a flexible fee model based on the hourly rates of the architects working on the developer's project (hopefully, from the developer's perspective, with a "not to exceed" cap on the overall fee). The architect's contract should clearly state which compensation method is used to determine the architect's fee and when that fee is to be paid (for example, monthly progress payments on an "as incurred" basis, incremental fees payable at the conclusion of each phase of the design process, or a lump sum fee payable on the completion of the architect's services).

There are two other issues related to the architect's compensation scheme that merit further discussion. The first issue is what happens to the architect's fee arrangement if the developer rejects the architect's project design and instructs the architect to "go back to the drawing table"? Is the architect entitled to an additional fee to compensate it for the time and effort spent on the redesign of the project or does the architect have to eat all of its additional redesign costs? The answer to that question is customarily tied to the reason underlying the developer's rejection of the architect's initial design proposals—that is, was the design rejected because of the developer's imposition of a new program requirement (in which event the architect has a strong argument for its receipt of an additional redesign fee) or was the design rejected because it failed to satisfy the specified program requirements or the developer's aesthetic sensibilities (in which event the developer has a sound argument that the architect should do the redesign work for no additional fee).A second issue is whether the architect is entitled to be reimbursed for the business expenses it incurs during the course of its design work and, if so, which business expenses are reimbursable and at what rate? It is fairly typical for the design contract to permit the architect to recover certain of its out-of-pocket expenses, such as copying charges, delivery fees, postage, airfare, hotel charges, and the cost of materials used in producing architectural renderings and models of the project. The careful real estate development lawyer should, however, insist that those reimbursable expenses be limited to the actual amount of the incurred expense—thereby preventing the architect from marking up the amount of its business expenses in an effort to cover the architect's back-office overhead.

4. Ownership of Plans

At common law, the construction drawings, plans, and specifications prepared by the architect for a particular project remain the property of the architect.[31] The principle that the architect owns the plans is also reflected in the AIA's form documents and most other standard pre-printed forms used in the construction industry.[32]

The issue of who owns the design plans involves the clash of two very legitimate, but conflicting views held by the developer and the architect. The developer argues that it has paid for the plans and, therefore, it should have the right to own the plans and use them in any way that it deems appropriate. The architect, on the other hand, asserts that the plans represent its unique work product and that the developer's re-use of those plans would unfairly deprive the architect of its pecuniary interest in the project design and could potentially subject the architect to increased liability. The developer does not want to see the unique design features of its project replicated in competing buildings and the architect is loath to accept the possibility that its created design might appear on a building developed by the developer in another location, without the architect being compensated for the developer's re-use of that design.

The resolution of the issue of who owns the plans turns on the uniqueness of the project design and the relative negotiating leverage of the developer and the architect. At the bare minimum, the developer should require the inclusion in the design contract of the confirmation of three points—(1) the right of the developer to use the plans to complete construction of the project in the event the architect's role in the project is voluntarily or involuntarily terminated, (2) the right of the developer's lender to use the plans if it takes over ownership of the project due to the developer's default under its construction loan, and (3) the right of the developer to use the plans in connection with any future alteration or expansion of the project.[33]

5. Allocation of Risk

There are two primary design risks that should be addressed during the negotiation of the design contract—(1) the risk that the condition of the site (for example, the existence of bad soils) renders the project design infeasible or makes the construction of the designed project more costly

---

[31] *See* Hastie *supra* note 22, at 8.

[32] *See e.g.*, AIA DOCUMENT B101—STANDARD FORM OF AGREEMENT BETWEEN OWNER AND ARCHITECT (2007), §§ 7.1–7.3. *But see* CONSENSUSDOCS 410—OWNER/DESIGN-BUILDER GMP AGREEMENT (2007), which contains provisions transferring ownership of design plans created in the context of a design-build arrangement to the developer upon the developer's making of its final payment to the architect. Note, however, that CONSENSUSDOCS 410 still does not permit the developer's unfettered re-use of the plans for another project without the architect's authorization. *See* Beck, *supra* note 8, at 4–45.

[33] *See* Hastie, *supra* note 22, at 8; and Circo, *supra* note 29, at 2.

than anticipated, and (2) the risk that the project design does not comply with applicable governmental requirements (for example, local building and zoning codes or the Americans with Disabilities Act). Architects typically seek to allocate those risks to the owner, while the owner returns the favor and argues that the architect should indemnify the owner against such risks. A common resolution of this issue is for the architect to assume responsibility for the governmental compliance risk and for the owner to assume (and then try to pass on to the general contractor) the site condition risk.

6. Insurance

An architect is generally liable at common law for all damages incurred by the owner as a result of the architect's negligent performance of its design services.[34] The owner's protection against the architect's negligence is, however, only as good as the architect's credit standing. It is, therefore, crucial that the real estate development lawyer incorporate into the design contract a requirement that the architect maintain professional errors and omissions insurance coverage throughout the duration of the construction process and for a fixed period after the final completion of the project (to give the developer sufficient time to discover any design defects). The real estate development lawyer should consult with the developer's insurance carrier to get a sense of the precise scope and amount of the architect's required insurance coverage. The real estate development lawyer should also make sure to exclude the architect's errors and omissions insurance premiums from the list of "reimbursable expenses" that the architect is contractually permitted to charge back to the owner.

7. Termination

Virtually every design contract contains a provision expressly permitting the developer to terminate the contract if the architect defaults in the performance of its contractual obligations (a "for cause" termination). The owner may, however, also want to terminate its contract with the architect for reasons other than the architect's non-performance. By way of example, the owner may simply decide that the architect, while technically in compliance with its contractual obligations, does not possess the level of creativity, core competency, or communication skills that the developer wants for its project. In such a situation, it may be in the long-term best interests of the project for the developer to terminate the design contract and hire a new architect to provide the project design.

---

[34] *See generally* CAMERON, *supra* note 5, at Chapter 7.

A contract termination that falls outside of the "for cause" category is commonly known as a ***for convenience termination***.[35] The developer should always seek to reserve the right to terminate the architect's contract for convenience. Doing so gives the developer the flexibility to respond to a situation where the developer no longer has confidence in the design capabilities of the original selected architect. The price the developer has to pay for preserving the right to effect such a for convenience termination may be its payment to the architect of a negotiated break-up fee.

C. KEY LEGAL ISSUES IN CONSTRUCTION CONTRACT

The dynamic nature of the construction process creates a number of issues that the real estate development lawyer must take into consideration when crafting the contract that governs the general contractor's construction of the developer's project. The discussion that follows touches on those issues that are most frequently the topic of vigorous negotiations between counsel for the developer and the general contractor. Because it is common for the owner's contract with the general contractor to contain a "flow-through" clause that "requires the . . . general contractor to tie the subcontractors to provisions of the prime contract that affect their work,"[36] the substantive points negotiated by the real estate development lawyer in the developer's contract with its general contractor typically define the entirety of the construction work, including the performance of components of the work by the general contractor's subcontractors and suppliers.

1. Construction Pricing

The most important issue that needs to be addressed in the construction contract is the setting of the price that the developer has to pay the general contractor to complete construction of the project. There are three components of the construction price—(1) the actual cost of completing the project (that is, the cost of all labor and materials paid to trade general contractors and suppliers), (2) the general contractor's cost of administering the project, including temporary utilities, trash removal, and job supervision costs (the ***general condition costs***), and (3) the general contractor's fee (which is intended to cover both the general contractor's unreimbursed overhead expenses and its profit on the project). For the purpose of the following discussion, the "actual cost of the work" refers to the sum of items (1) and (2), above.

The central question that must be resolved when describing the price in the construction contract is who bears the risk and who receives the

---

[35] *See generally* discussion of "for convenience" terminations of the architect's contract in Lynn R. Axelroth, *The Owner's Perspective*, in FUNDAMENTALS OF CONSTRUCTION LAW 1, 18 (Carina Y. Enhada, Cheri Turnage Gatlin and Fred D. Wilshusen, eds., 2001).

[36] SWEET, *supra* note 4, at § 28.04.

reward if the actual cost of the work differs from the developer's budgeted cost of the work. A difference between the actual and budgeted cost of work numbers can be produced by a variety of circumstances—for example, an increase in the cost of construction materials or labor after the date of the execution of the construction contract or an error made by the parties when establishing the initial budget for the cost of the work.

The three pricing mechanisms used in construction contracts are (1) a *stipulated sum*, (2) the *cost of the work, plus a fee*; and (3) a *guaranteed maximum price*.[37] The developer's selection of the pricing method it wishes to use for a particular project is largely dependent on: the status of the plans and specifications when the construction contract is executed; the project delivery system being utilized for the project; the projected construction schedule; and the developer's tolerance for risk. The pros and cons of each of the three construction pricing mechanisms are discussed below.

a.   Stipulated Sum

The stipulated sum method is the simplest way of establishing the construction price to be paid by the developer. In a *stipulated sum contract*, the parties agree to a fixed construction price (for example, $20 million) that is paid by the developer to the general contractor regardless of the actual cost of the work. In a stipulated sum contract, the general contractor assumes the risk that the actual cost of the work is greater than the stipulated contract price (thereby putting in jeopardy the general contractor's anticipated profit from the job). However, the general contractor also gets to retain the additional profit that is produced if the actual cost of the work is less than the stipulated price.

Stipulated sum pricing is attractive to a developer because it fixes the construction cost component of the overall project costs. However, the stipulated sum pricing model only works when the scope of the general contractor's work is tightly defined and the project plans and specifications are complete. If that is not the case, the parties will likely not be able to reach agreement on a stipulated price because the general contractor will, quite rightly, inflate its offered price by adding in a large fudge factor to compensate for the uncertainty surrounding the scope and design of the project. The general contractor's risk-adjusted price is usually unacceptable to the developer. For this reason, the stipulated sum pricing model works best in a design-bid-build arrangement and does not work well at all for projects that are being fast-tracked in a design-build or construction management structure.

---

[37] *See generally* Axelroth, *The Owner's Perspective, supra* note 35, at 20–24; Stanley P. Sklar, *What You Should Know Before You Start the Construction Project—Tips for Dirt Lawyers,* in ACREL PAPERS 1, 5–7 (Spring 2005); and CAMERON, *supra* note 5, at 8–120 through 8–124 of the 2009 Supplement.

b.   Cost of Work, Plus a Fee

Cost plus pricing is often utilized when the precise scope and design of the project has not yet been defined. In a *cost of work, plus a fee contract*, the developer is responsible for reimbursing the general contractor for its actual construction costs (labor and materials provided by trade general contractors and suppliers and the general contractor's general condition costs), plus a fee that is typically calculated as a percentage of the project's construction costs (for example, 3% of the total costs). A cost plus pricing structure places the risk that the actual cost of the work is greater than the budgeted costs entirely on the developer who is required to pay the general contractor its full fee, plus reimburse the general contractor for whatever the general contractor's actual construction costs turn out to be.

If the construction price is set using a cost plus approach, the developer must retain a right to review and verify all of the general contractor's construction cost records. One issue that demands the real estate development lawyer's special attention is the identification of those general conditions costs that fall within the definition of "reimbursable costs" that the developer is required to pay to the general contractor. The general contractor wants to recover as reimbursable costs as much of its home office and overhead expenses as possible (for example, a portion of the salaries and benefits payable to its accounting staff and other personnel having a limited role in administering the general contractor's construction of the project). The developer, on the other hand, strives to limit the general contractor's reimbursable costs to those general contractor-incurred expenses that are specifically attributable to the developer's project (for example, the direct cost of furnishing temporary utilities and trash removal services to the jobsite). A compromise that is commonly reached on this issue is either for the cost of the general contractor's general conditions to be expressed as a fixed number (for example, $100,000) or for the entire concept to be jettisoned with a concomitant increase in the amount of the general contractor's fee.

While the cost plus pricing mechanism has the advantage of permitting the developer to kick off its construction project before the design and scope of the project are fully-developed, the disadvantages of the cost plus method far outweigh that single advantage. From the developer's perspective, a pure cost of work, plus a fee pricing model has two principal disadvantages—(1) it does not provide the developer with certainty concerning the level of the project's construction costs, and (2) it does not create an incentive for the general contractor to lower its costs through competitive bidding or the efficient prosecution of the work. For these reasons, a pure cost plus pricing structure is seldom used for private commercial real estate projects.

c. *Guaranteed Maximum Price*

The guaranteed maximum price model is a hybrid of the cost of work, plus a fee arrangement discussed under the prior heading. In a guaranteed maximum price model, the parties acknowledge that the construction price is equal to the lesser of (1) the actual cost of the work, plus the general contractor's fee, and (2) a fixed sum agreed to by the general contractor (the *guaranteed maximum price* or *GMP*). The GMP can be set either at the time of the execution of the construction contract (the developer's preference) or at a later date in the construction process when the project scope and design is sufficiently well-defined for the general contractor to make a reasonable estimate of its construction costs (the general contractor's preference). In either circumstance, the GMP is usually pegged at a cost level that the general contractor is relatively confident can be achieved for the project—in other words, it includes an added cushion over the general contractor's best estimate of the project's cost of work.

The guaranteed maximum price model provides for a sharing between the owner and the general contractor of the risk that the actual cost of work exceeds budget. The general contractor assumes the risk that the actual cost of work exceeds the agreed-upon GMP and the developer takes the risk that the general contractor, lacking any financial incentive to keep project costs below the GMP, eschews cost savings that would otherwise be achievable for the project. Developers often try to create an incentive for the general contractor to keep construction costs as low as possible by agreeing to increase the general contractor's fee by an agreed-upon percentage (typically in the 25 to 50% range) of the excess of the GMP over the actual cost of work. Construction incentives of this type are known as *shared savings clauses*.

The use of a GMP pricing arrangement raises a few practical issues that the lawyer representing the developer must address when negotiating the construction contract.

- If the GMP is not set at the time of contract execution, the contract should include a default method for dealing with a situation where the owner and the general contractor cannot reach mutual agreement on the GMP. In such a circumstance, the developer should reserve the right to either terminate the construction contract or proceed with the contract with the added requirement that all subcontract work must be awarded to the low bidder as part of a competitive bidding process.[38]

---

[38] *See* Joyce K. Hackenbrach and Clark Whitney, How to Control the Owner's Risk in a Commercial or Industrial Construction Contract, 23 No. 6 PRACTICAL REAL ESTATE LAWYER 3, 5 (November 2007).

- The GMP can be phrased as either an overall cap on the total cost of the work or as a series of caps on individual components of the work (for example, $4 million for steelwork, $2 million for site work, etc.). Most general contractors resist the developer's request for line item GMPs because the general contractors want to be able to use cost savings on one line item to cover costs overruns on another line item. The developer should, in all events, try to fix or otherwise put a cap on the general contractor's general condition costs so that the general contractor is not tempted to augment its profit on the project by charging additional general condition costs to the project until the GMP threshold is met.[39]

- If the developer agrees to share cost savings with the general contractor, the general contractor has a strong incentive to set the GMP at an artificially high number thereby creating a very real prospect that it can add its share of the savings to its profit on the project. It is, therefore, incumbent on the developer to closely scrutinize the general contractor's offered GMP to try to make sure that the GMP is set at a realistic number and is not inflated simply to augment the general contractor's fee on the project. As one author/practitioner has noted, "if the developer finds that the general contractor is heatedly negotiating for a savings clause, it is time for the developer to put an estimator on the developer's payroll."[40]

The guaranteed maximum price model is the pricing mechanism most commonly used on projects where the plans and specifications are not fully complete on the date the construction contract is signed by the general contractor and the owner. While a GMP approach can be used in connection with any of the three project delivery systems discussed earlier in this chapter, it is most frequently linked with fast track construction projects utilizing a construction management or design-build delivery system.

2. Method of Payment

Once the construction price is determined, the next question that needs to be addressed in the construction contract is how and when that price is paid to the general contractor. In most construction projects, the construction price is paid monthly based upon the portion of the work completed (in a stipulated sum contract) or the construction costs incurred (in a cost plus or GMP arrangement) during the prior month.

---

[39] *See* Axelroth, *The Owner's Perspective*; *supra* note 35, at 23.

[40] *See* Hastie, *supra* note 22, at 12.

The developer should require the general contractor to provide the developer with a schedule describing the general contractor's best estimate of the timing and amount of the monthly progress payments that the general contractor anticipates requesting during the construction phase. The developer should closely review that schedule to prevent the general contractor from front-loading its receipt of the construction price. "Front-loading" is an attempt by the general contractor to better its cash flow position (and worsen the developer's) by receiving a greater portion of the construction price than is warranted in the early months of the construction process.[41]

The developer's counsel should also include in the construction contract a statement of those procedures that must be followed to permit the developer to verify that the work has progressed sufficiently to merit the making of each monthly payment to the general contractor. The construction contract should specifically recite that the general contractor must use the monthly progress payments it receives from the developer to make timely payment of all amounts then owed to its subcontractors and suppliers. Otherwise, the developer runs the risk of having a subcontractor or supplier file a mechanics' lien against its project. The payment procedures typically followed by the developer to protect its interests and those of its construction lender are discussed at length in *Chapter 9—Stage 5: Obtaining Construction Financing*, at pages 422–424. The real estate development lawyer should also make sure that the construction contract and all related subcontracts contain payment provisions that are fully consistent with the requirements set forth in the construction loan agreement.

Construction contracts typically contain provisions permitting the owner to withhold a stated percentage (normally 5–10%) from each monthly progress payment made to the general contractor. Similar provisions are also included in the general contractor's agreements with its subcontractors and suppliers. The withheld amounts (known as *retainage*) are typically not disbursed to the general contractor and its subcontractors and suppliers until the project is completed, thereby providing all those firms working on the construction project with an added incentive to complete construction on a timely basis. General contractors frequently request (and developers often agree) to eliminate retainage once the construction of the project is 50% complete, based on the theory that the developer's risk that the project is not completed on time and on budget is significantly lessened once the project reaches that stage of completion. It is also quite common for the developer and its lender to agree to disburse a subcontractor's share of the retainage upon the full completion of that

---

[41] *See* Hastie, *supra* note 22, at 5.

subcontractor's portion of the work (even though substantial completion of the entire project has not yet been achieved).

3.   Construction Schedule

A principal business objective of the developer during Stage 6 is the on time completion of its development project. In an attempt to create expectations and avoid unintended construction delays, the real estate development lawyer should include in the construction contract a clear statement as to when construction must begin and when it must be completed. The concept of completion has two distinct components—(1) "substantial completion," which is generally defined as the stage in the progress of the work when the project is sufficiently complete so that the owner can occupy or utilize the project for its intended use,[42] and (2) "final completion," which is the date on which all aspects of the general contractor's performance are fully completed.

A delay in the general contractor's completion of construction can produce serious and sometimes devastating financial consequences for the developer. A delay can result in the developer having to pay additional interest on its construction loan and could endanger the financial health of the entire project if, for example, the project leases contain provisions permitting the tenants to terminate their leases if the project is not contemplated by a certain date Although the focus of this text and this chapter is on the developer's plight, I would be remiss if I failed to mention that a construction delay can also prove costly to the general contractor. One practitioner correctly writes that "On the general contractor's side, delays translate into additional home office overhead, as well as increased jobsite overhead and supervision ('general conditions'), additional labor costs, and delays in transferring resources to another project or endeavor."[43]

The developer has several options at its disposal to prevent a construction delay. First and foremost, the developer should select a general contractor that has both a solid reputation for completing projects on time and the financial wherewithal to take whatever remedial measures may be necessary to avoid a delay (for example, the scheduling of a second construction shift or the payment of overtime to its trade general contractors). The developer should also closely monitor the progress of construction so that it can detect any early warning signs that the general contractor may have trouble meeting its completion deadline. Finally, the developer should, if possible, establish a completion deadline that is realistic and that has at least a modicum of flexibility.

---

[42] *See e.g.*, AIA DOCUMENT A201—GENERAL CONDITIONS FOR THE CONTRACT FOR CONSTRUCTION § 9.8 (2007).

[43] Beck, *supra* note 8, at 4–63.

The real estate development lawyer can provide additional comfort to the developer by inserting language in the construction contract that is designed to incentivize the general contractor to complete the project on time and to mitigate the financial impact to the developer of a construction delay. The following are examples of contractual techniques that the real estate development lawyer can employ to combat the prospect of a construction delay.

- *Written Notice of Delay*—The developer is often not in a position to independently discover the existence of a potential construction delay. The real estate development lawyer should consider adding a provision to the construction contract that requires the general contractor to provide the developer with written notice of a potential construction delay within a stated number of days following the occurrence of the event that gave rise to the delay. The inclusion of such a notice requirement permits the developer to learn of the potential delay when there is still time to take remedial measures to overcome the delay. The general contractor's right to receive an extension of the completion deadline or an increase in the construction price should be conditioned upon its delivery of the required written notice to the developer.[44]

- *Milestone Dates*—It is in the best interest of the developer to discover the potential for a construction delay as early as possible in the construction process. One way that the developer can accomplish that goal is to set forth in the construction contract interim milestone dates for the completion of certain portions of the work (for example, site excavation, foundation work, or steel erection). If the general contractor fails to meet one of the milestone dates, then the owner can reserve a contractual right to require the general contractor, at its expense, to take whatever actions are required to get the project back on schedule, including furnishing additional labor and working overtime or multiple shifts.

- *Liquidated Damages*—Finally, the real estate development lawyer should consider including a requirement for the general contractor's payment of liquidated damages to the developer if construction of the project is not completed by the

---

[44] *See* Dugan & Meyers Construction Co. v. Ohio Department of Administrative Services, 113 Ohio St.3d 226 (2007), for a case holding that a contractor's right to receive a construction extension is conditioned upon its full compliance with the notice of delay provisions of the construction contract (even if the owner has actual knowledge of the potential delay and orally informs the contractor that no extension will be forthcoming). *See also* Thomas L. Rosenberg, *Essential Construction Contract Terms: Avoiding Future Problems by Addressing Key Issues*, REAL ESTATE FINANCE JOURNAL 50, 54 (Spring 2007).

deadline date specified in the construction contract. Liquidated damage clauses in construction contracts typically provide for the payment of a per diem charge for each day after the targeted completion deadline that the general contractor fails to achieve substantial completion of the construction project. The lawyer's objective when drafting a liquidated damages clause is to include a per diem damages amount that is high enough to catch the general contractor's attention and incentivize the general contractor to complete the project on schedule, but not so high as to make the liquidated damages clause an unenforceable penalty.[45]

General contractors generally resist an attempt by the developer to make the general contractor responsible for a delay that is caused by events or circumstances that are beyond the general contractor's control (often referred to as an "excusable delay"). While the developer is often willing to accept that distinction, its view of what constitutes an excusable delay is usually light years away from the general contractor's view.

The two generally accepted categories of excusable delays are (1) delays caused by the owner, and (2) *force majeure* delays (meaning delays caused by unforeseen events beyond the general contractor's control, including severe weather and other acts of God). The negotiations over owner-caused delays generally involve a heated discussion concerning the precise obligations to be placed on the owner during the construction phase, with the owner typically taking the position that its only obligation is to pay the construction price and the general contractor vigorously arguing that the developer is responsible for everything from the accuracy and completeness of the plans and specifications to its warranty that the site conditions are appropriate for the construction of the project.

The parties also take markedly different positions as to what constitutes an excusable *force majeure* delay. The general contractor wants the list of *force majeure* events to be "broad and long," while the developer wants that list to be "specific and short." By way of example, the general contractor often seeks to have "inclement weather" treated as an excusable delay, while the developer insists that only "abnormal and unusually severe weather conditions for the season and location" be included within the definition of an excusable delay. Heated negotiations frequently also take place over the issue of whether the general contractor should be held responsible for delays caused by labor disputes or subcontractor bankruptcies (with the developer asserting that those events could

---

[45] *See* CAMERON, *supra* note 5, at 8–34 and 8–35 of the 2009 Supplement. Generally speaking, a liquidated damages clause is enforceable if "at the time of contracting, the provisions were intended not to establish a penalty but rather to reasonably estimate the amount of actual damages that would result from a delay but would otherwise be difficult to ascertain and prove." *See* Beck, *supra* note 8, at 4–66. *See also* Rosenberg, *supra* note 44, at 53.

reasonably have been anticipated by the general contractor and, hence, should have been taken into consideration by the general contractor when it agreed to the project completion deadline).

The resolution of what events and circumstances are treated as excusable delays for which the general contractor is entitled to an extension of time or additional compensation (or both) ultimately comes down to which side has the most "juice" in the negotiations. The tighter the construction schedule, the more heated those negotiations become.

4. Unforeseen Site Conditions

A particularly sensitive topic in the owner-general contractor negotiations is the treatment of the risk that "unforeseen site conditions" delay completion of construction or increase the cost of the work. In this context, unforeseen site conditions generally mean those site conditions that are not readily detectable by a visual inspection of the site. Examples of site conditions that can dramatically affect the project's schedule and costs are the presence on the site of bad soils, environmental contamination or protected wetlands.

The general rule is that the general contractor is responsible for the risk of bad site conditions. As noted by the Supreme Court in the landmark case of *United States v. Spearin*, "one who undertakes to erect a structure upon a particular site assumes ordinarily the risk of subsidence of soils."[46] The parties to a construction contract are, however, free to allocate the risk of unforeseen site conditions in any specific manner they see fit.[47]

The construction contract should clearly state whether responsibility for the condition of the site falls on the general contractor or the owner. Whichever party is assigned that responsibility should conduct thorough due diligence of the project's site conditions (by obtaining an environmental assessment, wetlands report, soils test, and other site reviews certified by qualified, licensed professionals) to provide it with comfort that the site conditions are suitable for the proposed project.

In most situations, the developer seeks to place the risk of unforeseen site conditions on the party that it considers to be an expert on all construction matters—the general contractor. If the developer is successful in that effort and adverse site conditions are subsequently unearthed, then the general contractor is the party responsible for paying the excess construction costs needed to solve the problem and get the project back on schedule. If the developer expressly assumes the site condition risk in the construction contract (and it is not unusual for it to do so), then the general contractor is entitled to an extension of the outside date for the completion

---

[46] United States v. Spearin, 248 U.S. 132, 136 (1918).

[47] *See* CAMERON, *supra* note 5, at 9–25.

of construction and additional compensation if adverse site conditions are discovered during the construction phase.[48]

5.   Changes in the Work

Change is the norm in the construction of commercial real estate projects. In a typical project, there are tens and maybe hundreds of changes made to the original plans and specifications. The owner may simply change its mind about the desired look or composition of the project. The general contractor may determine that there is a better way to go about completing the project. Finally, circumstances beyond the control of both the owner and the general contractor may dictate the need for a change in the scope of work, the project schedule, or the construction price.

It is the real estate development lawyer's job to include provisions in the construction contract that are designed to give the parties clarity and guidance about the manner in which changes to the work may be made and the impact that such changes have upon the construction schedule and pricing. In drafting the changes to work provisions of the construction contract, the lawyer needs to deal with three categories of potential changes—(1) *change orders*, (2) *change directives,* and (3) *constructive changes*. The developer's goals and objectives with respect to each of those change categories are discussed below.

- *Change Orders*—A change order is a modification to the general contractor's scope of work that is voluntarily agreed to by the general contractor and the owner. A request for a change order can be issued by either the general contractor or the owner. The contract should specifically provide that all change orders must be in writing and will not be effective until signed by both the general contractor and the owner. The written change order should specify the nature of the agreed-upon change and the schedule and cost implications of those changes.

- *Change Directives*—In certain situations, the owner may want to reserve the unilateral right to compel the general contractor to make changes to its scope of work even if all of the terms associated with that change have not yet been agreed to by the general contractor. This is especially true in fast-track projects where the owner cannot tolerate a work stoppage while the parties haggle over the precise terms of a formal change order. To deal with this type of scenario, the real estate development lawyer often includes a provision in

---

48   *See* Edward Neal Pollard, *Changes in the Work*, in FUNDAMENTALS OF CONSTRUCTION LAW, 227, 230–232 (Carina Y. Enhada, Cheri Turnage Gatlin and Fred D. Wilshusen eds., 2001); and Beck, *supra* note 8, at 4–80 through 4–84.

the construction contract that empowers the owner to issue a change directive compelling the general contractor to proceed with the changed work in advance of the parties' mutual execution of a formal change order. If the contract authorizes the owner to issue a change directive, then the contract should also establish general parameters for determining the modifications to be made to the contract price and schedule if the owner and the general contractor are not able to agree to the terms of a written change order. For example, the contract might recite that the contract price will be increased by an amount equal to the actual cost of the changed work, plus a fee equal to a fixed percentage of such cost.[49]

- ***Constructive Changes***—A constructive change is a change in the scope of the general contractor's work that is caused by the occurrence of unforeseen events or circumstances occurring after the date of the parties' execution of the construction contract. The two most obvious examples of constructive changes are those changes caused by the existence of excusable delays or unforeseen site conditions. If the nature of the general contractor's work performance is delayed or made more costly as a result of the occurrence of either of those two circumstances, then the general contractor wants to receive the owner's acknowledgement that the completion deadline will be extended or the construction price increased (or both).

The general contractor is customarily entitled to an increase in the construction price only if the excusable delay is an owner-caused delay (and not a delay caused by an event beyond the control of both parties to the construction contract). Developers often attempt to further augment this point by inserting into the construction contract a so-called "no damage for delay provision" that expressly states that the general contractor's sole and exclusive remedy for the occurrence of an excusable delay is an extension of the completion deadline (and specifically not an increase in the construction price). Courts are sometimes hesitant to enforce a no damages for delay provision against a general contractor with clean hands, based on the theory that such a provision is unconscionable and works an extreme hardship on the general contractor.[50]

---

[49] *See* Pollard, *supra* note 48, at 228.

[50] *See* CAMERON, *supra* note 5, at 17–8 through 17–10; Rosenberg, *supra* note 44, at 53; and Beck, *supra* note 8, at 4–9 through 4–73.

The best way for the lawyer to protect the developer from constructive change requests is to include very tight, restrictive language in the construction contract that (1) limits the scope and number of the general contractor's excusable delays, and (2) transfers the risk of unforeseen conditions to the general contractor. The developer's lawyer should also place a provision in the construction contract that waives the general contractor's claims for any constructive change if the general contractor fails to submit a written change order to the developer within a relatively short period of time after the occurrence of the event that supports the general contractor's claim for a constructive change.

General contractors are famous for seeking to profit from work changes (be they change orders, change directives, or constructive changes) by asking for a percentage mark-up on change costs that is higher than the fee the general contractor charges on the base cost of the work. Owners prefer to fix the mark-up on work changes at the same percentage fee that is applicable to the remainder of the general contractor's work. The developer's lawyer should include a provision in the construction contract that specifies the percentage fee that the general contractor is entitled to for all changes in the work.

HIBC Case Study—Design and Construction Issues

One of the primary factors contributing to the overall success of the HIBC project was The Pizzuti Companies' ability to put together a quality team of design and construction professionals and to then keep that team intact throughout the ten-year duration of the HIBC project. Pizzuti's objective when assembling its design and construction team was to select seasoned and highly talented professionals and to assign them responsibility and authority commensurate with their respective core competencies. While Pizzuti encouraged collaboration among all the team members, it was extremely careful not to permit blurred lines of authority or tolerate overlapping or redundant responsibilities.

Pizzuti believed that aesthetics would be an important driver for the project's profitability, so it selected an architect (Hunton Brady Architects) that was well-known in the Orlando market for its crisp and inventive architectural designs. Pizzuti was also well aware that the sheer size and complexity of the project would place incredible financial, manpower and logistical demands on whichever construction firm was selected as the general contractor of record for the project. After interviewing a number of qualified general contractors, Pizzuti hired Brasfield & Gorrie, a construction firm headquartered in Birmingham, Alabama, that had very deep financial pockets and a reputation for consistently bringing its projects in on time and on budget. Finally, Pizzuti was adamant that it wanted to be an active participant in and retain control over every aspect of the design and construction of the HIBC project. Given this desire, Pizzuti hired three seasoned professionals to head up its in-house development team—a senior executive to be responsible for all aspects of the HIBC project, a construction manager to supervise all vertical improvement projects, and a project manager to oversee Pizzuti's land development activities at HIBC.

Once its team members were selected, Pizzuti's senior executives conveyed three principal messages to the selected design and construction professionals: the architect is responsible for design; the general contactor is responsible for construction; and Pizzuti is in charge of everything. Because it realized the importance of maintaining continuity throughout the project's history, Pizzuti promised (in the moral, not the legal sense) Hunton Brady and Brasfield & Gorrie that they would serve in their respective roles on the HIBC project for as long as their performance merited their retention—which, as it turned out, would be for the entire ten-year history of the project.

That is more than enough discussion of what the business people did to dictate the success of the HIBC project during Stage 6. What you all want to know is what the real estate development lawyer did to contribute to the project's good fortune. The short answer to that question is fairly obvious— not too much. Having said that, Pizzuti's legal team (yours truly and two much more qualified legal professionals—one in-house and one out-house), were responsible for selecting a project delivery system and negotiating design and construction contracts that, at the very least, facilitated Pizzuti's implementation of the sage business decisions made by the company during Stage 6 of the development process. That is, after all, the essence of the real estate development lawyer's job—paving the way for the developer to achieve its business objectives.

The following are the mundane (but, hopefully, somewhat instructive) details regarding the actions taken by Pizzuti and its lawyers during Stage 6 of the HIBC project.

- All design and construction professionals who worked on the HIBC project were selected through negotiation (and not by a competitive bidding process). Pizzuti believed that this approach fostered a greater sense of teamwork among the selected professionals and produced a higher quality product.

- Pizzuti adopted a traditional design-bid-build delivery system for every project it developed in HIBC. The design and construction phases were implemented in a sequential order, thereby insuring that (1) the architectural design of each building would be given paramount importance, and (2) the *general contractor could establish its construction price based on its review of a full set of completed plans and specifications. The depth and sophistication of Pizzuti's in-house development staff permitted it to appropriately coordinate the design and construction silos that characterize the design-bid-build structure.*

- *The lawyers representing Pizzuti, Hunton Brady, and Brasfield & Gorrie agreed that they would use standard AIA forms to document their contractual relationships. The AIA contract format was selected because all the parties were familiar with the substantive provisions of the AIA documents. The contract negotiations on the first office building developed by the Pizzuti-Hunton Brady-Brasfield & Gorrie team were quite spirited and took a fair amount of time to complete. The end product was a set of contract documents that clearly articulated the authority, responsibility, and risk of each of the players and served as a template for the contracts used on all the HIBC construction projects.*

The following are several of the negotiated features of the owner-architect contract used for all HIBC projects.

- *The architect's compensation was stated as a fixed fee (thereby giving Pizzuti the certainty that it desired concerning its project design costs).*

- *The architect's reimbursable costs were tightly defined and the architect's ability to mark up any of those costs was eliminated.*

- *The contract deleted all of the standard AIA references to the architect providing construction cost estimates for the project (because Pizzuti knew that asking an architect to estimate project costs is like asking an artist to fix a car).*

- *All provisions seeking to give the architect a primary role in arbitrating owner-general contractor disputes, setting the terms of change orders, and communicating the owner's thoughts to the general contractor were excised from the contract.*

- *The contract included a "termination for convenience" feature, with no requirement that the owner pay the architect a break-up fee as a condition to its exercise of such feature.*

- *Pizzuti was given the unfettered right to use the design plans on any other project of its choosing as long as it paid Hunton Brady a relatively small fee each time it re-used the plans (approximately one-third of the fee paid for the initial set of design plans).*

The owner-general contractor agreement used for all HIBC projects contained the following features.

- *A guaranteed maximum price (without any contingency factor) was established on the date of contract execution. Brasfield & Gorrie was given the right to augment its construction fee by an amount equal to 25% of any actual cost savings below the stated GMP.*

- *A liquidated damages clause was inserted into all of the contracts requiring Brasfield & Gorrie to pay a per diem amount to Pizzuti for every day that it was late in achieving substantial completion.*

The amount of the per diem charge varied from project to project based on the tightness of the construction schedule and the contractual demands of the project tenants. In those situations where a tenant lease included a liquidated damages clause, Pizzuti always included a mirror image of that liquidated damages clause in its construction contract with Brasfield & Gorrie.

- *The definition of "excusable delays" was phrased in a very restrictive fashion to eliminate adverse weather and labor conditions that were reasonably foreseeable by the general contractor.*

- *The risk of unforeseen site conditions was placed on the owner (and not the general contractor)—an allocation of responsibility that was acceptable to Pizzuti because of the rigorous soils tests and other site-wide due diligence tests Pizzuti performed on all its Florida projects;*

- *Pizzuti retained the right to issue unilateral change directives and agreed to pay the general contractor a fee of 5% of the cost of all such directives (1% higher than the percentage fee paid to Brasfield & Gorrie on the base work).*

- *Retainage was set at 10%, until the project was 50% complete, at which time retainage on all subsequent construction disbursements was eliminated.*

The end result of the lawyers' work during Stage 6 of the HIBC project was the creation of design and construction contracts that specifically delineated the respective rights, responsibilities, and liabilities of the owner, architect, and general contractor. The fact that those contracts were used for the development of more than 1 million square feet of commercial space without a single lawsuit or lien ever being filed against Pizzuti or the HIBC project stands as a testament to the ultimate fairness of the contracts and the professionalism of the players that were parties to such contracts.

VIII. SUMMARY

The real estate lawyer's primary assignment during Stage 6 is to craft contracts that advance the developer's goals of completing its project on time, on budget, and in accordance with sound design and construction practices. In order to properly do that job, the lawyer must gain a sound working knowledge of the dynamics of the construction process and the roles served by all the players in that process. The lawyer must then use that base of knowledge to put together a set of contract documents that require and empower the architect, general contractor, and developer to effectively work together as a team to turn the developer's 20-page business plan into a fully operational building. In doing so, the lawyer must keep in mind the following advice offered up by a practicing construction lawyer:

> Building financial incentives and disincentives into a contract often tends to be more practical and effective than simply drafting stringent "commandments" to act in a particular way.[51]

Stated in a more colloquial fashion, you can catch more flies with honey than you can with a fly swatter.

---

[51] Hackenbrach, *supra* note 38, at 3.

CHAPTER 11

STAGE 7: NEGOTIATING THE PROJECT LEASE

■ ■ ■

I. INTRODUCTION

The first six stages of the real estate development process are all focused on the cost side of the developer's business—how much the project costs and how the developer funds its project costs. Stage 7 is where the developer makes its money by leasing its project to rent-paying tenants.

The lawyer's role in the leasing stage also undergoes a significant change of focus. The previous chapters of this book have focused on the lawyer's role in helping the developer preserve the integrity of the project's cost structure by managing the risks inherent in the real estate development process. During the leasing stage, the real estate development lawyer's attention turns to the income side of the developer's business. The lawyer's job is to carefully negotiate and draft the terms of the project lease to enhance the predictability and stability of the income stream generated from the developer's leasing of space in its project.

The manner in which the lawyer approaches the representation of the developer also shifts in a subtle, but extremely important way during the leasing stage. It is at this stage of the development process that the lawyer acts as a member of the developer's marketing team. While the lawyer may not be on the front lines in seeking to identify and entice prospective tenants to lease space in the developer's project, the manner in which the lawyer approaches the preparation and negotiation of the lease has a significant impact (hopefully a positive one) on the developer's ability to lease its project in a timely fashion.

Consistent with the approach taken in previous chapters of this book, this chapter begins by examining the competing business objectives of the parties involved in the leasing stage of the development process—primarily those of the landlord and tenant, but also the interests of the mortgage lender and the equity investor. It then touches on the types of leases used in the commercial real estate world. The remainder of the chapter is devoted to an analysis of the key provisions of a multi-tenant, office lease, with particular emphasis being placed on the varying perspectives of the landlord and tenant on each of those provisions. While the focus of this chapter is on the provisions typically found in a multi-tenant office lease, I will, where appropriate, comment on those lease clauses that are uniquely found in other types of leases—especially retail leases.

The Form Office Lease used by the author for the Heathrow International Business Center project in Orlando, Florida serves as the primary frame of reference for the discussion of those lease provisions (referred to in this chapter as the "Form Office Lease—see Document #6 in the *Document Appendix* at pages 709–731).

II. BUSINESS OBJECTIVES OF LEASE PARTIES

Let's start by setting some ground rules for the terminology to be used to identify the parties to a lease. The person who owns the real estate project and is trying to lease it to third parties is generally referred to in the commercial world as either the *landlord* or the *lessor*. The person who wants to lease space in the project is generally referred to as either the *tenant* or the *lessee*. Because the similarity of the "lessor" and "lessee" references creates the potential for confusion and error, the terms "landlord" and "tenant" are used throughout this chapter—and should also be used when drafting the lease.

A. BUSINESS OBJECTIVES OF THE LANDLORD

The developer/landlord has three business objectives during the leasing stage of the development process.

- The project should be leased at rents that are consistent with or better than those set forth in its financial projections for the project.

- The project should be leased as soon as possible and, in all events, within the time frames set forth in the project's initial business plan.

- The project should be leased on business and legal terms that are consistent with the expectations and requirements of the institutional investor community.

The profitability of the developer's project is determined by how well the developer fares in its attempt to achieve these three objectives.

B. BUSINESS OBJECTIVES OF THE TENANT

Unlike the landlord, the prospective tenant has no specific "real estate" business objective. The tenant's goal is to conduct its business as efficiently and productively as possible to foster the growth, profitability, and stability of its business operations. The prospective tenant simply wants to make sure that its leasing decision does not detract from its ability to meet its overall business goals.

In this regard, it is important to keep in mind why companies typically opt to satisfy their space needs by leasing and not owning real estate. First, it generally costs less to lease real estate than it does to own real estate (at least in the short-term). Most companies prefer to preserve their financial resources to fund the operation and growth of their core businesses, rather than to use those resources to pay for the development or acquisition of real estate. Similarly, companies are also reluctant to deploy their human resources to deal with the operational and financial risks associated with the ownership of real estate. Shareholders and directors want the companies' employees to spend their working hours formulating strategies to satisfy the demands of the companies' customers and not responding to complaints about leaky toilets and faulty HVAC systems.

In the context of the negotiation of the project lease, the tenant has the following goals.

- The tenant wants to lease space that permits it to further its enterprise mission. The space should be conveniently located to its targeted customer base and targeted labor pool and should be configured and sized to fit its business model. Finally, the look and feel of the building in which its leased space is located should be consistent with the corporate image that the tenant desires to project to its customers and employees.

- The tenant wants to negotiate *occupancy costs* that are consistent with the operating budget for its business. The tenant's occupancy costs refer not just to the fixed rental payment that the tenant is required to make each month to the landlord, but also to all other costs that are directly associated with its occupancy of the leased space. Those other occupancy costs include: its reimbursement of the landlord's building expenses; utility charges; parking fees; the cost of making improvements to its leased space; and the benefit of any tax or economic incentives tied to its occupancy of the project in question. The fact that the tenant's fixed rent payment at Location A might be lower than that at Location B is of little importance to the tenant if its all-in occupancy costs at Location B are higher than those for Location B (because, for example, the cost of making tenant improvements to its space in Location B is significantly higher than the cost of making comparable improvements to its space in Location A).

- The tenant wants to avoid economic surprises with respect to its occupancy of its leased space. Once the tenant determines that its occupancy costs at a particular location are within its budget, the last thing that the tenant wants to have happen is for an unanticipated event to occur that permits the landlord to exact additional charges that increase the tenant's actual costs of occupying the leased space above its budgeted amount.

- Finally, the tenant wants the lease document to maximize its flexibility to make space decisions that are responsive to its business needs. By way of example, if a tenant needs to hire new employees to respond to a spurt in its business growth, it wants to be able to expand the size of the space it leases in its current location to maximize the control and business synergy generated from having all of its employees located under the same roof.

All of the above goals have a central theme—the tenant does not want its leasing decision to hinder its ability to independently conduct its business operations. The tenant's quest to reach its leasing goals is made more challenging by the fact that an office lease customarily is for a term of anywhere from three to 20 years—a period of time in which any number of changes can occur with respect to the tenant's underlying business operations.

C. BUSINESS OBJECTIVES OF LENDER AND EQUITY INVESTOR

When negotiating the project lease, the landlord needs to be mindful of the interests of its lender and equity investor. The lender and equity investor share the following business objectives with respect to the leasing of the project by the landlord.

- They want to enhance to the maximum extent practicable the income stream generated from leases of space in the project. Their focus is not only on making sure that the project leases provide for rentals that are consistent with the project's financial projections, but also that such leases are with creditworthy tenants and do not allow the tenants to unilaterally trigger a reduction in their rent obligations or an increase in the landlord's operating costs.

- Under certain circumstances, a lender or equity investor might succeed to the leasehold interest of the landlord—for example, if the project mortgage is foreclosed on by the lender or if the equity investor buys out the landlord's ownership interest in the project. The lender and the equity investor are focused during the leasing stage on making sure that the lease documents permit each of them to step into the landlord's shoes without any diminution in the obligations that the tenant owes to the titular landlord.

In order to protect their business interests, lenders and equity investors usually insist that any lease executed by the project owner must either (1) be pre-approved by the lender/equity investor, or (2) conform to leasing guidelines agreed to in advance by the project owner and the lender/equity investor as to rent, term, tenant creditworthiness, etc.

III. TYPES OF COMMERCIAL LEASES

The term "lease" encompasses a wide variety of commercial transactions. In its broadest sense, a lease can cover either real or personal property, including intangible personal property. As befits the nature of this book, the focus of this chapter is on the leasing of space in a commercial building.

There are three principal types of commercial leases. While all commercial leases present the same core business and legal issues, each type of lease involves issues that are unique to the type of building in which the leased space is located.

- *Office Lease*—Because its provisions are generally applicable to all types of space leases, the office lease is the platform used throughout the remainder of this chapter to discuss the key provisions of a commercial lease. The substantive provisions of an office lease vary based on the type and location of the landlord's building (for example, a one-story suburban office building vs. a downtown skyscraper).

- *Industrial Lease*—The most common form of industrial lease is the lease of space in a warehouse building. Industrial leases can, however, also involve the leasing of space for the conduct of more intense uses, such as manufacturing, light assembly, and research and development. The heightened nature of the use of industrial space gives rise to unique environmental, safety, and noise issues that must be addressed by the lawyers representing the landlord and the tenant.

- *Retail Lease*—A retail lease is a broad category that includes the lease of space in regional shopping malls, lifestyle centers, neighborhood strip centers, and entertainment districts. Retail leases often include provisions that are not found in other types of space leases—for example, percentage rent, exclusive use, co-tenancy, and continuous operation clauses. Those retail-specific clauses are discussed in some detail later in this chapter at pages 531–533 and 549–554.

A commercial space lease (be it an office, industrial, or retail lease) is further subject to classification based on whether the tenant is leasing the entirety of the building or only a portion of the building. A *multi-tenant lease* is a lease where a building is leased to two or more separate and distinct tenants, while a *single tenant lease* is a lease where one tenant leases the entirety of the available space in a building. For the most part, this chapter centers on a multi-tenant office lease. Occasional note is, however, taken of the unique construction and operational issues presented by a single tenant lease (see pages 506–508).

IV. INTRODUCTION TO KEY LEASE PROVISIONS

The focus of the remainder of this chapter is on an analysis of the key provisions found in a typical multi-tenant office lease. For this purpose, the provisions of an office lease have been slotted into the following broad categories.

- *Parties*—This subsection focuses on the description of the parties involved in the leasing transaction, including the landlord, the tenant, and any guarantor of the landlord's or tenant's lease obligations.

- *Space*—This subsection explores the identification, measurement, and improvement of the space that is being leased to the tenant.

- *Term*—This subsection addresses the time period during which the tenant has the right to possess and occupy the leased space.

- *Rent*—This subsection addresses the various rental payments to be made to the landlord by the tenant and how those rental payments are calculated.

- *Use*—This subsection deals with the contractual parameters established for the tenant's use of its leased space, including provisions that govern what the tenant can and cannot do in the leased space and provisions that address the nature and scope of the services that the landlord is obligated to furnish to its tenants.

- *Tenant Flexibility Provisions*—This subsection focuses on those provisions that a tenant can insert into the lease to provide it with the needed flexibility to respond to a change in the size or nature of its business operations.

- *Risk Allocation and Other Leasing Issues*—Finally, this subsection addresses those provisions of the typical office lease that seek to allocate certain risks between the landlord and tenant, including the risks associated with the occurrence of a default, casualty, or condemnation. The discussion of the key provisions of a lease concludes with an examination of other contractual clauses that are unique to a commercial leasing transaction.

The discussion of each of these lease provisions begins with an analysis of the competing perspectives of the landlord and the tenant with respect to the subject matter of each provision. The focus of that discussion is on why the landlord and the tenant adopt their respective positions—in other words, what business purpose is being served by the stances taken by the landlord and the tenant. Suggestions are then offered about possible compromises available to the parties to resolve their differences.

Where the parties land on each of the key lease provisions is, of course, dependent both on the skill of their respective negotiators and the relative leverage that they bring to the lease negotiations. There is no one right or wrong answer as to what should be contained in a particular lease clause. In this regard, I am reminded of the following quote from a book authored by a seasoned practitioner:

> There are form books aplenty. How to draft clauses, with examples. They all assume there is nobody to negotiate against. I have always found it to be great fun to negotiate with oneself. . . . One is never troubled with arguments this way. And one makes the most brilliant deals, as long as there is no one on the other side."[1]

The Form Office Lease included in the *Document Appendix* as Document #6 serves as the platform for the examination of the import of the various provisions of an office lease. Parenthetical reference is made in the caption describing each of the key provisions of a commercial lease to the section of the form Office Lease where the subject provision is addressed. Document #6 of the *Document Appendix* also sets forth a lengthy list of *Pro-Tenant Lease Modifications* that a lawyer representing a tenant might want to consider making to the Form Office Lease.

The Form Office Lease is a relatively short and succinct form that I designed to lease space in the Heathrow International Business Center in Orlando, Florida. A description of the thought process that went into my development of the HIBC lease form follows.

---

[1] *See* MARTIN A. ZANKEL, NEGOTIATING COMMERCIAL REAL ESTATE LEASES ix–x (2001).

HIBC Case Study—A User-Friendly Lease Form

As mentioned earlier in this book, The Pizzuti Companies (where I served as general counsel for 13+ years) owned a 350-acre tract of office land located in Orlando, Florida that was known as the Heathrow International Business Center. The first lease deal done at HIBC was a single-tenant lease with Cincinnati Bell Information Services ("CBIS"). Because I had precious little experience in doing lease deals in the State of Florida and because I was at the time bogged down in closing the acquisition and equity financing for the HIBC land, I asked a senior lawyer from my former law firm to take the lead on preparing the first draft of the CBIS lease. The lawyer was a partner at a national law firm and was a card-carrying member of the prestigious American College of Real Estate Lawyers. As I expected, the lawyer produced a first-rate lease draft that was approximately 50 pages long. Over the next several months, I spent countless hours haggling with counsel for CBIS over every single line of that 50-page document. The negotiations were long, painful, and frequently confrontational. Somehow, with the help of the lawyer I had retained for the CBIS job, we finally got the CBIS lease signed ten long months to the day after the letter of intent with CBIS was first signed.

With the CBIS deal behind it, Pizzuti decided that it was time to build its first speculative multi-tenant office building in HIBC. It was my job to put together the standard form lease that Pizzuti would use to market space in its HIBC office buildings. I had the CBIS lease in hand and also asked a number of prominent Florida lawyers to send me their standard office leases, so that I could synthesize the various forms and come up with a workable standard lease form for the HIBC project. The first thing I noticed about all the lease forms that I received from my Florida lawyer buddies is that all the leases were long—really long (the shortest being 25 pages). My life flashed before my eyes as I envisioned the hours of pain and misery I would be forced to endure while negotiating a 50-page lease on each leased space in the 15 or so office buildings that were planned for the HIBC project. My gut reaction was that life was too short and office leases were too long.

I decided to test the validity of my gut by talking to the folks who really mattered in the leasing process—leasing brokers, office developers, property managers, the heads of corporate real estate departments and institutional investors (you will note that I decided not to talk to any more lawyers). What I heard from my eclectic discussion group was really quite interesting. The consistent theme voiced by the group was that they were all sick and tired of having to deal with 50-page lease forms. The brokers and developers bemoaned the fact that the length and complexity of the lease forms slowed down the deal, ticked off the tenants, and inevitably caused bad feelings and project delays for all involved. The property managers and institutional investors said that the sheer length of the leases made it incredibly difficult for them to review and administer the leases once the tenants were in the building. Finally, the heads of the corporate real estate departments (who are basically the developer's customers) expressed unending frustration with having to deal over and over again with lawyers for the landlord demanding that they sign 50-page lease documents, every line of which tried to hammer home the point that the interests of the landlord were supreme in every respect to those of the tenant.

With all these thoughts in mind, I decided to see if I could dramatically shorten the office lease forms without adversely affecting the developer's legitimate business interests. What I found when I looked through the various office lease forms was that they all suffered, in varying degrees, from three basic drafting maladies:

- They said the same thing over and over again using different words each time;

- They contained overreaching provisions that the landlord's lawyer would almost always agree to delete from the lease if ever asked to do so by tenant's counsel; and

- They spent page after page dealing with lawyer-invented complexities and so-called "legal issues" that had only marginal importance to the business deal.

I was surprised by how easy it was to reduce the length and complexity of an office lease by simply remaining faithful to the proposition that I would not fall prey to the above-noted drafting errors. The result of my efforts was the Form Office Lease that is included in the Document Appendix. The lease form that I used for the HIBC project actually appeared to be quite a bit shorter than the lease document included in the Document Appendix because, for marketing optics, I used a small font (10 pt.) and also reduced the spacing between sections and paragraphs.

I will let you judge for yourself whether I successfully achieved my drafting objectives—with the most important of those objectives being the preparation of a short user-friendly lease form that fully serves and protects the legitimate business interests of the landlord. The facts that Pizzuti used the shorter lease form to lease over 20 million square feet of office and industrial space over a period of ten years and then sold the entirety of its real estate portfolio to high-end institutional investors serves as at least anecdotal support for my view that "shorter is better."

V. PARTIES TO THE LEASE
(¶¶ B and C of Lease Summary)

The lease must set forth the full name and mailing address of the landlord and the tenant. If a party to the lease is an entity, the lease should also recite the jurisdiction in which the entity was formed (for example, a Delaware corporation). The landlord should search the public records to make sure that the lease accurately recites the entity's legal name and that the entity is in good standing and authorized to do business in both the jurisdiction of its formation and, if different, the jurisdiction in which the landlord's building is located. A landlord who makes a sloppy mistake and fails to verify this most basic information will be hard-pressed to enforce the provisions of the lease in the courts of the state where its property is situated.

One of the landlord's primary objectives is to lease space in its building to creditworthy tenants—that is, to tenants who can afford to pay the rent recited in the lease. In order to verify a prospective tenant's creditworthiness, the landlord should closely scrutinize the tenant's financial statements prior to its execution of the lease. The landlord's review of the tenant's financials should not only confirm the acceptability of the net worth and income numbers disclosed in the financial statements, but should also verify that the entity that is signing the lease is the same entity identified in the financial statements.

If the landlord determines that the credit standing of the prospective tenant is not to its liking, the landlord should require the involvement in the lease transaction of a third person—a *guarantor* who will personally guaranty of the tenant's obligations under the lease.[2] The guarantor is usually a high net worth entity or individual who is affiliated with the tenant named in the lease and who executes a written lease guaranty pursuant to which the guarantor agrees to guarantee the performance of all or a designated portion of the tenant's lease obligations. The landlord wants the guarantor to personally guarantee both the payment and performance of all of the tenant's obligations under the lease. The guarantor, on the other hand, routinely seeks to limit its obligations by placing a cap on the amount of the guaranteed obligations or limiting the duration of the guaranty.

If a third party guaranties the tenant's obligations, the lease should recite the guarantor's legal name and mailing address. The landlord should take the same precautions concerning the accuracy of the proposed

---

[2]   *See generally* Andrew R. Lubin, *Lease Guaranties—A Practical Approach*, 17 No. 3 PRACTICAL REAL ESTATE LAWYER 27, 28 (May 2001); Joshua Stein, *Model Lease Guaranty*, 32 No. 1 PRACTICAL REAL ESTATE LAWYER 29 (May 2016); and Susan Fowler McNally, *Get Guaranty When Renting Space to Limited Liability Entity,* in COMMERCIAL LEASE LAW INSIDER 5–6 (July 2008).

guarantor's name and financial statements that were described earlier in this section with respect to the identity and financial wherewithal of the tenant. The landlord should include the following provisions in the lease guaranty—(1) a clear statement that the landlord may pursue an action against the guarantor prior to and independent of any action it elects to take against the tenant, and (2) a confirmation that the guarantor's liability is not affected by any lease amendment, release of security, or dissolution or reorganization of the named tenant.

VI. LEASED SPACE
(¶ D of Lease Summary, § 6, Exhibit A)

Once the parties to the lease are properly named, the next issue that needs to be addressed is the identification of the space that the tenant is leasing from the landlord. In the context of a multi-tenant office building, the lease provides the tenant with the right to use two separate spaces— (1) the tenant's *leased premises* (sometimes referred to as the "demised premises") and (2) the building's *common areas* (referred to by more professorial types as "appurtenances"). The location, dimensions, and character of each of these space elements need to be precisely described in the lease.

The leased premises is the space over which the tenant has the exclusive right of possession. In an office lease, it is the space located within the four corners of the tenant's office suite. The leased premises can either be described by reference to a specific suite number (for example, Suite 101) or by the attachment to the lease of a floor plan establishing the exact dimensions and configuration of the space. The goal in either such event is to specifically identify the space that is reserved exclusively for the tenant's conduct of its business.

The common areas are those spaces within the landlord's project that the tenant may use in common with other tenants in the building. Common areas include both *building common areas* and *site common areas*. Building common areas are further broken down into two categories—(1) building-wide common areas, such as the first floor lobby, freight elevators, mechanical equipment rooms, and other spaces that are used by all building tenants, and (2) single floor common areas, such as the restrooms and corridors located on a particular floor of the building that are available for use only by the tenants whose leased premises are located on that floor. Site common areas refer to those areas located outside of the landlord's building that a tenant can use in common with other tenants, such as a parking lot, driveways, sidewalks, and patios.

The lease should describe, at least in general terms, the tenant's right to use the building and site common areas. Section 6 of the Form Office

Lease achieves that objective by reciting that "Tenant will also have the non-exclusive right to use the common areas that serve the Building, including, without limitation, the Building's common lobbies, hallways, elevators, risers, restrooms, parking areas, and sidewalks"(see the second to the last sentence of § 6 of the Form Office Lease).

The common area issue that is most frequently debated by counsel for the landlord and tenant is the standard provision contained in most landlord leases that reserves a right for the landlord to reconfigure the common areas after the tenant's execution of the lease (see the last sentence of § 6 of the Form Office Lease). The landlord wants to reserve a right to reconfigure the common areas to respond to changes in the real estate market and to attract new tenants to its project. By way of example, a landlord might decide that it needs to dramatically increase the size of its surface parking lot to lure a new tenant to the project and that its only option for doing so is to eliminate the building's green space and picnic area—a feature that may have attracted certain of its existing tenants to the building in the first instance. Similarly, a landlord might want to take advantage of a hot real estate market by constructing a new building in the area immediately adjacent to its existing building, with the result that the number of parking spaces serving the existing building is permanently reduced by 20% and the views from the existing building are totally obstructed by the newly-constructed edifice. To the extent the landlord has reserved in its lease a broad right to change the building's common areas, the existing tenants in the above scenarios are probably be out of luck even if they can, with a straight face, make the argument that they never would have moved into the landlord's building if the common area changes had been in place prior to lease execution.

The tenant often seeks to limit the landlord's open-ended right to reconfigure the common areas because the tenant fears that such a reconfiguration could have an adverse effect on its conduct of business in its leased premises. The best way for the tenant to accomplish that goal is (1) to attach a site plan to the lease that specifically identifies the location, size, and configuration of all existing common areas, and (2) to then expressly prohibit the landlord from changing the depicted common areas without the tenant's consent (see *Pro-Tenant Modification #6* at page 735).

A one-sided clause of that type is, however, seldom acceptable to a well-represented landlord. The best that the tenant can usually hope to achieve is to render off-limits those changes to the specific common area characteristics that are most important to the tenant (for example, a parking lot containing not less than 200 parking spaces—see *Pro-Tenant Modification #7* at page 735) and to include soft language in the lease that further precludes the landlord from making other common area changes to the extent "such changes would materially interfere with the Tenant's ability to conduct its business operations in the Leased Premises"—a standard that the landlord's lawyer promptly tries to modify to address only those "changes that would permanently deprive the Tenant of the substantial benefit and enjoyment of the Leased Premises" (see the last sentence of § 6 of the Form Office lease).

A. MEASUREMENT OF LEASED PREMISES

Most commercial leases contain prominent statements of the number of square feet contained within the leased premises. The landlord insists on this because it quotes and calculates its rent on a per square foot basis— for example, rent of $20 per square foot. The tenant wants the lease to recite the number of square feet contained within its leased premises so that it can make a rational determination of whether the size of the leased premises appropriately supports the conduct of its business operations. The tenant, of course, is also interested in determining the number of square feet in its leased premises because it has been told by the landlord (and every other landlord it has ever talked to) that its rent is calculated based on the number of square feet contained within the leased premises.

Having agreed that the lease should recite the number of square feet contained within the leased premises, the next challenge facing the landlord and tenant is to figure out how to measure the leased premises. That task is not nearly as clear-cut as it might seem. The square footage of an office building can be expressed in terms of its gross area, its usable area or its rentable area.

- ***Gross area*** of a building includes all the constructed space within a building's footprint. To measure a building's gross area, one practitioner suggests that one should "wrap a tape measure around the building's exterior."[3] A popular measurement standard adopted by the Building Owners and Managers Association (the ***BOMA Standard***) states that "gross building area is computed by measuring the outside finished surface of permanent outer building walls."[4] Gross area includes both building common areas and the leased premises of all building tenants and is calculated without any deduction for stairs, elevator shafts, flues, pipe shafts,

---

[3] *See* Theodore I. Yi and Dov Pinchot, *Space and Term Issues in Commercial Leases*, in THE PRACTICAL REAL ESTATE LAWYER'S MANUAL ON COMMERCIAL LEASING IN TROUBLED TIMES— FORMS, CHECKLISTS, AND ADVICE 3, 5 (2009).

[4] *See* BUILDING OWNERS AND MANAGEMENT ASSOCIATION INTERNATIONAL, STANDARD METHOD FOR MEASURING FLOOR AREA IN OFFICE BUILDINGS, ANSI/BOMA Z65.1, 10 (1996). The Building Owners and Managers Association International issued a new measurement standard in 2010. *See* BUILDING OWNERS AND MANAGERS ASSOCIATION INTERNATIONAL, OFFICE BUILDINGS: STANDARD METHODS OF MEASUREMENT, ANSI/BOMA Z65.1 (2010). The 2010 standard may one day supplant the 1996 BOMA standard as the measurement standard most widely referred to in commercial leases. However, as of the date of the writing of this chapter (the first quarter of 2017), the 1996 BOMA standard still remains the favored space measurement standard for tenants (presumably because of its familiarity to tenants and their legal counsel).

vertical ducts, atria, lightwells, and similar penetrations above the finished floor.

- *Usable area* is the space within the four walls of each tenant's leased premises or, as one author puts it, "the space for which a tenant might buy carpet."[5] The usable area of a building is the sum of the usable areas of the leased premises of all building tenants and expressly excludes any space devoted to building common areas.

- *Rentable area* of a building is equal to the sum of the building's usable area, *PLUS* an allocation for the building's common areas. Rentable area is a fictional number used by the landlord to calculate the amount of a tenant's rent. The rentable area of a building is always greater than the building's usable area, but is not necessarily equal to the building's gross area. The difference between the square footage of a building's rentable and usable space is known as the *common area load factor*. The common area load factor is typically expressed as a percentage that is calculated in accordance with the following formula: [rentable square feet − usable square feet] ÷ rentable square feet. A building with a high common area load factor is labeled an "inefficient" building because a higher percentage of the building's constructed space is devoted to common areas than is the case in a building with a lower common area load factor.

The interplay of the three space measurement modes is illustrated in the following example.

Example 11-1: Building A is a three story office building. The gross area contained on each floor is 10,000 square feet. The usable area of the tenant space located on each of the three floors measures 8,000 square feet, leaving 2,000 square feet on each floor to lobby corridors, restrooms, and other common areas.

The above assumptions produce the following space calculations for Building A:

- Gross area = 30,000 square feet;

- Usable area = 24,000 square feet;

- Common area = 6,000 square feet;

---

[5]   *See* MARK A. SENN, COMMERCIAL REAL ESTATE LEASES: PREPARATION, NEGOTIATION AND FORMS 4–18 (5th ed. 2012). The 2010 BOMA standard referred to in note 4, *supra*, substitutes the term "occupant area" for "usable area." The term "usable area" is used in this chapter because that is the term most practitioners and developers continue to use despite the introduction of the new term in the 2010 BOMA standard.

- Rentable area = 30,000 square feet; and

- Common area load factor = 20%.

So why do lawyers have to know all this stuff (it seems like it should be discussed in an engineering text and not in a law book)? As noted earlier, most landlords compute their tenants' rent based on the number of rentable square feet contained within the tenant's leased premises. Charging rents based on a building's rentable square footage theoretically permits the landlord to receive a rental return on *ALL* space located in the building and not just the usable space located within the four walls of the tenants' suites (or at least that is the common justification proffered by landlords for why they charge rents on a per rentable square foot basis). From a more practical perspective, it allows the landlord to quote lower per square foot rents than it would if it were quoting rents on a usable square foot basis—because there are always more rentable square feet in a building than there are usable square feet. Thus, if the landlord in Example 11-1 needs to collect $600,000 per year in rent from its tenants in order to meet its targeted financial goals, it could meet those goals by charging rent of either $20 per rentable square foot or $25 per usable square foot. Logic tells the landlord that using rentable square feet as a basis for its rent quotes produces a better marketing optic for its building. In addition, because the concept of rentable space is a fiction, the landlord is afforded greater flexibility in calculating its tenants' rent obligations on the basis of rentable area than it would if it were forced to calculate rents on the basis of the more exacting usable area method of space measurement.

It should be clear by now that the use of rentable square feet to measure a tenant's leased premises does not serve the tenant's goal of making sure that the leased premises is properly sized for the conduct of its business operations. Moreover, having its rent computed based on the fictional number of rentable square feet contained with its leased premises provides the tenant with little solace that it is paying a competitive rent for its leased space.

So what should a tenant do when it receives a proposal from a landlord to lease 10,000 square feet of rentable space at a rent of $20 per rentable square foot (other than to call someone who has read this chapter and actually understands all this space measurement mumbo jumbo)? The first thing that the tenant should do is ask the landlord how many usable square feet are contained within the tenant's leased premises. Getting the answer to that question (which, ideally, should be provided in the form of a landlord representation in the lease—see *Pro-Tenant Lease Modification #2* at page 733) permits the tenant to consult its operations people to determine if the leased premises are right-sized for its business.

The tenant should next try to unearth the precise method used by the landlord to calculate the rentable square footage of the tenant's leased premises—that is, exactly how much space in the building is devoted to common areas and what percentage of that space is being allocated to the tenant. Discovering the method behind the madness of the landlord's rentable space calculations permits the tenant to compare the landlord's lease proposal on an "apples to apples" basis with proposals made to the tenant by other property owners. The best way to achieve that objective is to require the landlord to make a certification in the lease that the landlord calculated the usable and rentable square feet contained within both the building and the leased premises in accordance with a well-recognized measurement benchmark, such as the BOMA standard referred to earlier in this chapter. The tenant should then reserve the right to re-measure its leased premises in accordance with the selected standard and to adjust its rent downward if its re-measurement of the leased premises shows that the leased premises contain less rentable square feet than initially certified by the landlord (see *Pro-Tenant Lease Modification #1* at page 733).

The following example illustrates the benefits that redound to the favor of a tenant who successfully adopts the suggested negotiating tactic.

Example 11-2: Tenant receives lease proposals from two local landlords (Landlord A and Landlord B). Each proposal calls for the tenant to lease 10,000 square feet of rentable space for an annual rental of $20 per rentable square foot (producing a total rent payment under each of the proposals of $200,000 per year). Tenant asks for and receives the following certifications from Landlord A and B concerning their respective calculations of the rentable square footage of tenant's leased premises.

Calculation Components	Landlord A	Landlord B
Rentable square feet in building	30,000	30,000
Rentable square feet in leased premises	10,000	10,000
Usable square feet in leased premises	8,000	9,000
Square feet in building common areas	6,000	3,000
Common area load factor	20%	10%

Based on this information, the tenant knows that, while its rent is the same for both buildings ($200,000 per year), the usable square footage of its leased premises in Landlord B's building is significantly greater than in

Landlord A's building (9,000 vs. 8,000 square feet). The usable square footage variance between the two buildings is attributable to the higher level of common area space found in Landlord A's building (hence, the higher common area load factor applicable to Landlord A's building). With this information in hand, the tenant can make an "apples to apples" comparison of the two buildings to determine if the additional common area amenities provided in Landlord A's building outweigh the relative inefficiency of that building.

The above example nicely portrays a theme that runs throughout the rest of this chapter—that is, the tenant's desire for transactional transparency and the landlord's preference for obfuscation.

HIBC Case Study—The Use of a "Modified BOMA Method"

The Form Office Lease makes no reference whatsoever to any standard of measurement (be it the BOMA standard or any other benchmark). Rather, all that the Standard Office Lease says is that the "Leased Premises is deemed to contain ___ square feet of rentable space" (see ¶ E of the Lease Summary to the Form Office Lease). I did not want to invite an argument with the tenant about the manner in which rentable space was calculated— hence, the reference to the "deemed" rentable square footage of the leased premises.

My desire to wholly avoid the rentable space controversy was regularly met with derision from tenant's counsel who would insist that the lease include provisions (1) confirming that the rentable area of the leased premises had been calculated in accordance with the BOMA standard, and (2) requiring a rent adjustment if the tenant's measurement of the leased premises produced a rentable square footage number that was different from that recited in the lease. My first reaction when braced with such a tenant-sponsored request was to point out to the tenant's lawyer that the landlord used a "modified BOMA standard" in its calculation of the rentable area of the building and the leased premises. This usually satisfied the tenant's lawyer, even though there is no specific benchmark defining what is meant by a "modified BOMA standard." I used that term simply to buy my client flexibility in the way it performed its rentable space calculations. In those rare instances where the modified BOMA standard ploy did not work, I would agree that the space would be measured in strict accordance with the BOMA standard, but would then argue till my last dying breath that the tenant's monthly rent payment would remain as recited in the lease and would not be adjusted in any fashion. In other words, the monthly base rent would be $20,000, regardless whether the tenant's leased premises contained 10,000 rentable square feet or 9,500 rentable square feet. My reluctance to give the tenant a rent adjustment had *less to do with my natural stubbornness than it did with my desire to protect the landlord's projected rental stream from its building (which was based on the project's costs and not any space calculation).*

———

B. TENANT IMPROVEMENTS
(¶ O of Lease Summary, § 9, and Exhibit D)

When the landlord and tenant sit down to begin their lease negotiations, the leased premises are seldom in move-in condition. Significant improvements and modifications invariably have to be made to the physical condition of the leased premises to render them suitable for the tenant's conduct of its business. This is true for both space that has not previously been occupied by a tenant (so-called "virgin space") and space that has previously been occupied by a tenant or tenants (so-called "second generation space"). The improvements and modifications that must be made to fit the tenant's planned use of the space are known as ***tenant improvements*** or ***TI***.

Tenant improvements are in addition to those core structural improvements that the landlord makes to the leased premises as part of its construction of the overall building—that is, those improvements that the landlord must make to facilitate the occupancy of the leased premises by any user and not just the specific tenant's planned occupancy. Those core structural improvements are commonly referred to as ***base building improvements*** and typically include, at a minimum, load-bearing walls, carpet-ready floors, life safety systems, windows, and stubbed-in utilities. Because the landlord bears the sole economic responsibility for constructing the base building improvements, it is in the tenant's best interests to define base building improvements in as expansive a manner as possible.

A commercial lease usually includes lengthy provisions addressing the tenant improvements for the leased premises. Those provisions can either be included within the text of the base lease or in a separate agreement often referred to as a ***work letter***. Regardless which drafting technique is utilized, the tenant improvement clause must address and answer all of the following questions.

- What specific improvements must be made to the leased premises?

- Who is responsible for designing and constructing the tenant improvements?

- Who is responsible for paying the costs of designing and constructing the improvements?

- When must the improvements be completed?

In the typical office lease, the landlord is designated as the person responsible for designing and constructing the leased premises. It is in the best interests of the landlord to control that process because it wants to make sure that the improvements enhance the long-term value of its office building. In addition, the landlord has a vested interest in seeing to it that the tenant improvements are completed ASAP because the completion of the tenant improvements is the usual trigger for the commencement of the tenant's rent obligation. Finally, the tenant seldom has either the expertise or the inclination to immerse itself in the intricacies of designing and constructing the tenant improvements.

Answering the remaining three tenant improvement questions is relatively straightforward if detailed plans and specifications showing the desired tenant improvements are in place in advance of the lease negotiations. If that is the case, the landlord can secure pricing and scheduling commitments from its selected design and construction professionals and then instruct its counsel to complete the tenant improvement clause by stating that (1) the improvements must be constructed in accordance with a specified set of plans and specifications, (2) the landlord assumes the cost of constructing the tenant improvements, and (3) the landlord must use its reasonable efforts to complete construction of the tenant improvements by a mutually agreeable target date. An arrangement of this type is commonly referred to as a ***turnkey build-out***—meaning that the landlord does all of the work and all the tenant has to do is "turn the key, open the door and commence business."[6] A turnkey arrangement is most often used for single tenant build-to-suit projects where the tenant has expended the time and effort needed to determine in advance of its execution of the lease precisely what type of build-out is needed to serve the tenant's operational needs (see *Practice Tip #11-2: The Build-to-Suit Lease*, at pages 506–508).

Unfortunately in the customary office lease transaction, the tenant does not enter the lease negotiations with a fixed sense of the precise nature and scope of its tenant improvement package. As such, the lawyers representing the landlord and the tenant must draft a tenant improvement clause that describes the process to be followed to determine the specifics of the tenant improvements to be made to the leased premises. That process typically involves the tenant's delivery to the landlord of its general program requirements for the space (for example, ten exterior offices, two conference rooms, and a reception lobby); the landlord's preparation of preliminary design plans implementing the tenant's program

---

[6] See ZANKEL, *supra* note 1, at 13.

requirements; and, once the preliminary plans are approved by the tenant, the landlord's preparation of final plans and specifications that are also subject to the tenant's approval (although the tenant's right to disapprove the final plans and specifications is often limited to matters that are inconsistent with the previously-approved preliminary plans—see the second paragraph of § 9 of the Form Office Lease).

The tenant improvement clause drafted by landlord's counsel usually imposes a timeline for all of the above actions—for example, the tenant's delivery of its program requirements to landlord within 30 days after lease execution, tenant's approval of the preliminary plans within 15 days after the landlord's submission of the preliminary plans to the tenant, and tenant's approval of the final plans within ten days after the landlord's submission of the final plans to the tenant. Once the final plans are approved by the tenant, the landlord then assumes responsibility for constructing the tenant improvements in accordance with the approved final plans.

While it is fairly easy to describe the process that governs the design and construction of the tenant improvements, it is a much tougher task to determine the economic consequences of a tenant improvement build-out when the specific nature of that build-out is not known when the parties sign the lease. When the landlord quotes a rent figure to a tenant, the landlord necessarily takes into account the budgeted costs for constructing tenant improvements to the tenant's leased premises. Similarly, when the tenant determines what rent it is willing to pay for particular space, it does so in anticipation that the landlord will improve the space in a manner that is designed to fit the operational needs of the tenant's business. All is well as long as the cost of the build-out needed by the tenant is less than or equal to the landlord's budgeted tenant improvement costs for the space. The issue that comes to the fore in every negotiation is what happens if the actual cost of the build-out exceeds the landlord's tenant improvement budget for the leased space. Who is responsible for the payment of the excess costs?

1.   Tenant Improvement Allowance

Landlords attempt to respond to the economic issue presented by an uncertain scope of the tenant improvement work by agreeing to pay tenant improvement costs up to a stipulated level (the ***tenant improvement allowance***), with the tenant then being responsible for the payment of any costs in excess of the allowance amount ("excess TI costs"). This contractual arrangement permits the landlord to fix its maximum lease costs and preserve the integrity of its financial returns even though the landlord does not have a firm handle on the precise amount of the tenant improvement costs on the date of its execution of the lease.

The TI allowance arrangement works well for the landlord, but it does not protect the tenant against the risk that the actual cost of the build-out exceeds the amount of the TI allowance. There are a number of tactics that the tenant can employ to attempt to mitigate its risks under a typical pro-landlord TI allowance provision. The most obvious thing that the tenant can do when presented with a lease draft that includes a TI allowance clause is to delay execution of the lease until the scope of the tenant improvement work has been finalized and, hence, the actual cost of the tenant improvement work has been bid out and finalized.

The option of deferring lease execution until the TI costs are finalized is usually rendered impractical due to (1) the time pressure felt by both the landlord and the tenant to lock in their lease deal ASAP, and (2) their shared reluctance to spend the time and money needed to prepare, review, and approve the tenant improvement plans and specifications without first having reached a definitive enforceable agreement on the tenant's leasing of the designated space from the landlord. If the circumstances surrounding the lease transaction make it impractical for the parties to defer lease execution until the TI costs are finalized, then the tenant is well-advised to retain the services of a design professional to try to get a preliminary sense as to whether what the tenant has in mind for the build-out of its leased premises can be designed and constructed at a cost that is consistent with the TI allowance being offered by the landlord. If the tenant hears back from the design professional that the offered TI allowance is insufficient to build out the leased premises as originally contemplated by the tenant, then the tenant should consider either downsizing its build-out expectations (for example, using carpet squares instead of granite tile in the lobby) or asking the landlord to increase the amount of the TI allowance (which, as one might expect, is usually a futile inquiry).

There are, however, a variety of tactics that the tenant's counsel can employ to try to chip away at the issue of the insufficiency of the stated TI allowance. By way of example, the tenant's counsel could try to negotiate provisions that (1) limit the landlord's ability to charge a supervisory fees and overhead costs against the TI allowance, (2) require the landlord to competitively bid out the tenant improvement work once the final plans are approved by the tenant, and (3) force feed as many construction costs as possible into the category of base building improvements that are not charged against the TI allowance (see *Pro-Tenant Modification #3* at page 734 and *Pro-Tenant Modification #4* at page 734).

2.   Rent Amortization of Excess TI Costs

Once it has done everything it can to try to properly align the scope of the anticipated build-out with the amount of the landlord's TI allowance, the tenant should next consider asking the landlord to absorb any excess TI costs in exchange for an increase in the tenant's future rental obligations. The standard landlord-oriented TI allowance provision states that all excess TI costs must be paid in cash by the tenant (see the first sentence of § 9 of the Form Office Lease). Such an upfront cash payment can be overly burdensome to a tenant, particularly one whose liquidity is not boundless. Asking the landlord to amortize the excess TI costs as a rent increase can significantly ease the tenant's cash flow burden if the actual cost of the build-out substantially exceeds the amount of the established TI allowance (see *Pro-Tenant Modification #5* at page 734). The landlord's willingness to agree to a rent amortization option depends largely on the landlord's own liquidity position and the amount of the rent increase that the tenant is willing to accept for the landlord's agreement to front the payment of the excess TI costs. If a landlord has the funds available to pay the excess costs and if the tenant agrees to a rent amortization equation that increases the landlord's financial returns for its project, then the landlord may well look kindly upon the tenant's request for a rent amortization option.

The setting of a ***rent amortization factor*** (that is, the percentage number by which the excess TI costs are multiplied to determine the tenant's annual rent increase) is a fairly complicated task that involves an analysis of the genesis of the excess TI costs against the backdrop of the landlord's financial return expectations. Too many lawyers fail to appreciate the nuanced nature of the negotiations over the setting of the rent amortization factor and, instead, spend their time simply trying to negotiate a high amortization factor for the landlord or a low amortization factor for the tenant (without having any real clue as to the logical underpinning of the rent amortization factor).

The tenant's starting point in the negotiation is to assert that the landlord should receive the same return on the excess TI costs that it does on any other project cost. Based on that assertion, the tenant might expect its annual rent to increase by somewhere between 8–12% of the excess TI costs (depending on the then prevailing conditions in the real estate marketplace). The landlord's counterpoint is that the landlord is simply extending a loan to the tenant to pay the excess TI costs and all principal and interest on that loan must be repaid over the initial term of the lease. That argument produces a rent amortization factor far in excess of that produced on the basis of the tenant's "just another project cost" argument (somewhere in the 25% range assuming an initial lease term of five years and an interest rate of 8%).

The ultimate resolution of this issue is dependent on the amount of the excess TI costs and the nature of the tenant improvements that gave rise to the existence of such excess costs. The way the math works on the rent amortization issue is illustrated by the following example.

Example 11-3: Assume that the excess tenant improvement costs are $100,000 and that the tenant is paying annual rent of $200,000 during each year of its five-year lease. If the "just another project cost" approach is adopted, the landlord will agree to pay the $100,000 of excess TI costs in exchange for the tenant's agreement to increase its annual rent by $10,000 (computed using a rent amortization factor of 10%). If the landlord treats its payment of the $100,000 of excess TI costs as a "loan" to the tenant, then the tenant's annual rent will increase by $25,000 (assuming the use of a rent amortization factor of 25% that is designed to pay off the "loan" in five years at an interest rate of 8%). The upshot of these varying treatments of the excess TI costs is that under the "just another project cost" approach, the tenant will pay $50,000 of additional rent over the five-year term of its lease, while it will pay additional rent of $125,000 over the five-year term under the "loan" perspective—a sizable difference that certainly merits the attention of the lawyers for both the landlord and the tenant.[7]

If the excess TI costs are relatively small in amount and are attributable to the construction of improvements that are likely be re-used by a future tenant (for example, a high-efficiency HVAC system), then the tenant should be in a relatively strong position to argue for the setting of the rent amortization factor in the 8–12% range (on the theory that the excess costs are "just like any other project cost"). If, however, the excess TI costs are significant in amount and are triggered by exotic improvements that will in all likelihood need to be demolished before the next tenant assumes occupancy of the space, then the landlord should prevail in it argument that it is simply acting as a lender and the rent amortization factor should be set at a percentage that results in the excess TI costs, plus interest, being repaid over the initial term of the tenant's lease. There is, obviously, plenty of room for negotiation between the two noted extremes and it is not uncommon for the landlord and the tenant to strike a compromise whereby the landlord agrees to amortize a portion of the excess TI costs at one percentage and another portion of such costs at a much higher percentage, with an overall cap then being placed on the amount of the excess TI costs that are required to be funded by the landlord. Any excess TI costs above the agreed-upon cap must then be paid in cash by the tenant.

---

[7]   *See* ZANKEL, *supra* note 1, at 15–17 for an interesting and entertaining take on this point.

VII. THE LEASE TERM
(¶¶ H–J of Lease Summary)

The *lease term* is the period during which the tenant has the right to exclusive possession of the leased premises. A typical lease term for a commercial lease is five to ten years. The length of a commercial lease term stands in sharp contrast to the usual six to 12 month term of a residential lease. The longer term of the commercial lease is driven by two factors—(1) the tenant's need for continuity in its business location, and (2) the landlord's desire to lock in a financial return on its capital investment for as long a period as possible.

The "commencement date" of the lease term is the date on which the tenant first gains the right to exclusively possess the leased premises and the "termination date" is the date when the tenant's right to possess the leased premises ends. The commencement date can be expressed either as a date certain (for example, January 1, 2018) or as the date on which certain conditions are satisfied (for example, the date on which construction of the tenant improvements is completed). It is important to keep in mind that the commencement date is almost never the same date as the date of the parties' execution of the lease (due primarily to the landlord's need to make tenant improvements to the space before delivering possession of the space to the tenant) and only sometimes the same as the date on which the tenant's rent obligation commences or the date on which the tenant first opens for business in the leased premises. The termination date is usually described as being a number of years/months/days after the commencement date (for example, sixty calendar months after the commencement date).

The lease should specifically recite both the commencement and termination dates of the lease term. The term of the lease recited in the lease is typically referred to as the *initial lease term* and may be extended or renewed for an additional term or terms by the agreement of the parties. The lease should also specify what the tenant's obligations are on the termination of the lease term—specifically, in what condition the tenant is required to re-deliver the leased premises to the landlord and whether the tenant is obligated to remove any improvements made by it in the leased premises.[8]

---

[8]   *See e.g.,* § 18 of the Form Office Lease. *See also* the discussion of the tenant's termination obligations in Ruth A. Schoenmeyer and Michelle M. McAtee, *Surrender Dorothy: Restoration Obligations in Office Leases*, 23 No. 3 PRACTICAL REAL ESTATE LAWYER 17 (May 2007).

A. DELIVERY OF POSSESSION—
AMERICAN VS. ENGLISH RULES

The biggest issue that arises concerning the lease term is what happens if the landlord is not able to deliver possession of the leased premises to the tenant on the commencement date specified in the lease either because another tenant is holding over in the leased premises or because the landlord has not yet completed construction of the leased premises. This topic necessarily begins with the discussion of two contrasting common law rules—the "American rule" (the minority position) and the "English rule" (the majority position).[9] Under the American rule (which is mentioned first solely for patriotic reasons), the landlord is only obligated to deliver "legal possession" of the leased premises to the tenant on the commencement date. The landlord is not required to put the tenant in "actual possession" of the leased space. As such, the tenant has no legal recourse against the landlord and must begin paying rent on its leased space even though a holdover tenant or trespasser is in possession of the leased premises—a crazy result, but one that is still followed in a number of states.

The English rule more appropriately requires the landlord to deliver both legal and actual possession of the leased premises to the tenant on the commencement date. If someone other than the tenant is in actual possession of the leased premises, then the tenant can withhold its rent, terminate its lease, or sue the landlord for damages.

The most important thing to remember about the American and English rules is that both rules can be abrogated by contract. A lawyer representing a landlord should exercise the "power of the pen" to make it clear that the tenant cannot sue the landlord for damages if the landlord is unable to deliver actual possession of the leased premises to the tenant on the scheduled date. The lawyer for the tenant might then want to also pick up a pen to draft a provision that provides that the tenant's rent obligation is abated if the tenant is prevented from taking possession of the leased premises by the act of a third party.

Practice Tip #11-1: Drafting Around the Law

The prior section's admonition that a lawyer should rely on "the power of the pen" when negotiating a commercial lease reminds me of a lunch meeting I had with a senior professor shortly after I agreed to join the law school faculty at The Ohio State University. The professor, an expert in contract and commercial law, asked me, "Are there a lot of cases that you

---

[9]   *See generally* Yi, *supra* note 3, at 6; and SENN, *supra* note 5, at 5–6 to 5–7.

can use in teaching your course on Real Estate Development Law"? My reply (which was received in a less than accepting manner by the commercial law professor) was "not really." I tried to explain to the professor that a business lawyer's job is not merely to research and understand the applicable case law, but, much more importantly, to "draft around it."

One of the hardest things for law students and young lawyers (and apparently most law school professors) to understand is that it is a business lawyer's job is to CREATE the law by spelling out in a contract exactly what obligations, rights, and remedies are available to serve the client's interests. There are no immutable legal principles on which the lawyer can rely for the client's protection. In the very first law school class I taught at Ohio State, I held up a 30-page lease document and told my students "this is my law." I recognized the looks on their faces as being the same stunned, uncomprehending visage that I saw when I talked to the senior professor about the need to draft around case law. It took my students the entire semester (and some probably even longer) to gain an understanding of what I was talking about in that first class.

B. TENANT IMPROVEMENT DELAYS
(§ 9)

The source of most commencement date problems is the landlord's failure to complete construction of the tenant improvements by the commencement date contemplated by the lease. While both parties are naturally motivated to cause the tenant improvements to be completed by the commencement date, any number of things can go wrong to thwart the timely completion of the landlord's construction efforts. The following are several of the more common reasons for the occurrence of a construction delay:

- The tenant improvement plans and specifications are not finalized in a timely fashion;

- The landlord fails to secure a building permit on the date contemplated in its construction schedule;

- The landlord sets an overly optimistic construction schedule that its contractor cannot meet;

- The contractor simply messes up and misses its completion deadline;

- The tenant requests changes to the work that delay construction;

- The materials called for in the specifications are on back order;

- A trade contractor files for bankruptcy or goes on strike; or

- Bad weather or other acts of God slow down the progress of construction.

The consequences of a construction delay can be severe for both the tenant and the landlord. If a tenant cannot open for business on the targeted date, it may suffer a loss of profits and almost certainly will incur additional costs triggered by it having to stop and later re-start the process of moving into its new space. In addition, the tenant may have to pay a penalty rent to hold over in its existing leased space or, worse yet, have no place whatsoever to conduct its business.

The impact on the landlord of a construction delay can be equally disastrous. At best, the landlord's rental stream is deferred until construction of the tenant improvements is completed. At worst, the landlord's lease with the tenant might be terminated, thereby forcing the landlord to go back in the market to find a replacement tenant. Even if it fortunate enough to secure a replacement tenant, the landlord will lose rent for a period of time and will likely have to pay additional leasing commission and tenant improvement costs to secure the new tenant.

The construction delay issue should be tackled head on in the text of the lease and not left to the vagaries of the American, English, or other common law rules dealing with delays in the delivery of possession of the leased premises. The landlord and the tenant normally stake out polar opposite positions when the issue of possible construction delays is first raised during the lease negotiations. The landlord graciously (and somewhat disingenuously) acknowledges that the American rule probably does not make a lot of sense in the context of a tenant improvement construction delay (unless, of course, the delay was the tenant's fault, in which event the landlord does a lot of flag-waving). The landlord's proffered solution is to stipulate that the only consequence of a construction delay should be the deferral of the commencement and termination dates by the number of days of the construction delay. The tenant, on the other hand, insists that (1) it be given the right to terminate the lease if the tenant improvements are not completed by the deadline specified in the lease, and (2) the landlord be held responsible for the payment of liquidated damages for each day of the construction delay.

The lawyers for the landlord and tenant then embark on a negotiation that is very similar to the owner-contractor negotiation concerning construction delays discussed in Chapter 10 of this book (see pages 465–471). Some of the issues that are discussed during the course of that negotiation and the lawyers' respective takes on those issues are summarized below.[10]

- ### Definition of Completion

  o **Landlord's take**—The tenant improvements should be deemed complete on the earlier of (1) the date on which the landlord's architect certifies that the improvements are sufficiently complete to permit the tenant to occupy the leased premises, or (2) the date on which the local building department issues a **temporary certificate of occupancy** for the leased premises. A temporary certificate of occupancy permits the tenant to occupy the leased premises on the condition that the landlord completes certain additional improvements within a fixed period of time established by the local governmental authorities. A temporary certificate of occupancy is, therefore, a revocable occupancy permit.

  o **Tenant's take**—The tenant improvements should be deemed complete only upon the occurrence of both of the following events (1) the issuance by the local building department of a **permanent certificate of occupancy**, and (2) the tenant's inspection and acceptance of the leased premises (subject to a small construction punchlist authored and agreed to by the tenant). A permanent certificate of occupancy is a final, irrevocable authorization for the tenant to assume occupancy of its leased premises for the conduct of its business.

- ### Liquidated Damages

  o **Landlord's take**—Liquidated damages should not apply to any excusable delay; should be in a fairly nominal amount; and should be imposed only after the expiration of a lengthy grace period (for example, 60 days after the completion deadline specified in the lease).

  o **Tenant's take**—Liquidated damages should be charged without regard to excusable delays; should be in an amount sufficient to incentivize the landlord to complete the project on time; and should be imposed immediately upon the passage of the completion deadline (see *Pro-Tenant Modification #13* at page 738).

---

[10] *See generally* Lisa Rosen, *Construction Issues in Leases: The Landlord's Perspective*, in LEASE NEGOTIATION HANDBOOK 93 (Edward Chupack ed., 2003); and Ray Kwasnick, *Construction Issues in Leases: The Tenant's Perspective*, 20 No. 2 PRACTICAL REAL ESTATE LAWYER 51 (March 2004).

- *Excusable Delays*

  o *Landlord's take*—Excusable delays should be a long, broad, and non-exclusive list of both foreseeable and unforeseeable events that are beyond the landlord's control.

  o *Tenant's take*—Excusable delays should be a short, specific, and all-inclusive list of unforeseeable events beyond the landlord's reasonable control (to the extent the tenant even recognizes the concept of an excusable delay).

- *Standard of Performance*

  o *Landlord's take*—The landlord should be required to pursue the completion of the tenant improvements "in the due course," with no requirement that it take any extraordinary measures to meet the completion deadline.

  o *Tenant's take*—The landlord should be required to use "all commercially reasonable efforts" to meet the completion deadline (specifically including the payment of overtime).

- *Consequences of Tenant-Caused Delays*

  o *Landlord's take*—The landlord and the tenant usually can agree on what constitutes a "tenant-caused delay" in the construction of the tenant improvements. The two most commonly cited types of tenant-caused delays are the tenant's failure to review design submissions within the time period stated in the lease and the tenant's requests for changes in the final TI plans. While the definition of a tenant-caused delay is seldom a topic of controversy in the landlord-tenant negotiations, the consequence of the occurrence of a tenant-caused delay certainly often becomes a matter of contention, with the landlord taking the position that a tenant-caused delay should result in the tenant being required to pay its rent effective as of the regularly-scheduled commencement date regardless when construction of the improvements is actually completed.

  o *Tenant's take*—After reaching agreement on the definition of a tenant-caused delay, the tenant's lawyer typically asserts that a tenant-caused delay should result in a deferral of the commencement and termination dates (and nothing more).

- **Termination Remedy**

  o **Landlord's take**—No way, no how (except after the passage of an extremely lengthy grace period and extensions granted for excusable delays).

  o **Tenant's take**—The tenant must have the right to terminate the lease if the work is not done within a reasonable period of time after the targeted commencement date (see *Pro-Tenant Modification #13* at page 738).

The ultimate resolution of the above issues depends on how important the schedule is to the tenant, how achievable the schedule is by the landlord, and what, if any, other leasing options are available to the landlord and the tenant. The negotiation of the construction delay provisions are particularly important in the context of the landlord's development of a build-to-suit project that is 100% occupied by a single tenant (see below, *Practice Tip #11-2: The Build-to-Suit Lease*).

Practice Tip #11-2: The Build-to-Suit Lease

*A **build-to-suit lease** typically refers to a lease that requires the landlord to construct a new building (be it an office building, warehouse, or retail building) from the ground up and lease the entirety of the completed building to a single tenant for an extended term (ten to 20 years being the norm). In most situations, the timely completion of the build-to-suit project is integral to the prospective tenant's achievement of its overall business objectives (think corporate headquarters or a new distribution hub).*

At its essence, a build-to-suit lease is part lease and part construction contract. It is the perfect storm where all the topics discussed in Chapter 10—Stage 6: The Design and Construction of the Project and this Chapter 11 merge into one commercial real estate transaction. The tenant wants a specialized building tailored to its business needs in accordance with detailed programmatic design requirements and construction time lines provided by the tenant to the landlord. Stated in the simplest terms, the tenant dictates that "I want this specific building constructed in this specific location and completed by this specific date."

Developers, of course, love build-to-suit leases because build-to-suit leases eliminate one of the primary risks faced by the developer of a new real estate project—that is, the risk that the project does not lease up at the rental rates and within the time frames contemplated in the developer's project pro forma. All that the developer has to do to reap the economic benefits inherent in a build-to-suit lease is complete the project on time and on budget—no small task given the magnitude, complexity, and time constraints that characterize most build-to-suit deals.

Both the landlord and the tenant face enormous risks under a build-to-suit lease. During my career as a practicing real estate lawyer, I have represented the landlord on well over a hundred build-to-suit projects. In every single one of those deals, the tenant made it clear to the landlord at the outset of the lease negotiations that the tenant would suffer catastrophic business losses if the project was not completed on time and in strict accordance with the tenant's approved plans and specifications. Those catastrophic losses range from the tenant's payment of egregious holdover rent at its existing building, to the loss of sales revenue if the tenant's big box store is not open for business in time for the holiday season, to the tenant's loss of a major logistics contract if a distribution facility is not operational by a specific date.

The landlord's risk of a failed build-to-suit project is equally significant. If the landlord fails to complete construction of the building at or below the projected level of development costs, then the landlord may find itself locked in to a project that hemorrhages cash for the duration of the long-term build-to-suit lease. Even worse, if the landlord fails to complete construction of the project by the deadline exacted by the tenant, then the tenant might walk from the deal, leaving the landlord with the ownership of a specialized single tenant project without a paying tenant.

It is, therefore, no surprise that the work letter component of a build-to-suit lease is the subject of very complex, laborious, and often highly-contentious negotiations between counsel for the landlord and counsel for the tenant.[11] The lawyers need to address and resolve all those issues mentioned in the earlier discussion in this chapter concerning the design and construction of tenant improvements (see pages 494–499 and 502–506)—for example, what happens if (1) the actual cost of the improvements exceeds the landlord's construction budget, or (2) the construction of the improvements are not completed by the commencement date of the lease term specified in the lease. While the construction and design issues presented by a build-to-suit lease are largely the same as those presented by a garden variety 5,000-square-foot lease in a multi-tenant building, the significance of an inappropriate resolution of those issues by the landlord or the tenant is astronomically greater in the context of a build-to-suit transaction.

The following are several construction and design issues that merit heightened attention in the context of a build-to-suit lease.[12]

---

[11] *See e.g.*, Richard R. Goldberg, *Complex Work Letter*, in ALI-ABA COURSE OF STUDY MATERIALS, COMMERCIAL REAL ESTATE LEASES: SELECTED ISSUES IN DRAFTING AND NEGOTIATING IN CURRENT MARKETS Course No. SN–013, 155 (May 2008).

[12] *See generally* Michael E. Rothpletz, Jr., *Build-To-Suit Leases: "Security," Contingencies, Rights and Remedies in the Event of Delay, Shifting the Risk, Warranties, and Other "Special Considerations"—Avoid the Pitfalls*, in ACREL PAPERS, Tab 9 (Spring 2015); and Loretta M. Kelly,

- *Does the tenant have a right to approve the selection of the project architect and general contractor?*

- *Who is responsible for insuring that the design and construction of the project complies with the requirements of governmental incentive programs, such as LEED certifications or other green building practices?*

- *What are the timelines and mandated processes for the landlord's submission and the tenant's approval of design plans and specifications?*

- *What is the impact on the amount and commencement of the tenant's rent obligation of (1) a change order requested by the tenant, or (2) a constructive change triggered by unforeseen site conditions?*

- *What is the definition of "completion of construction" as it pertains to the commencement of the lease term and the start of the tenant's rent payment obligation?*

- *What is the definition of an "excusable delay" that results in a deferral of the commencement date of the lease term without any penalty being imposed against the landlord?*

- *What is the definition and consequence of a "tenant-caused delay"?*

- *What are the tenant's remedies for the landlord's failure to complete construction by the date required by the lease—for example, liquidated damages, self-help rights, termination of lease?*

McGraw Hill Build-to-Suit-"Open Book" Pricing

Pizzuti developed several HIBC building that were ultimately leased to a single tenant. However, all of those buildings (other than the CBIS project, which has already been discussed ad nauseum in this book) were initially designed and launched as speculative multi-tenant buildings. The supply-demand curve prevailing in Central Florida during Pizzuti's ownership of HIBC was sufficiently favorable that Pizzuti was able to find tenants to lease 100% of a building on pricing and terms that were generally applicable to tenants in a multi-tenant building. For that reason, the single tenant leases that Pizzuti inked in HIBC are not overly instructive or interesting for the purpose of this book.

Build-to-Suit Leases: Pre-construction and Construction Issues (with Forms), 32 No. 1 PRACTICAL REAL ESTATE LAWYER 29 (January 2016).

A build-to-suit project that Pizzuti developed for McGraw Hill is, however, both interesting (at least to me) and instructive as to how deals might be structured in the future between sophisticated landlords and tenants. McGraw Hill decided that it needed a new warehouse in Central Ohio to streamline the distribution chain for its book publishing business. McGraw Hill reached out to Pizzuti because of Pizzuti's reputation as a leading industrial developer and negotiations were kicked off for a build-to-suit lease having an initial lease term of 20 years.

What made the McGraw Hill deal stand out was the approach that McGraw Hill took to the pricing of the deal. McGraw Hill's corporate real estate department (easily one of the most sophisticated in-house groups with which I ever had the privilege of working) took the position that the tenant's rent for the project should be calculated based on "open-book pricing." What McGraw Hill meant by "open book pricing" was that Pizzuti would share all of its project development costs with McGraw Hill on a fully transparent basis and that the rent would then be calculated by applying a fixed rent constant percentage against the project's development costs. McGraw Hill's theory was that an open book pricing methodology would operate to produce both a fair market rent for the tenant and a fair return on investment to the landlord. Once the initial shock of having to share information with a tenant wore off, Pizzuti began marching down the road of collaborating with McGraw Hill on an "open book" build-to-suit deal.

As negotiations on the deal proceeded, two significant obstacles to the "open book pricing" concept arose.

- First, McGraw Hill quickly realized that open book pricing would not work unless McGraw Hill was empowered to regulate Pizzuti's project development costs. Otherwise, Pizzuti would effectively be incentivized to overprice its development costs because it would be receiving a fixed percentage return on every dollar it threw at the project no matter how unjustified the costs might be (for example crazy high developer and contractor fees). After a fair amount of haggling over this issue, Pizzuti and McGraw Hill agreed to a guaranteed maximum price for the project that specifically included development and construction fees that were acceptable to Pizzuti and its contractors. The agreed-upon GMP served as a cap on the amount of the project development costs that could serve as the basis for the calculation of the tenant's rent. In order to incentivize Pizzuti to keep its development costs as low as possible, McGraw Hill agreed to pay Pizzuti a fixed percentage (30%) of any demonstrable cost savings on the project (that is, the excess of the GMP over the actual development costs).

- *Pizzuti and McGraw Hill were quickly able to agree on the percentage rent constant to be used for the calculation of the tenant's rent—10.4% of the lesser of the GMP or the actual project development costs, with the 10.4% figure being determined by assuming that: (1) 80% of the project costs would be funded with debt at a cost of 50 basis points over the yield for ten-year U.S. Treasury Notes; and (2) 20% of the project costs would be funded by equity priced at 17%. The tougher issue was how the tenant's rent should be adjusted if McGraw Hill requested changes to the agreed-upon plans that resulted in additional costs being added to the project's GMP. McGraw Hill's suggested resolution of this issue was that the rent should simply be increased by multiplying the amount of the added costs by the same 10.4% rent constant used to calculate McGraw Hill's base rent number. Pizzuti asserted (and McGraw Hill ultimately conceded) that those additional costs likely could not be funded on the same 80-20 debt-to-equity ratio that the GMP costs were funded and, therefore, the percentage rent constant that should be used to calculate McGraw Hill's rent on the additional costs should be increased to 11.5% for additional "base building costs" and 13.7% for additional "tenant improvement costs."*

The end product of the Pizzuti-McGraw Hill negotiations was a warehouse project that accomplished the two goals established by McGraw Hill at the outset of the project—a fair market rent for McGraw Hill and a fair return on investment for Pizzuti. In actuality, Pizzuti received a better than "fair" return on the project not because it hoodwinked McGraw Hill on the rent calculations (the talent of the McGraw Hill negotiating team made that possibility a non-starter), but because Pizzuti correctly anticipated how McGraw Hill's operations staff would react once they became involved in the project—specifically, by constantly asking for "more and better" additions to the project design on which the agreed-upon GMP was based. Every "more and better" request made by McGraw Hill's staff resulted in McGraw Hill's rent being increased by more than the agreed-upon base rent constant of 10.4% (11.5% for added based building costs and 13.7% for added tenant improvement costs). Pizzuti cashed in on this above market income stream by selling the McGraw Hill project to an institutional investor immediately following the project's completion at a beneficial fixed cap rate that did not distinguish between the rental attributable to the GMP costs and the rental attributable to the additional project costs triggered by McGraw Hill's change orders.

The transparency and collaboration that characterized the McGraw Hill deal is certainly not the norm for build-to-suit deals. However, on those rare occasions when a smart, open-minded landlord hooks up with an equally smart, open-minded tenant, the use of an open-book pricing model can prove to be a mutually rewarding development strategy.[13]

VIII. RENT
(¶¶ K–N of Lease Summary, §§ 1–3, and Exhibit B)

The developer's primary objective during stage 7 is to lease the project to creditworthy tenants who agree to pay rent at or above the rent level projected in the developer's operating budget for the project. While the real estate development lawyer needs to understand the economic drivers behind the developer's establishment of its quoted rent levels, the lawyer is rarely assigned the task of negotiating the per square foot rental rates that are included in the lease. The lawyer is, however, responsible for structuring a rent clause that is designed to protect the landlord against a potential reduction of its rental income from either (1) an unbudgeted increase in the landlord's building expenses, (2) the existence of inflation in the general economy, or (3) a tenant's failure to pay its agreed-upon rents.

Conversely, it is the job of the tenant's lawyer to craft a rent clause that protects the tenant against economic surprises and keeps the tenant's rent at or below the level contemplated in the operating budget for the business that the tenant conducts in the leased premises. Once again, it is not the job of the tenant lawyer to negotiate the per square foot rental rates recited in the lease, but rather to make sure that the tenant does not have to make additional payments under its lease that are inconsistent with the financial parameters set forth in the tenant's operating budget.

The next portion of the discussion focuses on the tactics and techniques at the lawyers' disposals to help their respective clients achieve their rent objectives. The following simple example is used as a touchstone for that discussion.

> **Example 11-4:** Landlord owns an office building containing 100,000 square feet of rentable space. Landlord's total development costs for the building were $20 million (or $200 per rentable square foot—"prsf"). In order to achieve its desired total return on costs of 10%, Landlord needs to produce an annual net operating income for the building of at least $2 million (or $20 prsf). Landlord's projections also call for its building expenses during the building's first full year of operation to be $1million ($10 prsf).

Note: For reasons that will become obvious as the remainder of this section unfolds, I have opted to use the term ***building expenses*** in lieu of the more

---

13   *See* Kelly, *supra* note 12, at 37–38.

commonly used term "operating expenses." The building expenses for a multi-tenant office project typically include the following categories of expenses: real estate taxes; insurance premiums; utility charges; maintenance and repair costs; capital expenditures to replace or add to existing project improvements; janitorial fees; property management fees; landscaping, snow removal, and trash disposal costs; legal, accounting, and other professional service fees; and other miscellaneous expenses and project reserves.

A. RENT STRUCTURES

The primary economic issue presented during stage 7 is, Can the landlord structure a rent clause that preserves the stability of its net operating income if its operating expenses are greater than projected? Providing a satisfactory resolution of this issue is paramount to the landlord's achievement of its desired financial returns because (1) the tenant's annual rent obligation is set at a fixed amount during each year of the lease term, and (2) the landlord's building expenses will fluctuate from year-to-year based on market conditions, project needs, inflation, and a variety of other circumstances. In the context of Example 11-3, the issue that the real estate development lawyer needs to answer is, What can be done to maintain the project's net operating income at or above $2 million if the building's expenses in any year exceed the $1 million projected threshold?

Answering this question requires an understanding of the three fundamental types of rent structures—(1) gross, (2) net, and (3) expense stop rents.[14] The three rent structures provide different answers to the basic question of who bears the risk that landlord's building expenses are greater than projected by the landlord.

Each of the three rent structures involves the tenant's payment of a fixed amount of rent (commonly known as **base rent**) that is payable by the tenant regardless of the level of the landlord's building expenses. Two of the structures contemplate the tenant's payment of an additional sum tied in some measure to the level of the landlord's building expenses. The variable component of the tenant's rent obligation is referred to as ***additional rent***. The levels of base and additional rent paid by the tenant under the gross, net, and expense stop rent structures are discussed below.

---

[14] Different people use different labels to describe these three rent structures. Additional terms used to describe the rent structures include "full service gross" (comparable to "gross" in the above discussion), "triple net ("net" in the above discussion), and "modified gross" (the "expense stop" arrangement in the above discussion). *See e.g.,* Terry L. Barger and Marc A. Maiona, *Operating Cost Escalation Theory and Practice under Commercial Leases,* in ACREL PAPERS 159, 161 (Spring 2007). As is the case with most things in life, it is the substance of the arrangements (and not the labels used to describe those arrangements) that is important.

1. Gross Lease

In a ***gross lease***, the tenant pays a fixed amount of base rent that is not tied in any way to the level of the landlord's building expenses. The tenant is not required to pay any additional rent whatsoever. If the landlord in Example 11-3 were to lease space in its building under a gross lease, it would need to charge each of its tenants annual base rent of $30 prsf in order to generate net operating income of $20 prsf (assuming that the landlord's actual building expenses are equal to the landlord's projected expense load of $10 prsf). In a gross lease, all the risk that the landlord's actual building expenses are greater than the budgeted expenses is placed on the landlord because the tenant's rent payment remains fixed at the $30 prsf level, regardless whether the actual building expenses are $10, $15, or $20 prsf.

2. Net Lease

In a ***net lease***, the tenant makes two rental payments—(1) a fixed base rent payment, *PLUS* (2) an additional rent payment equal to the tenant's share of the landlord's actual building expenses—whatever those expenses may be (see pages 523–527 for a discussion of how the tenant's share of the building expenses is calculated). If the landlord in Example 11-3 were to lease space in its building under a net lease, it could satisfy its financial goals by charging each of its tenants fixed base rent equal to $20 prsf and then further requiring each such tenant to pay additional rent equal to its share of the landlord's actual building expenses. In a net lease, the risk that the landlord's actual building expenses exceed the landlord's budgeted expenses is placed on the tenants because the tenants are required to reimburse the landlord for 100% of the actual building expenses regardless whether the actual expenses come in at $10, $15, or $20 prsf.

3. Expense Stop Lease

An ***expense stop lease*** is a hybrid of a gross lease and a net lease. As is the case in a net lease, the tenant in an expense stop lease makes two rental payments—(1) a fixed base rent payment, *PLUS* (2) an additional rent payment that fluctuates based on the level of the landlord's actual building expenses. The difference between an expense stop lease and a net lease is that, in an expense stop lease, the tenant is required to pay additional rent only if and to the extent that the actual building expenses exceed a pre-determined base amount (the ***expense stop***). As such, the tenant's additional rent payment is defined as its share of any *INCREASE* in the building expenses over the applicable expense stop. The expense stop can be defined either as a ***stipulated sum*** (for example, $10 prsf) or, more commonly, as the "actual building expenses incurred by the landlord in a specified base year" (a ***base-year expense stop***), with the selected ***base*** *year* typically being the first calendar year during which the tenant occupies its leased premises.

If the landlord in Example 11-4 were to adopt an expense stop rent structure (with a base-year expense stop equal to the landlord's actual building expenses during the first 12 months of the tenant's lease term), then the tenant's annual rent obligation would be equal to the sum of (1) fixed base rent of $30 prsf, plus (2) for all years subsequent to the base year, the tenant's share of any increase in the actual building expenses over the amount of the base-year expense stop. For example, if the actual building expenses in the base year were $12 prsf and the building expenses increased in the next year to $14 prsf, then the tenant would be required to make an additional rent payment in that next year equal to $2 prsf. In an expense stop lease, the risk that the landlord's actual building expenses exceed its budgeted building expenses is shared by the landlord and the tenant. The landlord assumes the risk that its actual building expenses in the base year are greater than the budgeted $10 prsf figure and the tenant bears the risk that the building's expenses increase after the base year.

The operation of the gross, net, and expense stop structures can best be shown through the use of an example.

Example 11-5: Assume the same facts used in Example 11-4 (that is, Landlord has a projected NOI goal of $20 prsf and projected building expenses for the first year of $10 prsf), plus the following additional facts:

- Actual Year 1 building expenses—$10 prsf (the same as budgeted);
- Tenant's annual base rent: Gross lease—$30 prsf;
  - o   Net lease—$20 prsf; and
  - o   Expense Stop—$30 prsf (with an expense stop = actual Year 1 building expenses).

The financial results produced for the landlord and the tenant under each of the three rent structures are shown in the following table (with all numbers being shown on a per rentable square foot basis).

Year 1 Operating Results	*Gross*	*Net*	*Expense Stop*
Base Rent	$30	$20	$30
Additional Rent	$0	$10	$0
Less: Actual Building Expenses	($10)	($10)	($10)
Landlord's Net Operating Income	$20	$20	$20

The above table illustrates that the three rent structures produce identical results for both the landlord (an NOI of $20 prsf) and the tenant (a total rent payment of $30 prsf) when the landlord's actual building expenses equal its budgeted building expenses. But, as the next example shows, the three alternative rent structures produce markedly different results when the actual building expenses exceed budget.

Example 11-6: Assume all of the same facts as used in Example 11-5, except that the actual building expenses in Year 1 are $12 prsf and the actual building expenses in Year 2 are $15 prsf.

The financial impact of the changed assumptions under each of the three rent structures is indicated in the following table.

Operating Results	Gross	Net	Expense Stop
Year 1 Operating Results			
Base Rent	$30	$20	$30
Additional Rent	$0	$12	$0
Less: Actual Expenses	($12)	($12)	($12)
Landlord's Year 1 Net Operating Income	$18	$20	$18
Year 2 Operating Results			
Base Rent	$30	$20	$30
Additional Rent	$0	$15	$3
Less: Actual Expenses	($15)	($15)	($15)
Landlord's Year 2 Net Operating Income	$15	$20	$18
Landlord's Total Net Operating Income	$33	$40	$36

This table shows that the three rent structures produce different financial results for the landlord and the tenant when the landlord underestimates the amount of its building expenses. Based on the facts assumed in Example 11-6, the landlord's total net operating income for Years 1 and 2 is: $40 prsf under a net lease; $36 prsf under an expense stop lease; and $33 prsf under a gross lease. Conversely, the tenant's total rent payments in Years 1 and 2 are: $60 prsf under a gross lease; $63 prsf under an expense stop lease; and $67 prsf under a net lease. The clear narrative produced by those numbers is that the risk that the actual building expenses exceed the budgeted expenses is placed on the tenant under a net lease, placed on the landlord under a gross lease, and shared by the landlord and the tenant under an expense stop lease.

B. SELECTING THE RIGHT RENT STRUCTURE

A gross lease is seldom used in a commercial transaction (despite the obvious attraction it holds for the tenant). There are a couple reasons why commercial leases so infrequently adopt a gross rent structure. The first reason is fairly obvious—the commercial leasing process remains largely landlord-controlled and landlords do not like gross leases because they place all the risk of an unbudgeted expense increase squarely on the landlord's shoulders.

The second, less obvious reason that gross leases are viewed with general disfavor has more to do with human nature than it does with economic theory. When asked to provide a rent quote under a gross lease arrangement, a landlord's natural inclination is to include a fudge factor in its quote to insulate it against the risk that the actual amount of its building expenses outstrips the level of those expenses included in its project budget. A landlord who has budgeted an NOI of $20 prsf and building expenses of $10 prsf might well quote gross rents of $32 prsf in the first lease year and seek to bump the gross rent by $2–3 prsf for each subsequent year during the remainder of the tenant's lease term. The tendency of landlords to include a fudge factor in gross rent quotes runs directly counter to the tenant's primary objective of keeping its occupancy costs as low as possible. A tenant might, therefore, be better served by using a net or expense stop lease and instructing its lawyers to vigorously negotiate lease changes designed to protect the tenant from an unwarranted increase in its additional rent obligation.

The selection of a net or expense stop lease is, to a large extent, predicated on the nature of the landlord's project. By way of example, net leases tend to be the favored choice for retail, industrial, and single-tenant office projects, while expense stop arrangements are more the norm for multi-tenant office buildings. The custom of the real estate market where the landlord's project is located also is a major factor affecting the selection of a rent structure. Some office markets, like Orlando, Florida, have a strong preference for expense stop leases (see the Form Office Lease that was prepared for use on the HIBC project), while others, like Columbus tend to favor the use of net leases for multi-tenant office projects.

To the extent market forces do not dictate the selection of a particular rent structure, most landlords tend to prefer the use of a true net lease structure because of the more ironclad protection a net lease affords a landlord against unbudgeted expense increases. Similarly, the expense stop arrangement is preferred by most office tenants because it gives a tenant a bit more predictability concerning the amount of its annual rent obligation and, if a base-year expense stop is used, forces a landlord to stand behind its projection of base-year building expenses.

It should be noted that most commercial leases are hybrids of the three basic rent structures. A lease may place an obligation on the tenant to reimburse the landlord for certain types of expenses (a net lease arrangement), but preclude the landlord from seeking reimbursement of other expenses (a gross lease approach). Similarly, a lease that generally adopts an expense stop structure might nonetheless require the tenant to pay 100% of certain specific expenses (for example, real estate taxes and insurance premiums). The lawyer's job, therefore, is only partly done when a general form of rent structure is selected. The lawyer must next determine whether each particular building expense merits a treatment that is disparate from the treatment otherwise contemplated by the selected rent structure.

C. TENANT'S SCRUTINY OF EXPENSE PASS-THROUGHS

As noted in the preceding section, most commercial leases contain a feature placing the financial responsibility on the tenant for the payment of at least a portion of the landlord's building expenses. Multi-tenant leases tend to contemplate that the landlord will pay those expenses in the first instance and then seek reimbursement from the tenants in the form of the payment of additional rent. Single-tenant leases usually require the tenant to pay the expenses directly to the person providing the subject service or materials to the building. In either event, the placement on the tenant of the ultimate financial burden for the payment of a certain building expense is colloquially referred to by leasing professionals as an *expense pass-through*.

Expense pass-throughs are an added component of the tenant's overall occupancy costs. Unlike base rent, the amount of the tenant's expense pass-through obligation is neither fixed, nor easily determinable and can vary widely from period-to-period based on unforeseeable fluctuations in the nature and amount of the building expenses being passed through to the tenant. The expense pass-through concept threatens the tenant's ability to meet two of its principal financial objectives in any lease transaction—(1) the avoidance of economic surprises, and (2) the maintenance of all-in occupancy costs at levels that are consistent with its overall operating budget. For this reason, the lease's purported treatment of expense pass-throughs draws closer scrutiny from tenant's counsel than any other provision of the lease.[15]

The primary goal of tenant's counsel when negotiating the expense pass-through clause is to limit the categories and amounts of those building expenses that the tenant is obligated to pay (see *Pro-Tenant Modification #16* at page 741). The tenant is legitimately fearful that the landlord will treat the expense pass-through provision as an "open checkbook" that permits the landlord to incur any costs of its choosing and then pass the financial obligation for the payment of those costs through to the tenant. As long as the ultimate financial responsibility for the expenses rests with the tenant, the landlord arguably has no incentive to keep its building expenses under control. The landlord's net operating income from the project remains stable even if the amount of its building expenses increase dramatically. With a full-bodied expense pass-through clause in hand, the landlord is free to increase the level and quality of its building services to attract new tenants to the project because the associated cost increases are subsidized by the expense pass-throughs paid by its existing tenants.

The tenant's lawyer has a variety of weapons in its arsenal to try to limit the adverse impact of expense pass-throughs on a tenant's finances. All those weapons (specifically, expense exclusions, caps, audit rights, and purpose clauses) share the same basic objective—limiting the amount of the tenant's additional rent obligation. Of course, any provision that limits the tenant's additional rent obligation has the automatic effect of decreasing the landlord's net operating income. When the lawyers sit down to negotiate the terms of the expense pass-through clause, they are doing battle over the one thing that is most near and dear to their clients' hearts—real money.

1. Exclusions

The prototypical landlord lease describes the pass-through expenses in an extremely expansive fashion (for example, "all expenses of any kind or nature related to the ownership, operation, management, maintenance, repair, and replacement of the building"), followed by a purely illustrative, non-exclusive listing of every conceivable category of expense conjured up by the landlord's lawyer. Tenant's counsel tries to slash the landlord's expense list to include only those specific expenses that must be incurred to provide the tenant with the level of service that it needs to efficiently conduct its business in the leased premises (see *Pro-Tenant Modification #16* at page 741). The tenant's lawyer also usually tries to limit the

---

[15] For detailed examinations of the tenant's perspective on expense pass-through clauses, *see* Thomas C. Barbuti and Alan A. Lascher, *CAM/Operating Expenses: Devil or Angel . . . So Whose Clause Is It Anyway?*, in ACREL PAPERS 518 (Spring 2004); Marc E. Betesh, *Rent Escalation Clauses in Office Leases*, in ACREL PAPERS 148 (Spring 2007); Barger, *supra* note 14; and Gary Goldman, *Tenant Triage: Operating on a Landlord's Operating Expense Clause*, 16 No. 2 PRACTICAL REAL ESTATE LAWYER 19 (March 2000).

permitted pass-throughs to those expenses that are classified as "operating expenses" under generally accepted accounting principles.

Landlord's counsel customarily agrees to exclusions for the landlord's debt service costs, income tax payments, leasing commissions, and tenant improvement costs (because those costs are either personal to the landlord or have already been factored into the landlord's project development costs). The battle then focuses on whether expenses such as the following will be passed through to the tenant—for example: capital expenditures; payments to affiliates of the landlord; corporate overhead; art purchases; real estate tax increases triggered by a building sale; property management fees; terrorism insurance; professional fees; and building promotion costs.[16] The landlord's lawyer counters tenant's counsel's assertion that "we can't give you an open checkbook," with the parry that "if you don't agree to pay for it, we won't do it." The end result is often a complex and very specific listing of expense inclusions and exclusions that are often internally inconsistent and, on occasion, flat out contradictory.

2.   Caps

A less artful, but often more effective, way of limiting the tenant's additional rent exposure is to include a cap on the amount of the tenant's annual additional rent payments (see *Pro-Tenant Modification #18* at page 742). The cap can be expressed either as an absolute number (for example, no more than $5 prsf in any one calendar year) or as a limited increase over the amount of the prior year's expenses (for example, an increase of no more than 3% over the prior calendar year's expenses). In either event, the use of a cap is the tenant's attempt to use a machete rather than a stiletto to reduce the potential for a dramatic increase in the tenant's additional rent obligation. If the landlord agrees to a cap (and the landlord typically does so only if it has limited leverage in the lease negotiations or if the negotiated cap provides it with a substantial cushion over its projected future expenses), its counsel should resist the imposition of a cap on any expense that is not within the landlord's control (so-called ***uncontrollable expenses***), such as real estate taxes, insurance premiums, and utility charges.

3.   Audit Rights

The practical reality is that landlords often err in the calculation of pass-through expenses. This is especially true in a multi-tenant project where the landlord is faced with the prospect of trying to keep track of the intricate details of the many separate pass-through clauses negotiated by

---

[16] For a representative sample of a tenant's wish list of expense exclusions, *see* Mark S. Hennigh, *Office Lease Operating Expense Exclusions*, in ALI-ABA COURSE OF STUDY MATERIALS, COMMERCIAL REAL ESTATE LEASES: SELECTED ISSUES IN DRAFTING AND NEGOTIATING IN CURRENT MARKETS Course No. SN–013, 129 (May 2008).

the landlord with its roster of tenants. Tenant's counsel frequently seeks to guard against landlord errors in the calculation of its pass-through expenses by inserting a clause into the lease that gives the tenant the right to audit the landlord's expense records (see *Pro-Tenant Modification #19* at page 742). The tenant may also have certain rights at common law to review the landlord's expense records.[17] However, the well-represented tenant should not rely on common law rights, but should instead seek to include an express audit right in the lease.

The following schematic highlights issues that are often the subject of negotiation when a tenant asks for an audit right and the initial positions staked out by the landlord and tenant when each issue is first broached.

- ***What level of information must the landlord provide to the tenant's auditors?***

    o ***Landlord's position***—A one-page summary of the general categories of expenses incurred by landlord.

    o ***Tenant's position***—A complete ledger of each and every individual expense incurred by landlord.

- ***Who can perform the audit on the tenant's behalf?***

    o ***Landlord's position***—Only a certified public accountant from a Big 4 accounting firm (and never a contingent fee auditor who gets paid only if the auditor finds a landlord error).

    o ***Tenant's position***—Contingent fee auditors are great because the tenant only has to pay a fee if the auditors find an error (and, if they do find an error, the tenant usually can get other tenants in the building to kick in to help pay the auditor's fee).

- ***Who pays for the costs of the audit?***

    o ***Landlord's position***—The tenant.

    o ***Tenant's position***—The landlord (but only if the auditor finds a significant landlord error—for example, a tenant overpayment of more than X% of the expense pass-through amount that the tenant should have paid)

- ***When can the audit be performed?***

    o ***Landlord's position***—Only within a short period of time (for example, 30 days) after the tenant's receipt of

---

[17] *See e.g.*, P.V. Properties, Inc. v. Rock Creek Village Associates Limited Partnership, 549 A.2d 403 (Md. App. 1988), where a Maryland appeals court effectively held that a tenant has an implied right to audit the landlord's books. *See also* Barbuti, *supra* note 15, at 7; and SENN, *supra* note 5, at 7–48 and 7–49.

landlord's notice quantifying the amount of the tenant's expense payments.

  o *Tenant's position*—Whenever.

 • *Where will the audit be conducted?*

  o *Landlord's position*—In the landlord's offices so that the landlord can closely monitor the auditor's activities and make sure that the auditor does not copy any of the landlord's records.

  o *Tenant's position*—Wherever.

 • *Does the tenant have to sign a confidentiality and non-disclosure agreement before it conducts the audit?*

  o *Landlord's position*—Absolutely.

  o *Tenant's position*—No way.

An interesting aspect of the tenant's audit right is that neither the landlord, nor the tenant really wants the right to actually be exercised. The landlord is leery of an audit because an audit burdens the landlord's property management staff and could potentially result in a refund of an overpayment. The tenant does not want to take the time to conduct a thorough audit of the landlord's books and records because doing so distracts the tenant from its real focus—successfully conducting its business operations in the leased premises. The real purpose of the insertion of an audit right in a commercial lease is the creation of an *in terrorem* effect that is intended to incentivize the landlord to calculate the tenant's pass-through obligations in a careful manner and in full compliance with the negotiated provisions of the tenant's lease.

4. Purpose Clause

One of the more useful tools available to tenant's counsel when negotiating the expense pass-through clause is a so-called "purpose clause." The purpose of a purpose clause is to impose general guidelines and limitations on the landlord's calculation of its pass-through expenses. The following is a representative example of a pro-tenant purpose clause (see *Pro-Tenant Lease Modification #17* at page 741):

> *The following general principles will apply with respect to the calculation of Landlord's Building Expenses:*
>
> A. *Landlord will not recover the cost of any item more than once, nor will Landlord seek reimbursement from Tenant for an amount greater than the actual cost incurred by Tenant with respect to any item; it being expressly acknowledged by Landlord that it is not the intention or purpose of this section*

*of the Lease to generate an economic profit or windfall to
Landlord;*

B.   *Landlord will operate and maintain the Building in a fair,
commercially reasonable, and cost-effective manner;*

C.   *Any additional costs incurred by Landlord due to its adoption
after the Commencement Date of any change of policy or
practice related to its operation of the Building (including,
without limitation, increased premiums for new or different
insurance coverages or additional costs related to any change
in the frequency or level of any service provided by Landlord)
will be excluded from the definition of those Building
Expenses for which Tenant is financially responsible under
this section;*

D.   *All services rendered and all materials supplied to the
Building will be of a nature and scope that are consistent with
those rendered or supplied to comparable buildings and the
cost of such services and materials will be of a cost no greater
than those charged in arm's length transactions for
comparable services or materials rendered or supplied for
comparable purposes to comparable buildings; and*

E.   *In determining the nature, amount, and allocation of any cost
to be included as a Building Expense, Landlord will comply
with and respect generally accepted accounting principles,
consistently applied.*

Landlords object to a purpose clause for several reasons: (1) it limits
the landlord's discretion in determining how best to operate its building;
(2) it fosters a "lowest common denominator" approach to building
operations by creating unfair and limiting comparisons with other
buildings; (3) it restricts the landlord's prerogative to respond to changed
market conditions by constraining its right to upgrade the building's
physical plant and services; and (4) the use of soft and ambiguous terms
like "fair," "commercially reasonable," and "cost-effective" creates
inappropriate opportunities for the tenant to second guess the landlord's
operational decisions. These are, of course, precisely the reasons why a
tenant wants to include a purpose clause in its lease. While a landlord is
hard-pressed to resist the tenant's entreaties to include clauses A (no mark-
up of expenses) and E (the use of generally accepted accounting principles),
it typically instructs its counsel to excise the remaining elements of the
purpose clause.

D. TENANT'S SHARE OF EXPENSES
(¶ N of Lease Summary and Exhibit B)

In a multi-tenant building, the amount of the tenant's additional rent obligation is determined by multiplying the total amount of the landlord's pass-through expenses by a percentage that represents the **tenant's proportionate share** of those expenses. The tenant's proportionate share is generally calculated in one of two ways—either by comparing the square footage of the tenant's leased premises to the square footage of all "rentable" space in the building or by comparing the square footage of the tenant's leased premises only to that portion of the building which is actually "leased to" or "occupied by " tenants.

The following example illustrates the consequences of determining the tenant's proportionate share under the two methods described in the preceding paragraph.

Example 11-7: Landlord owns an office building that contains 100,000 square feet of rentable space. There are only two tenants in the building—Tenant A who leases 10,000 rentable square feet and Tenant B who leases 30,000 rentable square feet of rentable space. The remaining 60,000 rentable square feet of space is unleased and unoccupied. Landlord's total pass-through expenses in Year 1 are $500,000. Each tenant is obligated to pay its proportionate share of all pass-through expenses under a net rent structure.

The following table shows how financial responsibility for the payment of the pass-through expenses is allocated among Tenant A, Tenant B, and Landlord.

Responsible Party	*"Rentable" Allocation*	*"Leased/Occupied" Allocation*
Tenant A	$50,000 (10%)	$125,000 (25%)
Tenant B	$150,000 (30%)	$375,000 (75%)
Landlord	$300,000 (60%)	$0 (0%)

What a difference a word makes! Under the "rentable" allocation method, Landlord bears the burden of paying the expenses allocable to the building's vacant space. Under the "leased/occupied" allocation method, Tenants A and B are allocated responsibility for paying all of the building's expenses, including the expenses attributable to the vacant space. Because it is difficult for the landlord to logically maintain that the tenants should bear the economic risk of a vacancy in the building (when the tenants have no ability to control the vacancy factor), most commercial leases calculate the tenant's proportionate share based on the "rentable" method—that is, the tenant's proportionate share is deemed to equal the number of rentable square feet contained in the tenant's leased premises, divided by the rentable square feet contained in the entire building.[18]

There is, however, one circumstance where allocating building expenses in accordance with the "rentable" method produces an illogical result.

Example 11-8: Assume all of the same facts of Example 11-7, except that included in Landlord's pass-through expenses are $100,000 of janitorial fees, all of which are attributable to the cleaning of the space leased by Tenant A ($25,000) and Tenant B ($75,000).

If the tenants' proportionate shares were to be calculated in accordance with the "rentable" method: Tenant A would pay $10,000 for janitorial fees; Tenant B would pay $30,000; and Landlord would bear the ultimate financial responsibility for the remaining $60,000 of janitorial fees—even though janitorial fees are not tied in any way to any of the building's vacant space. In Example 11-8, a more logical result would be for each of Tenant A and Tenant B to pay the janitorial fees incurred to clean its leased space—that is, $25,000 for Tenant A and $75,000 for Tenant B.

The desired result (at least from the landlord's perspective) is achieved by the insertion in the lease of a ***gross-up clause***. A gross-up clause authorizes the landlord to increase the amount of its pass-through expenses to include those hypothetical expenses that the landlord would have incurred if the building had been fully leased and occupied. The breadth of the gross-up clause should be limited to those building expenses that fluctuate with occupancy (for example, janitorial fees and utility charges). The importance to the tenant of having a gross-up clause included in an expense stop lease is discussed in more detail in the next section of this chapter.

E. EXPENSE STOP ISSUES

A stipulated sum expense stop lease is essentially nothing more than a net lease in disguise. If the landlord sets its stipulated sum expense stop at $5 prsf and its base rent at $15 prsf, then the landlord achieves the same financial results that it would have achieved if it used a net lease arrangement with a base rent equal to $10 prsf. The only exception to that

---

[18] *See* ZANKEL, *supra* note 1, at 68–70; Barger, *supra* note 14, at 167–168; Barbuti, *supra* note 15, at 521; and Mark S. Hennigh, *Office Leases*, in COMMERCIAL REAL ESTATE TRANSACTIONS HANDBOOK 15–40 through 15–43 (Mark A. Senn ed., 4th ed. 2016).

rule is when the stipulated expense stop turns out to be higher than the landlord's actual building expenses (a circumstance that I have seldom seen during my 40+ years in the practice). In that rare circumstance, the landlord's net operating income is decreased to the extent the stipulated sum stop exceeds the landlord's actual expenses.

For the reason noted above, smart tenants reject out of hand an expense stop lease that is premised on a stipulated sum expense stop. Tenants greatly prefer a base-year expense stop lease—which is why the base-year expense stop is the subject of the remainder of this section.

There are certain issues that are unique to base-year expense stop leases.[19] Those issues are triggered by the natural incentives and singular opportunities created by the expense stop structure for the landlord to manipulate its base-year expenses to enhance its net operating income (and increase the tenant's all-in rent burden). A landlord can significantly boost the value of an expense stop lease by (1) keeping its base-year expenses artificially low, and (2) selecting a base year that the landlord knows will likely produce an expense stop that is less than the expense load included in its base rent quote.

The following example illustrates how a landlord can use a base-year expense stop to its advantage.

> **Example 11-9:** It is July 2018 and Landlord and Tenant are diligently trying to finalize the terms of a base-year expense stop lease for Tenant's leasing of space in Landlord's new office building (which was completed in December 2017). When its lease term begins on December 1, 2018, Tenant will be the first tenant to assume occupancy of space in Landlord's new office building. Landlord's lawyer designates the "2018 calendar year" as the lease's "base year" after speaking to Landlord's property management staff and learning that: (1) Landlord's building should be fully occupied by no later than February of 2019; (2) Landlord's budgeted building expenses for a fully-occupied building are $10 prsf; and (3) Landlord's actual building expenses for the calendar year 2018 should be no more than $4 prsf (because the building will be vacant for most of the 2018 calendar year, the real estate taxes for 2018 have not yet been updated to reflect the existence of an office building on Landlord's property, and Landlord plans to defer payment of a number of its expenses until January, 2019).

The impact of the lawyer's insertion in the lease of the simple statement that "the expense stop will be equal to the actual expenses incurred by Landlord during the 2018 calendar year" is that Tenant will

---

[19] *See generally* Phil Skinner, *The Use of "Base Year" Provisions in Leases*, in LEASE NEGOTIATION HANDBOOK 201 (Edward Chupack ed., 2003).

likely be obligated to make additional rent payments during calendar year 2019 of somewhere around $6 prsf. Because additional rent is ordinarily paid in advance based on the landlord's estimate of what its actual building expenses will be for the upcoming calendar year (see § 2 of the Form Office Lease), Landlord could begin charging Tenant additional rent as early as January 2019 in a monthly amount equal to $.50 prsf (Landlord's estimate of the amount by which the 2019 expenses will exceed the 2018 base-year expenses—that is, $6 prsf divided by 12).

Tenant's counsel could have protected its client from the indignities it suffered in Example 11-9 by adding the following provisions to the lease (see *Pro-Tenant Modification #15* at page 740):

- The designation of the base year as "calendar year 2019";

- A requirement that the landlord calculate its building expenses in accordance with generally accepted accounting principles; and

- A gross-up clause.

A tenant should always seek to select a base year that is as far in the future as possible. Doing so forces the landlord to assume the risk that its actual building expenses are greater than its budgeted expenses (something that Landlord in Example 11-9 did not have to do). The selection of a base year that concludes well after the commencement date of the tenant's lease term also serves to defer the tenant's obligation to begin paying additional rent. The usual formulation of a tenant-friendly, base-year definition is "the first full calendar year following the commencement date of the lease term."

The insertion in the lease of a "generally accepted accounting principles" provision prevents the landlord from inappropriately accelerating or deferring the payment of an expense from one calendar year to another. Under generally accepted accounting principles, the landlord must use the accrual method of accounting to allocate each expense (regardless when actually paid) to the period in which the services or materials giving rise to such expense were actually provided.[20]

In the context of an expense stop lease, a gross-up clause is a lease provision that requires the landlord to increase its base-year expenses to include those hypothetical expenses that the landlord would have incurred in the base year if the building had been fully occupied and fully assessed for tax purposes. As is the case with respect to the net lease gross-up discussed earlier in this chapter, the gross-up clause in an expense stop lease should only cover real estate taxes and those variable expenses that

---

[20]   *See* Barger, *supra* note 14, at 170.

fluctuate with occupancy (for example, janitorial fees, utility costs, and the like).

The inclusion of a gross-up requirement in an expense stop lease serves two purposes—(1) it places the economic risk of a building vacancy on the landlord, and (2) it creates a more apt "apples to apples" comparison of the expense loads incurred during the base year and later years of the lease term (often referred to in commercial leases as "comparison years"). Tenants try to buttress the "apples to apples" comparative between the base and comparison years by requiring the landlord to retroactively gross up its base-year expenses to account for any added expenses incurred in a comparison year that are attributable to a landlord decision to either upgrade the nature, scope, or frequency of its building services (for example, the addition of a concierge desk or an increase in the frequency of window washing from once a month to once a week) or otherwise change its methods of operating the building (for example, the lowering of its property insurance deductibles, which, in turn, results in an increase in its insurance premiums).[21]

At the risk of stating the obvious, the landlord's lawyer seldom voluntarily includes these tenant-protective measures in the landlord's standard lease form. However, when braced with a need to include something in the lease to prevent the landlord from artificially keeping its base-year expenses low and its comparison-year expenses high (which, after all, is precisely what the landlord wants to do), the landlord's lawyer often makes a few concession to partially respond to the tenant's concerns. By way of example, the lawyer representing Landlord in Example 11-9 might agree to a "GAAP accounting" clause, a gross-up of base-year expenses, and, if the lawyer is in a good mood, a re-set of the base year to calendar year 2019 (although a sound argument could be made that a re-set of the base year is not needed if a gross-up clause is included in the lease). Landlord's lawyer should respectfully decline to go along with the tenant's request that the base-year gross-up be retroactively adjusted to reflect the added expenses incurred in any comparison year due to an upgrade in building services or another change in the landlord's mode of operation on the theory that doing so unduly limits the landlord's ability to respond to changes in the marketplace. Finally, Landlord's lawyer should assert that "what's good for the goose is good for the gander" and insist that the landlord's building expenses in each comparison year also be grossed up to account for any unanticipated decline in the building's occupancy rate.[22]

---

[21] *See* Michael Pollack, *Base Year Issues: "More Is Less,"* in LEASE NEGOTIATION HANDBOOK 217 (Edward Chupack ed., 2003); and Barger, *supra* note 14, at 181–183.

[22] *See* RODNEY J. DILLMAN, THE LEASE MANUAL—A PRACTICAL GUIDE TO NEGOTIATING OFFICE, RETAIL AND INDUSTRIAL LEASES 59–61 (2007) (especially the last sentence of clause #8 on p. 61).

HIBC Case Study—An Aggressive Use of Base-Year Economics

In the early years of the HIBC project, Pizzuti was extremely concerned about its ability to control the expenses of owning and operating office buildings in the HIBC park. Expense control is a challenge on any new development project because the landlord is forced to predict the unknown— that is, both the speed at which its project leases up and the expense load that is required to efficiently operate the building. Pizzuti's dilemma at the outset of the HIBC project was compounded by the fact that it had limited experience in operating suburban office buildings in Florida and, hence, did not have a raft of historical cost data that it could rely on when trying to project its HIBC building expenses.

The author's recommendation to solve Pizzuti's expense problem was simple—Pizzuti should use a net lease that passed all building expenses through to the tenant regardless of what those expenses actually proved to be. That solution, while theoretically sublime, was practically useless because Orlando was an expense stop market. Pizzuti was already pushing the development envelope by introducing a product with an innovative design in a pioneering market. Trying to further change the market dynamic by introducing a new lease structure was not a viable option.

Left with the singular choice of using an expense stop rent structure, I crafted a lease that sought to protect the landlord as best it could from the economic risk of an underestimation of its building expenses. The standard lease form that Pizzuti used in the marketing of its first HIBC office building contained the following provisions—(1) a gross-up of expenses only for the comparison years (and not the base year), (2) the designation of the base year as the first calendar year following completion of construction (annualized to the extent the first calendar year consisted of less than a full 12 calendar months), (3) an express reservation of the landlord's right to change its operating policies and practices at any time after the commencement date of the initial lease term, and (4) the establishment of separate caps on the base-year expenses for real estate taxes and electricity. These provisions were designed to permit Pizzuti to keep its base-year expenses as low as possible and to shift the risk of the volatility of the real estate tax and electricity expenses to the tenant (by effectively making the rent "net" for the purpose of determining the tenant's share of the building's real estate taxes and electricity costs).

The inclusion of the above provisions in Pizzuti's standard lease form was met with less scorn than I anticipated. A few tenants insisted that wholesale changes be made to the expense stop provisions (for example, the inclusion of a full gross-up for base-year expenses and the deferral of the base year until the first full calendar year after the commencement date).

However, many other tenants either accepted the provisions as is or required only minor tweaks in the lease language. As a result, Pizzuti was able to maintain a stable stream of income despite the fact that its expense projections were often significantly understated (particularly in the early years of its development efforts at HIBC). Pizzuti's concern over the management of its expense load lessened as it gained experience in operating office buildings in the HIBC environment. As a result, the lease provisions noted in this case study became less important over time and I was eventually able to revise the standard HIBC lease to be a bit more user-friendly on the topic of the computation of the tenant's base-year expenses. The Form Office Lease incorporates the "kinder, gentler" expense stop provisions.

I decided to discuss Pizzuti's treatment of base-year expenses in this case study to underscore two important lessons that the real estate development lawyer must learn. First, the lawyer's drafting approach needs to be adapted to fit the norms and customs followed in the market in which the developer is engaged (hence, Pizzuti's use of an expense stop lease when it would have preferred to use a net lease). Second, there is nothing intrinsically wrong with a lawyer's inclusion in the lease of unusually aggressive provisions if those provisions are designed to protect the client against real world risks. In drafting and negotiating a lease, the lawyer should not worry about whether a particularly provision is "fair," but rather whether its inclusion (or exclusion) helps the landlord achieve its stated business objective of leasing its building as soon as possible and on rental and other terms that are consistent with its business plan.

F.   COUNTERING THE RISK OF INFLATION

The last several sections of this chapter concentrated on how a landlord can structure an additional rent provision to mitigate the risk that the actual expenses of operating the landlord's building prove to be greater than the landlord's advance estimate of such expenses. Inflation is a second economic risk that the real estate development lawyer must take into consideration when drafting the rent provisions of a commercial lease.

The inflation risk is not directly linked to the operation of the landlord's specific building, but rather is a function of the overall condition of the economy. Inflation is generally defined as a loss of purchasing power due to a general increase in the cost of goods and services. In the context of a commercial real estate project, inflation can negatively impact the landlord either as a result of an increase in interest rates on real estate mortgage loans or a general increase in the cost of living in the locale where the landlord resides. In either case, even though the net operating income generated from the landlord's project remains stable (due to the appropriate use of a net lease or expense stop rent structure), that net operating income simply does not buy what it used to buy.

So how can a landlord protect the value of its base rent against the potential ravages of inflation? The simplest way for the landlord to mitigate the risk of inflation is to include a cushion in the amount of the base rent it charges its tenants (for example, by charging base rent of $21 prsf instead of $20 prsf). Market forces, however, seldom let the landlord hedge its inflation risk by overstating its base rent (and if they do, landlords view that cushion as a profit to which they are entitled and not a protection from the risk of inflation).

There are three ways that the landlord's lawyer can structure the base rent provisions to provide the landlord with a modicum of comfort that inflation does not adversely affect its net operating income.[23] All three techniques involve a future increase (or *rent bump*) in the base rent payable by the tenant at the inception of the lease term.

- *Fixed Bumps*—The most direct way that a landlord can try to deal with inflation is to establish fixed base rent increases at scheduled times during the tenant's lease term (for example, base rent of $20 prsf in Year 1, $20.60 prsf in Year 2, $21.22 in Year 3, etc.). This approach requires the parties to guess what the rate of inflation will be during the lease term. The fixed bump strategy works from the landlord's perspective only if the actual rate of inflation is less than the amount of the negotiated rent bump (3% per year in the above example).

- *Indexed Bumps*—A technique commonly used to combat the risk of inflation is to periodically adjust the tenant's base rent to reflect increases in a cost of living index, such as the Consumer Price Index. The use of indexed bumps is favored by many practitioners because the bumps are not merely the parties' guesses of future inflation (as is the case with fixed bumps), but rather are tied to an objective measure of inflation. The only negative associated with the use of cost of living adjustments is that there is no published index that accurately measures inflation in the commercial real estate industry.[24]

- *Market Bumps*—Adjusting base rent periodically to reflect the change in market rents is viewed by some practitioners as theoretically the best way to deal with the prospect of

---

[23] *See* Edward Chupack, *Rent*, in LEASE NEGOTIATION HANDBOOK 189, 195 (Edward Chupack ed., 2003); and DAVID GELTNER, NORMAN G. MILLER, JIM CLAYTON AND PIET EICHHOLTZ, COMMERCIAL REAL ESTATE ANALYSIS AND INVESTMENT 809–811 (2nd ed. 2006).

[24] *See* SENN, *supra* note 5, at 6–12; and DILLMAN, *supra* note 22, at 63.

inflation. Under the market rate method, the parties agree that the base rent will be reset at a specific point during the lease term to reflect the then fair rental value of comparable properties in the market in which the building is located. The fair rental value is customarily determined by an appraiser or real estate broker designated in the lease. The problems associated with market rent bumps are threefold—(1) the fair rental value of a property may increase for reasons other than inflation (for example, for external reasons of supply and demand), (2) the process of appraising the fair rental value of a leased space is time-consuming and costly, and (3) the appraisal of a leasehold interest is more art than science and can produce an unexpected result that may be extremely prejudicial to either the tenant or the landlord. For these reasons, market rent bumps are seldom used to adjust base rent during the initial term of a commercial space lease.

Landlords generally take the position that base rent should never increase during the lease term, but may increase based on indexed or market rent adjustments. In order to counter the economic uncertainty associated with indexed or market rent bumps, counsel for the tenant frequently requests (and often receive) the establishment of a ceiling on the amount of any base rent adjustment (for example, an increase of not more than 3% in any one year).

G. PERCENTAGE RENT

The discussion thus far in this chapter has centered on the office tenant's obligation to pay base and additional rent. A third type of rent that is peculiar to retail leases is *percentage rent*.

Percentage rent is the portion of a retail tenant's rent obligation that is equal to a percentage of the *gross sales* produced from the tenant's conduct of retail operations in its leased store. The concept of percentage rent was created to ease the fixed rental burden of a retail tenant when it first opens its store. A retail lease involves a higher degree of site-specific risk than does an office or warehouse lease because the success of the retail tenant's business operations is as dependent on the location and quality of the landlord's retail center as it is on the sustainability of the tenant's business model.

For this reason, the retail landlord is often willing to reduce the tenant's fixed base rent obligation (but not the tenant's additional rent obligation) in exchange for the tenant's commitment to pay the landlord a percentage of its store revenues. The landlord hopes that if the tenant's store is profitable, the landlord will be able to recoup the entirety of the fixed rent discount *AND MORE* from the tenant's payment of percentage rent. Percentage rent is, therefore, basically a risk-reward allocation model, where the landlord takes a little more risk on the front-end of the deal in exchange for its potential receipt of an above market rate of return on the backside of the lease transaction.

The following is a typical phrasing of the retail tenant's percentage rent requirement:

In addition to its payment of Base Rent and Additional Rent, Tenant will pay Percentage Rent in an amount equal to the product of (a) the amount by which the Tenant's Gross Sales exceeds its Breakpoint, multiplied by (b) ___%.

The calculation of the tenant's percentage rent obligation requires the landlord and the tenant to agree on the answers to three key questions.

- What revenues are included in the tenant's gross sales?[25]

- What is the tenant's **breakpoint**?

- What is the percentage used to compute the tenant's percentage rent?

The tenor of the negotiations over the revenues that are included in and excluded from the tenant's "gross sales" is similar to that of the negotiations concerning the categories of expenses that can be passed through to the office tenant as additional rent—in other words, they are very detailed, nuanced, and frequently strident. The landlord's objective is to define gross sales as broadly as possible to include every single penny of revenue that ever touches the tenant's store in any way. The tenant, on the other hand, strives to limit the revenues included under the gross sales umbrella by specifically excluding any receipts that do not produce a direct profit to the tenant (for example, sales taxes, vending machine receipts, lottery ticket sales, employee discount sales, returned merchandise, and the like).[26] An issue that is the subject of much current debate is whether internet sales should be included in gross sales.[27]

A tenant's "breakpoint" is the maximum level of gross sales that the tenant may attain without having to pay percentage rent. In this respect the breakpoint is akin to the expense stop, in that the tenant is only

---

[25] Net income is seldom used as the basis for a percentage rent clause for two reasons—(1) the calculation of net income can be manipulated by the tenant to produce little or no income even though the tenant's store is very successful, and (2) the use of a net income standard to compute the tenant's rent obligation serves as a disincentive for the tenant to efficiently operate its business in the leased premises. *See* SENN, *supra* note 5, at 6–32.

[26] *See* ZANKEL, *supra* note 1, at 52–53.

[27] *See generally* Julian Rackow, *Implications of E-Commerce for Commercial and Retail Leasing Transactions*, in ALI-ABA COURSE OF STUDY MATERIALS, COMMERCIAL REAL ESTATE LEASES: SELECTED ISSUES IN DRAFTING AND NEGOTIATING IN CURRENT MARKETS, Course No. SL–017, 1169 (June 2006); and John C. Murray, *Percentage Rent Provisions in Shopping Center Leases: A Changing World?*, 35 REAL PROPERTY, PROBATE AND TRUST JOURNAL 731, 747–752 (Winter 2001).

required to pay percentage rent if the gross sales produced from its store operations exceed the breakpoint. The tenant's breakpoint can be any number selected by the parties, but is most commonly set at what is called a **natural breakpoint**.[28] A natural breakpoint is equal to the volume of gross sales determined by dividing the tenant's base rent by the percentage used to calculate its percentage rent. Therefore, the natural breakpoint of a tenant that pays base rent of $200,000 per year and percentage rent at a 4% rate is $5 million.

The final component of the percentage rent calculation is the percentage that is used as a multiplier against the tenant's excess gross sales. The landlord obviously wants to select a high percentage, while the tenant prefers a low percentage. A useful rule of thumb to keep in mind when negotiating the economic terms of a retail lease is that high volume/ low profit margin stores (for example, a grocery store) usually merit a low percentage, while low volume/high profit margin stores (for example, a jewelry shop) typically draw a high percentage.[29]

In an effort to bolster the prospects for its receipt of substantial percentage rent payments, the retail landlord usually includes in its lease a series of provisions that are designed to maximize the level of gross sales produced in its center by dictating the manner in which the center's tenants conduct their retail businesses. Restrictive use clauses, continuous operation covenants, and radius restrictions are examples of provisions that are intended to augment the landlord's receipt of percentage rent. Those provisions and other clauses that are unique to a retail lease are discussed in greater detail later in this chapter at pages 549–554.

H. PAYMENT OF RENT

(§§ 2 and 3)

The lease must also cover the following practical considerations associated with the tenant's rent obligations.

- When will the tenant's base rent be paid? (Answer—usually monthly on or before the first day of each calendar month during the lease term).

- How should tenant's rent be paid? (Answer—either in cash or by an electronic wire transfer of same day funds).

- Where should the tenant's rent payments be sent? (Answer— usually to the landlord's primary mailing address or, if the

---

[28] See ZANKEL, *supra* note 1, at 53.

[29] See SENN, *supra* note 5, at 6–48 and 6–50, for a table showing the range of percentage rental rates commonly paid by various types of retail stores.

payment is to be made electronically, to a bank account designated in the lease).

- What happens if the tenant does not pay its rent by the due date specified in the lease? (Answer—typically the tenant is charged a late fee and interest accrues on the delinquent rent until it is paid).

- Is the tenant entitled to withhold any portion of its rent if the tenant is dissatisfied with the landlord's performance of its lease obligations? (Answer—"no way" for the landlord and "yes way" for the tenant).

The landlord typically requires the tenant to pay additional rent monthly in advance based on the landlord's estimate of its building expenses for the then current year. This payment method allows the landlord to make an approximate match between the date on which a particular expense is incurred and the date on which the landlord receives tenant's reimbursement—thus bowing to the time value of money concepts discussed in more detail in Chapter 3 of this book (see pages 67–69). If additional rent is paid in advance, the lease should include a clause providing for an annual reconciliation of the tenant's estimated payments and the actual amount of the pass-through expenses that the tenant is responsible for under the terms of the lease (see the second paragraph of § 2 of the Form Office Lease). The tenant's lawyer should also consider limiting the amount of the tenant's advance expense payments—for example, no more than 103% of its actual expense payments in the prior calendar year.

IX. USE

The prior sections of this chapter centered on three fundamental themes that drive the drafting and negotiation of a commercial lease—(1) the *SPACE* that is leased by the tenant, (2) the *TERM* of tenant's leasing of the designated space, and (3) the *RENT* that the tenant must pay to the landlord. The fourth leg of the leasing table relates to the following provisions of the lease that seek to regulate the tenant's *USE* of its leased space.

- The general use clause;

- The compliance with laws clause;

- The alterations clause;

- The maintenance clause; and

- The building services clause.

The shared objective of the landlord and tenant when negotiating all of the above clauses is to clearly delineate what the tenant can and cannot do in its leased premises and what, if anything, the landlord must do to facilitate the tenant's use of its leased premises. The landlord wants the use provisions to be structured in a fashion that permits the landlord to control its building expenses and preserve and enhance the value of its project. The tenant's objective is to negotiate a set of use provisions that allows the tenant to operate its business in a manner that is fully consistent with its business plan—both as that plan exists at the outset of the lease term and as it evolves over the course of the lease term.

A. GENERAL USE CLAUSE
(¶ F of Lease Summary and § 6)

If the lease is silent on the issue of the tenant's use of the leased premises, common law provides that the tenant may use the leased premises for any purpose that is not illegal.[30] Because commercial landlords are seldom willing to sanction such a broad range of the tenant's use of the landlord's building, the landlord's lawyer must clearly articulate in the lease the purpose for which the tenant may use the leased premises. The tenant's use may be prescribed in one of two ways—in a (1) *permissive use clause,* or (2) a *restrictive use clause*

A permissive use clause empowers the tenant to use the leased premises for a specified purpose, but does not expressly limit the tenant's use to the specified purpose. An example of a permissive use clause is "tenant *MAY* use the leased premises for the operation of an accounting firm." The use of a permissive lease clause is favored by the tenant because it accomplishes the tenant's two-pronged goal of blessing its present intended use and preserving its option to change its use in the future.

A restrictive use clause limits the tenant's use to the purpose specified in the lease. The following is an example of a restrictive use clause— "tenant *WILL* use the leased premises for the operation of an accounting firm and *FOR NO OTHER PURPOSE*." The landlord prefers a restrictive use clause because such a clause permits the landlord to retain control over the manner in which its project is used by its tenants.

Given the opportunity, the courts interpret a use clause as being permissive and not restrictive.[31] Therefore, to the extent the landlord

---

[30]   *See* SENN, *supra* note 5, at 11–6.

[31]   *See* SENN *supra* note 5, at 11–6 through 11–13; and Milton R. FRIEDMAN AND PATRICK A. RANDOLPH, JR., FRIEDMAN ON LEASES 27–9 through 27–14 (5th ed. 2010). By way of example of the courts' general inclination to interpret use clauses in favor of the tenant, an Ohio court ruled that a provision that said that "the leased premises may be used for the purposes of . . . a supermarket" permitted a successor tenant to use the leased premises as a karate school. *See* Juhasz v. Quik Shops, Inc., 55 Ohio App.2d 51 (1977). A lease stating that the leased premises were "to be used primarily as an auto dealership" was construed by a South Carolina court as authorizing the use of the leased premises as a saloon. *See* Chassereau v. Stuckey, 288 S.C. 368 (Ct. App. 1986).

prevails in its argument that the lease should contain a restrictive clause, it is imperative that the landlord's lawyer draft the tenant's use clause in a crisp and unambiguous fashion to make it clear that the leased premises will be used "solely" in the specified manner "and for no other purpose without the prior written consent of the landlord." Clauses incorporating that level of clarity are enforced by the courts as restricting (and not just permitting) the nature of the tenant's use of the leased premises.[32]

Landlord's counsel should endeavor to define the tenant's permitted use in as narrow a fashion as is reasonably practicable given the nature of the landlord's project. Tenant's counsel, conversely, should lobby in favor of a general description of the tenant's use of the leased premises in order to maximize the tenant's operational flexibility.

The following is a continuum of ways in which an office tenant's use of its leased premises can be described in the lease (listed in the order of the tenant's preference):

- Any lawful use (the common law default rule);

- General office use;

- Use as a law firm;

- Use as a patent law firm; and

- Use as a patent law firm with no more than seven practicing attorneys and five support staff.

The first choice provides the landlord virtually no control over the tenant's ultimate use of the leased premises, while the last choice probably provides the office landlord more control than it realistically needs. The landlord should determine just how much control it needs over the activities of its tenants. For example, does the landlord of a suburban office building really care if a tenant uses its space for the purpose of operating a law firm rather than an advertising agency? Once the landlord determines precisely how restrictive it needs to be in describing the tenant's use, it can then turn its lawyer loose in an effort to try to get even more control than it actually needs (on the theory that control is always a good thing, even if it is not actually exercised to its fullest extent).

Although a landlord may not really care if a particular office suite is used as a law firm or an advertising agency, it likely does not want to see the space used as a call center, governmental office, ticket brokerage, massage parlor, or other use that might unduly tax the building's systems or potentially detract from the quality of the building's tenant roster—all of which would presumably be permitted under a clause restricting the tenant's use to "general office use." A landlord whose lease broadly describes the tenant's permitted use (for example, "general office use") can

---

[32] *See* SENN *supra* note 5, at 11–7; and FRIEDMAN, *supra* note 31, at 27–8.

exert additional control over the tenant's use of the leased premises by including in the lease a listing of those uses that are expressly prohibited in the leased premises. The "prohibited uses" can be specifically listed (for example, "the operation of call center") or described in a more generic fashion (for example, "any use that could unreasonably interfere with the business operations of other tenants in the building or that could adversely affect the character or reputation of the building as a Class A office building").

A tenant faced with what it believes is an unduly restrictive description of its permitted use can attempt to ease the restriction by introducing into the lease the concept of "incidental uses." By way of example, if the landlord's initial draft of the lease provides that the "tenant will use the leased premises solely for the operation of a law firm," tenant's counsel might suggest that the phrase "and all other incidental or related uses" be added at the end of the landlord's restrictive use clause. The incorporation of such "incidental use" language provides the tenant with additional flexibility should it decide at a later time to add to or change the nature of its business operations (for example, the law firm's decision to open a title insurance agency in the leased premises). To the extent the tenant is aware of a potential change in its business model, it should give that information to its counsel, so that the lawyer can try to enhance the tenant's position under the lease by adding the following language at the end of the incidental use clause mentioned above—"including, without limitation, the following uses. . . ."

Landlords often try to impose additional use restrictions against the tenant by incorporating into the lease a set of building rules and regulations that delineate specific "dos and don'ts" associated with their tenants' business operations—for example, prohibitions on smoking or the installation of vending machines in the leased premises. The tenant and its lawyers should carefully review the rules and regulations to determine whether the rules and regulations present an obstacle to the tenant's operation of its business in the contemplated fashion. The tenant's lawyer should also ask for written confirmation that the rules and regulations cannot be modified without the tenant's consent and that the landlord will enforce the rules and regulations in a consistent manner as to all of the building's tenants (see *Pro-Tenant Modification* #22 at page 743)—two propositions that run directly counter to the provisions contained in most landlord-authored rules and regulations (including § 6 and Exhibit C of the Form Office Lease).

B. COMPLIANCE WITH LAWS CLAUSE
(§ 7)

The compliance with laws clause deals with the issue of who is responsible for making sure that the condition of the leased premises complies with all applicable legal requirements. The legal requirements that are the proper subject of this clause are not those rules that govern the licenses and governmental approvals that a tenant is required to secure as a precursor to its conduct of its business in the leased premises (clearly a tenant responsibility), nor are they the building codes applicable to the landlord's initial construction of its building (clearly a landlord responsibility). Rather the crux of the issue at this stage of the lease negotiations is who is responsible to make those repairs and improvements to the leased premises that are required to be made as a result of a specific governmental requirement—for example, the Americans with Disabilities Act,[33] the Comprehensive Environmental Response, Compensation, and Liability Act,[34] or a state statute imposing indoor air quality standards. Because the dollars at stake can be substantial (easily running into six or seven figures), the compliance with laws clause is one of the most heavily negotiated provisions of a commercial lease.

The starting point in the negotiation is usually a clause in landlord's standard lease form that purports to place the obligation on the tenant to comply with all laws and other governmental requirements affecting the leased premises in any way (specifically including the obligation to make any repairs or improvements mandated by governmental requirements). The tenant's knee-jerk response when it reads that clause is to point out to the landlord that "you own the building, so it's your problem not mine." The landlord's equally pithy response is "if it has to do with the leased premises, it is your problem."

The resolution of the landlord-tenant conflict over the proper allocation of the legal compliance risk requires the negotiators to address the following three questions:

- Was the law enacted before or after the lease was executed?

- Is the application of the legal requirement triggered by the tenant's unique use of the leased premises or is the legal requirement generally applicable to all owners of real property?

---

[33] *See* 42 U.S.C. §§ 12101–12213 (2016).

[34] *See* 42 U.S.C. §§ 9601–9675 (2016). For a provision attempting to allocate the responsibility for compliance with environmental laws, *see e.g.,* § 17 of the Form Office Lease. *See also* Dillman, *supra* note 22, at 125–129.

- Does the required legal compliance require the construction of permanent improvements that can be re-used by the landlord after the expiration of the tenant's lease term?

A well-represented tenant with bargaining power comparable to that of the landlord should be able to get the landlord to agree to assume responsibility for making those repairs and improvements to the leased premises that satisfy all of the following requirements: (1) the repairs or improvements are attributable to the imposition of a legal requirement that was in place prior to the tenant's execution of the lease; (2) the legal requirement is generally applicable to all owners of real property; and (3) the improvements are permanent, increase the value of the landlord's property, and are likely re-usable by the landlord after the expiration of the tenant's lease (see *Pro-Tenant Modification #23* at page 743). Similarly, the landlord is often successful in its efforts to place the obligation on the tenant to make those repairs and improvements to the leased premises that are directly tied to the tenant's unique use of the leased premises and that are required as a result of the enactment of a governmental requirement after the parties' execution of the lease.

The normative allocation of risks described in the preceding paragraph leaves an ample stable of legal compliance risks that remain to be negotiated by the landlord and the tenant—principally who is responsible for making those repairs and improvements to the leased premises that (1) are required as a result of the enactment of a law after the date on which the lease was executed, and (2) are not directly linked to the tenant's unique use of the leased premises? The following are tactics that can be employed by the tenant's lawyer (often successfully) in an effort to allocate some of the unresolved risks back to the landlord:[35]

- Requiring the landlord to provide the tenant with a representation confirming that the building is in full compliance with all laws in place as of the date of the execution of the lease (see *Pro-Tenant Modification #24* at page 744);

- Limiting the tenant's obligation to the making of non-structural improvements that exclusively serve the leased premises;

- Placing a cap on the amount of any costs that the tenant has to incur in making improvements to the leased premises;

- Granting the tenant a right to terminate its lease if the costs of the required legal compliance exceed a specific number or if the required compliance takes place in the last year of the tenant's lease term; or

---

[35] *See* Hennigh, *Office Leases, supra* note 18, at 15–48 through 15–50

- Requiring the landlord to amortize the cost of any required improvement over the useful life of such improvement (determined in accordance with generally accepted accounting principles),with the tenant then assuming responsibility for the payment of only that portion of the amortized cost that is allocable to its lease term.

As always, the outcome of this negotiation is dependent on the knowledge and guile of the competing lawyers and the relative bargaining strength of their respective clients. However, the landlord's lawyer has the upper hand in the negotiations if the tenant occupies the entirety or a substantial part of the landlord's building and if the initial term of the tenant's lease is ten years or more.

C. ALTERATIONS CLAUSE
(§ 10)

At some point during the lease term, the tenant may have a desire to alter the physical condition of the leased premises to better suit the needs of its business operations. For example, a tenant might want to replace the carpeting in its reception area with granite tiles, build a new conference room, or install a new technological advance throughout the leased premises. The issue addressed in the alterations clause is whether and under what circumstances the tenant may make such alterations.

The landlord wants to retain the right to approve each and every alteration that the tenant proposes to make to the leased premises. The landlord does not want the tenant to have the right to make any alteration that could adversely impact the value of the landlord's reversionary interest in the building—by either affecting the structural integrity of the building or hindering the landlord's ability to attract and retain other building tenants.

For this reason, most landlord lease forms contain an absolute prohibition against the tenant making any alterations to the leased premises. A standard tenant-sponsored incursion on that prohibition permits the tenant to make non-structural alterations up to a fixed dollar limit (for example, $10,000—see the definition of "minor alterations" in § 10 of the Form Office Lease).

The tenant next asks that the landlord agree to not unreasonably withhold its consent to any tenant-requested alteration. While most landlords (at least the reasonable ones) accede to that request, they often do so only with the following attached conditions:[36]

---

[36] *See generally* David L. Grobart, *Alterations*, in LEASE NEGOTIATION HANDBOOK 349 (Edward Chupack ed., 2003)

- The tenant is required to provide the landlord with complete plans and specifications depicting the proposed alteration;

- The landlord retains the right to either construct the alteration itself or approve the contractor selected by the tenant to perform the alteration work;

- The tenant is obligated to promptly pay all costs of constructing the alteration and to immediately discharge any mechanics' lien filed against landlord's reversionary interest in the building (see § 11 of the Form Office Lease); and

- If requested by landlord, the tenant will remove the alteration at the end of the lease term and repair any damage to the leased premises caused by such removal.

D. MAINTENANCE CLAUSE
(§ 5)

The landlord and the tenant share a goal of wanting the leased premises to be maintained throughout the lease term in the same approximate physical and operating conditions that existed as of the commencement date of the lease term. The landlord wants the leased premises to be properly maintained to preserve the value of its reversionary interest in the leased premises, while the tenant is focused on making sure that the leased premises are maintained in a manner that is conducive to the effective conduct of the tenant's business. Given the fact that the landlord and the tenant share the same overall objective, the principal issue to be addressed in the maintenance clause is not what has to be done, but who has to do it.

The maintenance clause is one of the least understood provisions of a commercial lease. The mistake that most practitioners make when drafting the clause is that they try to allocate responsibility for maintaining the leased premises, without first accurately identifying the various components of the maintenance obligation. There are two separate aspects of the maintenance obligation that a lawyer needs to take into consideration when negotiating the maintenance clause—specifically (1) what functions have to be performed to properly maintain the leased premises, and (2) what elements of the leased premises have to be so maintained?

The maintenance obligation consists of three distinct functions:[37]

- *Maintenance*—Keeping the leased premises in the same condition that existed as of the commencement date, subject to ordinary wear and tear;

- *Repair*—Fixing what is broken in the leased premises; and

- *Replacement*—Improving the condition of the leased premises by removing something that is irretrievably broken and substituting in its place something that is new or better.

The maintenance function is the least costly to perform, while the replacement function is the most costly.

Once the component functions of the maintenance obligation are identified, the next thing that the practitioner must do is to prepare a listing of what needs to be maintained and, potentially, repaired and replaced. The following are the subjects of the maintenance obligation:

- *Common areas*—including both building common areas (for example, lobbies, hallways, elevators, and other building-wide mechanical systems) and site common areas (for example, landscaping, parking lots, and sidewalks); and

- *Leased premises*—including both base building improvements (for example, floors, windows, load-bearing walls, and mechanical systems located in the leased premises) and tenant improvements (for example, carpeting, painted surfaces, light fixtures, and demising walls); and

- *Tenant's furniture, fixtures, and equipment* (for example, computers, copiers and conference room furniture).

Once all of the functions and subjects of the maintenance obligation are properly identified, the lawyers representing the landlord and tenant should then allocate responsibility for the performance of each of the functions (maintenance, repair, and replacement) as to each component of the tenant's leased space (the common areas, the base building improvements, the tenant improvements, and the tenant's FF&E). The key to the preparation and negotiation of a workable maintenance clause is for the lawyers to "close all the gaps"[38] and clearly and thoughtfully assign responsibility for the performance of each component of the maintenance obligation to either the landlord or the tenant.

In the context of a multi-tenant office lease, the landlord is usually allocated the responsibility for maintaining, repairing, and replacing all of the building's common areas, as well as the base building improvements located within the leased premises. The tenant customarily assumes

---

[37]   *See* Hennigh, *Office Leases, supra* note 18, at 15–52 and 15–53.

[38]   *See* SENN, *supra* note 5, at 19–11.

responsibility for maintaining, repairing, and replacing its furniture, fixtures, and equipment. The allocation of responsibility for the maintenance, repair, and replacement of the tenant improvements located within the leased premises is where the action is really at during the negotiation of the maintenance clause (see *Pro-Tenant Modification #28* at page 746). Factors that influence the outcome of that negotiation are the type of the project (with the tenant being more likely to assume all or a portion of the maintenance obligation in a warehouse or single tenant lease) and the length of the tenant's lease term (with the tenant being more likely to assume responsibility for the maintenance obligation in a long-term lease).

Finally, the practitioner needs to keep in mind that the allocation to the landlord of responsibility for performing a particular maintenance obligation does not necessarily mean that the landlord must bear the financial responsibility for paying the costs associated with such performance. As noted earlier in this chapter at pages 517–518, it is quite common for the landlord to pass through to its tenants some or all of the costs it incurs in connection with the performance of the landlord's maintenance obligation (including not only maintenance and repair costs, but also replacement costs) If the landlord opts to pass through some of those expenses to its tenants, landlord's counsel should be careful to eliminate any unintended inference that the performance provisions of the maintenance clause somehow override any inconsistent financial provision of the expense pass-through clause.

E. BUILDING SERVICES CLAUSE

(§ 4)

In a multi-tenant office building, the landlord customarily provides most, if not all, of the building services that the tenant requires to conduct its business in the leased premises. The basic services typically required by the tenant include: utilities (water, electricity, and heating, ventilating, and air conditioning services); elevator service; window washing; parking; landscaping, and snow removal; trash pick-up; and janitorial services. Landlords of high-end office buildings are increasingly providing the following additional services and facilities to entice new tenants to choose their buildings—concierge services; valet parking; state of the art video conferencing and telecommunication services; on-site fitness centers; and 24/7 security (although some office landlords try to avoid acknowledging in the lease that they have any obligation to provide security to the tenants out of a concern that doing so will subject them to liability if a tenant is attacked or its property is stolen).[39] Office tenants are generally

---

[39] *See* Hennigh, *Office Leases, supra* note 18, at 15–11.

responsible for handling their own telephone and other telecommunication services.

The following are three issues that the lawyers must resolve when drafting and negotiating the building services clause.

- What services is the landlord required to furnish to the tenant?

- How will the tenant pay for the cost of such services?

- What are the consequences of an interruption in the provision of any such service?

The answers provided by counsel for the landlord and the tenant are, understandably, quite different. The divergent positions of the landlord and tenant on the building services issue, as well as some commonly adopted compromises, are discussed below.

1.   List of Building Services

The landlord's required provision of any service to a tenant has two consequences to the landlord—(1) it increases the landlord's building expenses, and (2) it subjects the landlord to potential liability for failing to provide the contemplated service to its tenants. As a result, the landlord's lawyer first objective is to minimize the number of the services the landlord is required to provide to its tenants and to negate any exacting standards related to the nature, scope, or frequency of the required services. The landlord's lawyer accomplishes this goal by putting together a skimpy, but exclusive listing of the general building services that the landlord is required to furnish to its tenants (for example, electricity, water, HVAC, elevator, and janitorial services) and then stating that all of the listed services "will be furnished as required for the use of the leased premises for general office purposes during normal business hours" (see the first sentence of § 4 of the Form Office Lease). The specific designation of what constitutes "normal business hours" varies by building.

The lawyer representing the tenant has a decidedly different agenda concerning the description of the building services that the landlord is required to provide to the tenant. First, the tenant's lawyer seeks to incorporate into the lease a very long and non-exclusive list of the specific services that the landlord must provide to the leased premises (see *Pro-Tenant Modification #25* at page 745). Tenant's lawyer concludes that list with a catch-all concerning the landlord's provision of "all such other services that are reasonably required to permit the tenant's efficient operation of its business in the leased premises." Tenant's counsel then endeavors to introduce the landlord to the reality of a 24/7 economy by asking the landlord's lawyer to strike the "normal business hours" limitation from the building services clause. Finally, tenant's counsel attempts to insert into the building services clause detailed performance standards for each of the listed building services—for example, the provision of HVAC service to continuously maintain a specific range of temperatures inside the leased premises regardless of the outside temperature.[40]

Well-represented landlords and tenants usually end up with a lease that describes with reasonable specificity the nature, scope and frequency of those services that the landlord intends to furnish to all of its tenants during the building's normal business hours. The landlord should make sure that the delineated levels of building services are consistent with (1) the building's capabilities (for example, whether the building is designed to provide electrical service to meet the watts per square foot standard specified in the lease), and (2) the levels of building services contemplated in the landlord's lease quotes and operating budget for the building. It is then left to the best graces of the lawyers for the landlord and the tenant to determine whether the landlord's standard list of building services is acceptable to the tenant and, if not, what, if anything should be done to rectify that situation. If the landlord is capable of ramping up or otherwise changing its building operations to satisfy the tenant's needs, then the next question that arises is who bears the economic burden of paying the increased costs associated with such change—a topic that is addressed under the next subheading.

2.   Allocation of Cost of Providing Building Services

The tenant can pay its share of the landlord's cost of furnishing the required building services in one of three ways—either as (1) part of its base rent obligation, (2) an expense pass-through or (3) a direct payment to the vendor that provides the service. The determination of which of these methods is employed for a particular cost is generally resolved as part of the rent structure negotiation discussed earlier in this chapter at pages 512–517.

The key economic issue that must be resolved in the content of the building services clause is who pays the increased costs triggered by the tenant's excessive use of a particular building service. For this purpose, a tenant's use of a building service is viewed by the landlord as being "excessive" if such use is greater than the baseline use projected by the landlord for its general tenant population. The two most common examples of a tenant's excessive use of a building service are (1) the tenant's consumption during normal business hours of a higher level of service than

---

[40]   *See e.g.,* LAWRENCE EISENBERG, JONATHON MECHANIC AND DAVID ALAN RICHARDS, THE OFFICIAL COMMERCIAL OFFICE LEASE HANDBOOK 263 (2003). Commercial office leases often also include specific performance standards for the provision of electrical and janitorial services. *See* John S. Hollyfield, *Landlord's Services,* in ALI-ABA COURSE OF STUDY MATERIALS, COMMERCIAL REAL ESTATE LEASES: SELECTED ISSUES IN DRAFTING AND NEGOTIATING IN CURRENT MARKETS, Course No. SL–017, 189, 191 (June 2006).

that consumed by the landlord's remaining roster of tenants (for example, the tenant's excessive use of electricity due to its operation of a computer help desk in its leased premises), and (2) the tenant's required use of a service outside of the normal business hours for the building (for example, the tenant's operation of a call center on a 24/7 cycle).

Conceptually, most landlords and tenants agree that the increased costs associated with a tenant's excessive use of a building service should be paid by the tenant. It is, however, much tougher for them to reach a consensus on either the definition of an excessive use or the calculation of the increased costs attributable to the excessive use. The landlord wants to retain wide latitude to both identify the existence of an excessive use and measure the amount of the surcharge that is imposed on the tenant to reimburse the landlord for the increased costs produced by the tenant's excessive use. The tenant, on the other hand, wants the excessive use concept to be very narrowly defined and for the related costs to be objectively measured to prevent the landlord from profiting from the service surcharge imposed on the tenant. Counsel for the landlord and the tenant seek to bridge the gap between their clients' diametrically opposite positions by (1) agreeing on a compromised definition of "normal business hours" (something greater than "9 to 5" and less than "24/7"), (2) specifying performance standards for each building service that the landlord is required to provide to the tenant (thereby providing an objective benchmark to identify the tenant's excessive use), and (3) stipulating a fixed amount of the surcharge for the tenant's excessive use of a building service (for example, $__ per hour for after-hours HVAC service provided to the tenant's leased premises—see *Pro-Tenant Modification #26* at page 745).[41]

3. Interruption of Service

The final question that counsel for the landlord and the tenant must answer as part of their negotiation of the building services clause is, What happens if the provision of a required building service is interrupted for some reason? What, if anything, can the tenant do to protect itself from the burden placed on its business operations due to the elevators being out of service for an hour on a Tuesday morning, the parking garage being closed for two weeks while the landlord renovates the parking decks, or electric service being cut off to the building for a week due to a windstorm? The

---

[41] *See* SENN, *supra* note 5, at 9–8 through 9–10, for an excellent discussion of the options available to measure the tenant's use of electricity in its leased premises. The best way to deal with the tenant's excessive use of electricity is to install a separate meter in the tenant's leased premises that measures the exact amount of the tenant's actual electrical consumption. If the installation of a separate electrical meter is not an option (and, for a variety of technical reasons, it often is not), then the landlord and the tenant are left with the challenge of negotiating an excessive use provision that balances the competing interests discussed in the text.

remainder of this section discusses the common law and contractual remedies available to the tenant to deal with an interruptions of service.

Based on the common law doctrine of independent covenants that is followed in the majority of states, a tenant's sole remedy for the interruption of a required service is the filing of a damages action against the landlord.[42] Absent a specific provision in the lease to the contrary, the tenant does not have the right to suspend its rent obligation or terminate its lease unless the interruption of service is so severe that it amounts to a constructive eviction of the tenant's right to occupy and use the leased premises.

The common law doctrine of constructive eviction affords only limited protection to a tenant faced with the interruption of a required building service. In order to establish that an interruption of service has resulted in the tenant's constructive eviction from its leased premises (thereby permitting the tenant to terminate its lease and its ongoing obligation to pay rent), the tenant must establish that (1) the landlord caused the interruption of service, (2) the interruption permanently deprived the tenant of its use and enjoyment of the leased premises, and (3) the tenant vacated the leased premises within a reasonable period of time following the occurrence of the landlord-caused interruption of service.[43] Few tenants can satisfy this burden of proof and even fewer are willing to move out of the leased premises and take the risk that the landlord later sues the tenant for a breach of its lease obligations. The doctrine of constructive eviction is, therefore, useful to a tenant only in the most egregious of settings.

The courts in a minority of states have declined to follow the doctrine of independent covenants. In those states, a tenant may have the right to terminate its lease or suspend its payment of rent if the landlord breaches a "promise that was a significant inducement to the tenant's entering the lease in the first instance"[44]—a lower burden of proof than that customarily placed upon the tenant in a constructive eviction action. A few states have also hinted at the possibility that the tenant might have the right to withhold its rent based on the landlord's breach of an implied warranty of suitability of the leased premises for its intended use.[45] The dependent covenant rule and the implied warranty of suitability are, however, clearly minority positions and, hence, do not provide any comfort to most commercial real estate tenants. In addition, because they apparently have application only to those significant interruptions of service that are caused

---

[42] *See* FRIEDMAN, *supra* note 31, at 1–21.

[43] *See* David H. Fishman, *Get Me Out of This Lease*, 24 No. 2 PRACTICAL REAL ESTATE LAWYER 13, 14 (March 2008).

[44] *See* Wesson v. Leone Enterprises, Inc., 437 Mass. 708, 722. *See also* Richard Barton Enterprises, Inc. v. Tsern, 928 P.2d 368 (Utah 1996).

[45] *See* Fishman, *supra* note 43, at 17–18; and SENN, *supra* note 5, at 5–57 through 5–62.

by a material breach of the landlord's performance obligations, the doctrine of dependent covenants and the implied warranty of suitability also fail to provide the tenant with any useful means to deal with an interruption of service that is caused by a third party or one that does not rise to the level of significance contemplated by those minority rules.

The tenant can override all the common law strictures by including a provision in the lease that provides it with specific remedies to deal with an interruption in service (see *Pro-Tenant Modification #27* at page 745). The following constitutes the tenant's wish list of remedies to address the impact of an interruption of service:

- The right to abate its rent during the continuance of the interruption of service;

- The self-help right to do whatever is necessary to cure the interruption and then offset the costs of the cure against its rent obligation (see *Pro-Tenant Modification #30* at page 746); and

- The right to terminate the lease if the service is not reinstated within a stated period of time.

As noted above, the tenant does not have any of these remedies unless its lawyer is successful in expressly including such remedies in the lease document.

The landlord, of course, strenuously objects to the inclusion in the lease of any rent abatement, self-help, or termination remedy. The landlord wants to continue to receive the full benefit of its negotiated rental stream despite the occurrence of an interruption of service. In the landlord's view, the only remedy that the tenant needs to protect itself against a service interruption is the right to file a damages action against the landlord. The grant to tenant of any additional remedies significantly shifts in tenant's favor the negotiating leverage over a service dispute. Suddenly, a tenant who feels that it is "just way too hot" in its leased premises might avail itself of its rent abatement or self-help remedy to reduce the rent it pays to the landlord and then force the landlord to file a legal action against the tenant to try to recover the full amount of the rent that the landlord believes was due in the first instance. Worse yet, the tenant might actually try to get out of its lease by exercising its termination remedy.[46]

The following are factors that color the parties' determination of the remedies available to the tenant to deal with an interruption of service.

---

[46] *See* the last sentence of § 4 of the Form Office Lease for an example of a provision that attempts to eliminate any landlord liability for an interruption of service that is caused by a reason beyond Landlord's reasonable control. For a more aggressive, pro-landlord provision that wholly eliminates any tenant remedy for a service interruption (including one caused by the landlord), *see* *Form 1–1, Office Lease with Modifications*, in THE COMMERCIAL LEASE FORMBOOK: EXPERT TOOLS FOR DRAFTING AND NEGOTIATION 8, 32 (Dennis M. Horn ed., 2004).

- Does the service interruption prevent the tenant from conducting its business in the leased premises (or is the interruption simply an inconvenience for the tenant)?

- How long does the interruption last (for example, one hour versus one month)?

- Was the landlord at fault in causing the interruption or was the interruption caused by an event or circumstance beyond the landlord's control?

- Is the event or circumstance giving rise to the interruption covered by the tenant's business interruption insurance or the landlord's rent loss insurance?

In most situations, the landlord is extremely reluctant to give the tenant a right to terminate the lease as a result of the occurrence of an interruption of service, (no matter how long or how severe that interruption may be). Most landlords are also hesitant to give a tenant a self-help remedy because of the negative impact that a tenant-sponsored corrective action can have on the building's residual value. Landlords tend to be more willing to entertain the grant of a limited rent abatement right to the tenant as long as that right is exercisable only if the interruption was caused by the landlord and then only after the expiration of a substantial grace period (for example, an interruption lasting more than ten consecutive days).

F. UNIQUE USE ISSUES IN A RETAIL LEASE

Before leaving the "use" topic, some mention should be made of the unique provisions found in the use clauses of retail leases. The following are retail-specific provisions that are discussed in this subsection:

- A restrictive use clause;

- An exclusive use clause;

- A radius restriction;

- A continuous operation covenant;

- A go dark right; and

- A co-tenancy requirement.

The genesis of all these clauses is the reality that a retail lease is significantly different from other commercial leases in two principal respects—(1) the profitability of a tenant's store is inextricably linked to the vibrancy and success of the landlord's center as a whole, and (2) a significant portion of the landlord's financial returns (specifically the income stream represented by the tenants' percentage rent obligations) is tied to the sales revenues generated in the tenants' stores. As a result, the retail landlord and tenant have a shared goal of maximizing the customer traffic to and the sales generated from the tenant's store and the landlord's retail center. The restrictive use clause, the continuous operation covenant, and the radius restriction are tools used by the landlord to enhance the sales revenues produced from the operation of the center as a whole, while the exclusive use clause, the go-dark right, and the co-tenancy requirement are the means used by the tenant to aid the profitability of its particular store.

1.   Restrictive Use Clause

The retail landlord knows that having the right mix and balance of tenants is the key driver for increasing customer traffic to its center. The best way for the landlord to achieve the optimal tenant mix is for it to employ a ***restrictive use clause*** of the type mentioned earlier in this chapter relative to the discussion of the use clause of a multi-tenant office lease (see pages 535–537). A retail landlord must clearly articulate in a retail lease exactly what the tenant can and cannot sell in its store. The landlord's consistent use of tightly worded restrictive use clauses helps the landlord (1) create and maintain a synergistic mix of tenants, and (2) avoid the unfortunate circumstance of having multiple tenants selling the same product line (for example, five candle stores in the same center) or mismatched tenants being located in close proximity to each other (for example, a discount liquidation store situated next to a high-end fashion retailer).[47]

The tenant has an entirely different perspective on the use clause of a retail lease. The retail tenant desires to maintain maximum flexibility to change its retail operations and introduce new product lines if it determines that doing so will increase the profitability of the retail business. A retail tenant's clear preference is a use clause that says that "the leased premises may be used for any lawful retail purpose." This stands in stark contrast to the landlord's desire to have the tenant's use clause restrict the tenant to the use of the leased premises for the sale of a specific type of product—for example, the "sale of women's shoes." The tug of war that ensues between the lawyers for the landlord and the tenant is frequently resolved by the inclusion in the lease of concepts designed to permit the tenant to introduce new product lines in its store as long as the "primary use" of its store is for a specific retail use (which will likely be defined more broadly than the landlord would prefer and more narrowly than the tenant would prefer).

---

[47] *See generally* Joel R. Hall, *Use Clauses*, in ALI-ABA COURSE OF STUDY MATERIALS, COMMERCIAL REAL ESTATE LEASES: SELECTED ISSUES IN DRAFTING AND NEGOTIATING IN CURRENT MARKETS, Course No. SN–013, 499 (May 2008).

2. Exclusive Use Clause

Major retailers are occasionally successful in negotiating the right to be the only tenant in the landlord's center that can engage in a particular retail business (for example, the operation of a bookstore). In those situations, the landlord expressly grants to the tenant the exclusive right to sell a particular product line in the center and agrees to prohibit all other tenants from selling products covered by the granted exclusive. The receipt of an *exclusive use clause* gives the retail tenant a mini-monopoly and permits it to grow its revenue base without fear of competition from any other tenant in the center.

The landlord views the grant of an exclusive use as marketing handcuffs that unduly limit its ability to attain the desired mix of tenants in the center.[48] As such, the landlord resists the grant of an exclusive to anyone other than the most powerful of destination tenants whose presence is considered to be a crucial factor in driving the level of the customer traffic in the landlord's center. If the landlord feels that it has no choice but to grant an exclusive to a particular tenant, then its next battle is to define the scope of the exclusive in a fashion that does not totally tie the landlord's hands in its efforts to lease space in the center. The landlord prefers to phrase the exclusive use by stating that the landlord will not lease any other space in its center to a tenant whose "primary business is the operation of a bookstore." This description of the tenant's exclusive use permits the landlord to lease space in its center to other tenants who sell books as long as their sale of books is incidental to the conduct of their primary businesses.

3. Radius Restriction

A *radius restriction* is the landlord's version of an exclusive use clause. A radius restriction limits the tenant's ability to operate a competing store within a specified proximity to the landlord's retail center. The radius restriction is designed to protect the landlord's percentage rent receipts from a reduction occasioned by the tenant's diversion of a part of its potential sales to a nearby store located in a center owned by a competitor of the landlord.[49]

There are two types of radius restrictions—(1) an absolute prohibition against the tenant's opening of another store within the designated radius, and (2) a requirement that any gross sales derived from the tenant's new

---

[48] *See generally*, Kathleen A. Crocco and Jeffrey H. Kaplan, *"Good for the Goose, Good for the Gander": The Interplay between Radius Restrictions and Exclusive Use Clauses in Shopping Center Leases*, in INTERNATIONAL SHOPPING CENTERS LAW CONFERENCE Tab 2 (2005); Joel R. Hall, Exclusive Clauses, in ALI-ABA COURSE OF STUDY MATERIALS, COMMERCIAL REAL ESTATE LEASES: SELECTED ISSUES IN DRAFTING AND NEGOTIATING IN CURRENT MARKETS, Course No. SN–013, 509, 515–516 (May 2008); and Theani C. Louskos, Unique Issues in Retail Leasing, 27 No. 3 PRACTICAL REAL ESTATE LAWYER 7, 10–11 (May 2011).

[49] *See generally*, Crocco, *supra* note 48, at 9–20; and Louskos, *supra* note 48, at 16–17.

store must be included in the base for the computation of the tenant's percentage rent in the landlord's center. The enforceability of a radius restriction and its acceptability to a prospective tenant are dependent on the geographic scope of the restriction (typically no more than five miles from the boundaries of the landlord's center) and the duration of the restriction (usually no longer than the length of the tenant's existing lease term).

4. Continuous Operation Covenant

In an effort to maximize the gross sales generated from its center (and, hence, the amount of its percentage rent receipts), a retail landlord routinely insists that each of its tenants agree to continuously operate its retail business in the leased premises during the center's normal business hours and to staff, fixture, and stock its store in a manner designed to maximize its gross sales.[50] The landlord's inclusion in the lease of a *continuous operation covenant* is a direct product of the landlord's grant to the tenant of a base rent discount in return for the tenant's agreement to pay percentage rent. If a tenant is not going full bore in the operation of its store, then it is unlikely that the landlord will ever receive percentage rent from that tenant.

Courts in certain jurisdictions have held that there is an implied covenant of continuous operation if (1) the lease provides for the payment of insubstantial base rent (when compared to the tenant's percentage rent obligation), or (2) the provisions of the lease make it clear that the tenant is economically interdependent with other tenants in the center.[51] Best practices call for the landlord and the tenant to expressly address the continuous operation issue in the lease and not leave the resolution of that important issue to the whim of the judicial branch.

5. Go Dark Right

The tenant's counterpoint to the continuous operation covenant is a *go dark right*.[52] Under a go dark right, the tenant expressly reserves the right to close or curtail its store operations at any time and for any reason. The tenant's exercise of its go dark right does not effect a termination of its lease, but simply eliminates the tenant's need to continue conducting business in its leased space. By closing a bad store, the tenant saves money by eliminating both its percentage rent obligation and the costs of staffing and stocking the store.

---

[50] *See generally,* Marie Moore, *Shedding Light on Going Dark: Continuous Operation Clauses,* in INTERNATIONAL SHOPPING CENTERS LAW CONFERENCE Tab 1 (2005) and Louskos, *supra* note 48, at 11–12.

[51] *See* SENN, *supra* note 5, at 11–64 through 11–73.

[52] *See generally* Moore, *supra* note 50.

The resolution of the continuous operations vs. go dark riddle boils down to a simple matter of which party to the lease is the most motivated to have the tenant lease space in the landlord's retail center. The landlord and tenant often compromise their competing positions by agreeing to limit the time period in which the tenant has the right to go dark (for example, only during the last year of the lease term) or conditioning the tenant's exercise of its go dark right upon the occurrence of an objectively verifiable event or circumstance (for example, the tenant's gross sales dropping below a threshold amount).

6.   Co-Tenancy Requirement

A *co-tenancy requirement* is a pro-tenant provision that conditions the tenant's obligation to perform its lease obligations upon the status of other tenants in the retail center.[53] Co-tenancy requirements come in two distinctly different forms—(1) an *opening co-tenancy requirement* that conditions the obligation of the tenant to open for business and begin paying rent on the occupancy status of the center as a whole, and (2) a *continuing co-tenancy requirement* that permits the tenant to terminate its lease or reduce its rent if the occupancy of the center falls below an agreed-upon standard. The co-tenancy requirement can be expressed in a variety of ways, including a requirement that "at least 80% of the retail center must be subject to binding written leases" or a requirement that "Barnes and Noble and Cheesecake Factory must be open and actively conducting business in the retail center." Regardless of how the co-tenancy requirement is phrased, the purpose of the clause from the tenant's perspective is always the same—the tenant wants to be relieved of the duty to fully perform its obligations in a dead or dying retail center.

If a landlord is willing to entertain the inclusion of a co-tenancy requirement in its lease (and with some national retail chains, it has no other choice), the landlord's lawyer typically attempts to limit the co-tenancy to an opening only requirement. If the tenant insists on a continuing co-tenancy requirement, then the landlord's lawyer can soften the impact of that requirement by inserting a provision in the lease that gives the landlord a right for a specified period of time (ideally six months or more) to cure the co-tenancy violation by replacing the closed or departed tenants with suitable new tenants. For that type of provision to produce the intended result, it is imperative that the landlord reserve the right in the co-tenant's lease to terminate its lease if the co-tenant closes its store. This right affords the landlord the opportunity to cure the breach of the co-

---

[53] *See generally*, Eric D. Rapkin, *Co-tenancy Provisions in Retail Lease Agreements*, in INTERNATIONAL SHOPPING CENTERS LAW CONFERENCE Tab 3 (2005); and Ira A. Meislik, *Retail Leases,* in COMMERCIAL REAL ESTATE TRANSACTIONS HANDBOOK 14–47 to 14–49 (Mark A. Senn ed. 2016).

tenancy requirement by finding a new tenant to take over the co-tenant's space.

7.   Interplay of Retail Use Provisions

A landlord of a regional mall or lifestyle center might have upwards of a hundred tenants. It is, therefore, crucial that the landlord use its best efforts to limit both the number and scope of the special use provisions it includes in its tenants' leases. If a landlord is not careful, the interplay of the special use provisions can cause irreparable financial harm to the landlord's center.

The following are a few illustrative examples of the traps that await the unwary retail landlord:

- The grant of an exclusive to one tenant, coupled with the inclusion in another tenant's lease of a permissive use clause permitting the tenant to use its leased premises for "any lawful retail use";

- The grant of opening co-tenancy requirements to two tenants, with each such requirement stating that the tenant's obligation to open its store is expressly conditioned upon the other tenant being open and operating for business (a classic "chicken or the egg" scenario); and

- The grant of a go dark right to a tenant named in another tenant's co-tenancy requirement.

A leading expert on retail leasing notes that because the special use provisions of a retail lease "can give rise to a house of cards that can come crashing down if one of the linchpin stores closes, it is vital that the landlord carefully control . . . remedies in order to avoid a catastrophic collapse of the property's rent structure."[54]

X. TENANT FLEXIBILITY PROVISIONS

This section explores lease provisions that give the tenant the flexibility to alter its lease arrangement to respond to changes in its business operations. The tenant flexibility clauses generally fall into one of three categories—(1) clauses that provide the tenant with a right to expand or contract the size of its leased premises, (2) clauses that give the tenant the right to shorten or extend the term of its occupancy of the leased premises, and (3) clauses that authorize the tenant to transfer its leasehold interests to a third party.

It should first be noted that any provision that is structured to provide the tenant with flexibility works to the landlord's disadvantage. The tenant

---

[54] *See* Meislik, *supra* note 53, at 14–49.

flexibility provisions all share one common characteristic—they provide the tenant with the *OPTION* (and not the *OBLIGATION*) to take an action in the future to change the nature of the landlord-tenant relationship. The tenant will exercise its flexibility only if that option produces a result for the tenant that is more favorable than that which characterizes its then existing lease arrangement. A result that is more favorable to the tenant is almost always unfavorable to the landlord.

Why then does the landlord permit the tenant to include flexibility options in the lease? The answer to that question is relatively simple—in some situations, the landlord has no other choice. Many tenants place paramount importance during the lease negotiations on their retention of flexibility to properly deal with changes in their business models and will not sign any lease that locks them into a rigidly defined business dynamic for the duration of the lease term. Because the tenants adopting that stance are typically the tenants that are most attractive to the landlord (for example, large national tenants who have deep pockets and are willing to sign leases for large spaces and long terms), the real estate development lawyer often has no realistic alternative other than to try to craft lease clauses that grant the tenant a measure of flexibility, while still protecting the landlord's overarching business interests.

Landlords seldom provide the requested flexibility to tenants whose importance to the project's financial success is marginal—either because of the size of their leased premises or the depth of their pocket books. Throughout the remainder of this section, it is assumed that the tenant asking for a flexibility option is a person that the landlord very much wants to have in its building (although, to keep the playing field level, it is also assumed that the landlord does not feel compelled to accede to each and every request made by the tenant).

A. SPACE FLEXIBILITY OPTIONS

Any number of changes can occur during the course of a tenant's lease term that might cause the tenant to want to change the size and configuration of its leased premises. If the tenant's business has grown, it may want to increase the size of its leased premises so that it can secure the efficiencies associated with having its employees working under the same roof. If its business has declined, the tenant may need less space than it originally contracted for when it signed its lease. Finally, if the tenant's business has been sold or closed, the tenant may have no need whatsoever for any leased space.

The following are alternative clauses that the tenant's lawyer can include in the lease to provide the tenant with a right to expand the size of its leased premises at some point after the date of the tenant's execution of the original lease. The alternatives are presented in order from the most to the least desirable from the tenant's perspective.

1. Expansion Option

The optimal way for a tenant to preserve the its right to increase the size of the leased premises is to negotiate for the inclusion in the lease of an **expansion option** (see *Pro-Tenant Modification #8* at page 735).[55] Under an expansion option, the tenant receives the right (but not the obligation) to lease additional space in the building at a designated time during the lease term. If the tenant has an option to lease all or a designated portion of the vacant space in a building, then the landlord has no choice but to keep that space vacant and off the market throughout the pendency of the tenant's option—which means that the landlord will not receive any rental income from that space unless and until the tenant exercises its expansion option. For that reason, landlords strenuously resist the grant of an expansion option to a tenant or, at the very least, endeavor to limit both the duration of the tenant's option (for example, only for the first 12 months of the lease term) and the identity of the space that is the subject of the option (for example, only the 10,000 square feet of contiguous space located on the same floor as the tenant's original leased premises). The landlord might also try to receive partial compensation for keeping the option space off the market by insisting that the tenant pay the landlord an annual fee to keep the option alive.

2. Right of First Refusal

A **right of first refusal (RFR)** permits the landlord to continue to market the vacant space in its building, but gives the tenant a priority right to match any third party offer to lease that space (referred to in this section as the "RFR Space").[56] If a third party offers to lease the RFR space, then the landlord is first required to tender that offer to the tenant who then has a fixed period of time to decide whether it wants to lease the RFR Space (see *Pro-Tenant Modification #9* at page 736). If the tenant exercises its right of first refusal, then the third party offeror is out of luck and the size of the tenant's leased premises is expanded to include the RFR Space.

Although a right of first refusal does not prevent the landlord from marketing its vacant space, it does have a decided chilling effect on the landlord's ability to do so. Few companies are willing to take the time and spend the money required to negotiate a lease if there is a realistic prospect that an existing tenant might swoop in at the end of the negotiations and pull the rug out from underneath it by exercising a right of first refusal on the targeted space. A landlord can try to limit the chilling effect of a right of first refusal by (1) limiting both the duration and the identity of the space

---

[55] *See generally* ZANKEL, *supra* note 1, at 22–24; and Yi, *supra* note 3, at 4.

[56] *See generally* ZANKEL, *supra* note 1, at 24; and Yi, *supra* note 3, at 4.

covered by the RFR, (2) requiring a very short turnaround time for the tenant's exercise of the RFR (for example, two business days after its receipt of the third party offer), (3) triggering the time period for the tenant's exercise of the RFR by the landlord's delivery to the tenant of a letter of intent or term sheet signed by a third party (rather than a fully-negotiated lease document), (4) requiring the tenant to match every part of the third party offer even if that offer applies to space in more than one building or imposes a condition that is impossible for the tenant to satisfy (for example, a minimum net worth covenant or a use prohibition), and (5) providing that the RFR automatically terminates if the tenant ever opts not to exercise such right.

A right of first refusal that automatically expires whenever the tenant declines to exercise that right is commonly referred to as a "one bite out of the apple right." That type of right of first refusal stands in sharp contrast to the type favored by the tenant (a so-called "evergreen right"—see *Pro-Tenant Modification #9* at page 736) that keeps the tenant's right of first refusal intact as to all other RFR space in the building even after the tenant declines to exercise its right of first refusal as to a specific portion of the RFR space.

3.   Right of First Offer

A *right of first offer (RFO)* is one step removed from a right of first refusal. In a right of first offer, the landlord is required to extend an offer to the tenant to lease certain space in the building before the landlord begins marketing that space to other prospective tenants (see *Pro-Tenant Modification #10* at page 736).[57] The existing tenant has a fixed period of time (for example, ten to 30 days) in which to decide whether to exercise the right of first offer and lease the subject space on the terms and conditions specified in the landlord's offer. If the tenant declines to exercise the right of first offer within the designated time frame, then the landlord is free to begin actively marketing the space for lease to third parties.

A landlord is more inclined to grant a right of first offer than it is an expansion option or a right of first refusal because the right of first offer simply requires the landlord to do something that it would likely do in any event—try to "pick the low hanging fruit" by contacting all of its existing tenants before marketing the space to third parties. This is especially true if the right of first offer does not impose any limitation on the terms on which the landlord can lease the space to a third party following the tenant's waiver of its right of first offer. Given the lack of such limitations, the landlord is free to present a high-ball offer to the holder of the right of first offer and then later lease the space to a third party at a much lower rent. For this reason, most tenants insist that the right of first offer contain

---

[57]   *See* ZANKEL, *supra* note 1, at 24–25; and Yi, *supra* note 3, at 3–4.

a re-offer requirement that precludes the landlord from leasing the space to a third party on terms less favorable to the landlord than those specified in the landlord's initial offer to the existing tenant unless the landlord first re-offers the space to the tenant on the less favorable terms.[58]

4.   "Must Take" Agreement

This last alternative is the only flexibility provision that actually places an obligation on the tenant to expand the size of its leased premise (and, hence, is the alternative that is the most palatable to the landlord). Under a *"must take" agreement*, the tenant is obligated to lease additional space in the building effective as of a specified date following the date of the parties' execution of the lease term (for example, the first anniversary of the commencement date of the lease term). A tenant is typically reluctant to agree to a must take provision unless the tenant is reasonably confident that an external force will trigger its need for additional space in the future (for example, a pre-existing arrangement for the transfer of a portion of the tenant's workforce to the landlord's building at a predictable future date).

5.   Negotiating Space Flexibility Provisions

Regardless which of the above space flexibility alternatives finds its way into the lease, the landlord and the tenant both want to make sure that the lease provision clearly describes all the terms that govern the tenant's leasing of the expansion space. One common way to deal with that issue is to say that the lease of the expansion space will be upon all the same terms and conditions that are set forth in the tenant's original lease, with the exception of certain specific terms such as the rent, lease term, and tenant improvement allowance that are newly applicable to the tenant's leasing of the expansion space. The tenant customarily wants to preserve the economic benefit of the bargain it struck in its initial lease by having the rent it pays for the expansion space set at the per square foot rental rates specified in the initial lease. The landlord, on the other hand, typically insists that the tenant's rental rate for the expansion space be tied to changes in market conditions, either by using the rental rate specified in the lease offer under the right of first refusal or right of first offer or by requiring that the rental be equal to the greater of (1) the then prevailing market rental rate for the expansion space, or (2) the rental rate specified in the original lease.

The landlord might also want to limit the impact of the tenant's space flexibility options by inserting provisions in the lease that:

- Condition the tenant's exercise of options on the tenant being in full compliance with all its lease obligations;

---

[58] *See* Hennigh, *Office Leases, supra* note 18, at 15–17.

- Make the options personal to the tenant by expressly stating that such options may not be exercised by any assignee or subtenant; and

- Subordinate the tenant's options to all options previously granted on the expansion space to other tenants and third parties.

6.   Contraction Option

The conservative tenant also wants to preserve flexibility to downsize its leased premises should the vitality of its business decline due to an internal or external force. The tenant's ability to downsize its leased premises is commonly referred to as a *contraction option (see Pro-Tenant Modification #11* at page 737*).* Under a contraction option, the tenant is given the option to terminate its obligations with respect to all or a portion of its leased premises. Landlords despise contraction options and grant them only when their backs are fully pressed to the wall by a tenant who wields incredible negotiating clout. The landlord's distaste for contraction options is driven by the landlord's fear that its project's net operating income will be adversely affected either because the contracted space remains vacant for an extended period of time or because the rent produced on the re-leasing of the contracted space is less than the rent specified in the tenant's original lease.

A landlord can ameliorate the negative impact of the tenant's exercise of a contraction option by including modifications to that option that:

- Limit the amount and location of the space that is the subject of the option;

- Make the contraction option a one-time right that can only be exercised during a short window of time (for example, only during the 36th month of the initial lease term);

- Condition the option's exercise upon the occurrence of an objectively quantifiable event (for example, the tenant's loss of a major customer contract);

- Preclude the tenant from leasing any other space in the market for a specified period of time after its exercise of its contraction option (so that the tenant cannot use the contraction option as a convenient means to get out of an unfavorable lease);

- Insist that the contracted space be of a location and configuration that can be readily marketed by the landlord;

- Require the tenant to provide the landlord with a long lead time between the date of the tenant's exercise of its contraction option and the date on which the contraction becomes effective (for example, 12 months after landlord's receipt of the tenant's written exercise of its contraction option) so that the landlord has sufficient time to locate a substitute tenant for the contracted space); and

- Mandate the tenant's payment to the landlord of significant dollars coincident with the tenant's exercise of its contraction option (for example, a payment equal to the sum of (1) the landlord's unamortized tenant improvement costs and leasing commissions, and (2) 12 months of base rent) to give the landlord a financial cushion to absorb the rental loss resulting from the tenant's exercise of its contraction option).[59]

7.   Relocation Clause

Before leaving the topic of a change in the tenant's leased space, note should be made of a pro-landlord space provision—specifically the *relocation clause* (see § 27 of the Form Office Lease). The relocation clause presents the landlord with the opportunity to utter hackneyed phrases such as "what's good for the goose is good for the gander" and "turnabout is fair play." At its essence, a relocation clause gives the landlord the contractual right to move the tenant's leased premises to another location in the landlord's building (or, for that matter, in another building owned by the landlord or one of its affiliates). The inclusion in the lease of a relocation clause provides the landlord with the flexibility it needs to reposition a tenant to make room for a bigger and better tenant. By way of example, assume that IBM Corporation is interested in leasing 20,000 square feet of space in the landlord's building and that the landlord has exactly 20,000 square feet of vacant space. Unfortunately for the landlord, its vacant space consists of 18,000 square feet on the top floor of its building and 2,000 square feet located on the second floor. The landlord's inability to provide IBM with 20,000 square feet of contiguous space could result in the landlord's loss of the IBM deal unless the landlord can figure out a way to move the tenant who occupies 2,000 square feet of space on the top floor to the vacant space located on the second floor—enter the relocation clause that permits the landlord to do just that.

The tenant views a relocation clause with as much disfavor as the landlord does an expansion option (see *Pro-Tenant Modification #12* at page 738). The tenant's concerns are threefold—(1) the move could disrupt its business operations and potentially reduce its profitability, (2) the space to which it is relocated could be inferior to the tenant's existing leased premises (due to the comparative size, configuration, or location of the two spaces), and (3) the tenant could incur significant costs to make the move,

---

[59] *See generally* Hennigh, *Office Leases, supra* note 18, at 15–20 and 15–21; and Yi, *supra* note 3, at 7–8.

order new stationery, send out notices to customers, etc. Large tenants are usually successful in having the relocation clause wholly deleted from the lease. Smaller tenants are frequently left to try to negotiate modifications to the relocation clause that condition the landlord's exercise of its relocation right upon (a) the tenant being moved into space that is comparable in all respects to its original leased premises, and (b) the landlord's prompt reimbursement of all costs reasonably incurred by the tenant in connection with the move. Tenants also regularly ask for assurances that the landlord will move the tenant over a weekend and will use its best efforts to minimize any disruption of the tenant's business operations.[60]

HIBC Case Study—A Matter of Too Much Flexibility

The rent rolls of Pizzuti's HIBC office buildings were dotted with dynamic high technology companies, all of which shared the same messianic conviction concerning the growth trajectories of their respective business units. In an effort to land these high-growth companies as tenants in its business park, Pizzuti routinely gave in to their demands for the inclusion in their leases of expansion rights (primarily rights of first offer and first refusal, with an occasional limited expansion option thrown in for good measure). From Pizzuti's vantage point, the grant of the expansion rights seemed like a small price to pay for the privilege of securing high net worth growth-oriented firms as tenants for its HIBC buildings.

The inherent danger in handing out expansion rights in a liberal fashion was brought home to me when I received a phone call from Pizzuti's in-house leasing broker giving me the "good news" that five of our existing tenants had expressed an interest in leasing the last 20,000 square feet of vacant space located in our newest HIBC office building. The "bad news" was that each of the tenants felt that it had a right to lease the vacant space under a specific provision contained in its lease—two rights of first refusal and three rights of first offer (which our leasing broker failed to trigger because she never sent the requisite written lease offers to the holders of the rights of first offer). My failure to track and properly prioritize the expansion rights of the HIBC tenants had resulted in the outbreak of a donnybrook among five of the park's most important tenants, with each of them pointing a finger at Pizzuti and accusing it of double-dealing and other nefarious acts. While I was ultimately able to calm everyone down and lease the last of our vacant space to two of the five tenants, that success came at a significant cost—both in terms of the general loss of goodwill and the specific lease concessions that I had to offer up to allay the concerns of the

---

[60] *See generally,* Yi, *supra* note 3, at 8–9; and SENN, *supra* note 5, at 4–77 through 4–79.

five affected tenants. From that point forward, I adopted a much more restrictive policy on the grant of tenant expansion rights and insisted that Pizzuti's leasing brokers at all times carry a laminated cheat sheet in their back pockets describing the scope and relative priorities of all expansion rights granted to HIBC tenants.

B.   TERM FLEXIBILITY OPTIONS

The tenant seeks to gain the flexibility to remain in its leased space after the expiration of the initial term by including an ***extension option*** in its lease. An extension option is simply a provision included in the original lease that gives the tenant the option (but not the obligation) to extend the term of its lease beyond the termination date specified for the initial term.

Practitioners tend to use the terms "extension option" and "renewal option" interchangeably. However, a renewal option is technically a new lease entered into by the landlord and the tenant to govern the tenant's leasing of the leased premises after the termination of the stated term of its lease. An extension option, on the other hand, is a continuation of the stated term of the tenant's lease pursuant to an express option set forth in the tenant's lease.[61]

A tenant will exercise an extension option only if all of the following conditions exist as of the end of the initial lease term—(1) the leased premises remain well-suited for the conduct of the tenant's business, (2) the tenant does not want to pay the added cost or put up with the hassle of moving to new space, and (3) the rent applicable to the extension term is satisfactory to the tenant. If all those conditions are not met, then the tenant will opt to move out of the landlord's building and into new space owned by a competitor of the landlord.

Because there is no way for a tenant to know when it signs its lease whether it will want to extend the lease beyond the initial term, it is customary for a tenant to request the inclusion in the lease of an extension option. The extension option, if exercised, permits the tenant to continue to possess and occupy the leased premises for an additional period of time after the expiration of the initial term (typically somewhere between three to ten years).

From the tenant's perspective, the ideal extension option identifies all salient terms that will govern the tenant's leasing of its space during the extension term and gives the tenant an unfettered right to exercise the option at any time prior to the expiration of the initial lease term (see *Pro-Tenant Modification #14* at page 739). If the tenant wants to stay in the

---

[61]   *See* Hennigh, *Office Leases, supra* note 18, at 15–64 and 15–65.

leased premises and likes the terms of the extension, then it will exercise its extension option. If the tenant wants to stay in the leased premises, but does not like the terms of the extension, then it will renegotiate the extension terms prior to the outside date for its exercise of the extension option. If the tenant fails in its attempt to renegotiate the extension terms or is otherwise unhappy with the leased premises, then it will not exercise its extension option and will find another spot to conduct its business.

The above description of the process that the tenant undertakes when making a decision to exercise its extension option speaks volumes as to why the landlord generally does not like extension options. While the landlord recognizes that the grant of an extension option is often a marketing necessity, the landlord is also very much aware that the essence of an extension option works to the tenant's advantage and the landlord's disadvantage. A landlord knows that if the tenant exercises its extension option as written, it is likely because the tenant has determined that the terms of the extension option are below market—otherwise the tenant would be knocking on the landlord's door seeking to renegotiate the rent and other business terms applicable to its leasing of the leased premises during the extension term.

1.   Extension Option—Key Issues

There are three issues that the lawyers must resolve when negotiating the terms of an extension option. Those issues and the resolutions favored by the landlord and the tenant are discussed below.

- *Issue #1—How and when must the tenant exercise its extension option?* The landlord and the tenant can usually agree on the proposition that the tenant's exercise of its extension option must be in the form of a written statement delivered to the landlord sometime prior to the expiration of the then existing term of the lease. However, agreement is not as easily reached on the issue of the specifics of the required timing of the tenant's exercise of its extension option. The tenant prefers to have the right to exercise its extension option at any time prior to the expiration of the initial lease term, so that it can make a real time determination as to whether the prevailing market conditions and the unique needs of its business merit its exercise of the extension option. The landlord, on the other hand, wants the tenant to be required to notify the landlord as far in advance as possible as to whether the tenant is exercising its extension option so that the landlord has adequate time to try to re-lease the space to another party if the tenants declines to exercise its extension option. The outside date for the tenant's exercise of its extension option usually falls somewhere between 30 days to a year prior to the scheduled expiration of the then existing term of the tenant's lease.

- *Issue #2—What conditions, if any, are placed on the tenant's right to exercise its extension option?* The tenant does not want any conditions to be placed on its right to exercise its extension option (although it often begrudgingly accepts a limitation that it may not exercise its extension option if it is currently in default in the performance of its lease obligations). In addition to the "no current default" condition, the landlord customarily tries to preclude the tenant from exercising its extension option if (1) the tenant has been late on the payment of its rent more than a proscribed number of times during the initial lease term, or (2) the tenant's net worth is appreciably below what it was as of the commencement date of the initial lease term. Landlords also try to prevent the tenant from shopping a favorable extension option by asserting that the extension option is personal to the named tenant and cannot be sold or otherwise transferred by the tenant to a third party.

- *Issue #3—What terms will govern the tenant's leasing of its leased premises during the extension term?* The extension option should specify the exact terms that will apply during the tenant's extension term. This goal is accomplished by the insertion into the lease of a clause that states that "the extension term will be upon all of the same terms and conditions set forth in this lease with respect to the initial lease term, except . . . ," followed by a specific listing of those provisions of the base lease that will not carry over to the extension term (typically, the TI allowance, the number of further extension options, and the base rent)—see ¶ 1 of Exhibit E of the Form Office Lease.

2.   Extension Term Rent

The key business point that needs to be addressed within the text of the extension option is the level of base rent that the tenant is required to pay during the extension term. The extension term rent can be expressed in one of three ways—as (1) fixed rent (for example, $20 prsf), (2) indexed rent (for example, the base rent payable during the initial term adjusted to reflect increases in the Consumer Price Index), or (3) market rent. The advantages and disadvantages of the fixed and indexed rent alternatives were addressed earlier in this chapter as part of a discussion of the ways in which a landlord can protect its rental income from being eroded by the onset of inflationary conditions in the general economy (see pages 529–531). The rest of this subsection focuses on the merits and demerits associated with the use of a market rent standard to determine the tenant's base rent obligation during the extension term.

The market rent standard is frequently used to set the base rent that the tenant will pay if it exercises its extension option. The primary advantage of a market rent standard is that it is difficult for either the landlord or the tenant to logically resist the contention that the tenant's rent should be tied to the then prevailing market rental rates for comparable properties. The disadvantage of using a market rent benchmark is that no one really knows what the term means and, hence, its use introduces a level of uncertainty into the computation of the tenant's base rent obligation.

There are three fundamental issues that need to be taken into consideration with respect to the determination of the market rent for a particular leased premises—specifically (1) what market is used as a comparative for the leased premises, (2) what is the prevailing rent in the designated market, and (3) who gets to make the market rent determination?

The identification of the comparable market for a tenant's office suite should take into account all of the following considerations—the specific location of the office building (for example, the Orlando central business district or the Lake Mary suburban market); the type of office building (for example, low-rise or high-rise, Class A or Class B, multi-tenant or single tenant, new or old, brick or glass curtain wall); and the nature of the leased premises (for example, its square footage, floor location and the quality of its tenant improvements). In theory, the lawyers should strive to put together a market narrative that permits the value arbiter to zero in on the specifics of "comparable space, in comparable buildings, in a comparable location."

The determination of the prevailing market rents in the designated comparable market is equally troublesome and complex. The estimation of market rent requires an analysis of each of the following factors as they relate both to the tenant's existing lease and all the leases that are being used as benchmarks to establish the market rent in the designated market—the rent structure (that is, gross, net, expense stop or a hybrid of those three structures); rent concessions; the quality and level of building services provided to the tenant by the landlord; the common area load factor; the tenant's creditworthiness; the amount of the landlord's contribution to the cost of the tenant improvements; the leasing commissions and other transactional costs paid by the landlord; and all other lease provisions that impact the lease's overall economic position (for example, expense pass-through caps or the existence of expansion and contraction rights).[62]

The final piece of the market rent puzzle involves the selection of the person who is responsible for setting the market rent for the tenant's leased premises. The choices are: (1) the landlord (seldom a palatable alternative for the tenant); (2) the landlord and the tenant (by mutual agreement); (3) a published source (for example, CBRE's annual report for the designated market); (4) a single expert (usually a licensed commercial real estate broker or appraiser identified in the lease or chosen by the mutual agreement of the landlord and the tenant); or (5) a panel of experts selected in accordance with a procedure established in the lease. If the decision is going to be made by a panel of experts (a fairly common circumstance), then the drafters of the extension option should address the following issues within the skin of the extension option clause: how will the experts be selected; what will be their minimum, required qualifications; and how will variances in their respective rent determinations be reconciled?[63]

One of the most common methods employed to determine market rent is something called a **baseball appraisal**, where each of the landlord and tenant submits its determination of market rent and an expert or panel of experts is then required to select one of the submitted determinations as the true market rent for the tenant's leased premises (see *Pro-Tenant Modification #14* at page 739). This appraisal method gets its name from the fact that it is closely patterned after the arbitration method used to establish the salaries of major league baseball players. In a baseball appraisal, the expert is compelled to choose either the landlord's or the tenant's market rent determination and is not permitted to average or otherwise compromise the differing rent determinations in any way.[64]

C. ASSIGNMENT AND SUBLEASING

(§ 12)

The assignment and subleasing clause is the tenant's final avenue for the creation of flexibility to deal with its leased space. That clause provides the tenant with an opportunity to transfer its lease rights to a third party if the tenant believes that it makes sound business sense to do so—either as an exit strategy (if the tenant wants to downsize, sell or close its business) or as a potential profit center (if the tenant's rent is below market and it wants to monetize the intrinsic value of its lease by selling it to a third party). The tenant wants as much freedom as possible to transfer its

---

[62] *See generally* Yi, *supra* note 3, at 12–13.

[63] *See* ZANKEL, *supra* note 1, at 45–46.

[64] *See* Hennigh, *Office Leases, supra* note 18, at 15–68.

leasehold interest to any person of its choosing and on whatever terms and conditions it deems appropriate.

The landlord's position on the assignment and sublease clause is antithetical to that of the tenant. The landlord wants to restrict to the maximum extent possible the tenant's ability to transfer its leasehold interest to a third party. In that respect, the landlord has two separate objectives—(1) it wants to retain the right to approve the identity of the tenant's successor who will be paying rent and using the leased premises, and (2) it wants to capture for its own account any profit attributable to a future increase in rental rates above those specified in the tenant's lease.

An assignment and a sublease are distinct legal transactions. An *assignment of lease* is a transfer by the tenant to a third party of all its rights and interests in the lease and leased premises. In an assignment, the tenant has no reversionary interest in the lease or the leased premises and the recipient of the assignment (the "assignee") has privity with the landlord. Unless the landlord and the assignee separately agree to be contractually bound to each other, an assignment creates only privity of estate (and not privity of contract) between the landlord and the tenant. Privity of estate allows the enforcement of only those covenants that are deemed to "run with the land" (such as those covenants related to the payment of rent, the use of the leased premises, and the restriction on the tenant's ability to transfer its leasehold interests), while privity of contract permits the enforcement of the entirety of the lease as written.[65]

A *sublease* is a transfer by the tenant to a third party of part of its rights and interests in the leased premises (but not the underlying lease). In a sublease, the tenant retains a reversionary interest in the lease and the leased premises and the recipient of the sublease (the "subtenant") has no privity with the landlord.[66]

To illustrate the legal difference between an assignment and a sublease, assume that Tenant A leases 10,000 square feet of space from Landlord and that Tenant A has four years remaining on its initial lease term. If Tenant A opts to transfer its interest in all of the space for the remainder of the term to Tenant B, then Tenant A's transfer is an assignment. If, however, Tenant B decides to transfer only its interest to use and occupy the space for two of the four remaining years of the lease term, then the transfer is a sublease.

While there is a clear legal distinction between an assignment and a sublease, both transactions accomplish the same basic purpose of facilitating a transfer by the tenant of all or a portion of its leasehold interest to a third party. The legal and contractual considerations impacting assignments and subleases are similar in most respects. For the

---

[65] *See* SENN, *supra* note 5, at 13–11 through 13–15.

[66] *See id.* at 13–6 through 13–11.

purpose of the discussion that follows, an assignment and a sublease are jointly referred to as a "transfer," the recipient of the transfer is referred to as the "transferee," and the portion of the tenant's interest in the lease and the leased premises that is being transferred to the transferee is referred to as the "leasehold interest."

1.   Case Law on Assignment and Subleasing

The lease transfer topic is somewhat unique in the commercial leasing universe because there is a well-developed body of case law addressing the scope of the tenant's right to transfer all or a part of its leasehold interest to a third party. That case law generally establishes the following three general rules: (1) the tenant has the right at common law to freely transfer its lease interest in any manner and to any person of its choosing; (2) the transferring tenant remains liable under the lease following the transfer; and (3) both of the above rules can be abrogated and limited by the specific contractual agreement of the landlord and the tenant.[67] Landlords and tenants have fully embraced rule (3) and almost always include a specific clause in the lease that addresses the right of the tenant to transfer its leasehold interest to another person. The focus of the remainder of this section is on the issues faced by the practitioner when crafting the assignment and sublease clause.

The case law in most states validates the ability of the landlord to include in the lease an absolute prohibition on the tenant's right to make any lease transfer whatsoever.[68] The parties could, therefore, theoretically include in the lease a simple statement to the effect that "the tenant will not assign its interest in the lease or sublease all or any part of its interest in the leased premises." Similarly, the courts in most states support the enforceability of a lease clause that requires the landlord's consent to any transfer and then permits the landlord to withhold its consent "arbitrarily," "capriciously," or "in its sole discretion."[69] Finally, the majority rule in the United States is that the landlord may withhold its consent in its sole discretion if the lease fails to set forth any standard for its consent—that is, the lease simply says that the "tenant may not assign this lease or sublease all or any part of the leased premises, without the prior written consent of the landlord." There is, however, an "emerging trend [that] requires the landlord to be reasonable if no standard is stated."[70]

In most instances, the landlord does not have sufficient bargaining strength to carry the day on its assertion that it should have the sole

---

[67] *See generally* Brent C. Shaffer, *Counseling the Client on the Reasonable Consent Standard to Assignments*, 19 No. 4 PRACTICAL REAL ESTATE LAWYER 7 (July 2003); and SENN, *supra* note 5, at 13–13; FRIEDMAN, *supra* note 31, at 7–10 to 7–11.

[68] *See* FRIEDMAN, *supra* note 31 at 7–39 through 7–41.

[69] *See* SENN, *supra* note 5, at 13–17 through 13–24.

[70] FRIEDMAN, *supra* note 31, at 7–42. *See also* SENN, *supra* note 5, at 13–19 through 13–26.

discretion to determine when, whether, and to whom the tenant may transfer its leasehold interest. The default position in most landlord-tenant negotiations is an assignment and sublease clause that provides that the tenant may not transfer its leasehold interest "without the prior written consent of the landlord, which consent may not be unreasonably withheld or delayed." The discussion in the remainder of this section assumes that the landlord may not unreasonably withhold its consent to a transfer of all or a part of the tenant's leasehold interest either because that is what the lease says or because the lease is silent on the standard and the landlord's building is located in a jurisdiction that follows the minority rule implying a standard of reasonable consent.

2.   The Reasonable Consent Standard

There is an abundance of case law analyzing what it means for a landlord to act reasonably when responding to a lease transfer request from its tenant.[71] There are three guiding principles adopted by the courts to measure the reasonableness of a landlord's action:

- The landlord cannot use its consent right to get a better deal than it had with its original tenant (that is, the landlord can deny consent only for reasons related specifically to the lease that is the subject of the proposed transfer and not to the landlord's broader economic or business concerns);[72]

- The landlord cannot deny its consent for reasons of "personal taste, sensibility or convenience"[73] (that is, only objective and not subjective factors may be taken into consideration by the landlord); and

- The reasonableness of the landlord's actions is determined by looking beyond the pretextual reasons for landlord's actions to the real reasons underlying the landlord's denial of a tenant's transfer proposal (that is, the landlord must act in good faith in determining the reasons for its denial of the tenant's transfer request and the landlord's conduct may belie its stated intentions to the contrary).[74]

On the all-important topic of who has the burden of proof on the subject of the reasonableness of the landlord's behavior, the rule followed in the

---

[71] *See generally,* FRIEDMAN, *supra* note 31, at 7–54 through 7–71; SENN, *supra* note 5, at 13–24 through 13–39; Shaffer, *supra* note 67, at 193; and Mark S. Hennigh, *Negotiating Assignment and Subletting Provisions,* in ALI-ABA COURSE OF STUDY MATERIALS, COMMERCIAL REAL ESTATE LEASES: SELECTED ISSUES OM DRAFTING AND NEGOTIATING IN CURRENT MARKETS, Course No. SN-013, 199, at Appendix 1 (May 2008).

[72] *See* Shaffer, *supra* note 67, at 13.

[73] *See* Broad & Branford Place Corp. v. J. J. Hockenjos Co., 39 A.2d 80, 82 (N.J. Sup. Ct. 1944); and SENN, *supra* note 5, at 13–25.

[74] *See* Toys R Us, Inc. v. NBD Trust Co, 1995 WL 591459 (N.D. Ill. 1995); and Economy Rentals, Inc. v. Garcia, 819 P.2d 1306 (N.M. 1991).

majority of the states is that the burden is on the tenant to prove that the landlord acted unreasonably. Most states also hold that the burden is on the tenant to provide the landlord with sufficient information to permit the landlord to make a reasoned decision on the tenant's transfer request.[75]

The following is a quick summary of some of the most prominent "reasonable" and "unreasonable" reasons cited by the courts for a landlord's denial of a tenant's request to transfer its leasehold interest to a third party.[76]

- *"Reasonable" Reasons:*
  - o   The creditworthiness of the proposed transferee calls into question the proposed transferee's ability to pay its rent;

  - o   The lack of business experience of the proposed transferee raises legitimate questions about the transferee's ability to perform its obligations under the transferred lease; and

  - o   The nature of the transferee's proposed use is markedly different from and more intense than that of the original tenant.

- *"Unreasonable" Reasons:*
  - o   The landlord just does not like the proposed transferee;

  - o   The tenant fails to meet a landlord demand that the proposed transferee agree to pay the landlord increased rent or a consent fee—that is, good old, all-American greed;

  - o   The tenant's rent is below market and the landlord wants to share in any profit that might be realized by the tenant on the transfer of the favorable lease to the proposed transferee;

  - o   The proposed transferee is an existing occupant of the landlord's building; and

  - o   The landlord wants the proposed transferee to lease vacant space in the landlord's building (and not take over the space of an existing tenant).

The cases divining the landlord's relative reasonableness are so fact-sensitive as to raise interpretive questions even on the "reasonable"

---

[75]   *See* Shaffer, *supra* note 67, at 9–10.

[76]   For a more detailed discussion of representative cases weighing in on the topic of the reasonable consent standard, *see generally* Shaffer, *supra* note 67; and SENN, *supra* note 5, at 13–26 through 13–340.

reasons mentioned above. By way of example, is the mere fact that the transferee's net worth is less than the tenant's sufficient grounds to support the reasonableness of the landlord's denial of its consent to the proposed lease transfer (even if the tenant is Bill Gates and the proposed transferee is Warren Buffet)? Is the fact that the proposed transferee has an unsavory business reputation (think Jeff Skilling) adequate reason for the landlord to disapprove the transfer request, even though the transferee has an established record of success in the business world? In determining the unacceptability of the proposed transferee's use, can the landlord take into consideration the actual use of the leased premises by its existing tenant (the operation of a law firm) or only the permitted use specified in the lease (any lawful use)?

There is a growing trend among lawyers representing commercial landlords to include expansive language in the assignment and sublease clause that specifically sanctions the reasonableness of certain grounds for the landlord's disapproval of its tenant's transfer request.[77] By way of example, the landlord's lawyer might try to resolve one of the uncertainties noted at the end of the prior paragraph by clearly stating that the landlord is deemed to be acting reasonably if it denies the tenant's transfer request because the proposed transferee's net worth (even though substantial) is less than that of the existing tenant. Similarly, the lawyer might attempt to move a couple of reasons from the "unreasonable" list noted above into the "deemed reasonable category"—most notably the landlord's right to say "no" to the transfer request if the proposed transferee is an existing occupant of the landlord's building or if the landlord is negotiating with the proposed transferee to lease vacant space in the landlord's building. Most practitioners believe that provisions of this type should be upheld by the courts.[78]

3. Assignment and Subleasing in Retail Leases

There is much more at stake in the battle over the landlord's reasonable consent standard in the context of a retail lease than there is in the context of an office lease. The landlord of an office building usually does not get too worked up over a potential lease transfer as long as the proposed transferee is a creditworthy entity and its proposed use of the leased premises is not something totally out of character for an office building. However, the success of a retail center is directly linked to the mix of the retail tenants doing business in that center and their respective abilities to generate customer traffic. The financial viability of the entire center can be

---

[77] *See, e.g.,* Hennigh, *Negotiating Assignment and Subletting Provisions, supra* note 71, at 1137–1138; SENN, *supra* note 5, at 13–42 and 13–44 (Form 13–5); and Richard R. Goldberg, *Retail Lease Agreement,* in ALI-ABA COURSE OF STUDY MATERIALS, COMMERCIAL REAL ESTATE LEASES: SELECTED ISSUES IN DRAFTING AND NEGOTIATING IN CURRENT MARKETS, Course No. SN–013, 223, 259–260 (May 2008).

[78] *See* Shaffer, *supra* note 67, at 6.

jeopardized if an existing tenant transfers its lease to a transferee whose operations do not fit with the rest of the center (for example, Saks Fifth Avenue transferring its lease to Dollar General or a jewelry store assigning its lease to a candle store when there are already three stores in the center selling candles). An inappropriate lease transfer can also significantly reduce the landlord's percentage rent revenues (under both the transferred lease and the leases of other tenants in the center) and potentially result in a violation of a co-tenancy or exclusive use provision found in the lease of one of the landlord's other tenants.

For these reasons, the negotiations over the assignment and sublease clause in a retail lease are often long and frenzied, with the landlord adopting the expansive drafting approach noted above to try to make it clear that the landlord, in all events, has the right to deny a proposed lease transfer on the grounds that the proposed transfer could (1) reduce the amount of the landlord's percentage rent receipts, (2) trigger a violation of the provision of another tenant lease, or (3) result in a reduction of customer traffic to the center (either due to a duplication of another tenant's use or the reduced drawing power of the proposed transferee's store). The retail landlord can obtain added protection against an unwanted lease transfer by including a tightly worded, restrictive use clause in its lease—for example, "the leased premises may be used for the operation of the retail sale of candles and for no other purpose."

4.   Additional Assignment and Subleasing Issues

There are three collateral issues that should also be considered by the lawyers for the landlord and the tenant during their negotiations over the content of the assignment and sublease clause. The first is whether the landlord's consent is needed for the tenant's transfer of a leasehold interest to one of its affiliates or for its transfer of a leasehold interest to an entity that is acquiring substantially all of the tenant's business operations by way of a merger, stock sale, consolidation, asset sale, etc. A tenant generally does not want a landlord to be able to stand in the way of the reorganization or sale of its business and, therefore, typically asks for a specific statement that the tenant may effect such a transfer without the landlord's consent (see *Pro-Tenant Modification #29* at page 746). Most commercial landlords grant such a request as long as the landlord receives prompt written notice of the transfer and the tenant (or a related entity having a comparable net worth) remains fully liable following the transfer.[79]

---

[79] *See* Joel R. Hall, *Assignment,* in ALI-ABA COURSE OF STUDY MATERIALS, COMMERCIAL REAL ESTATE LEASES: SELECTED ISSUES IN DRAFTING AND NEGOTIATING IN CURRENT MARKETS, Course No. SN-013, 613–618 (May 2008); and Hennigh, *Office Leases, supra* note 18, at 15–59 and 15–60.

The second collateral issue is who is entitled to receive any profit realized from the tenant's transfer of its leasehold interest to a third party. If the tenant's existing rent is below market, then the tenant may be able to generate a profit by either assigning its lease in exchange for a cash payment from the transferee (paid either upfront or over a period of time) or subleasing the leased premises to the transferee for a sublease rental that is greater than the rent provided in the tenant's lease with the landlord. The landlord can attempt to recover all or a part of the generated profit by including either a recapture or a profit-sharing clause in its original lease with the tenant. Under a *recapture clause*, the landlord reserves the right to terminate its lease with the original tenant and then capture any potential profit by entering into a new lease with the proposed transferee. A *profit-sharing clause* requires the tenant to share with the landlord a portion (for example, 50%) of any profit the tenant it derives from a lease transfer. If a tenant is willing to agree to the inclusion of a recapture or profit-sharing clause in its lease (and only those with inferior bargaining positions are), the tenant's lawyer needs to carefully address a wide variety of issues, including (1) the identification of the trigger for the landlord's exercise of its recapture right (for example, just the tenant' statement that it is contemplating a transfer of its leasehold interest or the tenant's actual receipt of an offer to acquire the leasehold interest from an interested third party), and (2) the manner in which the tenant's profit on the transaction is computed (this computation is particularly difficult when the tenant is also transferring other property to the transferee in addition to its leasehold interest).[80]

Finally, the parties should carefully think through the remedies that are available to the tenant if the landlord breaches its covenant to act reasonably. The financial loss experienced by a tenant due to a landlord's breach of the reasonable consent standard can be quite severe—particularly if the landlord's denial of its consent results in the demise of a much larger deal (for example, the sale of an entire business division). Landlords frequently seek to insulate themselves from liability for the tenant's financial loss by including a statement in the lease that equitable relief (for example, an injunction or declaratory judgment action) is the tenant's sole and exclusive remedy for the landlord's breach of its covenant to not unreasonably withhold or delay its consent to a proposed lease transfer. The well-advised tenant should resist such a landlord ploy or, at the very least, reserve a right to sue the landlord for damages if the landlord is found to have acted in bad faith in denying its consent to a proposed tenant transfer.

---

[80] *See generally* Hennigh, *Office Leases, supra* note 18, at 15–60 through 15–64; and ZANKEL, *supra* note 1, at 123–125.

XI. ALLOCATION OF RISK AND OTHER ISSUES

The concluding section of this chapter examines the provisions of a commercial lease that address the following topics:

- The consequences of a default by the tenant or the landlord;

- The impact of a casualty on the landlord-tenant relationship;

- The impact of a condemnation on the landlord-tenant relationship;

- The subordination of the tenant's leasehold interest to the mortgage lien of the landlord's lender;

- The allocation of responsibility for the payment of leasing commissions;

- The tenant's responsibility to provide the landlord with estoppel certificates confirming the status of the tenant's leasehold interest;

- The tenant's posting of a security deposit and its provision of periodic financial statements for the landlord's review; and

- Other so-called "boilerplate" matters.

A. DEFAULT CLAUSE
(§ 22)

The discussion of the tenant default clause starts with the definition of an "event of default." An event of default exists if an event has occurred or a circumstance has arisen that permits the landlord to exercise its remedies. In most situations, an event of default requires both the tenant's non-performance of a lease obligation *AND* the passage of a specified period of time without the tenant's cure of its non-performance.

The landlord's lawyer's job in structuring the default clause is threefold. First, the lawyer must identify all those events or circumstances (the "default") that can give rise to an event of default. Examples of such events or circumstances are: a tenant's failure to pay its rent by the due date; the tenant's use of the leased premises in a manner not permitted by the lease; and the death or bankruptcy of a lease guarantor. The lawyer's next task is to determine whether the tenant is given a period of time (called a "grace period") to perform the subject lease obligation. Finally, the lawyer must make a reasoned determination whether the tenant is entitled to receive written notice of the existence of the alleged default and an additional period of time (the "cure period") to cure such default before the landlord can declare an event of default and exercise its remedies under the lease.

The landlord's preference would be for the definition of "default" and "event of default" to be identical—that is, for the occurrence of each listed event or circumstance to immediately authorize the landlord to pursue its remedies against the tenant. Time is the enemy of the landlord when the tenant defaults. If the landlord senses that the tenant is having financial trouble, then the landlord wants to move immediately to oust the tenant from possession of its leased premises and pave the way for a new tenant to take over occupancy of the space. If the tenant is financially stable, then the landlord wants to get its hands on the money to which it is due as quickly as possible. In either event, the passage of time works to the landlord's detriment.

The tenant, on the other hand, wants to make sure that it is not in jeopardy of either losing its right to conduct its business in the leased premises or being penalized economically for the occurrence of an inadvertent or immaterial event of non-performance. As such, the tenant tries to require the landlord to provide tenant with written notice of the alleged existence of any default and an ample period of time to cure the alleged default.

The lawyers for the landlord and the tenant begin their efforts to bridge their client's differences by focusing on two different types of default—a "monetary default" versus a "non-monetary default." A monetary default is defined as any failure of the tenant to pay its base or additional rent on or before the due date specified in the lease. A non-monetary default is any default other than a monetary default.

The landlord is most concerned with the treatment afforded monetary defaults. Stated succinctly, the landlord wants its money and it wants it now. The landlord's lawyer typically adopts a firm stance that the tenant knows when its rent is due and that there is no need for any grace period, written notice or cure period for a monetary default. The tenant's lawyer, in turn, points out that it would be grossly unfair to penalize the tenant for a bookkeeping error or other inadvertent failure to pay its rent. When all the shouting is done, the lawyers usually craft a middle ground position that takes into account the landlord's need to get paid on time and the tenant's desire to not be penalized for an unintentional error. The following is a representative example of a compromise that might be reached on the topic of monetary defaults:

- The grant to the tenant of a grace period of three days before the landlord can impose a late fee on the delinquent payment;

- The imposition against the tenant of a late fee of 3–5% of the amount of the delinquent payment immediately upon the expiration of the grace period (without the need for any notice);

- A requirement that the landlord provide the tenant with written notice of a monetary default not more than once during any 12 month period; and

- The grant of a ten-day cure period in which the tenant can cure its non-payment (again subject to the not more than once during any 12 month period limitation noted above).[81]

The landlord is generally receptive to providing the tenant with written notice of a non-monetary default and the right to cure that default for a cure period of somewhere between ten to 30 days after the notice date. The tenant frequently asks for (and usually gets) a reasonable extension of the cure period for those defaults that are not readily susceptible of being cured within the normal ten to 30-day cure period—for example, a repair requiring a new part that is on back order for two months. Landlord's counsel often counters by seeking to eliminate the notice requirement and cure period for certain defaults that cannot be cured—for example, the death or insolvency of a guarantor. Tenants are usually amenable to exempting a limited number of such defaults from the general notice and cure period requirements of the default clause.

1. Remedies for a Tenant Default

Once agreement is reached on what constitutes an event of default under the lease, the parties next turn to a discussion of the remedies that are available to the landlord to respond to the event of default. Once an event of default has occurred, the landlord wants to have the rights (1) to regain possession of the leased premises so that the landlord can try to re-lease the premises to a new tenant, and (2) to collect rent or damages from the defaulted tenant so that the landlord can maintain its targeted financial returns for the project while it searches for a substitute tenant.

There are three ways that the landlord can go about regaining possession of the leased premises. First, it can try to convince the tenant to voluntarily surrender possession of the leased premises by returning the tenant's keys and removing tenant's property from the leased premises. This is by far the most cost-effective method for the landlord to recover possession of the leased premises. The landlord must, however, be careful to avoid releasing the tenant from its continuing rent obligations by accepting the tenant's voluntary surrender of the leased premises. A letter to the tenant from landlord's counsel confirming that the landlord will continue to hold the tenant liable for the payment of its rent and other financial obligations despite the tenant's voluntary vacation of the leased

---

[81] *See generally* Russell B. Bershad, *Default*, in LEASE NEGOTIATION HANDBOOK 531, 532–533 (Edward Chupack ed., 2003); Patrick G. Moran and Martin H. Orlick, *Litigating Commercial Leases, Default and Remedies: Those Pesky and Expensive Frequently Litigated Lease Issues*, in ACREL PAPERS 70 (Spring 20070; ZANKEL, *supra* note 1, at 153–157; and DILLMAN, *supra* note 22, at 107–109.

premises should be a part of the landlord's standard operating procedures following the occurrence of an event of default.

If the tenant refuses to gracefully surrender possession of the leased premises, the landlord has two remaining options. It can either institute an eviction proceeding against the tenant under the applicable state statute[82] or exercise its self-help remedy by changing the locks on the building or taking other affirmative action designed to prevent the tenant from continuing to possess the leased premises. Going the self-help route can, however, subject the landlord to an open-ended liability to the tenant for a wrongful eviction. A landlord should, therefore, avoid exercising its self-help remedies, except in those extreme situations where it is concerned that the tenant might deliberately damage the leased premises or otherwise engage in prohibited conduct that will have a deleterious impact on the value of the landlord's project.

In most situations, the occurrence of an event of default means that the tenant is out of money and does not have the financial wherewithal to continue to pay its rent. In those situations, the landlord's sole goal is to recover possession of the leased premises so that the landlord can find a new tenant and once again begin receiving rental income from the leased premises. If the lease guarantor is a creditworthy person, then the landlord has the added goal of collecting money from the guarantor to preserve the benefit of the economic bargain the landlord originally struck with the tenant.

Guarantors often seek to eliminate their obligation to guaranty the payment of rent after the tenant's voluntary surrender of possession of the leased premises by posting what is commonly referred to as a **good guy guaranty**. A good guy guaranty limits the guaranteed rent obligations to those that accrued prior to the date on which the tenant voluntarily vacates the leased premises.[83]

At common law, the tenant's obligation to pay rent terminates coincident with the termination of its right of possession.[84] This rule can, however, be overridden by the inclusion in the lease of a **survival clause**. A survival clause is an affirmative statement that the tenant's obligation to pay rent survives the termination of its right of possession of the leased premises (see clause (b) of § 22 of the Form Office Lease). It is essential from the landlord's perspective that the lease contain a survival clause to

---

[82] Most states have enacted statutes (commonly referred to as forcible, entry, and detainer or FE & D statutes) that are designed to facilitate the landlord's expeditious recovery of possession of the leased premises upon the occurrence of a tenant event of default. *See, e.g.*, the discussion of Illinois' and California's FE & D statutes in Moran, *supra* note 81, at 72–74, 77–78.

[83] *See* Lubin, *supra* note 2, at 2.

[84] *See* Robert Harms Bliss, *Mitigation of Damages and Calculation of "Future Rentals": The Difference between Rent and Damages* in ACREL PAPERS 1, 1–2 (Spring 2007)

preserve the landlord's right to collect rent or damages from the tenant/guarantor after possession of the leased space reverts back to the landlord.

The landlord has two contractual remedies that it can include in the lease to collect additional sums of money from the tenant after the landlord's recovery of possession of the leased premises. The landlord can either terminate the lease and sue for damages (the "termination remedy") or it can elect to maintain the lease in place and continue to hold the tenant liable for the payment of rent when and as it comes due (the "maintenance remedy").

When the landlord elects to terminate the lease, the tenant's obligation to make future rent payments automatically ceases (although the tenant continues to be liable for all accrued and unpaid rent through the date of the termination of the lease).[85] The landlord can, however, sue for damages based on the tenant's breach of the lease contract. The measure of damages is generally the difference between the present value of the rent reserved under the lease and the present value of the current fair market rental value of the leased premises (see clause (a) of § 22 of the Form Office Lease). In determining the fair market rental value of the leased premises, the courts typically adjust the value downward to reflect both the rent hiatus that the landlord experiences during the time it takes to re-lease the leased premises and the reasonable costs that the landlord must incur as part of its efforts to re-lease the leased premises (including additional tenant improvement costs and leasing commissions).

There are a few cases that seem to allow the landlord to collect the full accelerated amount of the rent provided in the lease, without giving the tenant any credit for the fair market rental value of the lease during the remainder of the lease term. Those cases are, however, in the clear minority and, in any event, would require the landlord to pay back to the tenant any rent the landlord subsequently collects from a new tenant.[86] Because a full rent acceleration clause (without any credit being given to the tenant for the fair market rental value of the leased premises) works an extreme hardship upon the tenant, most lawyers representing the tenant insist that the lease contain a damages remedy that is styled in the manner discussed in the prior paragraph.

If the landlord elects to maintain the lease in place (despite its termination of the tenant's ongoing right of possession), then the tenant remains liable for the payment of the rent specified in the lease, when and as such payments become due and payable under the lease. The landlord can either file legal actions to collect the rent periodically throughout the lease term (for example, every six months) or it can wait until the end of the lease term and file a single legal action covering all of the unpaid rent

---

[85] See Moran, supra note 81, at 72.

[86] See SENN, supra note 5, at 31–3 to 31–34.

for the entirety of the lease term. If the landlord re-leases the leased premises at any time during the defaulted tenant's original lease term, then the rental payments received by the landlord from such re-leasing (net of any tenant improvement costs, leasing commissions and other reasonable re-leasing costs incurred by the landlord) are offset against the rent owed to the landlord by the tenant.[87]

Once the landlord decides to exercise its lease remedies, it next needs to choose whether it will terminate the lease and sue for damages or maintain the lease and sue for accrued and unpaid rent at a later date. That decision is driven by a number of considerations including: the length of the tenant's remaining lease term; the prevailing conditions in the local real estate market; and the soundness of the tenant's credit (which, for this purpose, also includes the credit of any lease guarantor).

If the tenant is in clear, financial trouble and there is no financially viable guarantor, then the landlord should elect to terminate its lease as quickly as possible. Based on the old adage that "you can't squeeze blood out of a turnip," it is unlikely that the landlord is going to collect any money from the tenant regardless which remedy it selects. More importantly, if the tenant files for bankruptcy while its lease is still in force, the pro-tenant provisions of the federal bankruptcy laws will become fully applicable and the landlord's efforts to re-lease the leased premises may be frustrated for an extended period of time.[88]

2. Landlord's Duty to Mitigate Damages

The final topic that needs to be covered as part of the discussion of the tenant default clause is the landlord's duty to mitigate its damages. Most states, either by statute or common law, now impose a duty on the commercial landlord to mitigate its damages.[89] Moreover, the well-represented tenant is often successful in including an express covenant in the lease requiring the landlord to mitigate its damages even if the jurisdiction in which the landlord's building is located does not require the imposition of such a duty (see *Pro-Tenant Modification #31* at page 746).

If the landlord has a duty to mitigate its damages, then the landlord is generally required to use reasonable efforts to find a new tenant to take

---

[87]   *See* Bliss, *supra* note 84, at 3.

[88]   *See* Bershad, *supra* note 81, at 538. The impact of federal bankruptcy laws on the landlord-tenant relationship is an important topic, but one that is well beyond the scope of this chapter. Helpful and thorough discussions of the treatment of commercial leases under the bankruptcy laws are found in Steven E. Ostrow, *What You Need to Know about the Treatment of Commercial Leases under the Bankruptcy Reform Act,* 22 No. 1 PRACTICAL REAL ESTATE LAWYER 27 (January 2006); Trev E. Peterson, *The ABC's of Landlord Claims in Bankruptcy,* in ACREL PAPERS 47 (Spring 2009); and David L. Pollack, *Defaults, Landlord and Tenant Litigation and Bankruptcies,* in ALI-ABA COURSE OF STUDY MATERIALS, COMMERCIAL REAL ESTATE LEASES: SELECTED ISSUES IN DRAFTING AND NEGOTIATING IN CURRENT MARKETS, Course No. SN–013, 1255 (May 2008).

[89]   *See* FRIEDMAN, *supra* note 31, at Appendix 16A.

over the defaulted tenant's leased premises.[90] There are several relatively obvious measures that a landlord should adopt if it wants to satisfy its mitigation duty—for example, the landlord should: (a) advertise the space as being available "for lease"; (b) hire a leasing broker to market the space; (c) respond in a timely fashion to inquiries from prospective tenants; and (d) put the leased premises into a rentable condition. There are, however, a number of gray areas concerning the scope of the landlord's duty to mitigate damages. Specifically, the courts have not provided clear-cut answers to the following questions.[91]

- Is the landlord required to accept a below market rent from a new tenant?

- Is the landlord required to re-lease the space to a person whose credit standing is somewhat questionable (and worse than that of the defaulted tenant)?

- Is the landlord required to accept a new lease that has a term that is significantly shorter or longer than the defaulted tenant's term?

- Is the landlord required to spend significant dollars on additional tenant improvements and leasing commissions?

- Is the landlord required to re-lease the leased premises if it has other vacant space in its building (or in a nearby building)?

To the extent the tenant is successful in its efforts to impose a duty to mitigate on the landlord, the landlord may want to adopt a similar approach to that suggested in the earlier discussion of the assignment and sublease clause (see pages 571–573) and specify certain actions that the landlord need not take to satisfy the duty to mitigate (such as the gray areas noted above).[92]

3. Landlord Default Clause

The discussion of the default clause has now covered several pages without a single mention of the prospect or consequences of a default by the landlord. That topic is also notably absent from most landlord-authored lease forms. If the tenant does not request the inclusion in the lease of a specific landlord default clause (and it often fails to do so), then the tenant is left with the very limited remedies that are available to it under common

---

[90] *See generally* SENN, *supra* note 5, at 31–37.

[91] *See* FRIEDMAN, *supra* note 31, at 16–78 through 16–90; and SENN, *supra* note 5, at 31–37 through 31–49.

[92] *See* Bershad, *supra* note 81, at 539; and SENN, *supra* note 5, at 31–48 to 31–49 (Form 31–5).

law—quite possibly nothing other than the right to sue the landlord for damages.[93]

If the tenant convinces the landlord that it makes sense to include a landlord default clause in the lease, then counsel for the landlord and the tenant must address many of the same issues discussed previously with respect to the tenant default clause—most notably the existence of notice and cure rights. The most contentious part of the discussion focuses on the tenant's demand that it be given the rights to withhold its rent and terminate its lease if a landlord event of default occurs. The landlord's lawyer, of course, resists those demands and tries to effectively limit the tenant's recourse to the "go ahead and sue me" alternative provided at common law.

B. CASUALTY CLAUSE
(§ 19)

Virtually every commercial lease has a clause devoted to sorting out the impact on the landlord-tenant relationship of the occurrence of a building fire or other casualty. Because the subject of that clause is the occurrence of an unusual event, many practitioners go through their entire careers without ever having the efficacy of their casualty clauses tested in a real world application. For that reason, casualty clauses are often given short shrift during the lease negotiations. However, those landlords and tenants who have been unfortunate enough to experience the aftermath of the occurrence of a fire are quick to remind their respective counsel of the importance of drafting a thoughtful and thorough casualty clause.

The term "casualty" is often used in a commercial lease as a short-hand reference to the occurrence of a fire, explosion, storm, flood, earthquake, or other calamitous event that damages the landlord's building or interferes with the tenant's use of its leased premises. Common law places no obligation on the landlord to repair its damaged building, nor does common law afford the tenant the right to abate its rent or terminate its lease following the occurrence of a casualty. While a few modern courts have softened the application of these common law rules in the context of a total destruction of the leased premises, lawyers are well-advised, as always, to put their stock in the written word contained in their clients' leases and not in the wisdom of the judiciary. Several states have enacted legislation designed to explicate the consequences of a casualty. Practitioners practicing in those states should closely review the legislation

---

[93] *See generally* Ronald R. Pollina, *"So, Sue Me"—What is the Tenant's Recourse,* in LEASE NEGOTIATION HANDBOOK 583 (Edward Chupack ed., 2003).

to determine whether the provisions of the statute can be modified by contract and, if so, whether they believe it is appropriate to do so.[94]

Because common law is singularly unhelpful in addressing the consequences of a building casualty (at least from the perspective of the tenant), counsel for the landlord and the tenant are left with the task of crafting lease language that answers the following two questions: (1) Does the tenant's rent obligation abate as a result of the casualty; and (2) Does either the landlord or the tenant have the right to terminate the lease following the casualty?

The answers to those two questions are largely dependent on the severity of the damage caused to the landlord's building by the occurrence of the casualty. In the context of the total destruction of a multi-tenant office building, counsel for the landlord and the tenant are typically willing to stipulate that the landlord and the tenant will each have the right to terminate the lease. If neither party exercises its termination right, the landlord will then be obligated to reconstruct its building and the tenant's rent will be abated during the reconstruction period.

The questions become much tougher to answer when the casualty does not result in the total destruction of landlord's project. Should a tenant have the right to terminate its lease or reduce its rent if a fire damages a portion (but not all) of the tenant's leased premises? What if a flash flood results in the building lobby and parking lot being rendered unusable for a period of time? Should either the tenant or the landlord have the right to walk away from the lease if it will take the landlord 90 days and a projected expenditure of $200,000 to repair the damaged areas?

A significant portion of the casualty clause negotiations is devoted to an attempt to delineate when the damage is so severe that the tenant should have the right to abate its rent or terminate its lease. The severity of the damage caused by the casualty can be measured in a number of ways—by the nature and amount of the space damaged by the casualty (for example, more than 50% of the square footage contained in the leased premises is rendered untenantable); by the cost of repairing the damage (for example, the estimated cost of repairing the damage exceeds 20% of the building's replacement cost); or by the time it will take to repair the damage (for example, more than 120 days).

A landlord typically seeks to establish a high threshold quantifying the severity of the damage that permits the tenant to terminate its lease. By way of example, a landlord-oriented lease might provide that the tenant may terminate its lease only if "the tenant is wholly deprived of the beneficial use and occupancy of the leased premises and the landlord's

---

[94] *See* Richard E. Strauss, *Damage and Destruction*, in LEASE NEGOTIATION HANDBOOK 481, 481–482 (Edward Chupack ed., 2003).

contractor determines that the damage to the leased premises cannot be repaired within 365 days after the occurrence of the casualty."

The tenant, of course, wants the flexibility to exit from its lease if the damage produced from the casualty adversely affects its ability to operate its business in the leased premises for any significant period of time. As a result, tenant's counsel typically asks that the lease expressly state that the tenant may terminate the lease if all damage to the leased premises and the building's common areas is not repaired within a relatively short time frame (for example, 60 days after the date of the casualty)—see *Pro-Tenant Modification #32* at page 746.

Once the parties have agreed upon the damage standard that triggers their respective rights to terminate the lease (usually somewhere between the two extreme standards noted in the preceding two paragraphs), they next turn to the issue of the abatement of the tenant's rent during the repair period. The landlord sometimes agrees to the insertion of a clause that provides that the tenant's rent "will be equitably and proportionately abated to reflect the untenantable portion of the leased premises" (see § 19 of the Form Office Lease). The landlord's willingness to grant this concession is linked to its expectation that it will recover the full amount of any granted abatement under the rent loss insurance policy it maintains for the project.[95]

Two additional points should be made concerning the parties' respective rights to terminate the lease following the occurrence of a casualty. The tenant usually tries to negotiate for a heightened right to terminate the lease if the casualty occurs during the latter part of the lease term (for example, the last 12 months of the term). Absent such a right, the tenant could be forced to move back into the leased premises for a brief tail period after the completion of the repairs even if its business interests would be better served by a permanent relocation to other space.

The landlord, on the other hand, wants to condition its obligation to repair the leased premises on the availability of insurance proceeds to fund its repair efforts. If the casualty is not insured under the insurance policy that the landlord is required to maintain under the insurance clause of the lease, then the landlord should reserve the right to terminate the lease. Similarly, if the insurance proceeds are insufficient to fund the full cost of the repair, then the landlord should reserve the right to either terminate the lease or alter the scope of its repairs to fit within its insurance budget.[96]

---

[95] *See* Richard R. Goldberg, *Insurance*, in ALI-ABA COURSE OF STUDY MATERIALS, COMMERCIAL REAL ESTATE LEASES: SELECTED ISSUES IN DRAFTING AND NEGOTIATING IN CURRENT MARKETS, Course No. SN-013, 1313, 1321 (May 2006)

[96] A commercial lease typically includes a clause that identifies the various insurance coverages that the landlord and the tenant must maintain throughout the lease term. *See e.g.,* § 15 of the Form Office Lease. The insurance topic is quite technical and, as such, is beyond the scope of this chapter. For a thorough-going discussion of the insurance clause, *see generally* Goldberg,

C. CONDEMNATION CLAUSE
(§ 20)

The negotiation of the condemnation clause involves many of the same issues discussed above with respect to the casualty clause—specifically, the nature and scope of the tenant's right to receive a rent abatement and the respective rights of the landlord and the tenant to terminate the lease as a result of a taking by the government of all or part of the landlord's project through the exercise (or threatened exercise) of its eminent domain powers. There are, however, a few lease issues that are unique to the condemnation context.

A governmental taking permanently changes the nature of the landlord's project. This result is unlike the situation following the occurrence of a casualty where the parties are focused on the landlord restoring the leased premises and its building to the same condition that existed prior to the occurrence of the casualty. That is not possible in the context of a condemnation because a part of the landlord's project is permanently taken away. As a result, the lawyers assigned with the task of negotiating the condemnation clause must tackle two issues that are not present in their negotiation of the casualty clause—(1) is the portion of the leased premises and the common areas remaining after the condemnation sufficient to permit the tenant to conduct its business in the leased premises in a substantially similar manner to that which characterized its use of the leased premises prior to the condemnation (see *Pro-Tenant Modification #33* at page 746), and (2) is the tenant entitled to a permanent reduction in its rent to reflect the fact that the post-condemnation property is inherently different from the property the tenant was leasing before the condemnation? Because both of these questions rely on the evaluation of subjective considerations, the condemnation clause usually includes equally subjective standards to determine the impact of a condemnation on the landlord-tenant relationship—for example, does the condemnation "materially interfere with the tenant's use of the leased premises" and is the tenant entitled to an "equitable adjustment" of rent to reflect the changed condition of the leased premises after the condemnation?[97]

The other issue that the condemnation clause needs to address is how the landlord and tenant will split the monetary award paid by the condemning authority—particularly an award related to the taking of the entirety of the project? Most tenants ask for the right to share in the award to reflect the value of the tenant's leasehold interest that was taken by the condemning authority. The landlord responds that the tenant is free to

---

Insurance, supra note 95; and Raymond S. Iwamoto, *Insurance and the Commercial Lease*, in THE PRACTICAL REAL ESTATE LAWYER'S MANUAL ON COMMERCIAL LEASING IN TROUBLED TIMES— FORMS, CHECKLISTS, AND ADVICE 225 (2009).

[97] *See* ZANKEL, *supra* note 1, at 150–151.

make a separate application to the condemning authority for an award compensating the tenant for its moving expenses, but that the tenant is not entitled to any portion of the authority's award for the value of the taken property. This is one battle that is typically won by the landlord.[98]

Practice Tip #11-3—Focus on What Matters

During my ten-year stint teaching at The Ohio State University's law school, I always invited Brian Ellis, a prominent Columbus developer, to speak to my law school class and share his thoughts on what it takes to be a successful real estate development lawyer. The first words out of Brian's mouth every year were "YOU NEED TO FOCUS ON WHAT MATTERS." Brian drove homes this point by telling a story about a young lawyer who camped out in his office one day to complain about the difficulty he was having in trying to get the tenant's lawyer to agree to the substance of a condemnation clause. After listening for a few moments to the young lawyer's saga, Brian lost his patience and blurted out "IT DOESN'T MATTER!" Once he regained his composure, Brian calmly explained to his legal counsel that this particular tenant was negotiating to take space in a brand new downtown office building and that its lease term was only five years. The likelihood that the building would be condemned in the ensuing five years was so slim that the intricacies of the condemnation clause "JUST DIDN'T MATTER."

I relished hearing Brian's story every year because it provides me with the perfect opening to make the point to my class that the successful transactional lawyer first needs to understand what matters most to the client. Only once the lawyer has figured out what matters to the client can the lawyer then follow Brian's sage advice to "FOCUS ON WHAT MATTERS."

D. SUBORDINATION CLAUSE
(§ 13)

The subordination clause attempts to deal with the status of the tenant's lease following the foreclosure of a lender's mortgage on the landlord's building. Specifically, the question is, Does the tenant have the right or obligation after a foreclosure to continue to occupy the leased premises pursuant to the terms of the lease it negotiated with the landlord?

---

[98] *See* EISENBERG, *supra* note 40, at 138.

The tenant does not want its lease to be terminated or otherwise affected in any way by the landlord's failure to comply with the terms of its mortgage loan. The lender, on the other hand, wants the right to pick and choose those leases that it recognizes following the foreclosure of its mortgage—keeping the good leases in place and rejecting the bad leases. The lender also wants to make sure that its interest in any insurance or condemnation proceeds are superior to the interests of the project's tenants. Finally, in a rare show of apathy, the landlord really does not care one way or the other what happens to the tenant after the lender forecloses on the landlord's building. As a result, the landlord's sole motivation when negotiating the subordination clause is to arrive at language that is mutually acceptable to the tenant and the lender.

The rule established at common law is that the tenant has an unrestricted right to remain in possession of the leased premises following a foreclosure only if its lease is deemed to have priority over the lender's mortgage. If the lease is found to be subordinate to the lender's mortgage, then the lender has the right to terminate the tenant's lease and evict the tenant from possession of the leased premises. There is a split in jurisdictions as to whether a foreclosure automatically terminates all subordinate leases (the "automatic termination rule") or only terminates those leases designated by the foreclosing lender (the "pick and choose rule"). Under either rule, the tenant's leasehold interest is in danger of being eliminated if that leasehold interest is found to be subordinate to the lien of the lender's mortgage.[99]

A lease is deemed subordinate to the lien of the lender's mortgage if either (1) the mortgage was recorded prior to the tenant's execution of its lease, or (2) the lease expressly provides that the tenant's interest is subordinate to the mortgage.[100] To provide its lender with the maximum available protection, the landlord consistently includes in its standard lease a provision stating that, unless otherwise specifically elected by the lender, the lease automatically is deemed to be subordinate to the lien of any mortgage. The effect of such a provision is quite clear—if the landlord's lender ever forecloses on its mortgage, the lender (and not the tenant) has the right to determine whether the tenant's lease remains intact or is terminated.

If the tenant has any negotiating clout whatsoever, it should insist that the subordination of its leasehold interest to the lien of the lender's mortgage is expressly conditioned upon the tenant's receipt of a written agreement from the lender acknowledging that the tenant has the continuing right to occupy the leased premises as long as the tenant remains in compliance with the terms of the lease. Assuming that the

---

[99] *See* Thomas Arendt, *Subordination, Attornment and Nondisturbance*, in LEASE NEGOTIATION HANDBOOK 469, 471–472 (Edward Chupack ed., 2003).

[100] *See* SENN, *supra* note 5, at 25–7 through 25–10.

tenant making the above request is of a sufficient size and stature to merit the lender's respect, the tenant and the lender then set about trying to negotiate the terms of a comprehensive document (known in the parlance of the lending industry as a "subordination, non-disturbance and attornment agreement" or "SNDA") that contains the following general features (see *Pro-Tenant Modification # 34* at page 747):[101]

- The tenant's agreement to subordinate its leasehold interest to the lien of the lender's mortgage unless the lender expressly elects to grant priority to the tenant's lease (the *SUBORDINATION* feature);[102]

- The lender's agreement not to disturb the tenant's right to possess the leased premises as long as the tenant complies with all of its lease obligations (the *NONDISTURBANCE* feature); and

- The tenant's agreement to attorn to and recognize the lender as the "landlord" under its lease following the lender's foreclosure of its mortgage (the *ATTORNMENT* feature).

The lender customarily also requests that the subordination clause contain provisions relieving the lender from liability for and requiring the tenant to provide the lender with an opportunity to cure any pre-foreclosure landlord defaults.

A tenant who does not have the negotiating power to demand the execution of an SNDA remains at risk that the lender will decide to terminate its lease if and when the lender forecloses its mortgage. The lender's ultimate decision to keep or terminate a subordinate lease is driven by its perception of the vibrancy of the leasing market and the fair rental value of the leased premises. A foreclosing lender seldom elects to terminate a tenant's lease unless doing so is a necessary adjunct to the lender signing a new lease with a known user whose credit and rent are superior to those of the tenant. The lender, however, frequently uses its termination right as a bargaining chip in its effort to renegotiate the terms of an existing tenant's lease.

---

[101] *See* Arendt, *supra* note 99, at 472–477; and SENN, *supra* note 5, at 25–20 through 25–40 (including Form 25–3).

[102] A clause that gives the lender the unilateral right to grant the tenant's lease priority over the mortgage is routinely used in those states that follow the automatic termination rule mentioned earlier in the text. The use of such a clause effectively permits the lender to "pick and choose" those leases that it wants to survive the foreclosure by opting to subordinate the lien of its mortgage to the chosen, favorable leases. *See* Arendt, *supra* note 99, at 476.

E. LEASING COMMISSION CLAUSE
(¶ R of Lease Summary and § 26)

A commercial lease should contain a clause that (1) identifies the brokers who are entitled to receive a commission from the subject lease transaction and (2) assigns responsibility for the payment of the commission to either the landlord or the tenant. The brokerage commission clause typically also includes a mutual representation and indemnity comparable to the following provision:

> *Landlord and Tenant each represents that it has not dealt or consulted with any real estate broker or agent in connection with this Lease, other than [insert name of brokers retained by Landlord or Tenant]. Landlord and Tenant each indemnifies the other against any liability or loss occasioned by a breach of the foregoing representation.*

The inclusion of such a clause significantly lessens the landlord's concern that an unknown broker unexpectedly shows up with its hand extended looking for a commission after the lease is fully executed—a frightening prospect considering that leasing commissions on major lease transactions can easily run into seven figures.

F. ESTOPPEL CERTIFICATE CLAUSE
(§ 13)

As noted on numerous occasions throughout this text, the value of the landlord's real estate project is a direct product of the terms of its tenant leases. As such, any lender, buyer, or equity provider seeking to make an investment in a real estate project always asks for written confirmations from the tenants that the terms of their leases are as represented by the project owner. An ***estoppel certificate*** is a written statement made by a tenant confirming the terms of its lease and representing that its lease is in full force and effect without any default on the part of either the landlord or the tenant.

A tenant who balks at furnishing an estoppel certificate (or who seeks to get a "little something extra" in exchange for its provision of the required certificate) can jeopardize the viability of an entire loan, sale or equity transaction. In an attempt to protect the landlord against that scenario, the landlord's counsel normally includes a provision in the lease that requires the tenant to execute an estoppel certificate within a stated number of days after its receipt of the proffered certificate. Some landlords attempt to include language in the estoppel certificate clause that (1) affirms that the tenant is liable for consequential damages should it breach its obligation to provide an executed estoppel certificate within the time period specified in the lease, and (2) appoints the landlord as the tenant's attorney-in-fact to execute the certificate on the tenant's behalf if the tenant fails to provide the required certificate on a timely basis.[103] Although this latter provision is frequently found in commercial leases, my experience has been that it has no real practical significance because a lender/buyer/equity provider rarely, if ever, accepts an estoppel certificate signed by the landlord pursuant to an attorney-in-fact clause.

Tenants, of course, resist both those provisions as unnecessary and overly draconian remedies for a simple failure by the tenant to turn around the landlord's request for an estoppel certificate within the short time frame specified in the lease. Tenants should also be mindful of the frequent attempt by the landlord and its buyer/lender/investor to include substantive provisions in the estoppel certificate that are intended to effect a modification of the lease terms or a waiver of all claims that the tenant may have against the landlord. For this reason, tenants are well-advised to expressly limit the content of any required estoppel certificate to a confirmation that the lease attached to the estoppel certificate is in full force and effect without any known default by the landlord.

G. SECURITY DEPOSIT/FINANCIAL STATEMENT CLAUSES
(¶ P of Lease Summary and §§ 32 and 33)

The landlord customarily requires all but the most creditworthy of tenants to post collateral to partially secure the tenant's performance of its obligations under the lease. A *security deposit* can take any number of forms, with the most common being a cash deposit or a letter of credit. The amount of the security deposit is typically tied in some fashion to the level of the tenant's base rent obligation—for example, a deposit equal to one or two months base rent for a tenant with a decent credit standing and six months to a year or more for a tenant with questionable credit. Regardless of the type or amount of the security deposit, the landlord wants the lease to make clear that (1) the landlord can take the deposit down immediately upon the occurrence of an event of default, and (2) the tenant is obligated to promptly replenish the security deposit to its full original amount (see however *Pro-Tenant Modification #20* at page 742).[104]

In an effort to monitor the evolving financial position of each of its tenants, the landlord should include a provision in its standard lease form that requires the tenant and any guarantor to provide the landlord with at least annual financial statements documenting its then current financial condition. The landlord often couples such a provision with a covenant that

---

[103] *See* ZANKEL, *supra* note 1, at 162.

[104] *See* Ira Fierstein, *Security Deposits*, in LEASE NEGOTIATION HANDBOOK 545, 545–546 (Edward Chupack ed., 2003).

requires the tenant and the guarantor to maintain a minimum net worth at all times throughout the lease term (see however *Pro-Tenant Modification #21* at page 743).

H. BOILERPLATE CLAUSES

The commercial lease often contains a number of other clauses that landlords and tenants (but hopefully not their counsel) lump into the category of **boilerplate**—meaning clauses that one does not need to read or worry about. Example of lease clauses commonly referred to as "boilerplate" are the successors and assigns, no waiver, amendment, governing law, and notice clauses contained in the Form Office Lease (§§ 24, 25, 29, 30, and 31, respectively). It is essential that the lawyer heed the admonition that one should never include a clause in the lease without having a legitimate reason for doing so—even if it is commonly relegated to the scrap heap of so-called boilerplate clauses.

XII. SUMMARY

Leasing is all about the creation of value. The value of a commercial real estate project is not a function of the project's location, design, construction, or financing structure, but rather of the income stream generated from the project. As such, the leases signed by the developer during Stage 7 dictate whether its development project is a financial success or a bust.

The real estate development lawyer plays an important role in helping the developer create value for its project. While the lawyer certainly does not (and should not) become directly involved in setting the annual rental rates for the project, it is the lawyer's job to include provisions in the lease that are designed to enhance the predictability that the net rental income is actually received by the developer at the projected times and in the projected amounts. Similarly, while the lawyer is not out front marketing the project to prospective tenants, the lawyer's conduct during the course of the lease negotiations significantly affects how the prospective tenant views the landlord. Finally, the real estate development lawyer, as the preparer and primary negotiator of the lease document, serves as the gatekeeper to insure that the executed lease appropriately serves the landlord's business goals and insulates the landlord to the fullest extent reasonably practicable from the risks inherent in the landlord-tenant relationship.

I want to leave you with one concluding thought about the negotiation of a commercial lease. A successful negotiation has nothing to do with body language or polemics, but it has everything to do with knowledge and preparation. As noted by a well-known author on the topic of commercial leasing—"If you know the impacts on finances, risk, operations and services of all the sections of a typical sophisticated commercial lease and if you understand the needs of your client, negotiation is simply a default condition."[105]

---

[105] *See* JOHN BUSEY WOOD, OUTLINE FOR COMMERCIAL LEASES, SEMINAR FOR NEW YORK UNIVERSITY/REAL ESTATE INSTITUTE SCHOOL OF CONTINUING AND PROFESSIONAL STUDIES 1 (2010), available online at http://www.officeleasingusa.com/downloads/nyucourseoutline.pdf.

CHAPTER 12

STAGES 8–10: SELECTING
AN EXIT STRATEGY

▪ ▪ ▪

I. INTRODUCTION

The final chapter of this book takes a consolidated look at the final three stages of a development project—that is, Stage 8 (executing an interim exit strategy), Stage 9 (operating the project), and Stage 10 (selling the project). All three of these stages address the central question of what the developer should do once its development project is fully leased and cash flowing.

The real estate development lawyer's job during the final project stages is twofold—the lawyer must (1) counsel the developer on which of the potential exit strategies best serves the developer's overall business objectives, and (2) execute the exit strategy selected by the developer. Developers often opt to skip Stages 8 and 9 entirely and instead sell the project as soon as it is leased and cash flowing. For the purposes of this chapter, it is assumed that the developer has decided to adopt an interim exit strategy and operate the project for an extended period of time before selling it outright to a third party.

The specific tasks performed by the development lawyer during Stages 8 through 10 are similar in many respects to those tasks discussed in earlier chapters of this book (specifically, *Chapter 5—Stage 1: Gaining Control of the Site, Chapter 7—Stage 3: Forming and Capitalizing the Project Entity,* and *Chapter 9—Stage 5: Obtaining Construction Financing*). This chapter does not repeat the material covered in those earlier chapters, but instead focuses on the special factors that the lawyer must take into consideration when advising the developer during the final three stages of a real estate development project.

II. ALTERNATIVE EXIT STRATEGIES

The developer's goal is always to stabilize its project as soon as possible. A **stabilized project** is one that is leased and producing positive cash flow. Once that goal is achieved, the developer is faced with the question of what to do next—either (1) sell the project outright, or (2) retain full or partial ownership of the project for a further period of time. The answer to that question involves a balancing of the developer's desire to maximize its after-tax economic returns from the project against the developer's equally strong objective of limiting its exposure to ongoing real estate risk.

There are a host of considerations that the developer must weigh when making its "hold or sell" decision. The most salient of these considerations are summarized below.

- *Financial Performance*—The threshold question that the developer must answer is whether the project's stabilized financial performance is sufficiently robust to merit the developer's retention of a long-term ownership interest in the project. If the project's cash flow is marginal or the creditworthiness of the project's tenant roster is questionable, then the developer may want to offload all of its real estate risk by immediately selling the project to a third party.

- *Market Conditions*—The conditions prevailing in the real estate and capital markets also impact the developer's exit strategy choice. During the period from 2002 through 2007, institutional investors were so anxious to invest in real estate that they were willing to invest in stabilized commercial projects on terms that conjured up images of Don Corleone uttering his infamous statement in the Godfather that "I will make him an offer he can't refuse."[1] In the aftermath of the financial crash of 2008, investment in commercial real estate projects came to a screeching halt. As of the date of the writing of the second edition of this text (the first quarter of 2017), the commercial real estate market has stabilized at a level somewhere between the two extremes of the go-go days of the early 2000's and the lost years of 2008–2012. The lesson to be learned from studying the crazy real estate cycles of the last 15 years is that the real estate developer must always be prepared to drastically change its business model to adapt to changes in the marketplace.

- *Personal Risk Profile*—Some developers are simply more risk averse than others. Those developers (often referred to as *merchant builders*) seek to limit their exposure to real estate risk by selling their projects as soon as they reach stabilization. Other developers (so-called *portfolio builders*) are more inclined to try to maximize their after-tax financial returns by holding on to their projects for a longer term.

---

[1]   THE GODFATHER, screenplay by Mario Puzo, directed by Francis Ford Coppola (Paramount Pictures 1972).

- *Tax Considerations*—An outright sale of the project subjects the developer to the payment of federal income tax on the difference between the sales price and the project's cost basis. If the developer has held its project for more than 12 months after completion of construction, then, in most instances, the developer's sale profit is taxed as a capital gain at a current maximum tax rate of 20%.[2] If, however, the developer has an established track record of consistently selling its projects once they achieve stabilization, then the developer may be treated as a "dealer" and compelled to pay tax on the sale profit at ordinary income tax rates (currently 39.6% for those taxpayers in the highest marginal tax bracket).[3] A developer can defer the recognition of income on the project's profit component by choosing to hold the project for an extended period of time after stabilization.[4]

- *Contractual Restrictions*—A developer's hold vs. sell decision may, on occasion, be dictated by the content of the debt and equity documents that the developer signed during the course of its raising of the funds needed to pay the project's development costs. By way of example, an LLC operating agreement may require an outside equity investor's consent to a sale of the project or the refinancing of the project's mortgage debt. The real estate development lawyer's job is, of course, to limit both the number and scope of any contractual restrictions placed on the developer's decision-making authority.

There is no right or wrong answer to the question of whether a developer should hold or sell its project. The advantage of skipping Stages 8 and 9 and moving directly to a sale of the project is that doing so permits the developer to garnish a quick cash return of both its invested capital and the profit inherent in the stabilized project. The quick sale approach also fixes the developer's project profit by eliminating the risk that the occurrence of a future event could unexpectedly diminish the project's value (for example, a tenant bankruptcy or a general market decline).

On the other hand, the developer's decision to hold the project may permit the developer to enhance its financial returns by benefitting from (1) the ongoing positive cash flow generated from the project (which presumably is higher than the return generated from more conservative cash equivalent investments), (2) the future appreciation in the value of

---

[2] *See* I.R.C. § 1(h)(1)(d).

[3] *See* I.R.C. § 1(a)(2).

[4] *See generally* Stefan F. Tucker, and Tamara F. Langlieb, *Real Estate—A Focus on Preserving Capital Gains and "Dealer" Issues,* ALI-CLE MODERN REAL ESTATE TRANSACTIONS, Course No. SY006, 813 (August 2016).

the project, and (3) the deferral of the imposition of income tax on the project's incremental value. The long-term hold strategy does, however, subject the developer to the added risk that something happens in the future that negatively impacts the after-tax profitability of the project.

A developer's hold vs. sell decision varies by project and time. An ardent portfolio builder may adopt the stance of a merchant builder if it needs to raise cash to deal with other financial challenges. Similarly, a developer who, by natural inclination, is a merchant builder may decide to hold on to the ownership of a project because the project's long-term financial prospects are solid and the then prevailing capitalization rates are inordinately high.

The following is a listing of illustrative factors that might cause a developer to say "let's hold this one" or "let's sell it now":

- The project's return on equity is only 8% → SELL;

- The project's return on equity is a whopping 30% → HOLD;

- The project is 100% leased by Microsoft → HOLD;

- The project is 100% leased by Sears → SELL (if that is possible);

- The project is a multi-tenant building in San Francisco with a tenant roster loaded with AAA credits → HOLD;

- The developer is mega-rich and really liquid → HOLD;

- The developer is just starting out in the business and damn near broke → SELL;

- Interest rates are at a historically low level → HOLD;

- Interest rates are rising and it is questionable whether rents will keep pace → SELL

- Cap rates have never been lower → SELL;

- There is a new President and no one has a clue what he's going to do → SELL.

A really fun and intriguing aspect of the hold vs. sell decision is that different developers often reach totally different conclusions when confronted with identical fact patterns. By way of example, one developer might think that historically low interest rates means that it makes sense to lock in a permanent loan and hold the project for another ten years, while another developer might conclude that low interest rates expand the universe of buyers and weighs in favor of a "sell now" mentality.

———————

Practice Tip #12-1: Hold vs. Sell by the Numbers

The prior section of this chapter narratively explored the hold vs. sell dilemma that a developer faces once its development project attains the exalted level of stabilization. This Practice Tip takes a quick look at how the numbers play out in the context of a developer's hold vs. sell conundrum.

Example 12-1: Developer is delighted that its office building is 100% leased by the beginning of Year 1 (only six months after completion of construction). Even better yet is that 60% of the building is leased for ten years to Google. Developer's enthusiasm for the project is only slightly dampened by the fact that the remaining 40% of the building is leased for a three-year term to Here's Hoping it Works, a high-tech start-up company with a net worth in single digits.

The following are the financial details of Developer's office building project.

- *Project Cost = $20 million, funded by:*

  - *80% ($16 million) with a construction loan that matures in six months; and*

  - *20% ($4 million) with Developer's equity dollars.*

- *Annual NOI = $2 million.*

- *Project's Appraised Value = $30 million (at a 6.6% cap rate).*

- *Permanent Debt Proposal Made by Life Insurance Company:*

  - *Principal amount =$16 million;*

  - *Loan Term = Ten Years;*

  - *Annual Debt Service Payments = $1.2 million; and*

  - *Projected Annual Operating Cash Flow if Permanent Debt Is Put in Place = $800,000 (assuming NOI of $2 million per year).*

So, given these numbers what should Developer do—sell or hold? Let's look at what the comparative hold vs. sell numbers look like in three different scenarios:

Scenario A—Google stays in the building for ten years and then extends its lease for another ten years. Here's Hoping It Works really does work out and signs a new lease that extends its lease term for an added ten years. Developer's NOI remains stable at $2 million per year and the cap rate applicable to Developer's building in Year 11 remains at 6.6%.

Scenario B—Everything is the same as in Scenario A, except that the prevailing cap rate for office buildings in Year 11 soars to 10% (not a good thing because the higher the cap rate the lower the project's value—remember Chapter 3—What the Real Estate Development Lawyer Needs to Know About Project Economics).

Scenario C—Here's Hoping it Works does not work and it files for bankruptcy shortly after taking occupancy of its space in Year 1. Here's Hoping it Works' space remains vacant for five years (with the building producing NOI of only $1.2 million in each of Years 1 through 5) and is then backfilled at the end of Year 5 by a bunch of small mom and pop companies at a rent level well below that previously agreed to by Here's Hoping it Works (resulting in the building producing NOI of $1.5 million in each of Years 6 through 10). Worse yet, Google requires a 30% rent cut as a condition to its agreement to renew its lease for another five years. The end result is that in Year 11 the building is producing an annual NOI of only $1.4 million. To make things even worse, cap rates on office buildings are at 8% in Year 11.

The following table summarizes the Developer's numbers if it opted to sell or hold its project under each of Scenario A, Scenario B, and Scenario C (assuming that the building is sold in Year 11 based on the NOI and cap rates that are in place at that time).

Financial Results	Project Hold for Ten Years with Sale in Year 11	Project Sale in Year 1
Scenario A		
Operating Cash Flow	**$8 million** ($800K for ten years)	**$0**
Net Sales Proceeds	**$12 million** ($30 million sales price minus $18 million permanent loan)	**$12 million** ($30 million sales price minus $18 million construction loan)
Total Cash Flow	**$20 million**	**$12 million**
Scenario B		
Operating Cash Flow	**$8 million** ($800K for ten years)	$0
Net Sales Proceeds	**$2 million** ($20 million sales price minus $18 million permanent loan)	**$12 million** ($30 million sales price minus $18 million construction loan)
Total Cash Flow	**$10 million**	**$12 million**
Scenario C		
Operating Cash Flow	**$1.5 million** ($0 in Years 1–5, and $300K in Years 6–10)	$0
Net Sales Proceeds	**$(500,000)** ($17.5 million sales price minus $18 million permanent loan)	**$12 million** ($30 million sales price minus $18 million construction loan)
Total Cash Flow	**$1 million**	**$12 million**

The financial results summarized in the above table illustrate that under the assumed facts in Scenario A, Developer should have opted to hold its project, while under the assumed facts in Scenarios B and C, Developer would have been wise to sell its project in Year 1. Unfortunately, in the real world, a real estate developer does not have the benefit of being told the "assumed facts" when it has to make the real-time decision in Year 1 whether it will sell or hold the stabilized project.

The developer must rely on its "educated gut" to predict how its project will fare in the future and, hence, whether it should sell that project now or hold it for an extended period of time. The developer's decision is further confounded by the fact that it also needs to divine what the developer's personal and professional interests will be five to ten years down the road —will the developer: have more money than God; be on the verge of bankruptcy; just want to hit the links and play with the grandkids; or want to go into politics (there is after all now precedent for that career path choice).

III. STAGE 8: EXECUTING AN INTERIM EXIT STRATEGY

The remainder of this chapter assumes that the developer has opted to hold its project for an extended period of time (five to ten years) and to then sell it outright to an institutional investor. As such, the discussion that follows examines the business objectives of the developer and the roles played by the developer's lawyer during each of Stages 8, 9, and 10.

At the advent of Stage 8, the developer is faced with a good news/bad news conundrum. The good news is that its project is fully leased and generating positive cash flow. The bad news is that the developer's project is probably encumbered by a construction loan that includes the following unwanted features:

- A rapidly approaching due date for the repayment of the loan (typically only two to three years after the initial loan closing);

- An interest rate that fluctuates with changes in a financial index (for example, the prime rate or LIBOR); and

- The developer's personal guaranty that the construction loan will be paid in full at maturity.

The developer's primary business objective during Stage 8 is to devise an interim exit strategy that permits it to refinance the construction loan with a loan that is not characterized by any of these negative features—in other words, a loan that has an extended term and fixed interest rate and is fully nonrecourse to the developer.

A. PERMANENT MORTGAGE LOAN

A loan that is used to retire the construction loan is known as a *permanent loan*. Permanent loans generally fall into one of two categories—(1) a *portfolio loan* that is originated and held by a single mortgage lender (for example, a life insurance company, pension fund, bank, or other financial institution), or (2) a *securitized loan* that is originated by a mortgage lender and then pooled with other mortgage loans and sold off in pieces and parts to investors.

A permanent loan (be it a portfolio loan or a securitized loan) differs in many respects from a construction loan. The following are some of the principal ways in which a permanent mortgage loan is different from a construction loan.

- *Term*—The term of a permanent loan is generally five to ten years (as contrasted to the typical two or three-year term of a construction loan).

- *Payment Schedule*—A permanent loan typically calls for the borrower to make a fixed monthly payment of principal and interest based on a fixed interest rate and an amortization schedule of anywhere from 15 to 30 years. Because the term of a permanent loan is almost always less than the assumed amortization period, a permanent loan usually requires the borrower to make a sizable principal payment at the maturity of the loan (commonly referred to as a *balloon payment*). By way of example, a $10 million permanent loan that has a stated term of seven years, an assumed amortization period of 20 years, and a fixed interest rate of 8% will have a balloon principal payment due on the maturity date of the loan of approximately $8.1 million.

- *Nonrecourse Clause*—A permanent loan is typically nonrecourse to the borrower and its affiliates. The nonrecourse nature of the permanent loan is, however, frequently subject to a laundry list of exceptions (see pages 603–605 for a discussion of "nonrecourse carveouts").

- *Prepayment Restrictions*—A permanent loan usually contains a restriction on the ability of the borrower to pay off the loan prior to the loan's stated maturity date.

- *Due on Sale or Encumbrance Clauses*—A permanent loan also customarily limits the borrower's ability to sell or further mortgage the project that serves as collateral for the repayment of the loan.

The remainder of this section focuses on a discussion of the nonrecourse, prepayment, and due on sale/encumbrance clauses of a permanent mortgage loan.

1. The Nonrecourse Clause

The inclusion in the permanent loan documents of a nonrecourse clause is intended to insulate the borrower from any personal liability for the repayment of the permanent loan. The permanent lender's sole recourse in the event of a borrower default is to foreclose on the mortgage and any other collateral that secures the permanent loan. The borrower and its principals are free to toss the lender the keys to the project and return to work knowing that their personal assets (cash, cars, planes, artwork, etc.) are immune from the lender's treacherous reach.

The following is a representative sample of a nonrecourse clause.

Neither Borrower, nor any shareholder, member, or partner of Borrower, is personally liable for the payment of any principal, interest, or other sum evidenced by the Loan or for any deficiency judgment that Lender may obtain following the foreclosure of the mortgage. Lender's sole recourse for any default under the Loan is limited to the property encumbered by the mortgage and any other collateral given to secure the Loan.

A permanent lender is receptive to making a nonrecourse loan on any stabilized project that has (1) sufficient cash flow to cover the lender's debt service, and (2) a residual value in excess of the principal amount of the loan. Permanent lenders rely on underwriting standards, such as the loan-to-value ratio, debt service coverage test, and debt yield standard, to provide the requisite solace on the adequacy of a project's cash flow and residual value to service the permanent loan. The theory underlying nonrecourse financing is that if the permanent lender subjects a borrower's request for a permanent loan to exacting underwriting standards, then the borrower's project should provide the lender with all the security it needs to ensure that the permanent loan is serviced and paid off at maturity. Based on this line of thinking, permanent lenders have historically been willing to look solely to the real estate as collateral for the repayment of the permanent loan and to dispense with the need to have a creditworthy entity on the hook to repay the loan.

The financial disaster wrought by the Great Recession of 2008 has caused permanent lenders to re-examine the fundamentals of their lending practices. In the last several years, permanent lenders have begun to impose a number of exceptions to the nonrecourse clause. Those exceptions (commonly referred to as *nonrecourse carveouts*) have become so numerous and invasive as to cause one author to wonder whether "the exceptions have now come to swallow the rule."[5]

a.   Nonrecourse Carveouts

A nonrecourse carveout seeks to place personal liability on the borrower for the repayment of all or a part of a permanent loan upon the occurrence of certain proscribed events or circumstances.[6] The prevalence of nonrecourse covenants in today's lending arena is driven in large measure by the fact that most borrowers are now ***special purpose entities (SPEs)*** with no assets beyond their ownership of the real estate that is the subject of the permanent lender's mortgage. For that reason, permanent lenders now also demand that a creditworthy entity personally guarantee the borrower's liability under the nonrecourse carveouts.

Most permanent loans have long contained exclusions from the nonrecourse clause for so-called "bad boy" acts, where the borrower engages in a type of particularly blameworthy conduct. The following are examples of typical "bad boy" carveouts—(1) fraud or misrepresentation in securing the loan, (2) intentional waste of the lender's collateral, (3) the misapplication of project receipts to pay expenses not related to the project, and (4) the violation of environmental laws.

Permanent lenders are increasingly attempting to broaden their nonrecourse carveouts to include events or circumstances that might hinder the lender's ability to secure a quick and full repayment of its loan even though such events or circumstances are not the product of any egregious borrower wrongdoing. By way of example, permanent lenders now regularly seek to impose personal liability on the borrower or one of its affiliates due to the occurrence of the following events:

- The borrower's bankruptcy or insolvency;

- The borrower's assertion of defenses to the foreclosure of the lender's mortgage;

---

[5]   Marc S. Intrilligator and R. David Walker, *Nonrecourse Carveout Provisions in Mortgage Loan Documents—A Trap for the Unwary*, THE REAL ESTATE FINANCE JOURNAL 5, 6 (Summer 2010).

[6]   *See generally* Intrilligator, *supra* note 5; Gary Fluhrer, Scott Osborne, Jim Wallenstein, *Bad Boys, Bad Bay, Whatcha Gonna Do: How "Non-Recourse Is Your Loan?*, in ACREL PAPERS, Tab 5 (Fall 2012); Andrew A. Lance and Susan G. Talley, *Non-Recourse Provisions and Carve-Outs*, in ACREL PAPERS, Tab 10 (Fall 2011); James H. Schwarz and Linda A. Striefsky, *The Nuts and Bolts of Negotiating Nonrecourse Carve-outs (with Sample Provisions)*, 31 No. 1 PRACTICAL REAL ESTATE LAWYER 5 (January 2015); Portia Owen Morrison and Mark A. Senn, *Carving Up the "Carve-outs" in Nonrecourse Loans*, 9 PROBATE AND PROPERTY 8 (June 1995); Joshua Stein, *Lender's Model State-of-the-Art Nonrecourse Clause (with Carveouts)*, 43 No. 7 PRACTICAL LAWYER 31, 34–36 (October 1997); and Gregory M. Stein, *When Can a Nonrecourse Lender Reach the Personal Assets of Its Borrower*, 17 No. 2 PRACTICAL REAL ESTATE LAWYER 33, 51–55 (March 2001).

- The borrower's breach of a prohibition contained in the loan documents restricting the borrower's right to sell the borrower's project or secure additional project financing;

- The borrower's breach of its representations and warranties set forth in the loan documents; and

- The borrower's failure to provide the lender with the borrower's financial statements.

The contest between the lender and the borrower over the scope and breadth of the nonrecourse carveouts is grounded in the parties' disparate views of the purpose that should be served by such carveouts. The borrower ideally wants to be in a position to give the lender the keys to the project and eliminate all its loan obligations if the project proves not to be financially viable for any reason. While the borrower is normally willing to accept carveouts for its "bad boy" acts, it wants to make sure that the carveouts only cover those intentional overt actions that are deliberately taken by the borrower to decrease the value of the lender's collateral. The borrower believes that the lender should bear the risk of a decline in the financial performance of the borrower's project unless the borrower has deliberately done something designed to hurt that performance.

The permanent lender, on the other hand, "is less focused on culpability than it is on risk allocation."[7] The carveouts represent the lender's attempt to place as much liability as possible on the borrower for a decline in the value of the collateral that secures its loan—regardless whether that decline is directly attributable to a wrongful act by the borrower or the occurrence of an event or circumstance with respect to which the borrower has no culpability whatsoever.

The outcome of the negotiations over the scope of the nonrecourse carveouts largely depends on the economic risk assumed by the lender in making the permanent loan. If the permanent loan is made at a 50% loan-to-value ratio, then the lender is more likely to limit the nonrecourse carveouts to true "bad boy" acts than it is if the loan carries a loan-to-value ratio of 80%. The expansion of nonrecourse carveouts to include items other than true "bad boy" acts is also more prevalent in securitized financings such as collateralized mortgage backed securities (see pages 610–613 for a discussion of securitized financings).

b.   Liability for Breach of Nonrecourse Carveout

Once the identity of the nonrecourse carveouts is determined, the next issue that counsel for the borrower and the permanent lender must tackle is, What is the scope of the personal liability of the person who is standing

---

[7]   Portia Owen Morrison and Mark A. Senn, *Carving up the "Carve-outs" in Nonrecourse Loans*, 9 PROBATE AND PROPERTY 8, 12 (June 1995).

behind the carveouts (typically a creditworthy affiliate of the single purpose entity borrower)? Traditionally, the recourse party's liability was limited to the loss or expense suffered by the permanent lender as a direct result of the borrower's breach of the nonrecourse carveout. By way of example, if the borrower misappropriated rents to pay fees to an affiliate of the borrower, then the recourse party would be personally liable for the repayment to the lender of the full amount of the misappropriated rents. Similarly, if the borrower violated an environmental law, then the recourse party would be personally liable for all damages and costs associated with the remediation of the violation.

The trend in recent years is for permanent lenders to take the stance that a violation of any nonrecourse carveout makes the person standing behind the carveouts personally liable for the repayment of the entirety of the permanent loan (and not just for any damages actually sustained by the lender due to the carveout violation). The recourse party's full liability for the repayment of the loan is often referred to as a *springing guaranty*.[8] Under a springing guaranty, the violation of a nonrecourse carveout results in the entirety of the permanent loan being converted from a nonrecourse loan to a fully recourse loan where the recourse party is personally liable for the payment of 100% of the unpaid principal and interest due on the loan.

Numerous courts in the last ten years have upheld the enforceability of full recourse springing guaranties over the objections of the recourse party that springing guaranties are unconscionable penalties. The sum and substance of those court decisions are that permanent loans involve sophisticated players of relatively equal bargaining power and, as a result, the courts will enforce nonrecourse carveout liability provisions as written.[9]

The obvious lesson to be learned from recent case law by the real estate development lawyer is that the nonrecourse carveout is yet one more provision where the written words used by the lawyer really matter. By way of example, it is crucial that a lawyer representing a borrower in a permanent loan pay exceedingly close attention to the precise wording of (1) the scope of the nonrecourse carveout (the "borrower's filing of a voluntary petition for bankruptcy under the U.S. Bankruptcy Code" versus the "borrower's insolvency"), and (2) the consequences of a breach of each nonrecourse carveout ("the lender's actual loss" versus "full liability for the repayment of the entirety of the loan").

---

[8]   *See* generally John C. Murray, *Exploding and Springing Guaranties*, in ALI-ABA COURSE OF STUDY MATERIALS, MODERN REAL ESTATE TRANSACTIONS: PRACTICAL STRATEGIES FOR REAL ESTATE ACQUISITION, DISPOSITION AND OWNERSHIP, Course No. SS–012, 1457 (July 2010); Intrilligator, *supra* note 5, at 6; and Morrison, *supra* note 7, at 9.

[9]   *See* Fluhrer, *supra* note 6, at 67–89.

2. Prepayment Restrictions

The lender's motivation in making a permanent loan is notably different than that of the construction lender. The construction lender's primary goal is to mitigate its risk by getting the construction loan repaid as soon as possible. The permanent lender, on the other hand, faces much less risk than does the construction lender and, as a result, is primarily focused on maintaining a consistent return on its debt throughout the stated term of the loan. The lender's prospects of achieving that consistent financial return is threatened if the borrower is able to pay its loan at par and without penalty prior to the loan's stated maturity date—because the lender may not be able to invest the repaid funds in a fashion that produces a return equivalent to the percentage interest rate applicable to the permanent loan.

The permanent lender tries to preserve the consistency of its loan return by either (1) prohibiting the repayment of the permanent loan for a stated period of time (a *lock-out period*) or (2) requiring the borrower to pay a negotiated premium for the privilege of prepaying the loan prior to maturity (a *prepayment penalty*). A permanent lender often combines these two protective measures by prohibiting any prepayments for a lock-out period of two or three years and then requiring the payment of a penalty for any prepayment occurring after the expiration of the lock-out period.

A prepayment penalty can be expressed in a variety of ways, including as a fixed percentage of the prepaid amount (for example, 1% of the principal prepayment). The most common formulation of a prepayment penalty is the *yield maintenance penalty*. A yield maintenance penalty attempts to protect the lender from a loss of its investment yield by requiring the prepaying borrower to pay the lender an additional sum that is equal to the difference between (1) the present value of the yield that would have been produced had the loan been held to maturity (roughly equivalent to the loan's fixed interest rate), and (2) the present value of the yield that the lender would achieve by investing the prepaid amount in another investment vehicle. The yield differential is typically calculated by comparing the permanent loan's fixed interest rate to the rate of return payable on a U.S. Treasury instrument having a term comparable to the remaining term of the permanent loan. This formulation is often referred to as a "Treasury-flat penalty." Best practice (at least from the borrower's perspective) is to adjust the comparable yield calculation by adding to the Treasury-flat figure the *spread* that existed on the funding date of the permanent loan between the return on a comparable term U.S. Treasury note and the fixed interest rate payable under the permanent loan. If the yield maintenance differential is not adjusted to reflect the spread over the yield paid on the comparable term U.S. Treasury instrument, then the permanent lender receives a windfall from the prepayment if the lender is able to re-invest the prepaid amount in an instrument (for example, another permanent loan) that pays a return in excess of that payable on the Treasury instrument.[10]

The enforceability of a prepayment penalty has been the subject of a great deal of litigation in the past several years.[11] The general rule produced from those cases is that a prepayment penalty is enforceable in the context of a voluntary prepayment made by a borrower as part of its sale of the underlying collateral or the refinancing of the permanent loan. Courts have rejected the notion that a prepayment penalty should be viewed as an unenforceable penalty under a liquidated damages analysis and, instead, have embraced the concept that a prepayment penalty negotiated by sophisticated parties is enforceable as "bargained-for form of alternative performance."[12]

The courts are split on whether a prepayment penalty is enforceable in the context of an involuntary prepayment engendered due to a condemnation, casualty, or borrower default.[13] A borrower under a true nonrecourse loan (with no or very limited nonrecourse carveouts) is, of course, not particularly concerned about the enforceability of a prepayment penalty following a borrower default because it views the prepayment penalty as just "one more obligation of the borrower that cannot be collected."[14] The borrower should, however, seek to clarify in the loan documents that a prepayment penalty cannot be imposed on a prepayment triggered by the occurrence of a casualty or condemnation.

3.   Due on Sale and Encumbrance Clauses

Permanent loan documents typically contain prohibitions against the borrower's sale of an interest in the mortgaged property (a *due on sale clause*) and the borrower's placement of secondary mortgage financing on

---

[10] WILLIAM B. BRUEGGEMAN AND JEFFREY D. FISHER, REAL ESTATE FINANCE AND INVESTMENTS 395–396 (14th ed. 2008).

[11] *See generally* Rod Clement, *Turmoil in Prepayment Land: An Update of Recent Prepayment Cases*, in ACREL PAPERS 355 (ALI-ABA Fall 2007). *See also* River East, 498 F.3d 718 (7th Cir. 2007), where the Seventh Circuit Court of Appeals sustained the enforceability of a Treasury-flat yield maintenance penalty.

[12] *See e.g.,* River East, 498 F.3d at 721; Chillicothe Telephone Co. v. Variable Annuity Life Insurance Company, 2007 WL 397058 (S.D. Ohio, January 31, 2007); In re CP Holdings, 332 B.R. 380 (W.D. Mo. 2005), *aff'd per curiam* 2006 WL 3203751 (8th Cir. 2006); and United States v. Harris, 246 F.3d 566 (6th Cir. 2001). *See also* Dale A. Whitman, *Mortgage Prepayment: A Legal and Economic Analysis*, 40 UCLA LAW REVIEW 851, 890 (1993), where Professor Whitman notes that "a freely-bargained prepayment fee clause ought to be enforced against the borrower who makes a voluntary prepayment, irrespective of the amount of money that the lender's clause demands."

[13] *See* Clement, *supra* note 11, at 359–364; and Robert A. Thompson and Brian D. Smith, *Negotiating Loan Transactions*, in COMMERCIAL REAL ESTATE TRANSACTIONS HANDBOOK 9–40(Mark A. Senn ed., 4th ed. 2009).

[14] Thompson, *supra* note 13, at 9–40.

the mortgaged property (a *due on encumbrance clause*). The following are typical examples of those two clauses.

> *Due on Sale.* Borrower will not sell, transfer, or convey any part of the mortgaged property, without the prior written consent of Lender.

> *Due on Encumbrance.* Borrower will not mortgage, encumber, pledge, or grant a security interest in any part of the mortgaged property, without the prior written consent of Lender.

Both of these clauses are intended to preclude the borrower from taking an action that could adversely affect the security of the lender's collateral position under the permanent loan. While the lender's primary concern when making a permanent loan is the value of the mortgaged property, the lender is also focused on the business acumen and financial capacity of the borrower. A due on sale clause is designed to insulate the lender from the risk of a change in the identity of the borrower.

The lender includes a due on encumbrance clause in the permanent loan documents to combat its fear that the placement of additional debt on the property could render the project financially unsustainable and, hence, increase the likelihood of a payment default by the borrower. A due on encumbrance clause also works to allay the permanent lender's concern that the introduction of another lender to the project's capital stack might impede the permanent lender's exercise of its legal rights and remedies in the event of a borrower default.[15]

Due on sale and encumbrance clauses are anathema to the borrower because those clauses limit the borrower's flexibility to preserve and enhance the value of its project by responding to changes in market conditions. While a borrower is seldom successful in having due on sale and due on encumbrance clauses deleted in their entirety from the permanent loan documents, a borrower is often able to negotiate limited exceptions to the blanket prohibitions contained in such clauses. The following is a summary of several exceptions that a borrower might want to consider incorporating into the due on sale and due on encumbrance clauses.[16]

- *Due on Sale Exceptions:*
  - o   The sale of the mortgaged property to a "qualified buyer" (meaning a buyer who meets pre-negotiated parameters

---

[15] *See* Alan Wayte, *Selected Issues in the Negotiation of Real Estate Financing Documents*, in ALI-ABA COURSE OF STUDY MATERIALS, COMMERCIAL REAL ESTATE FINANCING: STRATEGIES FOR CHANGING MARKETS AND UNCERTAIN TIMES, Course No. SP–008, 1, 7 (January 2009),; and Thompson, *supra* note 13, at 9–76.

[16] *See generally* Charles L. Edwards, *Commercial Mortgage Loan Commitments: A Borrower's Perspective*, 8 PROBATE AND PROPERTY 28, 29–30 (August 1994); Patricia Frobes and Frank Crance, *Anticipating the Future in Loan Documentation*, 18 No. 2 PRACTICAL REAL ESTATE LAWYER 41, 48–51 (March 2002); and Thompson, *supra* note 13, at 9–70 through 9–72

concerning the buyer's financial condition and business experience);

o   The transfer of the mortgaged property to an affiliate of the borrower;

o   The borrower's substitution of collateral for the mortgaged property as long as the substituted collateral has an appraised value equal to or greater than the mortgaged property and the substituted collateral satisfies other lender-imposed performance tests (for example, a loan-to-value ratio, a debt service coverage test, and a debt yield standard);

o   The transfer of equity interests in the borrower as long as control of the borrower is not changed as a result of such transfers;

o   The lease of space in the mortgaged property to tenants in accordance with pre-determined standards as to the form and content of the leases and the creditworthiness of the tenants;

o   The grant of easements required to operate the mortgaged property; and

o   The sale of vacant land that is not needed to operate the mortgaged property as long as the borrower pays the lender a negotiated release price (for example, $100,000 per acre).

• ***Due on Encumbrance Exceptions:***

o   Secondary mortgage financing designed to refurbish, expand, or reposition the mortgaged property as long as stipulated loan-to-value and debt service coverage ratios are met for the combined loans;

o   Mezzanine financing in which equity interests in the borrower (but not a direct interest in the mortgaged property) are pledged as security to the mezzanine lender (see pages 613–615 for a further discussion of mezzanine financing); and

o   Equipment leasing and financing that is required to permit the operation of the mortgaged property in the ordinary course of the borrower's business.

If the permanent lender agrees to any of the above exceptions, it is likely to insist that the borrower may rely on such exceptions only if (1) the borrower is not in default in the performance of any of its loan obligations, and (2) the junior lender enters into an intercreditor agreement with the permanent lender that expressly subordinates the interests of the junior lender in the mortgaged property to those of the permanent lender.

4. Securitized Loans (CMBS)

A *securitized loan* is a permanent mortgage loan that is pooled with other similar mortgage loans, with interests in the combined mortgage pool then being sold to third party investors. The theory behind securitized loans (also referred to as *commercial mortgage backed securities* or *CMBS*) is summarized in the following excerpt from a brochure jointly published by the Commercial Mortgage Securities Association and the Mortgage Bankers Association.

> CMBS has become an attractive capital source for commercial mortgage lending because the bonds backed by a pool of loans are generally worth more than the sum of the value of the whole loans. The enhanced liquidity and structure of CMBS attracts a broader range of investors to the commercial mortgage market. This value creation effect allows loans intended for securitization to be aggressively priced, benefitting borrowers.[17]

The use of securitized loans for commercial real estate experienced dramatic growth in the early and mid-2000s. At its peak in 2007, the CMBS industry packaged over $230 billion of securitized commercial real estate loans in the U.S. The CMBS market collapsed in 2008 (along with the rest of the United States economy), with the CMBS loan volume falling to only $2.9 billion in 2009. The CMBS market has made a measured recovery in recent years, with the deal volume for 2016 coming in right around $70 billion.[18]

However, the CMBS market faces uncertainty in the coming years due to the adoption by the SEC and other federal agencies of a *Credit Risk Retention Rule* that requires the sponsor of a CMBS issuance to keep "skin the game" by retaining at least 5% of the credit risk of the securitized loans.[19] Prior to the adoption of the Credit Risk Retention Rule, lenders could transfer 100% of the risk associated with potential defaults under the securitized loans to the purchasers of the CMBS investments. Because a lender of a securitized loan bore no risk of a default on the loan, the natural tendency of the lender was to relax its underwriting standards and make a loan to any borrower who was willing to pay the lender a fee, regardless whether the prospective borrower had the financial wherewithal to repay

---

[17] COMMERCIAL MORTGAGE SECURITIES ASSOCIATION AND MORTGAGE BANKERS ASSOCIATION, BORROWER GUIDE TO CMBS 2 (2004).

[18] *See* Ellen M. Goodwin, *Debt Markets—Dead, Delayed or Dynamic? Developments in Mezzanine and CMBS Finance in 2016 and the Impact of New Regulatory Requirements on the Capital Markets Generally,* in ACREL PAPERS, Tab 3 (Fall 2016); and Joseph P. Forte, *Disruption in the Capital Markets: What Happened,* in ACREL PAPERS, TAB 1 (Spring 2008).

[19] *See* Credit Risk Retention, 79 Fed. Reg. 77.601 (December 24, 2014).

the loan. The absence of the lender's continuing "skin in the game" on CMBS packages was a direct contributing factor to the financial collapse embodied in the Great Recession of 2008 and a circumstance that Congress sought to remedy when it passed the Dodd-Frank Wall Street Reform and Consumer Protection Act in 2010[20] that, among other things, authorized the SEC and other federal agencies to promulgate what eventually became the Credit Risk Retention Rule.

The Credit Risk Retention rule became effective on December 24, 2016 (Merry Christmas to all you CMBS sponsors). It is not knowable at this point what impact the Credit Risk Retention Rule will have on the CMBS market. While the rule exempts CMBS issuances where all the securitized loans are *qualified commercial real estate loans (QCREs)*, it is doubtful whether many CMBS deals will take advantage of the QCRE exemption due to the extremely conservative underwriting standards that a securitized loan must met to qualify for that exemption—for example, a debt service coverage ratio of at least 1.5 and more often 1.7; a loan-to-value ratio of no more than 65%; a minimum term of ten years; a maximum amortization period of 25 years; and a fixed rate of interest. While the Credit Risk Retention Rule may result in a slow-down in the volume of CMBS deals (at least in the short-term), that rule is neither designed nor expected to result in the long-term marginalization of CMBS as an important financing tool for the commercial real estate industry.[21]

5.   Unique Features of a Securitized Loan

While a full discussion of securitized loans is beyond the scope of this chapter, it is important to take note of several ways in which a securitized loan differs from the more traditional portfolio loan.

- *Standardized Documentation*—CMBS issuers (as well as rating agencies like Moody's that rate the credit of the CMBS issuances) insist on the consistent use of standard documents to evidence each mortgage loan included in their mortgage pools. As a result, the originators of securitized loans are much less likely to respond favorably to borrower requests for changes to the permanent loan documents.

- *Bankruptcy Remote Borrowing Entity*—In order to lessen the risk that a borrower could file for bankruptcy for reasons unrelated to the operation of the mortgaged property, a securitized loan customarily requires the borrower to be a bankruptcy remote entity.[22] A *bankruptcy remote entity* is

---

[20]   Dodd-Frank Wall Street Reform and Consumer Protection Act, Pub. L. No. 111–203, 124 Stat. 1376 (2010).

[21]   *See* Goodwin, *supra* note 18, at 15.

[22]   *See generally* Eric M. Schiller, *Know Your Financing Sources: Difference in Loan Documentation and Closing Requirements*, in ALI-ABA COURSE OF STUDY MATERIALS,

a single purpose entity (usually an LLC) that is prohibited from having any assets or liabilities other than those directly related to the ownership and operation of the mortgaged property (see page 377 for a discussion of bankruptcy remote entities in the context of construction loans). The borrowing entity also is required to make a series of so-called *separateness covenants* that are designed to insure that the borrower is operated independently of any of its affiliated entities. Finally, most CMBS issuers and rating agencies require that the borrower appoint an independent director approved by the lender, whose consent is required prior to the borrower's institution of a bankruptcy proceeding.[23] It should be noted that the requirement that the borrower be a bankruptcy remote entity underscores the importance to the CMBS issuer that of a creditworthy entity standing behind the nonrecourse carveouts contained in the underlying loans.

• *Defeasance*—In order to preserve the consistency and predictability of the yield to CMBS investors, each securitized loan typically requires a prepayment lock-out period of at least two years. After the expiration of the lock-out period, the borrower still may not prepay the loan (either at par or accompanied by a prepayment penalty). The borrower may, however, obtain a release of the mortgage on its project through a *defeasance* of its loan.[24] Defeasance entails the borrower's posting of Treasury instruments in an amount sufficient to fund all principal and interest payments when and as they become due under the securitized loan. From the borrower's perspective, defeasance is a more costly and complex alternative to the borrower's right to prepay the loan with a yield maintenance penalty—but an alternative that the borrower needs if it opts to obtain financing through a securitized loan.

• *Lack of Lender Relationship*—Unlike a portfolio loan that is originated and held by a single lender, a securitized loan quickly becomes co-mingled with a pool of other mortgages, all of which are administered by a loan servicing agent who has no affiliation with the originator of the borrower's loan. The borrower's lack of a direct relationship with the loan

---

COMMERCIAL REAL ESTATE FINANCING: STRATEGIES FOR CHANGING MARKETS AND UNCERTAIN TIMES, Course No. SP008, 111, 119–120 (January 2009); Portia Owen Morrison and Peter B. Ross, *Financial Covenants and Bankruptcy Remote Structures in Real Estate Loan Transactions with Forms*, 17 No. 1 PRACTICAL REAL ESTATE LAWYER 7 (January 2001).

[23] *See* Thompson, *supra* note 13, at 9–134.

[24] *See generally* John C. Murray, *Defeasance Provisions in Securitized-Loan Documents*, in ACREL PAPERS 401 (March 2004); and Thompson, *supra* note 13, at 9–136.

servicer makes it much more difficult for the borrower to negotiate loan modifications or waivers after the loan is first funded—a definite disadvantage for most commercial borrowers.

For the above reasons, the securitized loan model may not be a fit for every real estate borrower. A borrower who values flexibility and creativity in the structuring and administration of its permanent loan might want to stay away from a securitized loan and instead stick with a traditional portfolio loan made by a single financial institution.

Practice Tip #12-2: Mezzanine Debt

A real estate developer's election to effect an interim exit strategy by refinancing its existing mortgage loan with a permanent mortgage loan presupposes that the developer is able to secure a permanent loan in an amount sufficient to fully retire the existing debt. If the underwriting practices then prevailing in the permanent loan market (for example, loan-to-value, debt service coverage, and debt yield restrictions) preclude the developer from obtaining a permanent loan to fully pay off its underlying project debt on the date of its maturity, then the developer has three basic choices:

1. *It can sell the project and hope that the sales proceeds are sufficient to fully retire the existing project debt;*

2. *It can fund the "debt gap" (that is the excess of the unpaid balance of the existing project loan over the principal amount of the new permanent loan) by contributing additional equity to the project (either with its own funds or with funds from the coffers of an outside institutional investor); or*

3. *It can fund the debt gap by getting a loan that is subordinate to the new permanent mortgage loan (either a second mortgage loan or, more likely, a mezzanine loan.*

As noted earlier in this chapter, a permanent lender is typically loath to permit its borrower to place a second mortgage on the real property that is the subject of the permanent lender's first mortgage. For that reason, if the developer chooses (or is forced to choose) to fund the its debt gap with debt and not equity, then the developer usually must do so with a loan that is not collateralized with a mortgage on the developer's project—enter the mezzanine loan.

*A **mezzanine loan** is a funding vehicle that is part debt and part equity. The key feature that distinguishes a mezzanine loan from other project financings is that a mezzanine loan is secured by a pledge of the* *equity interests in the entity that owns the real estate project. The mezzanine lender stands in the shoes of the equity owners and, hence, the mezzanine lender's interest in the project's cash flow is subordinate to the first mortgage lender's interest in that cash flow—because all the equity owners have to pledge to the mezzanine lender is the equity owners' interests in the "leftover cash flow" (see discussion of the competing interests of the debt and equity providers in Chapter 3—What the Real Estate Lawyer Needs to Know About Project Economics, at pages 57–60). For that reason, the mezzanine lender's primary remedy for a borrower's loan default is to foreclose on the owners' equity interests and take over control of the project entity.*

The primary attraction of a mezzanine loan is that the borrower can fund its debt gap with debt dollars instead of with more costly equity dollars. Many permanent lenders permit a borrower to secure a mezzanine loan as long as the mezzanine lender enters into an intercreditor agreement with the permanent lender that clarifies the respective interests of the permanent lender and the mezzanine lender following a borrower loan default under either the permanent loan or the mezzanine loan.[25] The permanent lender's primary objective in crafting the terms of the intercreditor agreement is to eliminate any obstacles or delays that the permanent lender might encounter when exercising its remedies under the permanent loan. The permanent lender also wants to make sure that the mezzanine lender (or its transferee) is a creditworthy and experienced entity that is capable of taking over control of the project and preserving the project's value in the event of the borrower's default under the mezzanine loan. Finally, the permanent lender will seek to condition the mezzanine lender's ability to take over control of the project entity on the mezzanine lender's provision of a creditworthy substitute guarantor on the permanent loan's nonrecourse carveouts.[26]

Because the mezzanine lender has a higher risk of repayment than the traditional permanent lender, the mezzanine lender requires a higher return on its debt than does a permanent lender. However, while mezzanine debt is pricy compared to permanent debt, it is still cheaper to the borrower than the type of preferred equity brought to the dance by an institutional investor. Most borrowers facing a debt gap prefer to close that gap, if possible, with a mezzanine loan and not additional equity from an outside equity investor.

Mezzanine loans are likely to become an important part of the developer's funding plans in the coming years as developers attempt to refinance permanent and CMBS loans funded during the years leading up

---

[25] *See* Richard Goldberg, *Mezzanine Loan Intercreditor Agreement (Sample)*, in ALI-CLE COURSE OF STUDY MATERIALS: MODERN REAL ESTATE TRANSACTIONS, Course No. SY006 935 (August 2016).

[26] *See generally,* Goodwin, *supra* note 18; and Marianne Ajemian, *Are Mezzanine Loans Really the Lesser of Two Evils?*, 31 No. 3 PRACTICAL REAL ESTATE LAWYER 35 (May 2015).

to the Great Recession of 2008. It is estimated that over $200 billion of commercial real estate debt will mature in 2017 alone.[27] Because the underwriting standards used by lenders pre-2008 were so lax compared to the underwriting standards now prevailing in the debt markets, the borrowers under many of those pre-2008 loans will be facing a significant debt gap that must be funded in one of the three ways mentioned at the outset of this Practice Tip—that is, either by selling the project, putting in new equity dollars, or securing a mezzanine loan. For the borrower who wants to continue to hold a project for an extended period of time (especially if the borrower has limited internal funding capabilities), mezzanine debt will be a very attractive option.

B. THE EQUITY PLAY

The prior section centered on the developer's use of debt (in the form of a permanent loan) to facilitate its decision to retain ownership of its project after stabilization. A developer can also make an equity play during Stage 8 by contributing the stabilized project to a joint venture formed with one or more institutional investors. The institutional investors make a cash contribution to the venture in an amount sufficient to retire the construction loan (if no permanent loan is secured) or in a lesser amount (if a permanent loan is part of the developer's interim exit strategy). The developer retains an ongoing interest in the project's cash flow measured by both the developer's relative capital split and, hopefully, a generous promoted profit split (see the discussion of capital and profit splits in *Chapter 7—Stage 3: Forming and Capitalizing the Project Entity*, at pages 259–260).

The developer's primary objective when implementing an equity play is to extract cash to return its equity in the stabilized project. For this purpose, the developer's "equity" consists of two separate components— (1) its actual cash contribution to the project (the 10–30% of the project development costs that were not funded under the construction loan), and (2) the developer's interest in the incremental value of the project over and above its development costs. The following example illustrates how a developer might extract its equity in the project by entering into a joint venture with an institutional investor.

Example 12-2: Developer constructs an office building at a total cost of $8 million, $6 million of which is funded with the proceeds of a construction loan and $2 million of which is funded by equity contributions made by Developer. The office building is fully leased and has a fair market value of $10 million. Developer

---

[27] *See* Thomas A. Hauser, *Debt Markets—Dead, Delayed or Dynamic: Current Factors Influencing Real Estate Finance,* in ACREL PAPERS, Tab 2, 1–2 (Fall 2016).

contributes the office building to LLC, a limited liability company in which Developer and Equity Investor are the sole members. Equity Investor makes a cash contribution to LLC of $9 million, $6 million of which is used to repay the construction loan and $3 million of which is distributed to Developer as a partial return of its equity in the project. Developer and Equity Investor agree to split all LLC cash flow 90% to Equity Investor and 10% to Developer.

Under the above example, Developer accomplishes its goal of retaining partial ownership of its project (its 10% membership interest in LLC), while at the same time putting $3 million in its pocket.

The next example shows how a developer can optimize its position by combining an equity play with the placement of a permanent loan on the stabilized project.

Example 12-3: Assume the same facts as Example 12-2, except that (1) LLC secures a nonrecourse permanent loan of $8 million to repay the construction debt, and (2) Equity Investor makes a cash contribution to LLC of $3 million, all of which is distributed to Developer as a partial return of its project equity. Developer and Equity Investor agree to split all LLC cash flow 75% to Equity Investor and 25% to Developer.

By introducing leverage as a component of its interim exit strategy, Developer increases its ongoing interest in the project's future cash flow from 10 to 25%, while still receiving a current payday of $3 million.

Developer's ultimate financial return on the above-described equity play is, of course, further dependent on the tax treatment afforded its $3 million cash distribution. The substance of the transaction described in Example 12-3 is that Developer has sold 75% of its interest in the project to Equity Investor for $3 million. If the equity play were to be treated as a sale for federal income tax purposes, then Developer would have a taxable gain of $1.5 million (the $3 million cash distribution, less Developer's $1.5 million cost basis in the 75% project interest it sold to Equity Investor). If taxed at the current capital gains rate of 20%, Developer's after-tax return would be reduced by $300,000 (the $1.5 million gain, multiplied by 20%). While a detailed discussion of the rules of Subchapter K of the Internal Revenue Code is well beyond the scope of this chapter, it is certainly worth mentioning that, under the right circumstances, a creative and diligent lawyer might be able to defer Developer's taxable gain on all or a substantial portion of the $3 million cash distribution.[28]

---

[28] See Blake D. Rubin, Andrea Macintosh Whiteway, and Jon G. Finkelstein, *Partnership Equity Extraction Techniques*, in ALI-ABA COURSE OF STUDY MATERIALS, CREATIVE TAX PLANNING FOR REAL ESTATE TRANSACTIONS, Course No. Cy004 1037 (September 2016).

An equity play of the type described above involves most of the same legal and business issues discussed previously in *Chapter 7—Stage 3: Forming and Capitalizing the Project Entity*. The following are some of the key issues involved in the formation of an equity joint venture to house the ownership of a stabilized commercial real estate project:

- The agreed value of the developer's capital contribution of its project to the owning entity;

- The preferred return payable on the investors' capital contributions;

- The promote or carried interest given to the developer;

- The allocation of decision-making control over the entity's operations;

- The fees, if any, payable to the developer; and

- The buy-sell and other negotiated exits available to the parties to end their relationship.

HIBC Case Study—An Interim Exit Strategy

The Pizzuti organization developed nine office projects in the Heathrow International Business Center. All nine of the projects produced above-market financial returns and were supported by a creditworthy roster of tenants. As such, the HIBC office projects were prime candidates for the execution of an interim exit strategy involving the placement of nonrecourse permanent debt to retire the construction debt that was then encumbering those projects.

However, Pizzuti had broader business concerns that weighed against the execution of a simple permanent debt strategy. The company had embarked on a development binge during the prior five years that had wholly exhausted its independent financial resources. In addition to the nine HIBC office buildings, Pizzuti had also developed and still owned 21 warehouses located in various cities throughout the Midwest, several suburban office buildings in Central Ohio, and a luxury condominium project in downtown Columbus. Moreover, Pizzuti believed (quite correctly) that its land holdings in Ohio, Florida, Indiana, and Illinois provided it with a golden opportunity to ramp up its development efforts even further in the upcoming years. For all those reasons, Pizzuti felt that it needed money—and a lot of it—in order to restore its liquidity and position the company to take advantage of future development opportunities.

For a period of approximately seven years, Pizzuti had funded the equity required for its development projects through a combination of its own cash resources and those provided by the principals of Newport Partners. However, Pizzuti's liquidity was largely depleted and Newport's capital was both limited in amount and more expensive than the equity typically provided by institutional investors (largely because of the lack of a developer promote in Pizzuti's favor—see discussion of this point at pages 250–251).

Pizzuti's challenge, therefore, was to devise an interim exit strategy that would facilitate its achievement of both the following objectives:

- *The repatriation to the organization of a significant portion of the equity it had previously committed to its development projects; and*

- *The securing of a readily available capital source for its future development efforts that was both "cheaper" and "deeper" than that available from Newport Partners.*

The interim exit strategy identified and then executed by Pizzuti's senior financial and legal team centered on the equity participation of Nationwide Realty Investors, Ltd., the real estate arm of Nationwide Mutual Insurance Company ("NRI"), in both Pizzuti's existing real estate assets and its future development projects. Pizzuti used its grant to NRI of an equity interest in Pizzuti's portfolio of stabilized real estate projects as a carrot to entice NRI to agree to contribute capital on the front-side of future development projects—a proposition that the typical risk-averse institutional investor would normally be reluctant to embrace.

NRI and Pizzuti agreed to form a new joint venture entity ("Pizzuti Properties LLC") to own Pizzuti's existing real estate portfolio and all its future development projects. NRI agreed in principal that it would (1) acquire an approximately 60% equity interest in Pizzuti's portfolio of Florida office and Ohio warehouse projects (an equity investment that would fund a return of equity to Pizzuti well into eight figures) and (2) provide 90% of the capital required for Pizzuti's future development projects in Columbus, Orlando, Indianapolis and Chicago. The final piece of the financial puzzle was provided by NRI's agreement to give Pizzuti and its senior executives a 5% promoted profits interest in the existing portfolio and a 35% promote on all new development projects.

One obstacle remained to Pizzuti's grand plan to solve all of its problems by entering into a new joint venture with NRI. Newport Partners owned a 25% equity interest in all of Pizzuti's warehouse projects and a 50% equity interest in the nine HIBC office buildings and the approximately 140 acres of undeveloped HIBC land—and Newport had no intention of consenting to the roll-up of its equity interests into the new Pizzuti-NRI entity. Newport's intransigence left Pizzuti with no choice but to negotiate what proved to be a very expensive exit from its relationship with Newport. After lengthy and occasionally hostile negotiations, Pizzuti and Newport agreed to structure a termination of their partnership relationship along the following lines—(1) the newly-formed Pizzuti-NRI would purchase Newport's 25% interest in Pizzuti's warehouse properties, (2) Pizzuti (acting alone and not in concert with NRI) would purchase Newport's 50% interest in the undeveloped HIBC land, (3) Pizzuti (but not Newport) would contribute its 50% interest in the HIBC office buildings to the new Pizzuti-NRI entity, and (4) Pizzuti would immediately retain a broker to try to sell the nine HIBC office buildings that would then be owned jointly by Pizzuti Properties LLC and Newport Partners.

The marketing for sale of the nine HIBC buildings was especially galling to Pizzuti because it viewed the HIBC office buildings as perfect candidates for a long-term hold by the Pizzuti-NRI venture. While the negotiated exit deal struck with Newport was far from ideal, Pizzuti believed that the consummation of that deal was a sacrifice worth making to serve its broader business goals of establishing a long-term relationship with a deep-pocketed and reputable investor like NRI. As noted later in this chapter (see HIBC Case Study—The Sale of the Project at pages 632–633), Pizzuti and NRI were later able to overcome this particularly distasteful component of the negotiated deal with Newport by getting Newport to agree to sell most of its interests in the HIBC buildings to the newly-formed Pizzuti-NRI joint venture.

IV. STAGE 9: OPERATING THE PROJECT

Once the developer makes the decision to execute an interim strategy to further its long-term ownership of an interest in a development project, its attention necessarily turns to Stage 9—the operation of the project. The developer's business objectives during Stage 9 are to:

- Keep the project full with tenants paying rents at or above the pro forma rents for the project;

- Hold the project expenses at or below budget;

- Keep its two customers happy—that is, its tenants and equity investors; and

- Maintain the project in good condition and order of repair.

The developer typically delegates the achievement of these objectives to two real estate professionals—specifically, a licensed real estate broker as to the first of the listed objectives and a property manager as to the remaining three objectives. These professional positions can be staffed either with in-house personnel or by the hiring of independent real estate firms. The issues that must be addressed by the real estate development lawyer when papering the owning entity's relationship with the broker and the property manager are the same regardless whether those roles are filled by affiliates of the developer or independent third parties—the only difference is the identity of the person who gets to keep the fees paid for the provision of those services.

A. LEASING BROKER AGREEMENT

A *listing broker* is an important player in any development project. The broker is typically tasked with primary responsibility for finding tenants to fill the developer's building and later securing replacements for those tenants that opt to relocate to another building. Good leasing brokers are indispensable to the leasing process due to their superior knowledge of both the space that is available for lease in a particular market and the potential users that might be interested in leasing that space.

The developer's relationship with a leasing broker can be structured in one of three ways—as (1) an *open listing*, (2) an *exclusive agency,* or (3) an *exclusive listing*. In an open listing, the developer agrees to pay a commission to any broker in the community who actually procures a tenant for its building. In an exclusive agency, the developer selects a particular broker to lease space in its building and agrees to pay the selected broker a commission on any lease that is signed for the building unless the developer, without the assistance of any other broker, is the procuring cause of the signed lease. Finally, an exclusive listing obligates the developer to pay the broker a commission on any lease even if that lease is procured directly by the developer or another broker.

Most good brokers refuse to undertake the leasing of space in a developer's building unless they receive the full protection afforded by an exclusive listing. The following are the key provisions that should be addressed in an exclusive listing agreement entered into by a developer and a commercial leasing broker.[29]

- *Term of Engagement*—The term of an exclusive listing agreement typically runs between three to 24 months. The broker wants a term that is long enough to permit it to work its contacts in the community and maximize its ability to earn commissions. The developer, on the other hand, wishes to keep the term as short as possible so that it can, if necessary, replace an ineffective broker.

---

[29] *See generally* John S. Hollyfield, *Property Management and Listing Brokerage Agreements: Part Two*, 1 PROBATE AND PROPERTY 55 (October 1987); GEORGE LEFCOE, REAL ESTATE TRANSACTIONS, FINANCE AND DEVELOPMENT 40–42 (6th ed. 2009); Bruce B. May, *Real Estate Brokers: Agreements and Conduct*, in COMMERCIAL REAL ESTATE TRANSACTIONS HANDBOOK 3–18 through 3–44 and 3–79 through 3–87; and Pearl A. Zager, *Brokerage Issues*, in PLI COURSE HANDBOOK, NEGOTIATING COMMERCIAL LEASE: HOW OWNERS AND CORPORATE OCCUPANTS CAN AVOID COSTLY ERRORS, Course No. 8608, 461, 470 (May 2006).

- *Definition of Commissionable Event*—Under common law, the general rule is that a broker is entitled to a commission if it procures a tenant who is "ready, willing, and able" to lease space in the developer's building even if a lease is never signed or the tenant never takes occupancy of the space.[30] Most developers seek to circumvent the operation of this common law rule by specifically stating in the exclusive leasing agreement that the broker is not entitled to any commission unless the developer and the tenant sign a fully binding lease. A collateral issue is whether the broker is entitled to a commission for the tenant's renewal or extension of its lease, with the broker, quite predictably, taking the position that a renewal or extension is a commissionable event and the developer adopting a totally contrary stance.

- *Exclusions*—If the developer has identified or contacted a prospective tenant prior to the execution of its listing agreement with the broker, the developer should specifically exclude a lease with that prospective tenant from the list of transactions on which the broker is entitled to a commission.

- *Commission for Post-Termination Leases*—The broker wants to make sure that its entitlement to a commission is protected if the landlord signs a lease after the expiration of the term of the listing agreement with a tenant introduced to the landlord by the broker during the term of the listing. If a clause affording the broker that protection is not inserted into the listing agreement, then the developer might be able to wholly avoid its commission obligation by simply deferring the date of its execution of the lease to a date that is beyond the last day of the listing term. The developer wants to limit the scope of its obligation to pay a post-termination commission to leases signed within a relatively short period of time following the expiration of the listing agreement (for example, 60 days) and then only to leases signed with tenant prospects "registered" by the broker before the expiration of the term of the listing agreement. The "registered" tenants should include only those tenants specifically noted on a written list of prospective users to whom the broker showed the property and made a marketing presentation during the term of the listing agreement. If the listing agreement fails to so limit the identity of the "registered" tenants, then the

---

[30] *See generally* May, *supra* note 29 at 3–60 through 3–64; and Zager, *supra* note 29, at 472–474. *But see* Ellsworth Dobbs, Inc. v. Johnson, 236 A.2d 843 (N.J. 1967), where the New Jersey Supreme Court rejected the majority rule and held that a broker is not entitled to a sales commission unless the sale is actually consummated.

broker will be sorely tempted to "register the phone book" by listing every conceivable user for the space even though the broker may not have had any contact whatsoever with the user during the term of the listing agreement.

• *Amount of Commission*—The commission payable to a commercial leasing broker is usually stated as a fixed percentage of the rent payable by the tenant during the lease term. The commission percentage varies by market and product type. Leasing commissions are typically (although not always) calculated against the base rent payable by the tenant, expressly excluding any indexed base rent bumps, expense pass-through payments, or amortization of excess tenant improvement costs. The percentage used to calculate the amount of the commission, if any, payable for a renewal or extension term is almost always less than the percentage used to calculate the commission for the initial lease term.

• *Timing of Payment of Commission*—The broker believes that its job is done and that it should be paid the entirety of its commission upon the tenant's execution of its lease. A provision to that effect in the exclusive listing agreement places the entire risk of a tenant default on the landlord. The landlord often tries to mitigate its exposure to the risk of a tenant default by providing that a portion of the leasing commission (typically 50%) is deferred until at least the date on which the tenant assumes occupancy of the leased space and begins paying rent.

• *Duties of the Broker*—Best practice calls for the listing agreement to specifically recite what the broker must do as part of its efforts to market the developer's property. By way of example, the property owner might want to include in the listing agreement specific requirements that: the broker advertise the property as being "for lease" in a specific business journal of wide circulation in the community in which the developer's building is located; list the developer's building in a multiple listing service; attend periodic marketing meetings with the developer's principals; provide regular written reports to the developer identifying the prospective tenants to whom the broker has shown the property or made a marketing presentation; and assign specific individual leasing agents to market the developer's building. The listing agreement must also specifically require the broker to cooperate with other brokers in the market and to pay all commissions that are payable to any *cooperating broker* involved in the transaction. If the listing agreement fails to place an obligation on the listing broker to pay all commissions owed to cooperating brokers, then the developer might find itself in the extremely unenviable position of owing two commissions on the same lease transaction—that is, a full commission to its listing broker and an additional commission to the cooperating broker who served as the procuring cause for the tenant's lease.

- **Duties of the Owner**—Finally, the exclusive listing agreement should recite exactly what the property owner is required to do to assist the broker in its efforts to procure tenants for the owner's building. The broker generally requires the owner to refer to the broker all prospective tenants that contact the owner about the available space. The owner should also be required to provide the broker with all written materials needed by the broker to market the space, (including, floor plans, building photographs, and a standard lease form) and to provide the broker with rent quotes and other approved parameters for the leasing of the space.

A copy of a pro-landlord Exclusive Listing Agreement is included in the *Document Appendix* as Document #7, at pages 749–752.

Practice Tip #12-3: The Lawyer's Relationship with the Broker

The relationship between the landlord's lawyer and its leasing broker is frequently characterized by terms such as "antagonistic" and "distrustful." The lawyer views the broker as nothing more than a matchmaker who cares only about making the deal happen so that the broker can get paid, and who cares nothing at all about whether the terms of the deal actually serve the developer's business interests. The lawyer often bemoans the fact that the broker is going to receive a crazy high commission for doing nothing other than making a phone call to a prospective tenant and then turning all the dirty work over to the developer's lawyer. The broker, on the other hand, frequently views the lawyer as a deal killer whose sole motivation is to raise a bunch of legal issues that have nothing to do with the economics of the deal and everything to do with costing the broker a hard-earned commission.

Unfortunately, the genesis of the above stereotypes of both the real estate development lawyer and the leasing broker is based on reality. During my years of practice, I noted that lawyers (regrettably, including me) and brokers often butt heads for no apparent reason. Instead of acting as an efficient team to consummate a quick and favorable lease transaction, the lawyer and the broker often spend an inordinate amount of time covering the same ground in different and frequently contradictory ways and then blaming the other if the deal falters or eventually blows up.

I tried to overcome the natural bias against brokers that is inbred in real estate lawyers by following three simple rules.

- ***Rule #1—Recognize the value that the broker brings to the deal.*** *The truth is that the value added to the deal by the broker's procurement of a tenant is much greater than the value added by the lawyer's negotiation of a pluperfect lease document. That is undoubtedly why the developer is happy to pay the broker a six figure commission, but consistently grouses about paying the lawyer a four figure fee.*

- ***Rule #2—Establish sensible ground rules for the roles to be played by the lawyer and the broker.*** *The broker and the lawyer should allocate responsibility for the lease transaction by acknowledging what they do best and what they do not do well at all. As such, the broker should be the person who keeps things together by taking primary responsibility for schmoozing the tenant and helping the developer maintain a cooperative (and not contentious) relationship with the tenant. The lawyer should be the person who gets the deal done by serving in the role of the primary negotiator of the lease document. If the lawyer and the broker embrace their separate roles, the lease transaction will proceed much more smoothly than if each of them tries to be all things to all people.*

- ***Build a reputation as a deal maker and not a deal killer.*** *If the broker knows that the lawyer is a deal maker, the broker will be much more likely to adopt the limited negotiating role noted in Rule #2 and stay out of the lawyer's way (which I have found is the best way to get the deal done).*

B. PROPERTY MANAGEMENT AGREEMENT

The ***property manager*** is the person charged with operating the developer's project once the project achieves stabilization. It is the property manager's job to make sure that the project is properly maintained, the rent is collected, and the bills are paid. While the property manager was once viewed as little more than a custodian and toilet cleaner, that is no longer the case. Developers and institutional investors are now acutely aware of the positive impact that a professional property manager can have on the financial viability of a stabilized commercial real estate project.

The need for quality property management has been heightened by the trend toward the ownership of stabilized real estate projects by financial institutions that have no operating presence whatsoever in the community where the project is located. The absentee institutional owner has no choice but to delegate responsibility for the operation of its project to a reputable, independent property manager. National firms such as CBRE, Cushman & Wakefield, and Jones Lang LaSalle all have strong property management divisions that are responsible for managing millions of square feet of commercial space throughout the United States.

Regardless whether a project is being managed by an affiliate of the developer or by a national property management company, the property management agreement entered into by the property owner should address all the following considerations.[31]

- *Status and Authority of Property Manager*—Most property management agreements contain a clear statement that the property manager is an independent contractor and not an agent of the property owner. As such, the property manager may act on the owner's behalf only to the extent it is expressly authorized to do so under the specific terms of the management agreement.

- *Duties of Property Manager*—The property manager is charged with responsibility for managing, maintaining, repairing, and operating the owner's project. The specific duties delegated by the owner to the property manager vary widely based on project location and type and the business philosophy of the person that owns the project. Among other tasks, the property manager may be assigned responsibility for entering into all service contracts related to the day-to-day operation of the project (for example, snow removal and window washing agreements); supervising the making of all required repairs and capital improvements (including tenant improvements); securing all requisite insurance policies; complying with applicable laws affecting the project's operation; and collecting all rents and otherwise administering and enforcing the provisions of the project leases. It is essential that the property management agreement specifically describe the nature, scope, and performance standards for all the services to be provided by the property manager.

---

[31] *See* Earl L. Segal and Michael A. Segal, *Dissecting the Commercial Property Management Agreement (with Checklist)*, 20 No. 1 PRACTICAL REAL ESTATE LAWYER 31 (January 2004); and John S. Hollyfield, *Property Management and Listing Brokerage Agreements: Part One*, 1 PROBATE AND PROPERTY 24, 25 (August 1987).

- *Compensation*—The property manager's fee is typically expressed as a percentage of the rents collected under the project leases (for example, 3% of collected rents). The property management agreement should specifically define all payments that are intended to be included within the definition of "rents"—for example, just base rent or all tenant receipts (including indexed rent bumps, expense pass-throughs, amortization of excess tenant improvement costs, parking charges, and late fees). The property manager is also frequently reimbursed for expenses it incurs in connection with its performance of the required services under the property management agreement. The categories of the manager's reimbursable expenses are often the subject of heated negotiations, with the owner taking the position that all such expenses should be subsumed within the percentage fee paid to the property manager and the property manager seeking to preserve its fee as a pure profit by passing through to the project owner all conceivable expenses, including the salaries paid to the property manager's on-site personnel and a portion of the manager's general administrative and overhead costs.

- *Budgets and Operating Statements*—The property manager is usually charged with responsibility for preparing an annual operating budget for the owner's approval. Once the operating budget is approved by the owner, the property manager is then authorized to incur and pay expenses in accordance with the approved budget. Any unbudgeted or excess expenses should, however, require fresh approval by the project owner. The property manager is also customarily required to furnish the project owner with periodic operating statements comparing the actual and budgeted financial results for the property.

- *Collection and Disbursement of Rents*—In most situations, the property manager is delegated responsibility for collecting all rents and other receipts from the project's tenants and depositing those receipts in an operating account maintained specifically for the owner's project. The property manager is usually empowered and directed to disburse funds from the operating account to pay those expenses that fall within the parameters established in the approved project budget (with the owner being required to fund any shortfalls between the project's collected receipts and the approved project expenses). Some project owners prohibit the property manager from paying its property management fees out of the operating account (based on a fear that the property manager may pay its fees before paying other more pressing project expenses).

- *Key Employees*—The owner may want the agreement to require the property management company to assign a specific person as its on-site property manager. If the named employee is no longer assigned to the project, the owner should reserve the right to terminate the property management agreement.

- *Term of Agreement*—From the owner's perspective, the ideal property management agreement is one that provides that it may be terminated by the owner on 30 days (or less) notice. The property manager wants the guaranteed term of its engagement to be as long as possible (at least a year or two) so that it has sufficient time to recover its start-up costs and maximize the profitability of its contract. The initial stated term of the agreement usually falls somewhere between those two extremes, with the agreement being automatically renewed for a like term unless either party to the agreement specifically opts to cancel the term by delivering a written cancellation notice to the other party prior to the expiration of the then existing term of the property management agreement.

A copy of a fairly balanced property management agreement is included in the *Document Appendix* as Document #8, at pages 753–757.

V. STAGE 10: SELLING THE PROJECT

Stage 10 is, alas, the end of the road for the developer's involvement in the development of a real estate project. The developer has decided, based upon the status of its project, the developer's personal financial condition, and the state of the overall economy, that it is time to sell the project. The developer's business objective at this stage is quite simple—it wants to maximize its profit by choosing the optimal time to sell the project.

A. TIMING THE SALE

The developer's selection of the right time to sell the project is a major contributing factor to the determination of the project's ultimate profitability. The following example illustrates how accelerating or deferring the sale of a project can affect the developer's bottom line.

Example 12-4: It is the spring of 2007 and the Developer has just leased the last available space in its office building. Developer knows that the sales market is hot (with capitalization rates hovering in the 5–6% range for Class A office projects), but is confident that things will only get better in the coming years (and certainly will not get worse). As a result, Developer makes a decision to defer the sale of its project for at least a couple of years and exercises its right to extend the maturity date of its mortgage loan until the spring of 2010. Now fast forward to the spring of 2010 when Developer's loan is due. Unfortunately for Developer, the unimaginable has come true in the wake of the financial crisis of 2008—that is, things really have gotten worse, with the prevailing capitalization rates for the sale of office buildings topping out at 8–9%. The following chart illustrates the financial impact to the developer of its decision to postpone selling its project until 2010.

Assumptions	Sale in 2007	Sale in 2010
Project Cost	$15 million	$15 million
Annual NOI	$1.5 million	$1.5 million
Capitalization Rate	6%	9%
Sales Price	$25 million	$16.67 million
Profit on Sale	$10 million	$1.67 million

The end result of Developer's decision to delay the sale of its project was a reduction in its profit on sale of $8.33 million—even though the project was producing the exact same NOI in 2010 as it was in 2007.

Practice Tip #12-4: Don't Mess with the Developer's Timing

Example 12-4 clearly points out the danger of the developer mistiming the market. But what does that mean for the developer's lawyer? The answer is that a real estate development lawyer should strive to craft legal documents that create sufficient flexibility for the developer to choose the optimal time to sell its project. A lawyer who acquiesces to an absolute lock-out period on the prepayment of a permanent loan, without advising the developer of the danger of doing so, might find that the last work the lawyer ever does for that developer is the closing of the permanent loan. The lawyer should always take into account the possibility of a future change in the real estate markets or in the financial condition or perspective of the developer and seek to infuse the developer's transactional documents with as many contractual exits as reasonably practicable. A permanent loan that includes a yield maintenance prepayment penalty throughout the loan term might, therefore, better serve the developer's interests than would a permanent loan with a three-year lock-out period and an unrestricted right to prepay the loan after the expiration of the lock-out period.

B. MAKING THE SALE HAPPEN

The sale of a stabilized development project involves many of the same legal issues that were addressed in *Chapter 5—Stage 1: Gaining Control of the Site.* The developer's view of those issues, however, takes on a decidedly different tack when the developer is the seller and not the buyer. For example, a developer who is selling a completed project wants to limit the scope and duration of the buyer's contingency and sell the project on an "as is" condition without any significant representations and warranties being made by the developer (just the opposite of the positions the developer took during Stage 1 of the development process).

In addition to switching sides of the negotiating table on those legal issues that are common to both the developer's initial purchase of the project site and its ultimate sale of the stabilized project, the real estate development lawyer must also address in the sales contract certain issues that are unique to the sale of improved real property. Those additional issues are triggered by the fact that the sale of a stabilized real estate project involves not just the sale of land and a building, but also the transfer of a living and breathing operating business.

The following are several unique issues that a real estate lawyer must consider when preparing and negotiating a contract for the sale of a stabilized commercial real estate project.

- *Sale of Personal Property*—The sale of a stabilized project typically involves the sale of two property components that are not part of the developer's initial land acquisition— specifically, the sale of (1) tangible personal property (for example, cleaning supplies, lobby furnishings, and window coverings), and (2) intangible personal property (for example, trade names, development rights, construction warranties, and occupancy permits). The buyer wants to use expansive language to describe the personal property it is buying (that is, all tangible and intangible personal property used in connection with the operation of the project), coupled with a specific listing of each known item of personal property that the buyer wants to acquire in connection with its purchase of the subject project (for example, the "Heathrow International Business Center" trade name or the Alexander Calder mobile hanging in the building lobby).

- **Assignment of Leases**—The sales contract should specifically list the tenant leases that are being assigned by the developer to the project buyer. Each lease should be identified by the name of the tenant, the date on which the lease was executed, and the location and size of the tenant's leased premises. The project leases are typically described in a rent roll prepared by the developer and attached to the sales contract as an exhibit. The sales contract should (1) require the developer to furnish the buyer with accurate and complete copies of all project leases, and (2) provide the buyer with a right to terminate the contract if its review of the leases disclose provisions that are inconsistent with the rent roll or are otherwise unacceptable to the buyer. The buyer is usually given a relatively short period of time to review and approve the project leases (for example, 30–60 days after the execution of the sales contract).

- **Loan Assumption**—The project buyer occasionally opts to assume the permanent loan that encumbers the project. If the permanent loan is going to be assumed by the buyer, then the sales contract should (1) specify the terms of the proposed assumption (including who will be charged with the obligation to pay any assumption fees charged by the permanent lender), and (2) condition the buyer's obligation to purchase the project upon the permanent lender's approval of the buyer's assumption of the loan.

- **Rent Prorations**—The sales contract typically contains detailed provisions concerning the manner in which rents (including both base and additional rent) will be prorated between the seller and the buyer. The principal questions that must be answered as part of the rent proration provisions are (1) who bears the risk that the tenants do not pay their rent for the month of closing (that is, will the rents be prorated based on "collected" or "accrued" rents), (2) how are any year-end, expense-pass-through reconciliations to be handled (that is, who is obligated to refund any tenant overpayment of expense payments and who is entitled to collect any tenant underpayments), and (3) who is obligated to collect any delinquent rent receivables that are outstanding as of the date of closing.[32]

- **Representations and Warranties on Physical Plant and Leases**—The developer resists making any representations

---

[32] For a representative sample of a rent proration provision, *see* Peter Aitelli, *Purchase and Sale Agreement for Real Property*, in ALI-ABA COURSE OF STUDY MATERIALS, MODERN REAL ESTATE TRANSACTIONS, Course No. SY006, 7, § 10(August 2016).

and warranties concerning the status or condition of the project, preferring, instead, to sell the project in an "as is, where is" condition. The buyer is equally forceful in seeking to include in the sales contract specific seller representations and warranties concerning (1) the conformity of the tenant leases with the rent roll attached to the sales contract, and (2) the soundness of the physical condition of the building and its operating systems and equipment. The gulf that exists between the positions adopted by the seller and the buyer on these issues is often bridged by the introduction of "materiality" and "knowledge" qualifiers to the seller's representation and warranty about tenant leases and the limitation of the seller's representation and warranty on the physical condition of the property to "latent, structural defects" that are not readily discoverable as part of a thorough engineering inspection of the project.

- *Tenant Estoppel Certificates*—The buyer demands that it receive written confirmation from the tenants that (1) the project leases are in full force and effect without any default by the landlord, and (2) the form and content of those leases are fully consistent with the rent roll attached to the sales contract and the lease documents previously furnished to the buyer by the developer. A point of contention that frequently arises during the negotiation of this provision is whether the seller is obligated to deliver acceptable signed estoppel certificates for every tenant in the building (the buyer's preference) or just a limited subset of the building's tenants— for example, those tenants occupying 80% of the rentable square feet contained within the building (the seller's preference).

- *Building Contracts and Employees*—Both the seller and the buyer want the sales contract to recite what, if any, building contracts will be assumed post-closing by the buyer (for example, a trash removal contract) and the identity of those seller employees, if any, who will be offered jobs post-closing by the buyer.

- *Interim Operating Covenant*—Finally, a provision should be included in the sales contract that requires the seller to continue to operate the project prior to closing in accordance with its past practices and to refrain from entering into any new leases or contracts or amending any existing leases or contracts, without first obtaining the buyer's written consent.

HIBC Case Study—The Sale of the Project

The Heathrow International Business Center has been the case study used throughout this book to examine the roles played by the real estate development lawyer during each of the ten stages of a development project. The time has now come to tie a bow around both this book and the HIBC case study by briefly mentioning the circumstances surrounding the Pizzuti organization's sale of the HIBC project to Colonial Properties Trust.

As noted earlier in this chapter, Pizzuti contributed its 50% interest in nine HIBC office buildings to a joint venture formed by it and Nationwide Realty Investors, Ltd. In order to obtain Newport Partners consent to the closing of the NRI-Pizzuti equity deal, Pizzuti had grudgingly agreed to retain a real estate broker to pursue the sale of all of the HIBC buildings. Part of that strategy was implemented later that same year when Pizzuti sold the two office buildings that were 100% leased by First USA to Lexington Properties Trust for $41.7 million.

Because Pizzuti and NRI were both extremely bullish on the HIBC project, an agreement was ultimately struck with Newport Partners for the joint venture's purchase of Newport Partners' remaining 50% interest in five of the remaining seven HIBC office buildings. It was further agreed that Pizzuti would indefinitely suspend its efforts to sell the two office buildings in which Newport Partners continued to own an interest.

The redemption/reorganization of Newport Partners' interest in the HIBC project was undertaken to facilitate a long-term hold of the HIBC office buildings by the Pizzuti-NRI joint venture. That venture was also committed to an aggressive schedule for the development of the undeveloped HIBC land, which consisted of approximately 140 acres of office and commercial ground. Promptly after the formation of the Pizzuti-NRI joint venture, Pizzuti Properties LLC kicked off its first new office development project by starting construction of a 192,000-square-foot office building on an approximately 20-acre tract in HIBC. It was then the anticipation of Pizzuti and NRI that the venture would complete development of ten additional office buildings within the HIBC park within a horizon of five to seven years. The expectation was that the HIBC buildings would be a long-term hold for the NRI-Pizzuti joint venture.

Pizzuti Properties' long-term investment strategy for the HIBC project came crashing to a halt a short 12 months later when Pizzuti experienced a severe liquidity crisis. While Pizzuti's financial crisis was wholly unrelated to the HIBC project (which was continuing to produce stable above-market rates of return),Pizzuti's desperate need for cash precipitated its request that NRI consent to an immediate sale of the entirety of the HIBC office building portfolio. NRI eventually consented to the sale of the HIBC portfolio and Pizzuti retained a real estate broker to find a buyer for both the eight office buildings still owned by the Pizzuti-NRI joint venture entity (two of which *were partially owned by Newport Partners) and the approximately 120 acres of undeveloped land owned outright by Pizzuti. Six months later, Pizzuti sold the HIBC property to Colonial Properties Trust, a real estate investment trust headquartered in Birmingham, Alabama, for a combined purchase price of $143 million.*

The sale of the HIBC project was a particularly bittersweet moment for me. I had been intimately involved in every aspect of Pizzuti's development of the HIBC project, dating from Pizzuti's acquisition of its first HIBC building through its sale of the project to Colonial Properties Trust ten years later. The HIBC project afforded me the opportunity to work with some extraordinary people and to put my knowledge and skills to the test in the context of an incredibly challenging real estate project.

The sale of the HIBC project brought an end to a wonderfully successful development project. It also served as the effective end to my career as a practicing lawyer. Later that year, I retired from The Pizzuti Companies (yes I owned a promote on the HIBC project and the rest of Pizzuti's cash-flowing real estate portfolio that Pizzuti had to sell to resolve its liquidity issues). I joined the faculty of the Moritz College of Law at The Ohio State University shortly thereafter and set about writing a book on real estate development law—a venture that, among other things, has permitted me to re-live the challenges and excitement presented by my participation in the development of the HIBC project.

VI. SUMMARY

The final three stages of a development project are an interesting time for a real estate development lawyer. During each of these stages, other real estate professionals pour over the documents created by the real estate development lawyer during the seven formative stages of a development project to determine whether the developer can refinance, operate, and ultimately sell its project on terms favorable to the developer. Stages 8, 9, and 10 are, therefore, the true test as to whether the lawyer did what the lawyer was hired to do—add value to the developer's project.

APPENDIX A

DOCUMENT APPENDIX

• • •

The following are the core legal documents that are included in this Document Appendix and referred to in the text of REAL ESTATE DEVELOPMENT LAW.

Document #1: *Letter of Intent for Land Acquisition*

Document #2: *Real Estate Purchase Agreement for Land Acquisition*

Document #3: *Operating Agreement for Delaware LLC*

Document #4: *Closing Statement for Land Sale*

Document #5: *Construction Loan Agreement for Ohio Development Project*

Document #6: *Office Lease—Expense Stop*

Document #7: *Exclusive Listing Agreement for New Office Building*

Document #8: *Property Management Agreement for Office Building*

These documents are standard form agreements that I used during my years in the active practice of real estate development law. I believe that they are representative samples of the types of documents that real estate development lawyers regularly encounter in their daily practices. However, three important caveats need to be made concerning these documents— (1) they are standard forms that must be tailored to reflect the specifics of the business deal struck by the parties to the agreements, (2) they have been modified to create some "teaching moments" for the Real Estate Development Law course that I taught at the Moritz College of Law at The Ohio State University, and (3) they all have a slight (but hopefully not unconscionable) developer bias. For these reasons, I strongly advise you not to use any of the forms in your practice until you have thoroughly read and vetted each and every provision of the subject document.

DOCUMENT #1

LETTER OF INTENT
FOR LAND ACQUISITION

■ ■ ■

_____, 20__

[Insert Seller's Name and Address]

Subject: Letter of Intent to Purchase **[insert general description of the property]**

Dear **[insert Seller's name]:**

We are interested in purchasing **[insert general description of the property]** ("Property"). The general terms upon which we would consider purchasing your Property are outlined below.

1. **Description of Property.** The Property contains approximately ___ acres and is located in _____, _____. A legal description of the Property is attached to this letter of intent as Exhibit A.

2. **Purchase Price.** The purchase price for the Property will be **[insert price or method for calculating the price]** and will be paid in cash at closing.

3. **Buyer's Contingency.** We will need a period of _____ days after the date of our mutual execution of a definitive purchase agreement in which to conduct our due diligence of the Property. We will have no obligation to purchase the Property, unless **[include specific statement of contingency].**

4. **Closing.** We will close on the purchase of the Property within _____ days after the satisfactory completion of our due diligence efforts under ¶ 3, above. You will be responsible for paying the following closing costs: **[insert list of closing costs, if any, to be paid by Seller and those closing costs, if any, to be paid by Buyer].** Real estate taxes for the taxable year of closing will be prorated through the date of closing.

5. **Non-Binding Nature of Letter of Intent.** This letter of intent is merely an expression of our general interest in pursuing a purchase of your Property and is not intended to create any obligation for either of us concerning the purchase and sale of the Property. Neither of us will be bound to the other in any way unless and until we both execute a definitive

purchase agreement that sets forth the detailed terms and conditions that will govern our purchase of the Property.

If you are interested in selling us the Property in general accordance with the terms outlined above, please so indicate by signing and returning a copy of this letter to us at your earliest convenience (but, in any event, by no later than the close of business on _____, 20__). Once we receive an executed copy of this letter of intent, we will see to it that a draft purchase contract is immediately prepared and submitted to you for your review and comment.

We look forward to working with you on this matter.

Sincerely,

_____

                    Accepted as of _____, 20__.

                    By:_____

DOCUMENT #2

REAL ESTATE PURCHASE AGREEMENT
FOR LAND ACQUISITION

■ ■ ■

REAL ESTATE PURCHASE AGREEMENT

This Real Estate Purchase Agreement (*"Agreement"*) is dated _____, 20__ (*"Effective Date"*), and is between _____, a(n) _____ (*"Seller"*) and _____, a(n) _____ (*"Buyer"*). For the parties' convenience in reviewing this Agreement, all defined terms are highlighted by *italicized boldface print* when first defined in this Agreement.

Seller and Buyer agree as follows:

§ 1. Sale of the Property. Seller will sell to Buyer the following described property (*"Property"*):

    (a)   The approximately ___-acre tract of land that is located off of _____ in _____, _____, and that is further described in the legal description attached to this Agreement as Exhibit A (*"Land"*); and

    (b)   All rights and interests related to the Land, including, without limitation, air rights, water rights, mineral rights, development rights, easements, licenses, tradenames, trademarks, warranties, permits, governmental entitlements and approvals, rights-of-way, and utility agreements (collectively the *"Intangible Rights"*).

§ 2. Deposit. On or before the date that is ___ calendar days after the Effective Date, Buyer will pay an earnest money of $ _____ to _____ (*"Escrow Agent"*) in immediately available funds. Escrow Agent will hold the earnest money deposit in an interest-bearing account. All references in this Agreement to the *"Deposit"* includes the principal amount of the earnest money deposit and all interest earned on that principal amount.

Escrow Agent will disburse the Deposit as follows:

    (a)   If the closing occurs in the manner contemplated in this Agreement, then Escrow Agent will pay the Deposit to Seller and Buyer will receive a credit against the Purchase Price payable at closing in an amount equal to the Deposit;

    (b)   If this Agreement is terminated by Buyer under any right granted to Buyer in this Agreement (specifically including, without limitation, the termination rights set forth in §§ 4, 7, 8, 11, and 14), then Escrow Agent will return the Deposit to Buyer, without prejudice to Buyer's right to pursue any legal or equitable remedy Buyer may have against Seller to redress a default by Seller under this Agreement; and

(c)   If the closing fails to occur as a result of Buyer's default under this Agreement, then Escrow Agent will pay the Deposit to Seller as liquidated damages in full and complete settlement of all claims Seller has against Buyer as a result of such default.

Escrow Agent is signing this Agreement for the sole purpose of confirming its obligations under this § 2.

§ 3. Purchase Price. The purchase price for the Property is $_____ (*"Purchase Price"*). Buyer will pay the Purchase Price to Seller at closing by means of a federal funds wire transfer of immediately available funds. Buyer's payment of the Purchase Price is subject to those prorations, credits, allowances, and other adjustments set forth in § 10 of this Agreement.

§ 4. Buyer's Contingency. Buyer's obligations under this Agreement are contingent upon Buyer determining on or before the date that is ___ calendar days after the Effective Date (*"Outside Contingency Date"*), that (a) the condition of the Property is suitable for Buyer's intended use, and (b) that Buyer's proposed development of the Property is economically feasible. If Buyer gives Seller written notice on or before the Outside Contingency Date that the contingencies set forth in clauses (a) and (b) of the prior sentence have been satisfied (*"Approval Notice"*), then Seller and Buyer will proceed to close on Buyer's purchase of the Property in the manner contemplated in this Agreement. If Buyer fails to give Seller an Approval Notice on or before the Outside Contingency Date, then Buyer's obligations under this Agreement will automatically terminate and the Deposit will be returned to Buyer as required under § 2.

§ 5. Buyer's Due Diligence. On or before the date that is ___ calendar days after the Effective Date, Seller will deliver to Buyer complete and accurate copies of all written reports in Seller's possession or control related to the condition of the Property (*"Written Reports"*), including, without limitation, all environmental reports, utility studies, access studies, surveys, title insurance commitments and policies, topographical studies, soils tests, seismic tests, flood plain analyses, zoning reports, and wetland delineations. If Buyer fails to close on its purchase of the Property for any reason other than a Seller default, then Buyer will return all the Written Reports to Seller on or before the date that is ___ calendar days after Buyer's receipt of a written notice from Seller requesting the return of the Written Reports.

Seller will also permit Buyer and Buyer's agents access to the Property at all times prior to closing, so that Buyer can conduct such tests, studies, inspections, and other due diligence of the Property that Buyer deems appropriate. Buyer will indemnify Seller from any loss or expense incurred by Seller as a direct result of Buyer's conduct of its due diligence activities on the Property.

§ 6. **Representations and Warranties.** For the purpose of inducing Buyer to enter into this Agreement, Seller represents and warrants as follows.

(a) **Seller's Authority.** Seller has the full right, power, and authority to sign this Agreement and consummate the transactions contemplated in this Agreement, without first having to obtain the consent of any other person or governmental authority.

(b) **Foreign Person.** Seller is not a "foreign person" within the meaning of Section 1445 of the Internal Revenue Code.

(c) **Off-Record Title Matters.** Seller owns fee simple title to the Property, free and clear of all liens and encumbrances (including without limitation, any easement, mortgage, restrictive covenant, lease, option, right of first refusal, right of first offer, or purchase contract), except for those liens and encumbrances that appear of public record in the real estate records of the county in which the Property is located.

(d) **Rights of Possession and Use.** Seller has not granted any person a license, lease, option, interest, or right to use or possess any part of the Property and no person has ever used or possessed any part of the Property in a manner that is adverse to Seller's interests.

(e) **No Proceedings.** No legal action, proceeding, or investigation relating to Seller or the Property is pending or proposed before any agency, court, or governmental authority.

(f) **Public Improvements and Taxes.** Seller has not received notice of: (i) any pending or proposed improvements to the Property by any public authority, the cost of which could be assessed as a special tax against the Property, or (ii) any pending or proposed increase in the valuation of the Property for real estate tax purposes.

(g) **Creditor Problems.** No attachment, execution, receivership, assignment for the benefit of creditors, or voluntary or involuntary proceeding in bankruptcy or under any other debtor relief law is pending or proposed against Seller or the Property.

(h) **Termination of Access/Utilities.** No fact, condition, or proceeding exists that could result in the termination or impairment of any current access from the Property to any road or utility line or facility that serves, adjoins, or is situated on the Property.

(i) **Mechanics Liens.** All bills and claims for labor performed or materials furnished for the benefit of the Property have been paid in full. No mechanics liens (whether or not perfected) are pending or proposed against the Property.

(j) **Hazardous Materials.** No Hazardous Materials are located on the Property and neither Seller, nor any previous owner of the Property, has ever violated or received any notice of a claimed violation of any federal, state, or local law or regulation relating to the health, safety, or environment, including, without limitation, the Clean Air Act, the Clean Water Act, the Federal Water Pollution Control Act, the Resource Conservation and Recovery Act, the Hazardous Materials Transportation Act, the Comprehensive Environmental Response Compensation and Liability Act, the Solid Waste Disposal Act, the Safe Drinking Water Act, and the Toxic Substances Control Act. No underground storage tank exists on the Property. The term *"Hazardous Material"* means any chemical, pollutant, contaminant, waste, toxic substance, polychlorinated biphenyl, or petroleum product defined in, governed by, or regulated under any of the laws or regulations referred to in the first sentence of this subparagraph.

(k) **Compliance with Laws and Private Restrictions.** The Property is not in violation of: (i) any law, regulation, ordinance, permit, or other governmental requirement; or (ii) any of the Intangible Rights.

(l) **Zoning.** The Property is zoned _____. Seller has not received notice of any pending or proposed change to the Property's current zoning classification or the enactment of any other governmental requirement that could affect or limit the future use of the Property.

(m) **Separate Tax Parcel.** The Property is a separate, free-standing tax parcel for real estate tax purposes.

(n) **Condemnation.** There is no condemnation or eminent domain proceeding pending or proposed against the Property.

   (o) **Wetland and Flood Hazard Areas.** The Property is not located in: (i) a wetland (as that term is defined or used in any applicable federal, state local law or regulation, including, without limitation, the Clean Water Act), or (b) a designated flood plain or flood hazard area.

Each representation and warranty set forth in this § 6 will be deemed remade by Seller on the closing date, with the same force and effect as if each such representation and warranty were first made on such date. Each representation and warranty set forth in this § 6 will survive the closing for the maximum period of time allowed by applicable law.

§ 7. Title Commitment and Survey. On or before the date that is ___ calendar days after the Effective Date, Seller will cause _____, _____ or another nationally-recognized title insurance company acceptable to Buyer ("***Title Company***") to furnish to Buyer a commitment for an ALTA Owner's Title Insurance Policy (20__) in the face amount of the Purchase Price, together with legible copies of all title exceptions noted in such commitment ("***Title Commitment***").

Also on or before the date that is ___ calendar days after the Effective Date, Seller will cause _____ or another licensed land surveyor acceptable to Buyer ("***Surveyor***") to furnish to Buyer a survey of the Property certified to Buyer and the Title Company and dated after the Effective Date ("***Survey***"). The Survey must be prepared in conformity with the Minimum Standard Detail Requirements for ALTA/NSPS Land Title Surveys (2016) and must show the location of all improvements, easements, roads, rights-of-way, encroachments, and other title matters affecting the Property.

At any time on or before the Outside Contingency Date, Buyer may send written notice to Seller of Buyer's objection to any exception to title shown in the Title Commitment or Survey ("***Title Notice***"). Any title exceptions appearing in the Title Commitment or Survey that are not objected to by Buyer in a timely delivered Title Notice will be treated as a "***Permitted Exception***" for the purpose of this Agreement.

If Buyer sends Seller a Title Notice at any time on or before the Outside Contingency Date, then Seller will have until the date that is ___ calendar days after Seller's receipt of the Title Notice ("***Title Review Period***") to cure the title objections set forth in Buyer's Title Notice. If Seller is successful in curing any of the title objections set forth in Buyer's Title Notice, then Seller will send Buyer written proof of such cure and will also cause the Title Company and the Surveyor to take all requisite actions required to cure such title objection in the manner prescribed in Buyer's Title Notice.

If Seller does not cure all the title objections set forth in Buyer's Title Notice on or before the last day of the Title Review Period, then Buyer may either:

(a) terminate its obligations under this Agreement by delivering written notice of termination to Seller on or before the date that is ___ calendar days after the last day of the Title Review Period, in which event, the Deposit will be returned to Buyer; or (b) proceed to close on the purchase of the Property despite the continued existence Buyer's title objections. If Buyer does not send Seller such a written termination notice on or before the date that is ___ calendar days after the last day of the Title Review Period, then Buyer will, for all purposes of this Agreement, be deemed to have elected to close the transaction pursuant to clause (b) of this § 7.

Despite the above provisions of this § 7, Seller will be obligated to pay and discharge at closing all mortgages, judgment liens, and other liens against the Property that are susceptible to being paid off and discharged by the payment of an ascertainable sum or money ("*Monetary Liens*"). If Seller does not pay and discharge all Monetary Liens prior to closing, then Buyer is entitled to receive a Purchase Price credit at closing in an amount equal to the sum of money required to pay and discharge the Monetary Liens.

§ 8. <u>Conditions to Closing.</u> Seller's obligation to sell the Property to Buyer is conditioned on Buyer's performance of all Buyer's obligations under this Agreement (or Seller's waiver of such performance), including, without limitation, Buyer's payment of the Purchase Price to Seller in the manner set forth in §§ 3 and 10 of this Agreement and Buyer's execution and delivery to Seller of all of those documents required to be executed and delivered by Buyer under § 10 of this Agreement.

Buyer's obligation to purchase the Property from Seller is conditioned on Seller's performance (or Buyer's waiver of such performance) of all Seller's obligations under this Agreement, including, without limitation, Seller's timely delivery of a Title Commitment and Survey to Buyer in the manner set forth in § 7, and Seller's execution and delivery of all of those documents required to be executed and delivered by Seller under § 10 of this Agreement. Buyer's obligation to purchase the Property from Seller is further conditioned upon the satisfaction of both of the following conditions:

    (a) Buyer's delivery of an Approval Notice to Seller on or before the Outside Contingency Date;

    and

    (b) Seller's representations and warranties under § 6 being true on both the Effective Date and the date of closing.

If any of the Seller or Buyer conditions noted in this § 8 has not been satisfied as of the Outside Closing Date specified in § 9 of this Agreement, then the party in whose favor such condition runs may terminate its obligations under this Agreement by delivering a written notice of termination to the other party to this Agreement any time on or before the date that is ___ calendar days after the Outside Closing Date. The legal effect of any such termination (that is, the prescribed disbursement of the Deposit and the existence of any remedies available to either party for the failure of a condition) will be determined under § 4 (with respect to the failure of the Buyer condition specified in subparagraph (a), above), or § 14 of this Agreement (with respect to the failure of all other conditions).

§ 9. <u>Date and Place of Closing.</u> The closing must occur, if at all, on or before the date that is ___ calendar days after Buyer's delivery of an Approval Notice to Seller under § 4 ("***Outside Closing Date***"). Unless otherwise agreed to by Seller and Buyer, the closing will take place on the Outside Closing Date at 9 a.m. ___ Standard Time, at the offices of Seller's legal counsel at _____, _____. If, however, either Seller or Buyer sends the other a written notice prior to the Outside Closing Date electing to have the closing occur by way of an escrow arrangement, then the closing will be effected by the delivery by Seller and Buyer of all funds, closing documents, and other required deliveries prescribed under § 10 into escrow with the Escrow Agent and the Escrow Agent's holding, recordation, and disbursement of all such funds, closing documents, and deliveries in accordance with written escrow instructions delivered to the Escrow Agent by each of Seller and Buyer.

Each reference in this Agreement to the "***closing***", the "***closing date***" or the "***date of closing***" means the consummation of Buyer's purchase of the Property at the time, place, and manner prescribed in this Agreement.

§ 10. <u>Closing Obligations/Procedures.</u> Seller's sale of the Property to Buyer will be effected by Seller and Buyer taking the following actions at closing. Possession of the Property will be transferred to Buyer upon the completion by Seller and Buyer of all the actions prescribed in this § 10.

(a) **<u>Purchase Price Payment.</u>** Buyer will pay the Purchase Price to Seller by means of a federal funds wire transfer of immediately available funds. The amount of the Purchase Price payment will be adjusted in to take into consideration those prorations, credits, charges, and other adjustments specified in subparagraphs (h), (i), and (j), below.

(b) **<u>Transfer of Property.</u>** Seller will execute and deliver to Buyer a general warranty deed, in recordable form, pursuant to which Seller will transfer to Buyer fee simple title to the Property, free and clear of all liens and encumbrances, except for the Permitted Exceptions.

(c) **<u>Closing Affidavits.</u>** Seller will execute and deliver to Buyer (i) an affidavit stating that Seller is not a "foreign person" within the meaning of § 1445 of the Internal Revenue Code, (ii) an affidavit with respect to off-record title matters that is sufficient to permit the Title Company to issue a title policy for the Property in the form contemplated in subparagraph (g), below, and (iii) an affidavit affirming the continuing truth and accuracy on the date of closing of all Seller's representations and warranties set forth in § 6.

(d) Entity Resolutions. Seller and Buyer will each deliver to the other (i) a current certificate of good standing affirming such party's authority to do business in the state of its organization and in the state in which the Property is located, and (ii) a current entity resolution affirming the authority of such party to enter into the transaction contemplated in this Agreement and further authorizing an individual officer or representative of such party to execute this Agreement and all closing documents in the name and on behalf of such party.

(e) Closing Statement. Seller and Buyer will each execute and deliver to the other a closing statement that sets forth the economics of Buyer's purchase of the Property from Seller, including, without limitation, the Purchase Price, all closing cost payments, and all prorations, credits, charges and other adjustments specified in subparagraphs (h), (i), and (j), below.

(f) Miscellaneous Closing Documents. Seller and Buyer will each execute and deliver to the other such other documents as are reasonably requested by Seller or Buyer to further evidence or effect the sale of the Property to Buyer in the manner contemplated in this Agreement.

(g) Title Policy. Seller will cause the Title Company to issue to Buyer an ALTA Owner's Title Insurance Policy (20__) in the face amount of the Purchase Price, insuring in Buyer fee simple title to the Property, free and clear of all liens and encumbrances, excepting only the Permitted Exceptions. The title insurance policy must expressly reflect the Title Company's deletion of the standard preprinted exceptions set forth in Schedule B–2 to such policy.

(h) Closing Costs. Seller will pay the following costs at closing: (i) all premiums and other charges required to permit the Title Company to issue the title insurance policy referred to in subparagraph (g), above; (ii) all costs required to permit the Surveyor to issue and certify the Survey in the manner required under § 7 of this Agreement; (iii) all state, municipal, and county transfer taxes, documentary stamps and other fees payable as a condition to Seller's transfer of the Property to Buyer; and (iv) the real estate commission owed to the broker identified in § 12 of this Agreement. Buyer will pay the following costs at closing: (v) all recording fees required for the recordation of the general warranty deed referred to in subparagraph (b) above; and (vi) all costs associated with Buyer's conduct of its due diligence under § 5. Seller and Buyer will each pay 50% of any escrow fees payable to the Escrow Agent. Seller and Buyer will each separately pay any attorney's fees incurred by it in connection with the preparation and negotiation of this Agreement and the consummation of the transactions contemplated in this Agreement.

(i) **Closing Credits.** Seller will pay or credit on the Purchase Price: (i) all amounts required to fully pay and discharge the Monetary Liens affecting the Property; and (ii) the amount of all special assessments and delinquent real estate taxes (including penalties and interest) that are a lien on the Property on the date of closing). Seller will also credit on the Purchase Price an amount equal to that portion of all non-delinquent real estate taxes for the Property that are attributable to the period of time prior to the date of closing. If a final real estate tax bill for the taxable year of closing has not been issued by the taxing authority by the date of closing, then the calculation of the Purchase Price credit to be given to Buyer under the immediately preceding sentence will be determined based upon the most recently available tax use, tax rate, and tax valuation for the Property. Buyer is entitled to have the amount of such Purchase Price credit recalculated once the final real estate tax bill for the taxable year of closing is issued by the taxing authority. Buyer may exercise such right by delivering a written recalculation notice to Seller at any time on or before the first anniversary of the date on which the final real estate tax bill for the taxable year of closing is first issued by the taxing authority. Seller will pay any additional amount owed to Buyer as a result of the recalculation of such Purchase Price credit no later than the date that is 30 calendar days after Seller's receipt of Buyer's written recalculation notice. The provisions of this subparagraph (i) will survive the closing.

(j) **Closing Prorations.** All other items of income and expense related to the Property will be prorated through the date of closing, with Seller being entitled to receive or obligated to pay, as the case may be, all items of income or expense attributable to the period prior to the date of closing and Buyer being entitled to receive or obligated to pay, as the case may be, all items of income and expenses attributable to the period from and after the date of closing. For the purposes of this subparagraph (j), the determination of whether an item is "*attributable to*" a particular period will be made in accordance with generally accepted accounting principles, consistently applied.

§ 11. Risk of Loss. The risk of loss to the Property from the occurrence of a casualty or a taking by any public authority under the power or threat of eminent domain is borne by Seller until the closing of Buyer's purchase of the Property. If any such casualty or taking occurs prior to the closing, then Seller will promptly send written notice to Buyer of the occurrence of such event and Buyer may either: (a) proceed with the closing and receive all insurance proceeds or condemnation awards payable as a result of such casualty or taking; or (b) terminate its obligations under this Agreement by delivering written notice of termination to Seller on or before the date that is ___ calendar days after Buyer's receipt of written notice from Seller of the occurrence of such event. If Buyer fails to make the required election under this § 11 on or before the date that is ten calendar days after its receipt of Seller's written notice of the occurrence of any such event, then Buyer will be deemed to have elected to close the transaction pursuant to clause (a) of this § 11.

§ 12. Brokerage Commissions. Seller will pay all commissions and other amounts owed to _____ in connection with the transaction contemplated in this Agreement. Except as provided above, Seller and Buyer each represents and warrants to the other that it has not entered into any contract or taken any other action that could result in any fee being due and payable to any real estate broker, finder, or other person with respect to the transaction contemplated in this Agreement. The breach by either Seller or Buyer of its representation and warranty under this § 12 will be treated as a default by such party under § 14 of this Agreement. The provisions of this § 12 will survive the closing.

§ 13. Interim Operations. During the pendency of this Agreement, Seller will refrain from taking any of the following actions without first obtaining the written consent of the Buyer:

(a) The sale, transfer, encumbrance, or other conveyance of any legal, beneficial, or equitable interest in the Property (including, without limitation, any easement, lease, option, purchase right, or license affecting the Property);

(b) Any excavation or construction activity that has the effect of disturbing the natural condition of the Property; or

(c) A rezoning of the Property or any application for or acquiescence in a rezoning of the Property.

Also during the pendency of this Agreement, Seller will cooperate with Buyer in in connection with Buyer's proposed future development of the

Property. Seller's obligation to so cooperate with Buyer extends to and includes, without limitation, Seller's execution and delivery of zoning, utility, governmental incentive, and other land use applications. Despite the provision of the prior sentence, Seller will not be required to take any action that would result in Seller incurring any out-of-pocket expense or that would be legally binding on Seller or the Property prior to the closing of Buyer's purchase of the Property.

§ 14. <u>Defaults/Remedies.</u> If Seller defaults in the performance of any obligation under this Agreement and if such default continues for a period of ___ calendar days after written notice of the alleged existence of such default is given to Seller by Buyer, then Buyer may pursue any remedy available to it at law or in equity to redress such default, including, without limitation, the right to specific performance. Except as otherwise provided in this § 14, Seller will be deemed to have defaulted in the performance of its obligations if it breaches any representation or warranty made by it under § 6 or § 12 of this Agreement (regardless whether such representation and warranty was made as of the Effective Date or remade as of the date of closing). Despite the provision of the prior sentence, Seller will not be deemed to be in default under this Agreement if (a) any fact or circumstance occurs after the Effective Date that renders a Seller representation or warranty false, and (b) the occurrence of such fact or circumstance is not within the reasonable control of Seller; provided, however, that, the post-Effective Date occurrence of any such fact or circumstance will nonetheless permit Buyer to terminate its obligations under this Agreement and receive a refund of the Deposit.

If Buyer defaults in the performance of any obligation under this Agreement and if such default continues for a period of ___ calendar days after written notice of the alleged existence of such default is given to Buyer by Seller, then Seller will be entitled to receive payment of the Deposit as liquidated damages, in full and complete settlement of all claims it has against Buyer as a result of such default; it being expressly acknowledged by Seller and Buyer that Seller's actual damages in the event of a default by Buyer under this Agreement would be difficult to ascertain and that the receipt of the Deposit represents Seller's and Buyer's reasonable estimate of the damages that would be caused by such default. Seller's right to receive the Deposit as liquidated damages is Seller's exclusive remedy to redress a default by Buyer.

§ 15. <u>Assignment of Agreement.</u> Neither Buyer, nor Seller may assign any part of this Agreement, without first obtaining the written consent of the other party to this Agreement; provided, however, that Buyer may assign this Agreement to an affiliate of Buyer, without having to obtain Seller's consent.

§ 16. <u>Governing Law.</u> This Agreement is governed by Ohio law.

§ 17. <u>Counterparts.</u> This Agreement may be executed in counterparts, which, when combined, will constitute a binding contract.

§ 18. <u>Attorneys' Fees.</u> If any legal action is commenced by either Seller or Buyer to enforce its rights under this Agreement, then the non-prevailing party in such legal action will pay all reasonable attorneys' fees and other expenses incurred by the prevailing party in such legal action. Any payment required to be made under this § 18 must be made on or before the date that is ___ calendar days after the issuance of a final non-appealable decision in such legal action.

§ 19. <u>Entire Agreement.</u> This Agreement may not be amended except by a written instrument executed by both Seller and Buyer.

§ 20. <u>Notices.</u> All notices required or permitted to be given under this Agreement must be in writing and must be delivered to Seller or Buyer at the address set forth after its respective name below. Any such notice must be personally delivered or sent by certified mail, overnight courier, facsimile transmission, or email. For the purposes of this Agreement, any such notice will be deemed "delivered," "given," "sent," "received" or "effective" only as specified below:

    (a) If personally delivered or sent by certified mail or overnight courier, on the date when the notice is received or refused by the intended recipient of such notice; or

    (b) If sent by email or facsimile transmission, on the date when the notice is sent, as evidenced by the sender's "sent e-mail box" or facsimile transmission report.

The parties' addresses for the delivery of all notices are as follows:

    Seller:

    Buyer:

§ 21. <u>Confidentiality.</u> Buyer and Seller will each keep the provisions of this Agreement confidential and neither of them will release those provisions to any other person (including, without limitation, the media or general public) without first obtaining the written consent of the other party. This § 21 will survive the termination of this Agreement.

§ 22. <u>Defined Terms.</u> For the purpose of this Agreement, the following terms have the meanings attributed to such terms in the noted sections of this Agreement:

"*Agreement*" is defined in the preamble.

"*Approval Notice*" is defined in § 4.

"*Attributable to*" is defined in § 10.

"*Buyer*" is defined in the preamble.

"*Closing*", "*closing date*" and "*date of closing*" are defined in § 9.

"*Deposit*" is defined in § 2.

"*Effective Date*" is defined in the preamble.

"*Escrow Agent*" is defined in § 2.

"*Hazardous Material*" is defined in § 6.

"*Intangible Rights*" is defined in § 1.

"*Land*" is defined in § 1.

"*Monetary Liens*" is defined in § 7.

"*Outside Closing Date*" is defined in § 9.

"*Outside Contingency Date*" is defined in § 4.

"*Permitted Exceptions*" is defined in § 7.

"*Purchase Price*" is defined in § 3.

"*Property*" is defined in § 1.

"*Seller*" is defined in the preamble.

"*Survey*" is defined in § 7.

"*Surveyor*" is defined in § 7.

"*Title Company*" is defined in § 7.

"*Title Commitment*" is defined in § 7.

"*Title Notice*" is defined in § 7.

"*Written Reports*" is defined in § 5.

All the meanings attributed to the above terms are equally applicable to both the singular and plural forms of such terms.

Seller and Buyer are signing this Agreement as of the Effective Date.

SELLER:

By: _____

(Name)   (Title)

BUYER:

By: _____

(Name)   (Title)

**ESCROW AGENT
(signing solely to
confirm its obligations
under § 2 of this
Agreement):**

_____

By: _____

(Name)   (Title)

EXHIBIT A
LEGAL DESCRIPTION OF LAND

DOCUMENT #3

OPERATING AGREEMENT
FOR DELAWARE LLC

■ ■ ■

_____ LLC

(A Delaware Limited Liability Company)

OPERATING AGREEMENT

_____, 20___

_____

This is a sample form of Operating Agreement for a limited liability company being formed under the Delaware Limited Liability Company Act. The form assumes that there are only two members—a developer and an institutional investor—and that all capital contributions made to the LLC will be made in cash. The form assumes that capital contributions will be made 75% by the investor and 25% by the developer, with the developer receiving an additional 25% "promote" in the LLC's profits. The form further assumes that the LLC will be "manager-managed," with management authority being vested in the developer (acting in the dual capacity of both a member and a manager), subject, however, to the requirement that the investor's prior approval must be obtained for certain "major decisions." Finally, the Operating Agreement is premised on the assumption that the developer and the investor have relatively equal bargaining power. The form admittedly has a slight pro-developer bias—representing developers is, after all, how I spent my 40+ years in the practice. By way of example, the Operating Agreement does not have (a) a squeeze-down if a Member defaults on its Additional Capital Contribution obligation, (b) any right of the Investor to remove the Manager, or (c) a clawback if Developer receives a distribution of Operating Cash Flow that exceeds its rightful share of the Company's profits. All those provisions are, however, discussed in detail in Chapter 7 of the REAL ESTATE DEVELOPMENT LAW text.

TABLE OF CONTENTS

_____ **LLC**

(A Delaware Limited Liability Company)

OPERATING AGREEMENT

This Operating Agreement ("Agreement") is dated _____, 20__ ("Effective Date"), and is between _____ ("Developer") and _____ ("Investor").

Developer and Investor agree as follows.

ARTICLE 1: ORGANIZATION

§ 1.1   Formation of Company. The Company is a limited liability company formed under the Act.

§ 1.2   Name of Company. The name of the Company is "_____ LLC."

§ 1.3   Names and Addresses of Members. The full names and addresses of the Members are as follows:

      [Name of Developer]   [Name of Investor]

      [Address of Developer]   [Address of Investor]

§ 1.4   Business Purpose. The business purpose of the Company is: (a) to own, develop, finance, lease, operate, and manage the Project as an investment for the production of income; and (b) to engage in all other incidental or related activities, including, without limitation, the ultimate disposition of the Project.

§ 1.5   Principal Office. The address of the Company's principal office is _____, _____, _____. The address of the Company's principal office may be changed from time to time by Developer.

§ 1.6   Registered Agent for Service of Process. The name and address of the Company's registered agent for service of process are _____, _____, _____, _____, Delaware. The name and address of the Company's agent for service of process may be changed from time to time by Developer.

§ 1.7   Governmental Filings. Coincident with the full execution of this Agreement, Developer will file with the Delaware Secretary of State a certificate of formation creating the Company as a limited liability company under the Act. Developer may make all other governmental filings that the Developer deems appropriate to qualify the Company to do business in any jurisdiction or to otherwise carry out the purposes and intent of this Agreement.

§ 1.8   Term. The term of the Company's existence begins on the date on which the Company's certificate of formation is filed with the Delaware Secretary of State. The Company will exist in perpetuity unless it is earlier terminated pursuant to the provisions of this Agreement.

§ 1.9.   Limited Liability. No Member will be personally liable for any debt, obligation, or liability of the Company, regardless whether that debt, obligation, or liability arises in contract, tort, or otherwise.

§ 1.10   Definitions. All capitalized words and phrases used in this Agreement (other than the full names and addresses of the Company, the Members, and governmental subdivisions and agencies) have the meanings set forth in Exhibit A to this Agreement.

ARTICLE 2: CAPITALIZATION

§ 2.1   Initial Capital Contributions. Coincident with the full execution of this Agreement, each Member will make a cash Capital Contribution to the Company in the amount set forth after its name below:

Developer—$_____ [25% of total Capital Contributions]

Investor—$_____ [75% of total Capital Contributions]

§ 2.2   Additional Capital Contributions. The Members acknowledge that the Company may from time to time need additional funds for the payment of cost overruns, operating deficits, and other costs related to the Company's business (collectively "Additional Funds"). If Developer determines that Additional Funds are needed by the Company and that such Additional Funds cannot be borrowed on commercially reasonable terms or otherwise drawn from the Company's cash reserves, then Developer may deliver written notice to Investor of the need for such Additional Funds ("Additional Funds Notice"). The Additional Funds Notice must specify the amount of the needed Additional Funds and the specific purpose for which the Additional Funds are needed. If the Additional Funds are needed for an Approved Purpose (as that term is later defined in this § 2.2), then, on or before the payment date specified in the Additional Funds Notice, Investor will make a cash Capital Contribution in an amount equal to 75% of the needed Additional Funds and Developer will make a cash Capital Contribution in an amount equal to 25% of the needed Additional Funds.

For the purposes of this § 2.2, "Approved Purpose" means the funding of any cost that (a) is included in an Approved Development Budget or an Approved Operating Budget, or (b) has otherwise been previously approved by Investor.

Except for those Additional Capital Contributions required to provide Additional Funds for an Approved Purpose, no Member will have any obligation to make any Additional Capital Contributions to the Company.

§ 2.3   **Defaulted Capital Contributions.** If any Member defaults in its obligation to make a Capital Contribution to the Company, then the Company and the other Member may each pursue all remedies against the defaulting Member that are available at law or in equity.

§ 2.4   **Loans.** As an alternative to its right to call for Additional Contributions under § 2.2, above, Developer may loan to the Company any funds that Developer determines are needed by the Company for use in the operation of the Company's business. Any loans made to the Company by Developer under this section will be payable upon demand and at an interest rate equal to the prime published lending rate of Bank of America (or any successor to Bank of America). The unpaid principal and accrued interest of any loans made to the Company by Developer under this section must be paid in full prior to the distribution of any Operating Cash Flow, Capital Proceeds, or Liquidation Proceeds to any Member. Despite the above provisions, Developer may not make loans to the Company that, in the aggregate, exceed $100,000, without first obtaining the prior written consent of Investor. Developer will promptly give Investor written notice of any loans that Developer makes to the Company under this section and any repayments of such loans made by the Company.

§ 2.5   **Withdrawal and Return of Capital Contributions.** Except as specifically authorized in this Agreement, no Member may: (a) withdraw or demand a return of any part of its Capital Contributions; or (b) receive property other than cash in return for its Capital Contributions.

§ 2.6   **Capital Accounts.** A separate Capital Account will be maintained for each Member in accordance with § 1.704–1(b) of the Regulations. Except as otherwise required under the § 1.704–1(b) Regulations, the Capital Account of each Member will initially be credited with the amount of its initial Capital Contributions under § 2.1, and will be increased by (a) the amount of any cash paid by the Member to the Company as an additional Capital Contribution under § 2.2, (b) the agreed-upon fair market value of any property contributed by the Member to the Company as an additional Capital Contribution under § 2.2, (c) the amount of any Company liability assumed by the Member, and (d) the Member's allocable share of the Company's Profits, and will be decreased by (e) the amount of any cash distributed to the Member, (f) the fair market value of any property distributed to the Member (g) the amount of any liability of the Member that is assumed by the Company, and (h) the Member's allocable share of the Company's Losses. If any Membership Interest is transferred in accordance with the terms of this Agreement, then the transferee will succeed to the Capital Account of the transferor Member.

The provisions of this section are intended to comply with § 1.704–1(b) of the Regulations and will be interpreted and applied in a manner consistent with those Regulations. If Developer determines that it is prudent to modify the manner in which the Capital Accounts are maintained in order to comply with such Regulations, then Developer may make such modification as long as such modification is consistent with the manner in which Operating Cash Flow, Capital Proceeds, and Liquidation Proceeds are required to be distributed to the Members under this Agreement.

ARTICLE 3: CASH DISTRIBUTIONS

§ 3.1   Distribution of Operating Cash Flow. Developer will distribute Operating Cash Flow for each Fiscal Quarter to the Members in the following manner and order of priority:

(a) First, pro rata to Developer and Investor in proportion to their relative unpaid Preferred Returns, until such time as each of them has received the full amount of its unpaid Preferred Return; and

(b) The remainder, if any, 50% to Developer and 50% to Investor.

§ 3.2   Distribution of Capital Proceeds. Developer will distribute Capital Proceeds to the Members in the following manner and order of priority:

(a) First, pro rata to Developer and Investor in proportion to their relative Unreturned Capital Contributions, until such time as each of them has received the full amount of its Unreturned Capital Contribution;

(b) Second, pro rata to Developer and Investor in proportion to their relative unpaid Preferred Returns, until such time as each of them has received the full amount of its unpaid Preferred Return; and

(c) The remainder, if any, 50% to Developer and 50% to Investor.

§ 3.3   Timing of Distributions. Developer will distribute Operating Cash Flow on a quarterly basis no later than 45 days after the end of each Fiscal Quarter. Developer will distribute Capital Proceeds no later than 45 days after the Company's receipt of the Capital Proceeds.

ARTICLE 4: PROFIT AND LOSS ALLOCATION

§ 4.1   General Allocation Scheme. Developer will allocate Profits and Losses for each Fiscal Year to the Members so that the Capital Account of each Member is, as nearly as possible, equal to the aggregate amount that would be distributed to each Member pursuant to § 3.2, if all of the Company's assets were to be sold for cash in an amount equal to the book value of those assets (determined in accordance with generally accepted accounting principles) and all of the Company's liabilities were to be satisfied at par.

§ 4.2   <u>**Tax Allocations.**</u> Developer will use reasonable efforts to cause all allocations of items of taxable income, gain, loss, deduction, and credit to be made in a manner consistent with both the provisions of § 4.1, above, and the tax rules that are set forth in § 704 of the Code and the Regulations promulgated under that section. If Developer, in consultation with the Company's tax accountants, determines that any allocation mandated by the aforementioned tax rules could produce a result that is inconsistent with the Members' intentions as stated in § 4.1, then Developer may alter the manner in which certain items of taxable income, gain, loss, deduction, or credit are allocated so as to produce the result stated in § 4.1.

ARTICLE 5: MANAGEMENT

§ 5.1   <u>**Management of Company.**</u> The Company is a "manager managed" limited liability company, with the Developer being designated as the Company's sole "manager" (as those terms are used in the context of the Act). In its capacity as the manager of the Company, Developer has full and exclusive authority over the management of the Company's business and may take all actions on behalf of the Company that a limited liability company may take under the Act, subject, only to those limitations and restrictions on its authority specifically set forth in § 5.2 of this Agreement. Developer will manage the business of the Company in good faith, in a manner it reasonably believes to be in the best interests of the Company, and with the care that an experienced, knowledgeable professional in a similar position would use under similar circumstances.

§ 5.2   <u>**Limitations on Developer's Authority.**</u> Despite the breadth of the authority granted to Developer in § 5.1, above, Developer may not take any of the following actions without obtaining the prior written consent of Investor, unless such action is either: (i) expressly authorized in an Approved Development Budget or a current Approved Operating Budget; or (ii) required by law or by the terms of any agreement previously approved by Investor, including, without limitation, any lease or financing agreement:

     (a)   Sell or otherwise dispose of all or substantially all of the Project;

     (b)   Merge or consolidate the Company with another Person;

     (c)   Acquire, commence development of, or otherwise invest in any new real estate project or other asset, other than any acquisition, development, or investment effected in the ordinary course of the Company's business for a total consideration of less than $_____$;

(d) File a voluntary petition in or otherwise initiate or consent to the institution of any proceeding against the Company under any law relating to the bankruptcy, insolvency, reorganization, or relief of debtors;

(e) Institute, voluntarily dismiss, terminate, or settle any litigation or arbitration against the Company or any other Person involving claims for damages and penalties in excess of $_____, other than any litigation instituted against any tenant that is in default under any lease of any part of the Project;

(f) Distribute any cash, property, or other assets to any Member, except in accordance with the provisions of this Agreement;

(g) Issue any new Membership Interest or any other equity interest in the Company (including any interest convertible into any equity interest in the Company);

(h) Enter into any Major Lease;

(i) Take any action that would cause the aggregate actual, development costs (exclusive of Uncontrollable Expenses) for the Project to exceed the aggregate budgeted development costs (exclusive of Uncontrollable Expenses) specified in the Approved Development Budget by more than __%;

(j) Take any action that would cause the aggregate operating expenses (exclusive of Uncontrollable Expenses) for the Project to exceed the aggregate budgeted operating expenses (exclusive of Uncontrollable Expenses) specified in a current Approved Operating Budget by more than __%;

(k) Incur or refinance any Company debt that either (i) is secured by a mortgage or other collateral pledge of the Project, or (ii) has a principal amount of more than $_____;

(l) Issue any press release or statement to any media outlet concerning the Project or the Company's business;

(m) Materially change the nature of the Company's business; or

(n) Take any act that contravenes the terms of this Agreement or that would make it impossible to carry on the ordinary business of the Company.

§ 5.3 **Specific Duties of Developer.** In addition to the general management duties placed upon Developer in § 5.1, above, Developer will have the following specific duties:

(a) File such documents and do such other acts as may be required to form and maintain the Company as a limited liability company under the Act and to qualify the Company to transact business in all those jurisdictions in which the Company does business;

(b) Serve as the "Tax Matters Partner" of the Company and, as such, exercise all of the rights and obligations given to a Tax Matters Partner under Subchapter C of Chapter 63 of the Code;

(c) Maintain at the principal office of the Company all books, records, and information required to be maintained by the Company under the Act, and make all such books, records, and information available for inspection and copying at the reasonable request and expense of any Member;

(d) Cause the Company to diligently prosecute the completion of the construction of the Project in a good and workmanlike fashion;

(e) Use reasonable efforts to comply with the financial parameters specified in the Approved Development Budget and the current Approved Operating Budget;

(f) Use reasonable efforts to cause the Company to secure on commercially reasonable terms (i) a mortgage loan for the acquisition and development of the Project, and (ii) a refinancing of any maturing mortgage loan,; and

(g) Maintain in full force and effect insurance coverage for the Project and the conduct of the Company's business that is consistent with sound commercial practices.

§ 5.4   Developer's Compensation. In consideration of its performance of services for the Company, Developer is entitled to receive the following fees and expense reimbursements from the Company:

(a) A development fee equal to ___% of the total budgeted development costs set forth in the Approved Development Budget;

(b) A property management fee equal to ___% of all rents payable under all leases of the Project;

(c) Fees for Developer's provision of services not otherwise covered by the fees payable under (a) and (b), above, but only to the extent that such fees are comparable in amount to fees that would be paid to an independent third party in an arm's length transaction for the provision of comparable services in the locale where the Project is located; and

(d) Reimbursement of all reasonable out-of-pocket expenses incurred by Developer in connection with the formation of the Company and the management and conduct of the Company's business.

The fees and reimbursements specified above will be paid to Developer prior to the distribution of any Operating Cash Flow, Capital Proceeds, or

Liquidation Proceeds to the Members and at commercially reasonable times selected by the Developer.

§ 5.5   Dealing with Affiliates. Developer may engage any of its Affiliates to provide services or materials to the Company as long as the terms and conditions governing the provision of and payment for such services and materials are comparable to those that would govern the provision by an independent third party in an arm's length transaction of comparable services and materials in the locale in which the Project is located. Despite the authority granted to the Developer in the prior sentence of this section, Investor may monitor performance, declare defaults, grant approvals, and exercise options and other rights and remedies on behalf of the Company under any agreement entered into by Developer with one of its Affiliates.

§ 5.6   Other Business Ventures. Any Member may engage or possess an interest in any other business venture of any type or description, independently or with others (including, without limitation, any venture that could be competitive with the Company's business), and neither the Company, nor the other Member will, by virtue of this Agreement, have any right, title, or interest in or to such venture or the income or other benefits derived from such venture.

§ 5.7   Development Budget. The Approved Development Budget for the acquisition and development of the Project is attached to this Agreement as Exhibit B. Developer may take any action that is consistent with the Approved Development Budget, without having to obtain any approval from Investor. Developer may not, however, amend the Approved Development Budget in any material respect, without first obtaining the Investor's written approval of such amendment.

§ 5.8   Operating Budgets. The Approved Operating Budget for the 20__ Fiscal Year is attached to this Agreement as Exhibit C. On or before October 1, 20__ and October 1 of each year thereafter during the term of the Company's existence, Developer will prepare and deliver to Investor a proposed operating budget for the Project for the next ensuing Fiscal Year. The format of each proposed operating budget must be consistent with the format used in the Approved Operating Budget for the 20__ Fiscal Year that is attached to this Agreement as Exhibit C.

Investor will have 30 days after its receipt of a proposed operating budget ("Budget Review Period") to deliver to Developer a written disapproval notice that specifies each line item of the proposed operating budget that is disapproved by Investor. If Investor fails to deliver a written disapproval notice to Developer on or before the last day of the Budget Review Period, then the proposed operating budget previously submitted by Developer will be deemed to be the Approved Operating Budget for the next ensuing Fiscal Year. If Investor delivers a written disapproval notice to Developer on or before the last day of the Budget Review Period, then Developer and Investor will work in good faith to reach agreement on each line item specifically disapproved by Investor in its disapproval notice. If Developer and Investor are unable to agree on all the disapproved line items of the proposed operating budget by December 1 of the year prior to the beginning of the Fiscal Year to which the proposed operating budget relates, then, until such time as final agreement is reached by Developer and Investor on all line items of the proposed operating budget, the Approved Operating Budget for the next ensuing Fiscal Year will be deemed to consist of: (a) the numbers applicable to all line items of the proposed operating budget that were not specifically disapproved in writing by Investor within the Budget Review Period, (b) 105% of the numbers contained in the prior Fiscal Year's Approved Operating Budget for all line items disapproved by Investor, other than Uncontrollable Expenses, and (c) the numbers actually incurred by the Company during the next ensuing Fiscal Year for all Uncontrollable Expenses.

§ 5.9   **Indemnification.** The Company will indemnify Developer to the fullest extent permitted by the Act against any loss or expense (including, without limitation, legal fees and litigation expenses) incurred by Developer by reason of a claim made against Developer by a third party related to Developer's service as the Company's manager. The Company's indemnification of Developer under this section will not extend to any claim against Developer that (a) is made against Developer by the Company or any Member, or (b) is based on Developer's fraud or willful misconduct.

§ 5.10   **Limitations on Investor's Authority.** Investor may not sign for or otherwise bind the Company in any manner.

§ 5.11   **Buy-Sell.** If at any time after the ____ anniversary of the Effective Date, a "Deadlock" occurs (as that term is defined later in this section), then either Member ("Electing Member") may deliver written notice of its desire to sell its Membership Interest ("Liquidity Notice") to the other Member ("Recipient Member"). Promptly after the delivery of the Liquidity Notice, the Electing and Recipient Members will negotiate in good faith to resolve the dispute that gave rise to the Deadlock.

If the Electing and Recipient Members fail to resolve the dispute that gave rise to the Deadlock on or before the date that is 30 days after the Recipient Member's receipt of the Liquidity Notice, then the Electing Member may give a written buy-sell notice ("Buy-Sell Notice") to the Recipient Member. The Buy-Sell Notice must set forth the gross value that the Electing Member places on the Project and all other Company assets ("Entity Value"). The Entity Value specified by the Electing Member in its Buy-Sell Notice may be any value selected by the Electing Member, without regard to the actual value of the Company's assets or the Electing Member's estimate of such actual value.

At any time during the 180-day period following the date of the Recipient Member's receipt of the Electing Member's Buy-Sell Notice, the Recipient Member may elect either (a) to sell the Recipient Member's entire Membership Interest to the Electing Member, or (b) to buy the Electing Member's entire Membership Interest. If the Recipient Member fails to deliver a written notice to the Electing Member within such 180-day period specifying whether the Recipient Member elects to buy or sell, then the Recipient Member will be deemed to have elected to sell all of the Recipient Member's Membership Interest. For the purposes of the balance of this section, "Seller" means the Member selling its Membership Interest to the other Member, and "Buyer" means the Member buying the other Member's Membership Interest.

The purchase price ("Buy-Sell Price") for any Membership Interest sold pursuant to this section will be equal to the amount of the cash distribution Seller would receive under § 3.2 of this Agreement if all the Company's assets were to be sold for the Entity Value specified in the Buy-Sell Notice and all the Company's liabilities were to be satisfied at par. The closing of the sale of Seller's Membership Interest to Buyer must occur on or before the date that is 210 days after the date of the Recipient Member's receipt of the Buy-Sell Notice. At the closing, Buyer will pay the Buy-Sell Price to Seller in immediately available funds, and Seller will execute and deliver to Buyer a written instrument that transfers Seller's Membership Interest to Buyer. Buyer will make a good faith effort to cause Seller and all of Seller's Affiliates to be fully relieved from all personal liability for any Company liability. Buyer will also pay off any loan made to the Company by Seller under § 2.4.

If either Seller or Buyer defaults in the performance of its obligations under this section, then the other Member may pursue all remedies that are available at law or in equity to redress such default, including, without limitation, the right of the non-defaulting Member to reverse its role under this section and become a Seller (if the non-defaulting Member was originally a Buyer) or a Buyer (if the non-defaulting Member was originally a Seller). The non-defaulting Member may elect to reverse its role in the manner contemplated in the immediately preceding sentence by delivering written notice of such election to the defaulting Member at any time on or before the last day of the Fiscal Year of the defaulting Member's default under this section. The closing of the sale of the Membership Interest resulting from the non-defaulting Member's election to reverse its role under this section must occur on or before the date that is ___ days after the defaulting Member's receipt of the non-defaulting Member's election notice.

For the purposes of this section, a "Deadlock" will be deemed to have occurred if Investor fails to approve Developer's taking of any action that requires Investor's approval under § 5.2 and such failure to approve continues for a period of ten days after Investor's receipt of a written notice from Developer specifying the nature of the action that Developer proposes to take. Developer may negate the existence of a Deadlock by delivering written notice to Investor that Developer is withdrawing its proposal to take the subject action at any time on or before the date on which a Recipient Member receives a Buy-Sell Notice under this section.

ARTICLE 6: ACCOUNTING AND FISCAL AFFAIRS

§ 6.1   <u>**Fiscal Year and Accounting Method.**</u> The Company's Fiscal Year ends on December 31.

§ 6.2   <u>**Financial Statements and Reports.**</u> Developer will deliver to each Member the financial statements listed in paragraphs (a) and (b), below.

> (a)   Within 90 days after the end of each Fiscal Year, the Company's balance sheet, income statement, cash flow statement, budget variance report, and statement of changes in the Members' capital balances for the most recently concluded Fiscal Year; and

> (b)   Within 30 days after the end of each Fiscal Quarter, the Company's balance sheet, income statement, cash flow statement, and budget variance report for the most recently-concluded Fiscal Quarter and for the Fiscal Year to date.

The annual and quarterly financial statements described above must be accompanied by the written certification of the chief financial officer of Developer that such statements were prepared in accordance with generally accepted accounting principles, consistently applied. At Investor's request, Developer will cause the Company's annual financial statements to be reviewed or audited by a nationally-recognized firm of independent public accountants selected by Developer and approved by Investor.

§ 6.3   <u>**Tax Information.**</u> As soon as reasonably practicable after the end of each Fiscal Year, Developer will cause to be delivered to each Member a statement showing all items of the Company's taxable income, gain, loss, deduction, and credit for the most recently-concluded Fiscal Year and each Member's allocable share of such items. Developer will cause all tax returns and reports required to be filed by the Company to be prepared and timely filed with the appropriate authorities. Developer will retain such tax returns and reports as long as is required by applicable law.

Developer is authorized and directed to file all documents and take all other actions required to elect the "Safe Harbor" described in IRS Revenue Procedure _____ *[the successor to IRS Notice 2005–43]*. Such election will be binding on the Company and all the Members. Each Member (will comply with the requirements of the Safe Harbor with respect to any

Membership Interest transferred to it in connection with its performance of services for the Company.

ARTICLE 7: TRANSFER OF MEMBERSHIP INTERESTS

§ 7.1   General Prohibition Against Transfer of Membership Interests. No Member may sell, assign, pledge, encumber, or transfer all or any part of its Membership Interest, without first obtaining the other Members' written consent to such transfer.

§ 7.2   Permitted Transfer to Affiliates. Despite the provisions of § 7.1, any Member may transfer all or any part of its Membership Interest to an Affiliate of such Member as long as such transfer does not effect: (a) a release of the transferring Member's financial and other obligations under this Agreement; or (b) a termination of the Company for federal income tax purposes under § 708 of the Code.

§ 7.3   Admission of Transferee as Substituted Member. A transferee of a Membership Interest will not become a substituted Member, unless and until the other Member consents in writing to such substitution. Neither the transferor of a Membership Interest, nor a transferee who is not admitted as a substituted Member, will be entitled to: (a) require any accounting of the Company's transactions; (b) inspect the Company's books and records; (c) require any information from the Company; or (d) exercise any privilege or right of a Member that is not specifically granted to a non-substituted transferee of a limited liability company interest under the Act.

ARTICLE 8: WITHDRAWAL OF MEMBERS

§ 8.1   No Withdrawal. No Member may withdraw from the Company.

§ 8.2   Death, Bankruptcy, Liquidation of a Member. A Member will not cease to be a "member" within the meaning of the Act upon the occurrence of any of the items listed in § 18–801(b) of the Act, nor will the occurrence of any such event cause the dissolution of the Company.

ARTICLE 9: DISSOLUTION, WINDING UP AND TERMINATION

§ 9.1   Dissolution. The Company will dissolve upon the occurrence of any of the following events:

(a) The agreement in writing of all the Members to dissolve the Company;

(b) The sale of all or substantially all of the Company's assets;

(c) The entry of a decree of judicial dissolution of the Company under § 18–802 of the Act; or

(d)   The occurrence of any event that results in there being no Member of the Company, unless the Company is continued at the time and in the manner required under the Act.

§ 9.2   <u>**Winding Up and Termination.**</u> Upon the dissolution of the Company, the affairs and business of the Company must be wound up and terminated, the Company's liabilities must be discharged, and the Company's assets must be liquidated and distributed in the manner prescribed in this section. A reasonable time is allowed for the orderly winding up of the affairs and business of the Company, so as to enable the Company to minimize the normal losses attendant to the winding up and termination period.

Developer will have the exclusive power and authority to act on behalf of the Company:

1.   To wind up and terminate the affairs and business of the Company;

2.   To sell and convey the Company's assets to such Persons (including, without limitation, any Member or any of Affiliate of a Member) for such consideration, and upon such terms and conditions as Developer deems appropriate;

3.   To discharge the Company's liabilities;

4.   To establish any reserves that Developer deems appropriate for any contingent or unforeseen liabilities or obligations of the Company; and

5.   To distribute the Liquidation Proceeds in the manner described in the remainder of this section.

Upon completion of the winding up of the affairs and business of the Company, Developer will distribute the Liquidation Proceeds in the following manner and order of priority:

(a)   First, to the payment of the Company's debts and liabilities (including, without limitation, any debts or liabilities owed to any Member or any of Affiliate of a Member), and then to the payment of the expenses of the winding up of the affairs and business of the Company;

(b)   Second, to the setting up of any reserves (to be held by Developer in an interest-bearing account) that Developer deems appropriate for any contingent or unforeseen liabilities or obligations of the Company, with the undistributed balance of such reserves being distributed by Developer in the manner described in subparagraph (c), below, at such time as Developer deems appropriate; and

(c)   Third, to the Members in accordance with the provisions of § 3.2.

§ 9.3   Final Accounting. Developer will furnish each Member with a statement identifying the assets and liabilities of the Company as of the date of the completion of the winding up and termination of the affairs and business of the Company. Upon completion of the distribution plan set forth § 9.2, Developer will file in those public offices required by the Act a cancellation of the Company's certificate of formation and any other documents that Developer deems appropriate to effect the dissolution and termination of the Company.

§ 9.4   Return of Contribution Nonrecourse to Other Members. Each Member will look solely to the assets of the Company for the return of its Capital Contributions. A Member will have no recourse against the Company, Developer, or any other Member if the Company's assets remaining after the payment of the Company's debts and liabilities is insufficient to return the Member's full Unreturned Capital Contribution. No Member will be required to restore a deficit in its Capital Account.

ARTICLE 10: MISCELLANEOUS

§ 10.1   Notices and Addresses. Each Member must give any notice, consent, or other communication under this Agreement in writing by one of the following methods of delivery: facsimile; email; overnight courier (with all fees prepaid); or registered or certified United States mail, return receipt requested and postage prepaid. Any such notice, consent, or communication will be deemed effective when received by the specified addressee. Any such notice, consent, or communication must be sent to the Company at the address of the Company's principal office and to the Members at the addresses set forth after their respective names in § 1.3. The Company and any Member may change its address for the giving of notices, consents, or other communications by delivering written notice to the Company and to the other Member of its new address for such purpose.

§ 10.2   Counterparts. The Members may execute this Agreement in several counterparts that, when combined, will constitute a binding contract.

§ 10.3   Applicable Law. This Agreement is governed by Delaware law.

§ 10.4   Successors. This Agreement binds the Members and their respective successors and permitted assigns.

§ 10.5   Severability. If any provision of this Agreement is held invalid or unenforceable, then the validity and enforceability of the other provisions of this Agreement will not be affected or impaired in any way.

§ 10.6   Exhibits. All exhibits attached to this Agreement are incorporated into this Agreement by this reference.

§ 10.7   <u>Amendment of Agreement.</u> This Agreement may not be amended, except by a written instrument signed by all the Members.

§ 10.8   <u>Entire Agreement.</u> This Agreement is the complete and exclusive expression of the Members' agreement on the matters contained in this Agreement. All prior and contemporaneous negotiations and understandings of the Members concerning the matters contained in this Agreement are merged into and superseded by this Agreement.

§ 10.9   <u>No Waiver.</u> No provision in this Agreement may be waived, except by a writing executed by the party against whom the waiver is sought to be enforced.

§ 10.10   <u>Waiver of Partition.</u> Each Member waives any right to partition the Company's assets or to compel any sale or appraisement of any Company Property.

§ 10.11   <u>Standard for Consents.</u> Except as otherwise expressly stated in this Agreement, all consents or approvals from any Member may be withheld in the sole and unfettered discretion of the affected Member.

§ 10.12   <u>Default.</u> For the purposes of this Agreement (including, without limitation, the purposes of §§ 2.3 and 5.11), no Member will be considered to be in "default" in the performance of its obligations under this Agreement unless such Member fails to cure any alleged default within the time period set forth below:

    (a)   As to any failure to make any Capital Contribution pursuant to § 2.2, within ten days after the subject Member's receipt of an Additional Funds Notice issued pursuant to § 2.2; and

    (b)   With respect to all other matters, within 30 days after the subject Member's receipt of written notice from the other Member alleging the existence of such default (or, if the alleged default is not readily susceptible of being cured within a 30-day period, then such longer period of time, not to exceed 90 days, as is reasonably required to effect such cure as long as the subject Member commences the cure of such alleged default within the aforementioned 30-day period and at all times thereafter diligently pursues such cure to completion).

If a default occurs within the meaning of this section, then the non-defaulting party (be it the Company or any other Member) may pursue all such rights and remedies as are provided in this Agreement and at law or in equity.

Each Member is signing this Agreement as of the Effective Date.

DEVELOPER: **INVESTOR:**

_____   _____

By: _____   By: _____

(Name)   (Title)   (Name)   (Title)

<u>**EXHIBIT A**</u>

<u>**DEFINITIONS**</u>

The capitalized words and phrases used in the Operating Agreement for _____ LLC have the following meanings (such meanings being equally applicable to both the singular and plural forms of each word and phrase).

1.   "**Act**" means the Delaware Limited Liability Company Act, as set forth in Delaware Code, Title 6, Sections 18–101 *et seq.*, as the same may be amended from time to time (or any corresponding provisions of any successor law).

2.   "**Additional Capital Contributions**" means all cash or property contributed to the Company by its Members under § 2.2.

3.   "**Additional Funds**" has the meaning set forth in § 2.2.

4.   "**Additional Funds Notice**" has the meaning set forth in § 2.2.

5.   "**Affiliate**" means, with respect to any Person: (i) any Person directly or indirectly controlling, controlled by or under common control with such Person (within the meaning of 17 CFR 230–405); (ii) any Person owning or controlling 10% or more of the outstanding voting or equity interests of such Person; (iii) any officer, director, or general partner of such Person; (iv) any Person, who is an officer, director, general partner, trustee, or holder of 10% or more of the voting or equity interests of any Person described in clauses (i) through (iii) of this subparagraph; or (v) the spouse or lineal descendant of any such Person or any trust established for the benefit of any of the foregoing.

6.   "**Agreement**" means the Company's Operating Agreement, as the same may be amended from time to time.

7.   "**Approved Development Budget**" means the development budget referred to in § 5.7 and attached to this Agreement as Exhibit B.

8.   "**Approved Operating Budget**" means the operating budget for Fiscal Year 20__ referred to in § 5.8 and attached to this Agreement as Exhibit C, and any Operating Budget approved (or deemed to have been approved) by Investor for any subsequent Fiscal Year under the provisions of § 5.8.

9.   "**Approved Purpose**" has the meaning set forth in § 2.2.

10.   "**Budget Review Period**" has the meaning set forth in § 5.8.

11.   **"Buy-Sell Notice"** has the meaning set forth in § 5.11.

12.   **"Buy-Sell Price"** has the meaning set forth in § 5.11.

13.   **"Capital Account"** means, with respect to any Member, the capital account maintained for such Member in accordance with § 2.6.

14.   **"Capital Contribution"** means, with respect to any Member, the amount of cash or the agreed-upon fair market value of any property contributed to the capital of the Company by such Member pursuant to § 2.1 and § 2.2.

15.   **"Capital Event"** means the following: (a) the sale of all or substantially all of the Company's assets; (b) the placement and funding of any debt that is secured by a mortgage on the Project (including, without limitation, the refinancing of any such secured debt); (c)the condemnation of all or any material part of the Project; or (d) any loss of any part of the Project due to the occurrence of a casualty or failure of title that results in excess proceeds after the restoration or repair of the Project.

16.   **"Capital Proceeds"** means the gross cash receipts of the Company produced from the occurrence of a Capital Event, reduced by the sum of the following: (a) all cash expenditures made by the Company in connection with the Capital Event, including, without limitation, any brokerage fees or commissions paid to any Person; (b) repayment of the principal and any accrued and unpaid interest on any debt being refinanced or retired as part of the Capital Event and (c) such cash reserves as Developer may decide to establish, with the consent of the Investor, to cover future occurrences and contingencies.

17.   **"Code"** means the Internal Revenue Code of 1986, as the same may be amended from time to time (or any corresponding provisions of any successor law).

18.   **"Company"** means _____ LLC.

19.   **"Deadlock"** has the meaning set forth in § 5.11.

20.   **"Default"** has the meaning set forth in § 10.12.

21.   **"Developer"** means _____ and any Person who becomes a successor to _____ under this Agreement.

22.   **"Effective Date"** has the meaning set forth in the preamble.

23.   **"Electing Member"** has the meaning set forth in § 5.11.

24. **"Entity Value"** has the meaning set forth in § 5.11.

25. **"Fiscal Year"** means: (a) the period beginning on the commencement date of the Company's existence and ending on the next succeeding December 31; and (b) each subsequent 12 calendar month period throughout the term of the Company's existence that begins on January 1 and ends on December 31.

26. **"Fiscal Quarter"** means: (a) the period beginning on the commencement date of the Company's existence and ending on _____; and (b) each subsequent three calendar month period throughout the Company's existence that ends on March 31, June 30, September 30, or December 31, respectively.

27. **"Investor"** means _____ and any Person who becomes a successor to _____ under this Agreement.

28. **"Liquidation Proceeds"** means the cash or other property distributable to the Members pursuant to § 9.2 upon the dissolution and termination of the Company.

29. **"Liquidity Notice"** has the meaning set forth in § 5.11.

30. **"Major Lease"** means any new lease of more than _____ square feet of rentable space in the Project

31. **"Member"** means Developer, Investor, any Person hereafter admitted to the Company as a "member," and any Person who becomes a successor to any of the foregoing Persons under this Agreement.

32. **"Membership Interest"** means a Member's ownership interest in the Company, including, without limitation, the rights and obligations of such Member under this Agreement and the Act.

33. **"Operating Cash Flow"** means, with respect to each Fiscal Quarter of the Company, the sum of the gross cash receipts of the Company from any source other than Capital Proceeds, plus the amount of any previously-established, but unused cash reserves, reduced by the sum of the following items paid by the Company: (a) all principal and interest payments and all other sums paid on or with respect to any Company debt; (b) all operating expenses incurred incident to the operation of the Project; (c) all capital expenditures incurred incident to the construction, repair, or replacement of the Project; (c) such cash reserves as Developer may from time to time decide to establish, with the consent of the Investor, to cover future occurrences and contingencies; and (d) all other cash expenditures made by the

Company related to the ownership, operation, or management of the Project and the Company's business (other than any expenditure made in connection with the occurrence of any Capital Event).

34.   **"Person"** means any individual, general or limited partnership, corporation, trust, limited liability company, or other entity.

34.   **"Preferred Return"** means, with respect to each Member, an amount equal to a return of ___% per annum, compounded daily, on the balance of such Member's Unreturned Capital Contribution. Any Preferred Return that has accrued, but remains unpaid under §§ 3.1(a) and 3.2(b), will bear interest at ___%, compounded daily, and will be considered part of the "Preferred Return" for all purposes of this Agreement.

35.   **"Profits"** and **"Losses"** means, for each fiscal period of the Company, an amount equal to the Company's taxable income or loss from all sources, determined in accordance with Code Section 703(a) and adjusted in the following manner: (i) the income of the Company that is exempt from federal income tax must be added to such taxable income or loss; (ii) any expenditure of the Company described or treated under Code Section 705(a)(2)(B) shall be subtracted from such taxable income or loss;.

36.   **"Project"** means the approximately _____-square-foot _____ building to be developed by the Company on the approximately ___-acre tract of land located in _____, _____.

37.   **"Recipient Member"** has the meaning set forth in § 5.11.

38.   **"Regulations"** means the Federal Income Tax Regulations (including Temporary Regulations) promulgated under the Code, as the same may be amended from time to time (including corresponding provisions of successor regulations).

39.   **"Uncontrollable Expenses"** means all costs and expenses of the Company that are not reasonably capable of being controlled by Developer, either as to the amount or the timing of the incurring of such costs or expenses, and expressly includes, without limitation, utility charges, insurance premiums, real estate taxes, debt service increases resulting from an increase in interest rates, costs associated with unforeseeable repairs or replacements required to be made to the Project, and the incurring of any other cost or expense that is required by law or under any agreement to which the Company is legally bound.

40. **"Unreturned Capital Contribution"** means, with respect to each Member, the amount of all Capital Contributions made by such Member to the Company, reduced by the amount of any distributions made to such Member under § 3.2(a).

EXHIBIT B

APPROVED DEVELOPMENT BUDGET

See attached Schedule B–1.

EXHIBIT C

APPROVED OPERATING BUDGET—FISCAL YEAR 20__

See attached Schedule C–1.

DOCUMENT #4

CLOSING STATEMENT
FOR LAND SALE

■ ■ ■

CLOSING STATEMENT

PROPERTY: Approximately 120 acres of undeveloped land located in the Heathrow International Business Center in Seminole County, Florida

SELLER: HIBC Development Company

BUYER: Colonial Realty Limited Partnership

ESCROW AGENT: First American Title Insurance Company

REAL ESTATE BROKER: Greenwich Group International LLC

SELLER'S COUNSEL: Holland & Knight

BUYER'S COUNSEL: Leitman, Seigal & Payne, P.C.

DATE OF CLOSING: August 1, 2002

This Closing Statement was prepared based on the sale of the HIBC land by The Pizzuti Companies to Colonial Real Properties Trust in August, 2002. The numbers used in the Closing Statement (other than the purchase price, which is a matter of public record) are, however, simply approximations of the actual costs incurred in connection with the land sale closing.

Seller's Statement

	Credits	(Charges)
Purchase Price	$13,000,000.00	
Deposit		($300,000.00)
Loan Pay-off		($4,000,000.00)
Title Insurance Costs		($25,000.00)
Documentary Stamps		($91,000.00)
Real Estate Commission		($84,500.00)
Real Estate Tax Proration		($130,000.00)
Legal Fees of Seller's Counsel		($20,000.00)
Total Credits (Charges)	$13,000,000.00	($4,650,500.00)
Net Cash Payable to Seller	**$8,349,500.00**	

Buyer's Statement

	(Credits)	Charges
Purchase Price		$13,000,000.00
Deposit	($300,000.00)	
Survey Costs		$10,000.00
Recording Costs		$200.00
Real Estate Tax Proration	($130,000.00)	
Legal Fees of Buyer's Counsel		Paid outside of closing
Total Credits (Charges)	($430,000.00)	$13,010,200.00
Net Cash Payable by Buyer	**$12,580,200.00**	

Disbursements/Reconciliations

Funds Available for Disbursement:

Net Cash Payable by Buyer $12,580,200.00

Actual Disbursements:

First Union National Bank

(Loan Pay-off) $4,000,000.00

First American Title Insurance Company

(Title Insurance Costs) $25,000.00

Greenwich Group International LLC

(Real Estate Commission) $84,500.00

Seminole County Clerk of Circuit Court

(Documentary Stamps) $91,000.00

Holland & Knight

(Legal Fees of Seller's Counsel) $20,000.00

Tinkelpaugh Surveying

(Survey Costs) $10,000.00

Seminole County Recorder

(Recording Costs) $200.00

HIBC Development Company

(Net Cash Payable to Seller) $8,349,500.00

Total Disbursements: **$12,580,200.00**

Notes to Closing Statement

1.   All closing credits, charges and prorations have been calculated in accordance with the provisions of the Real Estate Purchase Agreement entered into by Seller and Buyer as of May 26, 2002 ("Purchase Contract"). All capitalized terms that are used, but not defined in this Closing Statement, have the meanings attributed to those terms in the Purchase Contract.

2.   All prorations set forth in this Closing Statement have been calculated, apportioned, and prorated between Seller and Buyer as of 11:59 p.m. on the day prior to the Date of Closing.

3.   At closing, the Escrow Agent will pay the principal amount of the Deposit ($300,000) to Seller and will refund all interest earned on the Deposit to Buyer.

4.   Attached to this Closing Statement as Schedule 1 is the loan pay-off letter from First Union National Bank.

5.   Attached to this Closing Statement as Schedule 2 is the proposed real estate tax bill issued by Seminole County for the Property for the 2002 taxable year. Because the real estate taxes are not yet due and payable, Buyer has been given a closing credit for 212/365ths of the proposed real estate tax bill (the number of days included in taxable year 2002 prior to the date of closing). The real estate tax credit is subject to being reprorated at the time and in the manner specified in § 7(a) of the Purchase Contract.

6.   Attached to this Closing Statement as Schedules 3, 4, 5, and 6, respectively, are the invoices submitted for payment at closing by First American Title Insurance Company (title insurance costs), Tinkelpaugh Surveying (survey costs), Holland & Knight (legal fees for Seller's counsel), and Greenwich Group International LLC (real estate commission).

7.   The net cash payable by Buyer at closing (as set forth in this Closing Statement under the caption "Disbursements/Reconciliations") has been wire transferred by Buyer in advance to the account of Escrow Agent for disbursement at closing in accordance with the "Disbursements/Reconciliations" section of this Closing Statement. Upon its receipt of a fully-executed copy of this Closing Statement and its receipt of further specific telephonic, electronic or written confirmation from each of Seller and Buyer, Escrow Agent will disburse all available funds to the parties in the manner contemplated in this Closing Statement and otherwise in accordance with wiring or other funding instructions provided to Escrow Agent by the intended recipients of such disbursements. The Escrow Agent's wiring instructions are attached to this Closing Statement as Schedule 7.

Seller, Buyer, and Escrow Agent have each executed this Closing Statement as of the Date of Closing.

Seller: **Buyer:**   **Escrow Agent:**

By: _____   By: _____   By: _____

DOCUMENT #5

CONSTRUCTION LOAN AGREEMENT FOR OHIO DEVELOPMENT PROJECT

■ ■ ■

CONSTRUCTION LOAN AGREEMENT

Effective Date: _____, 20__

Lender: _____

Borrower: _____

_____

This document was provided for use in this text through the good graces of David Conrad, a partner of the Bricker & Eckler law firm headquartered in Columbus, Ohio. This particular Construction Loan Agreement is a version used by David prior to the financial meltdown known as the Great Recession of 2008. In the aftermath of the Great Recession, many lenders instructed their counsel (including David) to reject the straightforward simplicity of loan documents such as this Form Construction Loan Agreement in favor of a 100-page "killer" CLA replete with every imaginable pro-lender provision. I have opted to buck that trend by including David's shorter CLA in the Document Appendix for two reasons—(1) as a real estate development lawyer, I abhor draconian loan documents that are unduly long and complex, and (2) the Form Construction Loan Agreement more than adequately covers all the primary construction lending issues discussed in Chapter 9 of this book.

ARTICLE I

Particular Terms and Definitions/Terms of Loan

1.1 The following terms, as used herein, shall have the following meanings:

"Aggregate Change Order Amount"—_____ Dollars ($_____).

"Borrower's Architects"—The architects and/or engineers approved by Lender who are responsible for preparing the Plans and supervising construction of the Improvements, and any successor engaged with Lender's consent.

"Change Orders"—Any amendments or modifications to the Plans, General Contract or Subcontracts.

"Commitment Fee"—_____ Dollars ($_____).

"Completion Date"—_____.

"Construction Loan Checking Account"—A separate non-interest bearing checking account with Lender which shall not be drawn upon except to pay Hard Costs and Soft Costs approved by Lender.

"Draw Request"—A statement by Borrower on AIA Form G702/703 or other form acceptable to Lender and executed by Borrower's Requisition Agent setting forth the amount of the Loan advance requested in each instance and including:

(a) Lien waivers from the General Contractor for all work performed through the date of the Draw Request ("Lien Waivers");

(b) Lien Waivers from all Subcontractors for all work performed through the date of the immediately preceding Draw Request;

(c) Proof of payment of all Soft Costs covered by the immediately preceding Draw Request; and

(d) Bills or invoices for all Soft Costs covered by the Draw Request.

"Event of Default"—Any of the following shall constitute an "Event of Default":

(a) Borrower shall fail to pay any installment of principal or interest under the Note when and as the same shall become due and payable, whether monthly, at maturity, at a date fixed for prepayment or by acceleration or otherwise; or

(b) Borrower shall fail to make any other payment when due, and such failure shall continue for a period of ten (10) calendar days after written notice thereof from Lender; or

(c) any representation or warranty made in writing by or on behalf of Borrower in any Loan Document or in any writing furnished by Borrower to Lender in connection with the transactions contemplated hereby, proves to have been false or incorrect in any respect on the date as of which made; provided that if such false or incorrect statement is capable of being cured, an Event of Default shall not occur unless and until Borrower fails to cause such misrepresentation or breach of warranty to be cured within thirty (30) days after receipt of written notice thereof from Lender; or

(d) Borrower (i) is generally not paying, or admits in writing its inability to pay, its debts as they become due, (ii) files, or consents by answer or otherwise to the filing against it of, or fails to secure the dismissal within ninety (90) days after filing of, a petition for relief or reorganization or arrangement or any other petition in bankruptcy, for liquidation or to take advantage of any bankruptcy, insolvency, reorganization, moratorium or other similar law of any jurisdiction, (iii) makes an assignment for the benefit of its creditors, (iv) consents to the appointment of a custodian, receiver, trustee or other officer with similar powers with respect to it or with respect to any substantial part of its Project, (v) is adjudicated as insolvent or to be liquidated, or (vi) takes corporate action for the purpose of any of the foregoing;

(e) A court or Governmental Authority of competent jurisdiction enters an order appointing, without consent by Borrower, a custodian, receiver, trustee or other officer with similar powers with respect to it or with respect to any substantial part of its property, or constituting an order for relief or approving a petition for relief or reorganization or any other petition in bankruptcy or for liquidation or to take advantage of any bankruptcy or insolvency law of any jurisdiction, or ordering the dissolution, winding-up or liquidation of Borrower, or any such petition shall be filed against Borrower and such petition shall not be dismissed within ninety (90) days;

(f) Borrower shall fail to perform any obligation or comply with any term applicable to it contained herein or in any other Loan Document and such failure is not remedied within thirty (30) days after Borrower' receipt of written notice thereof from Lender; or

(g) Any Guarantor fails to perform any obligation or comply with any term applicable to it under the Guaranty and such failure is not remedied within thirty (30) days after such Guarantor's receipt of written notice thereof from Lender.

"Extended Maturity Date"—_____, 20__.

"Financial Statements"—Statements of the assets, liabilities (direct or contingent), income, expenses and cash flow of Borrower and each Guarantor, as required by the Mortgage.

"General Contractor"; "General Contract"—Any general contractor engaged by Borrower and approved by Lender under any General Contract; any contract (together with all riders, addenda and other instruments referred to therein as "Contract Documents") between Borrower and the General Contractor which requires the General Contractor to provide, or supervise or manage the procurement of, substantially all labor and materials needed for completion of the Improvements.

"Governmental Authorities"—The United States, the state in which the Premises are located and any political subdivision, agency, department, commission, board, bureau or instrumentality of either of them, including any local authorities, which exercises jurisdiction over the Premises or the Improvements.

"Guarantor"—_____, _____ and _____, or any one of them, each of whom has jointly and severally guaranteed payment and performance by Borrower of Borrower's obligations to Lender.

"Guaranty"—The guaranty of the performance of all or part of Borrower's obligations which shall be executed by each Guarantor.

"Hard Costs"—The aggregate costs of all labor, materials, equipment, fixtures and furnishings necessary for completion of the Improvements.

"Improvements"; "Project"—The _____.

"Initial Advance"—The first advance of Loan proceeds to be made hereunder.

"Leases"—Any leases for space of the rentable area of the Improvements.

"Loan"—The loan to be advanced by Lender to Borrower pursuant to the terms and conditions of this Agreement, as the same is further defined in Section 1.2.

"Loan Amount"—_____ Dollars ($_____).

"Loan Budget Amounts"—The portion of the Loan Amount set forth in the Project Budget to be advanced for each line item and category of Hard Costs and Soft Costs.

"Loan Documents"—This Agreement, the Note, Mortgage, Guaranty, the Assignment of Construction Documents, the Assignment of Design Documents, UCC Financing Statements and any other instrument, document, certificate or affidavit heretofore, now or hereafter given by Borrower evidencing or securing or by any Guarantor guaranteeing all or any part of the foregoing.

"Maturity Date"—_____, 200__.

"Mortgage"—That certain Open-End Mortgage, Assignment of Rents and Security Agreement to be made by Borrower to Lender to secure the Note and any sums in addition to the Loan Amount advanced by Lender for completion of the Improvements.

"Mortgaged Property"—The Premises and other property constituting the "Mortgaged Property," as said quoted term is defined in the Mortgage.

"Note"—That certain Mortgage Note for a principal sum equal to the Loan Amount to be made by Borrower to Lender to evidence the Loan.

"Option to Extend"—Borrower's option, subject to the terms and conditions of Section 1.2, to extend the term of the Loan from the Maturity Date to the Extended Maturity Date.

"Plans"—All final drawings, plans and specifications prepared by Borrower, Borrower's Architects, the General Contractor or Subcontractors, and approved by Lender, which describe and show the labor, materials, equipment, fixtures and furnishings necessary for the construction of the Improvements, including all amendments and modifications thereof made by approved Change Orders (and also showing minimum grade of finishes and furnishings for all areas of the Improvements to be leased or sold in ready-for-occupancy conditions).

"Premises"—The real property described on Exhibit "A" to the Mortgage, upon all or part of which the Improvements are to be constructed.

"Project Budget"—The statement attached hereto as Exhibit "A", setting forth, by line item and category, the Hard Costs and Soft Costs of completion of the Improvements.

"Requisition Agent"—_____ who is hereby authorized by Borrower to execute and deliver each Draw Request.

"Retainage Percentage"—_____.

"Retained Amounts"—The greater of the Retainage Percentage of the Hard Costs or the actual retained amounts specified on the Draw Request.

"Single Change Order Amount"—_____ Dollars ($_____).

"Soft Costs"—All costs of acquisition of the Premises and completion of the Improvements other than Hard Costs, including, without limitation, architects' and attorneys' fees, ground rents, interest, real estate taxes, survey costs and insurance premiums.

"Subcontractor"; "Subcontract"—Any subcontractor or supplier engaged by the General Contractor and any contractor other than the General Contractor or supplier engaged by Borrower, under one or more contracts or work orders; any such contract or work order.

"Title Insurer"—The issuer(s), approved by Lender, of the title insurance policy or policies insuring the Mortgage.

"Variable Rate"—The rate of interest equal to (a) .5% plus (b) Lender's "Prime Rate" in effect from time to time that serves as the basis upon which effective rates of interest are calculated for those loans making reference thereto (any change in the rate of interest on the Loan due to a change in the Prime Rate shall become effective on the date each change in the Prime Rate is announced by Lender).

1.2   Certain salient terms of the Loan are summarized below.

(a) The Loan. In connection with the construction of the Improvements on the Premises, Borrower desires to borrow from Lender a loan (the "Loan") in an amount equal to the Loan Amount, the proceeds of which are to be used for the payment of certain costs and expenses related to the Project, all as set forth in the Project Budget. Any amounts of the Loan disbursed by Lender shall not, in total, exceed the Loan Amount and shall be deemed evidenced by the Note and shall be payable to Lender on or before the Maturity Date or, if applicable, the Extended Maturity Date and shall bear interest at the Variable Rate.

(b) Commitment Fee. Borrower shall pay Lender the Commitment Fee in the amount set forth in Article 1. The Commitment Fee shall be deemed fully earned, payable and non-refundable upon the Borrower's execution of this Agreement.

(c) Loan Documents. Borrower shall deliver to Lender concurrently with this Agreement each of the Loan Documents, properly executed and, where applicable, in recordable form.

(d) Maturity Date. Except as otherwise provided in Subparagraph e., below, all sums due and owing under this Agreement, the Note and the other Loan Documents shall be repaid in full on or before the Maturity Date.

(e) Option to Extend. Borrower shall have the option to extend the term of the Loan from the Maturity Date to the Extended Maturity Date, upon satisfaction of each of the following conditions precedent:

(i) Borrower shall provide Lender with written notice of Borrower's request to exercise the Option to Extend not more than 90 days but not less than 30 days prior to the Maturity Date;

(ii) As of the date of Borrower's delivery of notice of request to exercise the Option to Extend and as of the Maturity Date, no Event of Default shall have occurred and be continuing, and no event or condition which, with the giving of notice or the passage of time or both, would constitute an Event of Default shall have occurred and be continuing, and Borrower shall so certify in writing;

(iii) On or before the Maturity Date, Borrower shall pay to Lender an extension fee in an amount equal to .5% of the Loan Amount; and

(iv) Borrower shall execute all documents reasonably required by Lender to exercise the Option to Extend and shall deliver to Lender, at Borrower's sole cost and expense, such title insurance endorsements as may be reasonably required by Lender.

ARTICLE II

Loan Advances

2.1 Subject to the provisions of this Agreement, Lender will advance and Borrower will accept the Loan Amount in installments as follows:

The Initial Advance will be made upon the satisfaction of the applicable conditions set forth in Article III hereof, and all subsequent advances shall be made monthly thereafter, upon satisfaction of the applicable conditions set forth in Article IV hereof, in amounts which shall be equal to the aggregate of the Hard Costs and Soft Costs incurred by Borrower through the end of the period covered by the Draw Request less:

(a) the Retained Amounts; and

(b) the total of the Loan advances theretofore made;

and, at the election of Lender, less any combination of the following further amounts:

(c) all or a portion of the amount by which any Hard Costs or Soft Costs are or are reasonably estimated by Lender to be greater than the respective Loan Budget Amounts for such costs; and

(d) any costs covered by the Draw Request not approved, certified or verified as provided in Section 2.2 hereof, any Soft Costs covered by a previous Draw Request for which proof of payment has not been received by Lender, and any Hard Costs covered by a previous Draw Request for which Lien Waivers have not been received by Lender.

2.2 Hard Costs are to be certified by the General Contractor. Verification of the monthly progress and Hard Costs and Soft Costs which have been incurred by Borrower shall be subject to the reasonable approval and verification by Lender. Lender reserves the right to utilize its own in-house engineers, architects and inspectors for purposes of such inspections, verifications and approvals, and to engage the services of independent contractors, engineers, architects or inspectors where Lender so desires, and Borrower agrees to assume and pay all costs, including, without limitation, fees and travel expenses, associated with each engineer, architect, contractor and inspector, in-house and independent.

2.3 All advances to Borrower are to be made at Lender's principal office or at such other place as Lender may designate and shall be deposited in the Construction Loan Checking Account. Draw Requests shall be received by Lender at least five (5) business days prior to the date of the requested advance. Lender may, at Lender's sole discretion and at

Borrower's expense, make any or all advances through the Title Insurer, in which case interest shall accrue to Lender from the time such funds are deposited with the Title Insurer.

2.4 Retained Amounts not advanced pursuant to Section 2.1 hereof during the course of construction of the Improvements shall be advanced upon the satisfaction of the conditions set forth in Section 4.2 hereof. Loan Budget Amounts for Soft Costs not advanced prior to completion of construction of the Improvements shall be advanced until exhausted, not more frequently than once a month, for Soft Costs as incurred after such completion.

2.5 Lender shall not make Loan advances for building materials or furnishings which are stored but not yet affixed to or incorporated into the Improvements.

2.6 Lender may, in its sole discretion, accelerate all or any portion of the amounts to be advanced hereunder without regard to Borrower's satisfaction of the conditions to its entitlement to Loan proceeds and no person dealing with Borrower or the General Contractor or any other person shall have standing to demand any different performance from Lender.

2.7 If at any time the undisbursed balance of the Loan Budget Amount for any line item or category of cost shown on the Project Budget is, in Lender's reasonable judgment, excessive, the excess may be reallocated to any other Loan Budget Amount balance which Lender reasonably deems to be insufficient.

2.8 A drawing under any letter of credit which Lender has issued or hereafter issues in connection with the Premises or Improvements, irrespective of the account party thereunder, shall constitute an advance of Loan proceeds under this Agreement and the amount thereof shall be evidenced and secured, respectively, by the Note and Mortgage. The issuance of any such letter of credit shall effect a reduction, by the amount and during the existence thereof, of available Loan proceeds and Lender, in its reasonable discretion, shall allocate such reduction to the Loan Budget Amounts which it deems most appropriate.

ARTICLE III

Conditions Precedent to Lender's Obligation to Make the Initial Advance

3.1 Lender shall not be obligated to make the Initial Advance until the following conditions shall have been satisfied:

(a) Lender shall have received and approved the items specified in Section 3.2 below;

(b) The representations and warranties made in Article V hereof shall be true and correct on and as of the date of the Initial Advance with the same effect as if made on such date;

(c) Existing improvements on the Premises, if any, shall not have been materially injured or damaged by fire or other casualty unless Lender shall have received insurance proceeds sufficient in the reasonable judgment of Lender to effect the satisfactory restoration of the said improvements and to permit completion of said improvements prior to the Completion Date pursuant to terms of disbursement satisfactory to Lender; and

(d) There shall exist no Event of Default, as therein defined, under the Note or Mortgage, or any event or state of facts which after notice or the passage of time, or both, could give rise to such an Event of Default.

3.2 The items to be received and approved by Lender prior to the Initial Advance shall be:

(a) The Commitment Fee, to be retained by Lender whether or not any advances are made under this Agreement;

(b) The executed Note, Mortgage, Guaranty, Borrower's Closing Certificate, this Agreement and UCC–1 Financing Statements relating to the Mortgaged Property and any other documents to be executed in connection with, or property given as security for the Loan;

(c) A paid title insurance policy, in the amount of the Note, in form approved by Lender, issued by the Title Insurer which shall insure the Mortgage to be a valid lien on Borrower's interest in the Premises free and clear of all defects and encumbrances except those previously approved by Lender, and shall contain:

(i) full coverage against mechanics' liens (filed and inchoate);

(ii) a reference to the survey but no survey exceptions except those theretofore approved by Lender; and

(iii) a pending disbursements clause in the form of Exhibit "B" hereto;

(d) A survey (current to within thirty (30) days of the Initial Advance) of the Premises certified to Lender and the Title Insurer;

(e) The policies of hazard insurance required by the Mortgage (together with evidence of the payment of the premiums therefor) which policies will contain an endorsement specifically providing that, in the case of any damage, all insurance proceeds will be paid to Lender in accordance with the terms and conditions of the Mortgage;

(f) If Borrower, any Guarantor or any general partner of Borrower or any Guarantor is a corporation, copies of the following documents with respect to each:

(i) a good-standing certificate from the state of its incorporation and, as to Borrower only, from the state in which the Premises are located;

(ii) certified copies of the articles of incorporation and by-laws or code of regulations;

(iii) resolutions, certified by the corporate secretary, of the shareholders or directors of the corporation authorizing the consummation of the transactions contemplated hereby or by the Guaranty; and

(iv) a certificate of the corporate secretary as to the incumbency of the officers executing this Agreement, the Guaranty or any of the other documents required hereby;

and, if Borrower, any Guarantor or any general partner of Borrower or any Guarantor is a partnership or venture:

(v) the partnership agreement and all amendments and attachments thereto, certified by the general partners to be true and complete;

(vi) any certificates filed or required to be filed by the partnership in the state of its formation and the state where the Premises are located in order for it to do business in those states; and

(vii) any consents by other partners required for the borrowing contemplated hereby, the consummation of this Agreement or the execution of the Guaranty, and an acknowledgment by each general partner of his continued membership in the partnership;

(g) An opinion of Borrower's counsel, which counsel shall have been approved by Lender, which opinion shall be in form and content satisfactory to Lender;

(h) Current Financial Statements and such other financial data as Lender shall require;

(i) Certified and correct copies of all Leases, Subordination and Attornment Agreements and Estoppel Certificates, in form satisfactory to Lender, from tenants under all Leases, and all contracts of sale for all or any portion of the Premises, together with the standard form of lease or contract of sale, as the case may be, Borrower intends to use in connection with the leasing of space in the Improvements or the sale of all or any portion of the Premises;

(j) A copy of the purchase agreement, closing statement and deed pursuant to which the Premises have been or will be acquired by Borrower;

(k) A copy of the following documents, each of which shall be in form and content acceptable to Lender: (i) General Contract; (ii) all Subcontracts requested by Lender; (iii) Borrower's agreement with Borrower's Architect;

and (iv) any management agreement or franchise agreement relating to the Premises and Improvements; and (v) _____;

(*l*) Assignments of all contracts from Borrower to Lender and acknowledgments of and consents to such assignments of all contracts required to be provided to Lender as set forth in subsection ((k)) of this Section;

(m) An appraisal of the Premises and Improvements and, if required by Lender, a market feasibility study;

(n) A progress schedule or chart showing the interval of time over which each item of Hard Costs is projected to be incurred or paid;

(o) The Project Budget;

(p) A Draw Request for the Initial Advance;

(q) The Plans;

(r) Evidence satisfactory to Lender, to the effect that: (i) the Plans have been approved by Governmental Authorities and all tenants under Leases and purchasers under sales contracts which contain any requirements or specifications in respect of construction of the Improvements; (ii) the Improvements as shown by the Plans will comply with applicable zoning ordinances and regulations; (iii) a General Contract and/or Subcontracts are in effect which satisfactorily provide for the construction of the Improvements; (iv) all roads and utilities necessary for the full utilization of the Improvements for their intended purposes have been completed or the presently installed and proposed roads and utilities will be sufficient for the full utilization of the Improvements for their intended purposes; and (v) the construction of the Improvements theretofore performed, if any, was performed in accordance with the Plans;

(s) Copies of all inspection and test records and reports made by or for Borrower's Architects;

(t) Copies of the applicable zoning resolutions, ordinances and map (marked to show the location of the Premises), certified by an appropriate official to be complete and accurate;

(u) Copies of any and all authorizations including plot plan and subdivision approvals, zoning variances, sewer, building and other permits required by Governmental Authorities for the construction, use, occupancy and operation of the Mortgaged Property or the Improvements for the purposes contemplated by the Plans in accordance with all applicable building, environmental, ecological, landmark, subdivision and zoning codes, laws and regulations;

(v) Letters from local utility companies or Governmental Authorities stating that gas, electric power, sanitary and storm sewer and water facilities and any other necessary utilities will be available to service the

Premises in adequate capacities upon completion of construction of the Improvements, and that the same shall enter the Premises through public rights-of-way or through recorded private easements reviewed and approved by Lender;

(w) A site plan (showing all necessary approvals, utility connections and site improvements);

(x) A soil-engineer's report;

(y) An environmental site assessment;

(z) A copy of the Notice of Commencement prepared in accordance with Ohio Revised Code Section 1311.04 and to be recorded with the _____ County Recorder's Office immediately following the recording of the Mortgage; and

(aa) UCC searches against Borrower or other owner of the Mortgaged Property or any portion thereof and advice from the Title Insurer to the effect that searches of proper public records disclose no leases of personalty or financing statements filed or recorded against the Premises, Borrower or other owner of any portion of the Mortgaged Property.

ARTICLE IV

Conditions Precedent to Lender's Obligation to
Make Advances After the Initial Advance

4.1 Lender's obligation to make Loan advances after the Initial Advance shall be subject to the satisfaction of the following conditions:

(a) Any requirement of Article III that has not been satisfied or waived in writing by Lender must be satisfied;

(b) Lender shall have received a Draw Request for the advance;

(c) Lender shall have received a continuation report or endorsement to the title policy insuring the Mortgage to the date of such advance, in the form approved by Lender and setting forth no additional exceptions except those approved by Lender;

(d) For any advance immediately subsequent to the completion of the foundation of any building, Lender shall have received a survey certified to Lender and the Title Insurer, indicating the location of each such foundation, and updated, with respect to all relevant requirements and information, to within ten (10) days of the advance;

(e) The representations and warranties made in Article V hereof shall be true and correct on and as of the date of the advance with the same effect as if made on such date;

(f) There shall exist no Event of Default, as therein defined under the Note or Mortgage, or any event or state of facts which after notice or the passage of time, or both, could give rise to such an Event of Default;

(g) Existing improvements on the Premises, if any, shall not have been materially injured or damaged by fire or other casualty unless Lender shall have received insurance proceeds sufficient in the reasonable judgment of Lender to effect the satisfactory restoration of the said improvements and to permit completion of said improvements prior to the Completion Date pursuant to terms of disbursement satisfactory to Lender; and

(h) Copies of any amended Notice of Commencement filed in accordance with Ohio Revised Code Section 1311.04.

4.2 In the case of the final Hard Costs advance as provided in Section 2.4 hereof, Lender shall also have received and approved:

(a) Evidence satisfactory to Lender to the effect that construction of the Improvements has been completed and any necessary utilities and roads have been finished and made available for use, in accordance with the Plans, and that all approvals have been received from all Governmental Authorities of the Improvements in their entirety for permanent occupancy, and of the contemplated uses thereof, to the extent any such approval is a condition of the lawful use and occupancy thereof;

(b) A current, final, "as built" survey of the Premises, certified to Lender and the Title Insurer, showing the completed Improvements;

(c) Certificate of substantial completion from Borrower's Architects; and

(d) Certificates by all tenants under Leases to the effect that the Improvements have been satisfactorily completed.

ARTICLE V

Borrower's Representations, Warranties and Covenants

5.1 Borrower represents and warrants that:

(a) If Borrower, any Guarantor or any general partner of Borrower or any Guarantor is a corporation, each such entity is duly organized, validly existing and in good standing under the laws of the state of its incorporation, has stock outstanding which has been duly and validly issued, is qualified to do business and is in good standing in the state in which the Premises are located with full power and authority to consummate the transactions contemplated hereby;

(b) If Borrower, Guarantor or any general partner of Borrower or any Guarantor is a partnership or venture, each such entity is duly formed and validly existing, is fully qualified under the laws of the state in which the

Premises are located to do business therein, and has full power and authority to consummate the transactions contemplated hereby;

(c) The Plans are satisfactory to Borrower, have been reviewed and approved by each Guarantor, the General Contractor, the tenants under any Leases which require approval of the Plans, the purchasers under any sales contracts which require approval of the Plans, Borrower's Architects and, to the extent required by applicable law or any effective restrictive covenant, by all Governmental Authorities and the beneficiary of any such covenant; all construction, if any, already performed on the Improvements has been performed on the Premises in accordance with the Plans approved by the persons named above and with any restrictive covenants applicable thereto; there are no structural defects in the Improvements or violations of any requirement of any Governmental Authorities with respect thereto; the planned use of the Improvements complies with applicable zoning ordinances, regulations and restrictive covenants affecting the Premises as well as all environmental, ecological, landmark and other applicable laws and regulations; and all requirements for such use have been satisfied;

(d) Financial Statements have been heretofore delivered to Lender which are true, correct and current in all respects and which fairly present the respective financial conditions of the subjects thereof as of the respective dates thereof; no material adverse change has occurred in the financial conditions reflected therein since the respective dates thereof and no borrowings (other than the Loan) which might give rise to a lien or claim against the Mortgaged Property or Loan proceeds have been made by Borrower, any Guarantor or others since the date thereof;

(e) There are no actions, suits or proceedings pending, or to the knowledge of Borrower, threatened against or affecting Borrower, any Guarantor, the Premises, the validity or enforceability of the Mortgage or the priority of the lien thereof at law, in equity or before or by any Governmental Authorities; neither Borrower nor any Guarantor is in default with respect to any order, writ, injunction, decree or demand of any court or Governmental Authorities;

(f) The consummation of the transactions contemplated hereby and performance of this Agreement, the Note, Mortgage and Guaranty have not and will not result in any breach of, or constitute a default under, any mortgage, deed of trust, lease, bank loan or credit agreement, corporate charter, by-laws, partnership agreement or other instrument to which Borrower or any Guarantor is a party or by which any of them may be bound or affected;

(g) All utility services necessary for the construction of the Improvements and the operation thereof for their intended purposes are available in adequate capacities at the boundaries of the Premises, including water supply, storm and sanitary sewer, gas, electric power and telephone facilities, and all of such utility services enter the Premises through public rights-of-way or through recorded private easements reviewed and approved by Lender;

(h) Each Draw Request presented to Lender, and the receipt of the funds requested thereby, shall constitute an affirmation that the representations and warranties contained in Sections 5.1 and 5.2 remain true and correct as of the respective dates thereof;

(i) Borrower has entered into no contract or arrangement of any kind the performance of which by the other party thereto would give rise to a lien on the Mortgaged Property except for its arrangements with Borrower's Architects, the General Contractor, and Subcontractors who have been paid in full and have provided Lien Waivers for all payment due under said arrangements as of the end of the period covered by the last Draw Request;

(j) All roads necessary for the full utilization of the Improvements for their intended purposes have either been completed or the necessary rights-of-way therefor have been acquired by appropriate Governmental Authorities or dedicated to public use and accepted by said Governmental Authorities, and all necessary steps have been taken by Borrower and said Governmental Authorities to assure the complete construction and installation thereof no later than the Completion Date or any earlier date required by any law, order or regulation, or any Lease;

(k) Each of the Leases is unmodified and in full force and effect, there are no defaults under any provision thereof and all conditions to the effectiveness and continuing effectiveness thereof required to be satisfied as of the date hereof have been satisfied;

(*l*) There exists no Event of Default, as therein defined, under the Note or Mortgage, and no event or state of facts exists which after notice or the passage of time, or both, could give rise to an Event of Default thereunder;

(m) The approved Plans referred to in subsection ((c)) of this Section are the same as the filed plans referred to in the building permits for the Improvements;

(n) Borrower advised the Title Insurer in writing prior to the issuance of the title policy insuring the Mortgage whether any survey, soils-testing, site development, excavation or other work related to construction of the Improvements was begun or done before the Mortgage was recorded;

(*o*) No assessments (except installments not yet due and payable) of any nature will remain unpaid after the last Hard Costs advance, including, without limitation, assessments relating to streets, roads, entrances, waterlines, sanitary and storm sewers, gas lines and all other utilities including, without limitation, acreage fees and trunk sewers;

(p) Borrower shall indemnify and hold Lender harmless from all claims of every kind, of every person, including, without limitation, employees of Borrower, contractors and employees of contractors, tenants of Borrower, subtenants or concessionaires of any tenants, and employees and business invitees of any tenants, which claims arise from or out of the construction, use, occupancy or possession of the Improvements or the Mortgaged Property;

(q) The Mortgaged Property has not been damaged or injured as a result of any fire, explosion, accident, flood, gasoline or chemical leakage or other casualty;

(r) Borrower shall prepare and file a Notice of Commencement and amendments thereto as required under Ohio Revised Code Section 1311.04. Borrower represents and warrants that a Notice of Commencement has not been and will not be recorded prior to the recording of the Mortgage. Borrower shall post and keep posted the Notice of Commencement and all amendments thereto in a conspicuous place on the Premises during the course of construction of the Project. Borrower shall serve a copy of the Notice of Commencement and all amendments thereto on the original contractor in accordance with Ohio Revised Code Section 1311.04. Borrower further represents and warrants to timely comply with all provisions of Ohio Revised Code Section 1311.04 and failure to do so shall be deemed an Event of Default as defined under the Note and Mortgage;

(s) General Contractor and all Subcontractors have performed all work in connection with the Project for which they have been paid and General Contractor and all Subcontractors have been paid for all work in connection with the Project performed through the cutoff date of the immediately preceding Draw Request; and

(t) Borrower shall provide Lender with a copy of each Notice of Furnishing (as defined in Ohio Revised Code Section 1311.05) received by Borrower during the course of construction of any Improvements on the Premises.

5.2 Borrower covenants and agrees with Lender that Borrower will:

(a) Promptly comply with all laws, ordinances, orders, rules, statutes and regulations of Governmental Authorities and promptly furnish Lender with reports of any official searches made by Governmental Authorities and any claims of violations thereof;

(b) Permit Lender and its representatives to enter upon the Premises, inspect the Improvements and all materials to be used in the construction thereof and examine all detailed plans and shop drawings which are or may be kept at the construction site; Borrower will cooperate and cause the

General Contractor and Subcontractors to cooperate with Lender to enable Lender to perform its inspections hereunder;

(c) Pay all Hard Costs and Soft Costs and expenses required for completion of the Improvements and the satisfaction of the conditions of this Agreement, including, without limitation:

(i) all document and stamp taxes, recording and filing expenses and fees and commissions lawfully due to brokers in connection with the transactions contemplated hereby;

(ii) the fees and expenses of Lender's counsel, in connection with the preparation for and consummation of the transactions contemplated hereby, and for any services of such parties which may be required in addition to those normally and reasonably contemplated hereby; and

(iii) any taxes, insurance premiums, liens, security interests or other claims or charges against the Mortgaged Property;

(d) Commence construction of the Improvements no later than thirty (30) days from the date hereof; submit a Draw Request for the Initial Advance within thirty (30) days after such commencement and subsequent advances on a monthly basis thereafter; cause the construction thus begun to be prosecuted with diligence and continuity in a good and workmanlike manner in accordance with the Plans; use only materials, fixtures, furnishings and equipment in connection with construction of the Improvements that are not used or obsolete; and complete construction of the Improvements, and the installation of all necessary roads and utilities, in accordance with the Plans, on or before the Completion Date, free and clear of defects and liens or claims for liens for material supplied or labor or services performed in connection with the construction of the Improvements;

(e) Promptly following the execution of this Agreement, place a sign, at Borrower's own expense, on the Premises at a location satisfactory to Lender indicating, inter alia, that Lender is providing the "Construction Financing" and containing Lender's address and otherwise conforming to Lender's reasonable sign specifications;

(f) Receive and deposit in the Construction Loan Checking Account all advances made hereunder; hold the same and the right to receive the same as a trust fund for the purpose of paying only Hard Costs and Soft Costs;

(g) Indemnify Lender against claims of brokers arising by reason of the execution hereof or the consummation of the transactions contemplated hereby;

(h) Deliver to Lender copies of all contracts, bills of sale, statements, receipted vouchers and agreements under which Borrower claims title to any materials, fixtures or articles incorporated into the Improvements or subject to the lien of the Mortgage, or under which Borrower has incurred costs for which Borrower is entitled to a Loan advance, and deliver to Lender such other data or documents in connection with the Improvements as Lender may from time to time request;

(i) Upon demand of Lender, correct any defects (structural or otherwise) in the Improvements or any departures from the Plans not approved by Lender;

(j) Deliver to Lender a certified and correct copy of all Leases of the Premises whether executed before or after the date hereof and keep all of same in full force and effect in accordance with the covenants of Borrower contained in the Mortgage;

(k) Not permit the performance of any work pursuant to any Change Order until Lender: (i) shall have received a copy thereof; and (ii) in the case of Change Orders which will result in (A) a change in the aggregate of the contract prices for the construction of the Improvements in excess of the Single Change Order Amount or which, together with the aggregate of Change Orders theretofore executed by Borrower (excluding those approved by Lender pursuant to this subsection) will result in a change in such prices in excess of the Aggregate Change Order Amount or (B) a change in the character of the Improvements, shall have given specific written approval thereof; it being understood that approval of any Change Order will not obligate Lender to increase or advance any Loan Budget Amount on account of any such Change Order;

(*l*) Require covenants from the General Contractor to the same effect as the covenant made by Borrower in the immediately preceding subsection; and Borrower will provide in every General Contract that the General Contractor will deliver to Lender upon request of Lender, copies of all Subcontracts, Change Orders and any other contract, purchase order or subcontract covering labor, materials, equipment or furnishings to or for the Improvements, and the names of all persons with whom the General Contractor has contracted or intends to contract for the construction of the Improvements or for the furnishing of labor or materials therefor;

(m) Employ suitable means to protect from theft and vandalism all portions of the Improvements and all tools and building materials stored on the Premises; and

(n) Comply with all restrictions, covenants and easements affecting the Premises or the Improvements and cause the satisfaction of all conditions of this Agreement.

5.3 Borrower covenants that the representations and warranties made by it in Sections 5.1 and 5.2 hereof, and by each Guarantor in the Guaranty, will be continuously true and correct.

ARTICLE VI

General Conditions

6.1 The following conditions shall be applicable at all times during the term of the Loan:

(a) Any advance by Lender of Loan proceeds hereunder made prior to or without the fulfillment by Borrower of all of the conditions precedent thereto, whether or not known to Lender, shall not constitute a waiver by Lender of the requirement that all conditions, including the non-performed conditions, shall be required with respect to all future advances;

(b) All documentation and proceedings deemed by Lender to be necessary or required in connection with this Agreement and the documents relating hereto shall be subject to the prior approval of, and satisfactory to, Lender as to form and substance. In addition, the persons or parties responsible for the execution and delivery of, and signatories to, all of such documentation, shall be acceptable to, and subject to the approval of, Lender;

(c) If at any time Lender notifies Borrower that, in Lender's reasonable judgment, the undisbursed balance of the Loan is insufficient to pay the remaining Hard Costs and Soft Costs, Borrower shall either: (i) deposit with Lender an amount equal to such deficiency which Lender may from time to time apply, or allow Borrower to apply, to such Hard Costs and Soft Costs; or (ii) pay for such Hard Costs and Soft Costs in the amount of such deficiency so that the amount of the Loan which remains to be disbursed shall be sufficient to complete the Improvements, and Borrower shall furnish Lender with such evidence thereof as Lender shall require. Borrower hereby agrees that Lender shall have a lien on and security interest in any sums deposited pursuant to clause (i) above and that Borrower shall have no right to withdraw any such sums except for the payment of the aforesaid Hard Costs and Soft Costs as approved by Lender. Any such sums not used as provided in said clause (i) shall be released to Borrower when and to the extent that Lender determines that the amount thereof is more than the excess, if any, of the total remaining Hard Costs and Soft Costs of completion of the Improvements over the undisbursed balance of the Loan; provided, however, that should an Event of Default occur under the Note or Mortgage, Lender may, at its option, apply such amounts either to the costs of completion of the Improvements or to the immediate reduction of outstanding principal and/or interest under the Note;

(d) Upon the occurrence of any Event of Default under the Note or Mortgage, Borrower does hereby irrevocably authorize Lender to advance any undisbursed Loan proceeds directly to the General Contractor, Subcontractors and other persons to pay for completion of the Improvements but Lender is under no obligation to do so. No further direction or authorization from Borrower shall be necessary to warrant such direct advances and all such advances shall satisfy pro tanto the obligations of Lender hereunder and shall be secured by the Mortgage as fully as if made to Borrower regardless of the disposition thereof by the General Contractor, any Subcontractor or other person;

(e) All conditions of the obligation of Lender to make advances hereunder are imposed solely and exclusively for the benefit of Lender and may be freely waived or modified in whole or in part by Lender at any time if in its sole discretion it deems it advisable to do so, and no person other than Borrower (provided, however, that all conditions have been satisfied) shall have standing to require Lender to make any Loan advances or to be a beneficiary of this Agreement or any advances to be made hereunder. Any waiver or modification asserted by Borrower to have been agreed to by Lender must be in writing and comply with the provisions of subsection (h) of this Section;

(f) Borrower hereby irrevocably authorizes Lender to disburse proceeds of the Loan to pay: (i) interest accrued on the Note as it comes due; (ii) any and all commitment or loan fees; (iii) travel and inspection fees of Lender; (iv) fees and expenses of Lender's counsel; and (v) to satisfy any of the conditions of this Agreement; notwithstanding that Borrower may not have requested disbursement of such amounts and whether or not Borrower may be in default under the Note or Mortgage. Any such disbursements shall be added to the outstanding principal balance of the Note and shall be secured by the Mortgage. The authorization granted hereby shall not prevent Borrower from paying interest, or satisfying said conditions, from its own funds and shall in no event be construed so as to relieve Borrower from its obligation to pay interest as and when due under the Note, or to satisfy said conditions, or to obligate Lender to disburse Loan proceeds for the payment of interest or the satisfaction of said conditions;

(g) All notices to be given hereunder shall be sufficient if given in accordance with the provisions contained in Section 23 of the Mortgage;

(h) No provisions of the Note, Mortgage, UCC–1 Financing Statements, Guaranty or this Agreement may be changed, waived, discharged or terminated orally, by telephone or by any other means except an instrument in writing signed by the party against whom enforcement of the change, waiver, discharge or termination is sought;

(i) Except as herein provided, this Agreement shall be binding upon and inure to the benefit of Borrower and Lender and their respective heirs, personal representatives, successors and assigns. Notwithstanding the foregoing, Borrower, without the prior written consent of Lender, which consent may be withheld in Lender's sole discretion, may not assign, transfer or set over to another, in whole or in part, all or any part of its benefits, rights, duties and obligations hereunder, including, without limitation, performance of and compliance with conditions hereof and the right to receive the proceeds of current or future advances; and

(j) Borrower acknowledges that Borrower has selected or will select all architects, engineers, contractors, subcontractors, materialmen, and others furnishing services or materials for the Improvements and that Lender shall have no responsibility whatsoever for them or for any inspection reports or for the quality of their materials or workmanship. It is understood that Lender's sole function is that of lender and that the only consideration passing from Lender to Borrower are the Loan proceeds in accordance with and subject to the terms of this Agreement. Borrower shall have no right to rely on any procedures required by Lender herein, such procedures being solely for the benefit and protection of Lender.

6.2 The cover page and the Exhibits annexed hereto are incorporated as a part of this Agreement with the same effect as if set forth in the body hereof.

IN WITNESS WHEREOF, the parties have executed this Agreement as of the day and year first above written, the execution hereof by Borrower constituting: (a) a certification by the party or parties executing on its behalf that the representations and warranties made in Article V are true and correct as of the date hereof and that each of them duly holds and is incumbent in the position indicated under his name; and (b) the undertaking of said party or parties that each Draw Request, whether or not personally made by any or all of them, shall constitute the personal affirmation on the part of each of them that at the time thereof said representations and warranties are true and correct.

LENDER: BORROWER:

_____   _____

A National Banking Association

By: _____   By: _____

Its: _____   Its: _____

EXHIBIT "A"
PROJECT BUDGET

EXHIBIT "B"

Pending disbursement of the full proceeds of the loan secured by the mortgage set forth under Schedule A hereof, this policy insures only to the extent of the amount actually disbursed, but increases as each disbursement is made up to the face amount of the policy. However, if disbursements are made which the holder of such mortgage was not obligated to make after holder's receipt of a written notice of a lien or encumbrance or of work or labor performed or to be performed or of machinery, material or fuel furnished or to be furnished as provided in Section 5301.232 of the Ohio Revised Code, said mortgage, to the extent of said disbursements, shall be subordinate to the lien or encumbrance specified in such notice or to a valid mechanic's lien for the work or labor actually performed or machinery, material or fuel actually furnished as specified in such notice.

DOCUMENT #6

OFFICE LEASE—EXPENSE STOP

■ ■ ■

LEASE

Landlord: _____

Tenant: _____

Office Building: _____

This form is based on an office lease that I used for the office buildings in the Heathrow International Business Center in Orlando, Florida during my stint as general counsel for the Pizzuti Companies. During the period when space in the Heathrow International Business Center was actively being offered for lease to prospective tenants, I intentionally used a small font and wide margins in an effort to keep the main text of the lease document under ten pages—a perceived marketing advantage in the Central Florida real estate environment.

This lease clearly has a pro-landlord bias—that is, after all the party I was representing when the lease was prepared. A list of 34 pro-tenant modifications that a lawyer representing a tenant might want to insert in the lease is appended at the end of this Document #6.

LEASE SUMMARY

For all purposes of this Lease, the following defined terms have the meanings attributed to them in this Lease Summary. For the parties' convenience when reviewing this Lease, each defined term is highlighted by **boldface print** and *italics* when first defined in this Lease Summary and in the text of the Lease that follows the Lease Summary.

A.   *Effective Date:* _____, 20__

B.   *Landlord:* _____

C.   *Tenant:* _____

D.   *Building:* The office building located at _____ in _____, _____, together with the approximately _____-acre tract of land on which the office is located and all Common Areas (as that term is defined in § 5 of the Lease). The office building contains approximately _____ square feet of rentable space.

E.   *Leased Premises:* That portion of the Building outlined on Exhibit A and known as Suite #_____. The Leased Premises is deemed to contain _____ square feet of rentable space.

F.   *Permitted Use:* _____

G.   *Initial Lease Term:* _____ years, beginning on the Commencement Date and ending on the Termination Date.

H.   *Lease Term:* The Initial Lease Term, plus the term(s) applicable to any extension options granted to and properly exercised by Tenant under Exhibit E to this Lease.

I.   *Commencement Date:* The later of (1) _____, 20__ (the **Target Commencement Date**, or (2) the **Substantial Completion Date** (as that term is defined in § 9 of the Lease).

J.   *Termination Date:* The later of (1) _____, 20__ (the **Target Termination Date**), or (2) the _____ anniversary of the Substantial Completion Date.

K.   *Base Rent:* $_____ for each month of the Lease Term.

L.   *Base Year:* The 20__ calendar year.

M.   *Base Expenses:* The sum of all **Building Expenses** (as that term is defined in § 2 of the Lease) actually incurred by Landlord during the Base Year.

N.　*Tenant's Proportionate Share:* _____%

O.　*Tenant Improvement Allowance:* $_____

P.　*Security Deposit:* $_____

Q.　*Guarantor:* _____

R.　*Real Estate Broker:* _____

The following exhibits are attached to and made a part of the Lease:

Exhibit A: Description of Leased Premises

Exhibit B: List of Building Expenses

Exhibit C: Rules and Regulations

Exhibit D: Landlord's Work

Exhibit E: Special Terms

THE PROVISIONS OF THIS LEASE SUMMARY (INCLUDING ALL TERMS DEFINED IN THIS LEASE SUMMARY) ARE INCORPORATED BY THIS REFERENCE INTO THIS LEASE.

LEASE

Landlord leases the Leased Premises to Tenant for the duration of the Lease Term. The leasing of the Leased Premises to Tenant is governed by the terms and conditions set forth in this Lease.

§ 1. **Base Rent.** Tenant will pay Base Rent in the amount set forth in the Lease Summary.

§ 2. **Excess Expense Payments.** For each full or partial calendar year included within the Lease Term after the Base Year identified in the Lease Summary (***Comparison Year***), Tenant will pay as additional rent Tenant's Proportionate Share of the excess, if any, of the Building Expenses incurred by Landlord during such Comparison Year over the Base Expenses identified in the Lease Summary (***Excess Expenses***). ***Building Expenses*** means those expenses that are described in Exhibit B. Tenant will pay the Tenant's Proportionate Share of such Excess Expenses monthly in advance based upon Landlord's estimate of the Excess Expenses that will be incurred during each Comparison Year. Landlord will use its best efforts to notify Tenant by December 1 of each calendar year during the Lease Term of the amount of the estimated Excess Expenses that Tenant is required to make for each month of the upcoming Comparison Year.

As soon as reasonably practicable after the end of each Comparison Year, Landlord will deliver to Tenant a written statement showing its actual Building Expenses for such Comparison Year and Tenant's Proportionate Share of any Excess Expenses. If the sum of the estimated Excess Expense payments paid by Tenant during a Comparison Year exceeds Tenant's Proportionate Share of the actual Excess Expenses incurred during that Comparison Year, then Landlord will refund the excess amount to Tenant coincident with Landlord's delivery of its written statement to Tenant showing the actual Building Expenses for that Comparison Year. If the sum of the estimated Excess Expense payments paid by Tenant during a Comparison Year is less than Tenant's Proportionate Share of the actual Excess Expenses incurred during that Comparison Year, then Tenant will pay the deficiency to Landlord within ten days after Tenant's receipt of Landlord's written demand for the payment of that deficiency. If the Lease Term begins on a day other than January 1 or expires on a date other than December 31, then Tenant's Proportionate Share of the Excess Expenses for each of the first and last Comparison Years will be prorated to take into consideration the number of days during each such Comparison Year in which the Lease Term is in effect.

§ 3. **Manner and Timing of Rent Payments.** Tenant will pay each monthly installment of Base Rent and Excess Expenses in advance on or before the first day of each calendar month during the Lease Term by electronic funds transfer to an account designated by Landlord (or by such other means as Landlord may designate from time to time). If the Lease Term commences on a day other than the first day of a calendar month or terminates on a day other than the last day of a calendar month, then the amount of the installment of Base Rent and Excess Expenses payable by Tenant for any such partial calendar month will be prorated to take into consideration the number of days during such calendar month in which the Lease Term is in effect. If any installment of Base Rent or Excess Expenses or any other sum payable under this Lease is not received by Landlord on or before its due date, then Tenant will pay a late payment charge of 5% of such past due amount to Landlord, with such late payment charge being due on or before the fifth day of any calendar month for which Tenant's payment of any monthly installment of Base Rent and Excess Expenses is late. In addition, if any such installment or sum is not received by Landlord within ten days after its due date, then the unpaid amount will thereafter accrue interest until paid at a rate equal to four percent in excess of the rate from time to time announced as its prime lending rate by the Bank of America (or its successor). Landlord's acceptance of any payment that constitutes less than all of the balance then owed to Landlord by Tenant will be treated as Landlord's receipt of a payment "on account" and not as an accord and satisfaction and Landlord may accept any such payment (regardless of the existence of any endorsement or statement to the contrary contained on any check or letter accompanying such payment) without prejudice to Landlord's rights to recover the balance of the amount owed to it by Tenant or to pursue any other remedy provided to Landlord under this Lease. Each installment of Base Rent and Excess Expenses and all other sums payable by Tenant under this Lease are payable without notice or demand and without reduction, abatement, counterclaim, or offset.

§ 4. **Building Services.** Landlord will provide Tenant with such electricity, sewer, water, HVAC, janitorial, trash removal, elevator, landscaping, snow and ice removal, and other services that Landlord determines are required for Tenant's use of the Leased Premises for general office purposes during normal business hours (7:00 a.m. to 6:00 p.m. Monday through Friday, and 8:00 a.m. to noon on Saturday, recognized national holidays excepted). Tenant will contract directly for and pay all costs related to the provision of telephone, internet, and other telecommunication services to the Leased Premises.

If Landlord determines that Tenant's use of any service is excessive when compared to the normal use of such service by other tenants in the Building or if the nature of Tenant's business requires the provision of any service outside of normal business hours, then, in either such event, Tenant will pay a service surcharge to Landlord in an amount that Landlord determines fairly reflects Tenant's excessive or after-hours use of such service, with such service surcharge being due on or before the date that is ten days after Tenant's receipt of written notice from Landlord establishing the existence of the service surcharge. Landlord will not be liable to Tenant, nor will Tenant be relieved of any obligation under this Lease by reason of constructive eviction or any other legal theory if any service to the Leased Premises is interrupted for any reason beyond Landlord's reasonable control, regardless how long such interruption continues.

§ 5. **Maintenance and Repair.** Landlord will maintain, repair, and replace the Common Areas and Base Building Improvements in good condition. For the purposes of this Lease: ***Common Areas*** mean the Building's common lobbies, hallways, elevators, restrooms, parking areas, sidewalks, and other areas located outside of the leased premises of any Building tenant that are intended to serve as amenities for use by other Building tenants; and ***Base Building Improvements*** mean those improvements located within the Leased Premises that are specifically designated as "Base Building Improvements" in Exhibit D. Landlord's costs of maintaining, repairing, and replacing the Common Areas and Base Building Improvements are reimbursable by Tenant as part of Tenant's obligation to pay Excess Expenses under § 2 and Exhibit B. Despite any provision to the contrary contained in this Lease, Tenant will be responsible for the direct payment to Landlord of 100% of Landlord's cost of maintaining, repairing, and replacing any Common Area or Base Building Improvement if such cost is necessitated as a result of the fault or negligence of Tenant or its agents, employees, invitees, or guests. Landlord will not be liable to Tenant, nor will Tenant be relieved of any obligation under this Lease if Tenant's use of the Leased Premises is interrupted (regardless how long such interruption continues) as a result of Landlord's required entry into the Leased Premises for the purpose of maintaining, repairing, or replacing any Base Building Improvement.

Tenant will maintain, repair, and replace the Tenant Improvements in good condition. For the purposes of this Lease, ***Tenant Improvements*** mean those improvements located within the Leased Premises that are specifically designated as "Tenant Improvements" in Exhibit D.

§ 6. **Use of Leased Premises.** Tenant will use the Leased Premises solely for the Permitted Use and for no other purpose. Tenant will not cause or permit any waste or damage to the Leased Premises or the Building and will not occupy or use the Leased Premises for any business or purpose that is unlawful, hazardous, unsanitary, noxious, or offensive, or that unreasonably interferes with the business operations of other tenants in the Building. Tenant will comply with the Rules and Regulations for the Building that are set forth in Exhibit C and with any modifications or additions to the Rules and Regulations that Landlord opts to make for the benefit of the Building after the Effective Date.

Tenant is entitled to the non-exclusive use of the Common Areas along with all other tenants of the Building. Landlord reserves the right to change the size, use, shape, and nature of the Common Areas and to construct additional improvements in the Common Areas as long as such action by Landlord does not permanently deprive Tenant of the substantial benefit and enjoyment of the Leased Premises.

§ 7. **Compliance with Law.** Tenant will, at its sole expense, comply with all laws, governmental requirements, and recorded covenants or conditions that are now or in the future in force related to Tenant's occupancy or use of the Leased Premises, including, without limitation, the Americans with Disabilities Act.

§ 8. **Signs.** Tenant will not place any sign or other advertising material on the exterior of the Leased Premises or the Building. Landlord will, at its expense, provide Tenant with the Building's standard graphics and signage for identification of Tenant on the first floor business directory and the entranceway to the Leased Premises.

§ 9. **Improvements to Leased Premises.** Attached to this Lease as Schedule D–1 to Exhibit D are the preliminary plans and specifications for the interior improvements to be made by Landlord to the Leased Premises (*Tenant Improvements*). Exhibit D also lists the Base Building Improvements (described in Schedule D–2 to Exhibit D) that have been or will be made to the Leased Premises by Landlord, but that are not chargeable against the Tenant Improvement Allowance provided to Tenant under this Lease (as the amount of such Tenant Improvement Allowance is set forth in the Lease Summary). For the purposes of this § 9, *Improvements* mean both the Tenant Improvements and the Base Building Improvements.

As soon as reasonably practicable after the Effective Date, Landlord will deliver final plans and specifications for the Tenant Improvements to Tenant for Tenant's review and approval. Tenant will review and either approve or specify its objections in writing to the final plans and specification within ten days after Tenant's receipt of the same. Tenant's right to object to anything contained in the submitted final plans and specifications is specifically limited to objections that are premised solely upon the fact that the submitted final plans and specifications are inconsistent with the preliminary plans and specifications that are attached as Schedule D–1 to Exhibit D. The final plans and specifications approved or deemed approved by Tenant under this § 9 are referred to in this Lease as the **Final Plans** and are incorporated by this reference into the Lease.

Landlord will cause the Tenant Improvements to be constructed in accordance with the Final Plans. If Landlord determines that the cost of constructing the Tenant Improvements in accordance with the Final Plans exceeds the amount of the Tenant Improvement Allowance identified in the Lease Summary (such excess being referred to as *Excess TI Costs*), then Tenant will pay the full amount of the Excess TI Costs to Landlord in cash on or before the date that is ten days after Landlord's delivery to Tenant of a written demand for the payment of the Excess TI Costs.

Landlord will use reasonable efforts to substantially complete construction of the Improvements by the Target Commencement Date identified in the Lease Summary, subject to delays caused by the occurrence of any event that is beyond Landlord's reasonable control, including, without limitation, a labor dispute, civil commotion, war or war-like operations, sabotage, governmental requirements, unseasonable weather, fire or other casualty, inability to obtain any material or service, or any act of God. If for any reason other than the occurrence of a Tenant Delay (as that term is later defined in this § 9) the Improvements are not substantially completed on or before the Target Commencement Date identified in the Lease Summary, then the Commencement Date will be deferred until the date on which the Improvements are substantially completed (*Substantial Completion Date*) and the Termination Date will be deferred by the number of days equal to the deferral in the Commencement Date. Despite any provision to the contrary contained in this § 9, if Landlord's failure to substantially complete the Improvements on or before the Target Commencement Date is attributable to a Tenant Delay, then despite the fact that the Improvements have not been substantially completed by the Target Commencement Date, the Commencement and Termination Dates will be the Target Commencement and Target Termination Dates identified in the Lease Summary and Tenant will, from and after the Target Commencement Date, pay Base Rent, Excess Expenses, and all other sums payable by it under this Lease and perform all Tenant's other obligations under this Lease. For the purposes of this Lease, a *Tenant Delay* means any delay in Landlord's construction of the Improvements that is caused by any Tenant act or omission, including, without limitation, (a) Tenant's failure to either approve or object in writing to any plans and specifications submitted to it by Landlord on or before that date that is ten days after Tenant's receipt of the submitted plans and specifications, (b) Tenant's requested change order to the Tenant Improvements, and (c) Tenant's failure to pay any Excess Costs to Landlord within ten days after Landlord's delivery to Tenant of a written demand for the payment of such Excess Costs. Also for the purposes of this § 9, the Improvements will be deemed *substantially completed* on the date on which a temporary or permanent certificate of occupancy for the Leased Premises is issued by the appropriate governmental authority.

§ 10. <u>Alterations.</u> Except for a Minor Alteration (as that term is later defined in this § 10), Tenant will not make any alteration, addition, or improvement to the Leased Premises. For the purposes of this § 10, a *Minor Alteration* means any alteration, addition, or improvement to the Leased Premises that costs less than $5,000 and that does not alter the exterior aesthetics, structural integrity, or value of the Building. All improvements, alterations, and additions made at one time in connection with any one overall job will be aggregated for the purposes of determining whether the $5,000 limit has been exceeded. All alterations, additions, or improvements made to the Leased Premises (expressly including those made pursuant to this § 10, as well as the Improvements made by Landlord pursuant to § 9 and

Exhibit D) are the property of Landlord and will remain as part of the Leased Premises upon the expiration of the Lease Term.

§ 11. <u>Mechanics Liens.</u> Tenant will indemnify Landlord from any loss or expense associated with Tenant's construction of any alteration, addition, or improvement to the Leased Premises. On or before the date that is ten days after any mechanics lien is filed against the Leased Premises or the Building in connection with any work performed by Tenant, Tenant will cause such mechanics lien to be discharged of public record.

§ 12. <u>Assignment and Subleasing.</u> Tenant will not assign this Lease or sublet all or any part of the Leased Premises, without the prior written consent of Landlord. Unless otherwise expressly agreed to in writing by Landlord, Landlord's consent to any assignment or sublease will not relieve the "Tenant" named in the Lease Summary from its obligations under this Lease.

§ 13. <u>Subordination/Estoppel Certificate.</u> Tenant's rights and interests under this Lease are subordinate to all mortgages and other encumbrances now or in the future affecting any portion of the Building; except that the holder of any mortgage or encumbrance will have the unilateral right to elect to grant priority to Tenant's rights and interests under this Lease over the rights and interests of such holder. Tenant will attorn to and automatically become the tenant of any successor to Landlord's interest in the Building by way of a foreclosure of a mortgage or other encumbrance, without change in the terms or conditions of this Lease. Such successor will not be liable for any act or omission of any prior landlord or subject to any offsets or defenses that Tenant may have against any such prior landlord. This paragraph is self-operative and no further instrument is required to effect the subordination of Tenant's rights and interests under this Lease. Tenant may not exercise any remedy because of a default under this Lease by Landlord unless (a) Tenant first gives written notice of the alleged default to any mortgagee of Landlord whose name and address have been provided to Tenant, and (b) such mortgagee fails to cure the alleged default within 30 days after the mortgagee's receipt of such written notice.

Tenant will execute and deliver to Landlord a written estoppel certificate certifying to Landlord and any other person designated by Landlord that the Lease is unmodified and in full force and effect, without any default on the part of Landlord. If Tenant fails to deliver an estoppel certificate to Landlord on or before the date that is ten days after Landlord's delivery to Tenant of a written request for Tenant's execution and delivery of an estoppel certificate, then Tenant will be liable to Landlord for all damages incurred by Landlord as a result of Tenant's failure to timely execute and deliver the estoppel certificate to Landlord, including, without limitation, loss of profits and consequential damages.

§ 14. <u>**Limitation of Landlord's Personal Liability.**</u> Tenant will look solely to Landlord's interest in the Building (including, without limitation, all insurance proceeds or condemnation awards paid with respect to the Building) for the recovery of any judgment against Landlord; it being the express intent of Landlord and Tenant that neither Landlord, nor any of its partners, members, affiliates, shareholders, officers or employees is personally liable for any such judgment. Landlord's obligations under this Lease are binding upon Landlord only for the period of time that Landlord is the fee simple owner of the Building. Upon termination of that ownership, Tenant will look solely to Landlord's successor-in-interest in the Building for the satisfaction of each and every obligation of the titular "Landlord" under this Lease.

§ 15. <u>**Indemnification and Insurance.**</u> Landlord will not be liable for and Tenant releases Landlord from any loss or expense associated with any damage or injury to any person or property (including any person or property of Tenant or anyone claiming under Tenant) that arises in connection with the Leased Premises or Tenant's use or occupancy of the Leased Premises or any Common Areas. Tenant will indemnify Landlord from any of the above-described losses and expenses.

Tenant will, at its sole expense, maintain in full force and effect at all times during the Lease Term: (a) commercial general liability insurance for personal injury and property damage with liability limits of not less than $2,000,000 for injury to one person, $5,000,000 for injury from one occurrence, and $1,000,000 for property damage; and (b) commercial property insurance (a Causes of Loss—Special Form policy, with coverage extended to cover floods and earthquakes) on all property stored or placed by Tenant in or about the Leased Premises in an amount equal to the full replacement value of such property. All insurance required to be maintained by Tenant under this section must be issued by insurance companies having a policyholder rating of at least "A" and a financial size category of at least "Class X" under the A.M/ Best's Key Rating Guide for insurance companies (or any comparable rating under any successor publication or index). The commercial general liability insurance policy required to be maintained by Tenant under this section must name Landlord as an additional insured and must specifically provide that such insurance policy cannot be terminated without giving at least 30 days prior written notice to Landlord. Prior to the Commencement Date, Tenant will furnish Landlord with a certificate of insurance showing compliance with the insurance requirements set forth in this section.

Landlord will, at its initial expense, but as a Building Expense reimbursable by Tenant under § 2 and Exhibit D of this Lease, maintain in full force and effect at all times during the Lease Term: (a) commercial property insurance (a Cause of Loss—Special Form policy, with coverage extended to cover floods and earthquakes) on the Building in an amount equal to the full replacement value of the Building; (b) commercial general liability insurance for personal injury and property damage with limits of not less than $2,000,000 for injury to one person, $5,000,000 for injury from one occurrence, and $1,000,000 for property damage; and (c) rental loss insurance. Any insurance required to be carried by Landlord may be provided under a blanket policy covering other properties of Landlord or its related or affiliated entities.

§ 16. **Waiver of Subrogation.** Landlord and Tenant each waives its right to receive damages against the other with respect to any loss or expense occasioned by the occurrence of any hazard or peril covered by any insurance policy required to be carried under the provisions of this Lease, except that the foregoing waiver is not applicable to the portion of any loss or claim that is not reimbursable by the damaged party's insurer because of any "deductible" under such insurance policy. Any insurance policy procured by either Tenant or Landlord under this Lease must contain an express waiver of the right of subrogation by the insurance company against Landlord or Tenant.

§ 17. **Hazardous Substances.** Tenant will not use, store, or dispose of any Hazardous Substance (as that term is later defined in this § 17) on or about the Leased Premises, except for immaterial amounts that are exempt from or do not give rise to any violation of applicable law. Tenant will indemnify Landlord from any loss or expense (including, without limitation, reasonable attorney's fees, court costs, and any other expense incurred in connection with the investigation settlement, or implementation of any environmental clean-up) incurred by or claimed against Landlord as a result of Tenant's breach of the covenant contained in this § 17. For the purposes of this § 17, *Hazardous Substance* means any "hazardous" or "toxic" substance (as those terms are defined in the Comprehensive Environmental Response Compensation Liability Act) "hazardous waste" (as that term is defined in the Resource Conservation Recovery Act), polychlorinated biphenyls, asbestos, radioactive material, or any other pollutant, contaminant, or hazardous, dangerous, or toxic chemical, material or substance that is regulated by any federal, state, or local law, regulation, ordinance, or requirement. All the indemnifications contained in this § 17 will survive the expiration or sooner termination of the Lease Term.

§ 18. **Surrender of Premises.** Upon the expiration or sooner termination of the Lease Term, Tenant will immediately (a) surrender possession of the Leased Premises to Landlord in good repair and "broom clean" condition, reasonable wear and tear and damage by fire or other casualty excepted, and (b) remove all Tenant's personal property and movable trade fixtures from the Leased Premises. Tenant will promptly repair any damage caused to the Leased Premises by the removal of any of its moveable trade fixtures or personal property.

§ 19. **Casualty.** Except as provided in this § 19, if the Building or the Leased Premises is damaged by fire or other casualty, then Landlord will proceed to repair the damaged area at its sole expense; provided, however, that Landlord will not be required to repair or replace any personal property or fixtures owned by Tenant or any Minor Alterations made to the Leased Premises by Tenant under § 10. If the Leased Premises are rendered untenantable in whole or in part as a result of a fire or other casualty, then all rent and other payments accruing after the occurrence of any such fire or other casualty and prior to the completion of the repair of the Leased Premises will be equitably and proportionately abated to reflect the untenantable portion of the Leased Premises. Landlord will not be liable to Tenant for any inconvenience or interruption to Tenant's business occasioned by a fire or other casualty or the concomitant repair of the damaged area.

If the occurrence of any fire or other casualty renders more than 50% of the rentable square footage of the Leased Premises untenantable and if Landlord reasonably determines that the damaged portion of the Leased Premises cannot be repaired within 180 days after the date on which all requisite permits and licenses for the repair of the damaged portion of the Leased Premises are obtained from the appropriate governmental authorities, then Tenant may terminate this Lease by delivering written notice of termination to Landlord on or before the date that is 30 days after Tenant's receipt of written determination from Landlord that the damaged portion of the Leased Premises cannot be repaired within such 180-day period; except that Tenant may not terminate this Lease if the fire or other casualty was caused by the negligence or willful misconduct of Tenant or any of its employees, agents, guests, or invitees. In addition, if the Building is substantially damaged (by fire or other casualty, then Landlord may terminate this Lease by giving written notice to Tenant at any time on or before the date that is 90 days after the occurrence of such fire or other casualty. For the purposes of this § 19, the Building will be deemed **substantially damaged** if Landlord reasonably determines that the cost of repairing the damaged area is greater than 50% of the replacement value of the Building immediately prior to the occurrence of such casualty.

§ 20. **Condemnation.** If a taking of a portion of the Building by or under threat of condemnation renders the Leased Premises wholly untenantable, then this Lease will automatically terminate as of the date of the vesting of title to such property in the condemning authority. If such taking does not render the Leased Premises wholly untenantable, then this Lease will not terminate and Landlord will promptly take all reasonably practicable steps to constitute the Building as a complete architectural unit. Landlord will not be liable to Tenant for any inconvenience or interruption to Tenant's business occasioned by any such taking. Landlord is entitled to receive the entire award made by the condemning authority for any such taking, except that Tenant may seek and receive a separate award for any damage to Tenant's personal property and moving expenses as long as that separate award does not diminish the amount of the award otherwise payable to Landlord.

§ 21. **Holding Over.** Tenant will not hold over in its occupancy of the Leased Premises after the expiration of the Lease Term, without the prior written consent of Landlord. If Tenant holds over in its occupancy of the Leased Premises after the expiration of the Lease Term (with or without the consent of Landlord), then, for each month of its holdover, Tenant will pay 200% of the Base Rent and Excess Expenses in effect for the last month of the Lease Term. Tenant will also be required to pay Landlord all damages sustained by reason of Tenant's holding over after the expiration of the Lease Term (including, without limitation, all damages caused by Landlord's loss of any prospective tenancy).

§ 22. **Default.** If Tenant fails to pay any installment of Base Rent or Excess Expenses or any other sum payable by Tenant under this Lease on or before the date that is ten days after Tenant's receipt of written notice from Landlord that any such installment or sum is due and unpaid, or if Tenant defaults in the performance of any of its other obligations under this Lease and such default continues for 30 days after written notice of the existence of such default is received by Tenant, then, in addition to any other legal rights and remedies available to Landlord at law or in equity, Landlord may: (a) terminate this Lease and all rights and interests of Tenant under this Lease (including Tenant's right of possession under this Lease) and declare immediately due and payable as liquidated damages the amount by which Landlord's commercially reasonable estimate of the aggregate amount of Base Rent, Excess Expenses, and other sums payable by Tenant under this Lease for the remainder of the Lease Term, exceeds Landlord's commercially reasonable estimate of the fair rental value of the Leased Premises for the same period (after giving effect to the time needed to relet the Leased Premises and the costs that Landlord might have to incur in connection with any such reletting, including, without limitation, brokerage commissions, tenant improvement costs, and other tenant allowances and concessions), with both amounts being discounted to present value using a discount rate of 4%; or (b) terminate Tenant's right of possession of the Leased Premises without terminating this Lease and re-enter and attempt to relet the Leased Premises, in which event Tenant will remain obligated to pay to Landlord any deficiency between all sums payable by Tenant under this Lease and any sums collected by Landlord from any reletting of the Leased Premises (net of any sums paid by Landlord in connection with such reletting, including, without limitation, brokerage commissions, tenant improvement costs, and other tenant allowances and concessions).

§ 23. **Prevailing Party's Fees.** If any legal action is commenced by either Landlord or Tenant to enforce its rights under this Lease, then all attorneys' fees, paralegal fees and other costs and expenses incurred by the prevailing party in such action will be paid by the non-prevailing party to the prevailing party on or before the date that is ten days after the entry of a final non-appealable judgment in such action.

§ 24. **Successors and Assigns.** This Lease is binding upon and inures to the benefit of the successors and assigns of Landlord and the permitted successors and permitted assigns of Tenant.

§ 25. **No Waiver.** No waiver of any covenant or condition of this Lease by either party is deemed to constitute a future waiver of the same or any other covenant or condition of this Lease. In order to be effective, any such waiver must be in writing and must be delivered to the other party to this Lease.

§ 26. **Brokerage Commissions.** Each of Landlord and Tenant represents and warrants that it has not dealt or consulted with any real estate broker or agent in connection with this Lease, other than those Real Estate Brokers specifically identified in the Lease Summary. The commissions payable to any Real Estate Broker identified in the Lease Summary will be paid by the party (that is, Landlord or Tenant) identified in Lease Summary. Each of Landlord and Tenant indemnifies the other from any loss or expense occasioned by a breach of the foregoing representation and warranty. The representations and warranties made under this § 26 will survive the expiration or sooner termination of the Lease Term.

§ 27. **Relocation.** Landlord may relocate Tenant to other space in the Building, so long as the size, configuration, improvements, and amenities of the new space are substantially similar to those of the Leased Premises. Landlord will pay all reasonable expenses incurred by Tenant in connection with the relocation of its space. Landlord will effect such relocation in a manner intended to minimize any interference with Tenant's business operations. If such a relocation occurs, this Lease will continue in full force and effect without any change in the terms and conditions of this Lease, except that the new space will be substituted as the Leased Premises for the purposes of this Lease and, if the new space is smaller or larger than the initial Leased Premises, then the Base Rent and Tenant's Proportionate Share of Operating Expense will be proportionately decreased or increased, as the case may be.

§ 28. **Reasonableness of Consent.** Neither Landlord nor Tenant may unreasonably withhold, delay, or condition any consent or approval that is required to be given by it pursuant to the terms of this Lease.

§ 29. **Amendment.** This Lease may not be amended except by a written instrument signed by both Landlord and Tenant.

§ 30. **Governing Law.** This Lease is governed by _____ law.

§ 31. **Notices.** All notices required or permitted under this Lease must be in writing and must be delivered to Landlord and Tenant at their addresses set forth in the Lease Summary (or such other address as may be designated by such party). Any notice must be personally delivered or sent by either registered or certified mail, fax, email, or overnight courier. For the purposes of this Lease, any such notice will be deemed "received," "delivered," "given," "sent," or "effective" as specified below:

(a) If personally delivered or sent by certified mail or overnight courier, on the date when received or refused by the intended recipient of such notice; or

(b) If sent by email or facsimile transmission, on the date when sent, as evidenced by the sender's "sent e-mail box" or facsimile transmission report.

§ 32. Security Deposit. Coincident with its execution of this Lease, Tenant will deposit with Landlord a Security Deposit in the amount identified in the Lease Summary. Landlord will hold the Security Deposit as partial security for Tenant's performance of its obligations under this Lease. If Tenant defaults in the performance of any of its obligations under this Lease, then Landlord may use all or a portion of the Security Deposit to cure such default. On or before the date that is ten days after Landlord's delivery to Tenant of written notice that Landlord has so used the Security Deposit, Tenant will deposit additional sums with Landlord in an amount sufficient to restore the Security Deposit to its original amount. Landlord will return to Tenant (without interest) any portion of the Security Deposit remaining unutilized following the expiration of the Lease Term.

§ 33. Financial Statements. On or before April 1 of each year during the Lease Term, Tenant will provide Landlord with complete and accurate copies of the current financial statements of Tenant and any Guarantor. The financial statements will include a balance sheet, profit and loss statement, and statement of cash flows, each of which must be certified as being complete and accurate by an authorized officer of Tenant and any Guarantor.

§ 34. Defined Terms. The following terms (capitalized, bolded, and italicized when first appearing in this Lease and the Lease Summary) have the meanings attributed to such terms in the noted sections of this Lease. All meanings are applicable to both the singular and plural forms of such terms.

- ***Base Building Improvements*** is defined in § 5 and Exhibit D.

- ***Base Rent*** is defined in ¶ K of the Lease Summary.

- ***Base Year*** is defined in ¶ L of the Lease Summary.

- ***Base Expenses*** is defined in ¶ M of the Lease Summary.

- ***Building*** is defined in ¶ D of the Lease Summary.

- ***Building Expenses*** is defined in § 2 and Exhibit B.

- *Commencement Date* is defined in ¶ I of the Lease Summary.

- *Common Areas* is defined in § 5.

- *Comparison Year* is defined in § 2.

- *Effective Date* is defined in ¶ A of the Lease Summary.

- *Excess Expenses* is defined in § 2.

- *Excess TI Costs* is defined in § 9.

- *Final Plans* is defined in § 9.

- *Guarantor* is defined in ¶ Q of the Lease Summary.

- *Hazardous Substance* is defined in § 17.

- *Initial Lease Term* is defined in ¶ G of the Lease Summary.

- *Improvements* is defined in § 9.

- *Landlord* is defined in ¶ B of the Lease Summary.

- *Leased Premises* is defined in ¶ E of the Lease Summary.

- *Lease Term* is defined in ¶ H of the Lease Summary.

- *Minor Alteration* is defined in § 10.

- *Permitted Use* is defined in ¶ F of the Lease Summary.

- *Real Estate Brokers* is defined in ¶ R of the Lease Summary.

- *Security Deposit* is defined in ¶ P of the Lease Summary.

- *Substantial Completion Date* is defined in § 9.

- *Substantially complete* is defined in § 9.

- *Substantially damaged* is defined in § 19.

- *Target Commencement Date* is defined in ¶ I of the Lease Summary.

- *Target Termination Date* is defined in ¶ J of the Lease Summary.

- *Tenant* is defined in ¶ C of the Lease Summary.

- *Tenant Delay* is defined in § 9.

- ***Tenant Improvement Allowance*** is defined in ¶ O of the Lease Summary.

- ***Tenant Improvements*** is defined in § 9 and Exhibit D.

- ***Tenant's Proportionate Share*** is defined in ¶ N of the Lease Summary.

- ***Termination Date*** is defined in ¶ J of the Lease Summary.

§ 35. Special Terms. Exhibit E sets forth those special provisions, if any, that supplement and modify the provisions of this Lease Agreement.

Landlord and Tenant are signing this Lease as of the Effective Date.

Landlord: _____

By: _____

    (Name)   (Title)

Tenant: _____

By: _____

    (Name)   (Title)

[Add witness or notary clauses if required in jurisdiction where office building is located]

EXHIBIT A

DESCRIPTION OF LEASED PREMISES

See floor plan attached to this Exhibit as Schedule A–1.

Initialed and Approved by Tenant:

_____

EXHIBIT B

LIST OF BUILDING EXPENSES

For the purposes of this Lease (including, without limitation, § 2), **Building Expenses** mean the following costs and expenses:

1. Costs of maintaining, repairing, and replacing the Building, Base Building Improvements, and Common Areas (expressly including the Building's roof and mechanical systems);

2. The cost of providing electricity, sewer, water, HVAC, janitorial, trash removal, elevator, landscaping, ice and snow removal, security, and other services for the Building and Common Areas;

3. Real estate taxes and assessments on the Building and Common Areas, including, without limitation, any assessments imposed by any property owner's association;

4. Insurance premiums for all insurance policies maintained by Landlord on or with respect to the Building and Common Areas, including, without limitation; insurance against liability for personal injury, death, and property damage; fire and extended coverage insurance on the Building; and rent loss insurance;

5. Salaries and related costs (including, without limitation, fringe benefits and payroll taxes) of personnel spending time associated with the ownership, operation, or management of the Building, including, without limitation, those paid to on-site property management and maintenance personnel;

6. A reasonable property management fee;

7. The cost of any new Building improvement that Landlord elects to make to operate the Building at levels of efficiency and quality that are comparable to those maintained by comparable buildings in the submarket in which the Building is located;

8. The cost of any new cost-saving utility device installed in the Building, but only to the extent of the actual cost-savings obtained from the installation of the device;

9. The cost of any new Building improvement that Landlord is required to make as a result of the enactment or promulgation of any governmental law or regulation after the Effective Date;

10. The cost of cleaning goods and supplies;

11. Accounting, legal, and other professional services rendered in connection with the ownership, operation, or management of the Building;

12. Fees and charges payable to Landlord's affiliates for the performance of any services for the Building;

13. The cost of securing and maintaining all licenses, permits, and inspections required in connection with the ownership, operation, or management of the Building;

14. The cost of successfully contesting any real estate tax assessment or the validity or applicability of any law or governmental requirement to the Building; and

15. All other costs related to the ownership, operation, or management of the Building.

The following costs and expenses are excluded from the definition of "Building Expenses":

1. Tenant improvement costs, leasing commissions, and advertising expenses incurred in connection with the lease of space in the Building other than the Leased Premises;

2. Any inheritance, estate, gift, income, or similar tax that is assessed against Landlord's entity; and

3. Debt service payments made on any financing in place with respect to the Building.

Building Expenses are computed for the Base Year and each Comparison Year during the Lease Term based upon the accrual method of accounting. If, during the Base Year or any Comparison Year, the Building is ever less than 100% occupied, then the Building Expenses for each such period will be grossed up and calculated as if the Building had been 100% occupied and the results will constitute Landlord's Building Expenses for such period for all purposes of this Lease.

Initialed and Approved by Tenant:

_____

EXHIBIT C

RULES AND REGULATIONS

Tenant will use the Leased Premises and the Common Areas in strict accordance with the following rules and regulation. These rules and regulations are in addition to and do not in any way modify the provisions of Tenant's Lease. Tenant acknowledges that it is responsible for ensuring compliance with these rules and regulations by all of Tenant's employees, agents, customers, clients, invitees, and guests.

[Insert building-specific rules and regulations governing the use of the office building and its common areas (typically drafted by the landlord's property management staff), including rules and regulations covering the following general topics:

- *Signage;*

- *Floor load restrictions;*

- *Obstruction of common areas;*

- *Parking areas;*

- *Freight elevator use;*

- *Keys and key cards;*

- *Building directory;*

- *Blinds and window coverings;*

- *Janitorial services;*

- *Flammable materials;*

- *Recycling programs;*

- *Utility usage;*

- *Cost-saving programs;*

- *Non-solicitation policy;*

- *Prohibited uses;*

- *Vending machines and food service;*

- *Restrooms;*

- *Noise;*

- *Security;*

- *Change in name and address of building;*

- *Telecommunication equipment;*

- *Wall hangings;*

- *Trash disposal;*

- *Safety and fire procedures;*

- *Bicycles;*

- *Pets; and*

- *Smoking.]*

Tenant acknowledges and agrees that Landlord may take any of the following actions related to the promulgation and enforcement of the rules and regulations set forth in this Exhibit C.

- Landlord may waive any one or more of the rules and regulations for the benefit of any tenant of the Building. Any such waiver will not constitute a waiver of the subject rules and regulations against any other tenant, nor will it prevent Landlord from later enforcing the subject rules and regulations against the tenant receiving the benefit of the initial waiver.

- Landlord may enact modifications to any of the rules and regulations set forth in this Exhibit C.

- Landlord may implement and enforce new rules and regulations that in Landlord's judgment are appropriate to enhance the safe and orderly use of the Building and its Common Areas. Tenant's required compliance with any new rule and regulation will become effective immediately upon Landlord's written delivery to Tenant of the new rule and regulation.

Initialed and Approved by Tenant:

_____

EXHIBIT D

LANDLORD'S WORK

The preliminary plans and specifications for the Tenant Improvements to be constructed by Landlord to the interior of the Leased Premises are attached to this Exhibit as Schedule D–1.

A description of the Base Building Improvements that have been or will be constructed by Landlord and that are not to be charged against the Tenant Improvement Allowance is attached to this Exhibit as Schedule D–2.

Initialed and Approved by Tenant:

_____

EXHIBIT E

SPECIAL TERMS

The following special terms modify and supplement the provisions of the Lease between Landlord and Tenant. All capitalized terms used but not defined in this Exhibit E have the meanings attributed to such terms in the Lease.

Extension Option: Tenant has the option to extend this Lease for one extension term of five years. Tenant may exercise its extension option by delivering written notice of exercise to Landlord at least 365 days prior to the scheduled expiration of the Initial Lease Term. Tenant's option to extend this Lease is conditioned upon this Lease being in full force and effect, without any default on the part of Tenant, both at the time of Tenant's exercise of such extension option and at the time of the scheduled commencement of the extension term. The extension term will be upon all of the same terms and conditions set forth in this Lease with respect to the Initial Lease Term, except that (a) Tenant will not have any further extension options, (b) Landlord will not be obligated to pay any tenant improvement or other allowances in connection with the extension term, and (c) the Base Rent payable during each month of the extension term will be equal to the greater of (i) the fair market rent for comparable space in comparable buildings in the _____ submarket during the extension term, and (b) 115% of the Base Rent payable by Tenant during the last month of the Initial Lease Term. Landlord will provide Tenant with Landlord's determination of the fair market rent applicable to the extension term on or before the date that is 30 days after Landlord's receipt of Tenant's written exercise of the extension option. If Tenant disagrees with Landlord's determination of the fair market rent, then, as its sole option, Tenant may rescind its exercise of the extension option by delivering a written rescission notice to Landlord on or before the date that is ten days after Tenant's receipt of Landlord's fair market rent determination.

[Insert any other additions, deletions, or changes to the Lease]

Initialed and Approved by Tenant:

_____

PRO-TENANT LEASE MODIFICATONS

The following are examples of provisions that a tenant might want to include in Exhibit E of the Lease (that is, those "Special Terms" that are intended to modify and supplement the provisions of the form Lease). While these provisions are representative of lease modifications that might be requested by a tenant, they are not intended to be an exhaustive listing of a tenant's desired modifications. There is literally no limit to the imagination of a tenant's lawyer when he or she takes on the task of negotiating changes to the landlord's standard form of lease. Moreover, each of the provisions listed below can be further modified to reflect the needs and desires of a particular tenant.

Finally, it should be noted that most landlords will resist (at least initially) the inclusion of any of the following provisions in the lease. If the landlord's lawyer is persuaded to include any of the suggested provisions in the lease, one can rest assured that those provisions will be massaged and manipulated in a number of ways to more appropriately address the landlord's business concerns and objectives.

1.   **BOMA Method of Space Measurement.** Landlord represents and warrants that the rentable areas of the Building and the Leased Premises (as set forth in the Lease Summary) have been determined using the method of measurement mandated in the Building Owners and Managers Association International's Publication ANSI Z65.1, copyright 1996 ("BOMA Method"). Tenant reserves the right to have such rentable areas remeasured and recalculated by a licensed engineer selected by Tenant. If Tenant's engineer determines that the rentable area of the Building or the Leased Premises (calculated in accordance with the BOMA Method) is different from that specified in the Lease Summary, then Tenant's annual Base Rent and its Proportionate Share of Excess Expenses will be adjusted to take into consideration the new rentable area calculations.

2.   **Usable Area of Leased Premises.** Landlord represents and warrants that:

    (a)   The Leased Premises contain ___ square feet of usable area;

    (b)   The Building's common area load factor is ___%; and

    (c)   The calculations made in (a) and (b), above, were made in strict accordance with the BOMA Method.

Landlord will indemnify Tenant from any loss or expense incurred by Tenant as a result of Landlord's breach of any of these representations and warranties.

3.   **GMP for Tenant Improvements.** Before commencing construction of the Tenant Improvements to the Leased Premises, Landlord will provide Tenant with a written notice setting forth Landlord's guaranteed maximum price for the construction of the Tenant Improvements ("GMP"). If the GMP exceeds the amount of the Tenant Improvement Allowance being provided to Tenant under this Lease, then Tenant may either:

   (a)   Cause Landlord to competitively bid the construction of the Tenant Improvements to at least three general contractors approved by Tenant, with Landlord then being required to award the contract for the construction of the Improvements to the low bidder; or

   (b)   Take over direct responsibility for the construction of the Improvements with a contractor of Tenant's choosing.

   Tenant may exercise either of the above rights by delivering a written election notice to Landlord on or before the date that is ten days after Tenant's receipt of Landlord's written GMP notice. If Tenant elects to proceed under alternative (b), above, then, on or before the date that is five days after Landlord's receipt of Tenant's written exercise notice, Landlord will assign to Tenant all Landlord's rights and interest in the Final Plans and will pay Tenant the full amount of the Tenant Improvement Allowance.

4.   **Modification to Leasehold Improvements Section of Lease.** Despite any provision to the contrary contained in § 9 of this Lease, the following rules apply in connection with Landlord's construction of the Improvements to the Leased Premises:

   (a)   Landlord will construct the Improvements (i) in a good and workmanlike manner, (ii) free of any defects in design, materials, or workmanship, and (iii) in compliance with all applicable laws, governmental requirements, and recorded covenants or conditions; and

   (b)   Landlord will not charge against the Tenant Improvement Allowance any construction, design, or other fee payable to Landlord or any affiliate of Landlord.

5.   **Amortization of Excess TI Costs.** Despite any provision to the contrary contained in § 9 of this Lease, if the cost of the construction of the Improvements to the Leased Premises exceeds the amount of the Tenant Improvement Allowance being provided to Tenant under this Lease (meaning that there are Excess TI Costs, as that term is defined in § 9), then Tenant may require Landlord to fund the upfront payment of all Excess TI Costs. The Base Rent payable by Tenant

during each year of the Lease Term will then be increased by an amount equal to __% of the Excess TI Costs.

6.   **Reconfiguration of Common Areas.** A site plan depicting the present location of the site Common Areas located outside of the footprint of the Building is attached to this Rider as Schedule ___. The attached site plan is a material inducement for Tenant to enter into this Lease and Landlord may not make any material change, alteration, improvement, or addition to any of the Common Areas shown on such site plan, without first obtaining Tenant's written consent.

7.   **Parking.** Tenant may use parking spaces in the parking lot located adjacent to the Building on a first come, first served basis in common with other occupants of the building and their respective employees, agents, guests, and invitees. Landlord represents and warrants that the parking lot located adjacent to the Building contains ____ regular parking spaces, ____ handicapped spaces, and ____ visitor spaces and that all such spaces are reserved for the exclusive use of occupants of the Building and their respective agents, employees, guests, and invitees. Without Tenant's prior written consent, Landlord may not (a) reduce the total number of parking spaces located in the Building's parking lot or the number of handicapped or visitor spaces (b) change the location or configuration of the parking lot, or (c) grant any right to use the parking lot to any persons other than occupants of the Building and their respective agents, employees, guests, and invitees. Finally, Landlord will reserve and designate _____ parking spaces for the exclusive use of Tenant's senior management, with all such reserved parking spaces being located where indicated on the parking plan attached hereto as Schedule ____or in such other areas of the parking lot as are specifically approved in writing by Tenant.

8.   **Expansion Option.** Tenant has the option to expand its Leased Premises to include the _____ rentable square feet of space that is located on the _____ floor of the Building and that is more particularly shown on the floor plan attached to this Rider as Schedule ___ ("Expansion Space"). Tenant may exercise its expansion option by delivering written notice of the exercise of such option to Landlord at any time on or before the ____ anniversary of the Commencement Date. If Tenant so exercises its expansion option, then its leasing of the Expansion Space will be upon all of the same terms and conditions set forth in this Lease with respect to the original Leased Premises (including, without limitation, the Termination Date of the Lease Term and the per rentable square foot amount of Tenant's Base Rent), except that (a) the Commencement Date applicable to Tenant's leasing of the Expansion Space will be the date on which all improvements to be made to the Expansion Space are completed and

a permanent certificate of occupancy is issued for the Expansion Space, (b) the Tenant Improvement Allowance for the Expansion Space will be $ _____ per rentable square foot contained within the Expansion Space, and (c) Tenant's Proportionate Share for the Expansion Space will be deemed to be ___%. If Tenant exercises its expansion option at the time and in the manner required in this paragraph, then Landlord and Tenant will execute an amendment to this Lease that reflects the terms and conditions applicable to Tenant's leasing of the Expansion Space (as such terms and conditions are described in the immediately preceding sentence of this paragraph).

9.   **Right of First Refusal.** Tenant has a right of first refusal on all vacant space located on the _____ floor(s) of the Building ("RFR Space"). If at any time during the Lease Term, Landlord receives a bona fide written offer from any third party ("Third Party Offer") to lease any space that includes all or any part of the RFR Space ("Offer Space") and if Landlord in good faith is willing to accept such offer, then Landlord will promptly provide Tenant with written notice of the terms and conditions of such Third Party Offer. Tenant will have ten business days after its receipt of Landlord's notice to provide Landlord with written notice that Tenant elects to lease such Offer Space upon the identical terms and conditions set forth in the Third Party Offer. If Tenant does not provide Landlord with such written notice within the aforementioned ten business-day period or if Tenant expressly declines to exercise its right of first refusal under this paragraph, then, in either such event, Landlord will thereafter have the unrestricted right for a period of 60 days to lease the Offer Space to the third party who submitted the Third Party Offer upon the identical terms and conditions set forth in such Third Party Offer. If Landlord does not so lease the Offer Space within such 60-day period, then Tenant's right of first refusal under this paragraph will be fully reinstated.

10.   **Right of First Offer.** Tenant has a right of first offer on all space that "becomes available" (as that term is hereinafter defined) on the _____ floor of the Building. For the purposes of this paragraph, the space on the _____ floor of the Building will be deemed to have "become available" only after that space has been leased to a third party and such third party's right to occupy the subject space terminates (other than as a result of any assignment or subleasing by any such tenant) and expressly excludes any space that has never been leased to a third party or any space that is subject to an expiring lease if the tenant then occupying that space extends or renews its lease pursuant to a right granted to it under its lease or pursuant to a separate agreement entered into by such tenant and Landlord.

If at any time during the Lease Term, any space on the _____ floor of the Building becomes available ("Available Space"), then Landlord will promptly provide Tenant with written notice of such availability ("RFO Notice"), specifying (a) the size, location, and configuration of the Available Space, (b) the projected commencement and termination dates for Tenant's leasing of the Available Space, (c) the improvements that Landlord proposes to make to the Available Space (or the tenant improvement allowance that Landlord proposes to make available to Tenant for the construction of such improvements), (d) the Base Rent that Landlord proposes that Tenant pay for its leasing of the Available Space, and (e) any other provisions that Landlord proposes to include in Tenant's lease of the Available Space that are inconsistent with the provisions specified in this Lease with respect to Tenant's leasing of the Leased Premises (all of the terms specified in clauses (a) through (e) being hereinafter referred to as the "RFO Terms"). Tenant will have 20 business days after its receipt of Landlord's RFO Notice in which to provide Landlord with written notice of Tenant's exercise of its right of first offer. If Tenant so exercises its right of first offer, then Landlord and Tenant will execute a lease for the Available Space that incorporates the RFO Terms and all those provisions of this Lease that are not inconsistent with the RFO Terms. If Tenant fails to provide Landlord with notice of its exercise of its right of first offer within that 20 business-day period or if Tenant expressly declines to exercise its right of first offer under this section, then, in either such event, Landlord will thereafter have the unrestricted right for a period of 60 days to lease the Available Space to any third party upon terms and conditions that are at least as favorable to Landlord as are the RFO Terms. If Landlord does not so lease the Available Space within such 60-day period, then Tenant's right of first offer will be fully reinstated.

11. **Contraction Option.** Tenant has the option to contract the size of the Leased Premises by canceling this Lease as to the _____ rentable square feet of space that is identified in the floor plan attached to this Rider as Schedule ____ ("Contraction Space"). Tenant may exercise its contraction option by delivering written notice of the exercise of such option to Landlord at any time on or before the _____ anniversary of the Commencement Date. The cancellation of this Lease as to the Contraction Space will be effective ____ days after the date on which Landlord receives Tenant's written notice of the exercise of its contraction option ("Contraction Date"). It is a condition to Tenant's exercise of such contraction option that Tenant pay to Landlord, at the same time as it delivers written notice to Landlord of the exercise of the contraction option, cash in a sum equal to (a) the unamortized balance of all leasing commissions and tenant improvement costs paid by Landlord with respect to the Leased Premises (with such unamortized balance being computed as of the Contraction Date based

upon an initial amortization schedule equal to the length of the initial Lease Term and an annual interest rate of ___% per year), multiplied by the percentage determined by dividing the rentable square feet contained within the Contraction Space by the rentable square feet contained within the entirety of the original Leased Premises, plus (b) a contraction fee of $_____. If Tenant exercises its contraction option at the time and in the manner required in this paragraph, then, prior to the Contraction Date, Landlord and Tenant will execute an amendment to this Lease that reflects the cancellation of this Lease as to the Contraction Space. Such amendment will be prepared by Landlord and will confirm (i) the size, location, and dimensions of the remaining Leased Premises, (ii) the Contraction Date, (iii) the reduction, from and after the Contraction Date, of Tenant's Proportionate Share to ___% and its monthly Base Rent to $_____, (iv) Landlord's right to enter the Leased Premises, at all reasonable times prior to the Contraction Date, to do all work necessary to separate the Contraction Space from the remaining Leased Premises, including, without limitation, the construction of demising walls and the reconfiguration of any of the mechanical and electrical systems serving the respective spaces, (v) Tenant's ongoing obligation, from and after the Contraction Date, to abide by all of the terms and conditions of this Lease as they relate to the remaining Leased Premises, (vi) the survival of all of Tenant's obligations with respect to the Contraction Space that accrued prior to the Contraction Date and (vi) such other matters as are required to properly reflect the effect of Tenant's exercise of its contraction option.

12.   **Deletion of Relocation Section.** Section 27 of the Lease is deleted in its entirety.

13.   **Tenant's Remedies for Construction Delays.** Despite any provision to the contrary contained in § 9 of this Lease, if the Improvements required to be constructed by Landlord are not substantially completed by the Target Commencement Date identified in the Lease Summary for any reason other than a Tenant Delay, then Landlord will pay to Tenant liquidated damages in an amount equal to $_____ per day for each day of delay beginning on the Target Commencement Date and ending on the date on which the Improvements are substantially completed. Such liquidated damages must be paid by Landlord on or before the date that is ten days after the date on which the Improvements are substantially completed. If Landlord fails to pay such liquidated damages to Tenant on or before the expiration of that ten-day period, then Tenant may offset the amount of any unpaid liquidated damages against its next succeeding installment(s) of Base Rent and Excess Expenses. Landlord and Tenant acknowledge that Tenant's damages in the event the Improvements are not substantially completed on or before the Target

Commencement Date will be difficult to ascertain and the receipt of the amount set forth above constitutes a reasonable liquidation of such damages and is not intended as a penalty.

Tenant may also cancel this Lease if (a) the Improvements are not substantially completed on or before the date that is __ days after the targeted Commencement Date, and (b) the delay in the substantial completion of the Improvements is not attributable to a Tenant Delay. Tenant may exercise such cancellation right by delivering written notice of cancellation to Landlord at any time on or before the date of the substantial completion of the Improvements.

14.   **Extension Option.** Tenant has the option to extend this Lease for _____ extension terms of _____ years each. Tenant may exercise its extension option by delivering written notice of exercise to Landlord on or before the date that is 45 days prior to the scheduled expiration of the then existing term of the Lease (be it the initial term or any subsequently-exercised extension term). Each extension term will be upon all of the same terms and conditions set forth in this Lease with respect to the initial lease term, except that (a) in lieu of the Tenant Improvement Allowance referenced in the Lease Summary, Landlord will pay Tenant a refurbishment allowance of $_____ for each exercised extension term; and (b) the annual Base Rent payable during each year of each extension term will be equal to 90% of the "Fair Market Rent" for the Leased Premises. For the purposes of this section, "Fair Market Rent" means the average annual rental rate (expressed in an amount per rentable square foot) then being charged in the _____ submarket for space comparable to the Leased Premises, taking into consideration (1) the specific provisions of the Lease that remain constant during the extension term, (2) the relative condition, quality, design, age and location of the Leased Premises and all comparable space, (3) the building amenities and services available to the tenants of all the subject buildings, (4) the creditworthiness of Tenant, and (5) the provisions of all leases of comparable spaces, including without limitation, the tenant improvement allowances, rent structures and concessions provided under such leases.

Landlord and Tenant will have 30 days after Tenant's exercise of its extension option in which to reach mutual agreement on the Fair Market Rent for the Leased Premises (and, hence, the amount of the Base Rent that is payable by Tenant during the exercises extension term). If Landlord and Tenant are not able to reach agreement on such Fair Market Rent within such 30-day period, then the Fair Market Rent for the Leased Premises will be determined in accordance with the appraisal procedures specified in the succeeding paragraph.

Within five days after the expiration of the 30-day period referenced in the preceding paragraph, Landlord and Tenant will each appoint a licensed real estate broker with at least five years' full-time commercial brokerage experience in the _____ submarket to appraise the Fair Market Rent for the Leased Premises. Within 30 days after the appointment of the last broker, Landlord and Tenant will each submit to the appointed brokers its written statement ("Rent Statement") of the Fair Market Rent for the Leased Premises (including whatever support for such contention the party wishes to have considered by the brokers). The appointed brokers will then have ten days to reach agreement on the selection of the Rent Statement that is nearest to their belief of the Fair Market Rent for the Leased Premises. The brokers must select either Landlord's Rent Statement or Tenant's Rent Statement and may not compromise the two Rent Statements or otherwise determine a Fair Market Rent for the Leased Premises that is different from that set forth in one of the two Rent Statements. If the brokers cannot agree upon the selection of one of the two Rent Statements, then the brokers will have an additional period of seven days in which to appoint a third real estate broker with at least five years' full-time commercial brokerage experience in the _____ submarket. The third broker will then have fifteen days to select which of the two Rent Statements he or she believes is closest to the actual Fair Market Rent for the Leased Premises. The selection of such Fair Market Rent by the third broker will be binding on Landlord and Tenant for all the purposes specified in this Lease.

15. **Gross-Up Adjustments.** The following rules govern the Building Expense gross-up adjustments required to be made under the last sentence of Exhibit B to this Lease:

   (a) Such adjustments must be made in accordance with industry standards and generally accepted accounting principles, consistently applied;

   (b) Only those Building Expense components that fluctuate based upon occupancy levels in the Building may be grossed up;

   (c) Landlord will include a reasonably detailed description of how the gross-up adjustments were calculated in the written Building Expense statement for each Comparison Year that Landlord is required to provide to Tenant under § 2 of this Lease;

   (d) If, during any Comparison Year, Landlord incurs additional costs because of a change of policy or practice related to its operation or management, of the Building (including, without limitation, increased premiums for new or different insurance coverages or additional costs related to any change in the frequency or levels of Building services provided by Landlord), then the Base Expenses must be increased to include those additional costs that Landlord would have incurred if such change in policy or practice had been in effect at all times during the Base Year;

(e)   If any portion of the Building was covered by a warranty during the Base Year, then the Base Expenses must be increased to include those additional costs that Landlord would have incurred if such warranty had not been in effect during the Base Year; and

(f)   If the Building is not fully assessed for real estate tax purposes during the Base Year, then the Base Expenses must be increased to include the additional real estate taxes that would have been incurred by Landlord if the Building had been fully assessed during the Base Year.

16.   **Replacement of Building Expense Exclusions.** The exclusions from the definition of Building Expenses set forth as items 1 through 3 of the next to the last paragraph of Exhibit B are deleted and replaced with the list of Building Expense exclusions set forth in Schedule ___ to this Exhibit.

17.   **Rules Governing Calculation of Building Expenses.** Notwithstanding anything to the contrary contained in § 2 or Exhibit B to this Lease, the following general principles govern the calculation of Landlord's Building Expenses and Tenant's Excess Expenses:

(a)   Landlord may not recover the cost of any item more than once, nor will Landlord seek reimbursement from Tenant for an amount greater than the actual cost incurred by Tenant with respect to any item; it being expressly acknowledged by Landlord that it is not the intention or purpose of this Lease to produce or generate an economic profit or windfall to Landlord;

(b)   Landlord will operate and maintain the Building in a cost-effective and economically responsible manner;

(c)   Landlord will calculate its Building Expenses in a fair, accurate, and commercially reasonable manner;

(d)   All services rendered to and all materials supplied to the Building must be of a nature and scope that are consistent with those rendered or supplied to comparable buildings and the cost of such services and materials must be of a cost no greater than those charged in arm's length transactions for similar services or materials rendered or supplied for similar purposes to comparable buildings; and

(e)   In determining the nature and amount of any costs to be included as Building Expenses, Landlord will comply with and respect generally accepted accounting principles, consistently applied.

18. **Cap on Controllable Expenses.** Despite any provision to the contrary contained in § 2 or Exhibit B of this Lease, the amount of "Controllable Expenses" taken in consideration when computing Tenant's Proportionate Share of Excess Expenses in the 20__ calendar year is capped at $_____ per rentable square foot contained within the Leased Premises. The amount of Controllable Expenses to be taken into consideration when computing Tenant's Proportionate Share of Excess Expenses for each calendar year subsequent to the 20__ calendar year is capped at 105% of the Controllable Expenses taken into consideration for such purposes during the immediately preceding calendar year. For the purposes of this Lease, the term "Controllable Expenses" mean those expenses referred to in paragraphs ____, ____, ____, and ____ of Exhibit B.

19. **Audit of Operating Expenses.** Tenant may audit Landlord's books and records with respect to Landlord's computation of its Building Expenses for any calendar year during the Lease Term (including, without limitation, all invoices, executed contracts, canceled checks, and general legers related to such Operating Expenses). Tenant may exercise its audit right as to a particular calendar year by delivering a written audit notice to Landlord at any time on or before the ____ anniversary of Tenant's receipt from Landlord of a written statement showing Landlord's actual Building Expenses for such calendar year. If any audit conducted by Tenant discloses an overage in the amount billed to Tenant over the amounts actually due from Tenant, then Landlord will reimburse Tenant for the amount of such overage, plus interest thereon at ___% from the date paid through the date reimbursed. If such overage exceeds 2% of the amount actually due from Tenant, then Landlord will also reimburse Tenant for all reasonable out-of-pocket costs and professional fees incurred by Tenant in connection with its auditing of Landlord's books and records. The payments referred to in the immediately preceding sentences must be made by Landlord to Tenant within ten days after Landlord's receipt of a detailed invoice identifying the amount of such payments. Except as provided in this paragraph, Tenant will bear all costs associated with the auditing of Landlord's books and records.

20. **Modification to Security Deposit.** Despite any provision to the contrary contained in § 32 of the Lease, the following provisions govern the posting, holding, and disbursement of the Security Deposit identified in the Lease Summary.

  (a) Landlord will hold any cash Security Deposit in a separate interest-bearing account and will not co-mingle the Security Deposit with any of Landlord's other funds.

(b) In lieu of a cash Security Deposit, Tenant may deliver to Landlord an irrevocable letter of credit issued by a FDIC-insured bank in the amount of the Security Deposit identified in the Lease Summary. Upon its receipt of such letter of credit, Landlord will promptly refund to Tenant any cash Security Deposit previously paid to it by Tenant.

(c) If, as of the _____ anniversary of the Commencement Date, Landlord has not yet drawn down on any portion of the Security Deposit to cure any default by Tenant under the Lease, then Tenant's obligation to post a Security Deposit will automatically terminate and Landlord will promptly return the Security Deposit to Tenant.

21. **Modification to Financial Statements.** Landlord acknowledges that it has received a copy of Tenant's most current financial statement as of the Effective Date. Landlord will hold Tenant's financial statement in the strictest of confidences and will not disclose the financial statement to anyone other than a lender who has executed a subordination, nondisturbance, and attornment agreement with Tenant. Tenant has no obligation to provide any further financial statements to Landlord. As such, § 33 of the Lease is deleted in its entirety.

22. **Administration of Rules and Regulations.** Despite any provision to the contrary contained in § 6 or Exhibit C to the Lease, Landlord will not issue any new rule or regulation that unreasonably interferes with Tenant's conduct of its business in the Leased Premises. Landlord will enforce the Building's rules and regulations against Tenant and all other tenants in the Building in a fair, consistent, non-discriminatory, and even-handed manner. If there is any conflict between any rule or regulation established by Landlord and any provision of this Lease, then the provision of this Lease controls.

23. **Limitations on Tenant's Compliance with Law Obligation.** Despite any provision to the contrary contained in § 7 of this Lease, Landlord will, at its sole expense, comply with all laws, governmental requirements, and recorded covenants or conditions that are now or in the future in force pertaining to the ownership or use of office buildings generally (and not solely to Tenant's specific use of the Leased Premises). Tenant's compliance obligation under § 7 of this Lease is further made subject to the following limitations:

(a) Tenant will not be required to spend more than $_____ in making any alteration, addition, or improvement to the Leased Premises;

(b)   Tenant will not be required to make any alteration, addition, or improvement to the Leased Premises during the last 12 months of the Lease Term; and

(c)   Tenant will not be required to make any alteration, addition, or improvement to the Common Areas or to any structural element or mechanical or electrical system that does not exclusively serve the Leased Premises.

Landlord will be required to pay all compliance costs in excess of the $_____ limit set forth in subparagraph (a) and will be further required, at its sole expense, to make all those alterations, additions and improvements described in subparagraphs (b) and (c).

24.   **Landlord's Representations and Warranties.** Landlord makes the following representations and warranties to Tenant for the express purpose of inducing Tenant to execute this Lease and occupy the Leased Premises. All such representations and warranties are deemed made by Landlord both as of the Effective Date and as of the Commencement Date.

(a)   The Building does not contain any Hazardous Substance (as that term is defined in § 17 of the Lease), except for immaterial amounts that are exempt from or do not give rise to a violation of applicable law.

(b)   The Building complies with all laws, governmental requirements, and recorded covenants and conditions that are applicable to the ownership, use, and operation of the Building, including, without limitation, the Americans with Disabilities Act.

(c)   The Permitted Use identified in the Lease Summary is permitted under applicable zoning and other laws and regulations.

(d)   There are no restrictive covenants, exclusive use provisions, or any other agreements that would prevent Tenant from occupying the Leased Premises for the Permitted Use

(e)   The Building has no latent structural defects and all mechanical and electrical systems serving the Building (including, without limitation, the HVAC system) are in good operating condition.

(f)   The Building's HVAC system complies with the minimum operating standards set forth in the Ventilation for Acceptable Air Quality Standard promulgated by The American Society of Heating, Refrigerating and Air Conditioning Engineers.

Landlord will indemnify Tenant from any loss or expense incurred by Tenant as a result of Landlord's breach of any of these representations and warranties.

25.   **Level of Building Services.** The level of services currently applicable to the Building (including, without limitation, HVAC, electrical, elevator, janitorial, landscaping, window cleaning, and security services) are described in Schedule ___ to this Rider ("Current Services"). Without first obtaining Tenant's written consent, Landlord will not take any action that results in the level of the Current Services being reduced or otherwise changed in a manner that could adversely affect Tenant's use of the Leased Premises.

26.   **After Hours HVAC Service/Separate Meter.** Despite any provision to the contrary contained in § 4 of the Lease, the agreed-upon surcharge for the provision of HVAC services to the Leased Premises outside of normal business hours is the lesser of (a) $___ per hour, or (b) the actual cost incurred by Landlord in providing such after-hour HVAC service to the Leased Premises, taking into account any discount Landlord receives for a high volume usage of such service. Tenant may elect to have electricity supplied to the Leased Premises directly from the public utility company that furnishes electricity to the Building and to have the level of Tenant's consumption of electrical service measured by an electrical meter installed in the Leased Premises. If Tenant notifies Landlord that it elects to have electricity supplied and measured in the manner set forth in the preceding sentence, then Landlord will, at its sole expense, promptly install all meters and additional wiring and equipment that are required to permit electricity to be supplied directly from such public utility company to the Leased Premises. From and after the completion of all the required installations, Tenant will pay all costs of providing electricity to the Leased Premises directly to the public utility company and Landlord will thereafter exclude all costs of providing electricity costs to the leased premises of any Building tenant from the calculation of Landlord's Building Expenses.

27.   **Interruption of Building Services.** Notwithstanding anything to the contrary contained in § 4 of the Lease, if the provision of any service required to be provided to the Leased Premises by Landlord (including, without limitation, HVAC, electrical, elevator, janitorial, window cleaning, landscaping, and security services) is interrupted for any reason other than the negligence or willful misconduct of Tenant and if such interruption substantially impairs Tenant's ability to conduct its business in the Leased Premises, then Tenant's obligation to pay Base Rent and Excess Expenses will fully abate throughout the period of the interruption. If an interruption continues for more than ___ consecutive days, then Tenant may cancel this Lease

effective as of the date of Tenant's delivery of a written cancellation notice to Landlord.

28. **Limitations on Tenant's Maintenance and Repair Obligation.** Despite any provision to the contrary contained in § 5 of the Lease, Tenant will not be obligated (a) to replace any item, component, equipment, or system located within the Leased Premises if the useful life of any such item, component, equipment, or system (determined in accordance with generally accepted accounting principles) extends beyond the Lease Term, or (b) to repair or replace any damage to the interior of the Leased Premises caused by the fault or negligence of Landlord or Landlord's other tenants, agents, employees, guests, customers, or invitees.

29. **Permitted Transfers.** Despite any provision to the contrary contained in § 12 of the Lease, Tenant may, without having to obtain Landlord's prior written consent, sublet the Leased Premises or assign its interest in the Lease to (a) any successor-in-interest to Tenant resulting from a merger, consolidation, or sale of Tenant's entire business, or (b) any subsidiary or affiliate of Tenant. Tenant will provide Landlord with written notice at least ten business days prior to the scheduled occurrence of any sublease or assignment sanctioned under this paragraph.

30. **Self-Help Remedy.** If Landlord fails to perform any of its obligations under this Lease on or before the date that is __ days after its receipt of written notice from Tenant of the non-performance of such obligation, then, in addition to any other right or remedy that Tenant may have at law or in equity to redress such non-performance, Tenant may perform such obligation on Landlord's behalf and offset Tenant's performance costs against Tenant's next succeeding installment(s) of Base Rent and Excess Expenses.

31. **Landlord's Duty to Mitigate Losses.** Despite any provision to the contrary contained in § 22 of the Lease, Landlord must at all times following any default by Tenant use commercially reasonable efforts to mitigate Landlord's damages.

32. **Modification to Casualty Section.** Despite any provision to the contrary contained in § 19 of the Lease, if the Leased Premises or any Common Area is damaged by fire or other casualty during the last 12 months of the Lease Term and such damage cannot be repaired in 30 days or less after the date of the occurrence of such fire or other casualty, then Tenant may cancel this Lease effective as of the date of Tenant's delivery of a written cancellation notice to Landlord.

33. **Modification to Condemnation Section.** Despite any provision to the contrary contained in § 20 of the Lease, Tenant may also cancel

the Lease if a taking of any Common Area (including any parking area or means of access) materially interferes with Tenant's ability to conduct its business in the same manner as it conducted that business immediately prior to such taking. Tenant may exercise its cancellation option by delivering written notice of cancellation to Landlord at any time on or before the date that is __ days after the date on which title to the taken area vests in the condemning authority. The effective date of the cancellation will be 30 days after the date of Tenant's delivery to Landlord of written notice of the exercise of Tenant's cancellation option.

34.   **SNDA.** Despite any provision to the contrary contained in § 13 of the Lease, Tenant's subordination and attornment obligations are expressly conditioned upon Tenant's execution with Landlord's lender of a subordination, non-disturbance, and attornment agreement that provides that Tenant's leasing and possession of the Leased Premises will not be disturbed by Landlord's lender as long as Tenant is in full compliance with the provisions of this Lease. The subordination, non-disturbance, and attornment agreement must otherwise be in such form and content as are reasonably acceptable to Tenant and Landlord's lender.

DOCUMENT #7

EXCLUSIVE LISTING AGREEMENT
FOR NEW OFFICE BUILDING

■ ■ ■

EXCLUSIVE LISTING AGREEMENT

This Exclusive Leasing Agreement ("***Agreement***") is dated _____, 20__("***Effective Date***"), and is between _____ ("***Owner***") and _____ ("***Broker***"). For the parties' convenience in reviewing this Agreement, all defined terms are highlighted in ***italicized boldface*** print when first defined in this Agreement.

Owner and Broker agree as follows:

§ 1. Appointment of Broker. Owner appoints Broker as Owner's exclusive agent to procure tenants to lease improved office space in the building located at _____, _____ ("***Property***"). Broker will use its best efforts throughout the term of this Agreement to procure tenants for the Property upon the terms and conditions specified in § 3. Broker will assign _____ ("***Listing Agent***") primary responsibility for performing Broker's services throughout the term of this Agreement. Owner may terminate this Agreement effective immediately if the Listing Agent is no longer actively working on Owner's account.

§ 2. Term of Agreement. The term of this Agreement begins on the Effective Date and ends on the earlier of: (a) the first anniversary of the Effective Date; or (b) the date on which all improved space in the Property is leased to tenants.

§ 3. Acceptable Lease Terms. Owner will from time to time during the term of this Agreement specify those terms and conditions that are generally acceptable to Owner with respect to the leasing of space in the Property. Broker may use the supplied terms and conditions in Broker's efforts to procure tenants for the Property. Broker acknowledges, however, that the supplied terms and conditions are in no way binding upon Owner and that Owner will not be obligated to lease space to any tenant on any particular terms and conditions until Owner executes a fully-binding written lease for space in the Property ("***Lease***").

§ 4. Broker's Compensation. Broker's right to receive leasing commissions is governed by the provisions of this § 4. The amount of any leasing commissions payable to Broker will be calculated in the manner set forth in § 5 of this Agreement.

   (a) **Occurrences During Term of Agreement.** Owner will pay Broker a leasing commission only upon the execution of a Lease by Owner and a tenant during the term of this Agreement.

(b) <u>**Occurrences after Expiration of Term.**</u> Owner will also pay Broker a leasing commission upon the Owner's execution of a Lease within __ days after the expiration of the term of this Agreement with any tenant who was identified as a "Prospect" in the list furnished to Owner by Broker pursuant to § 12 of this Agreement.

Despite any provision to the contrary contained in this Agreement, the term "Lease" does not include any amendment, renewal, extension, assignment, sublease, or transfer of an existing lease and Owner will not be obligated to pay a leasing commission to Broker in connection with Owner's execution of any document evidencing any such transaction.

§ 5. <u>**Commission Schedule.**</u> With respect to any Lease in which a "Cooperating Broker" is involved (as that term is defined in § 7, below), the commission payable to Broker under this Agreement is equal to __% of the "Base Rent" payable during the initial lease term of such Lease (as the term "Base Rent" is later defined in this § 5). With respect to any Lease in which a "Cooperating Broker" is not involved, the commission payable to Broker is equal to __% of the "Base Rent" payable during the initial lease term of such Lease. "Base Rent" means fixed "base rent" payable by tenants of the Property under the terms of Landlord's standard lease form and expressly excludes any building expense pass-through payments, security deposits, tenant improvement costs, parking charges, or escalators of any nature payable by any tenant of the Property.

§ 6. <u>**Payment of Commissions.**</u> Owner will pay any commission payable to Broker under this Agreement one-half upon the execution of the Lease by Owner and the tenant and one-half upon the occupancy of the leased premises by such tenant.

§ 7. <u>**Cooperating Brokers.**</u> Broker will cooperate with and share its commission with each licensed real estate broker who is working with any tenant interested in leasing space in the Property ("***Cooperating Broker***") Broker will pay a commission to a Cooperating Broker (in such amount as is negotiated by Broker) out of the commission payable to Broker under this Agreement. Broker will indemnify Owner from any loss or expense for a commission made by any Cooperating Broker; it being expressly understood by Owner and Broker that Owner will not under any circumstance be obligated to pay any commission or other sum to a Cooperating Broker.

§ 8. <u>**Specific Duties of Broker.**</u> Broker will do all of the following at Broker's sole expense: advertise the Property as being "for lease" in a commercial multiple listing service and a business journal of wide circulation in the community in which the Property is located; attend weekly marketing meetings with representatives of Owner; and provide Owner with a monthly written report identifying the prospective tenants to whom Broker has shown the Property, made a marketing presentation, or delivered written materials concerning the availability of the Property.

§ 9. <u>Duties of Owner.</u> Except as provided in § 19 of this Agreement, Owner will: (a) cooperate with and assist Broker in effecting Leases of the Property; and (b) refer to Broker all inquiries of any party interested in leasing any space in the Property.

§ 10. <u>Owner's Disclosure Obligations.</u> Owner will disclose to Broker all pertinent information that Owner has in its possession regarding the environmental condition of the Property, including, without limitation, the presence of asbestos, PCB transformers, underground storage tanks, or other toxic, hazardous, or contaminated substances. Broker is authorized to disclose all information furnished by it to Owner under this § 10 to prospective tenants of the Property. Owner represents and warrants that: (a) it is the sole owner of the Property and has the legal right and authority to enter into this Agreement and lease space in the Property; and (b) no person or entity who has an ownership interest in the Property is a "foreign person" within the meaning of the Foreign Investment in Real Property Tax Act.

§ 11. <u>Advertising and Signage.</u> Owner will erect a project sign on the Property that specifically includes the Broker's name and telephone number and the name of the Listing Agent. The location, size, and format of the project sign will be determined by Owner. Broker may not erect any sign on the Property.

§ 12. <u>Prospects List.</u> Within ten days before the expiration of the term of this Agreement, Broker will deliver to Owner a list of all those persons to whom Broker has made a marketing presentation and physically shown the Property during the term of this Agreement ("***Prospects***"). Such list will set forth the name, address, phone number, contact person, and status of each Prospect.

§ 13. <u>Non-Discrimination.</u> It is acknowledged by Owner and Broker that it is illegal for either Owner or Broker to refuse to lease the Property to any person because of race, color, religion, national origin, sex, marital status, sexual orientation, or physical disability.

§ 14. <u>Amendment</u>. This Agreement may not be amended except by a written instrument executed by both Broker and Owner.

§ 15. <u>Applicable Law.</u> This Agreement is governed by _____ law.

§ 16. <u>Successors and Assigns.</u> Broker may not assign or delegate its interest in this Agreement to any third party without the prior written consent of Owner.

§ 17. <u>Default.</u> In addition to any other remedy available to Owner at law or in equity to redress any default by Broker under this Agreement, Owner may terminate this Agreement if Broker defaults in the performance of any provision of this Agreement and Broker fails to cure such default within ten days after Broker's receipt of written notice from Owner of the alleged existence of such default.

§ 18. **Legal Documents.** Owner and its counsel are solely responsible for determining the legal sufficiency of any Lease or other document related to any transaction contemplated by this Agreement. Owner will include in any such Lease a recital concerning Broker's representation of Owner and a provision committing Owner to pay all commissions owed to Broker under this Agreement.

§ 19. **Tenant Exclusions.** Despite any provision to the contrary contained in this Agreement, Broker will not under any circumstance be entitled to receive a leasing commission if Owner executes a Lease at any time with any of the prospective tenants named below (or any of affiliate of any such prospective tenant).

Excluded Prospective Tenants: _____.

Owner and Broker are signing this Agreement as of the Effective Date.

OWNER: **BROKER:**

_____   _____

By: _____   By: _____

(Name)   (Title)   (Name)   (Title)

DOCUMENT #8

PROPERTY MANAGEMENT AGREEMENT FOR OFFICE BUILDING

■ ■ ■

PROPERTY MANAGEMENT AGREEMENT

This Property Management Agreement ("**Agreement**") is dated _____, 20__ ("**Effective Date**"), and is between _____ ("**Owner**") and _____ ("**Manager**"). For the parties' convenience in reviewing this Agreement, all defined terms are highlighted by *italicized boldface print* when first defined in this Agreement.

Owner and Manager agree as follows:

§ 1. Appointment of Manager. Owner appoints Manager to manage and operate the building located at _____, _____, ("**Property**"). Manager will assign _____ ("**Executive**") primary responsibility for performing Manager's services under this Agreement. Owner may terminate this Agreement effective immediately if the Executive is no longer actively working on Owner's account.

§ 2. Term of Agreement. The initial term of this Agreement begins on the Effective Date and ends on the first anniversary of the Effective Date. The term of this Agreement will automatically be extended for consecutive extension terms of one year each unless either Owner or Manger elects to terminate this Agreement by giving written notice of termination to the other party at least 60 days prior to the scheduled commencement date of the next extension term.

§ 3. Manager's Duties. Manager will perform all the duties set forth in this § 3 in a diligent and competent manner to protect and promote Owner's interest in the Property. Manager may not incur any cost without first obtaining Owner's prior consent unless (i) the incurring of such cost is consistent with an "Approved Budget" (as that term is defined in subparagraph (a) below), or (ii) the incurring of such cost is immediately required for the preservation and safety of the Property or to avoid the suspension of any essential service to the Property.

    (a) Operating Budgets. Manager will prepare and submit to Owner an operating budget for the Property for each calendar year during the term of this Agreement. The operating budget for the 20__ calendar year is attached to this Agreement as Exhibit A. The operating budget for each subsequent calendar year must be submitted to Owner for its review and approval at least 30 days prior to the beginning of such calendar year. The operating budget attached as Exhibit A and each subsequent operating budget approved by Owner is referred to as an "*Approved Budget*".

(b) <u>**Maintenance of Property.**</u> Manager will maintain the Property in good order and condition of repair. Manager may not, however, make any structural changes to the Property without first obtaining the written consent of Owner.

(c) <u>**Rent Collection.**</u> Manager will invoice tenants for and use its best efforts to collect all base and additional rent and other charges payable by tenants under leases of space in the Property. Manager will also collect all applicable sales tax and remit such taxes to the appropriate public authority.

(d) <u>**Services and Utilities.**</u> Manager will negotiate contracts on behalf of Owner for the provision to the Property of water, electricity, telecommunications, security, trash collection, janitorial, elevator, landscaping, snow removal, and other similar services and utilities. Each contract negotiated under this subparagraph must permit cancellation by Owner without penalty on 30 days' prior written notice.

(e) <u>**Leasing Files**</u>. Manager will establish and maintain complete files of all leases of space in the Property and all correspondence with existing and prospective tenants. Manger will make such files available for inspection by Owner throughout the term of this Agreement and will deliver such files to Owner within ten days after the termination of this Agreement.

(f) <u>**Operating Statements.**</u> Manager will prepare and submit to Owner a monthly operating statement for the Property for each calendar month during the term of this Agreement. Each operating statement must delineate in reasonable detail all items of income and expense flowing from the Property for such month and for the year to date and must also compare actual results with the estimates set forth in the applicable Approved Budget. Manager will submit a monthly operating statement to Owner no more than ten days after the end of each calendar month during the term of this Agreement.

(g) <u>**Personnel.**</u> Manager will hire, supervise, pay, and discharge all employees, contractors, and other personnel that Manger deems appropriate to properly manage and operate the Property. All persons hired by Manager will be deemed to be the employees or contractors of Manager.

(h) <u>**Tenant Improvements.**</u> Manager will supervise the making of all tenant improvements to the Property, including, without limitation, the preliminary design and preparation of working drawings and specifications for the tenant improvements and the supervision, scheduling, and accounting for the construction of such tenant improvements.

(i) **Insurance Review.** At Owner's request, Manager will review Owner's insurance policies for the Property, including without limitation, policies for fire, theft, public liability, plate glass, rent loss, elevator, boiler, and workers compensation. Manager acknowledges that the services provided by Manager under this subparagraph are advisory only and that the sole responsibility for placing, maintaining, and administering such insurance policies rests with Owner.

(j) **Additional Services.** Manager will perform such additional management, advisory, consulting, supervisory, design, construction, or other services as are requested by Owner. Manager's compensation for the provision of any such additional services will be determined based upon the hourly rate then in effect for the person who renders the services on Manager's behalf.

§ 4. Management Account. Manager has established a bank account at _____ for the sole benefit of the Property ("*Management Account*"). Manager will deposit all monies collected by Manager under this Agreement (including, without limitation, all rents and other payments collected from tenants) into the Management Account"). Owner and Manager are both named as authorized signatories on the Management Account. Owner may at any time during the term of this Agreement suspend Manager's status as a signatory on the Management Account or limit Manager's authority to withdraw funds from the Management Account. The amounts deposited in the Management Account may not be commingled with any other funds of Manager.

Manager may withdraw from the Management Account such amounts as are required to pay those costs that Manager is authorized to incur under the first paragraph of § 3 of this Agreement, but Manager may not under any circumstance withdraw from the Management Account any management fees payable to Manager under § 5 of this Agreement. Manager will disburse any funds in the Management Account that are not required for the payment of current Property expenses to Owner in accordance with Owner's instructions to Manager. If the funds in the Management Account are insufficient to permit Manager to pay all expenses required to be paid by it under this Agreement, then Manager will so notify Owner in writing and Owner will promptly deposit in the Management Account the funds required to pay all such expenses. Manager will deliver an accounting of the balance in the Management

Account to Owner on or before the tenth day of each calendar month during the term of this Agreement.

§ 5. <u>Manager's Compensation.</u> Owner will pay Manager a monthly management fee equal to ___% of the Base Rent actually collected from tenants of the Property during the preceding calendar month. *"**Base Rent**"* means fixed "base rent" payable by tenants of the Property under the terms of Landlord's standard lease form and expressly excludes any building expense pass-through payments, security deposits, tenant improvement costs, parking charges, or escalators of any nature payable by any tenant of the Property. Owner will pay the management fee to Manager on or before the tenth day of each calendar month during the term of this Agreement.

§ 6. <u>Indemnification of Manager.</u> Owner will indemnify Manager from any loss or expense incurred by Manager in connection with the Property or Manager's performance of services under this Agreement, including, without limitation, any such loss or expense arising under the Comprehensive Environmental Response, Compensation and Liability Act or any other federal, state, or local law or regulation pertaining to the environment, but expressly excluding any loss or expense occasioned by Manager's gross negligence, willful misconduct, or default in the performance of any provision of this Agreement. Manager will indemnify Owner from any loss or expense incurred by Owner arising out of Manager's gross negligence, willful misconduct, or default in the performance of any provision of this Agreement. The provisions of this § 6 will survive the termination of this Agreement.

§ 7. <u>Independent Contractor Status.</u> Manager is an independent contractor and is not to be treated as a partner, co-venturer, agent, or employee of Owner. Manager's authority to act on behalf of Owner is strictly limited to the duties expressly delegated to Manager in this Agreement.

§ 8. <u>Amendment.</u> This Agreement may not be amended except by a written instrument executed by both Manager and Owner.

§ 9. <u>Applicable Law.</u> This Agreement is governed by _____ law.

§ 10. <u>Successors and Assigns.</u> Manager may not assign or delegate its interest in this Agreement to any third party without the prior written consent of Owner.

§ 11. <u>Default.</u> In addition to any other remedy available to Owner at law or in equity to redress any default by Manager under this Agreement, Owner may terminate this Agreement if Manager defaults in the performance of any provision of this Agreement and Manager fails to cure such default within ten days after Manager's receipt of written notice from Owner of the alleged existence of such default.

Owner and Manager are signing this Agreement as of the Effective Date.

OWNER: **MANAGER:**

_____   _____

By: _____   By: _____

  (Name)   (Title)   (Name)   (Title)

APPENDIX B

GLOSSARY OF TERMS

▪ ▪ ▪

All of the following terms are highlighted in **boldface italic** print in the text of REAL ESTATE DEVELOPMENT LAW, 2ND EDITION. The page where each term is first defined is noted parenthetically. For the purposes of this Glossary of Terms, the term *"project"* refers to a commercial real estate product created by a developer and the term *"venture"* refers to the entity that owns a project.

Access and utility study: A report that confirms that the land has direct access to public roads and that utilities of sufficient size and capacity to service the developer's proposed project are available to the boundaries of the land (page 126).

Additional rent: The variable component of the tenant's rent payment that is tied to the level of the landlord's building expenses (page 512).

After-tax return: The before-tax cash flow distributed to a real estate investor by the venture that owns a real estate project, reduced by any income tax payable by the real estate investor due to its receipt of the distributed cash and its participation in the venture (page 215).

ALTA survey: An as-built survey prepared in accordance with the surveying standards jointly promulgated by the American Land Title Association and the National Society of Professional Surveyors (page 321).

Amortization period: The benchmark period of time selected by the lender for the repayment of a real estate loan. Most commercial real estate loans assume an amortization period that is significantly longer than the actual term of the loan (page 50).

Anti-sandbagging clause: A clause that precludes a buyer who learns of a seller's breach of a representation and warranty *BEFORE* the buyer acquires title to the land from filing a legal action against the seller for that breach *AFTER* the date of the buyer's acquisition of the land (page 137).

Application for payment: A form prescribed by a lender (often AIA Document G–702) for the borrower's submission of its draw requests (page 423).

Architect: The licensed professional principally responsible for the design of a real estate project (page 436).

As-built drawings: Drawings prepared by the architect at the completion of construction that reflect any modifications made to the original construction drawings during the construction period (page 454).

"As is" clause: A clause inserted into a purchase contract that states that the buyer is purchasing the real property in its "as is, where is" condition, without any representations or warranties from the seller concerning the condition or character of the real property (page 130).

Assignment of lease: A transfer by a tenant to a third party (the *assignee*) of all of its rights and interests in the lease and the leased premises (page 567).

Back-end equity: Capital contributions that are funded after the disbursement of all of the construction loan proceeds (page 351).

Balloon payment: The sizable principal payment that is payable on the maturity of a permanent loan (due to the use of an amortization period that is longer than the term of the permanent loan) (page 601).

Bankruptcy remote entity: An entity that is not permitted to own any assets other than a single real estate project (for that reason also sometimes referred to as a *single purpose entity* or *SPE*). The entity is structured to protect a lender from the possibility that the entity owning the real estate project might be forced into bankruptcy for a reason unrelated to the financial performance of the subject project (page 377).

Baseball appraisal: A method used to determine the fair market rental value of leased space, where the landlord and the tenant each submits a determination of the fair market rental value and an expert or panel of experts is then required to select one of the submitted determinations as the market rent applicable to the tenant's leased premises (page 566).

Base building improvements: Those core and structural improvements that the landlord must make to facilitate any occupancy of the leased premises. They typically include, at a minimum, load-bearing walls, carpet-ready floors, life safety systems, windows, and stubbed-in utilities (page 494).

Base rent: The fixed amount of rent payable by a tenant during each year of the lease term (page 512).

Basel III Final Rule: A rule issued by The Federal Reserve Board, the Office of the Comptroller of the Currency, and the Federal Deposit Insurance Corporation in July 2013 that is designed to discourage the risky loan practices followed by U.S. banks prior to the onset of the recession in 2008. The hallmark of the Basel III rule is the requirement that financial institutions must establish higher capital reserves for their risky real estate loans (labeled in the rule as "high-volatility commercial real estate loans") (page 355).

Basis point: A common unit of measurement for interest rates and other financial percentages. One basis point is equal to 1/100th of 1% or 0.01%. A ***point*** is a short-hand reference to 100 basis points or 1% (page 348).

Before tax cash flow: The cash distributed to an equity investor by the venture that owns a real estate project. It is, by definition, calculated before the investor's payment of any income tax on its receipt of the distributed cash and its participation in the venture (page 59).

Bill of sale: A document that transfers title to personal property to a buyer, including a seller's rights and interests in trade names, contractual rights, and other intangible property (page 330).

Boilerplate: A misnomer used to describe provisions that are customarily included in all real estate documents (page 161).

BOMA standard: A standard for the measurement of space in a commercial building adopted by the Building Owners and Management Association (page 489).

Book/tax disparity: The difference between the agreed value and the tax basis of property contributed to a pass-through entity (page 244).

Breakpoint: The maximum level of gross sales that a retail tenant can attain without having to pay percentage rent (page 532). A breakpoint can be either a ***natural breakpoint*** (that is, the result produced by dividing the tenant's base rent by the percentage used to calculate its percentage rent) or an unnatural breakpoint (any breakpoint other than a natural breakpoint) (page 533).

Bring-down certificate: A document signed by the seller that confirms that all of its representations and warranties remain true and accurate as of the closing date (page 331).

Brownfield: A parcel of real property whose expansion, redevelopment or reuse is complicated by reason of the presence of hazardous substances, pollutants, or contaminants—contrasted with ***greenfield*** properties that have no environmental problems whatsoever (page 192).

Builder's risk insurance: An insurance policy that insures the owner against damage caused to a development project during the construction period by fire, wind, explosion, lightning, hail and other causes beyond the owner's control (page 383).

Building expenses: A term often used by a landlord to expand the scope of the expenses to be reimbursed by the project's tenants to include expenses other than the traditional operating expenses sanctioned by generally accepted accounting principles (for example capital expenditures) (page 511).

Build-to-suit lease: A lease that requires the landlord to construct a new building (be it an office building, warehouse, or retail building) from the ground up and lease the entirety of the completed building to a single tenant for an extended term (typically at least ten to 20 years) (page 506).

"But for" test: A test used by governments to determine whether the provision of a governmental incentive to a private real estate project serves a public purpose—that is, the subject project would not have been developed "but for" the receipt of the incentive (page 201).

C corporation: A corporation taxed as a separate entity under Subchapter C of the Internal Revenue Code (page 222).

Capital interest: An equity interest received by an equity owner in exchange for its contribution of services to a venture that gives the equity owner an immediate share of the value of all the venture's existing assets (page 245).

Capital proceeds: The portion of an entity's cash flow that is attributable to the occurrence of certain capital transactions, such as the sale of all or a part of a project or the refinancing of the project debt (also referred to as *extraordinary cash flow*) (page 257).

Capital split: An equity owner's percentage share of all capital contributed to an entity (page 260).

Capitalization rate (cap rate): The percentage return that a buyer demands as a condition to its purchase of a particular property. A project's value is often estimated by dividing a project's stabilized net operating income by the capitalization rate then prevailing in the market for comparable properties. An *exit cap rate* is the capitalization rate used in a discounted cash flow model to determine the project's ultimate sales price (page 76).

Carried interest: Another name for the profits interest granted to an equity owner in exchange for its contribution of services to the venture. The "carried interest" nomenclature is most commonly used in the context of hedge fund deals (page 264).

Cash flow: All cash that is available for distribution to the equity owners of a project. It is equivalent to before tax cash flow and includes both operating cash flow and capital proceeds (page 257).

Cash on cash return: A financial return standard used to measure the return achieved by an investor on its equity investment in a project. It is equal to the investor's before tax cash flow, divided by the total equity contributed to the project by the investor (page 59).

Cash reserve: The portion of a venture's cash flow that is held back from distributions to the equity owners and deposited into a "rainy day" account to protect the venture against foreseeable and unforeseeable future contingencies (page 258).

Caveat emptor: The "let the buyer beware" doctrine that is generally applicable to commercial real estate transactions and that supports the dual proposition that (1) the seller has no obligation to disclose to the buyer any defects or other problems related to the condition of the real property being sold to the buyer, and (2) the buyer has no inherent legal right to sue the seller if the condition of the real property purchased by the buyer ultimately proves to be at odds with the buyer's expectations (page 129).

Certificate of good standing: A document issued by the state in which an entity is formed affirming that the entity exists and is in good standing under the laws of such state (page 331).

Certificate of occupancy (CO): A local governmental approval that allows a building tenant to assume occupancy of its leased space and begin doing business in that space. A certificate of occupancy can be either ***temporary*** (one that can be revoked if future conditions are not satisfied within a stated period of time) or ***permanent*** (a final and irrevocable CO) (page 504).

Change directive: A contractual right reserved by the developer to compel the contractor to proceed with a change in the nature or scope of a construction project before the parties reach final agreement on the substance of a change order (page 469).

Change order: A change in the nature or scope of a construction project. It typically requires the agreement of both the contractor and the owner and may result in an adjustment to the construction price or schedule (page 469).

Clawback: A contractual provision that permits one party to a contract to recover from the other party the intended, but unfulfilled financial benefit contemplated under the contract. A clawback clause is commonly used in two contexts—(1) a joint venture between a developer and an investor where the clause authorizes the investor to recover from the developer any excess cash distributions made to the developer (page 277), and (2) the grant of a governmental incentive to a developer where the clause authorizes the government to recover from the developer the financial benefit of the incentive if the developer fails to satisfy the conditions to the grant of the incentive (for example, the production of a stated number of new jobs in a stated period of time) (page 207).

Closing: The consummation of all the transactions contemplated in a purchase contract (page 147). The closing can be effected as either (1) a ***New York Style closing*** where all the principals and lawyers gather in one room to sign all requisite legal documents and pay the purchase price and all closing costs, or (2) an ***escrow closing*** where the principals sign the requisite legal documents in advance and send those legal documents and all funds required to pay the purchase price and closing costs to an escrow agent who then disburses the documents and funds at the time and in the manner described in written *escrow instructions* sent to the escrow agent by the principals' lawyers (page 151).

Closing bible: The compilation of all those documents that are pertinent to the closing of a real estate transaction (page 339).

Closing statement: The document that shows how much money the buyer needs to pay to close a real estate acquisition and to whom that money is to be disbursed (page 331).

Commercial mortgage backed securities (CMBS): A securitized loan made with respect to a commercial real estate project (page 610).

Commitment letter: A letter issued by a lender to indicate its intention to make a loan to a borrower upon the specific terms and conditions set forth in the letter (page 356).

Common areas: Those spaces within the landlord's project that the tenant may use in common with other tenants in the building. Common areas include both *building common areas* (those contained within the four corners of the building) and *site common areas* (those located on the land parcel on which the building is situated) (page 487).

Common area load factor: The difference between the square footage of a building's rentable and usable space. It is typically expressed as a percentage equal to [the building's rentable square feet − the building's usable square feet] ÷ the building's rentable square feet (page 490).

Completion guaranty: A promise made to a lender by a guarantor (typically a creditworthy affiliate of the borrower) that the guarantor will do whatever is necessary to completion construction of a project in accordance with the approved plans and specifications and by the outside completion date specified in the construction loan documents (page 379).

Covenants, conditions, and restrictions (CCRs): A recorded document that places restrictions on the manner in which a parcel of land may be used (page 320).

Construction loan agreement: The document that establishes the rules that will govern the construction lender's disbursement of loan proceeds under a construction loan (page 359).

Construction management-agency system (CMa): A project delivery system in which the developer adds a fourth person to the design and construction process (in addition to the developer, contractor and architect) by hiring an independent construction manager to provide the developer with advice concerning the design and construction of the a project (page 443).

Construction management at risk system (CM@r): A variation of the pure construction management-agency system in which the construction manager serves in two capacities—as (1) the owner's advisor during the planning and design phases, and (2) the contractor during the construction phase (page 443).

Constructive change: A change in the scope of the contractor's work that is caused by the occurrence of unforeseen events or circumstances (page 470).

Contingency: A clause that conditions a party's contractual obligation to the occurrence of a stated circumstance or event (page 115).

Contingency reserve: A line item in a development cost budget that allows for unforeseen costs that may have to be incurred to deal with the specter that "something bad may happen" during the construction period or the term of a loan (page 388).

Continuous operation covenant: A lease clause that obligates a retail tenant to continuously operate its retail business in the leased premises during the retail center's normal business hours and to staff, fixture, and stock its store in a manner designed to maximize its gross sales (page 552).

Contraction option: A lease clause that gives the tenant an option to terminate its obligations with respect to all or a portion of its leased premises (page 559).

Cooperating broker: A broker who is retained to represent the interests of a buyer (page 314) or a tenant and who shares in the commission paid to the listing broker (page 622).

Cost of funds: A convention used to determine the cost to a lender of securing the funds needed to make a real estate loan (page 55).

Cost of the work, plus a fee contract: A construction contract that requires the developer to reimburse the contractor for the contractor's actual cost of the work (regardless what that actual cost is), plus a fee equal to a stated percentage of the project's construction costs (page 461).

Co-tenancy requirement: A lease clause that conditions a retail tenant's obligation to perform its lease obligations upon the status of other tenants in the retail center. The requirement can either relate to the tenant's obligation to open for business (an *opening co-tenancy requirement*) or to the tenant's ongoing obligation to perform its lease obligations after it opens for business (a *continuing co-tenancy requirement*) (page 553).

Credit Risk Retention Rule: A rule adopted by the SEC and other federal agencies in the aftermath of the Great Recession of 2008 that requires the sponsor of a CMBS issuance to keep "skin the game" by retaining at least 5% of the credit risk of the securitized loans (page 610).

Crowdfunding: A digital investment platform that offers a data base of wealthy accredited investors the opportunity to invest online in institutional-grade real estate projects (page 236).

Date-down endorsement: A title policy endorsement issued by a title insurance company confirming that no mechanics' lien has been filed against a project since the date of the construction loan closing (page 426).

Deal maker: A lawyer who has a reputation for doing that which is required to consummate a transaction in a manner that serves a client's stated business objectives—contrasted with a lawyer who becomes a *deal killer* by placing "the law" and his or her personal competitive interests above the interests of the client (page 23).

Deal momentum: A circumstance where the parties to a transaction feel committed mentally and emotionally to doing a deal, even though they are not legally committed to do so—often produced by the execution of a non-binding letter of intent (page 93).

Deal risk: The risk that a developer's proposed project on a particular land parcel proves to be infeasible for a reason unrelated to the physical condition of the land parcel (for example, the developer's inability to obtain debt or equity financing for the project or the developer's financial projections not "penciling out.") (page 106).

Debt service coverage ratio: A test used by a lender to limit the principal amount of a loan by requiring that the projected income stream produced from the project must be a fixed multiple of the debt service payable on the loan. The maximum loan amount sanctioned by the application of a debt service coverage test is determined by dividing the project's maximum debt service by the mortgage constant applicable to the loan (page 49).

Debt yield ratio: A test used by a real estate lender to limit the principal amount of a loan by dividing the project's annual projected net operating income by a fixed percentage yield (page 49).

Defeasance: An alternative to a borrower's prepayment of a securitized loan involving the borrower's posting of Treasury instruments in an amount sufficient to fund all principal and interest payments when and as they become due under the loan (page 612).

Design-bid-build system: A traditional project delivery system in which the developer assigns responsibility for the design function to the architect under one contract and the responsibility for the construction function to the contractor under a separate contract (page 441).

Design-build system: A project delivery system in which the design and construction functions are combined and delegated to a single entity known as the *design-builder* (page 445).

Design development drawings: Detailed architectural drawings that incorporate the general features of the approved schematic drawings, plus add new detail concerning the building's architectural design and the specifics of the building's structural, mechanical, and electrical systems (page 433).

Development costs: The aggregate costs that a developer incurs in connection with its construction, leasing, and operation of a commercial real estate project during the period beginning on the date of the developer's acquisition of the project land and ending on the date that the project produces cash flow sufficient to cover all project expenses (including debt service on the project loan) (page 47).

Discounted cash flow model: A real estate valuation methodology that takes into consideration both the volume and timing of future cash flows generated from a real estate project (page 69).

Double taxation: The taxation of the income stream generated by a commercial real estate project twice—once to the venture that owns the project and then again to the equity owners of the venture when the project's net cash flow is distributed to the equity owners (page 214).

Drag along: The right of an equity owner to sell its equity interest to a third party and to compel its fellow equity owners to similarly sell their equity interests to the designated third party (page 306).

Draw request: A written request periodically delivered to a construction lender by a borrower asking the lender to disburse loan proceeds to pay those development costs incurred by the borrower during the preceding period (page 422).

Due diligence: An investigatory process conducted by a buyer to determine whether a particular parcel of real property is suitable for its intended use (page 125).

Due on sale and due on encumbrance clauses: Prohibitions contained in permanent loan documents against the borrower's sale of an interest in the mortgaged property (a ***due on sale clause***) (page 607) and the borrower's placement of secondary mortgage financing on the mortgaged property (a ***due on encumbrance clause***) (page 608).

Earnest money deposit: Cash paid or property delivered by a buyer to partially secure its commitment to purchase real property (page 109).

EB–5: An immigration program that grants a residency visa to a foreign investor who invests a minimum of $500,000 in a real estate project that creates a statutorily-required number of jobs (page 237).

Economic development: A principle that supports the government's provision of assistance to a real estate project if the development of the project will create new jobs and spur further development in the vicinity of the assisted project (page 181).

Entitlement: A governmental approval that is required to be issued to the developer if its proposed development plan complies with governmental rules applicable to all similarly situated projects (page 170).

Environmental assessment: A report prepared by an environmental engineer that identifies any environmental problems associated with a particular parcel of land (page 126). A *phase one environmental assessment* is one that is prepared based on a routine walk-through of the land and an examination of the public records of the state and federal environmental protection agencies, while a *phase two environmental assessment* involves an additional round of testing of the soils and ground water located on the land (page 323).

Equity: The cash or other property contributed by the owners of an entity to pay the portion of a project's development costs that are not funded with debt—also commonly referred to as *capital* (page 56).

Escrow agent: A neutral third party designated to hold and disburse the earnest money deposit and transactional documents placed in escrow by the parties to a contract (page 110).

Estoppel certificate: A written statement made by a tenant confirming the terms of its lease and representing that its lease is in full force and effect without any default on the part of either the landlord or the tenant (page 588).

Exclusive agency: A brokerage arrangement where a developer selects a particular broker to lease space in its building and agrees to pay the selected broker a commission on any lease that is signed for the building unless the developer, without the assistance of any other broker, is the procuring cause of the signed lease (page 620).

Exclusive listing: A brokerage arrangement where the developer is obligated to pay its selected broker a commission on any lease signed for the building, even if that lease is procured directly by the developer or another broker (page 620).

Exclusive use clause: A lease clause that gives a retail tenant the exclusive right to sell a particular product line in a retail center (page 551).

Exit strategy: The developer's plan to realize its profit and eliminate its ongoing risk by selling all or a part of a project to an institutional investor or placing permanent financing on the project (page 8).

Expansion option: An option granted to an existing tenant to lease additional space in the landlord's building (page 556).

Expense pass-through: A lease provision that places the ultimate financial burden for the payment of a building expense on the tenant (page 517).

Expense stop lease: A hybrid of a gross lease and a net lease where the tenant makes two rental payments—(1) a fixed base rent payment, plus (2) an additional rent payment equal to the tenant's share of the excess, if any, of the landlord's actual building expenses over a pre-determined base amount (the ***expense stop***). The expense stop can be expressed either as a fixed number (a ***stipulated sum expense stop***) or as the landlord's building expenses is a specified ***base year*** (a ***base-year expense stop***) (page 513).

Extension option: A lease clause that gives a tenant the option (but not the obligation) to extend the term of its lease beyond the termination date specified for the initial lease term (page 562).

Fast-track construction: A compressed construction process that is characterized by the commencement of construction of a portion of a project before the planning and design of the entirety of the project is completed (page 435).

FIRPTA affidavit: An affidavit confirming that the seller is not a "foreign person" subject to the withholding of taxes under the Foreign Investment in Real Property Tax Act (page 330).

Floating interest rate: A variable interest rate used on construction loans that is adjusted throughout the loan term to reflect changes in a specified financial index (page 347).

Forced sale: An entity dispute resolution method where one member reserves the right to compel the entity to market its assets for sale to a third party (page 306).

Force majeure: The risk of the occurrence of an event that is beyond a party's anticipation or control, but that nonetheless delays or prevents the construction of a real estate project (page 361).

For convenience termination: A clause that permits the developer to terminate the architect's contract for any reason and without cause (page 459).

Front-end equity: A construction lender's requirement that all capital contributions of the equity investors must be funded before the construction lender disburses any construction loan proceeds (page 351).

Full warranty sale: A purchase contract that contains an extensive litany of representations and warranties concerning the condition and character of the real property and the seller's authority and capacity to sell the real property, including a statement that the seller has completely and accurately disclosed to the buyer all material facts concerning the real property and the contemplated transaction (page 131).

Future advance or open-end mortgage: A mortgage that contemplates that advances of loan proceeds will be made periodically throughout the loan term and that affords such periodic advances priority over liens filed subsequent to the initial loan closing (page 367).

General condition costs: A contractor's costs of administering a construction project, including temporary utility, trash removal, and job supervision costs (page 459).

General contractor: The person responsible for constructing the project in accordance with the plans and specifications prepared by the architect and approved by the developer and for coordinating the activities of all firms providing construction services or materials for the project (page 436).

General partnership: An unincorporated organization in which two or more persons agree to share profits and losses associated with the conduct of a business or investment activity (page 225).

General warranty deed: A document that conveys title to real property and includes a warranty from the seller that it is conveying good title to the land and that the buyer may bring a cause of action against the seller if the title is defective regardless whether the title defect arose during or prior to the seller's ownership of the land (page 329).

Go dark right: A lease clause that expressly grants a retail tenant the right to close or curtail its store operations during the lease term (page 552).

Good guy guaranty: A lease guaranty that limits the guarantor's guaranteed rent obligations to those that accrue prior to the date on which the tenant voluntarily vacates the leased premises (page 577).

Gross area: All constructed space within a building's footprint (page 489).

Gross lease A lease where the tenant pays a fixed amount of rent that is not tied in any way to the level of the landlord's building expenses (page 513).

Gross revenues: The sum of all rents and other income received by the owner of a real estate project (page 44).

Gross sales: The benchmark used to determine a retail tenant's percentage rent obligation. Gross sales are generally considered to be all those revenues generated from the tenant's conduct of retail operations in its leased store (page 531).

Gross sales proceeds: The sum of all funds received by the seller from the sale of real property—usually represented by the property's purchase price page 45).

Gross-up clause: A clause that authorizes the landlord to increase the amount of its expense pass-throughs to include those hypothetical expenses that the landlord would have incurred if its building had been fully occupied (page 524).

Guaranteed maximum price (GMP): A ceiling placed on the construction price payable under a cost of the work, plus a fee construction contract (page 462).

Haircut: The grant of an option to the non-defaulting equity participants in a real estate venture to buy the equity interest of the defaulting equity participant at a discounted price (page 255) or the loss suffered by a lender when it is forced to write down the value of the collateral securing a defaulted loan (page 365).

Hard costs: Those expenses that are directly incurred in connection with the construction of a building, the build-out of tenant space and the making of other site improvements (page 47).

High-volatility commercial real estate loan (HVCRE): A commercial real estate loan for which the lender must create a higher than normal capital reserve. The heightened capital reserve requirement for HVCRE loans is mandated under the Basel III rule issued by The Federal Reserve Board, the Office of the Comptroller of the Currency, and the Federal Deposit Insurance Corporation in the aftermath of the 2008 recession (page 355).

Holdback: A provision of a venture agreement that permits the venture to establish a cash reserve as a partial hedge against the possibility of the venture's premature and unintended cash distributions to a developer (typically caused by the distribution to the developer of operating cash flow per the venture's profits splits, followed by a sale of the venture's project for a purchase price that does not permit a full return of the equity investor's contributed capital and preferred return) (page 277).

Hurdle rate: An investor's minimum acceptable rate of return for its investment in a particular real estate project (page 71).

Incentive: Governmental assistance provided to encourage a developer to move forward with its development of a particular project (page 170).

Incentive zoning: A phenomenon of recent vintage where a local government provides a developer with a zoning bonus (usually in the form of increased density for its project) in exchange for the developer agreeing to develop its project in a manner that advances a governmentally embraced agenda— for example, the adoption of green building practices (page 191).

Inspecting architect: The design professional assigned responsibility (by the developer, the construction lender, or both of them) for making regular jobsite visits to confirm that the progress of construction conforms to the approved construction drawings and that the general contractor's draw requests relate to work actually completed on the project (page 454).

Institutional controls: Limited clean-up standards sanctioned by state and local governments to encourage the development of brownfield sites. The most common example of a permitted institutional control is the elimination of a developer's obligation to remove mildly contaminated soils if those soils are capped with a concrete pad for a building or parking lot (page 193).

Institutional-grade property: A real estate project that is deemed worthy of investment by institutional investors because (1) the creditworthiness of the project's tenant roster is sufficiently solid as to give the investor comfort that the expected income stream will be realized, and (2) the project location, design and quality of construction are such that it is reasonable to assume that replacement tenants will be found if and when the existing tenants vacate the project (page 8).

Institutional investors: Life insurance companies, pension plans, equity funds, sovereign wealth funds, and other financial institutions, both domestic and foreign, who have huge sums of money to invest in real estate each year (page 5).

Integrated project delivery method: A hybrid project delivery system in which the developer, contractor, and architect collaborate at all times during the planning, design, and construction phases of the construction process (page 447).

Interest rate hedges: Techniques used to mitigate the risk to the borrower and the lender of a fluctuation in a loan's floating interest rate. ***Caps, collars,*** and ***swaps*** are types of interest rate hedges commonly used in the commercial real estate industry (page 397).

Internal rate of return: The percentage rate at which the present value of a series of future cash flows equals an investor's required equity investment (page 76).

Killer form: A legal form that is unduly long, complex, and overreaching in its efforts to eliminate every conceivable risk faced by a party to a real estate document (page 30).

Land costs: The component of a project's aggregate development costs that is equal to the costs incurred by the developer in connection with its acquisition and ownership of the land on which the developer's project is located (page 47).

Land risk: The risk that a developer's proposed project proves to be infeasible because the physical condition of the land on which the project is to be constructed is not suitable for its intended purpose (for example, the land's soils are not sufficiently compact to support the construction of the developer's proposed building or the land has environmental problems (page 106).

Landlord or lessor: The person who owns a real estate project and is trying to lease it to third parties (page 478).

Leased premises: The space over which the tenant has the exclusive right of possession (page 487).

Lease term: The period during which the tenant has the right to exclusive possession of the leased premises. The lease term includes the *initial lease term* specified in the lease and may be extended or renewed for an additional term or terms by the agreement of the parties (page 500).

Letter of intent (LOI): A short-form document (typically two to three pages in length) that is a preliminary expression of certain key deal points on which both parties to a transaction have reached consensus (page 93).

Leverage: The use of debt to pay the costs of developing or acquiring a real estate project. Leverage is *positive* to the extent that a project's return on total costs is greater than the mortgage constant of the project's mortgage loan and is *negative* to the extent the project's total return on costs is less than the mortgage constant (page 60).

LIBOR: The London Inter-bank Offered Rate is an index commonly used by construction lenders to measure the floating rate of interest payable on a construction loan (page 347).

Lien waiver: A written waiver executed by a contractor, subcontractor, laborer, supplier or material provider confirming that it has been paid for all work performed by it on a construction project and expressly waiving its right to file a mechanics' lien against the project to the extent of such prior or contemporaneous payments (page 426).

Limited liability company (LLC): An entity that blends the best of both the corporate and partnership worlds by combining the limited liability status of corporations with the pass-through tax status and operational and investment flexibility of partnerships. It is the entity of choice for most private real estate projects (page 228).

Limited liability limited partnership (LLLP): A limited partnership that elects under state law to negate the vicarious liability of each named general partner. LLLPs are recognized in less than half of the states (page 229).

Limited liability partnership (LLP): A general partnership that elects under state law to negate the vicarious liability of each named general partner. Some states limit the use of LLPs to professional service firms, such as accounting and law firms (page 229).

Limited partnership: An entity that possesses all of the attributes of a general partnership except that certain partners are afforded limited liability status as limited partners (page 226).

Limited warranty deed: A document that conveys title to real property and includes a title warranty from the seller covering only those title defects that arose during the seller's ownership of the land (page 330).

Listing broker: The broker hired by a seller (page 314) or landlord to find a buyer or tenants for its project (page 620).

Loan advance: A distribution by a construction lender to the borrower of a portion of the proceeds of a construction loan (page 374).

Loan assumption: A buyer's payment of a portion of a property's purchase price by the buyer's agreement to take over responsibility for the payment of an existing mortgage loan on the property (page 113).

Loan balancing provision: A construction loan provision that requires the borrower to contribute additional capital or post additional collateral if the lender determines that the construction loan is "out of balance"—that is, the costs of completing construction of a project are greater than the amount of the funds then reserved for the funding of such costs (page 401).

Loan-to-cost ratio: A test used by a real estate lender to limit the principal amount of a loan to a fixed percentage of a project's total development costs (page 49).

Loan-to-value ratio: A test used by a real estate lender to limit the principal amount of a loan to a fixed percentage of the appraised value of the project that serves as collateral for the lender's mortgage loan (page 49).

Lock-out period: A period during which an equity owner is prohibited from exercising a buy-sell right (page 305) or a borrower is prohibited from prepaying a permanent loan (page 606).

Lookback: A provision of a venture agreement that calls for the reduction of the capital proceeds payable to a developer to take into account any excess distributions of operating cash flow previously made to the developer (page 277).

Major decisions: Those fundamental actions and decisions that require the approval of all or a super-majority of an entity's equity participants (page 286).

Manager: The person assigned responsibility for the management and control of the business and affairs of a manager-managed LLC (page 287).

Manager-managed LLC: A limited liability company in which the management and control of the business and affairs of the limited liability company is centralized in one or more managers (who may or may not be members of the limited liability company) (page 285).

Marketable title: A state of title that is legally presumed to be acceptable to all owners of real estate—that is, title that permits the owner to possess, use, and dispose of the subject property without any unreasonable legal impediment (page 140).

Mechanics' lien: Right created by statute whereby a person who works on or provides labor or materials to a construction project can file a lien against that project if such person is not paid in full for its efforts (page 368).

Member: An owner of an equity interest (*membership interest*) in a limited liability company (page 239).

Member-managed LLC: A limited liability company in which the management and control of the business and affairs of the limited liability company is vested in its members (who may, in turn, delegate such management and control to a specific managing member) (page 285).

Merchant builder: A developer who customarily seeks to limit its exposure to real estate risk by selling its projects as soon as they reach stabilization (page 37).

Mezzanine financing (mezz debt): A loan intended to help a borrower defray its equity requirement in exchange for the borrower's agreement (1) to pay an above-market interest rate to the mezzanine lender (sometimes in the form of a profit participation), and (2) to pledge equity ownership interests in the borrower as collateral for the mezzanine loan (page 404).

Mini-perm loan: A construction loan that affords the borrower a right to extend the loan's maturity date for an additional term of years if certain conditions are satisfied by the borrower (page 413).

Monetary liens: Those real property liens that can be discharged by the payment of an ascertainable sum of money—for example, mortgages and judgment liens (page 146).

Mortgage (called a *deed of trust* in some jurisdictions): The primary collateral document used in both permanent and construction loans to evidence the borrower's grant to the lender of a lien on the borrower's real estate project (page 358).

Mortgage constant: The percentage of a real estate loan that must be paid every year to repay all principal and interest over the loan's assumed amortization period (page 50).

Multiple prime contractor method: A hybrid project delivery system in which the developer enters into contracts with the architect and each of the prime trade contractors involved in the construction of the project (page 447).

Multi-tenant lease: A lease where a building is leased to two or more tenants (page 482).

"Must take" agreement: A lease clause that obligates an existing tenant to lease additional space in the building effective as of a specified future date (page 558).

Net cash flow: The cash profit generated from a real estate investor's equity investment in a project. A real estate investor's aggregate "net cash flow" consists of the sum of (1) the investor's net cash flow from operations over the duration of the investor's ownership of the project, plus (2) the net sales proceeds received by the investor following the sale of the project (page 45).

Net cash flow from operations: The cash available for distribution to the owners of a project that is equal to the project's net operating income minus the project's debt service payments and capital expenditures (page 45).

Net lease: A lease where the tenant pays a fixed base rent payment, plus an additional rent payment equal to the tenant's share of the landlord's building expenses (page 513).

Net operating income: The current operating profit produced from a real estate project, represented by the project's gross revenues minus its operating expenses (page 7).

Net sales proceeds: The cash available for distribution to the owners of a project that is equal the project's gross sales proceeds minus the pay-off of all project debt and selling expenses (page 45).

New markets tax credit: An income tax credit embodied in § 45D of the Internal Revenue Code that is intended to incentivize developers, lenders, and investors to fund commercial real estate projects located in low-income communities (page 186).

Nonrecourse: A feature common to permanent loans where the borrower has no personal liability for the repayment of the loan and the lender's sole recourse for a borrower default is a foreclosure on its mortgage (page 16).

Nonrecourse carveouts: Exceptions to the operation of a nonrecourse clause that seek to place personal liability on a creditworthy entity as a result of the occurrence of certain proscribed events or circumstances (page 602).

No shopping clause: A clause inserted into a letter of intent that seeks to place a legally binding limitation on a property owner's right to solicit or receive offers for the sale or leasing of its property from any party other than its counterpart under the letter of intent (page 97).

Notional amount: The principal amount covered by an interest rate hedge (page 398).

No work affidavit: An affidavit signed by a developer attesting to the fact that neither it, nor any contractor, subcontractor, supplier, or material provider has performed any work or provided any materials to the project site prior to the closing of the construction loan (page 426).

Obligatory advance: A loan advance that a construction lender is required to make to a borrower under the terms of the applicable loan documents. Such an advance is customarily afforded priority over mechanics' liens filed after the construction loan closing (page 370).

Occupancy costs: All costs associated with a tenant's occupancy of leased space, including not only its fixed rental payment, but also its reimbursement of the landlord's building expenses, utility charges, parking fees, the cost of making improvements to the leased premises, and the benefit of any tax or economic incentives tied to its occupancy of the subject project (page 479).

Open listing: A brokerage arrangement where a developer agrees to pay a commission to any broker who procures a tenant for the developer's building (page 620).

Operating agreement: The document that governs the relationship of the members of a limited liability company and the operation of the limited liability company's business (page 239).

Operating cash flow: The portion of an entity's cash flow that is attributable to the entity's day-to-day conduct of its rental and development operations (page 258).

Operating expenses: Those expenses that are paid to operate and maintain a real estate project, including real estate taxes, janitorial fees, maintenance and repair costs, insurance premiums, utility costs and property management fees. Principal and interest paid on project debt and capital expenditures (for example, leasing commissions and the cost of adding to or replacing the structural components of a project) are usually excluded from the definition of "operating expenses" (page 44).

Optional advance: A loan advance that a construction lender is not required to make to a borrower under the terms of the applicable loan documents. Such an advance is often held to be subordinate to a mechanics' liens filed after the construction loan closing, but prior to the date on which the optional advance is made by the lender (page 370).

Pari passu: A cash distribution scheme where the respective rights of the developer and its outside equity investors to participate in a venture's cash distribution category are placed on "equal footing" (which is what *pari passu* means in Latin) (page 273).

Pass-through tax entity: An entity formed to own a real estate project that does not pay any taxes on the income stream generated by the project, but rather passes all tax attributes and consequences on to the entity's equity owners (page 64).

Payment and performance bonds: Separate bonds pursuant to which a surety guaranties (1) the payment of all construction costs owed to subcontractors, laborers, suppliers, and material providers under a construction contract (the *payment bond*), and (2) the completion of construction of a project at the time and otherwise in accordance with the terms of the construction contract (page 380).

Payment guaranty: A promise made to a lender by a guarantor (typically a creditworthy affiliate of the borrower) that the guarantor will repay all or a designated portion of a real estate loan (page 359).

Payback period: A calculation of how long it takes a real estate investor to receive cash distributions from a project that are equal to the real estate investor's original equity contribution (page 78).

Percentage rent: The portion of a retail tenant's rent obligation that is equal to a percentage of the gross sales produced from the tenant's conduct of retail operations in its leased store (page 531).

Permanent loan: A mortgage loan placed on a real estate project to refinance a construction loan. A permanent loan typically has a term of five to ten years and is nonrecourse to the borrower (page 601).

Permissive use clause: A lease clause that empowers the tenant to use the leased premises for a specified purpose, but does not expressly limit the tenant's use to the specified purpose (page 535).

Permitted exceptions: Those liens, easements, restrictions and other exceptions to a perfectly clean title that are contractually deemed to be acceptable to the buyer (page 141).

Portfolio builder: A developer who, due to its financial position and innate disposition, is inclined to try to maximize its after-tax financial returns by holding on to its projects for a long term (page 37).

Portfolio joint venture: An equity arrangement between a developer and an outside equity investor that goes beyond the parties striking a deal for their co-investment in a single project and, instead, extends to their establishment of a complex set of upfront parameters for their joint investment in a portfolio of development projects (page 238).

Portfolio loan: A permanent loan that is originated and held by a single mortgage lender (page 601).

Preferred return: The required priority return payable to an equity investor on the amount of its contributed capital (page 266).

Prepayment penalty: A negotiated premium payable by a borrower for the privilege of prepaying a permanent loan prior to maturity. The most common formulation of a prepayment penalty is a *yield maintenance penalty* where the borrower is required to pay the lender an additional sum that is equal to the difference between (1) the present value of the yield that would have been produced had the loan been held to maturity, and (2) the present value of the yield that the lender could achieve by investing the prepaid amount in another investment vehicle (page 606).

Present value: The current value of a future payment, discounted to reflect time value of money concepts. A project's *net present value* is equal to the sum of the present values of all payments projected to be generated by the project (page 69).

Prime rate: A benchmark frequently used to set the floating interest rate payable by a borrower under a construction loan. It is generally viewed as the interest rate charged on loans made by a financial institution to its most creditworthy customers (page 347).

Profit and loss: An accounting and tax concept that measures the overall profitability (or lack thereof) of a real estate venture (to be contrasted with the financial measure of a real estate venture's cash flow) (page 257).

Pro forma: A developer's projection of the financial results that will be generated by a proposed development project, including the project's aggregate development costs, net operating income, before tax cash flow, and net sales proceeds (page 70).

Profit-sharing clause: A lease clause that requires a tenant to share with the landlord a portion of any profit it derives from an assignment of its lease or a sublease of its leased premises (page 573).

Profits interest: An equity interest received by an equity owner in exchange for its contribution of services to a venture that gives the equity owner an interest only in the profits that are attributable to the venture's future operations or a future appreciation in the value of the venture's assets (page 245).

Profit split: The ratio in which the developer and its equity investors share in a project's positive cash flow. The developer's profit split is typically greater than its capital split (the ratio of the cash and property contributed to the venture by the developer and its equity investors) because the developer is given a heightened profits interest in exchange for its contribution of past and future services to the venture (page 260).

Programmatic requirements: The developer's requirements concerning the design and function of a development project that the developer furnishes to its architect at the inception of the project (page 433).

Project delivery system: A method for assigning construction and design responsibility and authority to the developer, architect, and contractor (page 441).

Promissory note: A document evidencing a borrower's obligation to repay its loan that sets forth the loan amount, the maturity date of the loan, the borrower's interest rate, and the amount and timing of the periodic debt service payments due under the loan (page 358).

Promoted interest (promote): The portion of a developer's profits interest that is disproportionate to its share of an entity's contributed capital (page 266).

Property Manager: The person (who can either be an affiliate of the developer or an independent third party) assigned primary responsibility for collecting rents, maintaining and repairing the developer's project, and otherwise operating the developer's project (page 18).

Public-private partnership (PPP): A collaborative effort between a private developer and the public sector involving the government's provision of affirmative support for a particular project (page 208).

Purchase money financing: A loan made by a property seller to the buyer to wholly or partially fund the payment of the purchase price for the property (page 112).

Push-pull, buy-sell: A provision that provides deadlocked members with a mechanism they can use to go their separate ways, with one member acquiring the equity interest of the other member. Under this mechanism (also often referred to as a *Russian roulette* buy-sell), one member establishes the price to be paid for the equity interest, while the other member makes the decision whether to sell its interest at the established price or buy the other member's interest at that price (page 304).

Quitclaim deed: A document that conveys title to real property, but does not contain any title warranty whatsoever from the seller (page 330).

Radius restriction: A lease clause that limits a retail tenant's ability to operate a competing store within a specified proximity to the landlord's retail center (page 551).

Real estate investment trust (REIT): A creature of the federal tax laws that may be organized as either a corporation or an unincorporated trust having at least 100 shareholders. It is not subject to any entity-level tax as long as it satisfies a series of complex tests specified in the Internal Revenue Code, including the requirement that it distribute at least 90% of its qualifying income each year to its equity owners (page232).

Recapture clause: A lease clause that permits a landlord to terminate its lease with a tenant for the purpose of entering into a new lease with a proposed assignee or subtenant of the original tenant (page 573).

Reciprocal easement agreement (REA): A recorded document that creates easements that benefit more than one parcel of land (for example, a common parking area or driveway) and then allocates financial responsibility for the maintenance of the easement area among the affected landowners (page 320).

Recourse: A feature common to most construction loans where the borrower or a creditworthy affiliate of the borrower is personally liable for the repayment of the loan (page 16).

Relocation clause: A lease clause that gives the landlord a contractual right to move the tenant's leased premises to another location controlled by the landlord (page 560).

Remargining provision: A loan provision that obligates the borrower/guarantor to make additional capital contributions or post additional collateral if the lender determines that the financial performance of a development project is less that that projected at the inception of the lender's underwriting of the loan (page 413).

Rentable area: A fictional number used by a landlord to calculate a tenant's rent that equals the usable area of a designated space, plus an allocation of the building's common areas (page 490).

Rent amortization factor: The percentage number by which excess tenant improvement costs (that is, those in excess of the agreed-upon tenant improvement allowance) are multiplied to determine the tenant's annual rent increase (assuming that the landlord is willing to front such excess costs in exchange for the tenant's agreement to increase its annual rent) (page 498).

Rent bump: An increase in the tenant's base rent intended to provide the landlord with a modicum of comfort that inflation will not adversely affect the landlord's net operating income. A rent bump may be expressed either as a fixed rent increase (a *fixed bump*) or tied to an increase in a financial index (an *indexed bump*) or a change in the fair market rental value of the leased premises (a *market bump*) (page 530).

Representation: An affirmative statement made by a party to a contract concerning a current fact (page 128).

Residual value: The net cash produced on the sale of the project, represented by the gross sales proceeds minus any selling expenses (page 7).

Resolution: A document certified by an authorized officer of an entity confirming that all requisite action has been taken by the entity to authorize its participation in the subject transaction and that the person who is signing the closing documents on behalf of the entity is duly authorized to do so (page 331).

Restrictive use clause: A lease clause that limits the tenant's use of the leased premises to the purpose specified in the lease (page 535).

Retainage: Amounts withheld from advances made under a construction loan until a contractor completes its work on a project (page 382).

Return: The financial benefits produced to a person committing funds (debt or equity) to pay a project's development costs. A distinction is commonly made between a return *OF* an investment (the repatriation to the investor of the principal amount of its initial investment) and a return *ON* an investment (the investor's profit component (page 45).

Return on debt: A financial return standard used to measure the lender's return on its advancement of the principal amount of a construction loan. It is roughly equal to the interest rate payable on the loan, plus the amount of any fees received by the lender that are not in the nature of a reimbursement of a lender's transactional costs (page 59).

Return on equity: A financial return standard used to measure an investor's return on the equity it contributes to a real estate project (also referred to as an investor's cash on cash return). It is equal to the investor's before tax cash flow, divided by the total equity contributed to the project by the investor (page 59).

Return on total costs: A financial return standard used to measure the overall productivity of a real estate project. It is equal to the project's net operating income, divided by the project's total development costs (page 58).

Right of first offer (RFO): A lease clause that requires the landlord to extend an offer to an existing tenant to lease space in the building before the landlord begins marketing that space to other prospective tenants (page 557).

Right of first refusal (RFR): A lease clause that permits an existing tenant to lease additional space in the building by matching any lease offer received by the landlord from a third party (page 556).

Risk-adjusted return: The financial return payable to an investor after taking into consideration the relative risk inherent in a particular investment opportunity (page 66).

S corporation: A corporation that is exempt from most (but not all) entity level income taxes under Subchapter S of the Internal Revenue Code (page 223).

Schedule B–2 title exceptions: The exceptions to coverage set forth in a title commitment or title insurance policy, including those exceptions that are applicable to all properties (*standard preprinted exceptions*) and those exceptions that are applicable only to the specific insured parcel (*special exceptions*) (page 319).

Schematic drawings: General design drawings and guidelines prepared by the architect for the developer's review at the earliest stage of the design phase (page 433).

Securitized loan: A permanent loan that is originated by a mortgage lender and then pooled with other mortgage loans and sold off in pieces and parts to investors (page 601).

Security deposit: Collateral posted by a tenant to partially secure the performance of its obligations under a lease (page 589).

Selling expenses: Those transactional costs that reduce the amount of cash available for distribution to the project participants following a sale of the project—for example, real estate brokerage commissions, legal fees, and title insurance premiums (page 45).

Separateness covenants: A series of covenants made by a borrower that are designed to insure the bankruptcy remote status of the borrowing entity by requiring that the entity must be operated independently of any affiliate (page612).

Shared savings clause: A clause pursuant to which the developer agrees to increase the contractor's fee by an agreed-upon percentage of the excess of the guaranteed maximum price over the actual cost of the work (page 462).

Single member LLC: A limited liability company that has only one member. It is often referred to as a *disregarded tax entity* because it is wholly disregarded for federal income tax purposes and is not required to file an informational tax return (page 233).

Single tenant lease: A lease where one tenant leases the entirety of a building (page 482).

Skin in the game: A colloquialism used to describe the developer's equity contributions to its development project (page 56).

Soft costs: All those costs, other than hard costs, that would not have been incurred but for the development of the project (page 47).

Soils report: A report that is intended to confirm that the soils located on the land will support the construction of the proposed project (page 126).

Spread: The difference between the lender's cost of funds and the interest rate charged by it on a mortgage loan (page 352).

Squeeze-down: A right granted to a non-defaulting equity owner to cause a venture to recalculate the ratios in which the equity owners share in the venture's profits and losses to take into consideration an equity owner's default in its obligation to make additional capital contributions to the venture. The exercise of this right typically seeks to punish the defaulting equity owner by reducing its share of future profits and losses below its share of the total contributed capital (page 255).

Stabilized project: A real estate project that is leased and producing positive cash flow (page 593).

Stair-stepping: The staggering over time of a buyer's payment of its earnest money deposit. Stair-stepping a deposit usually entails either (1) a buyer paying additional deposits periodically throughout the contingency period (for example, every 60 days), (2) a portion of a buyer's refundable deposit becoming nonrefundable at designated points of the contingency period (this is often referred to as the deposit "going hard"), or (3) a combination of (1) and (2) (page 123).

Standby letter of credit: A form of collateral posted to secure a party's performance under a contract (for example, a construction loan agreement or lease), whereby a financial institution provides its unconditional commitment that it will pay the letter of credit beneficiary a specified sum of money upon its receipt of a demand for payment specifying that a default has occurred under the contract (page 408).

Stipulated sum contract: A construction contract in which the developer agrees to pay the contractor a fixed construction price regardless of the actual cost of the work (page 460).

Structural reserve: A financial line item frequently inserted into the project pro forma by an institutional investor to reflect the impact on a project's net operating income of the future cost of repairing and replacing the project's structural components—for example, $.05 per square foot of space contained within the project (page 44).

Subcontractor: A person contracted by the general contractor to perform specialized components of the construction work (for example, a site excavator, steel erector, plumber, electrician, carpenter, or painter) (page 436).

Sublease: A transfer by the tenant to a third party (the ***subtenant***) of part of its rights and interests in the lease premises (but not the underlying lease) (page 567).

Subordination, nondisturbance, and attornment agreement (SNDA): A document entered into by a tenant and the landlord's lender that delineates the relationship of the tenant and the lender following the lender's foreclosure of its mortgage on the landlord's building (page 415).

Suitability or free look contingency: A clause inserted into a purchase contract that conditions the buyer's purchase obligation on the buyer's subjective determination that the real property is suitable for its intended use (page 116).

Survey: A document prepared by a licensed land surveyor that depicts the dimensions and boundaries of a land parcel (a *boundary survey*), A survey that also shows the location of any improvements, easements, roads, and encroachments affecting a land parcel is referred to as an *as-built survey* (page 321).

Survival clause: A clause inserted into a purchase contract that states that certain seller representations, warranties, and covenants will survive the closing of the sale of the real property for a stated period of time (page 135). The term is also used to refer to an affirmative statement in a lease that the tenant's obligation to pay rent will survive the termination of its right of possession of the leased premises (page 577).

Sweat equity: A colloquialism used to describe a developer's contribution of its past and future services to a real estate venture in exchange for the venture's grant to the developer of an equity interest in the venture's profits (page 259).

Take-out commitment: An upfront agreement by a permanent lender that it will close a permanent loan to the borrower and pay off the construction loan upon the occurrence of certain conditions (page 410).

Tax abatement: A governmental incentive pursuant to which a taxpayer's tax liability is reduced or eliminated for a fixed period of time (page 185).

Tax credit: A governmental incentive pursuant to which the taxpayer is provided with a credit to offset its existing tax liability (page 185).

Tax increment financing (TIF): A financing device used by state and local governments to provide a source for the developer's funding of a portion of its development costs. The *incremental taxes* or *increment* created by a project (that is, the taxes that would not exist but for the development of the subject project) are used to pay certain statutorily approved development costs. A tax increment financing arrangement can be either a *pay as you go TIF* (where the developer is responsible for fronting the development costs) or a *bonded TIF* (where the government is responsible for fronting those costs) (page 178).

Tax rebate: A governmental incentive pursuant to which the government refunds taxes previously paid by a taxpayer (page 186).

Tenancy in common: An ownership structure whereby two or more persons hold undivided interests in the same real estate (page 220).

Tenant or lessee: The person who wants to lease space in a project (page 478).

Tenant improvement allowance: A maximum dollar amount that the landlord will pay for the construction of tenant improvements to a tenant's leased premises (page 496).

Tenant improvements (TI): The improvements and modifications that must be made to the leased premises to fit a particular tenant's planned use of the space (page 494).

Tenant's proportionate share: The tenant's percentage share of an expense pass-through (page 523).

Time value of money: The economic concept that states that a dollar received today is more valuable than a dollar received in the future due to the associated concepts of ***opportunity cost*** (the lost opportunity to invest the dollar in an income-producing manner), ***inflation*** (a future increase in prices that results in a decline in purchasing power), and ***risk*** (the possibility that the future payment will not be received as projected) (page 68).

Title affidavit: A document that sets forth the seller's certification that there are no off-record title matters affecting the subject real property (page 330).

Title insurance commitment: A title insurance company's written promise to issue a title insurance policy on the terms and conditions stated in the commitment (page 126).

Title insurance policy: A contract in which a title insurance company indemnifies an owner of real property against any loss that the owner suffers due to the quality of the owner's title being other than that specified in the title insurance policy (page141).

Turnkey build-out: A method used for the design and construction of tenant improvements where the landlord does all of the work and all the tenant has to do is "turn the key, open the door and commence business" (page 495).

Uncontrollable expenses: Those expenses that are not susceptible to control by a manager (page 304) or landlord (page 519).

Underwriting: The process undertaken by a lender to determine whether it should make a loan to a particular developer on a particular project (page 345).

Usable area: The space within the four walls of each tenant's leased premises (page 490).

Vacancy allowance: A financial line item frequently inserted into the project pro forma by an institutional investor to reflect the impact on a project's net operating income of expected tenant vacancies and uncollectible rents—for example, 5% of the project's total projected gross revenues (page 44).

Vertical improvements: The buildings and other above-ground structures constructed on the project land (page 10).

Voluntary action program (VAP): State programs designed to encourage the development of brownfield sites through the provision of grants and other financial incentives and the issuance of covenants not to sue (page 193).

Warranty: A promise made by a party to a contract concerning a future fact (page 128).

Waterfall: A cash distribution scheme where an outside equity investor is given a right to participate in a venture's cash distribution category that is superior to the right of the developer (contrasted with a *pari passu* arrangement where the rights of the developer and its outside equity investor to participate in a cash distribution category are placed on equal footing) (page 273).

Wetlands report: A report prepared by a wetlands consultant that identifies the location, size, and nature of any protected wetlands located on the land (page 126).

Work letter: A supplement to a lease that addresses all aspects of the making of tenant improvements to the leased premises, including the scope and timing of the improvements and the party who will be responsible for designing, constructing, and paying for such improvements (page 494).

Zero-sum game: A public policy argument that says that governmental incentives should not be provided to a private development project if the benefits garnered from a developer's decision to locate its development project in jurisdiction A (and not jurisdiction B) are directly and fully offset by losses suffered by jurisdiction B (page 203).

Zoning report: A report that recites the current zoning classification of the land and states whether the development plans for the proposed project conform to the requirements imposed by the applicable zoning classification (page 126).

INDEX

References are to Pages